The Birth of the Prophet Muḥammad

In the medieval period, the birth of the Prophet Muḥammad (the *mawlid*) was celebrated in popular narratives and ceremonies that expressed the religious agendas and aspirations of ordinary Muslims, including women. *Mawlid* celebrations expressed the hope for salvation through the relationship of love and mutuality with the Prophet, rather than exclusively through obedience to Islamic Law.

The Birth of the Prophet Muḥammad: Devotional piety in Sunni Islam examines the *mawlid* from its origins to the present day and provides a new insight into how an aspect of everyday Islamic piety has been transformed by modernity. The book demonstrates that medieval popular Islam was coherent and meaningful, not just a set of deviations from scholarly norms. It gives a window into the religious lives of medieval Muslim women, rather than focusing on the limitations that were placed on them. Elite scholars attempted to co-opt and discipline these forms of piety, but were not able to control or suppress them, and popular narratives about the Prophet's birth remained a powerful counter-canon for centuries. In the twentieth century, social and economic change transformed the ways in which Muslims imagined the Prophet Muḥammad, and the celebration of his birthday was marginalized by political forces.

Combining textual and historical analysis, this book is an important contribution to our understanding of contemporary Muslim devotional practices and will be of great interest to graduate students and researchers of Islam, religious studies, and medieval studies.

Marion Holmes Katz is Associate Professor at the Department of Middle Eastern Studies, New York University, USA. Her research interests are Islamic law, ritual, and gender.

Culture and Civilization in the Middle East
Series Editor:
Ian R. Netton
University of Leeds

This series studies the Middle East through the twin foci of its diverse cultures and civilisations. Comprising original monographs as well as scholarly surveys, it covers topics in the fields of Middle Eastern literature, archaeology, law, history, philosophy, science, folklore, art, architecture and language. While there is a plurality of views, the series presents serious scholarship in a lucid and stimulating fashion.

1. **Arabic Literature – An Overview**
   Pierre Cachia

2. **Modern Arab Historiography**
   Historical Discourse and the Nation-State
   Youssef Choueiri

3. **The Philosophical Poetics of Alfarabi, Avicenna and Averroes**
   The Aristotelian Reception
   Salim Kemal

4. **The Epistemology of Ibn Khaldun**
   Zaid Ahmad

5. **The Hanbali School of Law and Ibn Taymiyyah**
   Conflict or Concilation
   Abdul Hakim I Al-Matroudi

6. **Arabic Rhetoric**
   A Pragmatic Analysis
   Hussein Abdul-Raof

7. **Arab Representations of the Occident**
   East-West Encounters in Arabic Fiction
   Rasheed El-Enany

8. **God and Humans in Islamic Thought**
   Abd al-Jabbār, Ibn Sīnā and al-Ghazālī
   Maha Elkaisy-Friemuth

9. **Original Islam**
   Malik and the Madhhab of Madina
   Yasin Dutton

10. **Al-Ghazālī and the Qur'ān**
    One Book, Many Meanings
    Martin Whittingham

11. **The Birth of the Prophet Muḥammad**
    Devotional piety in Sunni Islam
    Marion Holmes Katz

The Birth of the Prophet Muḥammad

Devotional piety in Sunni Islam

Marion Holmes Katz

Routledge
Taylor & Francis Group
LONDON AND NEW YORK

First published 2007
by Routledge
2 Park Square, Milton Park, Abingdon, Oxon, OX14 4RN

Simultaneously published in the USA and Canada
by Routledge
270 Madison Ave, New York NY 10016

Routledge is an imprint of the Taylor & Francis Group, an informa business

Transferred to Digital Printing 2009

Typeset in Times New Roman by
Newgen Imaging Systems (P) Ltd, Chennai, India

British Library Cataloguing in Publication Data
A catalogue record for this book is available
from the British Library

Library of Congress Cataloging in Publication Data
A catalog record for this book has been requested

ISBN10: 0–415–77127–7 (hbk)
ISBN10: 0–415–55187–0 (pbk)
ISBN10: 0–203–96214–1 (ebk)

ISBN13: 978–0–415–77127–6 (hbk)
ISBN13: 978–0–415–55187–8 (pbk)
ISBN13: 978–0–203–96214–5 (ebk)

Contents

Acknowledgments vii

Introduction 1

1 **The emergence of *mawlid* narratives** 6

An archaeology of mawlid *narratives 6*
Formal mawlid *texts 50*
Conclusion 61

2 **Gifts and reciprocity in the celebration of the *mawlid*** 63

Mawlid *banquets 67*
Pious utterances and the generation of merit 75
The exchange of merit and the economy of salvation 87
Conclusion 96

3 **Emotion, law, and the celebration of the *mawlid*** 104

Joy 104
Love 117
The salvific value of personal relationships 125
Standing as an expression of emotion 128
Conclusion 139

4 **Time and merit in the celebration of the *mawlid*** 143

The night of the mawlid *and* laylat al-qadr *146*
Special times and their uses 147
Homogeneous and non-homogeneous time 153
Conclusion 164

Acknowledgments

The first stage of research on this project was made possible by a fellowship from the Association for Religion and Intellectual Life, which provided room, board, and library access in New York City in the summer of 1998. The generous comments and encouragement of the ARIL staff and the other participants helped me to incubate the project and encouraged me to pursue it. A fellowship from the American Institute for Yemeni Studies allowed me to spend five months researching *mawlid*s in Sanaa in 2000–1. The AIYS staff and the other residents in the hostel (particularly Chris Edens and Maurice Pomerantz) helped me with the connections and expertise to make research in an unfamiliar country possible. I thank the staffs of the Maktaba al-Gharbīya and Maktabat al-Awqāf, Sanaa, and the Aḥqāf Library, Tarīm, for access to the manuscript collections there. Mr Ja'far Muḥammad al-Saqqāf of Tarīm allowed me access to his invaluable personal library, and his graciousness and erudition were of enormous help. I am also grateful to the Jam'īyat al-Munshidīn for their extensive and patient contributions to my project. The professional help and personal kindness of a number of women chanters made my stay in Sanaa a happy one; my work with them will be reflected in a future publication. In Damascus, I received kind and spontaneous help from the staff of the Abū Nūr madrasa and the women to whom they introduced me. For access to manuscript and published sources, I am also grateful to the patient and professional staffs of Dār al-Kutub, Cairo; the Asad Library, Damascus; the Topkapı and Süleymaniye libraries, Istanbul; the Rare Books collection at Princeton University; and the Library of Congress, Washington.

I received both moral support and intellectual input for this book from my colleagues at both Mount Holyoke College, where I began my research, and New York University, where I completed it. In particular, I thank Bernard Haykel for encouraging me to travel to Yemen and Everett Rowson for helping me with his notes, comments, and general erudition. My parents, Stanley and Adria Katz, have contributed in countless ways throughout the project. I owe this book, like all of my accomplishments, to them.

In the course of this project, I have received help both from people who wish to see *mawlid* celebrations vanish from Muslim practice and from those who find them deeply meaningful. I have listened to impromptu lectures about the evils of religious innovation, and met women (in a mosque in Damascus) who kissed my cheeks to partake of the *baraka* of my project. The generosity and tolerance of both groups has touched and humbled me. I am profoundly grateful to the people who have shared with me not only their knowledge, but also their religious lives and aspirations. *Mawlid* opponents and devotees alike may find material that both delights and offends them in this work. I hope it will prove interesting and informative to some with a personal stake in the religious debates it traces, as well as to those whose interest is purely intellectual. Devotees of the Prophet will note that in my translations of Arabic works, I have omitted the blessings and greetings upon the Prophet that have been invoked by authors or added by copyists after mention of his name. Although I found such interjections awkward to include in English translation, I hope that they will be supplied in practice by readers who feel so moved. Regardless of the specific stances of the many authors whose work I have studied and the people whose religious lives I have been privileged to glimpse, being exposed to the genuine (if protean) love that the Prophet Muḥammad inspires has not been the least of the blessings of this project.

Finally, I thank Bradley Marshall McCormick, whom I met and married over the course of this project. His love and encouragement have supported me in my work, and it is to him that I dedicate this book.

Introduction

The origins of the *mawlid* celebration are widely considered, both among Muslim and secular scholars, to be well known. Even the most avid supporters of the celebration admit that it is an innovation (*bid'a*) that originated centuries after the life of the Prophet; no serious efforts have been made to obfuscate the practice's belated origins, or to project it into the distant Islamic past. Furthermore, although many details remain obscure, there are a number of historical accounts, contemporary or near-contemporary in origin, that trace several stages of the celebration's early history.[1] These have been exhaustively discussed by N.J.G. Kaptein in his monograph *Muḥammad's Birthday Festival.* The Fāṭimid dynasty, which ruled Egypt from 358 AH/969 CE to 567 AH/1171 CE, is known to have celebrated the Prophet's birthday as a state occasion. The observance, which differed little from other festivals sponsored by the Fāṭimid dynasty,[2] involved the distribution of sweets to state and religious functionaries and a brief ceremonial viewing of the ruling Fāṭimid imām.[3] The celebration's obvious function, within the religious agenda of the Shī'ite Fāṭimid state, was simultaneously to exalt the Prophet's family and to emphasize the Fāṭimid imāms' status as members and patrons of that lineage. Thus, the birthday of the reigning imām was celebrated along with those of the Prophet's most important kin. The exact chronological limits of Fāṭimid celebration of the *mawlid* are unknown. Kaptein infers that they began no earlier than 415 AH, the end point of his last source that fails to mention them; the earliest preserved descriptions of Fāṭimid mawlid ceremonies describe events no earlier than the beginning of the sixth century AH/twelfth century CE, the only firm *terminus ante quem*.[4] Whether the celebrations ceased with the fall of the dynasty itself, or had gained sufficient acceptance among the Egyptian population to survive the return to Sunnī rule, is unknown.[5]

It is, however, known that some prominent Sunnīs observed the Prophet's birthday around the time of the fall of the Fāṭimid dynasty. These celebrations combined feasting and *ṣūfī* audition (*samā'*) with various kinds of literary production. The Syrian ruler Nūr al-Dīn (d. 569 AH/1174 CE) observed the Prophet's birthday with festivities including night-time feasting and illuminations and the presentation of poetry in honor of the occasion.[6] Nūr al-Dīn was the devotee (*muḥibb*) and patron of a holy man known as 'Umar al-Mallā', who enjoyed a wide following including many members of the scholarly and political elite. Despite his poverty, ʻUmar was known for his hospitality, which included receiving crowds at his *zāwiya* for a multi-day celebration of the Prophet's birthday.[7] ʻUmar al-Mallā' is also known to have been the author of a lengthy compilation dealing with the life and habits of the Prophet entitled *Wasīlat al-mutaʻabbidīn fī sīrat sayyid al-mursalīn*.[8] An incomplete manuscript of this work, written during the lifetime of *shaykh* ʻUmar, is provided with a notation that it was read in the presence of the author during several sittings, the last of which was held on Tuesday, the 6th of Rabīʻ al-Awwal, 569 AH/1174 CE.[9] The fact that *Wasīlat al-mutaʻabbidīn* was publicly presented in the month of Rabīʻ al-Awwal suggests a connection with the celebration of the *mawlid*. However, in terms of form and content the text is not a *mawlid* in the later sense of the term; it does not primarily consist of a narrative of the Prophet's pre-creation, lineage, and birth.[10]

The celebration of the *mawlid* in the later sixth century AH/twelfth century CE was not limited to northern Mesopotamia. The traveler Ibn Jubayr describes the celebration of the occasion in Mecca in 579 AH/1183 CE, which involved the opening of the holy places and the veneration of the site of the Prophet's birth.[11] However, the evidence (though sparse) suggests that the celebration of the *mawlid* continued to flourish in the region that had seen the festivities of Nūr al-Dīn and ʻUmar al-Mallā'. The next recorded Sunnī *mawlid* celebration was the *mawlid* of Muẓaffar al-Dīn Kökbürī, a member of the local Begteginid dynasty, held in Irbil in the opening years of the seventh century AH/thirteenth century CE. As Kaptein points out, these festivities occurred a mere 80 kilometers from ʻUmar al-Mallā's location in Mosul. A contemporary, and probably eyewitness, description of this celebration was preserved for posterity by the historian Ibn Khallikān (d. 681 AH/1282 CE), a native of Irbil. The celebration attracted huge numbers of people from the surrounding region and involved spectacular outlays of money on the part of its patron. The preparations involved the erection of multi-leveled pavilions for the accommodation of various notables, each of which also featured ensembles of musicians and entertainers. The celebration culminated with a night-time session of mystical audition (*samāʻ*) and a banquet where both invited guests and masses of the needy were fed.[12] Ibn Khallikān also notes the participation of the Andalusian poet and scholar Ibn Diḥya, who composed in honor of the occasion a work entitled *al-Tanwīr fī mawlid al-sirāj al-munīr al-bashīr al-nadhīr*.[13] Unfortunately, this work has not been preserved.

On the basis of this data, Kaptein hypothesizes that the celebration of the *mawlid* was initiated by the Fāṭimid dynasty and spread to Syria and the Jazīra by the time of its fall. The practice then swiftly spread among Sunnīs, probably due to its popularization by influential figures such as ʻUmar al-Mallā', Nūr al-Dīn, and Muẓaffar al-Dīn Kökbürī, whose lavish and well-attended celebrations attracted guests from many different places. The observation of the Prophet's birthday in Mecca would have come to the attention of even greater numbers of visitors, who may then be assumed to have disseminated it at home.[14] Authoritative Sunnī authors ignored the Fāṭimid antecedents of the celebration, of which they were almost certainly aware; thus, Abū Shāma (d. 665 AH/1268 CE) identifies ʿUmar al-Mallāʾ as the originator of the *mawlid* festival, while al-Suyūṭī (d. 911 AH/1505 CE) names Muẓaffar al-Dīn Kökbürī. This, Kaptein argues, was a fairly transparent effort by influential Sunnī supporters of the *mawlid* to elide the heterodox origins of the festival.[15]

The idea that the celebration of the *mawlid* originated with the Fāṭimid dynasty has today been almost universally accepted among both religious polemicists and secular scholars. With respect to some of the more public, lavish, and carnivalistic aspects of the observance of the Prophet's birthday, it may very well be accurate. The state-sponsored patronage distribution and conspicuous consumption involved in Kökbürī's famous *mawlid* celebrations are certainly reminiscent of the Fāṭimid example in a number of respects, even if they lack some of the latter's imperial pomp. The Fāṭimid precedent, however, does little to explain other dimensions of the celebration of the Prophet's birthday. While the *mawlid*'s celebration as a state ceremony featuring the distribution of patronage continued into the modern period, both medieval and modern *mawlid* celebrations were often domestic occasions focusing on private devotional practice. The Fāṭimid celebration also lacks any precedent for another central element of later *mawlid* observances, the ritualized remembrance of the Prophet's actual birth (and sometimes of his entire life story) through the recitation of narrative texts on the subject. The Fāṭimid celebrations, although they included Qurʾān recitation and a public sermon, do not seem to have involved narration of the events of the Prophet's birth.[16]

The private and devotional aspects of the observation of the *mawlid*, rather than originating with the Fāṭimids, appear to be more closely akin to the Imāmī Shīʿite tradition. As we shall see, Imāmī Shīʿites had a rich and deeply rooted tradition of devotional narrative about the births of the Prophet and the Imāms, although much of the relevant material seems to derive from a fluid and popular storytelling milieu with little regard for sectarian boundaries. Furthermore, influential Imāmī scholars advocated the private observance of the birth dates of the Prophet and the Imāms prior to the probable rise of Fāṭimid *mawlid* celebrations. One likely early advocate is the prominent Imāmī authority Abū Jaʿfar Muḥammad ibn ʿAlī ibn Bābawayh, known as al-Shaykh al-Ṣadūq (d. 381 AH/991–2 CE) who, as we shall see later, disseminated important narratives about the events of the Prophet's birth. Ibn Ṭāwūs (d. 664 AH/1266 CE) cites a comment by Ibn Bābawayh appended to a tradition stating that the Prophet was conceived on the night of the nineteenth of Jumādā al-Ākhira: "If this is the case, then it is appropriate to honor this radiant night and spend it awake in interior and exterior devotions (*iḥyāʾuhā biʾl-ʿibādāt al-bāṭina waʾl-ẓāhira*)."[17] Although I have not been able to locate a statement by Ibn Bābawayh specifically advocating the observance of the Prophet's *mawlid*, it does seem unlikely that he would have promoted the celebration of his conception and ignored the date of his birth.

The celebration of the Prophet's *mawlid* among Shīʿites is explicitly mentioned, unfortunately with very little descriptive detail, by the influential Imāmī scholar al-Shaykh al-Mufīd (d. 413 AH/1022 CE). Significantly, far from perceiving the observance of the day as a recent innovation, al-Mufīd already considers it a time-honored practice. al-Mufīd's remarks reflect the fact that the Imāmī consensus on the date of the Prophet's birthday differed from that accepted among Sunnīs (although the discrepancy was relatively minor). al-Mufīd writes:

> The seventeenth of [Rabī' al-Awwal] is the birthday (*mawlid*) of our master the Messenger of God, at the break of dawn on Friday in the Year of the Elephant. It is a noble day of great blessings; in early times, the Shī'ites always honored it, recognized its due, and respected its sanctity (*lam tazal al-shī'a 'alā qadīm al-awqāt tu'aẓẓimuhu wa-ta'rif ḥaqqahu wa-tar'ā ḥurmatahu*) by voluntarily fasting on it. It is transmitted from the Imāms of guidance of the family of Muḥammad that they said, "Whoever fasts on the seventeenth of Rabī' al-Awwal, which is the birthday of our master the Messenger of God, God will credit him with fasting for a year." It is also desirable to give alms, visit the shrines (*mashāhid*) of the imāms, perform supererogatory acts of charity, and give joy to the faithful.[18]

The statement that fasting on the Prophet's *mawlid* was worth a year of fasting seems not to be found in classical Shī'ite compilations. However, in his book *al-Muqni'a*, al-Mufīd presents a *ḥadīth* in which the Tenth Imām, 'Alī al-Naqī (d. 254 AH/868 CE), instructs a follower about the days of the year on which one should fast. One of them is "the day of [the Prophet's] birth, which is the seventeenth of Rabī' al-Awwal."[19]

Assuming that al-Mufīd is sincere in his conviction that the observation of the Prophet's *mawlid* is an ancient Shī'ite practice, it must have been well-established by his prime – that is, in the second-half of the fourth century AH/tenth century CE. Given the brevity of al-Mufīd's statement, it is unclear precisely what was involved in the observation of the day. Fasting was clearly a central feature, and shrine visitation was recommended, but al-Mufīd's references to "performing supererogatory acts of charity" (*al-taṭawwu' bi'l-khayrāt*) and "giving joy to the faithful" (*idkhāl al-surūr 'alā ahl al-īmān*) are more ambiguous. The most obvious "act of charity" would certainly be almsgiving. "Giving joy to the faithful" may also refer to some form of charitable giving, but suggests a more festive and celebratory tone; it may well refer to gift-giving and feasting that were not limited to those poor people entitled to alms. Both of these activities would be consistent with later celebrations of the *mawlid*, but neither can be confirmed without further information.

For al-Mufīd, the Prophet's *mawlid* is not a unique holiday, but merely one in a series of calendrical commemorations of joyful events. For instance, he remarks of the birthday of the Fourth Imām Zayn al-'Ābidīn in the month of Jumādā al-Ūlā that it is "a noble day on which it is desirable to fast and to perform supererogatory acts of charity."[20] Of the birthday of Fāṭima in Jumādā al-Ākhira he observes that "it is a noble day on which the joy of the faithful is renewed, and on which it is desirable to perform supererogatory acts of charity and give alms to the indigent."[21]

al-Mufīd's testimony suggests that the observance of the Prophet's *mawlid* among Imāmī Shī'ites predates the rise of Fāṭimid *mawlid* celebrations; al-Mufīd died soon before Kaptein's *terminus post quem* of 415 AH, and a good century before the first Fāṭimid celebrations of which we have concrete records.[22] Rather than being inspired by Fāṭimid state ceremonial, it seems likely that the practice was rooted within the Imāmī tradition, taking inspiration from the extensive cultivation of devotional narratives about the births of the Prophet and the Imāms. The observation of other commemorative occasions, such as 'Āshūrā' and Ghadīr al-Khumm, would have offered a model for the construction of a more comprehensive cycle of celebrations. al-Mufīd's book *Masārr al-shī'a* ("The joyful occasions of the shī'a"), a survey of the celebratory commemorations in the Shī'ite religious calendar, suggests that this process was well advanced by the beginning of the fifth century AH/eleventh century CE.[23]

There is similarly little evidence that the Fāṭimid celebration inspired the Sunnī observance of the date. As noted by Kaptein, the earliest documented Fāṭimid celebration of the *mawlid* was in 517 AH, while the first reference to a Sunnī celebration relates to the year 546 AH.[24] Given that neither of these celebrations is explicitly described by the relevant sources as being innovative or novel, it seems unlikely that either of these dates is to be regarded as the point at which the celebration was initiated in the religious circles in question. They both probably represent the rather arbitrary point at which a pre-existing practice happened to be mentioned in a surviving source. In light of this likelihood, the rather insignificant thirty-year discrepancy between the dates of the Fāṭimid and Sunnī celebration becomes a questionable indicator of the chronological priority of the Fāṭimid festival. Given the nature of the Fāṭimid state festival, which bears very little resemblance to Sunnī *mawlid* celebrations, it seems more likely that Sunnī practices are related to the Shī'ite (and possibly *ṣūfī*) devotional practice and popular forms of devotional narrative about the birth of the Prophet.

1 The emergence of *mawlid* narratives

An archaeology of *mawlid* narratives

Similar to the history of *mawlid* observance, the history of *mawlid* texts extends beyond the documented beginning of the *mawlid* celebration under the Fāṭimid dynasty. While the *mawlid* genre as a literary form appropriate for recitation on the occasion of the Prophet's birth appears relatively late, works thematically focused on the Prophet's birth and youth emerge far earlier. Although evidence is scant (and the earliest relevant works are not preserved), it would seem that scholarly works in this genre originated among Imāmī Shī'ites, and that the first holy birth thus commemorated may not have been that of the Prophet. A book entitled *Mawlid amīr al-mu'minīn* ("The birth of the Commander of the Faithful," that is, 'Alī ibn abī Ṭālib) is attributed to one Wahb ibn Wahb ibn 'Abd Allāh ibn Zam'a, Abū'l-Bukhturī (200 AH/815 CE), a Medinian judge who is credited with a number of works in the area of *akhbār* (historical reports), *faḍā'il* (material on the extraordinary qualities of important religious figures), and genealogy.[1] His authorship of the *mawlid* work is mentioned by two authors of the fifth-century AH, the Shī'ite biographer al-Najāshī (d. 450 AH/1058 CE) and the Sunnī al-Khaṭīb al-Baghdādī (d. 463 AH/1071 CE).[2] The content of the book is suggested by the longer title cited by al-Khaṭīb al-Baghdādī, "The birth of 'Alī ibn abī Ṭālib, his growing up, the beginning of his faith, and his marriage to Fāṭima" (*Kitāb mawlid 'Alī ibn abī Ṭālib wa-nash'ihi wa-bad' īmānihi wa-tazwījihi Fāṭima*). Based on the title, the work must have been a devotional biography emphasizing the First Imām's birth and youth. This distinctive thematic focus, which diverges sharply from a more conventional emphasis on 'Alī's martial prowess and his adult role as the Prophet's legatee and successor, anticipates the model that would prevail in later *mawlid* texts about the Prophet Muḥammad. Like this early *mawlid* of 'Alī, as we will see, such works often culminate in the marriage of their youthful protagonist and exclude his most important adult accomplishments.

The existence of a Shī'ite genre focusing on the births of the Imāms is also suggested by a title attributed by Ibn al-Nadīm to al-Wāqidī (d. 207 AH/823 CE), "The Birth of Ḥasan and Ḥusayn and the killing of al-Ḥusayn" (*Kitāb mawlid al-Ḥasan wa'l-Ḥusayn wa-maqtal al-Ḥusayn*).[3] The earliest Shī'ite *mawlid* text from which any citation is preserved would seem to be the *Mawlid mawlānā 'Alī* of Ibn

Bābawayh (d. 381 AH/991 CE). It is listed among his works by al-Najāshī,[4] and is cited by Ibn Ṭāwūs (d. 664 AH/1265 CE) in his work *al-Yaqīn*.[5] al-Najāshī also credits Ibn Bābawayh with a work entitled *Mawlid Fāṭima*.[6] A work entitled "The birth (*mawlid*) of the Prophet and the Imāms," or "The birth of the Prophet, the pure ones and the legatees" (*Mawlid al-nabī wa'l-aṣfiyā' wa'l-awṣiyā'*) is attributed to al-Shaykh al-Mufid (d. 413 AH/1032 CE), and cited in several later Shī'īte sources.[7] Ibn Ṭāwūs cites a work of his own, apparently not preserved, by the title *al-Ta'rīf li'l-mawlid al-sharīf*.[8]

None of these works survives, even in substantial citation; it may be that some of them focused on technical issues such as the dating of their subjects' birth, rather than on devotional narrative. At least some of these works contained substantial devotional narratives, however, as indicated by Ibn Ṭāwūs's citation from Ibn Bābawayh's *Mawlid mawlānā 'Alī*. The selection consists of a summary of a single tradition, which Ibn Ṭāwūs states he has abridged because the original is about five leaves (*khams qawā'im*) long. It begins with an *isnād* ending: "Jābir ibn 'Abd Allāh al-Anṣārī reported to us, and said: I asked the Messenger of God about the birth (*mīlād*) of the Commander of the Faithful ['Alī]." He said, "Ah, ah, you have asked about the best infant to be born (*khayr mawlūd*) after me, according to the manner of the Messiah (*'alā sunnat al-masīḥ*)." "Then," Ibn Ṭāwūs remarks, "he mentioned wondrous things about God's choosing our master (*sayyid*) the Messenger of God and our master (*mawlānā*) 'Alī." Ibn Ṭāwūs then summarizes a fragment of the narrative, which recounts that before 'Alī was conceived his birth was predicted by a pious monk.[9]

A long version of the Jābir *ḥadīth* that corresponds to these excerpts from Ibn Bābawayh is presented by al-Fattāl al-Nīsāpūrī (sixth-century AH/twelfth-century CE).[10] While it is impossible to know whether it is identical to Ibn Bābawayh's long Jābir narrative in all of its details, based on Ibn Ṭāwūs's summary of the latter, it covers the same basic story. After proclaiming the glad news of 'Alī's advent, the monk produces a plate of the fruits of paradise as proof of his prediction. Abū Ṭālib partakes of the fruit, and it becomes semen in his loins; it is from this heavenly seed that his wife conceives 'Alī. 'Alī's conception is accompanied by an earthquake that forces the Quraysh to flee to the mountains with their idols; only Abū Ṭālib's invocation of Muḥammad, 'Alī, and Fāṭima brings relief. On the night of 'Alī's birth, the sky becomes luminous and the stars increase their brightness. Abū Ṭālib returns to find the monk who predicted 'Alī's birth, who has since expired but arises from the dead to pronounce the three-fold Shī'ite confession of faith and question Abū Ṭālib about the circumstances of the boy's birth. Abū Ṭālib describes the birth in detail (an account which will be discussed later, pp. 38–9). The monk weeps, prostrates himself in thanks to God, and once again passes away.[11]

Based on this material, it is clear that Shī'ites cultivated a rich and elaborate narrative tradition surrounding the birth of the First Imām. In its overall themes (such as the prediction of the numinous birth in question by a holy man of a previous religious dispensation) and – as we shall see later – in some of its concrete details, it anticipates some of the features of the narratives about the birth of the Prophet Muḥammad that circulated among Sunnīs.

Separate *mawlid* works (in this case, focusing on the birth of the Prophet) seem to have originated somewhat later among Sunnīs than among Shī'ites. The earliest Sunnī figure to whom a work centrally featuring the Prophet's birth has been attributed appears to be Muḥammad ibn Salāma al-Quḍā'ī (d. 454 AH/1062 CE). al-Quḍā'ī was an Egyptian who lived under Fāṭimid rule – conceivably a significant fact, although (as we have seen) there is no concrete evidence that the Fāṭimids held *mawlid* celebrations at this early date. In addition to his activities as a Shāfi'ī judge, he was known as a historian and a preacher (*wā'iẓ*).[12] al-Quḍā'ī is the author of a manuscript preserved in Egypt entitled "The Prophet's genealogy, his birth (*mawlid*), his emigration (*hijra*), and his death."[13]

Without access to this unique manuscript, it is impossible to determine its precise nature or content. It represents the earliest case known to me in which the Prophet's birth becomes a focus of narrative attention sufficiently prominent to warrant mention in the title of a Sunnī *sīra* work. Although (as will be discussed later) early biographies of the Prophet do include narrative material that manifests a degree of pious interest in the Prophet's birth, it is not an event that commands significant attention or space in proportion to the other incidents of the Prophet's life. Ibn Hishām's (d. 213 AH/828 CE) coverage of the Prophet's birth, for instance, is trivial in magnitude compared with his coverage of his military campaigns. The title of al-Quḍā'ī's work adumbrates the shape and priorities of what may be termed the devotional model of the Prophet's biography, which emphasizes the major transitions of the Prophet's life cycle (birth, marriage, the initiatory experience of the *mi'rāj*, emigration, and death) almost to the exclusion of the events of his career as a politico-religious leader. The nature of the material disseminated by al-Quḍā'ī may be suggested by a comment of Ibn Taymīya, who complains about the *ḥadīth* collection *al-Firdaws* of Shīrawayh al-Daylamī that it contains baseless statements such as "that the Prophet was a star (*kawkab*), or that the whole world was created from him, or that he existed before his parents were created, or that he knew the Qur'ān by heart before Gabriel brought it to him."[14] al-Daylamī's *al-Firdaws bi-ma'thūr al-khiṭāb* is based on al-Quḍā'ī's *Shihāb al-akhbār fī'l-ḥikam wa'l-amthāl wa'l-ādāb*; thus, Ibn Taymīya's critique suggests the rich and mythic nature of the material about the Prophet that was circulated by the preacher al-Quḍā'ī.[15] However, another surviving work by al-Quḍā'ī, which deals with the history of the prophets and caliphs, suggests that the author also produced terse historical narratives; the nature of his biography of the Prophet remains to be determined.[16]

Despite the existence of a number of scholarly works focusing on the birth of the Prophet, the growth and circulation of narratives on this subject may not have been most fundamentally shaped by the titled works of identifiable scholars. There is reason to believe that the *mawlid* tradition drew from a rich and extensive body of narrative material that probably originated with popular preachers and storytellers and never achieved the level of formal authentication required for acceptance by the scholarly elite. Some of this material, while decried by many authorities, achieved a level of standardization and dissemination constituting a form of *de facto* canonicity. As we shall see, some narratives rejected by scholars working within the classical paradigm of textual criticism nevertheless remained strikingly stable and widely circulated over a period of many centuries. At an even more popular level, episodes and embellishments must have been continuously generated in the semi-extemporaneous performances of gifted storytellers. Such material, to the extent that it is preserved at all, remains accessible only through isolated samples or citations; much of it must have escaped textual fixation and (at least in its medieval forms) is forever lost to scholarship. However, enough material remains to provide the basis for some firm generalizations about the nature of the popularly circulated story of the Prophet's birth and life.

The most influential text in the development of the *mawlid* genre may well be one whose ostensible author is unknown to history, the *Kitāb al-anwār* attributed to one Abū'l-Ḥasan al-Bakrī. The provenance and content of this work have already been ably discussed by Boaz Shoshan.[17] Although the association of the work with the name of al-Bakrī is consistent, the author himself is unidentifiable and undatable. The earliest manuscript of the work dates to 694 AH/1295 CE; the earliest citation, which matches the text of preserved manuscripts, appears in a work whose author died in 289 AH/902 CE.[18] Judging from its content, Bakrī's *Anwār* seems to have been intended for a popular audience, or at least for purposes of edifying entertainment; its accounts of events in the Prophet's life are more remarkable for their dramatic and diverting qualities than for their fidelity to the best-authenticated sources. Individual incidents, laconically described by the normative sources, are expanded into lengthy and theatrical scenes with lavish details and long passages of dialogue.

A reference to the works of al-Bakrī in one of the *fatāwā* of Ibn Taymīya suggests that his name was associated with the activities of popular storytellers.[19] However, as it appears in citations and manuscripts over the course of centuries and across the Islamic world, the work is far from being the product of spontaneous and informal storytelling activities. Rather, it is a fairly stable text whose uniformity and consistency over many centuries of transmission suggest that it enjoyed a certain degree of authority with those who retold it.[20] The literary quality of the book may be reflected in a comment by al-Dhahabī, who complained of the wide popularity of al-Bakrī's works in the booksellers' market; at least some of them were clearly literary texts reproduced by copyists.[21] Nevertheless, al-Bakrī's *sīra* work was the object of a great deal of learned opprobrium; it was denounced by scholars as eminent as al-Dhahabī, Ibn Kathīr, Ibn Ḥajar al-'Asqalānī, Ibn Ḥajar al-Haytamī, al-Qalqashandī, and al-Ṣafadī.[22]

Given the early Shī'ite interest in the births of the Prophet and the Imāms, it is worth noting that al-Bakrī's *sīra* as a whole may be considered somewhat ambiguous from a sectarian point of view. In one of the stories leading up to the Prophet's birth, for instance, a soothsayer pointedly pairs the Prophet's mother with 'Alī's mother, Fāṭima bint Asad; he foretells the births of both Muḥammad and 'Alī. Despite this exaltation of 'Alī, which would surely appeal to Shī'ite listeners, the story carefully avoids overtly sectarian language; it hails 'Alī merely as a hero and a defender of Islam, which would be unlikely to alienate Sunnīs.[23] Conversely, the text does not contain any obviously Sunnī features.

There is no concrete evidence that al-Bakrī's work was originally produced in connection with the celebration of the Prophet's birthday. However, it reflects a model of the Prophet's biography in which the protagonist's origins, birth, and youth disproportionately dominate the narrative. The text's primary subjects are the pre-existence of the Light of Muḥammad, its migration through the generations of his ancestors, and his earthly birth. The narrative from the Prophet's primordial creation to his infancy occupies fully half of the preserved text, and the story culminates with his marriage to Khadīja – that is, before the beginning of revelation. The allocation of narrative space and detail in al-Bakrī's *sīra* thus diverges sharply from the patterns established by early and authoritative biographies such as that of Ibn Isḥāq. It reflects the devotional reframing of the Prophet's life, already noted earlier, in which priority is accorded to his major life-cycle crises, rather than to his public career as the Messenger of God.

Whether or not its preoccupation with the Prophet's creation and birth reflect an original link with the celebration of his birthday, the text suited later conceptions of appropriate *mawlid* narratives so well that it was adapted to the purpose of recitation during the season of the Prophet's birthday, apparently by both Sunnīs and Shī'ites. The seventeenth-century CE Imāmī scholar Muḥammad Bāqir al-Majlisī remarks of al-Bakrī's *sīra* that "it is well known among our scholars, who recite it (*yatlūnahu*) in the month of Rabī' al-Awwal in sessions and gatherings until the day of the noble *mawlid*."[24] An undated introduction to the text of Bakrī's *Anwār* similarly indicates its use as a *mawlid* text, perhaps in this case in Sunnī circles. The edition published by Muṣṭafā al-Bābī al-Ḥalabī in Cairo in 1379 AH/1959 CE, unfortunately without identification of the manuscript on which it was based, begins with an introduction linking the text with the observation of the *mawlid* in the month of Rabī' al-Awwal. The text offers itself "to be read in some of these gatherings that are held in these nights and days, so that the elite and common people who attend them can enjoy listening to it and the blessings of these reports reach all of the male and female believers."[25]

Not only was the text of *al-Anwār* itself well adapted for recitation in the context of *mawlid* celebrations, however; its contents provided one of the richest sources of material for later *mawlid* compositions. Countless exemplars of the *mawlid* genre contain passages from al-Bakrī's *sīra*, either in the form of verbatim citations (sometimes with explicit attribution to al-Bakrī) or in the form of recognizable paraphrases. Extensive passages from al-Bakrī's work are reproduced approvingly in the first preserved Sunnī text produced expressly in view of the annual celebration of the Prophet's birth, *al-Durr al-munaẓẓam fī'l-mawlid al-mu'aẓẓam*, by Abū'l-'Abbās al-'Azafī (d. 633 AH/1236 CE). It would perhaps be an exaggeration to see this individual text as the source of the central elements of the tradition of *mawlid* writing. As we shall see later, the text attributed to al-Bakrī represents only one particularly stable and well-established manifestation of a rich and fertile narrative tradition. Nevertheless, the text of *al-Anwār* is one of the earliest and most influential elements in the complex of narratives that underlies the *mawlid* genre.

Another text focusing on the Prophet's birth and early life seems to reflect a much more popular level of the storytelling tradition. Unlike the *Kitāb al-anwār*, its literary embodiment seems to appear only in an isolated (and incomplete) instance; it does not seem to have attracted the attention, or to have carried the weight, of the narrative associated with al-Bakrī. This is a narrative pseudepigraphically attributed to the early historian al-Wāqidī, which is extensively excerpted in the *Kitāb al-Faḍā'il* of Shādhān ibn Jibrā'īl al-Qummī. al-Qummī, whose precise dates are unknown, is believed to have been alive in 650 AH/1252 CE.[26] The work itself contains a narrative which it states was transmitted to the author in 633 AH.[27] While al-Qummī was a Shī'ite and the overall content of the work is frankly sectarian, the Wāqidī narrative's only clearly Shī'ite element seems to be the date of the Prophet's birth, which reflects the Shī'ite consensus.[28] The narrative, which begins and ends abruptly, may be a selection from a longer (and perhaps elastic) tale. As it stands, it begins with the betrothal and marriage of the Prophet's parents and ends with the orphaned Prophet being nurtured by his uncle, Abū Ṭālib.[29]

The narrative is presented in an engaging popular style, rich with colorful detail and devoid of scholarly touches such as chains of transmission. It displays an almost ethnographic interest in customs such as marriage preparation and mourning, and a noticeable lack of concern with normative strictures. Thus, for instance, the death of the Prophet's father is followed by the erection of a shrine (*qubba*) over his grave and the hiring of wailing women (*nā'iḥāt*), both folk customs of questionable status in the legal tradition.[30] The narrator carefully explains that Arab bridegrooms did not depart their brides until the traces of henna disappeared from their hands, and gives a detailed (if inaccurate) description of the dwellings of nomadic tribesmen.[31] All of this may suggest that the narrative reflects a fairly high degree of cultural distance from the protagonists in the story, possibly because the original listeners were not themselves Arab. The touchingly literal descriptions of fabulously luxurious clothing, food, and drink suggest the tastes of a popular audience. The narrative is unusually divergent from the normative sources in terms of its basic factual framework; for instance, the Prophet's mother Āmina apparently keeps him with her for the remainder of her life, and only after her death is Ḥalīma summoned as a nursemaid.

The fantastical tone of the tale may be suggested by one of the miraculous events which it recounts for each month of Āmina's pregnancy with the Prophet.

> al-Wāqidī said: When the Prophet had been in his mother's belly for eight months, there was in the sea of air (*baḥr al-hawā'*) a whale called "Ṭīnūsā." She was the mistress of the whales. The fishes moved, and the fish [Ṭīnūsā] moved. She stood upright on her tail; she rose up, and the waves rose up over her. The angels said, "O our God and Master, do You see what Ṭīnūsā is doing? She is not obeying us, and we cannot control her." The angel Istiḥyā'īl gave a mighty cry and said, "Be still, Ṭīnūsā! Do you not know who is below you?" Ṭīnūsā said, "O Isitiḥyā'īl, on the day that He created me my Lord commanded me that when Muḥammad ibn 'Abd Allāh is born I should ask

forgiveness for him and for his community; now I have heard the angels giving each other the glad tidings, and for that reason I rose up and moved." Istiḥyā'īl called to her, "Be still and ask forgiveness; Muḥammad has been born." So she lay down in the sea and began to glorify God, declare His unicity, and praise the Lord of the Worlds.[32]

The pseudo-Wāqidī text is interesting because it reflects the fact that, long after the crystallization of the text associated with the name of al-Bakrī, there were folk versions of the *mawlid* narrative in circulation that were completely independent of it. The Wāqidī text displays the robust creativity of the storytelling tradition, and is probably a rare surviving fragment of a large repertory of orally composed renditions of the *mawlid* story. The freedom of the retelling is suggested by comparison of the Ṭīnūsā incident with a parallel occurring al-Fattāl's *Rawḍat al-wā'iẓīn*. In a long report attributed to Ka'b al-Aḥbār, the latter recounts: "I have heard that one of the whales of the sea, called Ṭimsūsā – who is the master of the whales, has 700,000 tails, and walks on the back of 700,000 fishes (*yamshī 'alā ẓahr sab' mi'at alf nūn*), each of which is bigger than the world and each of which has 700,000 horns of green emerald, which he does not feel – was agitated with joy at [the Prophet's] birth, and if it were not that God steadied him, he would have turned [the world] upside down."[33] Despite the fluidity of the text, this example also suggests that the pseudo-Wāqidī text bears a clear relation to a somewhat more scholarly stratum of the tradition.

Another episode of the narrative, in which 'Abd al-Muṭṭalib visits the Yemeni king Sayf ibn Dhī Yazin, clearly parallels narratives presented by the fourth-century-AH preacher al-Kharkūshī, by the fifth-century-AH Sunnī scholar al-Bayhaqī, and by the fifth-century-AH Imāmī scholar al-Karājikī.[34] In the pseudo-Wāqidī version it is transformed by a wealth of entertaining detail and engaging embellishments of the plot.[35]

As the earlier examples suggest, the birth of the Prophet was an object of interest for scholars, and of embellishment for preachers and storytellers, long before the generally recognized rise of Sunnī *mawlid* celebrations. Cultivation of interest in the pre-existence and earthly birth of the Prophet occurred at all levels of authority and expertise, from that of elite scholars to that of the most popular storytellers. It also seems to have crossed or transcended sectarian lines. In the next section, we will examine the content of the traditions on this subject that informed – either by perpetuation or by reaction – the development of the later *mawlid* genre.

The pre-existence of the Prophet and the Light of Muḥammad

The idea of the pre-existence of the Prophet Muḥammad is deeply rooted in the Islamic tradition. In a *ḥadīth* transmitted in the canonical compilation of al-Tirmidhī (d. 279 AH/892 CE), Muḥammad is asked when prophethood was decreed for him; he replies, "When Adam was between the spirit and the body."[36] A more popular, but less well-authenticated, version of the tradition states that

Muḥammad was a prophet "when Adam was between the water and the mud."[37] These *ḥadīth* texts suggest that Muḥammad's prophetic mission was predetermined at some point in the process of Adam's creation. In another widely circulated early report, Muḥammad states, "I was the first of the prophets to be created, and the last to be sent."[38] The associated idea of a primordial light of Muḥammad, transferred upon conception from one generation to another of his ancestors, also has an extremely long pedigree; it is reflected in Ibn Isḥāq's *Sīra*, which describes how the light shone in the forehead of 'Abd Allāh before the conception of Muḥammad.[39] The motif of a supernatural light is also reflected in the widely accepted early report that when his mother was pregnant with him, she saw a light emanating from her belly that reached to the castles of Syria.[40]

Probably at some later point, it came to be believed that the prophethood of Muḥammad preceded not only the creation of Adam, but that of all other things in existence. In popular usage, the tradition that Muḥammad became a prophet "when Adam was between the water and the mud" was extended to state that he existed "when there was no Adam, no water and no mud."[41] *Ḥadīth* experts emphasized that this addition, which had no basis in the textual tradition, was in circulation primarily in non-scholarly circles.[42] It also came to be believed that the Light of Muḥammad was the primordial substance from which all other elements of creation were brought forth. Later sources, both Shī'ite and Sunnī, expand on these motifs to construct elaborate cosmogonic scenarios. It may very well be that, as more than one author has suggested, Shī'ites were the first to develop such narratives.[43]

Given the state of the sources, it would be difficult to determine with certainty whether Shī'ites originated the motif of the Light of Muḥammad before its appearance among Sunnīs. It is certainly the case that Shī'ites elaborated it to an unusual degree, and that related traditions often have a sectarian cast that is rebutted by analogous traditions from the Sunnī side. While the idea of a pure Light transmitted through the generations of the Prophet's ancestry was well suited to (and perhaps historically rooted in) Shī'ite belief in the immaculate descent of the Imāms, it was also articulated in Sunnī forms. In one tradition reflecting the Sunnī belief that authority resided in the Prophet's tribe, Ibn 'Abbās declares:

> Quraysh was a light before God two thousand years before He created Adam. That light glorified God, and the angels glorified God with it. When God created Adam, He cast that light into his loins. The Prophet said: God sent me down to earth in Adam's loins; He placed me in Noah's loins, and cast me into the loins of Abraham. Then God continued to transfer me through noble loins and pure wombs until He brought me forth from my parents, without [any of my foreparents] meeting in illicit congress.[44]

Ṣūfīs also seem to have played a central role in the development narratives on this subject. Among the earliest figures to whom significant ideas about the Light of Muḥammad are plausibly attributed is the Iranian mystic Sahl al-Tustarī

(d. 283 AH/896 CE). al-Tustarī is cited as interpreting the "light verse" of the Qur'ān (24:35), which likens God's light to a lamp in a niche, by stating that "the lamp in the niche is a likeness of the Light of Muḥammad, when it lay hidden in the loins [of his forefathers]."[45] A fourth-century AH/tenth-century CE source transmits from Sahl a report that

> when God willed to create Muḥammad He brought forth light out of His own light and diffused it throughout His kingdom. When it reached the (veil of) Majesty (*'aẓama*) it prostrated itself. God created from its prostration a column of light as dense as glass and as far across as the seven heavens; its interior was visible from its exterior. In it Muḥammad worshiped God for a million years, without a body or a form, but by the nature of faith and insight into the unseen. [This was] before the beginning of creation, which is Adam, by a million years. [God] created Adam from the light of Muḥammad; Muḥammad's body is from Adam, and Adam's clay is from the column in which Muḥammad worshiped his Lord. [God] created Adam from the light of Muḥammad; He created the mystical masters (*murādūn*) from the light of Adam, and the mystical seekers (*murīdūn*) from the light of the mystical masters.[46]

The idea of the pre-existence of the Prophet Muḥammad (or of his primordial light) was a controversial one. Perhaps surprisingly, given its early and lasting appeal to *ṣūfī*s, one of its most vigorous detractors was Abū Ḥāmid al-Ghazālī (d. 505 AH/1111 CE). In his *Nafkh al-rūḥ wa'l-taswiya*, he comments on the *ḥadīth* in which Muḥammad states that "I am the first of the prophets to be created (*khalqan*), and the last of them to be sent." al-Ghazālī argues that in this context the word *khalq* does not, in fact, have its ordinary meaning of "bringing into existence" (*takwīn*); rather, it refers to God's determining (*taqrīr*) the existence of Muḥammad. "Before [the Prophet's] mother gave birth to him," al-Ghazālī affirms, "he was not created and did not exist" (*lam yakun makhlūqan mawjūdan*). Al-Ghazālī likens the priority of the Prophet Muḥammad in God's plan to the image of a house that pre-exists its construction in the mind of the builder. Although the finished house is the last stage of its physical construction, it is the finished house that is first pre-figured in the imagination of the architect. Muḥammad has priority over all other prophets because of his unique relationship to the ultimate aim of human existence, which is eternal felicity.[47] Ibn Taymīya (d. 728 AH/1328 CE) also summarily dismisses the idea of the Prophet's pre-existence and that of his primordial light. "All of the prophets were not created from the Prophet [Muḥammad]," he states in a *fatwā*; "rather, each one was created from his parents, and God breathed the spirit into him."[48] Since Ibn Taymīya has already stated that he rejects the idea of the Prophet Muḥammad's pre-existing the birth of his own parents, it seems clear that he did not exempt him from this rule. The Prophet Muḥammad, like all other prophets and all other human beings, was born from two parents and ensouled by the divine breath.

Nevertheless, the idea of the Prophet's pre-existence did find influential scholarly supporters. In his *fatāwā*, Taqī al-Dīn al-Subkī (d. 756 AH/1355 CE) argues that "If what was meant... was simply the knowledge of what will exist in the future, [the Prophet Muḥammad] would have no special distinction in being a prophet 'when Adam was between the spirit and the body', because God knew of the prophethood of all of the prophets at that time and before it." To an imaginary interlocutor who objects that Muḥammad became a prophet, not only after his own physical creation, but after forty years of human life, al-Subkī responds that "It is reported that God created spirits before bodies; it may be that [Muḥammad's] statement 'I was a prophet' alludes to his noble spirit and to his [inner] reality (*ḥaqīqa*)."[49]

The pre-existence of the Light of Muḥammad, including its origination at the beginning of creation and its migration through the loins of the Prophet's ancestors, is an integral element of the paradigmatic *mawlid* narrative. Of the scores of authored *mawlid* texts and informally compiled *mawlid* manuscripts in existence, the vast majority begin with an account of the Light of Muḥammad. This fact may seem paradoxical, given that the Prophet's pre-existence would seem to diminish the significance of his physical birth in the sixth-century CE – the event commemorated by the *mawlid* celebration. However, the overwhelming consensus of the *mawlid* tradition is to treat the Prophet's birth, not as the beginning of the existence of a historical individual, but as an episode in an ongoing cosmic drama that began with the inception of creation. The Prophet's physical birth is not the beginning of his existence, but the point at which his manifold blessings become manifest on earth and available to humanity.

The pre-existence of the Light of Muḥammad is described or alluded to in many ways in *mawlid* texts, but their accounts are most often based on one or the other of two broadly disseminated narratives associated with the figures of two of the Prophet's Companions, Ka'b al-Aḥbār and Jābir ibn 'Abd Allāh al-Anṣārī. Neither of these narratives has received credence from *ḥadīth* scholars, and neither of them is plausibly associated with the historically opaque Companion to whom it is described. Nevertheless, for the sake of convenience we will identify the two narratives by the names under which they have now circulated for hundreds of years.

The narrative of Ka'b al-Aḥbār

The earliest datable work containing the creation narrative associated with the name of Ka'b al-Aḥbār is the *Kitāb bad' al-khalq wa-qiṣaṣ al-anbiyā'* of 'Umāra ibn Wathīma al-Fārisī al-Fasawī, who died in 289 AH/902 CE.[50] Although the relevant passage comes at the very end of al-Fārisī's book, it comprises the opening of al-Bakrī's *al-Anwār*.

The narrative begins with God declaring to the angels that He intends to create "a being whom I will honor and exalt over all other beings, whom I will make the master of the first and the last and the intercessor of the Day of Resurrection – I mean the Day of Judgment; if it were not for him, the Gardens would not have been adorned and the Fires would not have been kindled."[51] Unlike in the Qur'ān (2:30), where God proclaims His intention to create Adam and is questioned by the angels, here precedence is accorded to the Prophet Muḥammad. The angels having (in contrast with the scenario presented in the Qur'ān) docilely proclaimed their obedience to God's will, He proceeds to create the Prophet:

> Then God commanded the peacock of the angels, Gabriel, to bring him the pure and purifying white handful which is the splendor and the light of the world. Gabriel descended among the angels of paradise, the angels of the highest rank who stand in ranks and glorify God, and the cherubim – who are the heads of the angels – and took the handful of the Messenger of God (*qabaḍa qabḍat rasūl allāh*) from the site of his grave. At that time it was white and pure; it was the cleanest, purest, most radiant, and most immaculate spot on the face of the earth. It was kneaded (*'ujinat*) with the waters of Tasnīm and Salsabīl and swelled until it became like a white pearl;[52] then it was immersed in all of the rivers of heaven, and taken around all of the heavens, the earths, and the seas. So the angels knew Muḥammad and his merit before they knew Adam and his merit. When God created Adam, he heard a swishing like the sound of dust motes (*nashīsh ka-nashīsh al-dharr*) from the lines of the wrinkles in his forehead. He said, "Glory be to You, what is that?" [A voice] called to him, "O Adam, that is the glorification of the Seal of the Prophets and the master of the messengers among your descendents, Muḥammad, My servant, messenger, beloved, close friend, and chosen one from among My creatures; take him with a pact and covenant with Me to place him only in pure loins and resplendent channels (*qanawāt zāhira*)."[53]

The light beams from the forehead of Adam, and is transferred to the face of Eve upon the conception of Seth. After a pregnancy fraught with miracles, she gives birth to the baby and the light migrates to him. When he reaches majority, Adam makes him party to the pact he had made with God; Seth is married to a pure wife in a wondrous ceremony, with Gabriel contracting the marriage on behalf of the wife and the angels witnessing the contract.[54] The reiteration of the pact in each generation and the transmission of the light are traced through the generation of Noah. Here the Fārisī citation breaks off; in manuscripts of *al-Anwār*, however, the narrative proceeds continuously up to the birth of the Prophet.

In the text of *al-Anwār*, this narrative is not presented as the original composition of al-Bakrī himself; although devoid of the *isnād*s demanded by more scholarly standards of attribution, the story is preceded by references to three different early Islamic authorities: Ka'b al-Aḥbār, Wahb ibn Munabbih, and Ibn 'Abbās.[55] In later sources, the narrative of the "white handful" and the light in Adam's forehead is associated with the name of Ka'b; it may be that other elements in al-Bakrī's tale were associated with Wahb and Ibn 'Abbās.

The fact that this narrative existed by the early-fourth-century AH/tenth-century CE, and that it circulated in diverse circles, is further demonstrated by the book *Ithbāt al-waṣīya li'l-imām 'Alī ibn Abī Ṭālib*, which is attributed to the historian al-Mas'ūdī (d. 345 AH/956 CE). Doubts have been cast on its authorship, largely because no Sunnī source lists it as a work of al-Mas'ūdī (although there is some possibility that they mention it under an alternative name).[56] Despite the doubts over the work's authorship, the text itself ends with an indication of its date, which is stated to be 332 AH.[57] This work contains a lengthy version of the "white handful" narrative (although without attribution to Ka'b) that generally parallels the content of the corresponding portion of *al-Anwār*. The parallel portion of the text, which is occasionally interrupted by the insertion of explicitly Shī'ite reports, fills twenty-five pages in the text of the *Ithbāt*[58]; it extends from the "white handful" incident (which displays extensive verbal similarities with the text of *al-Anwār*) to the birth of the Prophet. There are significant differences between the two texts, but this often seems to be due less to a fundamental divergence in content than to the fact that each of the texts is expanded in some places and abbreviated in others. The flexibility of the narrative framework provided by the descent of the light through the generations of the Prophet's ancestors is suggested by the inclusion of additional episodes in the *Ithbāt's* version of the story. While *al-Anwār* presents the descent of the light from Adam's son Seth to the Prophet's great-grandfather Hāshim as a simple list of names, the *Ithbāt* presents vivid and elaborate episodes associated with several different figures in this genealogy. One deals with Ismā'īl's son Qaydhār, who falsely supposes that the woman in whom he must deposit the Light of Muḥammad is of the line of Isḥāq. By divine intervention he is finally directed to marry an Arab woman of the line of Ismā'īl, at which point the light is transferred to her womb.[59]

Interestingly, the *Ithbāt* introduces the narrative with the words "the elite and the commoners have transmitted" (*rawat al-khāṣṣa wa'l-'āmma*).[60] In the context of an Imāmī work, this is unlikely to be a reference to the dual literary and popular dissemination of the report; rather, it probably alludes to the fact that the story was current both among Imāmī Shī'ites (the "elite" in their own terminology) and among the Sunnī majority. The author of the *Ithbāt* appears to regard the story as one of general and intersectarian currency, rather than the work of a specific author; its content is not distinctively Shī'ite in character.

The Ka'b tradition, beginning with the story of the "white handful," is also found in a Sunnī source of the later fourth-century AH/tenth-century CE, the work *Sharaf al-nabī* of Abū Sa'd al-Kharkūshī.[61] The latter was known as an ascetic (*zāhid*) and as a preacher (*wā'iẓ*). A native of Nīshāpūr, he traveled widely and then returned to his home town, where he died in 407 AH. He was a person of at least modest learning in *ḥadīth* and *fiqh*, enjoyed a good reputation for piety and learning, and wrote several works. Unlike al-Bakrī or the author of the *Ithbāt*, al-Kharkūshī traces the report to the Prophet's Companion Ka'b al-Aḥbār through a complete *isnād*, in accordance with the conventions of *ḥadīth* scholarship.

In the version transmitted by al-Kharkūshī, the story is preceded by an introduction suggesting the esoteric and privileged quality of the information Ka'b is purveying. 'Amr al-Anṣārī, who transmits the report from Ka'b, states that Ka'b never met the Prophet, but was constantly describing him and providing information about his actions and character. One night on the road to Medina Ka‘b begins to weep and lament, stating that he has seen the doors of heaven opened to receive the Prophet. Upon arriving in Medina, where the Prophet has indeed just passed away, ‘Amr reports Ka‘b's statements; the people are astounded, and say that Ka‘b is a sorcerer. Ka‘b draws forth a small casket of white pearl, closed with a lock and a seal, and opens it to reveal a tightly wound scroll of green silk. "Do you know what this is?" he asks rhetorically. "It is the description (*ṣifa*) of Muḥammad." He then commences the narrative of the "white handful."[62]

The Ka‘b narrative presented by al-Kharkūshī is extremely lengthy, and the insertion of parallel or supplementary material associated with other authorities makes it difficult to define its contents precisely. Displaying extensive parallels (sometimes word for word) with both the *Anwār* and the *Ithbāt*, it follows the transmission of the light through the generations of Adam's progeny. At the same time, it illustrates the flexibility and fertility of the narrative framework. For instance, Kharkūshī's rendition of the narrative involves a chest (*tābūt*) bequeathed by Adam to his descendants – a motif that is mentioned in passing by the *Ithbāt* (suggesting that it was already in circulation), but without elaboration.[63] Kharkūshī recounts that when Abraham is lying upon his deathbed, he gathers his sons and displays to them the contents of Adam's chest. It contains images of all of the prophets, culminating with that of the Prophet Muḥammad, who is accompanied in prayer by Abū Bakr, ‘Umar, ‘Uthmān, and ‘Alī (each of whom is identified with a laudatory label).[64] Subsequently, when Qaydhār discovers that the light can pass only to an Arab woman, the descendants of Isḥāq demand the chest and Qaydhār ultimately surrenders it to them.[65] The story of the images of the prophets is an independent narrative element that here is inventively imported into a new context.[66] Nevertheless, it demonstrates how the Ka‘b narrative, with its basic schema of the descent of the light through successive generations, could provide a flexible frame attracting additional narrative elements.

The fact that such additions display a degree of stability as well as flexibility is reflected by the parallel narrative in *al-Muntaqā min siyar al-nabī al-muṣṭafā* by Muḥammad ibn Mas‘ūd al-Kāzarūnī, a *faqīh* and *muḥaddith* who died in 758 AH/1354 CE.[67] Here the additional narrative elements are more smoothly integrated into the Ka‘b narrative, which is provided, in correct scholarly style, with a detailed *isnād*.[68] Both a degree of consistency with al-Kharkūshī's material and a significant element of narrative productivity is reflected, for instance, in *al-Muntaqā*'s version of the episode of Abraham and the images of the prophets. Here Abraham sees that the figure of each prophet bears a staff and a whip; these insignia follow the line of Isḥāq. The Light of Muḥammad, on the other hand, passes through the line of Ismā‘īl.[69]

Despite the elasticity and fertility of the narrative, there is a striking degree of consistency in content that unites the versions of the *Ithbāt*, al-Bakrī, al-Kharkūshī, and al-Kāzarūnī. An example of this uniformity is the story of the Prophet's grandfather, ‘Abd al-Muṭṭalib, and the birth and youth of his father ‘Abd Allāh. The narrative involves a number of colorful and distinctive episodes that are repeated from source to source. It recounts a prophetic dream of

'Abd al-Muṭṭalib's in which the birth of the Prophet is symbolized by a chain emerging from his body and extending to the limits of the earth, followed by a green tree under which are two old men.[70] The story then tells of a white woolen garment dipped in the blood of John the Baptist, in the possession of (variously identified) opponents of the true faith; it was written in their books that when the blood liquefied and dripped, the Prophet's father 'Abd Allāh ibn 'Abd al-Muṭṭalib would be born. Having identified 'Abd Allāh, the opponents attempt to kill him, but in vain.[71] The tale then turns to the beauty of 'Abd Allāh, which was such that "he experienced with the women in his time what Yūsuf experienced in his time with the ruler's wife."[72] Then seventy (or ninety) monks conspire to kill 'Abd Allāh with poisoned swords. They ambush him when he is hunting alone; however, Wahb ibn 'Abd Manāf sees them attack him, and watches in wonder as a band of angels descends from heaven to defend him. Rushing home, he tells his wife the story, and they hasten to seek the young man's hand in marriage for their daughter Āmina.[73] Many (in some versions, two hundred) women of Quraysh expire of jealously when Āmina wins his hand.[74]

Ka'b's report seems to constitute an example of the genre of the "*mawlid* narrative," tracing the Prophet's career from primordial light through his human ancestry and early life, even though it cannot be known whether it was in any way connected with the celebration of the date of the Prophet's birthday. The existence of such a narrative is confirmed by a reference in the Qur'ān commentary of al-Tha'labī (d. 427 AH/1035 CE), who refers to "Ka'b al-Aḥbār's report about the Prophet's birth and his beginnings" (*ḥadīth Ka'b al-Aḥbār fī mawlid rasūl allāh ṣallā allāhu 'alayhi wa-sallam wa-bad' amrihi*).[75] Certainly in the first-half of the sixth-century AH/twelfth-century CE, a complete Ka'b narrative culminating in the birth and nursing of the Prophet was in wide circulation. One of the Islamic texts whose translation was commissioned by Peter the Venerable on the occasion of his journey to Spain in 536 AH/1142 CE was the *Liber generationis Mahumet et nutritia eius* (which Peter Kritzeck, in his study of the Toledan translations, recognizes as a *mawlid* text in content although "the *mawlid* genre as such . . . did not appear at so early a date"[76]). This work consists of a narrative, introduced by a chain of transmission ending with Ka'b al-Aḥbār, that closely parallels the Ka'b material familiar from the sources discussed earlier, including the story of the blood of John the Baptist and the attack by "seventy Jewish rabbis."[77] The text ends with the story of the Prophet's wet-nurse, Ḥalīma.[78]

The basic content of this narrative seems to have gained wide currency, among both Shī'ites and Sunnīs and in scholarly as well as popular circles. The Imāmī author Muḥammad ibn 'Alī al-Karājikī (d. 449 AH/1057 CE) includes in his work *Kanz al-fawā'id* a short treatment of the Prophet's *mawlid*, including an outline of the story of the Prophet's birth. It begins with the migration of the Prophet's light from Adam's forehead through the generations of his ancestors, emphasizing the pact requiring that each male approach his wife only in a state of purity and that each son choose only the purest woman of his generation. It continues with the story of the garment dipped in the blood of John the Baptist. It is also reported, al-Karājikī recounts, that the women of Quraysh were entranced with

'Abd Allāh to the point that they lay in wait for him in his path, and "he experienced with them what Yūsuf experienced with the 'Azīz's wife."[79] al-Karājikī's account of the Prophet's light is a faithful, if brief, synopsis of the narrative associated with the name of Ka'b al-Aḥbār.[80] (al-Karājikī, similar to the *Ithbāt*, presents its brief synopsis anonymously; it may be that the story was circulated among Shī'ites independently of the name of Ka'b or of al-Bakrī.)

At least by the sixth-century AH, the narrative also seems to have been widely accepted among Sunnīs. In his *al-Wafā' bi-aḥwāl al-Muṣṭafā*, Abū'l-Faraj 'Abd al-Raḥmān Ibn al-Jawzī (d. 597 AH/1200 CE) presents a faithful, if brief, summary of the same story:

> From Ka'b al-Aḥbār; he said: When God willed to create Muḥammad, He commanded Gabriel to come to Him. He brought Him the white handful that is the place of the Prophet's grave. It was kneaded with the water of Tasnīm, then immersed in the rivers of paradise, and carried around the heavens and the earth. So the angels knew Muḥammad and his merit before they knew Adam. Then the light of Muḥammad was visible in the blaze (*ghurra*) of Adam's forehead. He was told, "O Adam, that is the master of the prophets and messengers of your children." When Eve conceived Seth, [the light] was transferred from Adam to Eve; she used to give birth to two children at a time except for Seth, whom she bore singly in honor of Muḥammad. Then [the light] continued to be transferred from one pure person to another until [the Prophet Muḥammad] was born.[81]

The commonalities among the sources suggest that the basic outline and much of the concrete wording of a fairly standard narrative about the Light of Muḥammad and its migration up to his birth was in circulation at least by the end of the third-century AH/ninth-century CE, the date of al-Fārisī's citation from al-Bakrī. Given that al-Bakrī draws on a narrative already attributed to Ka'b al-Aḥbār, it seems reasonable to assume that the Ka'b narrative pre-existed the authorial activity of al-Bakrī. If al-Bakrī indeed composed his work before the end of the third-century AH/ninth-century CE, as suggested by its citation in the work of al-Fārisī, the Ka'b narrative may be very old indeed. What were the origins of this narrative? Its introduction has an esoteric tone that perhaps suggests Shī'ite provenance, but even as presented in the *Ithbāt*, it is strikingly lacking in explicitly Shī'ite content. It may be either that the storyteller sought to please the widest possible audience or that, below the scholarly level, sectarian doctrinal issues were submerged in the general veneration of the Prophet and his family.

Over time and in specific contexts, various episodes of the story could be co-opted to contrasting sectarian agendas. In one widespread elaboration of the story of Adam, God places the Light of Muḥammad in Adam's back (*ẓahr*, also meaning "loins"). When the angels mass behind him to venerate the light, Adam asks God to transfer it so that they will stand before him. God places the light in his forehead, but Adam is still not satisfied; he asks that it be placed where he can see it. God places the light in his index finger; he places the residual light from Adam's back in the remaining fingers of his hand. In the Sunnī rendition transmitted by Ibn al-Ḥājj (d. 737 AH/1336 CE), God "placed the light of Abū Bakr in the middle finger, the light of 'Umar in the ring finger, the light of 'Uthmān in the little finger and the light of 'Alī in the thumb."[82] The motif of the light of the first four caliphs being placed in Adam's fingers also appears in the seventh-century AH/thirteenth-century CE Andalusian scholar al-Qurṭubī's *mawlid* work *al-I'lām bi-mā yajib 'alā al-anām . . .*, where an almost identical narrative is attributed to Ka'b al-Aḥbār (without any other *isnād*).[83] Unsurprisingly, in Shī'ite sources the lights placed in Adam's fingers correspond to 'Alī, Fāṭima, Ḥasan, and Ḥusayn.[84]

Another early manifestation of the "white handful" tradition suggests a second context in which the narrative might have been circulated and developed. In his *'Arā'is al-majālis*, al-Tha'labī (d. 427 AH/1035 CE) presents a version attributed simply to "the [Qur'ānic] exegetes (*al-mufassirūn*)." Rather than finding its place within the larger narrative of the migration of the Prophet's primordial light, the "white handful" is here incorporated into the frame story of the creation of Adam. The narrative begins when God informs the earth that He is about to make from it beings, some of whom will obey Him and some of whom will disobey Him; those who obey will enter heaven, and those who disobey will enter hell. Then He sends Gabriel to bring a handful of earth, but the earth does not want to yield a piece of itself, some of which will burn in hell. The same thing happens when God sends Michael. Finally, God sends the angel of death, who takes the handful despite the earth's protests. The angel of death collects different qualities and colors of dust from all corners of the earth, which is why the children of Adam are of all kinds.

> Then the angel of death brought it up to God; He commanded him to make it into mud and ferment it. He kneaded it with brackish, sweet and salty water until he made it into mud, and he let it ferment. For this reason the characters [of the children of Adam] varied. Then [God] commanded Gabriel to bring him the white handful that is the heart, the radiance and the light of the earth in order to create from it Muḥammad. So Gabriel descended among the archangels of paradise who are drawn close [to the divine Presence] and the angels of the highest level and took a handful [of earth] from the site of the Prophet's grave, which at that time was white and pure. It was kneaded with the water of Tasnīm and swelled until it was like a white pearl. Then it was immersed in all of the rivers of paradise. When it emerged from the rivers, the Truth looked at that pure pearl and it trembled with the fear of God; 124,000 drops fell from it, and God created a prophet out of every drop. Thus, all of the prophets were created from the light of [Muḥammad]. Then it was carried around the heavens and the earth, and then the angels knew Muḥammad before they knew Adam. Then [God] kneaded it with the clay of Adam, then left it for forty years until it became sticky, soft clay (*ṭīnan lāziban layyinan*, cf. Qur'ān 37:11). Then he left it for forth [more] years

> until it became "ringing like earthenware" (*ṣalṣāl ka'l-fakhkhār* – Qur'ān 55:14) – that is, dry clay that resounds if you hit it with your hand.[85]

This version of the story appears as an example of aggadic exegesis, with passages of the narrative pegged on specific Qur'ānic references or vocabulary. For instance, the story about the creation of Adam from variegated dust gathered from the four corners of the world is linked to verse 30:22 ("Among [God's] signs are the creation of the heavens and the earth and the variety of your languages and colors"). Given the difficulty of dating individual texts and the unlikelihood that we are in possession of all the relevant works (even excluding the oral tradition), it would be difficult to say whether narrative exegesis is the "original" setting of the "white handful" narrative. Regardless of the origins of the "white handful" motif or of the distinctive literary form in which it seems to have crystallized, it was obviously a widely known component of the narrative tradition that could be integrated into the broader Islamic creation narrative in more than one fashion.

The Ka'b narrative is related not merely to other cosmogonic narratives, however. Through the figure of Ka'b, it is also linked to other elements of a rich and early Islamic storytelling tradition. Ka'b, a Jew who was a contemporary of the Prophet Muḥammad but (in the eyes of later Muslims) mysteriously failed to embrace Islam until after the latter's death, was widely believed to be the repository of a wide range of esoteric knowledge. An irresistible narrative hook for speculation about his arcane knowledge and the reasons for his late conversion is supplied by a very early and authoritative source, the *Kitāb al-ṭabaqāt al-kubrā* of Ibn Sa'd (d. 230 AH/845 CE). In his brief biographical entry on Ka'b, Ibn Sa'd recounts the following tale:

> Ibn 'Abbās said to Ka'b, "What prevented you from embracing Islam in the time of the Prophet and Abū Bakr, so that you have now become a Muslim in the time of 'Umar?" Ka'b said, "My father wrote me a book from the Torah and delivered it to me; he said, 'Follow this!' He sealed the rest of his books and took an oath from me by a son's duty to his father that I would not break the seal. When this time came, and I saw that Islam had appeared and I did not think it did any harm, I said to myself, 'Perhaps your father concealed from you some knowledge and kept it from you; what if you were to read it?' So I broke the seal and read it, and I found in it a description of Muḥammad and his community. So now I have come as a Muslim."[86]

This narrative offered an alluring opportunity to speculate about the exact content of the wonderful document Ka'b's father strove to conceal, and medieval sources confirm that this opportunity was richly exploited by generations of storytellers.[87] The story of Ka'b and the mysterious sealed document bequeathed by his father is in turn mirrored in the story of Bulūqiyā, an Israelite prince whose story is separately recounted by Kharkūshī,[88] and whose wonder-laden tale was immortalized in the *Arabian Nights*.[89] Steven Wasserstrom has masterfully illustrated the fruitful interplay between the Bulūqiyā narrative and the cycle of tales revolving around the Jewish convert ‘Abd Allāh ibn Salām, which ultimately “developed into the Masā’il literature, a question-and-answer genre in which Muhammad answers dozens of questions put to him by ‘Abdallah.”[90]

The precise origin of the narrative of the “white handful” is probably unrecoverable, if indeed it had a single original author. It may have originated in Shī‘ite circles, ultimately circulating across sectarian lines and attracting Sunnī adaptations. It may have been generated by the activities of unaligned storytellers, only later to be appropriated and adapted by both Sunnī and Shī‘ite sectarian interests. Alternatively, it may have originated in exegetical circles, and originally served to amplify and embellish Qur’ānic language about the creation of Adam from dust and the ethnic and moral variety of humankind. It may also have been generated by fascination with the occult rabbinic lore supposedly transmitted by Ka‘b. In the absence of unambiguous textual evidence, however (and our textual evidence for the early centuries of Islam will never be complete, even without regard for the oral storytelling tradition) it may be best to eschew the idea of separate developmental stages in the growth of the story. As Jonathan Berkey has observed, storytelling and Qur’ānic exegesis should not be considered “distinct genre[s],” whether in content or in social context.[91] Instead, we might think in terms of a fairly extensive and well-established vocabulary of narrative and verbal motifs associated with the story of the origins of the Prophet Muḥammad. Key phrases such as “white handful,” “kneaded with the water of Tasnīm,” and “carried around the heavens and the earth” formed the identifying features of a fairly well-defined story that could yet be modified and embellished with each new rendition of the tale.

While we may never be able to trace the development of the Ka‘b narrative in detail, the combination of uniformity and improvisation displayed by the sources’ different versions of the narrative suggests certain things about the process of storytelling. On the one hand, this narrative clearly was neither scrupulously copied from one written text to another, nor memorized verbatim, as *ḥadīth* were by this point in Islamic history. Variations in the selection and elaboration of episodes between texts such as al-Kharkūshī’s *Sharaf al-muṣṭafā* and *Ithbāt al-waṣīya* suggest a fairly high degree of flexibility in the rendition of the story. There must have been room for the narrative skill and artful selectivity of the individual storyteller. On the other hand, the degree of consistency in the various renditions of the tale suggests that the story carried a certain integrity of its own. It was not a narrative that could be whimsically altered, but one whose basic lineaments and distinctive verbal keys remained constant over a period of centuries. Its basic stability probably reflects one or both of two causes. One possible explanation is that the story retained its basic narrative content and verbal features because its tellers considered it true; it was not subject to serious alteration because it was, in some sense, authoritative. Another possibility is that, for its audience (and thus in the eyes of the skillful storyteller) the pleasure of the narrative lay partially in its familiarity and in the performance of a known repertory of plot points and key phrases. Although it is impossible to determine the precise influence of these two factors in the preservation of this particular narrative, it seems likely that both were in play. In the case of a central religious narrative such as the one at hand, and one that came to be performed in ceremonial contexts, it seems likely that the first option – that both listeners and tellers respected the basic lineaments of the story because they believed it to be true – played the more important role. For many Muslims of the middle ages, this probably *was* the accepted story of the genesis of their Prophet.

The narrative of Jābir

Another of the most elaborate and widespread cosmogonic narratives popularized in *mawlid* texts is associated with the name of the Prophet's Companion Jābir ibn 'Abd Allāh al-Anṣārī. In this narrative, the Light of Muḥammad is created before any of the other elements of the cosmos. After the creation of the Light, God places it within a series of divine veils (*ḥijāb*), each of which is associated with a specific divine attribute or spiritual state. The Light sojourns in each of these veils for thousands of years, uttering a pious invocation specific to that veil. God then divides the Light of Muḥammad into portions, creating from each portion an element of the cosmos; in each case, the final portion is further subdivided to create successive components of the world. This narrative is probably less old than the Ka'b narrative, although the chronological point of origin of each story cannot be determined with precision. Unlike the Ka'b narrative, which describes the creation of the Prophet against the background of an already created earth and an audience of angels, the Jābir narrative regards the Light of Muḥammad as the primordial substance of all creation. As it seems likely that the scenario in which the pre-creation of the Prophet roughly coincided with that of Adam preceded the scenario in which the Prophet was created before anything else, so the Jābir narrative may represent a somewhat later stage in the development of popular cosmology.

The earliest occurrence of this narrative in the literary sources appears to be in Kharkūshī's *Sharaf al-muṣṭafā*; it is brief, and is presented anonymously.[92] Early in the development of formal Sunnī *mawlid* texts, however, the narrative seems to have crystallized in a very consistent form and become attached to the name of Jābir. The *mawlid* attributed to Muḥyī al-Dīn Ibn al-'Arabī (d. 638 AH/1240 CE) includes a very long version of the Jābir tradition.[93] Extremely close parallels appear in the *Muntaqā* al-Kāzarūnī and in the *Ta'rīkh al-khamīṣ fī aḥwāl anfas al-nafīs* of Ḥusayn ibn Muḥammad al-Diyārbakrī (d. ca. 966 AH/1559 CE).[94] A more divergent version of the text, attributed to Ka'b al-Aḥbār rather than to Jābir, appears in a *mawlid* sermon by the Egyptian *ṣūfī* Shaykh al-Ḥurayfīsh (d. 801 AH/1398–9 CE).[95] The narrative runs as follows:

> From Jābir ibn 'Abd Allāh al-Anṣārī: I asked the Messenger of God about the first thing God created. He said, "It is the light of your Prophet, Jābir. He created it, then created every good thing from it, and after that He created everything [else].[96] When He created it He made it stand before Him in the station of closeness (*maqām al-qurb*) for twelve thousand years. Then He

divided it into four parts; He created the Throne from part, the Footstool from part, the bearers of the Throne from part, and the keepers of the Footstool from part. He made the fourth [part] stand in the station of love for twelve thousand years, then divided it into four parts. He created the cosmos (*al-khalq*) from part, the Tablet from part, and Paradise from part. He made the fourth part stand in the station of fear for twelve thousand years, then divided it into four parts. He created the angels from part, the sun from part, the moon and the stars from part, and made the fourth part stand in the station of hope for twelve thousand years. Then He divided it into four parts. He created the intellect from part, clemency and knowledge from part, infallibility and providence (*al-'iṣma wa'l-tawfīq*) from part. He made the fourth part stand in the station of modesty (*al-ḥayā'*) for twelve thousand years. Then He looked at it, and the light exuded sweat. 124,000 drops of light dripped from it, and God created from each drop the soul of a prophet or a messenger. Then the spirits of the prophets breathed (*tanafassat*), and God created from their breaths the light of the saints, the blessed, the martyrs, and the obedient among the believers until the Day of Resurrection. So the Throne and the Footstool are from my light, the cherubim are from my light, the spiritual ones (*al-rūḥāniyūn*) of the angels are from my light, the angels of the seven heavens are from my light, the Garden and the delights it contains are from my light, the sun, moon, and stars are from my light, the intellect, knowledge, and providence are from my light, the spirits of the prophets and the messengers are from my light, and the martyrs and the righteous are from the products of my light.

Then God created twelve veils, and made the light – that is, the fourth part – stand in each veil for a thousand years; they are the stations of servanthood (*maqāmāt al-'ubūdīya*). They are the veils of magnanimity (*karāma*), felicity (*sa'āda*), awe (*hayba*), compassion (*raḥma*), kindness (*ra'fa*), clemency (*ḥilm*), knowledge (*'ilm*), dignity (*waqār*), serenity (*sakīna*), patience (*ṣabr*), truthfulness (*ṣidq*), and certainty (*yaqīn*). That light worshiped God in each veil for a thousand years. When the light emerged from the veils, God mounted (*rakkaba*) it in the earth; it illuminated it from the east to the west like a lamp on a dark night. Then God created Adam in the earth and installed the light in him, in his forehead. Then it was transferred from him to Seth and from him to Enoch, and it continued to be transferred in this way from a pure one to a clean one until God brought it to the loins of 'Abd Allāh ibn 'Abd al-Muṭṭalib, and from him to the womb of Āmina. Then He brought me forth into the world and made me the master of the messengers, the seal of the prophets, a mercy to the worlds, and the leader of those with luminous blazes on their foreheads and extremities (*al-ghurr al-muḥajjalīn*). That is the way the creation of your prophet began, O Jābir."[97]

It is notable that this narrative shares certain key features with the accounts attributed to Sahl al-Tustarī, discussed earlier (p. 14). The succession of named stations and veils would seem to be related Tustarī's rather opaque reference to the light of Muḥammad prostrating itself within "*al-'aẓama*." Both present a multi-tiered schema in which the light of Muḥammad produces Adam and/or the other prophets, who in turn form the source for the souls of the mystics. The report has a distinctly ṣūfī tone. Its use of the word "station" (*maqām*) combines the literal meaning of "a standing place" with the mystical sense of a graded level in the hierarchy of spiritual advancement. The development of the narrative is also reflected in a version presented by Kharkūshī, which lists a similar series of "veils" where the Light of Muḥammad abides for thousands of years before the creation of the other elements of the cosmos.[98]

The three versions of the Jābir narrative examined earlier are strikingly uniform in content and wording. However, the narrative also clearly circulated in freer and more divergent renditions. al-Qasṭallānī (d. 923 AH/1517 CE), for instance, presents a version in which the fourth division of the Light produces "the light of the believers' eyes," "the light of their hearts (which is the knowledge of God)," and "the light of their tongues (which is the statement of God's unicity, 'there is no god but God, and Muḥammad is the Messenger of God')." al-Qasṭallānī describes the report as a *ḥadīth* (rather than, for instance, a *qiṣṣa*) and attributes it to 'Abd al-Razzāq.[99]

By al-Qasṭallānī's time, the narrative contained in this report must have enjoyed some degree of currency – among other things, he seems to expect his reader to be sufficiently familiar with the report that it is unnecessary to cite it in its entirety. However, it was not a uniform text consistently associated with a specific source, nor did it receive the approval of other scholarly authorities. In his *fatāwā*, al-Qasṭallānī's contemporary Jalāl al-Dīn al-Suyūṭī (d. 911 AH/1505 CE) responds to a questioner who enquires (among other things) about "what is reported in the *ḥadīth* that God created the Light of Muḥammad and divided it into four parts, then created the Throne from the first part, the Pen from the second part, and the Tablet from the third part; then divided the fourth part into four, and created the intellect from the first part, knowledge from the second part, the light of the sun, the moon, and vision from the third part, and stored up the fourth part under the leg of the Throne." With respect to this part of the enquiry, al-Suyūṭī responds tersely that "the *ḥadīth* mentioned in the question has no reliable chain of transmission (*laysa lahu isnād yu'tamad 'alayhi*)."[100] At least in this divergent and simplified form, al-Suyūṭī does not consider the narrative a documented *ḥadīth* at all.

The theme of the creation of all elements of the cosmos from the Light of Muḥammad is sometimes combined with another motif, that of the divine gaze, which agitates or liquefies its object or causes it to exude a creative sweat. This motif seems to have been in circulation by the seventh-century AH among popular storytellers, independently of a formal tradition attributed to Jābir. One of the *fatāwā* of Ibn Taymīya responds to a long query from questioners who are concerned with the material being circulated by storytellers (*qāṣṣāṣīn*) who ply their trade "at the foot of the Citadel and in the markets and mosques." They provide a long list of the fantastical tales in question, which deal with the life and war campaigns (*maghāzī*) of the Prophet. The storytellers depend for their material on "books containing this type of material composed by a man known as al-Bakrī." They close their inquiry with a final example of the kind of disreputable tale in question:

> They also transmit that God took a handful (*qabḍa*) of the light of His face and looked at it; it sweated and trickled. God created a prophet from every drop, and the handful [itself] was the Prophet [Muḥammad]. There remained a pearly star (*kawkab durrī*; cf. Qur'ān 24:35) and it was a light that was transferred from the loins of men to the bellies of women.[101]

Ibn Taymīya responds that this report is "a lie, by the agreement of those knowledgeable about [the Prophet's] *ḥadīth*" (*kadhib bi'ttifāq ahl al-ma'rifa bi-ḥadīthihi*).[102]

Yet another permutation of this motif is provided in some forms of the *mawlid* text apocryphally attributed to Ibn al-Jawzī, whose dating and attribution will be discussed later:

> Then [God] took a handful (*qabḍa*) of His light and said to it, "Be My beloved, Muḥammad" – and it was. It circumambulated the Throne for seventy thousand years glorifying God. Then [God] looked at the handful with the eye of majesty and might (*al-hayba wa'l-'aẓama*); one hundred and twenty-four thousand drops dripped from it. God created from every drop a prophet; then God inspired them to circumambulate the Throne, saying, "Glory to the Knower, Who is never ignorant! Glory to the Generous, Who is never stingy! Glory to the Clement, Who is never hasty! (*Subḥān al-'ālim al-ladhī lam yajhal*! *Subḥān al-jawād al-ladhī lam yabkhal*! *Subḥān al-ḥalīm al-ladhī lā ya'jal*!)" Then God commanded that handful to split into two halves. He looked at the first half with the eye of majesty and looked at the second half with the eye of compassion. The half which He looked at with the eye of majesty and might became running water; it is the water of the oceans, which never sleeps and never subsides out of fear of God. As for the half which He looked at with the eye of compassion, God created from it four things.[103]

These narrative elements could be recombined and rephrased in a number of ways; Kharkūshī's version of the Jābir narrative, for instance, presents a different permutation of many of the same narrative elements (creation of the light, circumambulation, prostration, uttering of invocations, creation of water from the light).[104] The mobility and versatility of the story's component motifs are suggested by a report presented without attribution of any sort by al-Kāzarūnī:

> It is said that [the Prophet's] spirit (*rūḥ*) was like a white bird below the sea of compassion, which is beneath the Throne. It was immersed in it for four thousand years, pronouncing four glorifications (*tasbīḥāt*): "Glory to the

> Knower, Who is never ignorant! Glory to the Powerful, Who never passes away! Glory to the Generous, Who is never stingy! Glory to the Clement, Who is never hasty!" When it emerged from the sea, it had 24,000 wings.[105] A drop dropped from each wing, and a prophet was created from that drop; God created from them the spirits of all of the prophets. That is [the meaning of] God's statement, "Then We bequeathed the Book" (Qur'ān 35:32) – that is, after We made your spirit the substance of the spirits of the prophets, We bequeathed the Book. It is [also] said that when his light arose from [the sea] it breathed 24,000 times minus one (*ghayr wāḥida*); the spirits of the prophets were from his breath. Then the spirits of the prophets breathed, and the spirits of the righteous ones (*al-ṣiddīqīn*) was from their breath; similarly, the spirits of the righteous ones [gave rise to] the ascetics (*al-zāhidīn*), then the spirits of the obedient ones, then the spirits of the disobedient. It is for this reason that the obedient loves the disobedient, and all of them love the Prophet. Then God divided that mud (*ṭīn*) into four; he created from one [portion] the sun, from the second the column (*al-'amūd*), from the third the moon, and from the fourth a lamp (*qindīl*); He attached to it the chains of subsistence, giving, and meeting (*al-baqā' wa'l-'aṭā' wa'l-liqā'*); annihiliation (*al-fanā'*) dropped from the peg of concern (*watad al-'ināya*), and a drop fell from it. [God] commanded Gabriel to take up that drop with the dust upon which it fell, and that was [the Prophet's] mud. Then God made it pass from loins to loins and from belly to belly; [this is the meaning of God's] statement "and your passing among those who prostrate themselves" (*wa-taqallubuka fī 'l-sājidīn*, Qur'ān 26:219).[106]

Comparison of the many versions of the narrative in which God creates the various elements of the cosmos from the Light of Muḥammad brings to mind Peter Burke's observation that "in oral tradition, . . . the same text is different, and different texts are the same."[107] That is, the "same" narrative can vary in different renditions or performances, while "different" narratives share common schemas and motifs. In the case of the Jābir narrative, of course, sometimes the same narrative is the same; in the versions recorded by Ibn al-'Arabī, al-Kāzarūnī, and al-Diyārbakrī, the story has taken on the fixity of a semi-canonized literary text. Compared with other variants, such as that in the *fatwā* of al-Suyūṭī, however, the "same" story presents an inextricable blend of uniformity and difference. A number of identifying features, some or all of which many be present in any given rendition (from the attribution to Jābir to the pearl, the divine gaze, the division into four, the creation of different components of the cosmos, and the veils) give the story an enduring consistency and render it recognizable from one rendition to the next. Nevertheless, the various constituent elements shift and morph. Not all of the typical components occur in all versions of the story, and many of them also appear in versions of "other" narratives.

It would be almost impossible to say whether al-Kāzarūnī's "white bird" narrative is a version of the "same" story as that presented by Ibn al-'Arabī, or simply a "different" narrative. It is linked to what we may term the "Jābir complex" by a number of different elements. The creation of the spirits of the prophets from the thousands of drops dripping from the Prophet is a common element, as is the idea of the creation of the spirits of prophets and saints from breaths. The two-tiered pattern in which the prophets are created from drops emanating from Muḥammad, while the saints are created from the breaths of the prophets, goes back to Ibn al-ʻArabī (and before him to Sahl al-Tustarī). The motif of division into four and the creation of different elements of the cosmos from the individual parts links the story with the Jābir narrative. Finally, as in the case of the Jābir narrative, the story ends with an account of the Prophet's essence (in this case, a drop rather than a light) passing from one to another of his ancestors. The series of invocations pronounced by the Prophet's spirit in this text is shared with the two preceding narratives about the Light of Muḥammad, but is not found in the Jābir narrative. The images of the "white bird" and the lamp are completely new.

The various versions of the Jābir report are part of a larger narrative complex about the events of creation that is not always associated either with the name of Jābir or with the idea of the pre-existence of the Prophet Muḥammad. Distinctive keywords and narrative elements link the Jābir traditions, for instance, with the creation narratives presented in the *Qiṣaṣ al-anbiyā'* of al-Kisā'ī.[108] The different stories share a common repertoire of keywords and narrative elements, as well as an overall vision of the events of creation that is far more physically concrete and far more fraught with mythic incident than anything suggested by the text of the Qur'ān.

The Prophet's conception and Āmina's pregnancy

As we have seen, the date of the Prophet's conception was cited by Ibn Bābawayh as an appropriate occasion for religious commemoration. The religious importance accorded to the Prophet's conception is reflected in the attention focused on this event in *mawlid* narratives. Interest in the subject seems to have emerged quite early. al-Qurṭubī and al-Qasṭallānī both cite the following report, which they state is transmitted from Sahl al-Tustarī by the traditionist al-Khaṭīb al-Baghdādī (d. 463 AH/1071 CE):

> When God willed to create Muḥammad in Āmina's belly on the night of Rajab, which was a Friday night, on that night God commanded Riḍwān, the keeper of the Gardens (*khāzin al-jinān*), to open paradise. A voice called out in the heavens and the earth, "Indeed, the stored and concealed light from which the Guiding Prophet will be made will come to rest this night in the belly of Āmina, where its formation will be completed, and he will come out as a bearer of glad tidings and a warner to the people."[109]

Another widespread narrative motif associated with the Prophet's conception deals with the impotent rage of Iblīs (Satan), who is cast into despair by the event. Iblīs gathers all of the devils together and proclaims to them the end of their dominion over humankind. A dialogue ensues, in which the devils insist that it will still be possible to lead people to perdition despite the advent of the Prophet, while Iblīs retorts that the community of Muḥammad will be very difficult to beguile. Finally, the devils propose that they will subvert the resolve of the believers through their own vain desires, and Iblīs is comforted.[110]

The events surrounding the Prophet's conception clearly formed part of the Ka'b narrative, although it does not seem to have included either of the two episodes cited earlier. The Ka'b narrative translated in the Toledo corpus recounts that God commanded that the gates of heaven be opened "in order that I may transfer the light of My messenger from the loins of 'Abd Allāh into the womb of Āmina."[111] al-Qasṭallānī cites a passage from "the transmission of Ka'b" recounting that a heavenly voice proclaimed the news of the Prophet's conception throughout the earth, idols toppled, and the drought that had afflicted Quraysh was replaced with fruitfulness and plenty.[112] The Ka'b narrative was not the only one that covered these events, however; al-Kāzarūnī presents this dialogue in the context of a longer narrative transmitted from the Prophet's uncle, al-'Abbās, through the latter's son 'Abd Allāh. Unlike other narratives (which often imply that the Prophet was conceived on his parents' wedding night), this story recounts that God does not permit the light to be transferred to Āmina's womb for a number of years. This variation, while historically unorthodox, suggests that the appeals of narrative tension could justify slight deviations from the accepted course of events. Meanwhile, divine guidance and the memory of prophecy perish from the earth; human beings are enmired in oppression and the worship of idols. God then sends the angels down to observe the condition of the earth. They find the earth denuded of her beauty and lamenting her desolate state. She implores God to fulfill His promise by sending a light after which there will be no darkness, and the best community sent to humankind. "O Lord!" she cries, "fill me with the light of his remembrance, and bring him onto me quickly!" God sends Gabriel to give her the glad tidings of Muḥammad's conception. The earth quiets herself and trembles with joy. Muḥammad is born, and an elaborate version of the dialogue between Iblīs and the devils ensues.[113]

Also attributed to Ibn 'Abbās is another widespread account of the wonders accompanying the Prophet's conception, one which was stabilized in the literary tradition and became widely known. There are enough preserved fragments of narrative to suggest that there may at one time have been a complete Ibn 'Abbās *mawlid* narrative, analogous to that associated with Ka'b al-Aḥbār. The Ibn 'Abbās account of the Prophet's conception is presented as a continuation of the Ka'b narrative by al-Kharkūshī (with a reference to Ibn 'Abbās, but without an *isnād*); it is also presented, with a full *isnād* to Ibn 'Abbās, by the traditionist and *ṣūfī* Abū Nu'aym al-Iṣfahānī (d. 430 AH/1038 CE).

> One of the signs (*dalālāt*) of the conception of the Prophet is that every domestic animal (*dābba*) belonging to Quraysh spoke on that night and said, "The Messenger of God has been conceived, by the Lord of the Ka'ba; he is the security of this world and the lamp of those who dwell in it." There was no priestess (*kāhina*) of Quraysh or of any tribe of the Arabs but that she was

separated from her familiar spirit (*ṣāḥibatihā*) and the art of soothsaying was withdrawn from her. There was no throne of any king in the world but that it was toppled and the king struck mute, not speaking all that day. The beasts of the east went to the beasts of the west with the glad tidings; likewise, the denizens of the sea congratulated each other. Each month that he [was in the womb], there was a proclamation (*nidā'*) on the earth and a proclamation in heaven saying, "Be of good tidings! The time has come for Abū'l-Qāsim to come forth to the world, auspicious and blessed." His mother used to speak of herself, saying: When six months of my pregnancy with him had passed, a being came to me (*atānī āt*), struck me with his foot as I slept, and said: "O Āmina, you are pregnant with the best of all beings in the universe. When you give birth to him, call him Muḥammad and tell no one about your situation."[114]

Popular narratives surrounded not only the Prophet's conception, but his mother's pregnancy with an aura of the supernatural. The idea that Āmina had a visionary experience during her pregnancy with the Prophet long precedes the emergence of the *mawlid* tradition, and is rooted in early classical sources. The *sīra* of Ibn Hishām (d. 213 AH/828 CE) recounts,

> They claim – among the things that people recount – and God knows best – that Āmina bint Wahb, the mother of the Messenger of God used to report that when she became pregnant with the Messenger of God [a being] came to her and said to her, "You have conceived the master of this community; when he falls to the earth, say, 'I commend him to the protection of the One, from the evil of every envier' (*u'īdhuhu bi'l-wāḥid min sharr kull ḥāsid*); then name him Muḥammad." When she became pregnant with him she saw that a light came forth from her by which she saw the castles of Buṣrā in the land of Syria.[115]

It is notable that the historian's attitude toward this report is dubious in the extreme.[116] His introductory remarks suggest that it is a report in popular circulation, rather than a text enjoying credence in strictly scholarly circles. Given the lack of a formal *isnād*, it seems safe to assume that in this case, "*mā yataḥaddath al-nās*" refers to the story's currency among the public at large, rather than to the scholarly transmission of *ḥadīth*. It is significant that the content of the report is a powerful protective formula, simple yet incantatory, which is delivered to Āmina by an unidentified and yet clearly supernatural agent. Its generic applicability to the protection of any infant suggests that it is offered to the listener as a useful charm to be repeated in everyday life.

The idea that this anecdote responded to the religious needs of ordinary people is reinforced by the fact that it was extensively reworked and elaborated over time, although these embellishments garnered little respect from scholars.[117] The text begins identically, but proceeds into a longer and more inscrutable series of invocations. The value of this version clearly lies in the mysterious nature of the formulae, which evoke the *saj'* of the Arabian soothsayer. Abū Nu'aym presents the following extended version of the report:

> Āmina bint Wahb, the mother of the Prophet, dreamed that someone said to her, "You have conceived the best of humankind and the master of the worlds; when you give birth to him, call Aḥmad and Muḥammad, and hang this on him." Then she awoke, and by her head there was a sheet of gold on which was written: "I commend him to the protection of the One, from the evil of every envier / And every prowling thing, standing or lying / Deviating from the path, striving for corruption / From a blower or a knotter, and every rebellious being / Lying in wait, on the paths to water. He forbade him to them by God Most High / And protected him from them with the uppermost hand / And the hand that is unseen / The hand of God is above their hands / And the screen of God blocks the one of them who commits aggression / They do not drive him away and do not harm him, sitting or sleeping / Walking or halting / On the first of nights and the last of days" – this four times.[118]

Not only has the protective invocation grown to an impressive length, but it is now accompanied with satisfyingly elaborate instructions for ritual use. It should not only be repeated four times, but written as an amulet and hung on the baby. The text is highly unstable; although the length and form are similar, even the version in the Ibn Kathīr's *mawlid* diverges from that in the text of *al-Bidāya wa'l-nihāya*.[119] Overall, this set of invocations gives the impression of a charm elaborated and transformed over many generations of popular use, rather than a text preserved by scholars for antiquarian purposes. This situation is reflected in the remarks of critical scholars, who felt compelled to reproduce the text despite their philological misgivings because of its prevalence in popular piety. Zayn al-Dīn al-'Irāqī (d. 806 AH/1404 CE) observes that "from the statement 'hang this on him' to the end is an interpolation by some storyteller *(ba'ḍ al-quṣṣāṣ)*." Muḥammad al-Ṣāliḥī al-Shāmī (d. 942 AH/1536 CE) states that Abū Nu'aym's chain of transmission for this report is extremely feeble; "I have mentioned it merely to call attention to it, because it is so well known in *mawlid* books."[120]

While it is impossible to determine whether these apotropaic formulae were ever in popular use among new mothers, they seem unusually well-suited to the practical religious needs of ordinary women. A response to the religiously questionable status of the practice of hanging amulets on children is reflected in a version of the report presented by al-Kāzarūnī, in which Āmina is merely instructed to pronounce the formula. Her women friends counsel her to hang amulets on herself, which mysteriously fall from her body; she then refrains from hanging amulets on her child.[121]

The Prophet's birth

The most widespread narrative about the actual birth of the Prophet is recounted in the voice of his mother, Āmina. The most authoritative and prevalent version from the point of view of the normative tradition is presented by Abū Nu'aym al-Iṣfahānī with a full *isnād* to Ibn 'Abbās:

> [Ibn 'Abbās] said: [Āmina] used to say: I began to have labor pains (lit. "there befell me what befalls women," *la-qad akhadhanī mā ya'khudhu'l-nisā'*), and no one, male or female, knew about my situation; I was alone in the house, and 'Abd al-Muṭṭalib was circumambulating [the Ka'ba]. She said: I heard a great crash and a mighty sound (*sami'tu wajba shadīda wa-amran 'aẓīman*), and it struck me with terror – that was on a Monday. I saw [a vision] as if the wing of a white bird stroked my heart, and then all the alarm, panic, and suffering that I had felt left me. Then I turned, and there was a white drink; I thought that it was milk. I was thirsty, so I took it and drank it, and a bright light radiated from me. Then I saw women like lofty palm-trees, resembling the daughters of 'Abd al-Muṭṭalib,[122] surrounding me. As I was wondering [over this] and asking myself, "Woe is me, how did these women know about me?" my labor became intense. I heard the crashing becoming louder and more fearsome all the time. Suddenly I saw a piece of white brocade stretched between the heavens and the earth, and a voice was saying (*idhā qā'il yaqūl*), "Take him where no one can see him." [Āmina] said: I saw men standing in the air, holding silver ewers in their hands; I was dropping sweat like pearls, sweeter smelling than fragrant musk. I was saying, "If only 'Abd al-Muṭṭalib had come to me" – but 'Abd al-Muṭṭalib was far away. She said: I saw a flock of birds that had come without my noticing from whence they came, until they covered my chamber. Their beaks were made of emerald and their wings of rubies. The veil was lifted from my sight (*fa-kushifa lī 'an baṣarī*) and at that moment I saw the eastern and western regions of the earth. I saw three banners raised, a banner in the east, a banner in the west, and a banner on the top of the Ka'ba. The labor pains seized me and I was in great distress. I felt as if I were leaning against the limbs of women; they became numerous, to the point that it was as if there were many hands in the house, but I did not see anything (*kuntu ka'annī mustanida ilā arkān al-nisā' wa-kathurna 'alayya ḥattā ka'anna al-aydī ma'ī fī'l-bayt wa-anā lā arā shay'an*). I gave birth to Muḥammad; when he came out of my belly I turned and looked at him, and lo and behold, I saw him prostrating himself, with his finger raised like one who was pleading and supplicating. Then I saw a white cloud that had come from the sky come down until it covered him and he was concealed from my sight; I heard a voice call out, "Take Muḥammad around the east and west of the world; take him into all of the oceans, so that they will know his name, his description, and his form, and they will know that in [the oceans] he is called '*al-Māḥī*' ('the Effacer'), because there is no polytheism but that it will be effaced by him in his time." Then [the cloud] revealed him again in the twinkling of an eye, and lo, he was clothed in a woolen robe that was whiter than milk, and underneath him was a piece of green silk. He was grasping three keys of brilliant white pearl, and a voice said, "Muḥammad has grasped the keys of victory, the keys of the wind, and the keys of prophecy."[123]

> Then another cloud, from which the whinnying of horses and the fluttering of wings could be heard, approached until it covered him and he was concealed from my sight. I heard a voice call out, "Take Muḥammad around the east and the west, and the birthplaces of the prophets; present him to every being with a spirit (*kull rūḥānī*), whether jinn, human, bird or beast. Give him the contentment (*ṣafā'*) of Adam, the tenderness (*riqqa*) of Noah, the friendship (*khulla*) of Abraham, the tongue (*lisān*) of Ishmael, the good tidings (*bushrā*) of Jacob, the beauty of Joseph, the voice of David, the patience of Job, the renunciation (*zuhd*) of John, and the magnanimity (*karam*) of Jesus. Immerse him in the moral qualities of the prophets." Suddenly a voice said, "Good! Good! Muḥammad has grasped all the world, and none of its people remain but that they have entered his grasp." Then I saw three people, in the hand of one of whom was a silver ewer, in the hand of the second a basin of green emerald, and in the hand of the third a piece of white silk. He unfolded it and took from it a seal that dazzled the eyes of its beholders. He washed it [with water] from that ewer seven times, then sealed between [Muḥammad's] shoulders with the seal and wrapped it in the silk. Then he picked him up and held him between his wings for a while, then returned him to me.[124]

Closely linked with Āmina's narrative is a continuation of the story, recounted in the voice of the Prophet's grandfather, 'Abd al-Muṭṭalib:

> It is transmitted from 'Abd al-Muṭṭalib that he said: On the night of the birth of my [grand-]son Muḥammad, I was at the Ka'ba, repairing part of the House. In the middle of the night, I suddenly saw that God's Sacred House had bent down with its four sides and prostrated itself in the Standing Place of Abraham (*maqām Ibrāhīm*). Then it straightened up as it had been before. I heard it call out loudly, "God is most great! God is most great, the Lord of Muḥammad, the Chosen One! Now my Lord God has cleansed me of the filth of the polytheists and the uncleanness of the Age of Ignorance." Then the idols collapsed like houses. It was as if I saw the greatest idol, Hubal, shattered into pieces. When I saw the House and what it did, I did not know what to say. I began to rub my eyes and say, "I'm asleep – no, I'm awake." Then I set out and fared forth to the valley of Mecca. There I saw [the hill of] al-Ṣafā' craning its neck and [the hill of] al-Marwa quaking, and I heard voices calling to me from every side, "O master of Quraysh, why do you appear fearful and anxious? Are you being chased?" I returned no answer; my only concern was to go to Āmina to see her son Muḥammad.
>
> Suddenly I saw the birds of the earth gathering around her [house], and I saw the mountains of Mecca looking down upon her [house], and I saw a white cloud over her room. When I saw that I approached the door and looked; I saw that Āmina had shut herself in. . . .[125] I knocked on the door, and she answered in a faint voice. I said, "Come quickly, and open the door!" The first thing my eye fell upon was her face, and I did not see the blaze of the Light of Muḥammad. I said, "Āmina, am I sleeping or awake?" She said,

"Awake! Why do you appear fearful and anxious? Is someone chasing you?" I said, "No, but all night I have been in a state of alarm and fear. Why is it that I do not see the light that I used to see beam from between your eyes?" She said, "I have given birth." I said, "How can that be? There is no sign of childbirth upon you, and you seem to be completely well." She said, "I have indeed given birth in the most perfect, pleasant and easy way. These birds that you see above me are trying to make me give him to them, so that they can carry him to their nests; this cloud is asking me for the same thing." 'Abd al-Muṭṭalib said, "Bring him to me, so that I can look at him." Āmina said, "You have been prevented from seeing him, because a being like a rod of silver or a lofty palm tree came to me and said to me, 'Look, Āmina; do not bring him out to any human being until three days after you have given birth to him'." 'Abd al-Muṭṭalib became angry at what she said, and said, "You will bring him out to me, or I will kill myself!" When she saw that he was in earnest, she said, "Do with him as you please. He is in that house, wrapped in a woolen garment whiter than milk, with a piece of green silk beneath him." 'Abd al-Muṭṭalib said: I went to go through the door, but before I could do so a man came to me from within it. He said, "Stop and withdraw! No human being can see him for three days, until the angels have finished their visit to him." ['Abd al-Muṭṭalib] said: My limbs trembled, and I hastened out to inform Quraysh of that. God took hold of my tongue, and I did not utter a word about it for seven days and nights.[126]

These reports may be said to constitute the most prevalent narrative of the birth of the Prophet, although they did not receive the approval of most scholars. In the later *mawlid* tradition, the narration of the events of the Prophet's birth is usually quite clearly based on these accounts. The narrative is sometimes reproduced verbatim, but also seems to have been retold with variant wording and some rearrangement of the component parts. Abū Nu'aym's canonization of the text clearly did not freeze the storytelling process. A paraphrase of the story by Muḥammad ibn Qāsim al-Raṣṣā' (d. 894 AH/1489 CE) illustrates both the stability of the narrative and the artistic latitude that storytellers enjoyed with respect to its details; for instance, the sequencing diverges from al-Bayhaqī's version and there are many discrepancies of detail (e.g., the keys grasped by the newborn infant are of emerald rather than pearl, and the second key is the "key of remembrance," *miftāḥ al-dhikr*). al-Raṣṣā' describes the wonders recounted by 'Abd al-Muṭṭalib as a "lengthy tale" (*qiṣṣa ṭawīla*), suggesting both the extensiveness of the material in circulation and its context in a storytelling milieu.[127]

One major area in which the narrative was embellished was the motif of the mysterious women who appear when Āmina goes into labor. Mentioned only in passing in the narrative presented by al-Bayhaqī, the women play a much more colorful role in other renditions of the tale. In the earliest manuscript of al-Bakrī, their musklike scent and lovely garments are described, and each one advances in turn to present glad tidings of Muḥammad's exalted station to his laboring mother.[128] Later works elaborate the motif even further, identifying each of the women as a figure from the sacred past. A *mawlid* entitled *Sharaf al-ʿālamayn* and attributed to Nūr al-Dīn ʿAlī ibn Nāṣir al-Shāfiʿī al-Ashʿarī al-Makkī (d. 915 AH/1509 CE) recounts the story as follows:

> When it was the twelfth night of the month of Rabīʿ al-Awwal I felt that the one who was in my belly wanted to come out; I began to cry, because I was alone in the house and no one was with me. I looked into the corner of the house; four women had appeared from it, tall, resembling moons, wearing white wrappers, emanating perfume from their bodies. I said to them, "Who are you whom God has bestowed upon me in my loneliness and by whom He has relieved my distress?" The first said, "I am Maryam the daughter of ʿImrān; the one who is to your left is Sarah the wife of Abraham; the one who calls to you from behind you is Hājar the mother of Ismāʿīl, the Sacrificed; the one who is in front of you is Āsiya the daughter of Muzāḥim, the wife of Pharaoh." I was cheered by their presence and rejoiced greatly. The first one came forward and said, "Be of good tidings, Āmina; who is like you? You are bearing the master of the people of earth and heaven, the lamp of this world, the seal of the prophets, the Beloved, the Chosen One (*al-muṣṭafā*)!" Then she sat down to my right. Then the second one came forward and said, "Who is like you, O Āmina? You are carrying the supreme Beloved, the one who is empowered to intercede for humanity on the Morrow (*al-mushaffaʿ fī'l-khalq ghadan*), the best who ever trod on soil or gravel!" Then the third one came forward and said, "O Āmina, we congratulate you on the master of humankind, the pride of Rabīʿa and Muḍar, for whom the moon will be split in two and trees and stones will speak!" Then the fourth one came forward – she was the greatest of them in majesty and the most glorious – and called, "O Āmina, who is like you; you have been honored with the one sent with virtues and exploits, possessor of miracles and great deeds!" Then she sat before me and said, "Lean yourself on me and bend all of yourself towards me."[129]

In a sermon by the Egyptian *ṣūfī* preacher al-Ḥurayfīsh (d. 801 AH/1398–9 CE), the scene is further dramatized. Alone in the house as her labor pains increase, Āmina recounts, "I extended the hand of entreaty to the One from whom nothing is concealed, and suddenly, there was the comforting sister, Pharaoh's wife Āsiya. Then I saw a light that illuminated the place, and lo and behold, it was Maryam the daughter of ʿImrān." When the baby is born, Āsiya hastens to apply kohl to his eyes, but finds them already adorned; Maryam wants to cut his umbilical cord, but finds it already cut.[130]

Other versions expand on the theme of Āmina's initial loneliness. An anonymous *mawlid* manuscript preserved in Cairo explains her lack of aid (familiar from the narratives in *Ithbāt al-waṣīya*, *Sharaf al-Nabī*, and *Rawḍat al-wāʿiẓīn*) by the fact that ʿAbd al-Muṭṭalib was at the Kaʿba:

> Āmina said, "It was a moonlit night without darkness; ʿAbd al-Muṭṭalib had taken his children and set out for the Sanctuary (*al-ḥaram*) to repair those of

its walls that had fallen down. No one, whether female or male, remained with me. I wept at my loneliness and said, 'Alas, how lonely I am! There is no woman to assist me, no friend to keep me company, no maidservant to support me!' "[131]

The ways in which the story could be molded and embellished by a skilled storyteller are best illustrated by the pseudo-Wāqidī narrative. Here the narrator dramatizes the situation by linking Āmina's isolation with her recent widowhood.

> al-Wāqidī said: When the Messenger of God had [been in the womb for] a full nine months, the Messenger of God's mother looked to her mother Birra and said, "Mother, I wish to enter the house to weep for my husband for a time, and shed tears for his youth and the beauty of his face; when I enter the house, let no one enter after me." Birra said to her, "Enter, Āmina, and weep; you are entitled to weep." So Āmina entered the house alone, sat, and wept. Before her was a burning candle, and in her hand was a spindle of ebony; on her spindle was a piece of red carnelian. Āmina was weeping and lamenting (*tanūḥ*) when she felt birth pangs; she got up and went to the door to open it, but it would not open. So she returned to her place and said, "Alas, how lonely I am (*wā-waḥdatāh*)!" She was seized by birth pangs and went into labor. Before she knew it, the roof split open and four houris descended from above; the house was illuminated by the light of their faces, and they said to Āmina, "Don't be afraid, girl (*jāriya*)! We have come to serve you, so don't worry about yourself." The houris sat down, one to her right, one to her left, one in front of her, and one behind her. Āmina nodded off and dozed a bit.[132]

The themes of Āmina's loneliness at the Prophet's birth and of the four "heavenly handmaidens," each of whom is identified as a great woman from salvation history, do not seem to be rooted in the reports on the subject accepted by Sunnī textual scholarship. Indeed, relevant reports suggest that Āmina was attended in her labor by human kinswomen.[133] The prototype for the narrative that was circulated and elaborated in later Sunnī *mawlid* works seems to be an Imāmī tradition about the birth of Fāṭima. In his *Āmālī*, Ibn Bābawayh presents a lengthy narrative about the birth of Fāṭima transmitted from Ja'far al-Ṣādiq; it will be remembered that he is also credited with a work entitled *Mawlid Fāṭima*. It recounts that after Khadīja marries Muḥammad she is ostracized by the women of Mecca. When the time comes for her to give birth, she sends word to the women of Quraysh to come and "do what women do for women." They send back the scornful retort that "you disobeyed us, did not accept our advice, and married Muḥammad the orphan of Abū Ṭālib, a poor man with no money. We will not come, and we will not do anything for you." Khadīja is depressed by this response, but suddenly "there came in to her four women, dark-skinned and tall like the women of Banū Hashim." She is alarmed, but one of them says, "Do not grieve, Khadīja; we are emissaries of your Lord (*rusul rabbiki*), and your sisters. I am Sarah; this is Āsiya bint Muzāḥim, who is your companion (*rafīqatuki*) in paradise; this is Maryam bint ‘Imrān, and this is Kulthum the sister of Mūsā ibn ‘Imrān. God has sent us to you to do what women do for women.” One of them sat to her right, another to her left, the third in front of her and the fourth behind her, and she gave birth to Fāṭima.[134]

The elaboration of the story of the “heavenly handmaidens” within the Shī‘ite tradition is apparent from a narrative about the birth of ‘Alī, which may also have been disseminated by Ibn Bābawayh:

> When a third of the night had passed, Fāṭima [bint Asad] went into labor (*akhadhat Fāṭima mā ya’khudhu al-nisā’ ‘inda al-wilāda*). [Abū Ṭālib said:] I said to her, “What is the matter with you, O queen of women (*sayyidat al-nisā’*)?” She said, “I feel a burning (*wahaj*).” I recited over her the name in which there is salvation (*qara’tu ‘alayhā al-ism al-ladhī fīhi al-najāt*), and she became quiet. I said to her, “I will go and get you some of your women friends to help you with your situation tonight.” She said, “Whatever you think is best, Abū Ṭālib.” When I got up to do that, suddenly a mysterious voice (*hātif*) cried out from the corner of the house, saying, “Stop, Abū Ṭālib; the intimate friend (*walī*) of God cannot be touched by an unclean hand (*yad najisa*)!” Suddenly I saw four women coming in to [Fāṭima’s] presence, wearing clothes that looked like white silk; their scent was more pleasant than fragrant musk. They said to her, “Peace upon you, O close friend (*walīya*) of God!” She responded to them. Then they sat in front of her; they had with them a covered vessel (*ju’na*) of silver. They kept her company until the Commander of the Faithful was born.

‘Alī prostrates himself and pronounces the three-fold confession of faith.

> Then one of them took him from the ground and placed him in her lap. When ‘Alī looked into her face he addressed her with an eloquent and articulate tongue, “Peace upon you, mother!” She said, “And upon you, son!” He said, “How is my father?” She said, “He is turning in God’s blessings and enjoying His company (*fī ni‘am allāh yanqalib wa-ṣuḥbatihi yatana“am*).” When I heard that I could not restrain myself from saying, “Son, am I not your father?” He said, “Yes, but I and you are both from the loins of Adam, and this is my mother Eve.” When I heard that, I covered my head with my cloak and cast myself into the corner of the house out of shyness of her. Then another [woman] approached, carrying a covered vessel, and took ‘Alī. When he looked into her face he said, “Peace upon you, sister!” She said, “And upon you, brother!” He said, “How is my uncle?” She said, “He is well, and sends you his greetings.” I said, “Son, what sister and what uncle are these?” He said, “This is Maryam the daughter of ‘Imrān, and my uncle is ‘Īsā the son of Maryam.” She perfumed him with perfume from the vessel. . . . Then the women disappeared and I saw them no more. I said to myself, “If only I knew who the other two women were!” God inspired ‘Alī and he said, “Father, as for the first woman, she was Eve; as for the one who held me in

her arms, she was Maryam bint ʿImrān, who kept herself chaste; as for the one who wrapped me in the garment, she was Āsiya bint Muzāḥim, and as for the one with the covered vessel, she was the mother of Mūsā ibn ʿImrān."[135]

Compared with most of the other narratives discussed here, the story of the "heavenly handmaidens" remains strikingly fluid. Even different versions that parallel each other very closely display differences in wording and sequencing that suggest that they are rather loose and extemporaneous renditions of the same basic story. Details accumulate over time; the identification of the individual women, for instance, seems to be an embellishment that was borrowed from the Shīʿite tradition about Fāṭima sometime after the development of the *mawlid* genre. New elements continue to emerge; for instance, in a modern rendition of the story appearing in a work by Aḥmad Zaynī Daḥlān (d. 1304 AH/1886 CE), Āmina recounts how the second woman (apparently Maryam) "rubbed my belly with her hand and said, 'In the name of God, come out with the permission of God!' "[136] Perhaps most strikingly, other than its attribution to Āmina the story of the "heavenly handmaidens" seems never to be supplied with an *isnād* (no matter how bad) or cited from a specific author (no matter how disreputable).[137] The story seems to have been (so to speak) in the public domain, freely reframed and retold by generations of storytellers. While we will never know the identity of the storytellers who elaborated the story or of the audiences to whom it was intended, it seems extremely plausible that it may have particularly appealed to women. From its touching depiction of Āmina's loneliness and apprehension to its comforting image of female solidarity, in which heavenly matriarchs arrive to surround the new mother and physically support her, it seems calculated to please an audience for whom the terrors of childbirth may have been all too familiar. Similar to the amulet text discussed earlier, the image of a heavenly midwife rubbing Āmina's belly and pronouncing a simple invocation for God's help in the emergence of the baby suggests an immediate practical application for a fraught moment in ordinary women's lives.

The story of Saṭīḥ

Another strand of narrative recounts the miraculous events of the night of the Prophet's birth from a more distant vantage point. This narrative gained currency in the classical historical tradition, appearing in the *Taʾrīkh al-rusul waʾl-mulūk* of al-Ṭabarī (d. 310 AH/923 CE) and other scholarly works. Rather than focusing on the intimate scene of Āmina's labor, it approached the Prophet's birth from the point of view of outsiders whose political and religious primacy would in time be challenged by his mission. Its original thematic context seems to be the broader genre of omens and prognostications of the Prophet's advent, which are usually associated with the religious authorities of the previous dispensation. It is thus probably rooted in the "sectarian milieu" in which the authenticity and supremacy of the Islamic dispensation were elaborated, rather than in the impulse of popular devotionalism. However, its glorification of the event of the Prophet's birth fit well with emerging devotional trends, and it was embraced and elaborated in the *mawlid* tradition.

al-Ṭabarī attributes the story to one Makhzūm ibn Hāni' al-Makhzūmī from his father, "who lived 150 years":

> On the night that the Messenger of God was born, the vault (*īwān*) of Chosroes quaked and fourteen of its battlements toppled; the fire of Persia was extinguished, not having gone out before that for a thousand years; the lake of Sāwa went dry; and the high priest saw [in a dream] unbroken camels leading pure Arabian horses, which had crossed the Tigris and spread throughout his lands. When Chosroes awoke, he was alarmed by what he had dreamed.[138] He calmed himself and took heart. Then he decided that he should not conceal it from his advisors and satraps; he donned his crown, seated himself on his throne, and gathered them in his presence.

While he is in this colloquy, news arrives of the fire's being extinguished. The high priest recounts his dream about the camels. Seeking an interpretation, Chosroes sends word to the Ghassanid king al-Nu'mān ibn Mundhir requesting that he dispatch a wise man. Al-Nu'mān sends one 'Abd al-Masīḥ, who in turn recommends his uncle Saṭīḥ, who dwells in the mountains of Syria. 'Abd al-Masīḥ travels to see Saṭīḥ, who is at the point of death. There ensues a long exchange in which 'Abd al-Masīḥ introduces himself in verse and Saṭīḥ prognosticates in rhymed prose, predicting that fourteen more Persian monarchs will reign before the Arab invasion.[139]

The figure of the soothsayer Saṭīḥ was the focus of a complex of narratives with a fantastical and entertaining dimension. Ibn 'Asākir (d. 571 AH/1176 CE) recounts a long narrative attributed to Ibn 'Abbās, in which Saṭīḥ presents a lengthy chiliastic prophecy tracing the history of the caliphate. The report begins, "It is transmitted from Ibn 'Abbās that a man came to him and said, 'We hear that you mention Saṭīḥ, and claim that God did not create any of the children of Adam similar to him?' " Ibn 'Abbās affirms this, and explains that Saṭīḥ was created as a mass of flesh without any bones but his skull, neck, and hands; he could be rolled up from the feet to his collarbone like a garment, and could move nothing but his tongue. (According to other informants, when enraged he swelled and sat up.)[140]

This riveting image of Saṭīḥ, which may be based on an imaginative extrapolation from his name (literally, "flat"), opens the vastly expanded narrative about the soothsayer in some versions of *al-Anwār*.[141] In addition to the description of Saṭīḥ, it parallels Ibn 'Asākir's report in an incident where the soothsayer correctly identifies members of Quraysh who have misrepresented their identity and describes a hidden gift. However, the body of the narrative is a completely independent and elaborate narrative of Saṭīḥ's reaction to the signs of the imminent birth of the Prophet Muḥammad, which he sees in the heavens from his horizontal position. He visits Mecca and prognosticates the births of Muḥammad and of his cousin 'Alī; his prediction of the end of paganism leads Quraysh to attack the Prophet's mother, Āmina, and violence is forestalled only by divine intervention. There follows a visit by Saṭīḥ's associate, the priestess al-Zarqā' of al-Yamāma, an uncanny woman with preternaturally sharp powers of vision. She bribes Āmina's hairdresser (*māshiṭa*) to stab her with a poisoned dagger. At the last moment, an unseen being stays the hairdresser's hand. al-Zarqā' escapes with nothing but her life. At this point there follows the narrative of the falling of the fourteen battlements, the extinction of the Persian fire, and the dream of the camels.

Even *mawlid* texts that do not include the entire narrative of Saṭīḥ often incorporate elements drawn from it, including the toppling of the battlements and the drying of the lake of Sāwa.

The story of Ḥalīma

The final component of what may be termed the "classical" *mawlid* narrative is the story of the Prophet's wet-nurse, Ḥalīma. The narrative is unusually well authenticated by the standards of the genre; it appears as early as the *Sīra* of Ibn Isḥāq, and is generally accepted by mainstream historians. Unlike the story of Saṭīḥ, which (at least in its original form) primarily serves to foreshadow the Prophet's mission and the triumph of Islam, Ḥalīma's narrative seems to reflect distinctively devotional religious impulses; it emphasizes the miraculous effects of contact with the infant Prophet, quite independently of any foreshadowing of the rise of Islam. By the standards of the historical tradition it is also quite a lengthy report; its sustained narrative arc and distinctive voice make it one of the most appealing and cohesive stories about the Prophet's early life.

Ibn Isḥāq recounts,

> Ḥalīma bint Abī Dhu'ayb al-Sa'dīya, the Messenger of God's [foster-] mother who nursed him, used to recount that she went out from her homeland with her husband and a young son whom she was nursing, among [a group of] women from the tribe of Sa'd ibn Bakr, seeking babies to nurse. She said: That was in a dry and barren year that had left us with nothing. She said: So I went out on a white she-ass of mine with an old camel mare of ours; by God, she did not trickle out a drop [of milk]! We did not sleep all night because of our boy who was with us, because of his crying from hunger; there was not enough in my breast to satisfy him, nor enough in our she-camel to nourish him.... But we hoped for rain and for deliverance.
>
> So I went out on that she-ass of mine; I kept on riding until [we] found it difficult to go on out of weakness and emaciation. Finally we came to Mecca seeking babies to nurse. Every single woman among us was offered the Messenger of God and rejected him, because she was told that he was an orphan. This is because we hoped for benefits from the father of the child [we nursed], so we said, "An orphan?! What can his mother and his grandfather do [for us]?" We disliked him for that reason. Every woman who had come

with me had found a nursling but I. When we decided to set out [for home], I said to my companion, "By God, I don't like to go home [as the only one] among my friends not having taken a nursling. By God, I will go to that orphan and take him." He said, "Why shouldn't you? Perhaps God will give us a blessing through him." She said: So I went to him and took him; the only thing that made me take him is that I couldn't find anyone else.

The good fortune that came to Ḥalīma: She said: When I took him, I returned with him to my saddle. When I put him into my lap, my breasts gave him as much milk as he wanted; he drank until he was satisfied, and his brother drank with him until he was satisfied. Then both of them went to sleep. Before that we were not able to sleep with [our child]. My husband went to that camel mare of ours and found that she was full of milk; he milked for himself to drink, and I drank with him until we stopped because we were satisfied and full. We spent a lovely night. She said: My companion said when we got up, "Do you know, by God, Ḥalīma, you have taken a blessed person." She said: I said, "By God, I hope so!"

She said: Then we went out and I mounted my she-ass and put him on her with me. By God, she covered ground as none of their donkeys could, to the point that my friends were saying to me, "O daughter of Abū Dhu'ayb, woe to you! Wait for us! Is that your she-ass that you went out on?!" I would tell them, "Yes, by God, it's the same one!" and they would say, "By God, there's something special about her!"

She said: Then we arrived at our homes in the territory of Banū Sa'd. I know no land on God's earth more barren than it. When we brought him there with us, my sheep would come back to me in the evening having eaten their fill and giving plenty of milk, and we would milk them and drink. No one [other than us] was getting a drop of milk, nor did they find it in the udders. It got to the point that those of our people who were present would say to their shepherds, "Woe betide you, graze where the shepherd of Bint Abī Dhu'ayb grazes!," but their sheep would come home in the evening hungry and not trickling out a drop of milk, and my sheep would come home in the evening having eaten their fill and giving plenty of milk. We continued to experience increase and blessings from God until his two years were up and I weaned him. He grew up in a way unlike other boys; by the time he was two years old he was a strapping lad.

Ḥalīma's return to Mecca for the first time. She said: So we took him to his mother; we were as eager as could be for him to remain among us, because of what we were experiencing of his blessings (*baraka*). We spoke with his mother, and I said to her: "If only you would leave my little boy with me until he grows strong; I fear for him from the diseases of Mecca." She said: We did not let up on her until she sent him back with us.

The account of the two angels who split open his belly. She said: So we took him back. By God, a month after we arrived he was with his brother with some lambs of ours behind our dwellings when his brother came dashing to us and said to me and his father, "Two men wearing white clothes

> took that Qurashite brother of mine, laid him down, and split open his belly; they are scourging him!" She said: I and his father went out towards him; we found him standing up, looking pale. I hugged him and his father hugged him, and we said to him, "What is the matter, son?" He said, "Two men wearing white garments came to me; they laid me down and split open my belly, and they looked for something – I don't know what it was." She said: So we returned to our shelter.
>
> Ḥalīma returns Muḥammad to his mother. She said: His father said to me, "Ḥalīma, I am afraid that this boy has been afflicted; bring him back to his family before the signs become apparent in him." She said: So we took him and brought him to his mother. She said, "What made you bring him, wet-nurse, when you were keen on him and on keeping him with you?" She said: I said: "God has brought my son to maturity and I have fulfilled my duty; I was afraid that something might befall him, so I delivered to him as you desire." She said, "That is not what you are up to; tell me your story truthfully." She said: She did not leave me alone until I told her. [Āmina] said, "Do you fear that the devil will harm him?" She said: I said, "Yes." She said, "No! By God, the devil has no power over him; my little boy is very special. Shall I tell you about him?" She said: I said, "Yes!" [Āmina] said, "When I conceived him I saw that a light came forth from me that illuminated the castles of Buṣrā in the land of Syria. Then I conceived him, and by God I have never experienced a pregnancy lighter and easier than his. When I gave birth to him he fell with his hands to the earth, lifting his head to the heavens. Leave him be, and go off wisely."[142]

The story of Ḥalīma, although its basic outlines remained largely consistent, was expanded into a number of lengthy and elaborate versions that amplified the emotional impact of the tale and increased its exaltation of the Prophet. The supernatural elements of the story are multiplied, and direct divine intervention in the form of disembodied proclamations becomes pervasive. Unlike the story found in Ibn Isḥāq's *Sīra*, these expanded narratives did not find favor with the more rigorous religious scholars. In his *Dalā'il al-nubūwa*, al-Bayhaqī first presents the "official" version familiar from Ibn Isḥāq and then remarks that

> Muḥammad ibn Zakarīya al-Ghilābī has transmitted this story with many additions through his chain of transmission from Ibn 'Abbās, from Ḥalīma; it has been transmitted to me (*hiya lī masmū'a*), except that this Muḥammad ibn Zakarīya is accused of forgery. Thus, it is more appropriate to limit oneself to what is well-known among the historians (*ahl al-maghāzī*).

However, al-Bayhaqī reports, he finally performed *istikhāra* to determine God's will with regard to the presentation of the expanded story; the ritual came out in favor of its presentation, and he appended it to the better-known narrative.[143] al-Bayhaqī begins al-Ghilābī's narrative at the point when the Prophet is weaned; it seems likely, however, that it originally covered the entire story of Ḥalīma.

al-Bayhaqī's Ghilābī narrative is paralleled by a lengthy version of Ḥalīma's story attributed to Ibn 'Abbās (without *isnād*) in al-Kāzarūnī's *Muntaqā*, which covers the Ḥalīma narrative from the beginning. Although the two texts are not identical, their close overall correspondence and the frequent appearance of identical wording suggest that they represent two – probably oral – renditions of the same narrative.[144] The same distinctive additional episodes appear in al-Bakrī's *Anwār*, which similarly shows extensive literal parallels.[145] Corresponding episodes, although much more freely rendered and embellished to a far more extreme degree, appear in the pseudo-Wāqidī *mawlid* transmitted by al-Qummī.

One of the ways in which Ḥalīma's story could be further dramatized was to elaborate on the direness of her plight before her encounter with the Prophet. In al-Kāzarūnī's Ibn 'Abbās narrative, Ḥalīma describes her own starvation in the most moving terms. Wandering the countryside in search of grasses and plants to eat, she never ceases to thank God even for the suffering and privation He has sent to her. Not having eaten for three days, she writhes in pain like a snake. She gives birth to a son, and does not know if her agony is caused by the birth itself or by the extremity of her condition. However, her desperate situation is alleviated by divine intervention. In her sleep she is visited by a mysterious man who carries her to a place where she is given sweet, white water to drink. He tells her to go to Mecca, where she will find abundant sustenance, and strikes her on her chest with an invocation of God to make her breasts flow. She returns to her people, whose bellies are emaciated and their faces pale, with breasts like overflowing waterskins. Looking like a princess, she conceals her secret. All the women of her tribe give birth to males, and all gray hair once again becomes black.[146]

In al-Bakrī's *Anwār*, Ḥalīma's dream is recounted very similarly. Rather than merely being given water to drink, she is cast into the river of Kawthar, "in which was white water that was sweeter than honey and more fragrant than musk and ambergris." Her physical transformation is differently, although just as vividly described.

> Halīma said: When I arose in the morning the weakness and hunger left me, and I found my breast like an ocean; my body filled out with fat and flesh, and I was enveloped in resplendence, light, comeliness and beauty; my condition became completely different than it was before. Ḥalīma said: When the women of my clan saw me in that state of loveliness, beauty, strength and energy, they were extremely astonished at me. They said to me, "O Ḥalīma, we are astonished at you and at this state in which you have arisen; if you had been eating bread, meat, dates and ghee behind our backs (lit., 'without us') you would not have attained all of this. You have become splendidly lovely and beautiful."[147]

Another embellishment of the story of Ḥalīma that is common to the various versions is the idea that, rather than nursing Muḥammad by default when all of the other women rejected him as an orphan, Ḥalīma was divinely pre-ordained as the Prophet's nurse. Although the theme of the Prophet's orphanhood remains (the *Anwār* presents an emotional exchange between Ḥalīma and her husband, in which the weeping wife finally extracts her husband's permission to accept the fatherless child), there are also abundant foreshadowings of Halīma's destiny and of the extraordinary status of the child. In the *Anwār*, a mysterious heavenly voice cries out "O Banū Sa'd, We have brought down blessings upon you and averted sorrows through the nursing of an infant who has been born in Mecca; his name is Muḥammad, and the Singular One has favored him. Happy is the one who goes to him and has the good fortune to suckle him." All the women of the tribe set out to gain this prize. When Halīma finally goes to the house of 'Abd al-Muṭṭalib, Āmina discloses that a heavenly voice (*hātif*) has revealed to her that only Ḥalīma should nurse her child.

The exaltation of Ḥalīma is carried to its logical conclusion in the version presented in the pseudo-Wāqidī narrative, where the motifs of drought and starvation disappear altogether. In this rendition of the tale, which (as usual) diverges from the normative historical tradition more than the others, a wet-nurse is sought for Muḥammad only after the death of his mother. He refuses to suckle from any woman of Quraysh, although 460 of them try to nurse him. 'Abd al-Muṭṭalib finally seeks counsel, having concluded that the child will nurse from no woman who has any fault. Ḥalīma is recommended to him as the best woman of the Arabs. With great ceremony, her father is summoned and agrees that she become Muḥammad's wet-nurse. A lengthy negotiation ensues, in which 'Abd al-Muṭṭalib offers her princely sums of money and luxurious food and clothing if she will dwell with Quraysh while suckling the child. He finally allows her to take him away, with lesser but still lavish payment.[148]

There are also additional incidents that are introduced into the story following the "opening of the chest" (*shaqq al-ṣadr*) episode. In the Bayhaqī/Kāzarūnī version, following that event people counsel Ḥalīma to consult a soothsayer (*kāhin*) about Muḥammad's condition. Against her better judgment, Ḥalīma ultimately complies. Upon hearing the story, the soothsayer leaps to his feet and cries out, "O people of the Arabs (*yā āl al-'arab*), O people of the Arabs! Beware of an evil that has come nigh; kill this child and kill me, for if you leave him and he grows to manhood he will ridicule your dignity, give the lie to your religion, and call you to a lord you do not know and a religion of which you are ignorant."[149] Ḥalīma snatches the child back and tells the soothsayer to find someone else to kill him, as she has no intention of killing Muḥammad. She is finally persuaded to return Muḥammad to his relatives in Mecca. As soon as she arrives, she leaves him for a moment; when she returns, the child is gone. An old man offers to help, and takes her to the Ka'ba to consult the idol Hubal; the idols fall on their faces; the aged man drops his cane to flee, and emerges with chattering teeth and knocking knees. A lengthy and dramatically narrated search, involving 'Abd al-Muṭṭalib and all of Quraysh, ensues; Muḥammad is finally recovered, unharmed, with the help of a mysterious supernatural voice (*hātif*).[150]

This incident is recounted by the Qur'ān commentator al-Tha'labī (d. 427 AH/ 1035 CE); while the degree of correspondence does not suggest direct textual transmission, there are extensive verbal parallels.[151] The text of *al-Anwār* reflects a similar degree of consistency, and the same episodes appear in the Ka'b narrative of the Toledo corpus.[152] The pseudo-Wāqidī text is, as usual, far more divergent than any of the others; while more vivid and fanciful, however, it shares the basic motif of the loss and pursuit of the child Muḥammad. Typically of the pseudo-Wāqidī narrative, which frequently rearranges the sequencing of the standard elements of the tale, the placement of the search scene is changed; it is on the occasion of the "opening of the chest" that he is declared lost. Also typically, the emotional pitch of the tale is raised to melodramatic levels. The lengthy passage begins, "Ḥalīma arose, rent her garments, scratched her cheeks, and loosed her hair as she ran through the steppes, the deserts and the desolate lands, barefoot, with the thorns piercing her feet and the blood flowing from them."[153]

The motif of Ḥalīma's search for the mysteriously mislaid child is a very old one, appearing in a much simpler form as early as the *Sīra* of Ibn Isḥāq. Its probable origins in the narratives of the *quṣṣāṣ* (storytellers) is suggested by Ibn Hishām's dubious introduction to the anecdote: "people claim, among the things that they recount" (*wa-za'ama al-nās fīmā yataḥaddathūn*).[154] Like Āmina's birth narrative, it seems to have circulated on the periphery of the scholarly tradition. The motif of the child's disappearance very likely originated in an exegetical context; al-Tha'labī recounts the incident in the context of his interpretation of verse 93:7 ("And He found you wandering, and guided you"). Precisely when the story reached the form recorded (with slight variations) by al-Bayhaqī, al-Tha'labī, al-Bakrī, and al-Kāzarūnī is more difficult to determine. The apparent existence of al-Bakrī's *Anwār* in the third-century AH, similar to al-Bayhaqī's attribution of the story to al-Ghilābī, suggests that this version of the story originated quite early.

al-Tha'labī attributes his selection from the story of Ḥalīma to "Ka'b al-Aḥbār's report about the Prophet's birth and his beginnings (*ḥadīth Ka'b al-Aḥbār fī mawlid rasūl allāh ṣallā allāhu 'alayhi wa-sallam wa-bad' amrihi*)"[155]; thus, it was an element of the larger Ka'b narrative that we have already encountered earlier. As we have seen, it is also likely that a comprehensive narrative of the Prophet's origins and birth was associated with the name of Ibn 'Abbās (the source cited by al-Bayhaqī). The Ibn 'Abbās narrative presented by al-Bayhaqī follows the conventions of the scholarly tradition, although it does not meet its standards; al-Bayhaqī presents it with a full, if questionable, chain of transmission. Muḥammad ibn Zakarīyā al-Ghilābī, the Baṣran transmitter whom al-Bayhaqī suspects of putting the story into circulation, is supposed to have died in 280 AH.[156] Muḥammad ibn Ḥibbān al-Bustī (d. 354 AH/965 CE) describes him as a purveyor of "tales and (historical) reports" (*ṣāḥib ḥikāyāt wa-akhbār*); he considers his reports transmitted from reliable sources to be acceptable, but notes that he transmitted questionable material from unknown persons.[157] It is thus likely that by the end of the third-century AH, elaborate versions of the story of Ḥalīma were in circulation in scholarly circles – or on their periphery – under the names of two different Companions of the Prophet. The names of each of these Companions, as we have seen, were associated with a much longer and more comprehensive narrative of the Prophet's origins and birth. The extensive verbal parallels between the two versions suggest that they were not two separate and independent texts, but two rubrics under which a very cohesive body of narrative material was consolidated and circulated. Given that *al-Anwār* at various places cites narratives attributed by both Ka'b al-Aḥbār and Ibn 'Abbās, it seems likely that the narratives were known by the names of these two Companions before they were subsumed into the text of *al-Anwār*, which is simply the most widespread form in which they were known in later centuries.

The story of Ḥalīma can be regarded as a "sub-scholarly" narrative that (similar to several of the other stories discussed earlier) achieved a quasi-canonical status that lent it uniformity and durability, despite its general rejection by the scholarly elite. The pseudo-Wāqidī text reflects the basic structure of this alternative narrative by including such conventional components as the search for the lost child, but reflects a much freer and more imaginative storytelling technique. Although the true "folk" tradition – the oral performances that must have brought these stories to the ears of many illiterate (as well as educated) medieval Muslims – will remain forever inaccessible to us, in its loose and improvisational use of elements from the "sub-scholarly" version of the Prophet's life this narrative suggests how the folk storytelling tradition may have operated.

Even in the very early form presented by Ibn Isḥāq, and much more so in the various non-normative versions discussed here, the story of Ḥalīma exemplifies a number of the key elements that typify the religiosity associated with the *mawlid* genre. Most importantly, all versions of the narrative centrally emphasize the auspicious power – the *baraka* – of the infant Prophet. Contact with (or mere propinquity to) the Prophet is the cause of fertility and plenty. In his presence plants bloom, animals and humans give birth, and milk flows copiously from both women and livestock. Ḥalīma's physical transformation, from dire emaciation to buxom and radiant womanhood, exemplifies the child's supernatural aura. These elements of the narrative reflect a religious devotion to the infant Muḥammad that is distinct from his later, historical prophetic mission; as in the stories of his pre-existence and light, Muḥammad is a cosmic figure long before he receives revelation. The story of Ḥalīma also reflects the centrality of emotion in the religious world constructed by the narration of the Prophet's life. The pathos of her hungry and weeping baby and the joy of her delivery from want are involving even in the relatively sober version of Ibn Isḥāq; in the non-normative versions of the story, and most extremely in the pseudo-Wāqidī text, the emotions evoked by the narrative are raised to a fever pitch. It is difficult to imagine, for instance, that an audience heard the description of a starving Ḥalīma "writhing like a snake" or a distraught Ḥalīma rending her garments as she wailed for her lost foster-child without sympathetic groans and exclamations of its own.

The tradition of popular mawlid narratives

There is no reason to believe that the *mawlid* narratives contained in works such as *al-Anwār* represented "popular Islam" in the sense that they were distinctively associated with Muslims who were illiterate, rural, or impoverished. There is no evidence that any of these texts came from other than urban settings (al-Bakrī himself being traditionally identified as a Baṣran). While we know nothing about the socioeconomic status of the generators or audience of this material, there is reason to think that it crossed social strata. Certainly all of it was familiar to elite and learned Muslims of the period under discussion; however, some of them may have objected to it. It was sometimes sought out by the upper sociopolitical strata: al-Kāzarūnī accuses the purveyors of wild and fanciful *mawlid* tales of using them to extract wealth from the royal treasury, which suggests that they were presented at court to a warm reception.[158] In addition to their reproduction or denunciation in some scholarly works, occasional remarks also suggest that such tales were presented in circles frequented by scholars. After complaining about the activities of women storytellers at *mawlid* celebrations, Ibn al-Ḥājj laments, "I have heard that [a '*shaykha*'] did this in the house of one of the respected scholars of our time (*shaykh min al-shuyūkh al-mu'tabarīn fī 'l-waqt*) and no one corrected her; rather, they honored her and gave her [gifts]."[159] Speaking about the wild embellishments of the *mawlid* narrative that continued to be invented by popular preachers in his time, Ibn Ḥajar al-Haytamī (d. 974 AH/1567 CE) remarks that it is incumbent on the religious scholars and on any other knowledgeable person to set such storytellers straight or simply to arise and take leave of the gathering where they are holding forth.[160] Clearly scholars were sometimes present at such performances, and did not necessarily denounce them.

Peter Burke has argued that in Europe before 1500, "popular culture was everyone's culture." Everyone, regardless of status, was familiar with the culture of the carnival and the folktale; in addition, the learned had a second culture that was unavailable to the masses. The narratives associated with the *mawlid* seem to reflect just such a situation; scholars knew the stories circulated by less-learned storytellers and preachers (sometimes disseminating, and sometimes denouncing them), even as they cultivated a more exclusive historical tradition that may have held less immediate appeal for ordinary Muslims.

While the precise composition of the audience for popular *mawlid* narratives can never be known, one notable dimension of many of the non-normative *mawlid* narratives is their high degree of concern with female characters. The text of *al-Anwār* provides a striking illustration of this trend. From the point of Muḥammad's conception, the story is dominated by a series of women: first his mother Āmina, then his wet-nurse Ḥalīma, and finally his wife Khadīja. It is true that all of these women are fundamentally defined by their relationships to the Prophet; however, particularly in the case of Āmina and Ḥalīma, events are presented very much from their perspective. The story is narrated in their voices, and revolves around their experiences and concerns. In this rendition of the Prophet's life, gestation and lactation eclipse revelation; even the Prophet's own life culminates with courtship, marriage, and the recommencement of the cycle of birth. Episodes which in more normative renditions have exclusively male characters, such as that of the soothsayer Saṭīḥ, in *al-Anwār* are revised to include female leads: the devious Zarqā', absent in al-Ṭabarī's version of the tale, in *al-Anwār* takes a role as central and vivid as that of Saṭīḥ himself. Women are well represented even on the supernatural plane; the male angels who herald the Prophet's birth are balanced by the band of holy foremothers who attend it.

It might seem that the earlier portions of the tale, which focus on the transmission of the Light of Muḥammad through the spermatic substance of his forefathers, reflect classically patriarchal concerns. However, even in this section of the narrative significant attention is focused on female characters. The most notable example of this trend is the story of the Prophet's great-grandmother, Salmā, which occupies a disproportionate share of the story of the Prophet's ancestors. While the Vatican manuscript of *al-Anwār* does not include this episode, it appears in the version cited by Majlisī, and thus must have entered the tradition at least by the sixteenth-century AH. When the Prophet's great-grandfather, Hāshim, visits her father to seek her hand, he is informed that Salmā "is her own mistress" (*mālikat nafsihā*).[161] Consulted about the match, she agrees that Hāshim seems to be an ideal husband, but insists that "I must demand a bridal payment and everything else I deserve from him; I cannot sell myself short (*lā uṣaghghir ḥālī*)."[162] Meeting Hāshim unexpectedly, Salmā declares that she desires to marry him, and promises herself to repay any sums that he agrees to pay for her hand.[163] Despite Salmā's joy when the betrothal finally occurs, she tells Hāshim's brother the story of the stratagem by which she relieved herself of her previous husband, "so that he will know just what I am like and won't neglect me in favor of any of his other wives."[164] As a wealthy widow who takes a leading role in her own marriage negotiations, Salmā is in many ways a double of Khadīja, the heroine of the final third of al-Bakrī's work.

The female-centered nature of much of the narrative in *al-Anwār* does not, of course, necessarily indicate that women were involved in the generation or framing of the story. The text is associated with the name of a male figure, and regardless of the degree to which al-Bakrī may have been a historical individual or the "author" of these tales in a conventional sense, we have no justification for positing that the stories originated with women. The fact that the stories of the Prophet's birth and suckling are narrated in the voices of Āmina and Ḥalīma does not, of course, tell us anything about the gender or identity of the individuals who first produced the narratives. However, the discrepancy between the gynocentric nature of many of the non-normative narratives and the relatively androcentric nature of much (although certainly not all) of the normative material suggests that there is some kind of gender differential involved. Although no proof of this supposition is possible, it seems highly probable that women were well represented in the audience of the popular and semi-popular storytelling tradition, and that the stories' enhanced attention to the roles and perspectives of women reflects a desire to cater to this audience.

The non-normative *mawlid* narratives also reflect a distinctive religious worldview that distinguishes them from material of the more scholarly stratum, at least within the Sunnī context. In the world of semi-popular *mawlid* literature (i.e., non-normative narratives that are nevertheless stabilized in literary form), there is such a thing as Islamic cosmogonic myth. The luxurious growth of narratives in which lights, pearls, seas, fish, and the earth itself function as semi-personified actors in an eventful cosmic drama stands in stark contrast to the spare Qur'ānic schema of creation *ex nihilo*, in which God says to a thing, "Be!" and it is.[165] The sheer physicality of the narratives is striking; things glow, sweat, tremble, fissure, and give birth to other things.

The portion of the narrative dealing with the Prophet's earthly birth and life also reflects a distinctive religious vision. Particularly (but not exclusively) in the lengthy section devoted to Ḥalīma's tale, the story expresses a theology of fertility. The Prophet's auspicious power (his *baraka*) is expressed through fruitfulness of all kinds: the growth of crops, the flowering of trees, the fecundity of flocks, the miraculously swift growth of children, and the nourishing power of food (which is more filling in the presence of the Prophet than in his absence). Again, the physicality of the imagery is striking. Ḥalīma's experience of the Prophet's blessings is embodied in her physical regeneration, from a gaunt and starving sufferer whose dry breasts torment her languishing infant to a plump and radiant woman capable of nourishing two children. Perhaps the central symbol of the story is Ḥalīma's abundantly flowing breasts, which condenses the narrative's central themes of light/whiteness/purity, nourishment, and love. It is tempting to wonder whether this embodied theology, with its celebration of women's fertility and sustaining power, has something to do with the larger story's focus on women and its possible appeal to a female audience. However, this is not an issue that can be resolved on the basis of the text alone, which is all that remains to us of the storytelling process.

Although the precise chronological placement and socioreligious setting of each individual element of the story is probably impossible to determine, there is certainly a substantial body of narrative material about the pre-history and birth of the Prophet that significantly pre-dates the rise of the *mawlid* festival among Sunnīs (and, in many cases, even the celebration of the *mawlid* as a Fāṭimid state festival). The existence of such material suggests that the pre-formation, conception, and birth of the Prophet were the focus of religious interest and narrative elaboration long before the emergence of a yearly holiday commemorating the Prophet's birthday. The narratives on this subject reflect a lively concern with the Prophet as a cosmic figure whose auspicious power yielded good fortune and prosperity in this life and whose high station with God promised his followers a privileged status in the life to come. Significantly, none of them focus on the pre-figuration of the revelation of the Qur'ān or the anticipation of the normative dispensation of the *Sharī'a*. Rather, they exalt the status of the Prophet himself and emphasize his cosmic centrality.

Formal *mawlid* texts

Although narratives about the Prophet's birth had been recounted for centuries, a distinct genre of texts specifically devoted to the Prophet's birth emerges only in the sixth-century AH/twelfth-century CE – that is, in the era of the emergence of the Sunnī *mawlid* celebration. The circulation of the *mawlid* narratives discussed earlier, to the extent that it can be geographically located, seems to have been disproportionately concentrated in the eastern lands of Iran and Iraq. In the era of the rise of the Sunnī *mawlid* celebration, the pace and nature of *mawlid* production changed markedly, as did its geographical focus. Although the attribution of the earliest formal *mawlid* texts is in several cases uncertain, clear overall patterns do emerge. Geographically, no fewer than six of the earliest *mawlid* texts are attributed to scholars from Andalusia and the Maghrib; more speculatively, two more of the most important *mawlid* texts can also be traced to Andalusia (see Appendix).

A scholar known for his devotional work on the Prophet Muḥammad, ʿIyāḍ ibn Mūsā al-Yaḥṣubī (d. 544 AH/1149 CE) allegedly wrote a work entitled "*Risāla badīʿa fī bayān mawlid al-nabī (ṣ) wa-ajdādihi wa-miʿrājihi wa-wafātihi wa-baʿḍ muʿjizātihi*" ("Novel treatise elucidating the Prophet's birth, his ancestors, his ascent to heaven, his death, and some of his miracles"), or simply "*Risāla fī mawlid al-nabī.*" Two copies of this work are preserved in Saudi Arabia.[166] al-Qāḍī ʿIyāḍ, a maghribī who had a career as a judge in Grenada, was a Mālikī jurist with expertise in many areas of the religious sciences. Similar to the earliest Sunnī *mawlid* attributed to al-Quḍāʿī, his work would seem to be a devotional biography in which the Prophet's birth (and, in this case, his ascension to heaven) takes pride of place. Another possible *mawlid* text (this time, a specialized *mawlid* composition rather than a full biography of the Prophet) is attributed to ʿIyāḍ's Andalusian contemporary Aḥmad ibn Maʿadd al-Iqlīshi (d. ca. 550 AH/1155 CE). al-Iqlīshī is listed in *Īḍāḥ al-maknūn* as the author of *al-Durr al-munaẓẓam fī mawlid al-nabī al-aʿẓam* ("Arranged pearls on the birth of the greatest Prophet").[167] However, there is circumstantial evidence that this attribution may possibly be faulty.[168] Interestingly, al-Iqlīshī was the author of a *ḥadīth* work based on al-Quḍāʿī's *Shihāb.*[169]

The *mawlid* text often assumed to be the first of the genre, Ibn Diḥya's *Tanwīr fī mawlid al-sirāj al-munīr*, was produced by an Andalusian on a journey in the Muslim East. While his *mawlid* work is not preserved, the earliest extant *mawlid* text was produced by his exact contemporary, the maghribī Aḥmad al-ʿAzafī (d. 633 AH/1236 CE). Two preserved *mawlid* texts are attributed to the great Andalusian mystic Ibn al-ʿArabī (d. 638 AH/1240 CE), and one to the Andalusian Qur'ān commentator Muḥammad al-Qurṭubī (d. 671 AH/1272 CE). More speculatively, a *mawlid* work entitled *Ṭall* (or *Ẓill*) *al-ghumāma fī mawlid sayyid Tihāma* ("Dew / shadow of the cloud on the birth of the master of Tihāma") is attributed to one Aḥmad ibn ʿAlī ibn Saʿīd, apparently a Grenadan who died in 673 AH/1274–5 CE.[170]

While most of these works are either lost or obscure, there is some reason to think that it was in Andalusia in the seventh-century AH that two of the most widely circulated *mawlid* texts in history originated. Probably the most widely disseminated *mawlid* work in the Arab world, and the most prevalent version in preserved manuscripts, is best known under the title *Mawlid al-ʿarūs* ("*Mawlid* of the bride/groom"[171]) and attributed to the Ḥanbalī preacher Ibn al-Jawzī (d. 597 AH/1200 CE). It remains in print in pamphlet form, and can still be purchased for small change in Damascus today. This text exemplifies the structural and stylistic qualities of what may be called the "classical" prose *mawlid*, the model that dominated the genre from the late-middle ages until the twentieth century. It begins with an elaborate introductory passage (*dībāja*) in flowery rhymed prose. The rest of the text alternates passages of rhymed prose with interludes of devotional poetry, each of which in turn is punctuated or ended with the invocation of prayers upon the Prophet. The content of the body of the work is somewhat fluid, since it is subject to the addition, subtraction, and rearrangement of units of text.

The clearest marker of different versions of this text is its introduction, a highly distinctive and stable block of rhymed prose. It begins, "Praise be to God, Who brought forth from the blaze on the forehead of the bride of the Presence a luminous dawn, and made rise in the orbits of perfection from the constellations (*burūj*) of beauty a radiant sun and moon, and chose the Master of the Two Worlds as a beloved, a noble one, and an emissary in pre-eternity."[172] Very similar in style and content is the *mawlid* known as *Sharaf al-Ānām*, which remains in wide circulation without any attribution of authorship; its title ("Honor of humankind") is drawn, similar to that of *Mawlid al-'arūs*, from its opening passage of rhymed prose.

The true authorship of *Mawlid al-'arūs* and *Sharaf al-ānām* has long been obscure; their wide circulation under titles drawn from their opening lines suggests that their complete titles and correct authors disappeared over centuries of copying and recitation. The Yemeni scholar (and *mawlid* author) Ibn al-Dayba' (d. 944 AH/1537 CE) is supposed to have left a note in his own handwriting stating, "Praise be to God! The author of the book *Mawlid al-nabī* that begins with 'Praise be to God who honored humankind with the possessor of the highest station' is the *shaykh* and *imām* Shihāb al-Dīn Aḥmad ibn 'Alī ibn Qāsim al-Mālikī al-Bukhārī al-Andalusī al-Mursī al-Lakhmī, known as al-Ḥarīrī. This *mawlid* is the ninth section of his book that he composed on preaching and edifying religious discourses (*raqā'iq*)." Ibn al-Dayba' notes triumphantly that he located this text "after a lengthy search for the author of this work," whose identity is "not known by most scholars; this is a piece of information that is worth a journey!" Ibn al-Dayba''s biographer notes that this discovery disproves the work's widespread attribution to Ibn al-Jawzī.[173] Interestingly, this comment associates the name of Ibn al-Jawzī with the opening line of *Sharaf al-ānām*.

Ibn al-Dayba''s attribution is supported by the eighteenth-century *mawlid* author Fatḥ Allāh al-Bannānī, who attributes a characteristic passage of rhymed prose appearing in both *Sharaf al-ānām* and *Mawlid al-'arūs* to "the muftī of mankind" (*muftī al-anām*) Abū'l-'Abbās Aḥmad ibn Qāsim al-Mālikī al-Bukhārī al-Andalusī al-Lakhmī, "known as al-Ḥarīrī."[174] Although Ibn al-Dayba' and al-Bannānī together supply a remarkably thorough identification for al-Ḥarīrī, no such figure can be identified in biographical dictionaries covering either the Mālikī school of law or Muslim Andalusia. Nevertheless, there seems to be little doubt that this work can be traced to an Andalusian Mālikī. If al-Bannānī is correct in describing him as having moved from Bukhāra to Murcia (*al-bukhārī thumma'l-mursī*), he is unlikely to have done so later than the mid-seventh-century AH/thirteenth-century CE, when the latter city fell to the Christians. Certainly there must have been time for the work to become widely popular – and its true authorship to be obscured – by Ibn al-Dayba''s lifetime in the first-half of the tenth-century AH/ sixteenth-century CE.

The references by Ibn al-Dayba' and al-Bannānī appear to refer to the work now known as *Sharaf al-ānām*, although it too seems to have been associated with the name of Ibn al-Jawzī and to have shared some rhymed prose with *Mawlid al-'arūs*. Although the original author of the latter may never be conclusively identified, Ḥajjī Khalīfa tantalizingly observes that the *mawlid* of Aḥmad ibn 'Alī ibn Sa'īd began with the line "Praise be to God, Who brought forth from the blaze on the forehead of the bride of the Presence."[175] This is the characteristic opening line of *Mawlid al-'arūs*, from which it draws its popular title. Although it cannot be known how much of the text now known as *Mawlid al-'arūs* this author's work comprised, this opening line suggests that the most distinctive feature of this most popular of *mawlid* texts also originated in Spain in the seventh-century AH. Although the attributions of individual works are sometimes speculative, the cumulative evidence suggests that important elements of the *mawlid* tradition – including flowery passages of rhymed prose that were circulated and modified for centuries – originated in Spain, probably in the seventh-century AH/thirteenth-century CE.

Texts such as *Mawlid al-'arūs* and *Sharaf al-anām* straddle the boundary between authored compositions and the anonymous products of a shared tradition. It is clear that it was possible to borrow passages of rhymed prose and incorporate them into one's own work. Passages paralleling the texts of *Mawlid al-'arūs* and/or *Sharaf al-anām* appear, for instance, in a sermon on the Prophet's *mawlid* by Shaykh al-Ḥurayfīsh (d. 801 AH/1398–9 CE).[176] It is perhaps not coincidental that al-Ḥurayfīsh's work is presented in a work of precisely the same genre (*al-mawā'iẓ wa'l-raqā'iq*) that Ibn al-Dayba' attributes to the mysterious al-Ḥarīrī. It is in the field of preaching and exhortation, with its stylistic affinity for rhymed prose and its sacrifice of historical niceties in the pursuit of emotional response, where the literary and narrative conventions of the *mawlid* tradition were nurtured.

In content, the texts of the *Mawlid al-'arūs* tradition reproduce the major elements of the semi-popular cosmogonic and birth narratives familiar from *al-Anwār* and related sources. They feature versions of the Ka'b and Jābir narratives and of Āmina's account of the Prophet's birth, as well as elaborate versions of the story of Ḥalīma. They are distinguished from other examples of that narrative tradition mainly by their shorter length, which is appropriate for performance in a single sitting, and by their higher degree of literary ornamentation. Passages of loose, flowery rhymed prose alternate with narrative *ḥadīth* reports, which are presented in unrhymed prose. Devotional poetry is interspersed throughout, and may (as is the case in the modern period) have been recited or sung by participants in a *mawlid* ceremony.

Both the geographical focus and the literary and religious style of *mawlid* composition shifted sharply in the following century. No fewer than eleven authors who lived in Damascus and died between 727 AH/1327 CE and 842 AH/1438 CE (a period of little more than a century) are credited with the composition of formal *mawlid* works. *Mawlid* works were also produced by authors from other regions who lived in or visited Syria; over time, the production of *mawlid*s seems to have spread into other areas of the Islamic world. The *mawlid* texts produced by what may be termed the "Damascus school" share a number of distinctive features. One is their scrupulous avoidance of the expansive and fanciful cosmogonic narratives typical of the *mawlid* genre up to this point in time. No longer is the creation of the Prophet depicted in terms of radiant pearls, divine veils, or droplets of creative sweat. The texts do emphasize the chronological priority of Muḥammad's prophethood and the purity of his lineage, but only to the extent that these motifs had been incorporated into the mainstream scholarly tradition. The narrative elements in these *mawlid*s are similarly limited to the better-authenticated of the relevant texts. For instance, the story of the dream in which Āmina is instructed to protect her baby with a special apotropaic formula and to name him Muḥammad, and the motif of the light that beams forth to illuminate the castles of Syria, continue to appear. The story of the soothsayer Saṭīḥ, represented in the mainstream history of al-Ṭabarī, is frequently featured. The more elaborate narrative familiar from such sources as al-Bakrī and al-Bayhaqī, in which Āmina is attended by heavenly handmaidens and the newborn instantly seized by angels, is consistently excluded. The Ḥalīma narrative, when it appears at all, is limited to the relatively sober version presented by Ibn Isḥāq.

To a certain extent, the scholarly *mawlid* tradition seems to represent a reaction to the lush storytelling tradition associated with the Prophet's *mawlid* and to the extra-canonical accounts of creation featured so prominently in that tradition. The *mawlid* of Ibrāhīm ibn 'Umar al-Ja'barī (d. 732 AH/1332 CE) is a case in point. "Praise be to God," it begins, "who originated the creation of human beings from clay, then breathed into it His spirit and made the closest of the angels prostrate themselves before him; then He made his progeny from an extract of base water, and deposited his sperm in a secure resting place. Then He changed it into a clot of blood, then into a clump, then into bones which He covered with flesh in the best of forms. Blessed is God, the best of creators!"[177] Given the centrality of the theme of the pre-existence of Muḥammad in the *mawlid* tradition as a whole, it seems implausible that al-Ja'barī was unaware of the expectation that a narrative celebrating the Prophet's birth would begin with the creation and migration of the Light of Muḥammad. al-Ja'barī's detailed evocation of the Qur'ānic account of human creation appears as an obvious, if tacit, rebuke to those who circulated noncanonical creation narratives in the name of the *mawlid*.

In a somewhat similar vein, Ibn Kathīr opens his *mawlid* work as follows: "Praise be to God, who illuminated the world with the appearance of the Master of Messengers and dispelled the shadows of falsity with the light of manifest truth, when people had been passing in ways of ignorance."[178] Following the first section of the text, which (in accordance with the classical sources) mentions the radiance of 'Abd Allāh's forehead and the light that shone from his mother to the castles of Syria, Ibn Kathīr begins the second section as follows: "When God wished to bring forth His servant and messenger Muḥammad into this world, and to make manifest the light of His guidance to all in existence…"[179] In Ibn Kathīr's *mawlid*, the light of the Prophet is not the primordial substance from which the elements of the cosmos were brought forth, but the light of guidance and truth. Unlike in the more popular tradition of *mawlid* narrative, the motif of the Prophet's light is firmly linked to his role as a recipient of revelation and a teacher of right guidance.

In the Damascus *mawlids*, the traditional framework in which *mawlid* narratives focused on the events of the Prophet's birth and childhood and ended before he reached adulthood (or, at the latest, with his marriage to Khadīja) is abandoned. In some cases, the Damascus *mawlids* have no narrative structure at all; pursuing edification rather than entertainment, they simply enumerate facts about the Prophet. This is true of the *mawlid* of al-Ja'barī. Although al-Ja'barī explicitly states that his work was composed in honor of the Prophet's birthday,[180] he carefully avoids the prevalent narratives about the Prophet's actual birth in favor of a didactic enumeration of facts about the Prophet's life. Much of the work takes the form of lists. It includes sections on the meaning of prophethood (*nubūwa*), the impeccability (*'iṣma*) of the prophets and whether they are superior to angels; the Prophet's birth; his names; his lineage; his physical appearance; his moral qualities; his food and clothing; his early life; the beginning of his prophetic mission; various facts about the revelation of the Qur'ān; the Prophet's night journey to heaven; his emigration to Medina; events that occurred in Medina; the Prophet's death; prophecies about Muḥammad from previous scriptures; prophecies from soothsayers and *jinns*; and the Prophet's miracles.

Even when they do involve substantial narrative, the scholarly *mawlids* that begin to appear in the eighth-century AH routinely involve discussions of factual and interpretive questions that interrupt any narrative flow. The narrative portion of a *mawlid* by the Damascene scholar Muḥammad ibn 'Alī al-Zamlakānī (d. 727 AH/1327 CE) ends with Ibn Isḥāq's account of Ḥalīma's story. However, this is far from being the culmination of the text. He follows the story with a detailed discussion of several relevant points. After explaining the reasons why the Prophet was confided to the care of a wet-nurse in the first place, al-Zamlakānī provides an alternative account of the incident of the "opening of the chest." He explains that the two narratives recount different incidents, one of them occurring when the Prophet was in the care of his wet-nurse and the other preceding his night journey to heaven, in his adulthood. al-Zamlakānī, a *ṣūfī* as well as a jurist, provides a thorough symbolic interpretation of the details of each version.[181] The remainder of the *mawlid*, about a third of the whole, comprises an enumeration of the various ways in which the Prophet Muḥammad was distinguished from all previous prophets. Similarly, Ibn Kathīr's *mawlid*, although it does narrate the Prophet's birth and early life up to Ibn Isḥāq's account of Ḥalīma's story, culminates with a substantial section on the physical and moral attributes of the Prophet.[182]

A similarly pedantic approach, and a similarly scrupulous avoidance of the more popular narratives about the Prophet's birth, is discernible in a *mawlid* composed by the distinguished Qur'ānic scholar Muḥammad ibn Muḥammad al-Jazarī (d. 833 AH/1429 CE). al-Jazarī offers thoughtful factual discussions of the number of generations between the Prophet's ancestors Ismā'īl and 'Adnān and of the dates of his conception and birth.[183] He debates whether Muḥammad was the only prophet to be born circumcised and with his umbilical cord cut.[184] In connection with the report that eavesdropping spirits were pelted with shooting stars after the birth of Muḥammad, he ponders whether being hit by a shooting star would kill a *jinnī*.[185] Al-Jazarī's *mawlid* provides a concise account of the Prophet's biography, providing more narrative interest than al-Ja'barī's but avoiding popular narratives such as those associated with al-Bakrī.

The *mawlid* texts of the "Damascus school" are also distinctive in that they seem to be specifically intended for ritualized public reading. It is not clear at what point the custom of *mawlid* recitation (*qirā'a*) became prevalent. While the existence of *mawlid* narratives can be documented at quite an early period, it is not clear that they were intended for ritual recitation or not. A text such as *al-Anwār* could be read aloud (or orally reproduced) in multiple sessions, as is demonstrated by later practice, but it is unclear whether its original *Sitz im Leben* was devotional practice during the month of the Prophet's birth or simply non-seasonal popular amusement. The first surviving work explicitly associated with the celebration of the Prophet's birthday, al-'Azafī's *al-Durr al-munaẓẓam*, is more a sourcebook than a script; it is too lengthy and too eclectic to be recited in full in the context of a *mawlid* celebration. Of course, the oral presentation of scholarly works was the norm in the premodern period, but such scholarly dictation does not constitute the kind of pious performance associated with later *mawlid* works. By the time that *mawlid* production flourished in eighth-century AH Damascus, however, the genre seems to have been adapted to oral performance in the context of *mawlid* celebrations. One sign of this is the modest dimensions of the *mawlid* texts produced in this period, most of which could easily be read aloud in a single sitting. Occasional references to the reading or recitation (*qirā'a*) of the *mawlid* also begin to appear. In one of the several *mawlid* texts he composed, the Syrian jurist and litterateur al-Ḥasan ibn Ḥabīb (d. 779 AH/1377 CE) writes that if time allowed, "we would read a *mawlid* on every day or night."[186] Ibn al-Jazarī (d. 833 AH/1429 CE) describes various elements of the celebration of the Prophet's birthday, including "the reading/recitation of [the Prophet's] noble *mawlid*."[187]

The recitation of formally composed, scholarly *mawlid* texts was probably an alternative and a response to more informal storytelling on the occasion of the *mawlid* celebration. Ibn al-Ḥājj states that women

> gather for a *mawlid*... only with a woman in attendance whom they claim is a teacher (*shaykha*) according to their custom (*'alā 'urfihinna*). She may be – and this is usually the case – one of those women who enters into the interpretation of the Book of God; she interprets, tells the stories of the

> prophets, and adds and subtracts. Sometimes she falls into explicit disbelief (*al-kufr al-ṣarīḥ)* without being aware of it, and there is no one to prevent her or set her straight.[188]

Ibn al-Ḥājj associates his disapproval of such women with the general condemnation of the activities of popular storytellers (*quṣṣāṣ*); however, he considers female storytellers particularly pernicious because of their limited access to books and their lesser ability to distinguish sound from forged material.[189] Based on Ibn al-Ḥājj's description, it does not seem that the Prophet's birth was the exclusive subject of such storytelling on the occasion of the *mawlid*. However, it seems very likely that the lush material on the Prophet's birth represented part of the "stories of the prophets" that were presented at such gatherings.

Against this background, the major objective of the scholarly *mawlid*s that began to appear in Damascus in the eighth-century AH/fourteenth-century CE was to replace the copious popular narratives surrounding the Prophet's birth with material deemed more legitimate. Narratives such as those associated with al-Bakrī, although "canonical" in the sense that they clearly enjoyed wide acceptance and careful cultivation over a period of many centuries, were replaced in the newer *mawlid*s by narratives from the official scholarly canon. This agenda is clear from the content of the *mawlid* texts of the Damascus school, which consistently present the relevant narratives from *ḥadīth* compilations and from the mainstream historical works of Ibn Isḥāq and al-Ṭabarī, while shunning the ubiquitous narratives associated with figures such as al-Bakrī. The essential problem addressed by these texts was the circulation of spurious stories. As much is suggested by the text of Ibn Kathīr's *mawlid*, which begins with striking emphasis: "This [work] mentions some of the *ḥadīth* and historical texts relating to the birth of the Messenger of God which are transmitted and accepted by the accomplished, accurate scholars and by the masters of textual criticism" (*dhikr al-aḥādīth wa'l-āthār al-manqūla al-maqbūla 'inda al-ḥuffāẓ al-mutqinīn wa'l-a'imma al-nāqidīn*).[190] The continuing vitality of the storytelling tradition is clear from a much later *mawlid*, that of Ibn Ḥajar al-Haytamī (d. 973 AH/1565 CE). Among the reprehensible features of the *mawlid* celebration in his time, al-Haytamī lists the fact that

> in those *mawlid*s, they bring someone who reads to them the noble *mawlid* according to the manner to which the preachers (*al-wu''āẓ*) have become accustomed in these times. That is objectionable in the extreme, because most of it is lies, falsehoods, and inventions; what is more, they continue to generate even more objectionable and offensive material for it (*lam yazālū yuwallidūna fīhi mā huwa aqbaḥ wa-asmaj*), which is not licit to transmit or to hear.[191]

Indeed, there is a clear correlation between the composition of scholarly *mawlid* texts and the expression of opposition to the more popular traditions of storytelling and preaching (*wa'ẓ*). As we have seen, several scholarly *mawlid* authors are also on record as having denounced al-Bakrī's *Anwār* (see earlier, p. 9).

Others produced separate works critiquing the activities of storytellers and preachers. The *mawlid* author Zayn al-Dīn al-ʿIrāqī (d. 806 AH/1404 CE) wrote a composition warning of the deviations of the *quṣṣāṣ*.[192] The most zealous defender of the legal legitimacy of the *mawlid* celebration, Jalāl al-Dīn al-Suyūṭī, also produced a work in denunciation of popular storytellers. The incident that precipitated the composition gives some idea of the kind of material that aroused the ire of scholars. al-Suyūṭī was moved to action when he was consulted about the statements of a particular *qāṣṣ*. Among other things, the latter was relating that when verse 21:107 of the Qur'ān was revealed, which states that "We sent you only as a mercy to the worlds," the Prophet asked the angel Gabriel whether he had received any of this mercy. Gabriel replied in the affirmative. Before his own creation, God had created thousands of angels named Gabriel; when God asked each one, "Who am I?" it did not know the answer and melted away. The present angel Gabriel survived only because the Light of Muḥammad instructed it to reply, "You are God, than whom there is no other deity."[193] The themes of this story, the pre-existence of the Light of Muḥammad and the Prophet's cosmic salvific role, are of course also the predominant motifs of the *mawlid* genre.

The degree of respectability and authentication of a given narrative, of course, was very much in the eye of the beholder. As we have seen, the *Muntaqā* of al-Kāzarūnī includes a rich selection of the more elaborate "popular" narratives about the Prophet's pre-existence, birth, and nursing. However, in the introduction to his work he presents the following lament: "What are these lying *mawlid*s (*mā hādhihi al-mawālīd al-akādhīb*)? What are these mockeries and wonders? What are these inventions, fables, and falsehoods that have no basis at all, consisting of forged reports?"[194] He presents his own work, in contrast, as "the most truthful of *mawlid*s" (in his terminology, *mawālīd*, singular *mīlād*). The reports contained in it are rational and acceptable (*maʿqūla, maqbūla*) and have been transmitted from trustworthy persons.[195]

al-Kāzarūnī, a student of the great *ḥadīth* specialist al-Mizzī,[196] cannot have been unaware that there existed criteria according to which his own material was unacceptable. Its comparative respectability clearly resulted from the contrast with far more disreputable stories. While the bulk of al-Kāzarūnī's *mawlid* material is "popular" or noncanonical with respect to the more rigorous standards of his Damascene contemporaries, it is clear that there was a far more wild and unruly form of storytelling in contrast to which it appeared sober and scholarly. As is demonstrated by the textual comparisons above, it is certainly true that much of the narrative tradition preserved by al-Kāzarūnī was fairly textually stable and widely circulated in written form; it is unsurprising that the oral practice of storytelling was far freer and produced results of an even more vivid character. It may be that the pseudo-Wāqidī *mawlid* text is the closest we will ever come to encountering such orally improvised premodern narratives.

Mawlid narratives such as the Kaʿb and Jābir traditions and the text of *al-Anwār* (as well as the material transmitted by al-Kāzarūnī) may be regarded as examples of "midcult," a level of medieval Islamic culture "situated between the great and little traditions and drawing on both."[197] The narratives often display knowledge of Qur'ān, *ḥadīth*, and the scholarly historical tradition, while molding and embellishing their base materials in ways that reflect folkloric storytelling techniques. They also represent a median level in terms of the continuum between written and oral culture. They are available to us because they were committed to writing, and al-Dhahabī's lament about the prevalence of al-Bakrī's works in the booksellers' market suggests their entrenchment in the world of literacy. The plasticity of the stories and the fairly free circulation of episodes and motifs suggest, however, that they were also sustained and reproduced in the context of oral performance. In these ways, they resemble what Peter Burke has described as "chapbook culture" in early modern Europe.[198] The cheap pamphlets in which such materials continue to circulate in the present day may indeed be the equivalent of chapbooks.

The more scholarly and sober *mawlid* texts of the Damascus school did not succeed in displacing the more exuberant *mawlid* narratives that we have surveyed earlier in this chapter. Unlike the *mawlid* of Ibn Kathīr, which was rediscovered fairly recently in an apparently unique manuscript located outside of the Islamic world, al-Bakrī's *Anwār* exists in multiple manuscripts and is currently in print in several different editions; it can be bought cheaply and easily in Cairo today. The manuscript record, and the appearance of excerpts in texts from various eras, indicates that narratives from *al-Anwār* were reproduced and circulated in every century until the present. The narrative contained in *al-Anwār* has also been perpetuated in popular *mawlid* chanting. A text currently in circulation under the title *Mawlid al-Nūr* recounts episodes from the biography of the Prophet that are distinctive to *al-Anwār*.[199]

al-Anwār is not, however, the only representative of the non-normative tradition that continued to flourish after the rise of scholarly *mawlids*. *Mawlid*s continued to be composed within the semi-popular storytelling tradition,[200] and earlier literary *mawlid*s of a more flowery devotional cast continued to be circulated and redacted. For instance, an undated manuscript entitled *Kitāb sharaf al-anām fī mawlid man ẓallahu al-ghumām* ("The honor of humankind on the birth of the one who was shaded by the cloud") presents an unusually complete version of the text known as *Sharaf al-anām*, attributed to the famous Shāfi'ī jurist Tāj al-Dīn al-Subkī (d. 769 AH/1368 CE).[201] It is not inconceivable that al-Subkī might have produced a version of this work, although none is ascribed to him in the bio-bibliographical sources; in terms of his lifetime, his residence in Damascus, and his membership in the Shāfi'ī school, he fits neatly into the overall pattern of *mawlid* authorship. In any case, the manuscript suggests continuing efforts to disseminate this influential *mawlid* text and provide it with a respectable provenance – one that, given al-Subkī's favorable attitudes toward some forms of devotional practice, offered a somewhat plausible figurehead for a popular but controversial text. The manuscript contains several other narratives of a pious but entertaining character, suggesting the context in which *Sharaf al-anām* continued to flourish.

Similarly, a version of the text of *Mawlid al-'arūs* appears in a manuscript entitled *Durar al-biḥār fī mawlid al-mukhtār* ("Pearls of the seas on the birth of the Chosen One").[202] The manuscript is an autograph copy by its author, Aḥmad ibn ʿAbd al-Raḥmān ibn Makkīya, dated the thirteenth of Rabīʿ al-Awwal, 876 AH/1471 CE. Ibn Makkīya, a native of Nablus, was a man of some scholarly training who achieved renown as a preacher (*wāʿiẓ*) at the Umayyad Mosque of Damascus.[203] While Ibn Makkīya almost certainly originated little (if any) of the material presented in this *mawlid*, its compilation was clearly a sufficiently honorable accomplishment to warrant presentation under his own name and title.

Although it is impossible to determine with certainty the audiences that sustained the popularity of works such as *Mawlid al-ʿarūs*, the texts themselves are sometimes suggestive. In particular, there is reason to believe that some of the most influential *mawlid* texts may have been shaped by the interests of women, and more particularly by performance in the context of women's life-cycle rituals. It is known from textual references that at least by the ninth-century AH/fifteenth-century CE, *mawlid*s were sometimes performed as elements of wedding celebrations (see Chapter 2); while this argument must remain speculative, it is tempting to infer that this may have been a context that helped to shape the text of *Mawlid al-ʿarūs*. In the context of the work *Mawlid al-ʿarūs* as a whole, the image of Āmina parallels that of the Prophet himself. Each is depicted as a figure of radiant beauty; like the bride Āmina, the Prophet is characterized as an "*ʿarūs*," a gender-neutral term that in classical Arabic can refer to either a bride or groom. A distinctive feature of the *mawlid* is a lengthy interlude of verse vividly evoking Āmina's luminous and triumphant appearance at her wedding. This poetry appears in various different manuscripts of the text; its variability suggests oral transmission and popular use.[204] Its content suggests the strong possibility that it was modeled on the actual wedding practices of the era in which it was produced. It describes Āmina's performance of a wedding procession, or *zaffa*, which remains a prominent feature of such celebrations in many parts of the Islamic world until today. The bride's appearance in gowns of various colors (often on successive days of the festivities) is also a widely known custom. Sitting on a throne (*kursī*) on a dais (*manaṣṣa*) is similarly widespread. The poem's use of distinctive vocabulary, such as the verb *naqqaṭa* (to give *nuqūṭ*, bridal gifts) also suggests that it evokes actual wedding festivities. Although it is impossible to determine the actual composition of the text's original audiences, it seems plausible to infer that – like Āmina's account of her labor with the Prophet – the loving evocation of Āmina's nuptials represented a numinously heightened rendition of a widespread facet of female experience.

The centrality of the wedding in *Mawlid al-ʿarūs* is not unique to that text. It is reminiscent of the fulsome treatment of Khadīja's wedding to Muḥammad in the popular narrative of the Prophet's life, represented in the text of al-Bakrī. Shīʿite *mawlid*s (for instance, those of ʿAlī and Fāṭima) also typically culminate with the main character's marriage. A modern published *mawlid* of ʿAlī (of unknown authorship and date) ends with a loving evocation of his marriage festivities, centering on Fāṭima's successive appearances in different sets of finery and the poetry that was recited in each case.[205] The role of the wedding as a focal point of popular narratives need not be of unduly profound significance; a wedding is an appropriate "happy ending" for a diverting narrative, or (in the case of Āmina's wedding) an engaging set piece likely to maintain the interest of a popular audience. Given that popular *mawlid* narratives are a form of religious expression as well as a kind of folk entertainment, however, it is worth unfolding the possible religious significance of this motif. Āmina's marriage to 'Abd Allāh, similar to Ḥalīma's loving encounter with the infant Prophet and Khadīja's wedding with her beloved Muḥammad, all represent moments when women become the recipients of extraordinary divine favor through their connection with the person of the Prophet. They all do so through traditional female roles (bride, mother, wet-nurse, wife) that would have been familiar and accessible to women in *mawlid* audiences. Through empathetic listening to stories of these women's encounters with the numinous reality of the Prophet, ordinary women (and men) may have hoped to access the auspicious power of these events. The contagiousness of *baraka* may in some sense have operated through narrative, as well as through the more conventional means of physical contact with the holy.

Conclusion

The checkered history of *mawlid* narrative suggests a complex interplay among various levels of Islamic society and culture. It supports neither a unilateral "trickle-down" model nor its inverse, a model in which the agendas and beliefs of ordinary Muslims operated independently of the input and direction of scholarly elites. On the one hand, the most "popular" material available to us through the written record shows evidence of extensive knowledge drawn from the normative tradition. The basic factual framework of the story (as well as many of its details) is familiar from scholarly sources such as the *Sīra* of Ibn Isḥāq; even the more exotic narratives, such as the cosmogony revolving around the Light of Muḥammad, reflect the influence of religiously sophisticated figures such as Sahl al-Tustarī. However, despite the wide prevalence of factual conventions and narrative and exegetical motifs from the scholarly tradition, scholars were clearly incapable of unilaterally guiding or controlling the material circulating in the broader society. Non-canonical *mawlid* narratives preceded the composition of scholarly *mawlid* texts in time and exceeded them in popularity. *Mawlid* texts such as those of al-Ja'barī and Ibn Kathīr, which were written as elite responses and alternatives to the more objectionable material in popular circulation, generally failed to achieve wide currency; they have been re-introduced into public consciousness only by the efforts of parties to the modern *mawlid* debate, who revisited isolated manuscripts to highlight the participation of distinguished scholars in the *mawlid* tradition. Non-canonical material was so successful that it eventually penetrated the preserve of elite scholarship; by the time the distinguished scholar al-Barzanjī composed his *mawlid* in the eighteenth-century, motifs such as the "heavenly handmaidens" attending Āmina were acceptable even to many respected authorities. If any distinctive social or professional group exercised disproportionate control over the dissemination of *mawlid* narratives, it was probably the *wu"āẓ* (preachers) and *munshidūn* (chanters) whose performances delighted broad audiences. The female *shaykh*s deplored by Ibn al-Ḥājj and the preachers whose activities are described by Ibn Ḥajar al-Haytamī were the immediate agents whose choices and proclivities shaped the *mawlid* tradition. They themselves, however, must have been influenced both from "above" and from "below," drawing basic facts and motifs from books and scholars while catering to the desires of their audiences.

2 Gifts and reciprocity in the celebration of the *mawlid*

As a new religious practice, the celebration of the Prophet's birthday required justification by scholars who encouraged or condoned it. The observance of the occasion of the Prophet's birth was often conceptualized by jurists as a form of reciprocation for God's bestowal of the Prophet Muḥammad. In this view, the Prophet himself was a gift conferred on the Muslim community and, indeed, on all of humanity; the bestowal of such a momentous gift required thanks, which were constituted by the celebration of the *mawlid*. The Damascene Shāfiʿī Abū Shāma (d. 665 AH/1268 CE) justifies the celebration of the *mawlid* on the basis that, in addition to involving charity toward the poor and the expression of love for the Prophet, it constitutes "thanks to God for what he has bestowed [upon His creatures] by creating His Messenger, whom He sent as a mercy to the worlds."[1]

Ibn Rajab al-Ḥanbalī (d. 795 AH/1392 CE) presents a longer and more rigorous exposition of the same idea. He bases his discussion on a *ḥadīth* tradition in which the Prophet is questioned about his custom of fasting on Monday and replies that "that is the day on which I was born, and on which prophecy was [first] revealed to me." Ibn Rajab argues that this text indicates that it is desirable to fast on the anniversaries of God's benefactions upon His servants.

> The greatest of God's benefactions towards this community is bringing forth Muḥammad to them, commissioning him as a prophet and sending him to them, as God said, "God did confer a great favor on the believers when He sent among them a messenger from among themselves" [Qur'ān 3:164]. The benefaction towards the community in sending him as a prophet is greater than the benefaction towards them in creating the heavens and the earth, the sun and the moon, the winds, the night and the day, sending down rain, bringing forth vegetation, etc.; all of these benefactions included people who disbelieved in God, His messengers, and the meeting with Him and exchanged His benefactions for ingratitude/disbelief (*kufr*). As for the benefaction of sending Muḥammad as a prophet, by means of it are completed the welfare of this world and the next, and because of it is perfected God's religion which He desires for His servants, and whose acceptance is the cause of their felicity in this world and the next. To fast on a day on which these benefactions from God towards His servants are renewed is right and good

> (*ḥasan jamīl*); it falls under the rubric of reciprocating benefactions with thanks at the times when they are renewed.

Ibn Rajab continues his discussion with an oblique reference to a *ḥadīth* text in which the Prophet finds the Jews of Medina fasting on 'Āshūrā'. Asked why they are fasting, they reply that they are doing so in thanksgiving for God's delivering Moses from Pharaoh.

> Similar to this is fasting on the day of 'Āshūrā', because on it God delivered Noah from drowning and on it He delivered Moses and his people from Pharaoh and his armies and drowned them in the sea, so Noah and Moses fasted on it in thanks to God, and the Messenger of God [Muḥammad] fasted on it in emulation of God's [other] prophets. He said to the Jews, "We are more worthy of Moses than you are," and fasted on ['Āshūrā'] and ordered [the Muslims] to fast on it.[2]

Whereas the "thanks" envisioned by Ibn Rajab appear to be limited to the pious practice of fasting in commemoration of the Prophet's birth, a legal opinion attributed to Ibn Ḥajar al-'Asqalānī (d. 852 AH/1449 CE) uses a similar argument to justify a much wider range of celebratory activities. The textual basis of his position is the *ḥadīth* about the Jews and the fast of 'Āshūrā' already cited by Ibn Rajab. Ibn Ḥajar's statement resembles that of Ibn Rajab closely enough to suggest dependence, although his wording seems to imply that his argument is novel. Whether or not the passage represents unacknowledged borrowing from Ibn Rajab, the conception of "thanks" is broadened considerably. "Thanks to God," writes Ibn Ḥajar, "are constituted by the various forms of worship, such as prostration, fasting, almsgiving, and [Qur'ānic] recitation." Later in the *fatwā*, he reiterates and expands on this point:

> As for what is performed on [the day of the *mawlid*], one should limit oneself to what expresses thanks to God, such as the things that have already been mentioned: [Qur'ānic] recitation, serving food, almsgiving, and recitation of praise [poems] about the Prophet and asceticism which motivate people to perform good deeds and act in view of the next world (*al-madā'iḥ al-nabawīya wa'l-zuhdīya al-muḥarrika li'l-qulūb ilā fi'l al-khayr wa'l-'amal li'l-ākhira*).

Ibn Ḥajar's only rigorous limitation on the forms of celebration is that they be neutral (*mubāḥ*) under the *sharī'a*; anything that is forbidden (*ḥarām*) or objectionable (*makrūh*) should be forbidden.[3]

Jalāl al-Dīn al-Suyūṭī (d. 911 AH/1505 CE) discovers another textual basis for the celebration of the *mawlid* that similarly rests on the principle of *shukr al-ni'ma*. This is a *ḥadīth* stating that the Prophet made a birth sacrifice (the *'aqīqa*, ordinarily offered seven days after the birth of a child) on his own behalf after the beginning of his prophetic mission. al-Suyūṭī argues that it is known that the Prophet's grandfather performed the *'aqīqa* for him in his infancy. Since the *'aqīqa* is not ordinarily performed a second time in a person's lifetime, the only reasonable explanation for the Prophet's repetition of the sacrifice is that he did so

> in order to express thanks for God's creation of him as a mercy to the worlds and as an honor to his community, just as he used to invoke blessings upon (*yuṣallī 'alā*) himself. Thus, it is desirable (*mustaḥabb*) for us as well to express thanks for his birth by the gathering of brethren, the serving of food (*iṭ'ām al-ṭa'ām*), and similar forms of pious activity (*wujūh al-qurubāt*) and expressions of delight (*iẓhār al-masarrāt*).[4]

Opponents of the *mawlid* celebration also invoked the concept of reciprocity in support of their critiques. Ibn al-Ḥājj (d. 737 AH/1336 CE), who regards the Prophet's birthday as an unusually blessed time of year, nevertheless (as we shall see) objects to the institution of celebratory activities in commemoration of the event. His rejection of the practice is based not only on its classification as a *bid'a* (innovation) but also on the idea that it is a perverted form of reciprocity. The underlying logic is most thoroughly expressed in his discussion of the night of the *mi'rāj*, believed to have occurred on the twenty-seventh of the month of Rajab. Ibn al-Ḥājj states that the exemplary early generations of Muslims (*al-salaf*) glorified this night in honor of the Prophet by increasing their devotions, lengthening the "standing" during their prayers, and engaging in supplication and weeping (*al-taḍarru' wa'l-bukā'*), in addition to other good customs. All of this constituted "the glorification of that which God has glorified" (*ta'ẓīm mā 'aẓẓamahu allāh*) as well as obedience to the *sunna* of the Prophet, who commanded the believers to "expose themselves to the fragrant waftings (*nafaḥāt*) of God." This blessed night, on which God multiplied the reward for the five daily prayers to equal fifty or even seven hundred, is surely one of these "fragrant waftings."

> This is great favor from One Who is generous and without need (*hādhā huwa'l-faḍl al-'aẓīm min ghanī karīm*); when [that night] came, they reciprocated it (*qābalūhā*) with what has just been mentioned, as thanks from them to their Lord for what He bestowed upon them and rendered to them (*shukran minhum li-mawlāhum 'alā mā manaḥahum wa-awlāhum*).[5]

The proper reciprocity of the early Muslims, however, had been replaced by more recent generations of Muslims by a distorted form of thanks. Speaking of another popular holiday, Ibn al-Ḥājj remarks that "this is a night of exceeding virtue (*hādhihi'l-layla zādat faḍīlatuhā*), and what follows from an increase in virtue is an increase in the thanks that it merits through the performance of acts of obedience (*al-ṭā'āt*) and the like. [However], some people, instead of increasing thanks, have increased innovations on it." This is "the reverse of reciprocating that with thanks for the increase in virtue" (*'aks muqābalat dhālika bi'l-shukr li-ziyādat al-faḍīla*) and "the opposite of giving thanks for benefactions, like for like" (*ḍidd shukr al-ni'am sawā'an bi-sawā'*).[6] Similarly, Ibn al-Ḥājj argues, the celebration of the Prophet's birthday represents a misguided form of reciprocation. "It would have been obligatory for [people] to increase their devotions and good works in [the month of Rabīʿ al-Awwal] in thanks to the Lord for these great blessings that He has bestowed upon us," he writes; instead, people engage in sinful and disruptive innovations.[7]

A similar understanding of the underlying rationale of the *mawlid* celebration is reflected in a *fatwā* by the North African jurist al-Ḥaffār (d. 811 AH/1408 CE). He argues that property whose income a woman had assigned to the celebration of the *mawlid* should be re-allocated to the aid of the indigent. This would fulfill the woman's underlying intent in endowing the *mawlid* celebration in a more legally suitable manner, al-Ḥaffār reasons, because it would be done by way of "thanking God [for] His benefaction towards His servants in the birth of the Noble Prophet, who was the means of saving them from hellfire; this is occasion for thanks, and that can only be in the legally valid manner."[8] Here again, the jurist suggests replacing an inappropriate form of thanks with a more fitting act of reciprocation.

The idea that favors require reciprocation is deeply rooted in the Islamic tradition. As discussed by Kevin Reinhart in his landmark study *Before Revelation*, "thanking the benefactor" is one of the fundamental principles of Muslim moral thought. Reinhart argues that the application of this principle underwent a transformation between 400 and 600 AH. While early Muslim thinkers such as al-Ḥasan al-Baṣrī defined the "thanks" owed to the divine benefactor as obedience to the divine command, by the sixth century, Reinhart argues, "Thanking is intellectual (or emotional . . .). Thanks is no longer a response implying action."[9] Reinhart roots this putative shift in the transformation of Islamic theological attitudes. "It seems clear," he writes, "that in the period 450–550 AH the transactional nature of the human-divine relationship is lost. . . . Thanking God becomes something categorically different from thanking another human being."[10]

Reinhart's insightful reading of the theological literature, however, does not encompass all of the domains in which ideas of reciprocity and thanking were applied by late-medieval Muslims. The debate over the legitimacy of the *mawlid* illustrates that thanks could still be deployed as a "response requiring action." In arguing that the celebration of the *mawlid* (with all of its component acts of worship, giving, and rejoicing) constituted thanks for the divine gift of the Prophet, Ibn Ḥajar used the principle of *shukr al-munʿim* as a productive legal precept justifying substantively novel forms of Islamic piety. It should be emphasized that the idea that the Prophet is a gift for which we may thank God with any pious action expressive of gratitude and joy departs quite sharply from more limited understandings of adherence to the *sunna*. The believer's relationship with God and the Prophet, rather than being strictly limited to obedience and emulation, becomes one of reciprocity and exchange.

The conceptualization of the Prophet as a gift, and of the celebration of his *mawlid* as a form of thanks, reflects an overall model that also informs devotees' understanding of the individual components of the *mawlid* celebration.

A transactional model emphasizing relationships of reciprocity and exchange underlies supporters' understanding of activities as externally diverse as the donation of money, the serving of food, and the composition and performance of *mawlid* texts. Because it involved monetary expenditure and the serving of a meal, *mawlid* recitation was concretely linked with these other forms of piety. Because it created a relationship of reciprocity that elicited rewards from God, it was structurally equivalent to them. All three in some sense represented counter-gifts for God's supreme gift of the Prophet Muḥammad, and were expected to evoke further divine bounties in return.

al-Qāri' al-Harawī (d. 1014 AH/1606 CE) expresses the interrelationship of the various components of the classical model of *mawlid* piety explicitly in the introduction to his *mawlid* text *al-Mawrid al-rawī fī mawlid al-nabī*. He begins the passage by citing Ibn Ḥajar's argument that the *mawlid* celebration legitimately involves all licit activities expressing thanks (*shukr*) to God for the bestowal of the Prophet. Citing the example of a religious scholar who prepared and distributed food in celebration of the Prophet's birthday, al-Qāri' al-Harawī remarks, "As I myself am incapable of providing physical hospitality (*al-ḍiyāfa al-ṣūrīya*), I have written these pages so that they may become a luminous spiritual hospitality (*ḍiyāfa ma'nawīya nūrīya*) that lasts continually over the pages of time."[11]

Mawlid banquets

Whether on the level of large-scale public festivities or of modest domestic celebrations, the observance of the Prophet's birthday seems to have featured two central components: feasting and recitation. Early public celebrations of the *mawlid* seem to have involved an almost potlatch-like level of conspicuous consumption. Sibṭ ibn al-Jawzī (d. 654 AH/1257 CE) reports of the celebration sponsored by Muẓaffar al-Dīn Kökbürī – the first Sunni *mawlid* celebration of which we have a detailed description – that "somebody who had been present at the banquet of al-Muẓaffar during one of the *mawlid* celebrations said that for that banquet he served 5000 roast [sheep], 10,000 chickens, 100,000 dishes (*zabdīya*) and 30,000 platters of sweetmeats."[12] According to Ibn Khallikān (d. 681 AH/1282 CE), the number of camels, cows, and sheep that were paraded to the slaughter to the accompaniment of drumming and singing was simply "beyond description."[13] The overall cost of the annual celebration is said to have reached 300,000 *dirhams*.[14] More than a century later, Ibn al-Jazarī estimates the cost of the *mawlid* festival held by the Mamlūk sultan al-Ẓāhir Barqūq in 785 AH/1383 CE at around 10,000 *mithqāl*s of gold. The expenses included gifts bestowed on Qur'ān reciters and other participants, robes of honor, food, drink, and incense.[15]

N.J.G. Kaptein has convincingly argued that the presence of guests and the distribution of largess at early Sunnī *mawlid* festivals performed "an important social and political function."[16] By concretizing ties of patronage and dramatizing the benevolence of the ruler, they must have served to consolidate and legitimize power relationships. However, such epic expenditures also carried religious significance. As reported by Sibṭ ibn al-Jawzī, Kökbürī's lavish spending on the *mawlid* celebration was only one in a range of pious expenditures including the maintenance of a guest-house for travelers, the ransoming of Muslim prisoners of war, and the upkeep of facilities for pilgrims to Mecca. As Ibn Khallikān notes, "nothing in this world was dearer to him than almsgiving." His daily routine included the personal distribution of prodigious quantities of bread to the needy; he distributed garments and coins to supplicants at his home.[17] These expenses reportedly depleted Kökbürī's funds to the point that he himself wore a cheap cotton garment worth less than five *dirhams*.[18] Kökbürī's benevolence, whether or not it literally impoverished him, presumably played a role in his political legitimation. However, it also reflects a model of pious expenditure that was applied by laypeople of modest means as well as by wielders of power.

*Fatwā*s addressing the legitimacy of the festival suggest that in private *mawlid*s as well, the serving of food and the associated expenditure of money were central. Issues of spending and feeding were pivotal both to the religious and social function of the celebration and to the objections it raised. Muḥammad ibn Yūsuf al-Ṣāliḥī al-Shāmī (d. 942 AH/1536 CE) records the following opinion from Naṣīr al-Dīn al-Mubārak, known as Ibn al-Ṭabbākh:

> If someone spends money (*anfaqa al-munfiq*) on that night, gathers a group of people to whom he feeds licit things and makes them listen to licit things (*aṭʿamahum mā yajūzu iṭʿāmuhu wa-asmaʿahum mā yajūzu samʿuhu*), and gives the performer who arouses people's longing for the next world something to wear, all of this out of delight in [the Prophet's] birth, all of this is permissible and the one who does it will be rewarded if his intention is good. This is not limited to the poor to the exclusion of the rich [i.e., as recipients of food], unless he intends to comfort those who are most needy, in which case the poor yield greater rewards.[19]

The *shaykh* Naṣīr al-Dīn also said, "This is not a *sunna,* but if one makes expenditures on this day and displays delight out of joy in the entrance of the Prophet into this world," and performs licit *samāʿ*,

> this is a good gathering, and anyone who intends that and performs it will be rewarded for it, except that asking people for what they possess for this reason alone, and without necessity and need, is a disapproved request (*suʾāl makrūh*). The gathering of righteous people (*al-ṣulaḥāʾ*) simply to eat that food, remember God, and invoke blessings upon the Prophet will multiply good deeds and rewards for them.[20]

al-Mubārak ibn ʿAlī ibn al-Ḥusayn, Abū Muḥammad ibn al-Ṭabbākh (d. 575 AH/1178–9 CE) was a Baghdādī Ḥanbalī who settled in Mecca and served as the Ḥanbalī prayer leader in the sanctuary (*imām al-ḥanābila bi'l-ḥaram*). He was a distinguished *muḥaddith*, considered the foremost traditionist of Mecca in his time, as well as a *faqīh*.[21] While there is no way of determining the date of his *fatwā* on the celebration of the *mawlid*, his date of death suggests that the private celebration of the *mawlid* had become an issue (at least in Mecca) at approximately the same time as the first public Sunnī celebrations of the holiday. Ibn al-Ṭabbākh's emphasis on mystical audition (*samā'*) suggests that the celebration was popular in *ṣūfī* circles. A central feature of the gathering was the serving of food. The significance of the meal lay in the expression of joy in the Prophet's birth, but a key element was clearly the expenditure of money; Ibn al-Ṭabbākh refers to the host as "the one who makes an expenditure (*al-munfiq*)." However, unlike in the case of a dignitary such as Kökbürī, this cannot always have been a display of means by a person of substantial wealth. Ibn al-Ṭabbākh's disapproving reference to the practice of "asking people for what they possess for this reason alone" suggests that the host solicited donations to defray the costs of the celebration.

A positive insider's view of the custom of holding *mawlid* banquets is provided in another passage cited by al-Ṣāliḥī, apparently from a lost *mawlid* text:[22]

> Those who love the Prophet have given banquets out of joy in his birth; among these are the great banquets that were given in Cairo by the *shaykh* Abū'l-Ḥasan, known as Ibn Qufl, may God sanctify his innermost being, the *shaykh* of our *shaykh* Abū 'Abd Allāh Muḥammad ibn al-Nu'mān. This was done earlier by Jamāl al-Dīn al-'Ajamī al-Hamadhānī. Among those who did this to the extent of his means (*'alā qadr wus'ihi*) was Yūsuf al-Ḥajjār in Egypt. He saw the Prophet in a dream, urging the aforementioned Yūsuf to do so.
>
> He said: I heard Yūsuf ibn 'Alī ibn Zurayq, who was of Syrian extraction but born in Egypt, al-Ḥajjār, say in Egypt in his home there where he used to celebrate the Prophet's *mawlid*, "I saw the Prophet in a dream twenty years ago. I had a brother in religion (*akh fī Allāh ta'ālā*) called the *shaykh* Abū Bakr al-Ḥajjār, and I dreamt that I and this Abū Bakr were sitting before the Prophet; Abū Bakr grasped his own beard and separated it into two halves, and mentioned something to the Prophet that I did not understand. The Prophet said in answer to him, 'If not for this, it [i.e., the beard] would be in the Fire.' He turned to me and said, 'I am going to beat you!' – there was a staff in his hand. I said, 'For what, O Messenger of God?' He said, 'So that you will not abandon (*tubṭil*) the *mawlid* or the *sunnas*'." Yūsuf said, "So I have performed it for twenty years, until today."
>
> He said: I heard the aforementioned Yūsuf say: I heard my brother Abū Bakr al-Ḥajjār say: I heard Manṣūr al-Nashshār say, "I saw the Prophet in a dream saying to me, 'Tell him not to abandon it!' – meaning the *mawlid*; 'It is not your fault who eats and who does not eat' " (*mā 'alayka mimman akala wa-mimman lam ya'kul*). He said: I heard our *shaykh* Abū 'Abd Allāh ibn abī Muḥammad al-Nu'mān say: I heard the *shaykh* Abū Mūsā al-Zarhūnī say, "I saw the Prophet in a dream and mentioned to him what the *fuqahā'* were saying about the holding of banquets for birthday, and he said, "Whoever rejoices in us, we rejoice in him."[23]

With the exception of the two *shaykh*s, whose dates allow us to place these events in the seventh-century AH/thirteenth-century CE, the individuals mentioned in this passage are unidentifiable.[24] However, this interlocking set of anecdotes provides several clues to the social setting of early private celebrations of the *mawlid*. First of all, the setting is clearly ṣūfī. The individuals involved are represented as "brothers" in a spiritual confraternity and as disciples of named ṣūfī *shaykh*s. The text does not, however, necessarily imply a high degree of mystical depth to the celebrations. They seem to consist simply of festive meals, whether presented by the *shaykh* himself or (on a smaller scale) by his individual followers. The names of the followers, interestingly, point to a specific (and rather humble) social stratum. Both Yūsuf and his "brother" Abū Bakr bear the cognomen al-Ḥajjār, "the stonemason." Abū Bakr's informant Manṣūr is called al-Nashshār, "the sawyer." Thus, all three men would seem to have been artisans (although such cognomens were sometimes inherited). The celebrations themselves seem to have ranged from rather grand banquets given by recognized ṣūfī *shaykh*s to more modest meals in the homes of individual devotees. The text specifies that Yūsuf ibn 'Alī's banquets took place in his own home (*manzil*) and suggests, by remarking that he held the celebration "to the extent of his means," that his resources may not have been lavish.

As we have already seen, hosts might be aided in defraying the costs of a *mawlid* by monetary contributions from their guests. The idea that private individuals collected money for the celebration of the *mawlid* is also suggested by a *fatwā* produced by Ṣadr al-Dīn Mawhūb ibn 'Umar al-Jazarī, an Egyptian Shāfi'ī *qāḍī* who died in 675 AH/1274 CE.[25] In response to a query about the celebration of the *mawlid*, he responds:

> This is an innovation, but it is an unobjectionable innovation. However, it is not permissible [for the host] to ask the people [for money]; rather, if he knows or has good reason to suspect that the person who is asked is happy to give what he gives him, it is allowed (*mubāḥ*) to ask – I hope that it does not lead to anything [legally] repugnant (*arjū an lā yantahī ilā al-karāha*).[26]

The possibility of coerced giving at *mawlid*s is one of the most prominent recurrent themes in early *fatwā*s and discussions on the celebration. The problem is featured in one of the earliest anti-*mawlid fatwā*s preserved, that of Tāj al-Dīn al-Fākihānī.[27] al-Fākihānī, an Alexandrian Mālikī who died in 731 AH/1331 CE, highlights the centrality of eating in the observation of the *mawlid* by dismissing it as "an innovation invented by idlers and a sensual indulgence to which gluttons (*al-akkālūn*) are devoted." Because the celebration of the *mawlid* is a religious innovation (*bid'a*), its status under the *sharī'a* may be either undesirable (*makrūh*) or forbidden (*ḥarām*). It is *makrūh* if a man holds it at his own expense for his family, friends, and children (*ahl*, *aṣḥāb*, *'iyāl*), and they do nothing but gather to eat without committing any sins. It is *ḥarām* if people are constrained to contribute money to it when they would rather not, or if it involves musical instruments, or the mixing of men and women, or dancing. al-Fākihānī strongly emphasizes the possibility that guests will feel shamed into making donations, which he equates with the false expropriation of wealth; he notes that "the religious scholars have said that 'taking money by means of shame is tantamount to taking it by means of the sword.' "[28]

al-Fākihānī's contemporary Ibn al-Ḥājj al-'Abdarī, another Mālikī who resided in Egypt, shared his misgivings about the celebration of the *mawlid*. Similar to al-Fākihānī, he perceived the most basic (and the least controversial) element of the celebration to be the serving of food to guests. Even this elementary (and in itself innocuous) activity, however, was religiously suspect.

> If [the performance of the *mawlid*] is free [of *samā'*] and [a person] simply prepares food, makes the intention of [celebrating] the *mawlid* (*nawā bihi al-mawlid*), and invites his friends (*ikhwān*) to it..., it is an innovation by virtue of his intention alone, because that is an addition to the religion and is not something that was performed by the exemplary Muslims of the past (*wa-laysa min 'amal al-salaf al-māḍīn*).[29]

Also like al-Fākihānī, Ibn al-Ḥājj critiques the elements of social and financial coercion involved in holding *mawlid* celebrations. Supporters of the *mawlid*, he complains, consider those who do not perform it to be stingy (*bakhīl*).[30] He also contends that the hosting of a *mawlid* could be an occasion for the veiled extortion of money, suggesting that the banquet might cost less than the total of the contributions made, thus leaving a net gain for the host.

Ibn al-Ḥājj suggests that a person might use a *mawlid* as a pretext to recoup the money (lit., silver, *fiḍḍa*) that he had distributed to people on previous festive occasions, such as weddings and holidays. He observes that guests might contribute money out of more than one motive. Sometimes the donation might be made in consideration of the poverty of the host, either real or feigned for the purpose of encouraging contributions. On the other hand, attending *mawlid*s and contributing to their costs might be motivated by fear of the spite of a host known for his sharp tongue or malicious character. Ibn al-Ḥājj paints a fearsome picture of the hazards of refusing an invitation to an acquaintance's *mawlid*, ranging from personal enmity to denunciation to the authorities. He further suggests that some people hold *mawlid*s as a way of seeking social approval (*thanā' al-nās*), a motive which he regards as flatly contradictory to the proclaimed religious purpose of the celebration. Here again, the social aspect is primary.[31] Although Ibn al-Ḥājj regards the *mawlid* celebration's entanglement in the web of social obligation and exchange in a purely negative light, his comments suggest that it played a role in the consolidation of social relationships and the enactment of prestige. The holding of *mawlid*s seems to have played a role in the economy of gifts that cemented relationships and defined social networks in contemporary Cairo.

Regardless of the ethical and legal scruples of some jurists, the holding of banquets was clearly the central element of the *mawlid* celebration. The identification of *mawlid*s with food distribution was so strong that the Shāfi'ī scholar Abū Zur'a ibn al-'Irāqī (d. 826 AH/1423 CE) responded to an enquiry about the legitimacy of the *mawlid* celebration by affirming that "banquets and the distribution of food (*al-walīma wa-iṭ'ām al-ṭa'ām*) are desirable at all times," and even more so when combined with the manifestation of joy on the occasion of the Prophet's birth.[32] The same assumption emerges from the similar, but more oblique, comments of Ibn Taymīya (d. 728 AH/1328 CE). Asked whether it was legally desirable (*mustaḥabb*) to hold a complete reading of the Qur'ān (*khatma*) each year on the night of the Prophet's birth, he responded with a review of the occasions on which it is religiously commendable to distribute food and give gifts to reciters. He writes that it is *sunna* to gather people for festive meals on the two *'Īd*s and during the last three days of the ḥajj pilgrimage (*ayyām al-tashrīq*), and to distribute food to the poor during Ramaḍān; it is meritorious to aid needy Qur'ān reciters at any time of the year. However, designating a festival (*mawsim*) in addition to those mandated by the *sharī'a* is a religious innovation (*bid'a*).[33]

The diarist Ibn Ṭawq gives a matter-of-fact and non-polemical sense of the role of domestic *mawlid* celebrations in Damascus in the fifteenth-century CE. His passing references suggest that *mawlid*s formed an integral part of the networks of religious sociability and neighborly gift exchange. The serving of food was certainly a feature of *mawlid* celebrations. Ibn Ṭawq describes a *mawlid* held in Rabī' al-Awwal of 887 AH/1482 CE that brought together about twenty people at the home of a confectioner (*sukkarī*) by the name of Muḥammad ibn Waṭfa. Before the recitation, sweets were served. After the *mawlid*, there was a meal consisting of a bean dish, couscous with chicken and meat, sweet rice with sugar and almond oil, and an apricot dish (*mishmishīya*). Scent (*mashmūm*) and rosewater were also provided.[34] Women also held domestic *mawlids*.[35] The kind of contribution that might be made by a participant is suggested by Ibn Ṭawq's comment that he attended the *mawlid* of one of his neighbors in Rabī' al-Awwal of 888 AH/1483 CE, taking "a large gilded candle."[36] As Ibn al-Ḥājj implies, *mawlid* contributions seem to have been similar in magnitude and kind to those associated with wedding celebrations; Ibn Ṭawq records almost identical contributions – in each case, a candle and a monetary gift – made for a *mawlid* and for a wedding.[37]

The recitation of *mawlid*s could also be incorporated into other festive occasions, particularly the celebration of marriages. It is not clear when the custom of holding *mawlid*s in this context emerged. By the late-ninth-century AH/fifteenth-century CE, Ibn Ṭawq treats it as a matter of course; *mawlid*s are a common, although far from universal, component of wedding celebrations.[38] In 917 AH/1511 CE, Ibn Ṭūlūn al-Ṣāliḥī similarly records the identity of the *mawlid* reciter as a routine piece of information about a marriage, along with the names of the witnesses.[39] He also records a celebration that occurred a few years later, when a man engaged his two sons to marry a pair of sisters; the happy father gave a banquet attended by the religious court judges, and a *mawlid* was recited by a preacher (*wā'iẓ*).[40] In Jumādā al-Ākhira of 926 AH/1520 CE, an official held a *mawlid* performed by a *mu'adhdhin* when he circumcised his three youngest sons, a festive occasion attended by the notables of the city that included a banquet for which eighty sheep (in addition to other livestock) were slaughtered.[41]

The incorporation of *mawlid* performances into the celebration of joyful occasions (particularly life-cycle celebrations) is probably founded on the understanding of the *mawlid* as both an expression of gratitude for divine favors and as a source of religious merit (thus adding to the auspiciousness of a happy day and perhaps conducing to good luck). Because *mawlids* ordinarily were associated with festive meals, they were also a natural accompaniment to special occasions (such as weddings) that in any case involved banquets.

The expenditure of money on festive banquets was not, however, the only way in which *mawlid* celebrations were incorporated into an economy of merit. It is clear that in North Africa, at least, bequests for the support of *mawlid* ceremonies became a widespread (if controversial) phenomenon. Several *fatwās* address this custom in the Maghrib in the eighth-century AH/fourteenth-century CE. The *Mi'yār* of Aḥmad al-Wansharīsī records *fatwās* addressing three such cases, issued by the jurists Abū Isḥāq al-Shāṭibī (d. 790 AH/1388 CE) and Muḥammad al-Ḥaffār (d. 811 AH/1408 CE). In one case addressed to al-Shāṭibī, the deceased had designated one-third of his or her estate – the legal maximum for testamentary bequests – for the celebration of the night of the *mawlid* (*iqāmat laylat al-mawlid*). The other two bequests involved the grain crop from a piece of land and the fruit of a mulberry tree. While the last mentioned may have been of rather modest value, the other two suggest that the celebration of the *mawlid* was a pious act of very high priority for the individuals involved. The jurists imply in their responses that the beneficiaries of such bequests were organized groups of *ṣūfīs*. In all cases, the jurists argue that the celebration of the *mawlid* is an illegitimate innovation, that expending money on innovations is impermissible, and that the bequest is thus void.[42]

The fact that bequests were made for the celebration of the *mawlid* demonstrates that such gatherings had a religious significance that transcended the holding of a party or the reinforcement of social ties; they were expected to produce religious merit. The generation of religious merit had continuing (indeed, perhaps enhanced) relevance after an individual's death, hence its attractiveness as a continuing post-mortem activity supported by bequests and *waqf* endowments.

The extent to which the feasting and celebration associated with the *mawlid* were embedded in the social and economic relationships of the community is suggested by a question addressed to the jurist Ibn Ḥajar al-Haytamī (d. 974 AH/1567 CE). The questioner wishes to clarify the forms of financial support that may licitly be accepted by a judge. In the absence of a central authority, a treasury, or an individual patron to pay a judge's salary, is it permissible for the community leaders to impose a tax on agricultural produce marketed in the town? Is it permissible for a judge to accept vows (*al-nadhr*) or gifts (*al-hiba*), or to attend banquets held in honor of the Prophet's birthday? Ibn Ḥajar replies that a judge may not be supported by noncanonical taxes or accept vows or gifts. It is permissible for a judge to attend banquets, although ideally he should refrain from doing so.[43] Ibn Ḥajar's questioner outlines an array of benefits potentially bestowed upon a judge, ranging from the purely financial issue of tax-financed salary to the religiously laden transactions of oaths and *mawlid* banquets. As has already emerged from the jurists' concern over the issue of coerced giving, the holding of a *mawlid* celebration was simultaneously an issue of pious action and one of financial ethics.

The importance of feasting and pious expenditure in the celebration of the Prophet's *mawlid* is suggested by a story that has been reproduced in *mawlid* texts over many centuries. It was in circulation as early as the eighth-century AH/ fourteenth-century CE, appearing in the *mawlid* text of Ibn Jābir al-Andalusī (d. 780 AH/1377–8 CE).[44] Its wide dissemination was insured by its inclusion in the *mawlid* text known as *Sharaf al-anām*.

> 'Abd al-Wāḥid ibn Ismā'īl said: In Egypt there was a man who used to hold a *mawlid* in honor of the Prophet every year. Living next to him was a Jewish man; his Jewish wife said, "Why is it that our Muslim neighbor spends such quantities of money in this month of every year?" Her husband said to her, "He claims that his prophet was born in it; he does that to rejoice in him, and to honor him and his birth." Then they fell silent. That night they slept, and the Jew's wife dreamt of a beautiful, majestic man of great stateliness, nobility and dignity. He entered the house of their Muslim neighbor, surrounded by a group of his companions who honored and exalted him. She said to one of the men, "Who is this man who is so fair of face?" He said to her, "This is the Messenger of God, may God bless him and grant him peace! He has entered this house to greet its inhabitants and visit them because they rejoice in him." She said to him, "Will he speak to me if I speak to him?" He said, "Yes!" She came to him and said, "O Muḥammad!" He replied, "Here I am, at your service!" She said to him, "You answer thus to a person like me, a follower of another religion and one of your enemies?" He said to her, "By the One who sent me as a prophet with the truth, I answered your call only when I knew that God Most High had guided you!" She said, "Indeed, you are a noble prophet, and your character is lofty![45] Wretched are they who disobey your commands, and losers are they who are ignorant of your station. Stretch out your hand [to take my oath of allegiance]; I bear witness that there is no god but God, and that you are Muḥammad, the Messenger of God." Then she vowed to God in her heart that when she awoke she would give all she owned in charity and hold a *mawlid* for the Prophet out of joy in her conversion and gratitude for the dream that she had dreamed.
>
> When she awoke she saw that her husband had [already] prepared the feast and had busied himself mightily. She said, "How is it that I see you busying yourself with a good work?" He replied, "It is for the sake of him at whose hand you converted last night!" She said, "Who is it who revealed to you this well-guarded secret, and who is it who informed you of it?" He replied, "The one at whose hand I converted after you [told me], just as he told me about God and called me to Him. He is empowered to intercede on the Morrow [i.e., the Day of Judgment] for those who bless and greet him."[46]

This narrative is interesting in a number of ways, and we will have occasion to discuss it again. For our current purposes, however, a few features of the story are central. From the point of view of the Jewish man and his wife, the most prominent (and mysterious) feature of their neighbor's celebration of the *mawlid* is the annual expenditure of copious amounts of money. For them his generous spending is the subject of wondering comment, possibly (although not explicitly) because they have assumed themselves to be stingy. That the object of this expenditure is a banquet becomes clear when the Jewish couple converts to Islam as a result of their dream encounter with the Prophet; the husband's first act is to prepare a festive meal. The expenditure of money on the celebration is either associated or conflated with the giving of charity. The wife vows to "give all she owns in charity" and to hold a *mawlid*; it is not clear whether these are two separate acts of devotion, or whether she is determined to expend all of her resources on the *mawlid* itself. In any case, the strong interrelation of spending, feasting, and the celebration of the *mawlid* is unmistakable.

al-Qāri' al-Harawī provides an insight into the financial and religious dynamics of the celebration of the *mawlid* at a somewhat later period. He notes that the Persians (*'ajam*) hold splendid gatherings with recitation and singing where food is served to Qur'ān reciters and ṣūfīs; "even some old ladies collect from [the money earned with] their spinning and weaving the means to gather prominent men and dignitaries (*al-akābir wa'l-a'yān*) and provide hospitality to the extent of their ability at that time [i.e., the beginning of Rabī' al-Awwal]."[47] Much like a wedding feast, the *mawlid* was an invitation that could not be declined. al-Harawī describes how a ruler compelled an unwilling *ṣūfī* shaykh to honor him with a visit by inviting him to a *mawlid*, an invitation he could not refuse.[48] It activated the obligations of gift-giving and hospitality, with both the social benefits and the elements of coercion that they implied.

Like other forms of gift-giving, the holding of *mawlid*s was based on an underlying concept of reciprocity. The ultimate recipient was God, and the gift that *mawlid*s were intended to elicit (not as a due recompense, but as a gracious divine benefaction) was personal salvation. "Whoever spends a *dirham* on [the celebration of] his *mawlid*," declares one version of *Mawlid al-'arūs*, "al-Muṣṭafā [the Chosen One, that is, the Prophet Muḥammad] will be his intercessor whose mediation is accepted, and God will recompense him for every *dirham* ten." It continues,

> What felicity is enjoyed by the one who performs a *mawlid* for Aḥmad [i.e., the Prophet Muḥammad]! He experiences well-being, honor, wealth and renown, and he will enter the Gardens of paradise wearing diadems of pearl beneath which are robes of green. He will be given palaces [in heaven] that none can describe or count, in each of which is a virgin houri. So invoke blessings on the best of humankind, for the best fate has been unfolded through his *mawlid*![49]

Pious utterances and the generation of merit

In addition to the serving of lavish meals, the celebration of the *mawlid* is also associated with a number of different forms of verbal production and performance. In keeping with the *ṣūfī* context of many of the earliest sunnī *mawlid* celebrations, the performance of mystical verse was frequently featured. Such poetry was not necessarily thematically connected with the Prophet's birth, but was drawn from the *ṣūfī* repertoire and revolved around the usual ambiguous tropes of divine and profane love. It was accompanied by ecstatic behavior that drew the condemnation of the more sober jurists. This is clear from several early *fatwā*s, which express reservations about the content of the poetry as well as the abandonment with which it was performed. Ibn al-Ṭabbākh, although he endorses the observation of the *mawlid* itself, objects to celebrations "involving the taking of hashish, the gathering of young men, the rejection of the singer if he has a beard, the singing of [songs] arousing longing for worldly pleasures, and other forms of degradation (*al-khizy*)." He condones only "*samā'* that is free of the gathering of young men and the singing of love poems (*'ishqīyāt*) that arouse the fire of desire and things that induce longing for worldly pleasures, like [poems that mention] the stature, the cheek, the eye, and the brow [of the beloved]." Acceptable themes include "things that induce longing for the next world and renunciation of this world."[50] Ja'far al-Tizmantī (d. 682 AH/1283 CE) condemns "the gathering of rowdies (*ra'ā'*), the performance of *samā'*, dancing, and casting robes upon the singer (*qawwāl*) for the sake of his youthful charm (*murūdīyatihi*) and the beauty of his voice."[51] Tāj al-Dīn al-Fākihānī similarly condemns singing accompanied by dancing to reed flutes and drums.[52] Ibn al-Ḥajj provides a vivid description of the excesses involved in *samā'* sessions held in honor of the *mawlid*.[53]

The celebration of the *mawlid* also involved less ecstatic verbal performances. These included Qur'ānic recitation and the "remembrance of God" (*dhikr*), usually the repetitive recitation of selected names of God. As we have seen, Ibn Taymīya responds to a question about the custom of holding a complete recitation of the Qur'ān (*khatma*) on the night of the Prophet's birthday.[54] Ibn al-Ḥajj writes that persons too scrupulous to hold *samā'* sessions in honor of the *mawlid* invited reciters of the Qur'ān, while yet others held readings of the *Ṣaḥīḥ* of al-Bukhārī.[55] Most typically and distinctively, however, the celebration of the *mawlid* featured the invocation of blessings on the Prophet Muḥammad. These more sober recitations, free of the scandalous abandon that was perceived to characterize *ṣūfī samā'*, were often condoned by jurists. While Ibn al-Ṭabbākh expresses reservations about some manifestations of the *mawlid* celebration, for instance, he affirms that "the gathering of pious people (*al-ṣulaḥā'*) simply to eat that food, remember God, and invoke prayers upon the Prophet will multiply good deeds and rewards for them."[56] Similarly, Ẓahīr al-Dīn Ja'far al-Tizmantī states that the *mawlid* "is a good innovation (*bid'a ḥasana*) if the one who performs it intends the gathering of pious people (*al-ṣāliḥīn*), the invocation of prayer upon the Prophet, and the feeding of the poor and the indigent."[57]

Unlike the performance of *samā'*, the invocation of blessings on the Prophet is a devotional practice that is not distinctively *ṣūfī* in character. It is rooted in verse 33:56 of the Qur'ān, which states that "God and His angels bless the Prophet; o you who believe, invoke blessings upon him and greet him often." Both linguistically and theologically, the use of the verb "*ṣallā ʿalā*" (here translated "to bless" or "to invoke blessings") is somewhat opaque. The ordinary meaning of the verb *ṣallā* is "to pray," although this meaning cannot literally be predicated of God. Despite the inherent incommensurability of the divine and human capacities to bestow blessing or to perform prayer, however, the invocation of blessings upon the Prophet (*ṣalāt ʿalā al-nabī*) is established by this verse not only as a commanded action, but as one performed in emulation of the angels and of God Himself.

In practice, it consists of pronouncing the phrase *ṣallā allāhu ʿalayhi wa-sallam* ("may God bless [the Prophet] and greet him/grant him peace"), or of some equivalent. The invocation of God's blessings upon the Prophet is a ubiquitous expression of Islamic piety. It is considered religiously meritorious to pronounce the *ṣalāt ʿalā al-nabī* every time the Prophet's name or title is mentioned, whether verbally or in print, and unmannerly or impious to neglect to do so. The invocation of blessings upon the Prophet is also a component of the canonical prayer ritual. Over time, it also became an important form of Islamic piety in its own right.[58] al-Suyūṭī records that blessings on the Prophet were added to the evening call to prayer in 781 AH/1379 CE; ten years later it was added to every *ādhān* except the maghrib.[59]

The earliest preserved *mawlid* text, al-ʿAzafī's *al-Durr al-munaẓẓam*, contains a chapter discussing the virtues and rewards of performing the *ṣalāt ʿalā al-nabī*. Although it provides no information about the form in which the invocation of blessings on the Prophet was to be incorporated into the *mawlid* celebration, it does reveal important aspects of the framework within which this act of piety was valorized and understood. al-ʿAzafī begins by invoking upon the Prophet "a continuous *ṣalāt* that is accepted [by God], by means of which our great debt to [the Prophet] is discharged" (*ṣalātan dāʾiman maqbūlan tuʾaddā bihā ʿannā ḥaqquhu al-ʿaẓīm*).[60] This opening statement immediately highlights an important aspect of al-ʿAzafī's framing of the *ṣalāt ʿalā al-nabī:* it is a form of payment by which a debt is defrayed. The idea that the invocation of prayers upon the Prophet is a form of expenditure is underlined by the *ḥadīth* with which al-ʿAzafī illustrates his point.

> An example of this (*min dhālika*) is what was transmitted by ʿĀʾisha. She said: I was sewing something at dawn; I dropped the needle, and the lamp went out. The Prophet came in; the house was illuminated by the light of his face, and I found the needle. I said, "How bright your face is, O Messenger of God; may God bless you" (*ṣallā allāhu ʿalayka*). He said to me, "Woe betide the one who does not see me on the Day of Resurrection." She said: I said, "And who is the one who will not see you, O Messenger of God?" He said, "The stingy one." I said, "And who is the stingy one, O Messenger of God?" He said, "The one who, when I am mentioned in his presence, does not invoke blessings upon me (*lam yuṣalli ʿalayya*)."

To this report al-ʿAzafī adds others in which such a person is termed "the stingiest of people" or "the stingiest of the stingy."[61] We have already encountered Ibn al-Ḥājj's complaint that *mawlid* supporters labeled those who refrained from such celebrations stingy (*bakhīl*). Like the holding of banquets, the invocation of blessings on the Prophet was clearly understood by its advocates not merely as an act of piety, but more specifically as an act of generosity. The withholding of blessings, like the withholding of money, was a sign of avarice. The invocation of blessings thus appears as an intangible form of expenditure that parallels the material expenditure involved in *mawlid* banquets.

Muḥammad al-Sakhāwī (d. 902 AH/1497 CE), the author of a *mawlid* that survives only in short citations, also composed an entire monograph on the virtues of invoking blessings upon the Prophet.[62] Interestingly, he cites al-ʿAzafī's discussion of the topic in *al-Durr al-munaẓẓam* in a number of places; his treatment of the *ṣalāt ʿalā al-nabī* is thus rooted in the *mawlid* tradition.[63] Unlike al-ʿAzafī, however, al-Sakhāwī is also interested in the theoretical and theological dimensions of the practice. He is concerned to define precisely what one is doing when one invokes blessings upon the Prophet, and what one hopes to achieve by doing so. One of the authorities he cites on this question is al-Ḥusayn ibn al-Ḥasan al-Ḥalīmī (d. 403 AH/1012 CE), who argues that the words "O God, bless Muḥammad" really constitute a plea that God raise the Prophet's repute, establish his religion in this world, and grant him intercession in the next. All of these things, of course, are believed by Muslims already to have been granted to the Prophet Muḥammad. al-Ḥalīmī argues, however, that they may be subject to "ranks and degree"; thus,

> it may be possible that if one of his community invokes blessings upon him and his prayer is granted, the Prophet may receive an increase in the rank and degree of all of the things we have mentioned by means of that prayer. For this reason, prayer [upon him] is one of the things by means of which one may seek to discharge one's obligation to him (*qaḍāʾ ḥaqqihi*) and by whose performance one may seek closeness to God (*yutaqarrabu bi-adāʾihā ilāʾllāh*).[64]

al-Sakhāwī also cites the opinion of Ibn ʿAbd al-Salām (d. 660 AH/1262 CE), who said:

> Our prayer upon the Prophet is not intercession by us for him; the likes of us cannot intercede for the likes of him. Rather, God has commanded us to requite those who do a favor to us and confer a benefit upon us (*amarana biʾl-mukāfaʾa li-man aḥsana ilaynā wa-anʿama ʿalaynā*). [Even] if we are incapable of [reciprocating the favor], we requite [our benefactor] by praying [for him]. Because He knew that we were incapable of requiting our Prophet, God guided us to invoke blessings upon him so that our blessings upon him could be a requital for his favor and benefaction to us, since there is no favor more beneficent than his.[65]

While al-Ḥalīmī and Ibn ʿAbd al-Salām seem to disagree about the possibility of a believer's blessings actually benefiting the Prophet in any way, they concur in regarding the invocation of blessings as a form of recompense (*qaḍā' ḥaqq, mukāfa'a*), however inadequate, for the benefits conferred on believers by the Prophet. Thus, the invocation of prayers upon the Prophet is a form of reciprocation where true reciprocity is impossible. The inequality between the infinitely exalted rank of the Prophet and his infinitely great beneficence toward us on the one hand, and our paltry ability to recompense him on the other, is such that we cannot benefit him in any meaningful way.

The point of invoking blessings upon a personage whose religious status is beyond further exaltation lies, perhaps unsurprisingly, in the potential to elicit further benefits in return. According to another authority cited by al-Sakhāwī, "since the benefit of your prayer upon [the Prophet] actually returns to you, you are actually praying for yourself." al-Sakhāwī similarly quotes Ibn al-'Arabī as remarking, "The benefit of praying upon him returns to the one who invokes prayer upon him, because that [action] indicates the sincerity of his belief, the purity of his intent, and the manifestation of love and continuous obedience" toward the Prophet.[66]

In fact, allusions to the invocation of blessings upon the Prophet in *mawlid* texts routinely refer to the copious rewards that will accrue to the person who engages in it. al-'Azafī himself provides particularly vivid reports to this effect, although not all of them were popular in later *mawlid* texts. "Whoever invokes blessings upon me one hundred times every day, a hundred needs will be met for him, thirty for this world and the rest for the next world." "Whoever invokes blessings upon me ten times at the beginning of the day and ten times at the end of the day will receive my intercession on the Day of Resurrection." The folk (and possibly sectarian) origins of devotional concern with the invocation of blessings upon the Prophet are suggested by the longest and most colorful of al-'Azafī's reports on the subject:

> 'Alī ibn Abī Ṭālib reported that the Messenger of God said to him, "Invoke blessings on me frequently when I have died." 'Alī said: I said, "Will blessings reach you from us after you have become scattered [bones]?" [The Prophet] said, "God has forbidden the earth to eat the flesh of the prophets; I am too precious in the eyes of God for him to give [the earth] dominion over me. God has placed an angel in charge of my grave whose name is Ṣalṣā'īl. He is in the form of a rooster. The curve of his neck is beneath the Divine Throne, and his talons are in the seven limits (*tukhūm*) of the earth. He has three wings: a wing in the east, a wing in the west, and a wing with which he fans my grave. If a person invokes blessings upon me, wherever he may be …, he pecks [the words] from his mouth as a bird pecks up grain. Then he says, "O Muḥammad, so-and-so the son of so-and-so from such and such a place has invoked blessings upon you and sends greetings to you." Then he writes it on a parchment of light in fragrant white musk and places it at my head so that I can intercede for [the person] with it on the Day of Resurrection and he will be raised 20,000 degrees, 20,000 good deeds will be recorded for him, 20,000 sins will be erased from [his record], 20,000 trees will be planted for him on the banks of the [river of] al-Kawthar.[67]

There ensues a dramatic account of the Day of Judgment. When the (good) actions of a person who has invoked many blessings on the Prophet are placed in the balance and prove unequal to his sins, the Prophet cries out that "I owe him a deposit and a favor (*lahu 'indī wadī'a wa-ṣanī'a*)." When the scroll is placed in the scale, the Prophet prays that it will outweigh his sins; of course, his prayers are answered.

Most reports about the rewards of the invocation of blessings upon the Prophet are less elaborate and colorful than this one. However, reports on this subject are ubiquitous in *mawlid* texts, particularly those dating from later centuries. The best authenticated and most frequently encountered *ḥadīth* states that "whoever blesses the Prophet one time, God will bless him for it ten times." al-Sakhāwī supplies literally dozens of citations and variations for this *ḥadīth*.[68] A version of *Mawlid al-'arūs* declares:

> [It is transmitted] from Ibn 'Abbās from the Prophet that he said: "Whoever blesses me one time, God will bless him for it ten times; whoever blesses me ten times, God will bless him for it one hundred times; whoever blesses me one hundred times, God will bless him for it a thousand times; whoever blesses me one thousand times, God will make his hair and his body forbidden to the Fire." [The Prophet also] said: "Whoever invokes the most blessings upon me will have the most wives in Paradise." [The Prophet also] said: "I am live and fresh in my grave; whoever blesses me, I will bless him, and whoever greets me, I will greet him."[69]

The salvific power of the invocation of blessings on the Prophet was such that it could be understood as a major objective of *mawlid* recitation. The Egyptian *faqīh* and *ṣūfī* 'Abd al-Salām ibn Ibrāhīm al-Laqānī (d. 1078 AH/1668 CE) states modestly near the beginning of one of his *mawlid* texts that "I am not one of the knights of this arena, nor the specialists in this area (*rijāl hādhā al-sha'n*), but I hoped that [my *mawlid*] would be the occasion for the invocation of blessings upon [the Prophet] when he was mentioned." He goes on to recount a story attributed to Wahb (probably, Ibn Munabbih):

> A man of the Children of Israel disobeyed God for a hundred years. Then he died, and they threw him onto the rubbish heap. God revealed to Moses, "Go out and pray over him!" [Moses] said, "O Lord, the Children of Israel witnessed that he disobeyed You for a hundred years!" God revealed, "So it was; however, every time he unrolled the Torah and looked at the name of Muḥammad he kissed it and placed it against his eyes. I have thanked him for that, forgiven him, and married him to seventy houris."

al-Laqānī follows this story with a series of *ḥadīth* texts about the virtues of blessing the Prophet. Significantly, his final remarks emphasize that invoking prayers on the Prophet may help the participants to gain God's forgiveness for their sins.[70] Sins are, of course, the debits that people hope to offset with the merits earned by their devotional activities.

Over time, as the recitation of formal *mawlid* texts became a central feature of *mawlid* celebrations, the invocation of blessings upon the Prophet became an integral part of such texts. In what may be termed "classical" *mawlid*s, the narration of the events of the Prophet's birth is broken into sections interspersed with invocations of blessings on the Prophet. When al-Bakrī's *Kitāb al-Anwār* was adapted for performance as a *mawlid* text, for instance, it was not merely supplied with an introductory passage dealing with the Prophet's *mawlid*; the invocation of blessings upon the Prophet was also inserted into the text at regular intervals. In more literary *mawlid* compositions, the invocation of blessings upon the Prophet is not merely a reproduction of the canonical formula but a rhymed couplet. Such couplets serve as distinctive refrains to the *mawlid* texts in which they appear. The refrain of the *mawlid* of Ja'far ibn Ḥasan al-Barzanjī (d. ca. 1177 AH/1764 CE), one of the texts most widely performed and revered in many parts of the Islamic world, likens the invocation of blessings upon the Prophet to the offering of incense or perfume to his grave: "O Lord, perfume his noble grave / With fragrant scents of prayer and greeting" (*'Aṭṭir Allāhumma qabrahu 'l-karīm / bi-'arf shadhin min ṣalāt wa-taslīm*). Probably as a result of the wide popularity of al-Barzanjī's *mawlid*, such refrains came to be known as "*ta'ṭīra*" (perfuming).[71]

It is difficult to know precisely how premodern *mawlid* ceremonies were conducted, or how *mawlid* texts were performed. Only rarely do early texts provide stage directions indicating such elements as audience participation or responsive reading. However, it seems reasonable to extrapolate from later practice that the invocation of blessings upon the Prophet was a participatory element of *mawlid* performance. A passage from a nineteenth-century commentary on al-Barzanjī's *mawlid* describes the practice as it exists until today. After the recitation of the Qur'ān, "the reciter (*qāri'*) of the *mawlid* begins to recount the way in which the noble birth occurred, while those present listen reverently and humbly. When the reciter comes to one of these *ta'ṭīra*s, they lift their voices in prayers and greetings (*al-ṣalāt wa'l-salām*) for the master of the people of earth and the heavens."[72]

Like the distribution of food, the invocation of blessings on the Prophet was an act of piety that was expected to yield copious rewards. The dynamic underlying the exchange was one of reciprocity, although a highly asymmetrical reciprocity in which the modest offerings of humble believers were requited with vast amounts of divine reward. Ultimately, despite the external dissimilarity of food distribution and the repetition of pious formulae, the two were functionally equivalent in the economy of merit envisioned by *mawlid* practitioners. The figurative equation between the uttering of blessings and the expenditure of money also features in an anecdote that appears in many different *mawlid* texts.[73] Although the story seems to lack any authentication acceptable to scholars, its repeated appearance in the more popular *mawlid* narratives suggests that it was meaningful to a broad audience. It recounts that after the creation of Eve, Adam asked God, "O Lord, how can I make her permitted to me?"

> [God] said, "Seek her hand in marriage from Me." Adam said, "O Lord, give me Eve in marriage!" God, exalted is He, said, "It is for your sake that

> I created her, Adam. What will you give me as a bridal payment (*mahr*)?" [Adam said, "O Lord, you are Most High and All-Knowing!" [God] said, "[Her bridal payment] is that you bless My Beloved, Muḥammad, ten times." Adam did so; the Truth [i.e., God] wrote their marriage contract, and the angels witnessed it.[74]

The invocation of blessings on the Prophet is a clear example of a speech act whose efficacy was more important than its meaning. Like the expenditure of money for *mawlid* banquets, such blessings served primarily as media of exchange within a complex economy of merit. Sincere as the sentiments of love and devotion expressed by the blessings might be (and devotees' love for the Prophet Muḥammad was presumably very genuine), the use of blessings on the Prophet as a bridal payment illustrates that they also figuratively had purchasing power. Like the Qur'ānic recitations which also frequently accompanied the presentation of *mawlid* texts, the invocation of blessings upon the Prophet was understood primarily as a means of eliciting bounteous rewards from an infinitely generous and responsive deity.

Another form of verbal performance associated with the celebration of the *mawlid* is, of course, the recitation of *mawlid* texts containing narratives of the Prophet's birth. Although (as we have seen in Chapter 1) devotional narratives on this subject long predated the rise of the Sunnī *mawlid* celebration, it is not clear precisely when such readings became a formal part of *mawlid* ceremonies. It must have been a fairly early development in the history of Sunnī *mawlid* celebrations, however, because it is referred to as an established custom by Ibn al-Jazarī (d. 833 AH/1429 CE). He writes that "the Muslims have continued to celebrate the month of [the Prophet's] birth, holding banquets for it, giving different kinds of alms on its nights, manifesting joy, increasing their acts of beneficence and concerning themselves with the recitation of his *mawlid*."[75] The objectives of such recitations, unlike those of the *ṣalāt 'alā al-nabī*, were not extensively discussed by scholars. The invocation of blessings upon the Prophet is a practice grounded in the text of the Qur'ān and referenced in many *ḥadīth* texts; it was thus an integral part of the normative model of pious action that was discussed by religious scholars. The recitation of *mawlid* texts, in contrast, is a custom that developed centuries later. As a consequence, it is neither mentioned in the *ḥadīth* nor analyzed in the classical scholarship that addresses such authoritative texts. Occasional references in the *mawlid* literature, however, do provide some indication of the beliefs surrounding *mawlid* recitations.

Like the invocation of blessings on the Prophet, it seems that the recitation of *mawlid* narratives was understood primarily in terms of the generation of religious merit, the activation of the Prophet's auspicious power (*baraka*), and the expectation of copious divine rewards. Ibn al-Jazarī himself writes in the introduction to his abridgment of his *mawlid* text,

> The blessings (*barakāt*) of that auspicious book [i.e., his *mawlid* text] have been experientially tested, and its blessings proved to be many, not paralleled

> or shared by other [books]. Among them is [the fact] that it is never read in a house but that its owner experiences security for himself, his wealth, and his family and is not harmed in that year and until the same time [of the next year]. Among them is [the fact] that no house where it is found has been afflicted by disaster (*nukibat*), no caravan where it is found has been plundered, and no ship where it is found has sunk. By the blessings (*barakāt*) of the one who is mentioned in it [i.e., the Prophet] it fulfills needs, and by means of it the favor of the Lord of the heavens is sought. This is something that has been experienced and become common knowledge (*jurriba wa-shā'a*).[76]

Baraka, like reward (*thawāb*), is a central concept in *mawlid* piety. The concept of *baraka*, an auspicious power that affects all that is associated with the Prophet Muḥammad and other sacred persons and things, is more amorphous than that of *thawāb*; *baraka* is communicated by association, rather than elicited by exchange. However, in his presentation of the components of the *mawlid* celebration Ibn al-Jazarī links *mawlid* recitation with the holding of banquets and the distribution of alms; all are acts of piety that activate the Prophet's *baraka*, and their efficacy is manifested in concrete signs of well-being.

A sense of the ways in which *mawlid* recitation was understood by ordinary practitioners is supplied by texts that circulated at a more popular level, and were unconstrained by scholarly standards of authentication. One such text is a set of statements about the virtues (*faḍā'il*) of the *mawlid* that seems to have circulated widely, both as a separate text and as an introduction tacked on to several different *mawlid*s. The statements are ascribed to authorities of the highest caliber, without the slightest concern for the historical plausibility of the attributions. While the identity of the authorities reveals a decided *ṣūfī* bias, there is no mystical component to the text; rather, it seems to reflect a *ṣūfī*-influenced folk religiosity.

> [The Prophet] said: Whoever glorifies my birthday (*mawlid*), I will be his intercessor on the Day of Resurrection, and whoever spends a *dirham* on my *mawlid*, it is as if he had spent a mountain of red gold in the path of God. Abū Bakr al-Ṣiddīq said: Whoever spends a *dirham* on the Prophet's *mawlid* will be his companion in Paradise. 'Umar said: Whoever glorifies the Prophet's *mawlid* has revived Islam (*qad aḥyā al-islām*). 'Uthmān said: Whoever spends a *dirham* on the recitation of the Prophet's *mawlid*, it is as if he participated in the battles of Badr and Ḥunayn. 'Alī said: Whoever glorifies the Prophet's *mawlid* and causes it to be recited will exit this world only as a believer and enter Paradise without being called to account (*bi-ghayr ḥisāb*). al-Ḥasan al-Baṣrī said: If I had as much gold as Mount Uḥud, I would spend it on the recitation of the Prophet's *mawlid*.

These statements emphasize the vast merit that accrues from the recitation of the Prophet's *mawlid*. Interestingly, they treat the recitation of the *mawlid* as an object of monetary expenditure. This may reflect either the fact that *mawlid* hosts spent money on the banquets at which the recitations occurred, or that the *mawlid* was recited by paid professionals and was thus itself an object of pious expenditure.

A statement fathered on the mystic Junayd al-Baghdādī (d. 298 AH/910 CE) attributes complete faith to the one who attends the recitation of the Prophet's *mawlid*, and one ascribed to Ma'rūf al-Karkhī (d. 200 AH/815–16 CE) promises a resurrection with the first rank of prophets and saints to the one who prepares food for the recitation of the *mawlid*, lights lamps, adorns himself with new clothes and perfumes himself with incense in honor of the Prophet's birthday. The text continues:

> The [scholar] unique in his age and unparalleled in his time, the imām Fakhr al-Dīn al-Rāzī,[77] said: If anyone recites the Prophet's *mawlid* over salt, wheat, or some other foodstuff, auspicious power (*al-baraka*) will be manifested in it and in everything that salt or wheat – or other thing – touches. Anyone who has one of those things in his stomach, it will be agitated – that is, it will move – and not settle down in his stomach until God forgives the one who eats it. If the Prophet's *mawlid* is recited over pure water, a thousand lights and mercies will enter the heart of anyone who drinks from that water, and a thousand spites and ills (*ghill wa-'illa*) will depart from it; that heart will not die on the day when hearts die. Whoever recites the *mawlid* over minted *dirhams*, whether of silver or of gold [*sic*], and mixes those *dirhams* with others, blessings will enter into them, their owner will not suffer poverty, and his hand will never be empty of them, by the auspicious power (*baraka*) of the Prophet.

Here, as in Ibn al-Jazarī's statement, the *mawlid* is a medium of *baraka*. Its powerful blessings are contagious, and can be transferred through foodstuffs, drink, and currency. As in the larger complex of practices involved in the celebration of the *mawlid*, food, money, and pious utterance are linked in a larger economy of blessing. Money can generate blessings through its expenditure on food or recitation for the *mawlid* celebration; the recitation itself generates blessings which can then be transferred to food or money.

The text concludes with further statements emphasizing the vast salvific power of the recitation of the *mawlid*:

> The imām al-Shāfi'ī said: Whoever gathers brethren for [the celebration of] the Prophet's *mawlid*, prepares food, makes space for it, engages in almsgiving, and causes [the *mawlid*] to be recited, on the Day of Resurrection God will raise him up with the righteous, the martyrs, and the pious (*al-ṣiddīqīn wa'l-shuhadā' wa'l-ṣāliḥīn*), and he will dwell in the gardens of Paradise. al-Sarī al-Saqaṭī[78] said: Whoever sets out for a place where the Prophet's *mawlid* is being recited has set out for one of the gardens of Paradise, because he has set out for that place only out of love for the Prophet, and [the Prophet] said, "Whoever loves me will be with me in Paradise." The sultan of the gnostics, Jalāl al-Dīn al-Suyūṭī, may God illuminate his tomb, said in his

> book entitled *al-Wasā'il fī sharḥ al-shamā'il*: Any house, mosque, or quarter (*maḥalla*) where the Prophet's *mawlid* is recited, the angels surround that house, mosque, or quarter, the angels invoke blessings on the people in that place, and God envelops them with [His] mercy and satisfaction. As for those [angels] who are encircled with light (*muṭawwaqūn bi'l-nūr*), that is, Jibrā'īl, Mikā'īl, Isrāfīl, and 'Azrā'īl, they invoke blessings on whomever causes the Prophet's *mawlid* to be read. He also said: Any Muslim who recites the Prophet's *mawlid* in his house, God removes drought, pestilence, fire, flood, blights, afflictions, hatred, envy, the evil eye, and thieves from the people of that house; when he dies, God eases the questioning of Munkar and Nakīr for him, and he is "in an honorable seat in the presence of a mighty king" [Qur'ān 54:55].[79]

Despite the blatant spuriousness of the quotations contained in this text, it seems to have enjoyed wide circulation. Presumably, it was popular in circles unconcerned with (or unaware of) its blithe disregard for scholarly standards of authentication; surprisingly, however, it seems to have been embraced by authors of some respectability. It is reproduced in full in the *mawlid* text of the nineteenth-century CE Moroccan *ṣūfī* Fatḥ Allāh al-Bannānī.[80] It is also incorporated into a commentary on the *mawlid* of al-Barzanjī by the Indonesian scholar Muḥammad Nawawī al-Bantanī (d. 1316 AH/1898 CE), a Shāfi'ī jurist who settled in Mecca and exercised wide influence in his time.[81] The stability of the text suggests that it was faithfully reproduced by individuals who regarded it with some respect. In some cases, it was supplemented with additional passages including the following anecdote:

> A story is told about a man in the time of Hārūn al-Rashīd [the fifth 'Abbasid caliph, ruled 170–193 AH/786–809 CE] in the city of Baṣra who was a sinner and squandered money on himself. The people of the city held him in contempt because of his vile actions, except that when the month of Rabī' al-Awwal arrived he washed his clothes, perfumed himself, gave a feast and had the Prophet's *mawlid* read at it. He continued to do this for a long time. When he died, the people of Baṣra heard a great voice saying, "O people of Baṣra, attend the funeral of one of God's intimate friends (*walī min awliyā' allāh*)." The people of the city attended his funeral and buried him. When night fell, they dreamt that he was in heaven wearing robes of the fine brocade of paradise. They said to him, "By what virtue did you acquire this honor?" He replied, "By glorifying the Prophet's birthday."[82]

The wondrous efficacy of the *mawlid* is also illustrated by an anecdote dealing with an unjust king who is saved from a would-be assassin by the power of the *mawlid*. After the assassination is miraculously averted, the king hears a supernatural voice (*hātif*) saying, "You have glorified the birthday of Our Beloved, Muḥammad, so We have saved you. If you do more, We will do more." The caliph repents of his oppression and injustice and begins to spend a third of his wealth every year on the [celebration of the] Prophet's birthday.[83] The statement that "if you do more, We will do more" precisely expresses the sense of reciprocity that underlies *mawlid* performance; the imbalance in magnitude between the performance of a *mawlid* and the saving of a life suggests that relatively small acts of devotion can access vast reserves of divine benevolence.

In a third anecdote, set in the time of the caliph 'Abd al-Malik ibn Marwān (ruled 65–86 AH/685–705 CE), a "comely youth" is riding through the streets of Damascus when his horse bolts and tramples to death the caliph's son.

> The news reached the caliph and he ordered that [the youth] be brought to him. When he came into sight [of the caliph], it occurred to him to say, "If God saves me from this catastrophe, I will give a great banquet and have the Prophet's *mawlid* recited." When he came before the caliph and [the caliph] looked at him, he smiled after his anger and said, "Can you perform sorcery, boy?" He said, "[No,] by God, o Commander of the Faithful!" [The caliph] said, "I pardon you; but you must tell me what you said when I sent for you." He said, "[I said that] if God saved me from this catastrophe and this grievous predicament I would give a banquet for the recitation of the Prophet's *mawlid*." The caliph 'Abd al-Malik said, "I pardon you; here are a thousand *dīnār*s for the banquet, and you are quit of my son's blood." He went out, having been pardoned and released from blood retaliation by the blessing (*baraka*) of the Prophet's *mawlid*.[84]

The prestige enjoyed by these stories is suggested by the fact that the Damascene Ḥanafī jurist Aḥmad Ibn 'Ābidīn (d. 1307 AH/1889 CE) cites this last anecdote as a real incident, using the fact that someone was delivered from peril "by virtue of the mere fact that performing the Prophet's *mawlid* occurred to him" as evidence for the efficacy of the *mawlid*.[85]

Passages from other *mawlid* texts similarly emphasize the efficacy of *mawlid* recitation in yielding security and blessings for the persons and homes of those who patronize or perform it, as well as its value for individual salvation. The recitation of the *mawlid* is not merely meritorious, but constructs a warm and personal relationship between the Prophet and the devotee that is expected to manifest itself in this life and the next. One nineteenth-century text reports,

> [It is reported] of a pious man (*ba'ḍ al-ṣāliḥīn*) that he wished to see the Prophet in a dream. The Prophet said to him, "What do you desire of me, O servant of God?" He said, "My desire of you is to visit you every year." The Prophet said to him, "If you want to see me every year, recite [the story of] my birth every year. If you do that, you will visit me every year" – that is, in a dream. He said, "God inspired me, and I said, 'O Prophet, what is the reward for [reciting] the story of the Prophet's birth every year?' " He said, "Whoever recites the story of my birth sincerely and solely for the sake of God, exalted is He, God will forgive him the sins of the past year, and he will remain in its blessing until the next year. God will ascribe to him a good deed for every

morsel of the *mawlid* food that is eaten, and ten good deeds for every *dirham* [he spends on the *mawlid*]. He will experience a light in his heart, health in his body, and well-being in his person. God will shed blessings on his sustenance, on the place where the story of my birth is recited, and on forty houses around the house where the story of my birth is recited. The one who recites it will remain under God's protection for forty mornings."[86]

Another *mawlid* text similarly assures its listeners,

> A scholar said, "Whoever recites the Prophet's *mawlid* in a home, the angels surround that home for seven days and it is pervaded by the Prophet's blessings for a complete year, until the same day on which the noble *mawlid* was recited. Whoever spends a *dirham* on [the Prophet's] *mawlid*, God will multiply it into ten, the Chosen One will take him by the hand on the Day of Resurrection, and he will rejoice in [the Prophet's] intercession in this world and the next."[87]

The recitation of the Prophet's *mawlid*, while meritorious in itself, could also be accompanied by other offerings that elicited further divine recompense. The author of the undated manuscript *Rawḥ al-nufūs fī mawlid rūḥ al-nufūs*, one Shaykh Yaḥyā, cites an obscure report that the Prophet Muḥammad forbade the killing of frogs. This is because when the Prophet Abraham was cast into the fire by the tyrant Nebuchadnezzar, frogs carried water in their mouths to sprinkle on the flames.[88] Shaykh Yaḥyā reasons,

> If the frog's salvation (*najāt*) from being killed is by reason of the drops of water that it sprinkled on the fire of Abraham, what is the situation of the believer who sprinkles rosewater and burns ambergris over [other] believers during the recitation of the *mawlid* of al-Muṣṭafā, whom God sent as a mercy to the worlds, and gives them water with sugar, musk, ambergris, and honey at the gathering for his birthday?

Shaykh Yaḥyā expresses the wish that God will give such a person the pure draughts of Paradise on the Day of Resurrection.[89]

The exchange of merit and the economy of salvation

The generation of merit through the recitation of the Prophet's *mawlid* was not a purely individualistic pursuit. We have already seen that *mawlid* gatherings were group endeavors supported partially by the monetary contributions of the guests. Presumably, such giving offered participants a lesser but still meaningful opportunity for the generation of religious merit. Although expressed purely in negative terms, Ibn al-Ḥājj's complaints about the social pressure to attend *mawlid*s reflects the fact that they must have played a role in the solidification of social networks. Both hard cash and spiritual benefits were implicated in this social practice, which must have generated bonds both material and intangible.

The social network involved in the celebration of *mawlid*s was not, however, limited to those present at the gatherings. Indeed, it was not limited to those currently alive. Rather, the generation and exchange of merit bound together an imagined community of Muslims, both dead and alive.

In his account of the events of Rabīʿ al-Awwal 926 AH/1520 CE, Ibn Ṭūlūn al-Ṣāliḥī presents an unusual incident that reflects the double role of the donation of merit as an expression of religious piety and a means of articulating and reinforcing interpersonal (or in this case political) loyalties. On the night of the Prophet's birthday, the provincial governor holds a *mawlid* that is performed by a preacher (*wāʿiẓ*) named Barakāt ibn al-Kayyāl. After the recitation of the *mawlid* and of a number of Qur'ānic verses (some of which seem to have been chosen for their political relevance), the *nā'ib* is asked whether it (presumably, the merit of the celebration) should be dedicated to his own account or to that of the Ottoman sultan Selim; he orders that it be donated to (*yuhdā li-ṣaḥā'if*) the Mamlūk sultan Qāytbāy.[90]

As is the case with other aspects of the *mawlid* celebration, the practice of donating merit is very difficult to date. It is reflected primarily in the texts of closing prayers appended to *mawlid* texts, and these additions are even more indeterminate in their dating and attribution than the *mawlid*s themselves. It seems likely that the oral presentation of *mawlid*s was often accompanied by the recitation of closing invocations (*duʿā'*) that were not included in the written texts, and it is impossible to know the content of most prayers that were recited in the premodern period.

A manuscript of one version of the *mawlid* text traditionally attributed to Ibn al-Jawzī, copied in 1259 AH/1843 CE, ends with an extensive closing prayer. It begins by "reminding" God of the meritorious act that has just been performed: "O God, we have attended the *mawlid* of Your Prophet and Your chosen one from among Your creatures; cast upon us from his *baraka* a robe of honor, and cause us to dwell beside him in the gardens of delight."[91] After a long series of invocations, the prayer implores:

> O God, place the reward for what we have presented of Your pre-existent speech and the blessings (*baraka*) of what we have recited, the *mawlid* of Your noble Prophet, in the records (*ṣaḥā'if*) of our parents and parents' parents; [give it also] to those who have taught us, and [place it] in the records of our masters (*mashāyikhinā*) and the records of the gentlemen who are present and their parents, and in the records of the one who was the cause of this auspicious gathering and his parents, and in the records of all of the Muslims.[92]

The closing prayer in the *mawlid* of Ibn al-Daybaʿ (d. 944 AH/1537 CE), which seems to be a stable component of the text, requests that deceased members of the group partake of the merit of the celebration. It ends by imploring,

> O God, by virtue of it/him [presumably, either the reading of the *mawlid* or the Prophet himself] forgive us, our fathers and mothers, our *mashāyikh*, our

teachers, those to whom we are obligated (*dhawī al-ḥuqūq 'alaynā*), the one who caused this good work to be performed at this time, all the male and female believers, and the male and female Muslims, both those of them who are alive and those who are dead.[93]

A *mawlid* attributed to'Alī ibn Nāṣir al-Shāfi'ī al-Ash'arī al-Makkī (d. 915 AH/ 1509 CE) also ends with an elaborate *du'ā'*, although it is impossible to know whether it is an integral part of the original text. It similarly includes a passage donating the merit of the *mawlid* and the accompanying Qur'ānic recitations to the Prophet Muḥammad and to God's other prophets; to the four Rightly Guided caliphs and the rest of the Companions of the Prophet; "and to those who follow them in righteousness until the Day of Judgment." It concludes by asking God to place the reward of the *mawlid* in the account of "him in whose presence we are and for the sake of whom we have gathered," the host and sponsor of the *mawlid* performance.[94]

An anonymous *du'ā'* to be recited at the end of the reading of the *mawlid*, published in booklet form, presents an even more elaborate distribution of merit beginning with the Prophet Muḥammad and proceeding through the other prophets and messengers and their families, companions and followers; the founders of the four classical schools of Sunnī law, the religious scholars, the jurists, the transmitters of *ḥadīth*, the Qur'ān reciters, the Qur'ānic exegetes, and the *ṣūfīs*; those on whose behalf the *mawlid* has been read and the Qur'ān has been recited; and all deceased Muslims, particularly those related to the ones on whose behalf the recitation has been performed.[95] The closing *du'ā'* of an undated *mawlid* preserved in Damascus requests "a bounteous reward and a blessed recompense" (*thawāban jazīlan wa-ajran mubārakan*) for the recitation that has just occurred, and prays that it be transferred "fully and in its entirety" to the Prophet Muḥammad and to a long list of other recipients, beginning with Adam and Eve and ending with "those by reason of whom and for whose intentions we have recited this noble *mawlid*."[96]

The donation of the merit accruing from the recitation of the Prophet's *mawlid* (and the accompanying Qur'ānic recitation) raises several religious issues. The first issue relates to the transferability of religious merit in general. The text of the Qur'ān contains a number of passages that, in a simple commonsense reading, would seem to suggest that both the merit of righteous actions and the penalties of transgressions accrue exclusively to the individual who has performed them. "A person is entitled to nothing but his own efforts," declares verse 53:39. "None will bear another's burden," affirm verses 6:164, 17:15, and 35:18. "[Each soul] is entitled to every good that it earns, and is liable for every bad thing it commits," states verse 2:286.[97] In general, the Qur'ānic ethic would seem to be stringently individualistic. Also frequently cited in the context of the debate over the transferability of merit is a *ḥadīth* stating that "When a son of Adam dies, his work ceases, except for three [kinds]: continuing charity (*ṣadaqa jāriya*), beneficial knowledge, or a righteous son who prays for him."[98]

Despite the apparent individualism of the Qur'ānic ethic, other textual and theological factors led most classical scholars to conclude that in some cases merit could indeed be transferred from one person to another. The clearest basis for this inference is the principle, accepted by three out of the four Sunnī schools of law, that one can under some circumstances perform the *ḥajj* on behalf of a deceased parent or another Muslim who has died or become physically disabled without performing this religious obligation.[99] This practice is supported by several *ḥadīth* texts in which the Prophet is consulted about the permissibility of performing the *ḥajj* in place of a feeble or deceased relative and replies in the affirmative.[100] *Ḥadīth* texts also affirm that it is possible to benefit one's deceased parents by performing other meritorious acts. Classical scholars generally agree that pious acts of a "financial" nature (*al-'ibādāt al-māliya*), such as almsgiving and the manumission of slaves, can be performed on behalf of deceased persons. Such actions are easily likened to other financial commitments, which are universally understood to be fulfilled by the heirs on behalf of the deceased. In another *ḥadīth* text, a Muslim approaches the Prophet wondering if it is appropriate to carry out a fast that her deceased mother had vowed to perform, and he answers rhetorically, "If she had a debt, would you pay it for her?"[101] If we discharge debts owed to human beings, debts to God – that is, acts of worship – are yet more worthy of being paid. There is greater ambiguity, however, with respect to "physical" acts of worship (*al-'ibādāt al-badanīya*). Such pious activities, unlike those in the previous category, have no monetary component at all. While Ḥanbalīs and Ḥanafīs hold that the merit of these acts is also transferable, a majority of Mālikīs and Shāfi'īs deny it.[102] With such actions, obviously, the analogy of payment of a debt becomes less directly applicable.

In order to benefit another person by one's pious act, it is not necessary that the act itself be credited to his account. Jurists envisioned several indirect modes by which pious actions might benefit persons other than the actor, including the deceased. The Shāfi'ī jurist Bahā' al-Dīn al-Ḥuwwārī (d. 889 AH/1484 CE) is cited as having enumerated three possible modes by which the merit of Qur'ānic recitation might be transferred to the intended beneficiary. First, the act itself might be credited to the deceased, precisely as if he himself had performed it. (Shāfi'īs – as well as Mālikīs, although not Ḥanafīs or Ḥanbalīs – traditionally reject this possibility.) Second, while the act itself is attributed to the person who has actually performed it, the merit of the act can be donated by the actor. This does not necessarily mean that the reciter can dispose of the merit as he desires; rather, he must pray that God accord the merit to the intended recipient. Third, even if neither the act itself nor the merit accruing from the act can be directly transferred to a second party, the deceased may benefit from the outflowing of divine mercy that accompanies the act of recitation.[103]

A commentator of the Mālikī jurist al-Qarāfī reproduces the arguments of jurists who argue that, despite the consensus that prayer can benefit the dead, no acts of worship are actually being transferred to them. The benefit conferred, rather than the prayer itself or even the reward for performing it, is first the divine response to the prayer (for instance, forgiveness), and second the blessings (*baraka*) associated with its performance. One can benefit from the prayers of a believer, the companionship of holy men, or the presence of a pious relative not because one receives the merit for their actions but because of the *baraka* generated by them all. *Baraka*, unlike merit, does not depend on the performance of actions or even on the ability to be addressed by divine commandments or prohibitions; thus, for instance, the Prophet's *baraka* is known to have passed into animals.[104] This principle, the Mālikī author argues, negates the contention of Aḥmad ibn Ḥanbal and Abū Ḥanīfa that if the Qur'ān is recited at a grave the deceased will receive the merit of listening to the Qur'ān; since the dead are not addressed by God's commandments and prohibitions, they are incapable of earning merit. They can, however, benefit from the *baraka* of the recitation.[105]

Despite some scholars' reservations about the possibility of literally transferring merit, others treat the merit or reward (*thawāb*) accruing from a pious action as itself equivalent to a monetary asset, one that can be expended on behalf of loved ones or of the Muslim community as a whole.[106] The Ḥanbalī Ibn al-Qayyim al-Jawzīya argues that "the merit belongs to the one who performs the action, and nothing prevents him from donating it to his Muslim brother, just as nothing prevents him from giving [him] his money during his life or forgiving him a debt after his death."[107] He even contemplates the possibility that merit can be distributed in precisely quantified shares; for instance, "If he were to give the whole to four [people], each of them would get a fourth of it; similarly, he could give a fourth to one person and keep the rest for himself."[108] Unlike monetary assets, however, distributing the merit of pious actions is not necessarily a zero-sum activity. One legal compendium urges the reader to donate his supererogatory devotions to all of the Muslims, male and female, "because it reaches them, and [the original actor's] recompense (*ajr*) is not decreased at all."[109] The scholar Ibn Ḥajar al-Haytamī is reported to have been asked about the merit of reciting the Fātiḥa for the benefit of those buried in a cemetery: is it divided into even shares among all those present in the graves? He is supposed to have replied that each of them received the entire merit of the recitation.[110]

Those who deny the possibility of transfer have a far less concrete conception of merit itself than those who advocate it. They argue, Ibn al-Qayyim reports, that

> acts do not necessarily yield merit, rather, it is merely God's favor and benefaction. How can a human being transfer a mere favor which is not incumbent on God, but which He will give him or not as He wills? It is as if a destitute person were to transfer the "debt" of someone he hopes will give him alms; such a thing cannot validly be given or donated.[111]

The Andalusian jurist al-Shāṭibī (d. 790 AH/1388 CE) records another argument with conflicting premises but identical conclusions. Opponents of the transfer of merit, he reports, argue that *thawāb* is to righteous action as effect is to cause (*ka'l-musabbabāt bi'l-nisba ilā'l-asbāb*); it automatically accrues by their performance. Just as in the case of any other chain of cause and effect, it is a necessary relationship that is not subject to the will or choice of the actor. The merit is, thus, not at his disposal and cannot be donated to another.[112] While the first argument represents merit as a free and incalculable expression of divine grace and the second as the automatic precipitate of human actions, they agree in denying that it is an asset available for gift or exchange.

The idea that religious merit was a transferable good appears to have triumphed on a popular level, at least in the premodern period. The ways in which it was understood in less scholarly circles may be suggested by the content of a manuscript preserved in the Great Mosque of Ṣan'ā' and compiled by one 'Alī ibn Aḥmad ibn Yūsuf al-Hakārī.[113] Entitled "The Gift of the Living to the Dead and the Merit that Reaches Them over the Course of Time" (*Kitāb hadīyat al-aḥyā' ilā'l-amwāt wa-mā yaṣilu ilayhim min al-thawāb 'alā mamarr al-awqāt*), it proposes to demonstrate "with clear proofs and illuminating evidence" "the correct belief (*al-i'tiqād al-ṣaḥīḥ*) that the merit (*thawāb*) of alms, prayers (*du'ā'*), recitation of the Qur'ān, and canonical prayers (*ṣalāt*) by a Muslim reach the dead in their graves and that the gifts of the living to the dead reach them and benefit them."[114] The form of the text is modeled on normative sources (for instance, each *ḥadīth* being introduced by a statement such as "by a sound chain of transmission to [name of Companion of Prophet]"), and the author is capable of producing standard Qur'ānic evidence for the transfer of merit to the dead.[115] However, the content of most of the *ḥadīth* reports seems to be purely apocryphal. The text consists largely of stories depicting in the most vivid and concrete terms the grateful reception of donations by the more fortunate among the deceased and the desolation of those who receive no such benefits.

One report states that

> When you give alms on behalf of your deceased [loved one], an angel brings it on a dish of light and calls, "O estranged denizen of the grave (*yā ṣāḥib al-qabr al-gharīb*), your relatives have given this to you as a present; accept it!" [The angel] puts it into his grave, and [the deceased] says, "May God reward my family on my behalf."

The inhabitant of the next grave bewails his lack of surviving children as the lucky recipient rejoices (*fariḥa*) in his good fortune.[116] In this (presumably spurious) *ḥadīth*, the performance of good works on behalf of the dead is not merely a one-sided transaction. Rather, it maintains a mutually beneficial relationship with the deceased, who asks God to reward the giver on his behalf. The entire exchange occurs in a context of neighborly admiration and envy very much resembling the social response to good fortune in the world of the living. Another section of the text extols the spiritual benefits of performing pious utterances and Qur'ānic recitations at a graveyard and donating the merit to the inhabitants of the graves. Such recitations bring "radiance and light, joy and delight" (*al-ḍiyā' wa'l-nūr wa'l-faraḥ wa'l-surūr*) to the dead, as well as resulting in lavish rewards (including a castle in paradise) for the reciter.[117] In other stories, the pious utterances and actions of the living are presented to the dead in the form of plates of food and clean clothes. In one, a dead man's son forgets his nightly practice of reciting the 112th chapter of the Qur'ān eleven times and donating the merit to his father; the father asks him through an intermediary, "Why did you leave me without dinner?"[118]

The stories presented in al-Hakārī's work suggest how the donation of merit to the dead fits into the larger complex of pious activities involved in *mawlid* celebrations. The donation of merit to the dead plays the same role as the distribution of food to the living; benefits circulate and multiply in a lively community of piety. The technical arguments of the scholars had their concrete correlates in the popular imagination; while scholars like Ibn al-Qayyim discussed the theoretical dimensions of merit transfer, ordinary people apparently envisioned in it more palpable terms. The issue of merit transfer did not merely reflect different ideas about the nature of merit and the degree to which it might be considered a possession at the disposal of its owner. Also at stake was the relationship between the individual and the community in the economy of salvation. Those who denied the possibility of merit transfer advanced a theology of individual responsibility. Despite his own views, Ibn al-Qayyim al-Jawzīya offers a surprisingly eloquent recital of the arguments of his opponents in the debate over the donation of *thawāb*. "They say," he reports

> that religious duties (*al-takālīf*) are a test and a trial which cannot be undergone by a substitute; their object is the responsible actor (*al-mukallaf al-'āmil*) who is addressed by commands and prohibitions, himself, and no one can be substituted for the responsible person who is being tested or act in his stead, because the objective is that he himself be obedient and submit himself to God as a worshiper. If it were possible for him to benefit from another's donating [merit] to him without his performing the action himself, it would be more fitting that the Supremely Beneficent [benefit him] in this way. However, [God] has decreed that he benefit only from his own efforts.... No one can take medicine on behalf of a sick person; if someone is hungry, thirsty or naked, no one can eat, drink, or don clothes on his behalf.[119]

Despite the Qur'ānic evidence to the contrary, scholars committed to a model of pious action in which merit can be donated flatly deny that individuals must work out their own salvation in isolation from their relatives and friends. Some authors, for instance, hold that verse 53:39 ("A person is entitled to nothing but his own efforts") is specified (*makhṣūṣ*), that is, that its field of application has been significantly limited by other verses with contrasting content.[120] Interestingly, despite his unswerving dedication to the principle of transfer of merit, Ibn al-Qayyim accepts the relevant Qur'ānic verses at face value. The text of the Qur'ān, the intellect,and innate human nature (*al-fiṭra*), he writes, all bear witness to both that a person is not punished for another's offence and that he achieves salvation only through his own acts and efforts.[121] Ibn al-Qayyim's belief in the possibility of donating merit rests on an understanding of the Islamic community as an organic whole in which no individual believer's strivings are truly separate from those of his fellow believers. He begins by citing the interpretation of the Ḥanbalī scholar Abū'l-Wafā' ibn 'Aqīl (d. 513 AH/1119 CE), who argues that "the individual, by his own efforts and his kindness towards others (*ḥusn 'ishratihi*), won friends, begot children, married spouses, performed good actions, and endeared himself to people, so that they had mercy on him and donated acts of worship to him; this was the effect of his own efforts."

Ibn al-Qayyim finds Ibn 'Aqīl's solution sound but incomplete. He expands on the idea as follows:

> By his faith and his obedience to God and His Prophet, the individual (*al-'abd*) has striven to benefit [religiously] from the works of his fellow believers along with his own works, just as he benefits from their works in [this] life. The believers benefit from each other's actions in the works they perform together, such as communal prayer. The prayer of each of them is multiplied twenty-seven-fold if another person performs the prayer with him; thus, the action of another caused his reward (*ajr*) to increase, just as his action caused the other's reward to increase. It is even said that the merit of prayer is multiplied by the number of people praying [together]. The same is true of their joining together in *jihād*, the *ḥajj* pilgrimage, enjoining good and forbidding evil, and cooperating in good works and piety (*al-birr wa'l-taqwā*). The Prophet said, "Believers are to each other like parts of a building that prop each other up" – and he laced together his fingers [in illustration]. It is obvious that this is even more true in matters of religion than in worldly matters; an [individual] Muslim's entering into the covenant of Islam with all the other Muslims is one of the greatest causes for the benefits of each Muslim to reach his fellow [Muslim], during his life and after his death.

Even the most apparently one-sided bestowal of favors is, if rightly understood, in fact a collaborative event in which the individual's efforts are commingled with those made on his behalf. Even in the absence of more substantial cooperation, it is by virtue of his own faith that any Muslim is capable of benefiting from the beneficence of holy personages, such as the angels' invocation of God's forgiveness on the believers; thus, "it is as if it were from his own efforts."[122] Ultimately, the efforts of the believers are indivisible. Within the Islamic community, including its heavenly and prophetic membership, pious exertion circulates ceaselessly, and the efforts of any individual are ultimately inextricable from this flow.[123]

Mawlid prayers seeking to bestow religious merit on deceased persons thus reflect a widespread, if disputed, element of Islamic piety. Some of the *mawlid* prayers cited earlier, however, involve an additional element that is far more religiously problematic: the donation of merit to the Prophet himself. At least in later centuries, the donation of merit to the Prophet was an established element of *mawlid* piety. Muḥammad Nawawī al-Bantanī (d. 1316 AH/1898 CE), an Indonesian scholar who lived and worked in Mecca, begins his commentary on the *mawlid* of al-Barzanjī by donating the merit (*thawāb*) that accrues from it to the Prophet "to increase his honor" (*ziyādatan fī sharafihi*) and in the hopes of God's forgiveness of his sins and of the Prophet's intercession on the Day of

Judgment.[124] An unidentified ṣūfī author by the name of Muḥammad al-Majdhūb directs that the reciter of his *mawlid* should begin by reciting verses from the Qur'ān; "the recitation of these chapters should be out loud, with the intention of donating their reward (*thawāb*) to the spirit of al-Muṣṭafā."[125] Here the difficulty lies not in the possibility of transfer (which is affirmed in the case of dead people as a class) but in its rationale. Why, precisely, would one give one's own meager acts of piety to the most perfect of humankind? Religious scholars are, naturally, at one in affirming that the Prophet cannot possibly be in need of the merit of his followers. Some of them even find such donation implicitly insulting.

The practice of donating merit to the Prophet was not an early one, but was prevalent by the period in which Sunnī *mawlid* celebrations flourished. Ibn al-Qayyim states that among the more recent jurists (*al-muta'akhkhirīn*) there are those who consider it desirable (*istaḥabba*) to donate merit of recitations to the Prophet and others who do not, on the grounds that it is an innovation unknown to the Companions and that the Prophet receives merit for all of the righteous actions of the believers in any case, because he is the one who guided them to perform such actions.[126] al-Sakhāwī was still acutely aware of the newness of the custom. Asked about someone who prays, "O God, take the merit of what I have recited to increase the honor (*sharaf*) of the Messenger of God," he answered: "This is an invention of the modern [Qur'ān] reciters (*muta'akhkhirī al-qurrā'*); I do not know of anyone who preceded them in doing this (*lā a'lamu lahum salafan fīhi*)."[127] al-Subkī (probably Tāj al-Dīn) is supposed to have considered it permissible to donate the merit of one's Qur'ānic recitation to the Prophet. However, he is supposed to have declared it objectionable to ask people to recite the Fātiḥa for the Prophet, "for obvious reasons (*li-mā lā yakhfā*)" – presumably, because it implied that the Prophet was in need of prayers for his salvation.[128] The Maghribī jurist al-Ḥaṭṭāb presents a lengthy discussion of the permissibility of donating the merit of Qur'ān recitation to the Prophet from a *mawlid* text entitled *Kanz al-rāghibīn al-'ufāt fī'l-ramz ilā al-mawlid wa'l-wafāt*.[129] Although al-Ḥaṭṭāb himself is unaware of the work's authorship, it is a work of Burhān al-Dīn al-Nājī, a Damascene Shāfi'ī who died in 900 AH/1495 CE. The fact that this issue was discussed in the context of a *mawlid* work suggests that the practice of donating merit to the Prophet may have been incorporated into *mawlid* performances by the eighth-century AH/fifteenth-century CE.

Another devotional practice associated with the *mawlid* ceremony reveals a similarly transactional model of piety. This is the practice of making a vow (*nadhr*) to perform a *mawlid* ceremony if a specific hope is fulfilled or harm is averted. Although it seems impossible to determine when ordinary believers first made vows specifically for *mawlid*s, the custom may have a lengthy history. The practice of making *mawlid* vows may be reflected in the story of the Jewish man and his wife, recounted as early as the *mawlid* text of Ibn Jābir al-Andalusī in the eighth-century AH; having dreamed of the Prophet, the wife "makes a commitment to God" (*'āhadat allāh*) to give her possessions as alms and hold a *mawlid*. The diarist Aḥmad al-Budayrī reports that in Damascus in 1161 AH/1748 CE, a prostitute vowed to hold a *mawlid* recitation if a Turkish slave boy she was in love with recovered from an illness. The ensuing celebration, which involved a procession of bare-headed prostitutes bearing candles and incense, clapping and beating drums, was certainly unusual; her vow probably was not.[130]

By the nineteenth century, jurists were clearly familiar with vows to perform *mawlid* ceremonies. The Damascene scholar Muḥammad ibn ʻĀbidīn (d. 1252 AH/1836 CE) objects in his commentary on the Shāfiʻī legal text *Radd al-muḥtār* to women's custom of vowing oil to a saint's tomb, which was used to light a lamp in the minaret. "More offensive than that" (*aqbaḥ minhu*), he writes, "is vowing to recite the *mawlid* in the pulpits – in addition to its involving singing and entertainment – and donating the merit (*thawāb*) of that to [the Prophet]."[131] The nineteenth-century Mālikī jurist Muḥammad ʻUlaysh (d. 1299 AH/1882 CE) received an inquiry that reveals the dynamics of the practice. "What is your opinion," his questioner asks,

> of a man who has a cow, and it falls ill while it is pregnant. He says, "If God heals my cow, I promise to slaughter what is in her womb for a *mawlid* for the Prophet." God heals the cow, and it gives birth to a female [calf]; then he delays slaughtering it until it grows up and [itself] becomes pregnant. Must he slaughter that specific cow, or may he slaughter a substitute for it, or is he not obligated to do anything?

ʻUlaysh responds that the man is under no obligation whatsoever, because the performance of a *mawlid* (*ʻamal mawlid li'l-rasūl*) is not recommended in the *sharīʻa*, particularly if it involves religiously objectionable activities.[132]

Although not all acts of devotion were considered fit objects of religious vows, the legitimacy of vows to perform supererogatory acts of piety was recognized by the classical schools of law. Similar to the donation of merit, the practice of vowing *mawlid* ceremonies in return for future acts of divine favor (whether the healing of the sick, the return of the absent, or the birth of a child) reflects a transactional model in which acts of devotion function as a response to signs of God's compassion. In the case of vows, this response is promised in anticipation of a future favor. Normative Islamic belief did not, of course, suggest that vows could induce God to produce the desired result; vows are not bribes directed to the divine, and God's will is sovereign. Nevertheless, such vows at least imply the hope of engaging God in an infinitely unequal relationship of exchange. Ibn ʻĀbidīn's observation that people vowed to donate the merit of the *mawlid* to the Prophet suggests that vows potentially involved multilateral relationships of gift-giving and obligation.

Conclusion

The model of pious action underlying classical *mawlid* celebrations is expressed with unusual eloquence in the work of the prolific and influential *mawlid* author Ibn Nāṣir al-Dīn, a prominent Damascene Shāfiʻī who died in 842 AH/1438 CE. He composed no fewer than three *mawlid* texts, one of them lengthy, and left a permanent mark on the tradition. Unlike more obscure *mawlid* authors, Ibn Nāṣir al-Dīn has left sufficient evidence of his ideas to provide some sense of his religious worldview and objectives. Unlike more famous authors who happen to have composed a *mawlid* text or expressed a view on the celebration of the *mawlid*, Ibn Nāṣir al-Dīn produced enough *mawlid* texts to represent a substantial proportion of his literary output; they were not merely incidental to his core agendas. The *mawlid* loomed large in his scholarly activities, just as he looms large in the history of the *mawlid*. For these reasons, it is worthwhile to examine in detail the main themes in his preserved works. They provide one insight into the religious milieu in which the Prophet's *mawlid* was disseminated and popularized.

Shams al-Dīn Muḥammad ibn Abī Bakr ʻAbd Allāh al-Qaysī, known as Ibn Nāṣir al-Dīn, was a native Damascene.[133] Trained in the discipline of *ḥadīth*, he attained considerable stature as a scholar, receiving high praise from several of his most prominent contemporaries. His sound scholarly reputation was rewarded with a prestigious teaching position; one of his preserved works consists of a long series of lectures delivered on the occasion of his installation as head of *Dār al-ḥadīth* al-Ashrafīya in 836 AH. Ibn Nāṣir al-Dīn was, thus, a respected elite scholar who excelled in one of the most important Islamic disciplines and engaged with the most important figures and issues of his day. However, the nature of his work suggests that he was also concerned with less scholarly objectives. Most of his compositions, based on the titles of lost works and the content of those that remain, address the religious needs of ordinary believers rather than the technical concerns of his learned peers. While much of his written output deals with the life of the Prophet Muḥammad, for instance, it reflects the priorities of the religious devotee more than those of the historian. In addition to his three *mawlid* texts, he composed at least two works on the *miʻrāj*, one on the *hijra*, and one on the Prophet's death. Ibn Nāṣir al-Dīn was also concerned with Islamic holidays, including those of noncanonical status; aside from his works on the *mawlid* and the *miʻrāj*, he is supposed to have produced compositions on the days of ʻĀshūrā' and ʻArafāt.

The themes of gift and reciprocation are at the heart of the lectures Ibn Nāṣir al-Dīn delivered upon assuming his post at the Ashrafīya. Ibn Nāṣir al-Dīn took as his theme for the series verse 3:164 of the Qur'ān, "God indeed gave a boon to the believers when He sent among them a messenger from among themselves." This passage elicited from him a complex series of reflections on humankind's indebtedness to God and the ways that it could be repaid. Like the jurists whose arguments have been discussed earlier, Ibn Nāṣir al-Dīn conceptualized the Prophet Muḥammad as a gift bestowed by God. The distinctive qualities of Ibn Nāṣir al-Dīn's agenda as a religious teacher perhaps best emerges from his work *al-Tarjīḥ li-ḥadīth ṣalāt al-tasbīḥ*, written in defense of a text describing how to perform a special prayer supposedly authorized by the Prophet. The text emphasizes the efficacy of pious utterance and the vast quantities of merit (*thawāb*) that can be reaped from rather modest devotional activities. It constructs the relationship of the individual believer with God and the Prophet in terms of asymmetrical reciprocity: it is based on mutual acts of giving, with reified utterances serving as media of exchange, but is based on a model of divine munificence in which modest outlays of effort on the human side are met with outpourings of reward from God.

Ibn Nāṣir al-Dīn then sets the stage for the main issue of his essay, the defense of a devotional practice based on a questionable *ḥadīth* text.

> Included in [God's] ample grace to His worshipers and His generosity that reaches those who seek Him, is [the fact] that if anyone hears that God [has promised] some kind of reward (*thawāb*) and acts on the basis of [that report] on the basis of faith and the anticipation of reward (*'alā ṭarīq al-īmān wa'l-itḥisāb*), God will give him that bounteous reward even if the report was not accurate.[134]

The author then cites a number of versions of a *ḥadīth* to this effect (which itself is open to criticism on the basis of its chain of transmission).[135] As for those that are merely weakly authenticated, many authors have argued that they should be treated leniently as long as they fall within the broad category of *al-targhīb wa'l-tarhīb* (enticing people with the pleasures of paradise and frightening them with the horrors of hell), *al-qiṣaṣ wa'l-amthāl* (narratives, usually elaborating the stories of the prophets, and parables), and *al-mawā'iẓ wa-faḍā'il al-a'māl* (admonitions and the merit of pious actions). Ibn Nāṣir al-Dīn cites several early authorities who are supposed to have transmitted poorly authenticated *ḥadīth* texts that fell within these subject areas. If it is permissible to transmit such reports, he further argues, it is also permissible to act on the basis of them; this, he states, is the position of the majority (of religious scholars: *al-jumhūr*).[136]

He then proceeds to the *ḥadīth* itself. It begins with the Prophet asking his uncle al-'Abbās ibn 'Abd al-Muṭṭalib,

> Shall I give you [something]? Shall I bestow [something] on you? Shall I present you with [something]? (*A-lā u'ṭīka*? *A-lā amnaḥuka*? *A-lā aḥbūka*?) Shall I make you do ten things (lit., "qualities," *khiṣāl*) that, if you do them, God will forgive you your sins, the first and last of them, the old and the new, the inadvertent and the intentional, the small and the large, the secret and the manifest – ten things?"

He then instructs al-'Abbās in the performance of a special prayer that involves four prostrations and many repetitions of Qur'ānic chapters and a set of pious formulae. He concludes, "If you are able to pray [this prayer] once a day, do so; if you don't, then [pray it] once every Friday; if you don't, then [pray it] once every month; if you don't, then [pray it] once every year; if you don't, then [pray it] once in your life."[137]

In this *ḥadīth*, the pious utterances prescribed for the "prayer of *tasbīḥ*" are represented as a gift from the Prophet to his uncle, as well as an offering to God that can be made by the individual who performs the prayer. That the "prayer of *tasbīḥ*" is an item of value bestowed by the Prophet emerges from the terminology of gift so strongly emphasized at the beginning of the report. The concrete implications of this language are made clear in variant versions of the *ḥadīth*, in which the Prophet's uncle comments that he expected a material gift; in one text he says that "I thought that he would give me [the weight of] the mountains of Tihāma in gold"[138] and in another "I thought that he would give me [the province of] al-Baḥrayn in fief."[139] Another prominent theme is the disproportionality between the prescribed pious action and the promised reward. The magnanimity of God, and the ultimate incommensurability between human action and divine reward, are emphasized in the dwindling number of prayers demanded at the end of the *ḥadīth*. Even a single repetition of the prayer is sufficient to yield the entire reward. This disproportionality is emphasized even more strongly in a version of the text in which the Prophet assures his uncle that he will be forgiven "even if your sins were as numerous as the stars of the sky, as the drops of rain, as the days of the earth, as the sand of 'Ālij, as the trees, the clods of earth, and the dust."[140]

Ibn Nāṣir al-Dīn gives many different chains of transmission and parallel or divergent texts for this *ḥadīth*, as well as reviewing the opinions of various scholars about the quality of its *isnād*s, and defends it from its critics.[141] Despite the fact that textual citations and *isnād* criticism occupy the bulk of the essay, however, it is clear that the author's interests are primarily oriented toward pious action, rather than textual critique. Ibn Nāṣir al-Dīn concludes his essay with a direct appeal to action: "So it is incumbent on every person of discernment not to neglect the prayer of *tasbīḥ* and to pray it, if only once in his lifetime, and to store it up for his day of need."[142] At least in this context, Ibn Nāṣir al-Dīn is ultimately less interested in textual criticism than in a golden opportunity for the generation of religious merit.

Ibn Nāṣir al-Dīn's interest in the ideas of merit and demerit are also reflected in another composition, his *Minhāj al-salāma fī mīzān al-qiyāma*. This short essay is a defense of the literal existence of the scales that will weigh the deeds of human beings on the Day of Judgment. It begins with an extremely elaborate, multi-stranded chain of transmission for a *ḥadīth* in which a hapless believer's good deeds are outweighed by his sins on the day of judgment, until a slip of paper recording his utterance of the *shahāda* tips the scales in his favor.[143] Like the ideas of gift and reward developed in his treatment of the texts on the "prayer of *tasbīḥ*," this *ḥadīth* (selected by the author from among many on the theme of the Scales) emphasizes the quasi-quantifiable nature of merit and demerit, the concretization of pious utterance, and the ultimate salvific value of small acts of piety through the infinite generosity of God.

Ibn Nāṣir al-Dīn's pervasive invocation of the concept of *thawāb* and the emphasis on the multitude of sins committed by even the most faithful believer suggest a basically economic model for Islamic ethics. It is possible, or in fact necessary, to "earn" merit in order to pay the "debt" for one's sins. What is emphasized is not primarily the overall moral or religious character of the individual, but the aggregate of the credits and debits generated by his or her good and bad actions. However, the calculation of merit and demerit is constantly overturned by the infinite profusion of God's rewards, overwhelming with merit any believer who is willing sincerely to perform the smallest act of supererogatory piety. Among the most basic media of exchange in this moral commerce are pious utterances, which appear as gifts in a cosmic circuit of exchange. Pious formulae are bestowed by God upon the believers (or by God upon the Prophet, who bestows them upon the believers), who return them to God in their own invocations. Because of the disproportionate magnitude of the reward, such simple pious actions (even if, technically speaking, textually ill-founded) can effect the salvation of the most deficient Muslim. Ibn Nāṣir al-Dīn's message ultimately has a strongly populist cast: salvation is available, at the price of small acts of devotion, to the simplest of believers.

The fact that much of the transactional content of *mawlid* ceremonies involves non-material media of exchange – specifically, pious utterances – means that the underlying model can be applied even by those with few financial resources to devote to the *mawlid*. The invocation of blessings upon the Prophet, such as the *ṣalāt al-tasbīḥ* advocated by Ibn Nāṣir al-Dīn, is a low-cost form of religious achievement in terms of both money and time. It requires neither financial outlay nor significant religious expertise. In this regard, it is interesting to note that Tāj al-Dīn al-Fākihānī's critique of women's *mawlid*s focuses on the excesses of their verbal performances, while his general critique of *mawlid* celebration – presumably based on the activities of males – focuses on banqueting practices and the monetary contributions that support them. The same discrepancy can be noted in the discussion by Ibn al-Ḥājj. These authors' failure to mention food or money in connection with women's *mawlid* celebrations does not decisively demonstrate that these elements were not involved, although their failure to denounce the women's handling of money would then be somewhat surprising. In any case, it is a distinct possibility that while men's *mawlid*s featured banqueting, women's centered more exclusively on verbal performance. If such a discrepancy existed, it probably reflected differential access to financial resources on the part of men and women. Recitation may well have been to women's *mawlid*s as money was to men's.

Indeed, the idea that pious utterance could be the religious currency of the poor is deeply rooted in the Islamic tradition. A well-known *ḥadīth* recorded in the *Ṣaḥīḥ* of al-Bukhārī recounts that

> The poor came to the Prophet and said, "The people with abundant wealth (*ahl al-duthūr min al-amwāl*) have taken the highest ranks and the abiding bliss. They pray as we pray and fast as we fast, and they have surplus wealth with which they make the major and minor pilgrimages, engage in *jihād* and give alms." [The Prophet] said, "Shall I tell you something that, if you take it, you will catch up with those who preceded you and no one who comes after you will catch you, and you will be the best of everyone around you, except those who do the same? You say *subḥān allāh* (glory be to God), *al-ḥamdu li'llāh* (praise God), and *allāhu akbar* (God is most great) after every prayer thirty-three times."[144]

In the version of the *ḥadīth* transmitted by Muslim, the poor then return to the Prophet to complain that the rich have overheard their prayer and use it themselves; the Prophet replies merely that "that is God's favor, which He gives to whomever He pleases." The way in which utterances could function as a pious offering for believers of limited resources is similarly suggested by another anecdote, presented at the end of a *mawlid* text within a discussion of the religious value of blessings on the Prophet. A man prepares a banquet (*walīma*) and invites the Prophet, the story recounts. The Prophet accepts the invitation; as he walks from the mosque to the house of his host, the man follows him and counts his steps. The host then frees a slave for every step the Prophet took on the way to his house. The Prophet's other Companions approach him and wistfully comment on the great religious merit that has accrued to his host. "The invocation of prayers upon me," the Prophet replies, "is better than the freeing of slaves."[145] While this narrative does not make the issue of financial means explicit, the force of the other Companions' lament is clear; they lack the resources to prepare banquets and free slaves. The invocation of blessings, in contrast, is a form of pious expenditure that is accessible to all.

*Mawlid*s also, of course, involved more material forms of gift and exchange. The transactional quality of the *mawlid* celebration is expressed, succinctly and rather naively, in lines of poetry presented in a *mawlid* work by Muḥammad ʻAlī ibn ʻAllān al-Bakrī, a Meccan Shāfiʻī scholar who died in 1057 AH/1646–7 CE:

> Hold a *mawlid* for Aḥmad
> And you will be given [your] objectives and right guidance
> Expend on it what you can
> Of gifts and preparations
> And know that for all of it You will be recompensed,
> Immediately and on the Morrow.[146]

The material medium of exchange in the premodern celebration of *mawlid*s was food. Food distribution (*iṭʻām al-taʻām*) was important as a strategy of piety among both organized ṣūfīs and ruling dynasties. It is worth noting that both in Mosul and in Sabta, two of the points of origination for the Sunnī celebration of the Prophet's *mawlid*, ṣūfī, and dynastic celebrations featured in tandem with parallel mass distributions of food. The example of Nūr al-Dīn and ʻUmar al-Mallā' has already been mentioned. In Sabta, the *mawlid* celebrations patronized by the ʻAzafid dynasty were mirrored by the lavish *mawlid* feasts of the ṣūfī master Abū Marwān al-Yuḥānisī (d. 667 AH/1269 CE). Francisco Rodriguez-Manas has speculated that the ṣūfī festivities may in fact have inspired those of the ruling authorities. In any case, "ruling elites, either imitating Sufi lodges or reproducing an ancient tradition of 'royal largesse', also resorted to the *iṭʻām* to commemorate officially sponsored feasts and to mark special events," including the *mawlid*, which "was an auspicious occasion to show generosity to those they ruled."[147] The lavish *mawlid* celebrations patronized by rulers and ṣūfīs would seem to exemplify Mauss's dictum that "to give is to show one's superiority."[148]

Yet *mawlid* piety also, and perhaps more integrally, involved a countervailing form of gift: that initiated by an inferior and bestowed upon a superior. While material expenditures on *mawlid* celebrations may have been immediately bestowed on human beings (whether Qur'ān reciters, preachers, or guests), they were fundamentally directed toward the Prophet, and ultimately toward God. The bestowal of such utterances perfectly exemplifies the blend of interest and disinterestedness that according to Mauss characterizes the gift.[149] Blessing the Prophet is simultaneously a sincere expression of devotion for a profoundly beloved guide and intercessor, and a transactional strategy to elicit reward. Neither God nor the Prophet can be subject to the moral obligations ordinarily involved in gift exchange, God because of His inherent immunity to need and the Prophet because his exalted spiritual status is (arguably) above enhancement by the prayers of the individual believer. Nevertheless, in each case the infinite magnanimity of the recipient guarantees the lavish reciprocation of the gift. The underlying logic is well expressed by Muḥammad al-Kattānī (d. 1345 AH/ 1927 CE), who writes in justification of the *mawlid* celebration that

> there is no doubt that the Prophet's recompense to someone who does something for him will be better, more momentous, more copious, greater and more abundant than [that person's] action, because gifts correspond to the rank of those who give them and presents vary according to their bestowers; it is the custom of kings and dignitaries to recompense small things with the greatest of boons and the most splendid treasures, so what of the master of the kings of this world and the next?[150]

While celebratory distributions of food served to enhance the legitimacy and prestige of both ṣūfī orders and the political authorities with whom they sometimes competed for the allegiance of the population, the widespread phenomenon of the domestic *mawlid* celebration suggests that the pious strategy of feeding was not limited to the institutional holders of socioreligious power. Rather, the activities of hosting and feeding enacted ideals of giving and mutuality that had deep religious roots. Whether rulers were ultimately emulating ṣūfīs or vice versa, and whether domestic acts of pious feeding were the models for royal and mystical food distribution or their imitators, the model of pious food distribution functioned at several different levels of social practice simultaneously. More relevant to the history of the domestic *mawlid* than the top-down models of patronage and legitimation may be the comments of Dina Rizk Khoury on modern Mosul, where "marriage and *mawlid*... rituals reinforced neighborhood ties through celebrations which functioned as redistributive mechanisms of wealth among neighbors."[151] Rather than genuinely redressing disparities in wealth, however, the relatively modest expenditures involved in *mawlid* celebrations probably contributed to the web of obligation and mutuality by which friends and neighbors were bound.

It is true that in some cases, specific classes of recipients are suggested. 'Alī al-Qāri's allusion to old women who save money from the proceeds of their domestic crafts in order to entertain male dignitaries in the season of the *mawlid* suggests that such persons could confer merit by their acceptance of food and hospitality. Certainly organized *ṣūfī* groups could perform such a function by accepting money to support the performance of devotional activities, including *mawlid* celebrations. Operating from a different social and religious location, the poor could also play this role by virtue of the meritorious quality of almsgiving. However, the devotional model of merit generation and exchange did not inherently require a distinct class of recipients. The holding of a *mawlid* did not necessarily require the participation of notables, *ṣūfī*s, or the economically deprived. Rather, individual participants might both contribute to and partake of a *mawlid* banquet. Although conditions inevitably varied, the bonds of social and religious obligation generated by *mawlid* celebrations were probably more often mutual and symmetrical than one-sided and hierarchical. The non-material acts of exchange involved in *mawlid* celebration, such as the donation of *thawāb*, involved a larger and more hierarchical cast of characters, involving God, the Prophet Muḥammad, and a range of possible merit recipients including prophets, bygone generations of Muslims, and the deceased relatives of the attendees.

3 Emotion, law, and the celebration of the *mawlid*

Some of the most central and time-honored justifications for the celebration of the *mawlid* revolve around the evocation and expression of appropriate emotions. Scholarly authors treat sentiments such as joy and love as concrete matters subject to regulation under the *sharīʿa* and to divine reward and punishment. Such emotions are understood both as subjective feelings and in terms of performative conventions whereby love, joy, and reverence for the Prophet are enacted in publicly recognized forms.

Joy

A *fatwā* attributed to Ibn al-Ṭabbākh (d. 575 AH/1178–9 CE) states that if someone holds a banquet in honor of the Prophet's *mawlid* and bestows gifts on the reciter who performs devotional poetry for the occasion, "all of this out of delight in [the Prophet's] birth," his actions are licit.[1] It is certainly a condition of the gathering's acceptability that the activities involved in the celebration themselves be within the limits of the *sharīʿa*; Ibn al-Ṭabbākh goes on to condemn licentious singing and the taking of hashish. However, the fundamental legitimacy of the gathering itself rests on the emotion which gives rise to it, the host's feelings of delight. Another opinion attributed to Ibn al-Ṭabbākh states that the celebration of the *mawlid* "is not a *sunna*, but if one makes expenditures on this day and displays delight out of joy in the entrance of the Prophet into this world . . . this is a good gathering, and anyone who intends that and performs it will be rewarded."[2] A century later, the Egyptian Shāfiʿī *qāḍī* Ṣadr al-Dīn Mawhūb ibn ʿUmar al-Jazarī (d. 675 AH/1274 CE) characterizes the celebration of the *mawlid* as "an unobjectionable innovation (*bidʿa lā baʾs bihā*)" because it is not in conflict with the *sunna*; furthermore, he remarks, "a person will be rewarded according to his intent (*qaṣdihi*) to manifest delight and joy (*al-surūr wa'l-faraḥ*) in the birth of the Prophet."[3] Abū Zurʿa Ibn al-ʿIrāqī (d. 826 AH/1423 CE), asked whether the celebration of the *mawlid* was approved or disapproved (*mustaḥsan* or *makrūh*) under Islamic law, replied that holding banquets and feeding people is always desirable (*mustaḥabb*); and, he rhetorically adds, "what if added to that is delight (*al-surūr*) at the appearance of the Prophet in this noble month?"[4]

In a similar vein, the ṣūfī Abū ʻAbd Allāh ibn abī Muḥammad al-Nuʻmān (d. 683 AH/1284–5 CE) recounts the following anecdote:

> I heard the shaykh Abū Mūsā al-Zarhūn say: I saw the Prophet in a dream and mentioned to him what the jurists say about giving banquets for the *mawlid*. He said, "Whoever rejoices in us, we will rejoice in him (*man fariḥa binā fariḥnā bihi*)."[5]

While this is a pointedly ṣūfī anecdote with an overt agenda to counter "what the jurists say," it reflects a basic concern with correct emotion that is shared by legal scholars such as Ibn al-Ṭabbākh and Mawhūb ibn ʻUmar al-Jazarī. The valorization of joy (*faraḥ*) is common to all. Here again, the point is not so much that the Prophet expresses himself on the subject of the celebration of the *mawlid*, thus incorporating it into the *sunna* and clearing it of the odium of *bidʻa*, as that he provides a devotional rationale for its performance. The practice is legitimized, not as an instance of obedience to or emulation of the Prophet, but as an expression of emotion, a manifestation of joy. The devotee's joy is reciprocated by the Prophet, who thus enters into a relationship of mutuality and closeness with the individual believer.

A more extensive discussion of the expressive rationales for the celebration of the *mawlid* is provided in the letters of the maghribī ṣūfī master Ibn ʻAbbād (d. 792 AH/1390 CE). Ibn ʻAbbād rejects some of the customary forms of observance of the day, which (among other things) involved mixed crowds of men and women; yet he staunchly defends the legitimacy of the celebration itself.[6] Although Ibn ʻAbbād was a mystical teacher, he was also trained in Mālikī *fiqh*; his arguments about the legitimacy of the *mawlid* are fundamentally juristic in nature, while reflecting Ibn ʻAbbād's values and agendas as a ṣūfī. Like his predecessors cited earlier, Ibn ʻAbbād justifies the observation of the *mawlid* fundamentally as an expression of joy. He writes,

> As for the *mawlid*, it seems to me that it is one of the holidays and festivals of the Muslims, and everything that is done on it out of joy and pleasure in that blessed birth, including the lighting of candles, the gratification (*imtāʻ*) of the sight and the hearing, adornment with fancy clothes and the riding of swift steeds, is a permissible thing for which no one should be censured (*lā yunkaru ʻalā aḥad*), based on the analogy with other times of rejoicing (*qiyāsan ʻalā ghayrihi min awqāt al-faraḥ*). To judge that these things are an innovation at this time when the secret of existence appeared, the banner of witnessing was raised, and the darkness of unbelief and denial was dispersed, to claim that this time is not one of the legitimate festivals of the people of the faith, and to compare it with [the Iranian festivals of] *Nawrūz* and *Mihrajān*, is a distasteful thing from which sound hearts recoil, and which sound opinions reject.[7]

In another letter Ibn ʻAbbād responds to his followers, who have forbidden the boys in the Qur'ānic schools from participating in *mawlid* festivities. He advises them to allow the boys to engage in "permissible entertainment or play" (*lahw mubāḥ aw la'b*) on the occasion of the *mawlid*. His followers should not marvel at his giving them this advice, because it has a basis (*mustanad*) in the *sunna*. It is that a woman once came to the Messenger of God on his return from one of his military expeditions and said to him, "I had vowed that if God returned you safely, I would beat a drum before you." The Prophet replied that she should fulfill her vow. Ibn 'Abbād states that he does not now remember which of the authorities on *ḥadīth* have presented this report, but affirms that it is considered well-founded and known through multiple chains of transmission (*thābit mashhūr*).

> There is no doubt that her beating the drum is a kind of entertainment (*lahw*). The Prophet directed her to fulfill her vow to do so because its cause was joy (*faraḥ*) at his safety, at which it was obligatory for her to rejoice (*allatī tajib 'alayhā al-faraḥ bihā*). He did not equate that to vowing something that is [merely] permissible (*mubāḥ*) or sinful, in that it is not obligatory to fulfill [such vows]. The same applies to someone who introduces (*aḥdatha*) a permissible entertainment on the occasion of his rejoicing at the time of [the Prophet's] birth, [even] without a commitment (*iltizām*) or vow.[8]

In making this argument, Ibn 'Abbād assumes that rejoicing in the Prophet is a religious act, one that can be captured by the categories of the *sharī'a* and deemed to be obligatory. However, rejoicing is an act which is itself impalpable, and which must find expression in other, external acts. It is rejoicing, and not drumming, which Ibn 'Abbād considers obligatory; yet the obligation to rejoice is not exhausted by mere subjective feelings of elation. Joy manifests itself in a range of outward activities including drumming, feasting, and the donning of festive clothes.

Among jurists as well as ṣūfīs, arguments in favor of the celebration of the Prophet's *mawlid* have thus been based on the principle that rejoicing in the Prophet is meritorious, or even obligatory. What is the basis for this claim? Interestingly, most early *fatwā*s assume rather than argue this fundamental point. They apparently see no need to cite textual evidence in its support, a fact which may reflect widespread agreement on the meritorious nature of religious rejoicing. However, some *mawlid* texts do provide at least tenuous textual support for this principle, at least as it applies to the celebration of the Prophet's birth. The most widely cited piece of evidence for the merits of rejoicing on the occasion of the Prophet's birth is an anecdote about the Prophet's uncle Abū Lahab, an intransigent opponent of Islam who died as an unbeliever and achieved the questionable distinction of being explicitly consigned to hell in the Qur'ān.[9] This anecdote, oddly transposed to the Prophet's uncle Abū Jahl, appears already in the first preserved *mawlid* text, the *Durr al-munaẓẓam* of Abū'l-'Abbās al-'Azafī (d. 633 AH/1236 CE). al-'Azafī recounts:

> It is transmitted (*wa-ruwiya*) from al-'Abbās that he said, "I had a fraternal and sincere relationship with Abū Jahl (*kuntu muwākhiyan li-Abī Jahl muṣāfiyan lahu*), may God curse him. When he died and God stated what

> He did about him I grieved for him and was concerned about him. For an entire year I asked God to let me see him [in a dream]. [Finally], I saw him burning in a blaze. I asked him about his condition and he said, "I have gone to Hell, [and am] in painful and constant torment which is not alleviated for me and which does not go away, except on Monday nights; then the torment is removed from me." I said, "Why and how is that?" He said to me, "When Muḥammad was born on that night, a maidservant of mine came and gave me the good tidings that his mother had given birth to him. I rejoiced at his birth and freed a slave girl of mine (*walīda lī*) because of my joy in him. God rewarded me for that to the point that He removed my torment every Monday night because of it."[10]

The roots of this story extend far beyond al-ʿAzafī and, indeed, far beyond the origins of the *mawlid* celebration itself. The motif of the alleviation of Abū Lahab's suffering goes back at least to the third-century AH, when it was recorded in the *Ṣaḥīḥ* of al-Bukhārī. It is presented by al-Bukhārī as an explanatory comment, transmitted without a full *isnād*, appended to a reference to the Prophet's wet-nurse Thuwayba:

> ʿUrwa said: Thuwayba is a freedwoman of Abū Lahab; Abū Lahab had freed her, and she nursed the Prophet. When Abū Lahab died, one of his relatives saw him [in a dream] in a sorry state (*fī sharr ḥayba*). He said to him, "What has happened to you?!" Abū Lahab said, "Nothing [good] has happened to me since [I saw] you, except that I was given to drink from this [that is, the hollow at the base of his thumb][11] for my freeing of Thuwayba."[12]

al-ʿAzafī's anecdote is clearly related to that transmitted by al-Bukhārī, since the core elements of the vignette (the uncle's appearance in a dream after his death and the alleviation of his torments in hell, which results from his freeing of a female slave) are identical. However, it is also clear that al-ʿAzafī is not drawing directly from al-Bukhārī. It would have been possible for him to do so, by linking Thuwayba's manumission to the occasion of the Prophet's birth (which does not figure in al-Bukhārī's report) and inferring a connection between Abū Lahab's reward and his rejoicing at the *mawlid*. Instead of resting his argument on the prestige of al-Bukhārī and drawing his own juristic inferences, however, al-ʿAzafī cites an anonymous report whose vivid narration suggests an origin in popular storytelling rather than in textual scholarship.

More importantly, the narrative cited by al-ʿAzafī has clearly already been adapted for the context of *mawlid*-centered piety. The freeing of the slave girl is associated specifically with the Prophet's birth, and it is precisely for his joy at this event – rather than for the manumission *per se* – that Abū Lahab is rewarded. Unlike the freeing of the Prophet's own wet-nurse, an act of piety that no later Muslim was in a position to perform, rejoicing at the Prophet's birth was an act of devotion that could be emulated by any believer. The idea that Abū Lahab was rewarded specifically for his joy is one that seems to be specific to the *mawlid* tradition. The fact that this anecdote was already in circulation in this form in al-'Azafī's time suggests that there was a popular pre-history to the concept of meritorious rejoicing at the birth of the Prophet. Because it specifies that Abū Lahab was rewarded on Mondays, rather than on the yearly anniversary of the Prophet's birth, it is conceivable that the story is related to weekly devotional activities (such as Monday fasting, which is explicitly linked in the *ḥadīth* to the Prophet's birth) rather than to the annual *mawlid* festival. However, it suggests that by the early-seventh-century AH/thirteenth-century CE there were *mawlid*-centered devotional materials in circulation that reflected the style and values of a broader, non-scholarly audience.[13]

Interestingly, the story of Abū Lahab's being rewarded specifically for his joy at the birth of the Prophet was known to Ibn Diḥya (the author of an even earlier, but now lost, devotional text in honor of the *mawlid*), complete with a piece of unattributed dialogue; yet it was not completely acceptable to this rigorous scholar. In his *Nihāyat al-sūl fī khaṣā'iṣ al-rasūl* he cites al-Bukhārī's version of the text and then remarks:

> [The story of] that is that [Thuwayba] came to him bearing the glad tidings; she said to him, "Are you aware that Āmina has given birth to a child?" He said to her, "You are free!" His torment is alleviated every Monday because of his delight in the Prophet's birth on that day and his freeing of the one who brought him the good tidings. [However,] it is more appropriate to say that it is a blessing that was communicated to Abū Lahab (*fa'l-awlā an yuqāla innahā baraka ta'addat li-Abī Lahab*).[14]

Even after the rise of *mawlid* celebrations, and even in the version transmitted by al-Bukhārī, the story remained subject to theological and textual reservations in scholarly circles. Even Ibn Ḥajar al-'Asqalānī, a known advocate of the meritorious nature of rejoicing at the memory of the Prophet's birth, regarded the anecdote with suspicion. First of all, he points out in his commentary on al-Bukhārī, while 'Urwa's comment implies that Abū Lahab freed Thuwayba before she nursed the Prophet, biographical sources place her manumission immediately before the *hijra*. Second, the anecdote's implication that unbelievers may be rewarded for their good actions contradicts the obvious meaning (*al-ẓāhir*) of passages in the Qur'ān; Ibn Ḥajar cites Qur'ān 25:23, which describes the unbelievers' (good) acts as "scattered dust." Ibn Ḥajar suggests first that the story is poorly authenticated (particularly as it recounts the dream vision of a person who may not have been Muslim when he made the report), and second that the reward of an unbeliever in the afterlife is an exceptional case reserved for those who helped the Prophet Muḥammad.[15] It may have been this theological point, the question of divine reward being bestowed on an unbeliever, that concerned Ibn Diḥya. Instead of reward (*thawāb*), he invokes the concept of *baraka*, an auspicious power that is automatically communicated to all who come in contact with it (and is thus presumably independent of the faith status of the individual in question).

Not all *mawlid* proponents had the intellectual rigor of Ibn Diḥya and Ibn Ḥajar, however, and by the latter's time other authors of some scholarly standing were lending it an air of legitimacy. The story's role in the *mawlid* genre was consolidated by Ibn al-Jazarī (d. 833 AH/1429 CE), who recounts the anecdote and comments:

> If Abū Lahab, the unbeliever whose condemnation was revealed in the Qur'ān, was rewarded (*jūziya*) in hell for his joy on the night of the Prophet's birth, what is the case of a Muslim monotheist of the community of Muḥammad the Prophet who delights in his birth and spends all that he can afford for love of him? By my life, his reward (*jazā'*) from the Beneficent God can only be that He graciously causes him to enter the gardens of bliss![16]

A similar comment appears in Ibn Nāṣir al-Dīn's (d. 842 AH/1438 CE) *Mawrid al-ṣādī fī mawlid al-hādī* in a list of the Prophet's wet-nurses. "Thuwayba is the first one who nursed him," he writes.

> She is a freedwoman of his paternal uncle Abū Lahab; he freed her out of delight (*surūran*) at the birth of the Prophet of spirits and humankind (*nabī al-thaqalayn*). For this reason, it is reliably reported that the punishment of hell is alleviated for him every Monday. If this was an unbeliever whose condemnation was revealed and whose hands perished eternally in hell [cf. Qur'ān 111:1–3] and it is reported that on Monday his [torment] is always alleviated because of his delight in Aḥmad, what do you think of the servant who delighted in Aḥmad all of his life and died as a monotheist?![17]

In a more homely vein, Ibn Makkīya (d. 903 AH/1497–8 CE) comments in his *mawlid Durar al-biḥār fī mawlid al-mukhtār* that if Abū Lahab was rewarded "despite his unbelief . . . , what do you think of a believing monotheist who manifests delight and joy in [the Prophet's] birthday among his family and neighbors at its proper time?" Ibn Makkīya follows this comment with the story of the Jewish man and his wife whose Muslim neighbor celebrates the *mawlid* (see Chapter 2). When the wife sees the Prophet Muḥammad in her dream visiting her neighbor's home and asks one of his companions who he is, the latter replies, "He is the Messenger of God, who has entered this home to greet and visit its inhabitants because they have rejoiced in his birth, and their delight has increased."[18]

The anecdote about Abū Lahab was admirably suited to the defense of *mawlid*s because of its close linkage to the actual event of the Prophet's birth. However, concerns about the accuracy and authority of the story made it a more effective element of devotional texts than of legal opinions.[19] It is another legal principle that most often appears in *fatwā*s, one that is rarely explicitly and rigorously invoked but whose terminology recurs with striking frequency. In texts supporting the celebration of the *mawlid*, the motif of meritorious rejoicing is frequently paired with the obligation to give thanks for benefactions (*shukr al-ni'ma*). *Mawlid* authors often juxtapose and intermingle the terminology of joy and thanks in their discussions of the *mawlid* without making explicit the link between the two. However, a direct linkage can be inferred both from texts directly concerned with *mawlid* celebrations and from the broader Islamic literature relating to the concept of *shukr al-ni'ma*.

Abū Shāma (d. 665 AH/1268 CE) endorses the celebration of the *mawlid* with "almsgiving, acts of charity (*al-ma'rūf*), and the display of adornments and delight (*iẓhār al-zīna wa'l-surūr*)," because, in addition to providing relief to the poor, all of this "expresses love for the Prophet, and his honor and greatness in the heart of the one who engages in it, and thanks to God for what He bestowed in creating His messenger whom He sent as a mercy to the worlds."[20] Here delight, love, veneration, and thanks are intimately linked; they are all expressed by the same displays of gaiety and kindness. Similar associations are established by Ibn Ḥajar al-'Asqalānī in his *fatwā* in support of *mawlids*. As we have already seen, Ibn Ḥajar justifies the celebration of the *mawlid* as a form of thanks for a benefaction, on analogy with the 'Āshūrā' fast. Among the various forms of thanking that Ibn Ḥajar envisions are licit music and entertainment, because they comprise "rejoicing in that day" (*al-surūr bi-dhālika al-yawm*).[21] (Nevertheless, such diversions are subsidiary to the central forms of thanking, which include recitation, food distribution, and almsgiving.) Suyūṭī understands thanks to God to include both "forms of pious activity" (*wujūh al-qurubāt*) and "expressions of delight" (*iẓhār al-masarrāt*).[22] Performing pious acts of charity and manifesting one's feelings of joy through licit festivities are both elements of "thanking the benefactor."

What is the relationship between joy and thanks? No *mawlid* text of which I am aware explicitly discusses the connection. However, a sense of the overall context of these motifs can be gained from the exhaustive treatment of this issue provided by al-Ghazālī in his *Iḥyā' 'ulūm al-dīn*. In this passage al-Ghazālī treats thankfulness (*shukr*) not as an obligation of the *sharī'a*, but as a stage in the mystical path (*min maqāmāt al-sālikīn*).[23] However, he does provide one of the most thorough and thoughtful expositions of the concept of *shukr* in medieval Islamic culture. According to al-Ghazālī, *shukr* consists of a knowledge, a state, and an action (*'ilm wa-ḥāl wa-'amal*). Each of the three gives rise to the next in succession: the knowledge generates the state, which in turn generates the action. The knowledge in question is knowledge of the benefaction and of its being from the benefactor. In the case of God, the requisite knowledge involves the recognition that all possible benefactions issue from Him, and the withdrawal of any feelings of gratitude from the persons or things by means of which He bestows them. The state derived from this knowledge is joy (*faraḥ*). This joy in itself constitutes thanks, just as the relevant knowledge constitutes thanks (*wa-huwa ayḍan fī nafsihi shukr 'alā tajarrudihi kamā anna al-ma'rifa shukr*).[24] The third stage of thankfulness is action in accordance with the joy resulting from one's knowledge. Such action is related to the heart, the tongue, and the limbs. With respect to the heart, it entails harboring good feelings and intentions towards all beings. The tongue verbally thanks God and utters His praises. The thanks of the limbs are constituted by their use in accordance with God's will and the avoidance of disobedience to Him.[25]

al-Ghazālī modulates his discussion of joy by arguing that it constitutes thanks only on the condition that it be joy in the benefactor, not in the benefaction itself or in the fact of its bestowal. While al-Ghazālī clearly advocates that one strive for this pure and disinterested kind of joy, he acknowledges that it may not be attainable for all believers: "If there are no camels, then a goat," he remarks philosophically.[26] al-Ghazālī's exposition of *shukr* reflects his ṣūfī outlook in its graded progression of the manifestations of thankfulness. For him true thanks, the culmination of this progression, consists in the selfless service of the divine benefactor. The devotionalist outlook underlying the *mawlid* genre does not aspire to such disinterested dedication; rejoicing in one's own delivery from hell through the divine bestowal of the Prophet Muḥammad is considered satisfactory. In al-Ghazālī's terminology, the *mawlid* literature is satisfied with a goat rather than a camel.

The question of meritorious rejoicing on the Prophet's birthday is complicated by the fact that he is generally understood to have died on the day of his own birth. Monday, the twelfth of Rabīʿ al-Awwal, was thus both the Prophet's birthday and the anniversary of his death, and its commemoration required a choice between rejoicing and mourning. The emotional valence of the occasion thus depended on a careful parsing of the comparative religious values of pious joy and grief. Opponents of the *mawlid* celebration sometimes argue that no reasoned choice is possible. Tāj al-Dīn al-Fākihānī (731 AH/1331 CE) argues in his *fatwā* against *mawlid*s that the rejoicing appropriate to the Prophet's birth is effectively canceled out by the mourning appropriate to his death. Referring to the common practice of celebrating the *mawlid* for the duration of the month, he writes that people celebrate "despite the fact that the month in which [the Prophet] was born, namely Rabīʿ al-Awwal, is the very same one in which he died. Therefore joy and happiness in [this month] are no more appropriate than sadness in it."[27]

Ibn al-Ḥājj (d. 737 AH/1336 CE) makes a similar but more elaborate and moralistic argument about the moral valence of the season of the Prophet's birth and death. "Consider this noble month . . . ," he writes, "how they play and dance in it, and do not weep and sorrow!" It would be more appropriate to grieve than to frolic, he argues, because of the burden of sin and the sorrow of the Prophet's loss. Weeping and sorrowing efface sins. In the hierarchy of emotions, Ibn al-Ḥājj privileges sorrow over joy because grief chastens the soul, while rejoicing indulges it. Nevertheless, if people were to lament the Prophet's death in a regular and organized fashion, this would also be an illegitimate innovation. Although it is incumbent on Muslims to mourn for the Prophet at all times, they must not gather to weep and grieve; their sorrow must remain in their hearts, although their sentiments may overflow in tears.[28] Here Ibn al-Ḥājj is in the somewhat odd position of endorsing an emotional response to a special time while objecting to any form of ritualization. Appropriate emotion is praiseworthy, but it must remain personal and spontaneous. This approach contrasts with those of many *mawlid* supporters, who implicitly assume that religiously meritorious emotions must be expressed performatively.

Mawlid supporters, of course, did not concur in valuing grief above joy. In rebuttal of al-Fākihānī's argument that rejoicing in Rabī' al-Awwal is no more appropriate than mourning, al-Suyūṭī argues as follows:

> [The Prophet's] birth is the greatest of benefactions to us, and his death is the greatest calamity to befall us. The *sharī'a* advocates that we give thanks for benefactions and that we practice patience endurance, silence, and restraint in the face of calamities. The [divine] Lawgiver commanded the performance of the *'aqīqa* sacrifice at the birth [of a child], which is a display of thanks and joy for the newborn. On the occasion of a death [, in contrast], He did not command the performance of a sacrifice or anything else; rather, He forbade lamentation and the display of grief. Thus, the principles of the *sharī'a* indicate that during this month it is good to manifest joy in [the Prophet's] birth, rather than sorrow at his death.[29]

Another approach for *mawlid* supporters was to deny that the death of the Prophet or any other great figure was an occasion for sadness at all. This was an attitude particularly attractive to mystics. In his *mawlid* text *al-Mawrid al-rawī fī mawlid al-nabī*, al-Qāri' al-Harawī (d. 1014 AH/1606 CE) adopts this distinctively ṣūfī approach to the convergence of the dates of the Prophet's birth and death. To him the Prophet's advent in this world is a painful and temporary exile from the divine presence, which the Prophet undertook only because it was the divine will. The Prophet's death, accordingly, is a welcome return to his only true home. It is one of the providential wonders of history that the two events (which he also refers to as "the two great blessings," *al-ni'matān al-'aẓīmatān*) occurred on the same date.[30] For al-Qāri' al-Harawī, the Prophet's birth and death are not contrasting events with opposite emotional valences; they are both wondrous blessings, the one a gift to humankind, the other a joyful homecoming for the Prophet, and their temporal convergence is a sign of divine benevolence.

In general, however, proponents of the *mawlid* celebration did not neglect the commemoration of the Prophet's death, and they commonly regarded it as an occasion for mournful reflection. Ibn Rajab al-Ḥanbalī (d. 795 AH/1392 CE) includes in the section of *Laṭā'if al-ma'ārif* devoted to the month of Rabī' al-Awwal, in addition to two pieces on the subject of the Prophet's pre-existence and birth, a moving sermon on his final illness and his demise.[31] Ibn Nāṣir al-Dīn composed a rather lengthy monograph (129 pages in the printed edition) on the Prophet's death that provides a largely chronological narrative of his final days and ends with a series of elegies composed upon his death.[32] al-Qasṭallānī (d. 923 AH/1517 CE), whose *Mawāhib al-ladunīya* includes an effusive endorsement of the celebration of the Prophet's *mawlid*, also wrote a work that dealt with both the birth and death of the Prophet.[33] While the death of the Prophet was clearly considered an appropriate subject for sorrowful contemplation, however, it does not seem to have rivaled his birth as a focus for ritual commemoration. Sermons or monographs inviting serious or even tearful meditation on the event clearly were not lacking, but the *mawlid* literature does not reflect a Sunnī tendency to institute any form of ritualized mourning comparable to the feasting and recitations commemorating the Prophet's birth.[34]

To understand the idea of meritorious rejoicing fully, we must also be attentive to another level of the religious context of the rise of *mawlid* celebrations. This is the level of inter-sectarian polemic and intra-sectarian self-understanding. In practice, any sectarian valence of the *mawlid* literature is usually strictly implicit. It is frequently observed (particularly by opponents of the *mawlid*) that *mawlid* celebrations first arose under the Shīʿite Fāṭimid dynasty. We have also presented evidence that Twelver Shīʿites observed the occasion of the Prophet's birth. However, it would be hasty to assume that Sunnī participants in the rise of the *mawlid* celebration were aware of these facts, or that they perceived the practice to carry any Shīʿite taint. Had the celebration of the *mawlid* been associated with Shīʿism in the minds of contemporary Sunnī Muslims, that fact would undoubtedly be reflected in polemics against the practice or in apologetics in its favor. In fact, this is not the case. In the first centuries of the *mawlid* celebration supporters defended it from the accusation of being a *bidʿa*, but not of being a Shīʿite *bidʿa*. N.J.G. Kaptein concludes from al-Suyūṭī's own works that the latter was familiar with copious information about the *mawlid* celebrations of the Fāṭimid caliphs, and that he probably intentionally suppressed this information in his *fatwā* in favor of the Prophet's *mawlid*.[35] Other authors may have been sincerely unaware of the festival's historical origins. Whatever the reason, a sectarian taint was not among the accusations routinely directed at the *mawlid* by its opponents until the modern period.

The absence of explicit references to sectarian issues in the premodern *mawlid* literature does not, however, mean that inter-sectarian dynamics did not play a role in the festival's development and cultivation. In fact, the idea of meritorious rejoicing, which underlies the most important defenses of the *mawlid* festival, was probably closely linked with Sunnī critiques of Twelver Shīʿite devotional practice. Specifically, it forms part of a complex of Sunnī responses to Shīʿite observance of the day of ʿĀshūrā'. As will be remembered, in the *mawlid* tradition, the ʿĀshūrā' fast is taken as the authoritative precedent for the commemoration of joyous occasions (see Chapter 2). This precedent was, however, enmeshed in a broader debate over sacred times and meritorious emotion. As is well known, Shīʿites commemorated ʿĀshūrā' as the anniversary of the slaughter of the Imām Ḥusayn and his companions on the plain of Karbalā'. They observed the day with funereal pomp and elaborate expressions of sorrow. Although the historical origins of the Sunnī response are obscure, by the time of the rise of the Sunnī *mawlid* celebration it was a well-established custom to invert Shīʿite practice by observing ʿĀshūrā' as a day of merriment and rejoicing. Ibn Taymīya (d. 728 AH/1328 CE) wrote a *fatwā* on this subject in response to a questioner who observes that it is customary for people to bathe, adorn themselves with kohl and henna, shake hands with each other, cook grains, and generally "manifest joy" (*iẓhār al-surūr*) on this day; he desires to know whether there is any basis for these observances in the *ḥadīth*.[36]

The *mawlid* author and advocate Ibn Nāṣir al-Dīn deprecates the festivities associated with the popular Sunnī observance of 'Āshūrā' and rejects several relevant *ḥadīth* texts as forgeries, although he cites several different paths of transmission for a text advocating festive spending on one's dependents.[37] Ibn Nāṣir al-Dīn also strongly emphasizes the special and auspicious nature of the day of 'Āshūrā'. The many reports he cites about the wondrous events that occurred on this day of the Islamic calendar reflect a basic dispute about the emotional coloring of the day of 'Āshūrā' in human history, an issue that was hotly contested by Sunnīs and Shī'ites. Sunnī rejoicing on this day of the calendar was supported by a set of traditions associating the day with a series of propitious and joyful events in salvation history. In Shī'ite reports the Imāms strongly object to this association. In a *ḥadīth* reported from the Imām 'Alī, it is predicted that "They shall fabricate a *ḥadīth* … claiming that it was on that date that God forgave Adam, but in fact, He forgave him during the month of Dhū-l Ḥijja … They shall assert wrongly that it was the day on which God accepted David's repentance, but that also was in Dhū-l Ḥijjah." The Shī'ite report goes on to deny that it was on 'Āshūrā' that Noah's ark came to ground after the flood and on which God parted the Red Sea for Moses.[38] The disputed *ḥadīth* about the fast of 'Āshūrā', with its identification of the day as the date of a joyous event and an occasion for thanksgiving, clearly fits into the Sunnī side of this controversy. Its use by scholars such as Ibn Rajab and Ibn Ḥajar as evidence for the legitimacy of the *mawlid* celebration reflects this sectarian background, once again using 'Āshūrā' as a model for thanks and rejoicing rather than for grief and lamentation.

The debate over the observance of 'Āshūrā' was not merely about the joyous or mournful nature of a specific day in the Islamic calendar, however. It also raised broader questions about appropriate religious emotion. Ibn Nāṣir al-Dīn denies that it is in principle appropriate to engage in mourning practices in commemoration of the great religious figures of the past. In his view, the Shī'ites "have exaggerated (*taghālā*) in their sorrow over this calamity and have made the day of 'Āshūrā' a funeral (*ma'tam*) for the killing of al-Ḥusayn."

> On its anniversary they perform mourning ceremonies, engage in prolonged lamentation and weeping, display sorrow and dejection, and behave as no right-thinking person would do (*yaf'alūna fi'la ghayr ahl al-iṣāba*). … Were it permissible to do such things among the Muslims, it would be more appropriate to mourn on the day on which the Muḥammad, the master of the prophets, passed away.[39]

He then cites the great Ḥanbalī ṣūfī master 'Abd al-Qādir al-Jīlī (d. 561 AH/1166 AH)[40] as critiquing the view that it is not permissible to fast on 'Āshūrā' because Ḥusayn was killed on it, and on it all people should mourn him. al-Jīlī retorts that "the one who says this is in error, and his opinion is repugnant and faulty, because God chose to bestow martyrdom on the grandson of His Prophet on the noblest, greatest, most glorious day in His eyes and the highest in rank." If any day should be taken as a day of mourning, "then Monday would be more worthy of that, because on it God gathered in His Prophet." On the contrary, however, "the Muslims have agreed on the nobility of Monday and the virtue of fasting on it."[41] Here, interestingly, al-Jīlī appears to assume that fasting is a celebratory activity that is incompatible with the observance of a day of mourning.

The emotional valence of fasting seems to have been very much at issue among scholars who pondered the celebration of the *mawlid*. Ibn Ḥajar's use of the precedent of 'Āshūrā' suggests that fasting can be regarded as an act of celebration, and equated with other pious or festive activities expressing thanks. The statement attributed by Ibn Nāṣir al-Dīn to 'Abd al-Qādir al-Jīlī similarly assumes that fasting is an expression of rejoicing (and thus offensive to Shī'ites observing 'Āshūrā'). Many scholars before and after his time, however, made the converse argument that fasting was inappropriate on the day of the *mawlid* because it was incompatible with the joyous mood of the day. The *locus classicus* for this position is in the letters of Ibn 'Abbād, who recounts the following anecdote:

> Once in the past I had gone out on the *mawlid* to the riverbank, and I happened to find there Sayyidī al-Ḥājj ibn 'Āshir[42] and a group of his companions; some of them had brought out different foods to eat them there. When they were ready to eat they wanted me to share their food. I was fasting at the time, and I told them, "I'm fasting." Sayyidī al-Ḥājj looked at me disapprovingly and said something to the effect that "today is a day of joy and delight (*faraḥ wa-surūr*), on the likes of which it is not considered appropriate to fast, equivalent to an *'īd*." I considered what he said and found it true; it was as if I had been sleeping and he woke me.[43]

The idea that the *mawlid* was a festive occasion on which fasting was inappropriate persisted over time, not only among ṣūfīs but among jurists. In later centuries, a number of Mālikī *furū'* works stated that it was undesirable (*makrūh*) to fast on the day of the *mawlid* because it is tantamount to an *'īd* (*ilḥāqan bi'l-a'yād*).[44]

In the *mawlid* celebration, the meritorious mourning of the Shī'ites was countered with the meritorious rejoicing of the Sunnīs. As indicated by the example of Ibn Nāṣir al-Dīn, however, even authorities who supported the celebration of the *mawlid* were sometimes uncomfortable with Sunnī celebration on the day of 'Āshūrā'; it was too much entangled with folk piety and egregiously spurious *ḥadīth* texts to win the approval of scholars. It is notable that many of the practices associated with the Sunnī counter-observance of 'Āshūrā' – including extra expenditures on one's family, the donning of festive garments, and the serving of special foods – are the same ones associated with the celebration of the Prophet's birthday. In both cases, the activities in question represent a standard repertory of socially recognized forms of "rejoicing." For a *mawlid* supporter such as Ibn Nāṣir al-Dīn, in many ways the celebration of the *mawlid* might be seen as a religiously legitimate alternative to the baseless festivities associated with the day of 'Āshūrā'.

However, the legal relevance of emotional expressions of joy or sorrow was itself subject to debate. Ibn Taymīya's response to the enquiry about Sunnī rejoicing on ʿĀshūrāʾ exemplifies a categorical rejection of meritorious emotion as a productive source of legal norms. The major thrust of Ibn Taymīya's arguments about the observance of ʿĀshūrāʾ is to de-emphasize the expression of emotion in favor of a strict construal of the boundaries of the *sunna*. Although Ibn Taymīya does not address the issue of the *mawlid* (which was not yet associated with the precedent of the fast of ʿĀshūrāʾ in his time), his attitude clearly resonates with that of a *mawlid* opponent such as al-Fākihānī. What they have in common is the denial that concrete religious activities can be justified by the claim that they arise from or express desired emotions, whether of sorrow or rejoicing. To start with, Ibn Taymīya reframes al-Ḥusayn's martyrdom as a divinely bestowed honor rather than a dreadful tragedy. In any case, Ibn Taymīya argues later in the *fatwā*, the appropriate response to bereavement is not extravagant mourning, but patient endurance and pronunciation of the Qur'ānic formula that "we belong to God, and to God we will return." This is what God has commanded with respect to fresh catastrophes; what, then, of those that are long past?[45] Conversely, those who celebrate on ʿĀshūrāʾ are either anti-Shīʿī zealots with an animus against al-Ḥusayn and his family (*al-nawāṣib al-mutaʿaṣṣibīn ʿalā al-Ḥusayn wa-ahlihi*) or "ignorant people who have met corruption with corruption, lies, with lies, evil with evil, and innovations with innovations." They have fabricated *ḥadīth* texts that recommend spending money on one's dependents, cooking special foods, and generally observing the day as a festival and an occasion of joy. For Ibn Taymīya, all of this is strictly an issue of the authenticity of *ḥadīth* and the content of the Prophet's *sunna*. Whereas mourning the death of al-Ḥusayn is an inappropriate display of emotion, celebrating on the anniversary of his demise is for Ibn Taymīya not a tasteless indulgence but a falsification of the *sharīʿa*. The point is not that merriment and glee are an inappropriate emotional response to the violent death of the Prophet's grandson, but that the Prophet simply did not instruct believers to do anything of the sort. "Neither the Prophet nor his rightly guided caliphs established any of these things as a *sunna* on the day of ʿĀshūrāʾ," Ibn Taymīya concludes, "neither the practices of sadness and grief nor the practices of delight and joy."[46]

At this point, Ibn Taymīya turns to the one practice which the Prophet did establish as a normative custom on the day of ʿĀshūrāʾ, that of fasting. He accepts this practice on the basis of the *ḥadīth* recounting the Prophet's exchange with the Jews of Medina. What is notable about Ibn Taymīya's discussion of the *ḥadīth* recounting the origin of the ʿĀshūrāʾ fast, particularly in light of its later role in justifying the celebration of the *mawlid*, is that he does not regard it in terms of commemoration or celebration at all. The fact that the Prophet chooses to fast on that date in response to the Jews' statement that it is the anniversary of a joyous deliverance in the past has no relevance to his analysis. The only material fact is that the Prophet does, in fact, both fast on that date and instruct others to do so. This is, of course, a rigorous but also selective reading of the text of the *ḥadīth*. To focus on the rationale for the fast, the manifestation of thanks to God for a past boon, would open the question of whether there are other means of expressing the same sentiments. For Ibn Taymīya, however, there is no expressive element in the act of fasting. It is not a mode of manifesting gratitude and joy, but a concrete act that means nothing beyond itself and can be extended only through its own repetition.[47]

Love

In addition to joy, the emotion most frequently invoked by *mawlid* proponents is love. After condemning the falsehoods of popular storytellers who preach about the *mawlid*, Ibn Ḥajar al-Haytamī suggests appropriate forms of celebration "for those who intend to do good and to manifest joy and delight in [the Prophet] and love for him."[48] The rationale of expressing love for the Prophet was so compelling that it occasionally forced even opponents of the *mawlid* celebration to qualify their disapproval. Ibn Taymīya remarks that people may celebrate the *mawlid* either in order to emulate the Christians' celebration of Jesus's birthday, or "out of love (*maḥabba*) and reverence (*ta'ẓīm*) for the Prophet." Although the first motive is manifestly invalid, Ibn Taymīya acknowledges the latter intention as legitimate; one who acts on this motivation may be rewarded for his love and his effort, although not for the sinful religious innovation in itself.[49]

Unlike rejoicing in the Prophet, love for him had a well-established and incontestable status in Islamic law. Love of the Prophet is not merely a natural response to his many exquisite qualities of person and character. Rather, it is universally recognized to be a legal obligation of Muslim believers. Authoritative *ḥadīth* texts establish that a true believer must love the Prophet more dearly than his spouse, his children, and even himself.[50] While the obligation to love is usually an underlying assumption rather than an explicit subject of *mawlid* texts, it is sometimes overtly invoked. "God has made the love [of the Prophet] an individual obligation (*min al-furūḍ al-'aynīya*)," remarks the anonymous author of a *mawlid* preserved in Damascus; "the one who has no love [of the Prophet] has no faith."[51] "Among the greatest of the individual obligations and the firmest requirements of the religion is the love of God's greatest Beloved ... " begins another *mawlid* text.[52] Muḥammad Ṣāliḥ al-Dasūqī (d. 1246 AH/1830 CE) argues that the more someone listens to the *mawlid*, "the more the love of the Prophet establishes itself in his heart; from [love of the Prophet] arises his veneration and exaltation (*ta'ẓīmuhu wa-ijlāluhu*), which are among the greatest branches of the faith."[53]

Muslim authorities never doubted that the Prophet was worthy of a surpassing love, because of his inherent beauty, his incomparable moral virtues, and his incalculable benefactions to humankind. However, these qualities could be grasped by the individual believer and translated into the requisite emotion only through exposure to knowledge about the Prophet's life and character. This line of reasoning is adumbrated in the *Shu'ab al-īmān* of Aḥmad ibn al-Ḥusayn al-Bayhaqī (d. 458 AH/1066 CE) which, although it predates the rise of Sunnī *mawlid* ceremonies, nevertheless suggests how the imperative to love the Prophet could justify the devotional recitation of tales about his life and birth.

al-Bayhaqī's fourteenth "branch of faith" is the love of the Prophet (*ḥubb al-nabī*). After presenting eleven *ḥadīth* texts illustrating that love of the Prophet is integral to true faith, al-Bayhaqī writes,

> al-Ḥalīmī[54] said: The root of this matter is that he ponder the praises (*al-madā'iḥ*) of the Messenger of God and his inherent good qualities, then his good deeds on behalf of God's religion and the debt that is owed to him by his community (*mā yajibu lahu min al-ḥaqq 'alā ummatihi*), both by custom and by divine law. Anyone who comprehends all of this and is of sound mind will realize that [the Prophet] is more worthy of love than a father who is inherently good, kindly, and tender towards his child, and than an inherently satisfactory teacher who devotes himself to teaching and exerts himself in educating.

There follows a list of the subjects of study or contemplation that one might use to achieve this level of awareness of the Prophet's lovable qualities; first in the list is "the nobility of his origins and the purity of his birth." al-Bayhaqī remarks that he composed his work *Dalā'il al-nubūwa wa-ma'rifat aḥwāl ṣāḥib al-risāla min waqt wilādatihi ilā ḥāl wafātihi* ("The Proofs of Prophecy and the Knowledge of the States of the Messenger from the Time of his Birth until the Circumstances of his Death") of reports that serve to elucidate the points set out by al-Ḥalīmī. Following these remarks, al-Bayhaqī inserts a section containing traditions about the Prophet's birth.[55] The material on this subject that he provides for contemplation anticipates to a large extent the content of later *mawlid* works.

A concern with the interdependence of knowledge and emotion somewhat analogous to al-Bayhaqī's is apparent in the earliest preserved *mawlid* text, al-'Azafī's *al-Durr al-munaẓẓam*. Unlike al-Bayhaqī, who emphasizes that knowledge generates emotion, however, al-'Azafī explores the way in which emotion motivates and consolidates the acquisition of knowledge. As described in the introduction of his *mawlid* text, al-'Azafī's fundamental concern is pedagogical. He is disturbed by the interest and concern for Christian holidays expressed by ordinary Muslims and even by religious scholars, which leads them to enquire into the birth dates of Jesus and of John the Baptist. In contrast to their eagerness to inform themselves about the birth dates of other holy figures, they neglect to ask about the birthday of their own prophet. Even scholars do not concern themselves with it, contenting themselves with the knowledge that the date is contained in their books. Muslims arrange sumptuous displays of fruits, nuts, and sweets for their families in honor of Christian festivals, and markets are closed for the occasion; large amounts of money are expended for these indulgences, and people believe that the celebration will ensure their prosperity in the coming year.[56]

The reason for Muslims' inappropriate concern with alien festivals is rooted in childhood, and it rests on the pedagogical power of pleasurable indulgences. al-'Azafī notes that on the birthdays of Jesus and John the Baptist and on the seventh day after Jesus's birth boys are given a holiday from Qur'ānic school, which inspires them with a love for such innovations.[57] Given the pleasurable customs surrounding such celebrations, al-ʿAzafī complains, it is inevitable that children grow up as confirmed devotees of these holidays.[58] Children, al-ʿAzafī observes, have better memories and are more receptive to admonition than adults; and the Qur'ānic schools (*makātib*) are their gathering place. al-ʿAzafī describes how he took it upon himself to visit schools and explain to the children and their parents the relevant facts about the Prophet's *sunna* and religious innovations. However, he "did not know of anything that would implant in their hearts acceptance of that." The solution arose from his realization that "festivals are an occasion of delight, joys, permissible play and licit amusement." Furthermore, "joyous occasions are most appropriate and fitting for boys, and the things they rejoice in are established in their minds[59] like engraving in stone."[60] In short, al-ʿAzafī proposes to create an alternative to the celebration of Christian festivals that will be just as memorable and endearing to the young, and the key to this is to elicit happiness and rejoicing. The joy experienced in such festivities in youth will then give rise to an enduring love for their occasions.

At this point a hypothetical questioner intervenes to ask whether the diversion of Muslims from the celebration of Christian holidays to that of the Prophet's birthday, while in itself praiseworthy, has any basis in the *sharīʿa*. Does al-ʿAzafī's method of enticement (*talaṭṭuf*) have any sound foundation that would include worship, delight, rejoicing, play, and amusement? al-ʿAzafī replies that it does. The *sharīʿa* provides guidance to the best means to various ends. The Prophet used the best means of guiding and forming his followers (*al-siyāsa, al-iyāla*), those which were conducive to the best results and were most likely to be accepted and met with a positive response. He declares, "Enticing hearts (*al-talaṭṭuf bi'l-qulūb*) and by this means making them forget their [illegitimate] desires is the objective."[61]

As evidence, al-ʿAzafī presents a series of *ḥadīth* texts illustrating that the Prophet condoned various forms of festive amusement and that in some cases they functioned as replacements for other celebrations. First he cites a report in which a Companion of the Prophet states that "The people of the Age of Ignorance had two days in every year on which they frolicked (*yalʿabūna fīhā*); God replaced them for you with better ones, the day of the breaking of the fast and the day of the sacrifice." Then he transmits a *ḥadīth* in which ʿĀ'isha recounts how her father, Abū Bakr, once entered the Prophet's apartment on a festival (*yawm ʿīd*) and admonished two slave girls who were singing about the exploits of the Anṣār on the Day of Buʿāth.[62] The Prophet replied, "O Abū Bakr, every people has its festival, and this is our festival."[63] al-ʿAzafī notes that alternative versions of the *ḥadīth* mention the slave women's beating on drums. Another version recounts how ʿĀ'isha watched Abyssinians play with spears, to the acclaim of the Prophet.

The pedagogical value of joyful celebration in inculcating love for the Prophet is also emphasized by the North African scholar and ṣūfī Muḥammad ibn Qāsim al-Raṣṣāʿ (d. 894 AH/1489 CE) in his book *Tadhkirat al-muḥibbīn fī asmā' sayyid al-mursalīn*.[64] Similar to al-ʿAzafī, he regards the celebration of the *mawlid* festival as a means of sowing the love of the Prophet in the hearts of the more impressionable and less learned sectors of the population, including children, women, and the uneducated. For al-Raṣṣāʿ, the *mawlid* is an instrument for the social reproduction of the devotion to the Prophet cherished by the pious adult male. Both wondrous stories and material consumption evoke delight in the hearts of the young, which in turn (it is implied) gives rise to the pious love of the mature believer. al-Raṣṣāʿ writes,

> It is part of the correct conduct (*ādāb*) of one who loves this noble Prophet to honor the night of his birth and the day on which God made manifest the final successor (*al-ʿāqib*) of His prophets. . . . Everyone who feels longing and love (*shā'iq wa-muḥibb*) [for the Prophet] ought to manifest delight and gladness (*al-surūr wa'l-bishāra*) on that night and the following morning, and treat his children and wife to whatever he can afford (*wa-yumatti'a awlādahu wa-ahlahu bi-mā amkana lahu*) in order to receive its blessings. [He should] entertain them (*yudkhila al-surūr 'alayhim*) and teach them that he did so simply out of love for that night, delight in it, and concern for its merit. [He should] explain to them that it is the noblest of nights in the eyes of God, because on it the Messenger of God was born, and mention to them the description of the Messenger of God, his beauty and comeliness, his perfection, virtues and moral qualities, his speech and eloquence, his generosity and magnanimity, his character and clemency, his forgiveness and tolerance, his miracles and signs, everything that endears him to their hearts and exalts him. [He should also] teach them poems praising and extolling him. I and every [other] person who loves [the Prophet] consider this to be judicious and well-considered (*min ḥusn al-ra'y wa'l-naẓar*), because teaching something [to a person] in his youth is like carving in stone – especially since youths are enamored of wonders, and [the Prophet's] miracles are among the most wondrous things.

The love of the Prophet is thus inculcated both through discursive means (description, narrative, and verse) and through more concrete delights. al-Raṣṣāʿ's recommendation that one should provide treats for one's family suggests that festive food or gifts would also contribute to the emotional impact of the *mawlid*. Such positive reinforcement is not limited to the domestic sphere. On that day schoolchildren should also be decked out in their finest, gifts should be presented to their teachers, and their schoolrooms should be decorated. The "common people" should share in the benefits of the *mawlid*, being instructed in the miracles of the Prophet's birth and receiving clothing and charity.[65]

al-Raṣṣāʿ also considers the perusal of narratives about the Prophet's birth to be part of the continuing spiritual self-cultivation of the mature Muslim. Studying stories about the Prophet's birth reinforces the affective foundation of an adult's religious practice, evoking feelings of happiness, love, and assurance. al-Raṣṣāʿ recommends that the believer "should frequently study (*muṭāla'a*) [the story of] his birth and take pains to memorize its date and to learn [the Prophet's] noble ancestry" and the ways in which God preserved him in his childhood. He should also "ponder the signs, wonders, prodigies and marvels that were manifested at his birth, so that his heart is gladdened (*yansharih ṣadruhu*), his love is increased even more, his faith is strengthened, and he follows [the Prophet's] *sunna* and path."[66]

Unlike joy, love was an emotion that was extensively theorized by Islamic scholars. Perhaps the most influential and widely cited discussion of the obligation to love the Prophet was produced in the sixth century AH by the North African scholar al-Qāḍī 'Iyāḍ, who is credited with one of the earliest *mawlid* texts. After discussing the obligation to love the Prophet and various manifestations of that love, al-Qāḍī 'Iyāḍ attempts to define the nature of love itself. First, he states that love is "the inclination (*mayl*) to that which agrees with a person (*mā yuwāfiqu al-insān*)," either because it is aesthetically or sensually pleasing or because it has abstract good qualities that can be perceived by the mind (as one loves religious scholars or righteous persons). Love also arises from the experience of benefit, because "souls are innately inclined to love those who do good to them" (*jubbilat al-nufūs 'alā ḥubb man aḥsana ilayhim*).[67] All of these different modes of love, al-Qāḍī 'Iyāḍ explains, are directly applicable to the case of the Prophet; he manifests beauty of form, perfection of moral qualities, and the utmost degree of kindness and beneficence. After expanding on the unique nature and scope of the Prophet's favors to the believers, which include saving them from hellfire and helping them to achieve eternal bliss, 'Iyāḍ concludes,

> If a person loves someone who does him a good turn one or two times in his earthly life, or who saves him from a pitfall or harm the suffering resulting from which would be small and fleeting – then someone who bestows on him a bliss that is everlasting and protects him from the undying torment of hell is more worthy of love.[68]

While *mawlid* texts are saturated with references to the love of the Prophet and (as we have seen) juristic justifications of *mawlid* celebrations often revolve around the issue of correct emotion, they very rarely present any explicit discussion of the nature of love or the factors from which it arises. Nevertheless, the content of typical *mawlid* texts displays a remarkable correspondence with the schema presented by al-Qāḍī 'Iyāḍ. The depiction of the Prophet as a divine boon whose presence showers blessings upon all in his presence – and whose loving intercession will bring salvation to sinners on the Day of Judgment – is the central element of most *mawlid* texts. The description of the Prophet's physical beauty and the enumeration of his moral virtues (with particular emphasis on his kindness and benevolence), while not mandatory elements of such texts, are widespread and integral to the genre. This is not to suggest that the *mawlid* genre was shaped specifically in view of the work of al-Qāḍī 'Iyāḍ. However, it does suggest a certain underlying continuity and consistency in ideas about devotion to the Prophet.

One of the most notable elements in al-Qāḍī 'Iyāḍ's discussion is his emphasis on the idea that love arises from the conferral of benefits. His passage on the love of the Prophet is saturated with the vocabulary of favor, gift, and obligation: *iḥsān, in'ām, ifḍāl, ijmāl, manfa'a, fā'ida, manaḥa*. The maxim that al-Qāḍī 'Iyāḍ cites in support of the idea that love naturally arises from benefits received, "souls (or hearts) are innately inclined to love those who do good to them" (*jubbilat al-nufūs/al-qulūb 'alā ḥubb man aḥsana ilayhim*), is actually a poorly attested *ḥadīth* which appears in a scattering of non-canonical collections.[69] A similar line of reasoning is presented by Ibn Ḥajar al-'Asqalānī. He begins by arguing that a person inherently loves himself, in the sense that he desires to subsist free from harm. "As for [persons or things] other than himself, if it applies to them it is only by reason of the acquisition of some benefit (*naf'*), in any of its different forms." He concludes that

> If he ponders the benefit which has accrued to him from the Prophet, who brought him forth from the darkness of unbelief to the light of faith either directly or by intermediation, he will realize that [the Prophet] is the cause of his own soul's eternal subsistence in unending bliss, and he will realize that the benefit he receives from this is greater than all the various kinds of [other] benefits, and that for that reason [the Prophet] deserves a share of his love larger than anyone else's, because the benefit that arouses love comes from him more than from anyone else. However, people vary in this respect according to [the degree of their] consciousness of that and their obliviousness to it; there is no doubt that the Companions' share of this element is most perfect, because this is the fruit of knowledge and they know most about it.[70]

The idea that the enumeration of the Prophet's benefactions will give rise to feelings of love is central, explicitly or implicitly, to many *mawlid* texts. Counseling his readers to devote themselves on the *mawlid* to poetry in praise of the Prophet, al-Raṣṣā' writes:

> On this noble day, remember all that characterized our Prophet and all the ways in which God honored him; [remember] everything that will endear him to our hearts and all the ways in which he benefited us (*mā kāna yuḥsinu bihi ilaynā*) so that our faith and love will increase. Hearts are naturally disposed to love those that benefit them (*inna al-qulūb majbūla 'alā ḥubb man aḥsana ilayhā*), and the Prophet benefited all created beings so that they were gladdened and hoped that their Lord would forgive their sins.[71]

One of the few *mawlid* texts explicitly to address the issue of the nature and origins of love is an anonymous manuscript preserved in Cairo. First of all, the author assumes that his composition's prospective listeners are already enamored of the Prophet. Those who are enamored of a thing constantly mention and remember it, and the reports about the Prophet recited in the *mawlid* will be a source of pleasure to his devotees.

> In addition, mentioning that and listening to it give rise to knowledge of [the Prophet's] beauty and beneficence (*ma'rifat ḥusnihi wa-iḥsānihi*). This is

a means of increasing [the listeners'] love for him and the perfection of their longing for him. The causes of love, although they are many, revolve around two things, beauty and beneficence. Souls are innately inclined to (*majbūla 'alā*) love of comeliness and beauty and the love of those who do them good in any way; God has combined these two things in our Prophet.

Following his division of the root causes of love into beauty and beneficence, the author first discusses the loveliness of the Prophet's external appearance and then turns to a description of the manifold benefits he has conferred on the believers, particularly his role in preserving them from hellfire.[72]

The *mawlid* genre's emphasis on the benefits conferred by or through the Prophet as the basis of love for him is a rather distinctive one within the classical Islamic literature on love. On the one hand, the maxim that "hearts are innately inclined to love those that benefit them" is widely cited by Islamic authorities of varying inclinations. Its underlying implications were widely accepted; as Joseph Bell has observed, "the disposition to love one's benefactor was generally considered by Muslim authors to be innate."[73] Commenting on a *ḥadīth* in which the Prophet states that "a person (*'abd*) does not [truly] believe until I am dearer (*aḥabb*) to him than his family/wife (*ahl*), his wealth, and all other people (*al-nās ajma'īn*)," al-Nawawī cites the opinion that "By this he did not mean innate love (*ḥubb al-ṭab'*); rather, he meant voluntary love (*ḥubb al-ikhtiyār*), because a person's self-love is innate, and there is no way to overthrow it."[74] On the other hand, however, the transactional and self-interested nature of the love implied by the maxim is sometimes judged unsatisfactory. al-Sakhāwī, who critiques a version of the saying in his *al-Maqāṣid al-ḥasana fī bayān kathīr min al-aḥādīth al-mushtahira 'alā 'l-alsina*, goes so far as to suggest that the questionable *ḥadīth* was circulated by an authority in connection with false praise of a corrupt judge.[75] The saying's dissemination was thus linked, unflatteringly, with the self-interested quality of its content.

Despite their acceptance that self-love was ineradicably rooted in human nature, some authors held that the self-interested love arising from favors received was the lowest form of the emotion. Ṣūfīs were particularly dismissive of the love arising from self-interest. However, unlike mystical authors such as al-Ghazālī, who analyzed various modes of love in terms of a hierarchy of increasingly ethereal values,[76] most *mawlid* authors seem to have been content with less exacting standards of emotional achievement. The implicit position of most *mawlid* texts is that love based on self-interest is a fully valid form of religious expression. It is desirable and meritorious to love the Prophet because of his manifest benefactions to humankind, and more particularly for his service in preserving one personally from hell. Unlike al-Ghazālī, most *mawlid* authors do not seem to privilege disinterested forms of love based on impalpable moral attributes. Instead, they represent the Prophet as a fully available patron and benefactor whose physical beauty is as concrete as his anticipated acts of intercession. By positing rarified forms of love that transcend innate human self-interest, al-Ghazālī adheres to the values of classical ṣūfism. *Mawlid* texts, in contrast, adopt a devotionalist stance in which the Prophet can rightly be loved as a benefactor.

Scholars were sufficiently aware of the role of *mawlid* texts in evoking religious sentiment that they occasionally expressed concern about the correct definition and channeling of such emotions. According to one report, a questioner asked Ibn Ḥajar al-ʿAsqalānī about "what some preachers (*wuʿʿāẓ*) do in *mawlid*s in their crowded gatherings, which include the elite, commoners, men, and women." Their performances, the enquirer stated, include "mentioning the Prophet in a way that detracts from perfect reverence for him, to the point that those who hear it display sorrow and tenderness, and [the Prophet] enters the realm of those who are pitied rather than held in awe." Examples of this include their statement that wet-nurses refused to foster the Prophet because he had no money, except for Ḥalīma, who wanted to nurse him out of compassion. Similarly, preachers give touching descriptions of the young Prophet's activities as a shepherd, reciting tender verses about his labors. All of this, the questioner states, impairs the awe in which the Prophet is properly held. Ibn Ḥajar replies that it is incumbent on those who recount narratives about the Prophet to omit anything that their listeners might imagine to be deficiencies; this is not a shortcoming, but a duty.[77] This exchange reveals some discrepancy between popular expressions of religious sentiment, in which pathos seems to have played an effective role, and a more normative model in which the preservation of the Prophet's dignity and the reinforcement of his exalted status were paramount.

While *mawlid* texts evoked love by presenting reports about the Prophet's luminous beauty, boundless beneficence, and tender concern for his community, they also used less discursive means of inducing emotional responses. Commenting on Ibn Ḥajar al-Haytamī's recommendation that devotional verses be performed in the context of the *mawlid*, one author remarks that "This is because among the strongest causes of love for [the Prophet] is listening to beautiful voices making music by chanting the praises [of the Prophet] if they meet a receptive locus; they create thankfulness and love in the hearer."[78] In the *mawlid* tradition, love of the Prophet appears as a feedback loop in which concrete actions such as the recitation of poetry in his honor and the repetition of blessings and greetings upon him performatively express one's devotion to his person, while in turn themselves producing the appropriate emotional dispositions.

Ideally, devotional activities do not merely perform the love of the Prophet, but produce a feeling of emotional intimacy with him. An anonymous *mawlid* author remarks that "mentioning and hearing" reports about the Prophet's beauty and beneficence offers

> pleasure and enjoyment for people's spirits in hearing the mention of their beloved. It may [also] be a sort of closeness to him and meeting with him when they bring him vividly to mind and concentrate their thoughts on him. While the eyes are deprived of the sight of him, ears are not deprived of listening to the loveliest reports. Anyone who is enamored of something and

infatuated with it constantly mentions it with his tongue and makes it present in his mind until his thoughts picture it for him and his memory brings it close to him.[79]

The salvific value of personal relationships

The importance of emotion in the devotional model underlying the *mawlid* celebration lies largely in the formation of relationships of mutual attachment and exchange. Rejoicing in God's benefactions is a form of grateful acknowledgment that is expected to consolidate the worshiper's relationship with the divine patron and elicit further blessings. The cultivation of feelings of love for the Prophet, in addition to motivating religious learning and fulfilling an explicit divine command, deepens the individual bond with this tender teacher and intercessor. The importance of an intimate and loving connection to the Prophet for personal salvation is underlined by the content of *mawlid* narratives, which (particularly in their less scholarly form) emphasize the divine favors enjoyed by individuals whose only claim to religious distinction is their loving personal relationship with the infant Muḥammad. Such narratives pointedly ignore (or heatedly dispute) the fact that such individuals' religious status may be questionable according to other criteria.

In the more popular *mawlid* texts, the Prophet's mother Āmina is an important focus of attention. The elaborate narratives about the miraculous happenings surrounding her labor are recounted in her voice, and her initial apprehension and ultimate joy lend emotional depth to the story. Similar to both the Prophet and his wet-nurse, Ḥalīma, Āmina appears in such popular *mawlid* texts as a person transfigured by divine favor. Each of them is captured by the narrative in a moment of transition. Āmina's marriage, the Prophet's birth, and Ḥalīma's transformation from a starving tribeswoman to a radiant font of auspiciousness and abundance are all parallel instances of the eruption of divine favor and blessing into the world. In the structure of the *mawlid* narrative, the birth of the Prophet plays the role that might be played by conversion in a more conventional religious biography. The advent of the Prophet is the central event from which the two women's blessings derive. The Prophet's birth is, it seems, a moment of passage not for the Prophet himself (who is timelessly radiant and beneficent) but for the world that receives his light. In each case, however, the *mawlid* narrative in some sense represents a rite of passage; birth, marriage, and deliverance from want are all key moments of transition that dramatize God's beneficent power as represented by the person of the Prophet.

Āmina's prominence in popular *mawlid* narratives is somewhat problematic from the view of normative Islamic thought, because Āmina died long before the beginning of her son's prophetic mission. This fact is quite irrelevant to the worldview of the popular *mawlid*, in which Muḥammad is a prophet from pre-eternity and chronological development is pre-empted by visions and dreams. In the world of popular narrative, Āmina was not merely a believer "before the letter" but a person of considerable religious stature. For textual scholars, however, it was less easy to ignore the historical context of Āmina's life. From the point of view of a historical framework in which the Prophet's mission began at the age of forty, it was difficult to affirm that his mother, who died in his childhood, was fully a believer. The same problem applied to his father, who according to the most prevalent accounts died during Āmina's pregnancy. This difficulty was exacerbated by the existence of problematic *ḥadīth* texts. It was particularly acute in the case of the Prophet's father, whose fate was addressed by a *ḥadīth* canonized in the authoritative *Ṣaḥīḥ* of Muslim. The report recounts that a man asked the Prophet, "Where is my father?" The Prophet replied, "In hell." When the man turned to go, the Prophet called him back and said, "My father and yours are in hell."[80] The tradition appears in a chapter entitled "Clarification that whoever dies as an unbeliever is in hell; he cannot receive intercession, nor does he benefit from his family relationships."

The textual evidence in the case of the Prophet's mother was less damning, but still sufficiently disturbing. In a report transmitted by Abū Dāwūd, al-Nasā'ī and Ibn Māja, the Prophet visits Āmina's grave and weeps so inconsolably that his companions also dissolve in tears. Explaining his grief, the Prophet states that "I asked my Lord's permission to seek forgiveness for her (*astaghfira lahā*), and He did not give me permission; I asked His permission to visit her grave, and He gave me permission. So visit graves; they will remind you of death."[81] Other, less well-authenticated traditions stated more directly that his mother had met a dire fate.[82] More obliquely, the Qur'ānic verse 2:119 ("You will not be asked about the denizens of hell") was sometimes read in the active voice to mean "Do not ask about the denizens of hell." One tradition about the occasion of revelation for this verse held that it was revealed after the Prophet mused, "I wonder what has become of my parents?"[83]

This textual evidence, combined with the sheer chronological inference that his parents had died without embracing Islam, convinced some authorities that they came to a bad end. The creed *al-Fiqh al-akbar*, attributed to Abū Ḥanīfa, states outright that "the parents of the Messenger of God died as unbelievers (*mātā 'alā al-kufr*)."[84] This statement was sufficiently controversial that it was deleted from some manuscripts of the work, and its attribution to Abū Ḥanīfa was disputed. However, it was strongly supported by a few scholars. Mullā 'Alī al-Qāri' wrote a monograph in its defense.[85]

Nevertheless, the idea that the Prophet's parents had failed to achieve salvation was discomfiting to many scholars. Some, like the Ḥanafīs who criticized Mullā 'Alī al-Qāri' for enlarging on the subject, felt that (regardless of the truth of the matter) it was potentially insulting to the Prophet and thus better left in obscurity.[86] Others enthusiastically advocated the opposing position that the Prophet's parents were indeed among the saved. Perhaps the most prominent proponent of this stronger position was al-Suyūṭī, who composed three essays in its support (and three more on closely related topics)[87]; Mullā 'Alī's work was composed specifically in refutation of al-Suyūṭī.[88] In addition to a concern for the dignity and status of the Prophet, the affirmation that his parents had achieved salvation was based on fundamental theological considerations. The Qur'ān states that God punishes no one who has not first been warned by a prophet (verse 17:15).

The Prophet's parents lived in a period of ignorance between the disappearance of one prophetic mission and the advent of the next. They were thus among the "people of the interim" (*ahl al-fatra*), and could not be subject to divine punishment.[89] This was distinctively the theological position of the Ash'arīs (and of the Shāfi'īs who largely followed their teachings), who denied the possibility (affirmed by the Mu'tazilīs) that the obligation to worship God could be known intellectually, independently of divine revelation.[90]

As illustrated by the example of Mullā 'Alī al-Qāri', a *mawlid* author who denied the salvation of the Prophet's parents, there was no perfect correspondence between authorship or advocacy of *mawlid*s and affirmation of the faith status of the Prophet's parents. However, 'Alī al-Qāri' is rare in this respect among *mawlid* authors (indeed, in his outspoken discussion of an embarrassing subject, he was rare among Islamic scholars in general). Overall, there is a strong positive correlation between *mawlid* authorship and enthusiastic support of the position that the Prophet's parents were saved. al-Suyūṭī, author of the most extensive defenses of both the Prophet's parents and the celebration of the *mawlid*, is the most obvious example. Separate works on the subject of the Prophet's parents were also composed by the *mawlid* authors 'Afīf al-Dīn al-Shīrāzī (d. 855 AH/1451–2 CE), Muḥammad al-Sakhāwī, and Ibn Ṭūlūn al-Ṣāliḥī (d. 953 AH/1546–7 CE).[91]

More pervasively, however, the salvation of the Prophet's parents became a recurring theme within the *mawlid* genre itself.[92] In many cases, *mawlid*s supported the most extreme (and perhaps fanciful) solution to the chronological problem of 'Abd Allāh and Āmina's early deaths. Basing themselves on *ḥadīth* texts of questionable provenance, they affirmed that the Prophet had brought his deceased parents back to life just long enough for them to formally embrace Islam. This story was reported by a number of sources, although none of them at the highest level of the canon.[93] Ibn Taymīya claimed that *ḥadīth* scholars were in agreement that it was "an invented lie."[94] Despite its somewhat dubious status, however, it was accepted by a number of authors. al-Qurṭubī argued in its favor that the revivification of the Prophet's parents was neither intellectually nor religiously (*shar'an*) impossible, particularly in view of the fact that God continued to add to the Prophet's distinctions until the day of his death.[95]

As in so many cases, the predominant verdict of the *mawlid* tradition was enunciated by Ibn Nāṣir al-Dīn. In a set of widely quoted couplets, he affirmed the incident of the parents' revivification, forthrightly concluding that "the Eternal One is capable of it, even if the *ḥadīth* is weak."[96] These verses were approvingly cited by both al-Suyūṭī and al-Sakhāwī.[97] Ibn Ḥajar al-Haytamī includes a lengthy discussion of the theological issues in his *mawlid* text, and also embraces the idea of the parents' revivification.[98] The verse rendition of the beloved *mawlid* of Ja'far al-Barzanjī (d. 1187 AH/1764 CE) incorporated Ibn Nāṣir al-Dīn's wording while enlarging on his point.[99]

Like Āmina, the other main female character in traditional *mawlid* narratives was similarly not known to have been a Muslim in the historical sense. Ḥalīma's case was less acute because her death date was unknown, and the possibility of her having converted during her natural lifespan thus remained open. A *ḥadīth* recounts the Prophet's gracious reception of his wet-nurse during his adulthood, although it is not completely clear that Ḥalīma is the woman in question.[100] Ibn Kathīr argued that she had probably not survived to see Muḥammad's prophetic mission, although other scholars disputed this inference.[101] A certain degree of perplexity over Ḥalīma's status is suggested by the case of the *muḥaddith* Mughulṭāy ibn Qilīj, who recounts that in 838 AH/1434 CE he saw Jesus in a dream and questioned him about her fate; Jesus assured him of her salvation.[102] Despite Ḥalīma's disputed faith status, however, her survival until the rise of Islam and acceptance of the faith do not become explicit subjects of discussion within the *mawlid* genre. Just as many *mawlid* texts assumed rather than argued for Āmina's salvation, they left Ḥalīma's religious identity implicit. Much more important than any overt theological judgment was the intrinsic logic of the *mawlid* narrative, in which Ḥalīma was inundated by blessings as a result of her contact with the infant Prophet. Indeed, the *mawlid* narrative has its own implied theology, in which proximity to the Prophet and loving devotion to him are the sources of salvation. This is not necessarily the logic of other forms of *sīra* narrative, in which (at least for the earlier part of the Prophet's life) there is a notable lack of correspondence between personal intimacy with the young Muḥammad and formal embrace of Islam. Like his parents and (perhaps) his wet-nurse, his loving guardian Abū Ṭālib enjoyed a tender and nurturing relationship with the child without ever becoming a Muslim. Although not relevant within the *mawlid* genre itself, the case of Abū Ṭālib also posed a conundrum from the point of view of a devotional understanding of Islam.[103] Within the *mawlid* genre, however, personal contact with the Prophet is a guarantor of salvation. Within this framework, it is necessary to affirm the blessedness of the Prophet's closest relatives and associates. As the modern devotee Yūsuf al-Nabhānī (d. 1350 AH/1932 CE) puts it in one of his poems, after affirming the revivification and faith of the Prophet's parents, "How is it possible to hope for salvation for [ordinary] people / From someone who did not bring salvation to his [own] parents?"[104]

Standing as an expression of emotion

Mawlid celebrations involved not only the evocation of feelings of love and gratitude for the Prophet and their expression in generally celebratory activities, but the conventionalized expression of emotion in certain specific ritual forms. The most important of these is standing (*qiyām*) at the culminating moment of the *mawlid* recitation, the birth of Muḥammad. The incident generally recognized as the first instance of *qiyām* in honor of the Prophet was not associated specifically with the *mawlid* celebration, but occurred in the same circles. It was performed by the illustrious Egyptian scholar Taqī al-Dīn al-Subkī (d. 756 AH/1355 CE) and is recounted in his biography by his son Tāj al-Dīn (d. 769 AH/1368 CE). Tāj al-Dīn relates,

> Once [Taqī al-Dīn] attended a full recitation [of the Qur'ān: *khatma*] in the Umayyad Mosque, and the judges and the notables of the town attended in

> his presence as he sat in the prayer-niche of the Companions. The chanter chanted al-Ṣarṣarī's ode beginning, "Writing in gold is but little for the praise of al-Muṣṭafā." When he reached [the hemistich] "and for noble men to stand up when it is heard" (*wa-an yanhaḍa 'l-ashrāfu 'inda samā'ihi*), a[n ecstatic] state came upon the master teacher, and he instantaneously got up and stood (*ḥaṣalat li'l-shaykh al-imām ḥāla wa-qāma wāqifan li'l-ḥāl*). All the people felt a need to stand up (*fa'ḥtāja al-nās kulluhum an yaqūmū*), and every one of them stood up. A delightful interlude ensued (*wa-ḥaṣalat sā'a ṭayyiba*).[105]

Tāj al-Dīn does not provide a date for this event; regardless of its precise date, however, it occurred in the place and era that produced the first flowering of the *mawlid* genre among Sunnī scholars: Damascus in the eighth-century AH.

It is difficult to determine when the *qiyām* became a standard component of *mawlid* ceremonies. Even *mawlid* texts with clear performative elements ordinarily lack specific directions for actions such as standing. It is clear that the practice of standing in honor of the Prophet's birth had become well entrenched as a popular custom by the first-half of the tenth-century AH, although it remained in dispute among scholars. As demonstrated by a fragmentary manuscript preserved in Berlin, by the time of Ibrāhīm ibn Muḥammad ibn Ibrāhīm al-Ḥalabī (d. 956 AH/1549 CE) the *qiyām* was sufficiently well established to place opponents on the defensive; it was even widely held to be a religious duty. In an essay entitled *al-Qawl al-tamām [fī al-qiyām] 'inda dhikr wilādatihi 'alayhi al-salām*, al-Ḥalabī writes: "Many people of our time believe that it is obligatory to stand up at the mention of the birth of the Prophet and his emerging into this world, to the point that a learned person (*ba'ḍ al-fuḍalā'*) has taken offense at this poor one's omitting to do so and calumniated me in certain ways (*wa shanna'a 'alayya bi-mā shanna'a*)."[106] It has even been claimed that the Ottoman *muftī* Abū al-Su'ūd (d. 982 AH/1574 CE) issued a *fatwā* placing persons who failed to perform the *qiyām* under suspicion of being unbelievers, because their inaction suggested a lack of respect for the Prophet.[107]

The widespread practice of the *qiyām* is corroborated by al-Ḥalabī's younger contemporary, the Egyptian *muḥaddith* and ṣūfī Najm al-Dīn al-Ghayṭī (d. 984 AH/1576 CE).[108] al-Ghayṭī represents it both as a custom associated with the practice of professional chanters and as a legitimate practice based on the authoritative precedent of an eminent scholar. He remarks in his *mawlid* text,

> Note: It is customary (*jarat al-'āda*) that when the preachers and praise-singers (*al-wu''āẓ wa'l-muddāḥ*) recite [the Prophet's] *mawlid* and mention his mother's giving birth to him, most people stand up at that point to express reverence for him (*ta'ẓīman lahu*). [This is] an innovation which has no [textual] basis, but there is no harm in it (*lā ba's bihi*) because of the reverence [which it expresses]. Rather, it is a good action (*fi'l ḥasan*) for anyone dominated by love and awe (*al-ḥubb wa'l-ijlāl*) for that gracious Prophet, upon him the best blessings and the noblest greetings.[109]

al-Ghayṭī then approvingly quotes the verses of al-Ṣarṣarī in full, and cites the example of Taqī al-Dīn al-Subkī.

If al-Ḥalabī's refusal to perform the *qiyām* was sufficiently distinctive to attract disapproving attention, however, he was not alone in his time in disputing its legitimacy. The practice was also rejected by his younger contemporary Ibn Ḥajar al-Haytamī. Although his work devoted to this subject, *Taḥrīr al-kalām fī 'l-qiyām 'an dhikr mawlid sayyid al-anām*,[110] does not seem to have been preserved, he alludes to the issue in his *Fatāwā ḥadīthīya*. With respect to "the standing that is performed by many people at the mention of [the Prophet's] birthday and his mother's giving birth to him," he states that "it is ... an innovation about which no [text] has been transmitted." While the practice is a *bid'a*, he concedes that its motivation is sound; "people do that merely in reverence for [the Prophet]. Thus, ordinary people are justified in doing so, unlike the elite; God knows best what is right."[111] Here, as in the case of the *mawlid* celebration itself, Ibn Ḥajar takes a middle path. He is clearly aware of the wide acceptance of the practice, and is loath to denounce it unconditionally. He also acknowledges the legitimacy of the sentiment from which the *qiyām* arises, the desire to honor the Prophet. However, his restrictive understanding of the *sunna* demands that he ultimately deny the legal foundation of the practice. While willing to allow the masses to continue in their well-intentioned ways, he hopes that scholars will set a better example of strict adherence to the *sunna*.

Rationales for the legitimacy of the *qiyām* generally revolve around two general themes, reverence and joy. Thus, like the *mawlid* itself, the *qiyām* is generally justified in terms of appropriate emotions or sentiments. Because of the simplicity of the *qiyām*, however, its interpretation is particularly conducive to micro-analysis of the relationship between emotion and action. Interpretations range from those in which the *qiyām* is the spontaneous result of emotional effervescence expressible only by springing to one's feet, to those in which it is a socially conventional signifier of deference.

The terminology chosen by Tāj al-Dīn Subkī in recounting his father's inaugural *qiyām* is distinctively ṣūfī in flavor; his father's "*ḥāla*" is a spontaneous state of spiritual exaltation familiar from many mystical works. However, it is also significant that the event did not occur in a strictly ṣūfī setting; it happened not in the context of a *dhikr* ceremony or a *ṭarīqa*-oriented gathering, but in an assemblage of "judges and notables" convened to hear the Qur'ān. This suggests how ṣūfī spirituality pervaded elite religiosity, and indicates the spread of mystical attitudes into broader currents of Islamic devotionalism. Although this incident would later become the classic model illustrating the acceptability of the *qiyām*, in this passage Tāj al-Dīn does not seem to be concerned with defensively justifying his father's action. Nevertheless, his description suggests a justification for the *qiyām*. The defining characteristic of the act of standing is its spontaneity; it is the unpremeditated expression of an irresistible emotional impulse. Just as Taqī al-Dīn acts in the throes of a wave of devotion, the rest of the company "feels the need" to stand.

Later discussions, particularly those with a ṣūfī flavor, do not lack allusions to the outpouring of emotion that gives rise to sincere *qiyām*. In a *mawlid* text entitled *al-Manhal al-awfā fī mīlād al-muṣṭafā*, Muḥammad Ṣāliḥ al-Dasūqī attributes the custom of standing at the mention of the Prophet's birth to "many people who have been enthralled by love (*man tayyamahu al-ḥubb*) and lost their wits out of passion for the Glory of Creation [i.e., the Prophet]."[112] However, the legitimacy and popularity of the practice were not ultimately dependent on a concept of spiritual "states" rooted in ṣūfī theory. The act of standing at the mention of the Prophet's birth is frequently seen as a conventional expression of respect or reverence (*ta'ẓīm*) whose authenticity does not in any way depend on a wave of spontaneous sentiment. Juristic authors discuss the permissibility of standing as a form of social etiquette. This raises important legal issues, as it is an unresolved question whether it is licit to stand in honor either of the Prophet or of distinguished living persons. Several widely circulated *ḥadīth* texts suggest that the Prophet forbade his Companions to stand at his approach, although others suggest that he encouraged the practice or engaged in it himself.[113]

The permissibility of standing in honor of another person was at issue not only in the context of the *mawlid* ritual, but in that of normative Islamic social behavior in general. Standing in honor of dignitaries seems to have remained a controversial practice in the century before al-Subkī's famous inaugural *qiyām* occurred, and one whose legitimacy was actively debated by scholars. A short monograph in defense of the practice was composed by the Damascene Shāfi'ī Abū Zakarīyā al-Nawawī (d. 676 AH/1277 CE).[114] The Cairene Mālikī Aḥmad al-Qarāfī (d. 684 AH/1285 CE) describes how he once addressed a query on this subject to the Damascene Shāfi'ī al-'Izz ibn 'Abd al-Salām al-Sulamī (d. 660 AH/1262 CE). al-Qarāfī describes al-Sulamī as a staunch defender of the *sunna* who had no fear of those in power (and would thus be unlikely to soften his opinion on a legal question about the display of social deference). In his enquiry, al-Qarāfī speaks of standing (*al-qiyām*) as something "newly introduced by the people of our time" and asks whether it is permissible. In reply, al-Sulamī issues a *fatwā* that opens by citing a *ḥadīth* in which the Prophet admonishes, "Do not hate each other, envy each other, treat each other with hostility, or sever relations with each other; be servants of God as brothers." At this time, he reasons, omitting to stand in someone's honor would lead to hostility and the severing of relations; thus (far from being impermissible) it would even be possible to rule that it was obligatory.

al-Qarāfī elaborates on this point to construct a general account of the relationship between the *sharī'a* and the evolving conventions of interaction in a given society. He argues that there are two forms of social deference (*ikrām al-nās*) permitted by the *sharī'a*. One consists of those courtesies explicitly mandated by the divine law, such as shaking hands upon meeting and asking permission to enter someone's dwelling. The second category comprises those social pleasantries that were neither mandated by the law nor practiced by the earliest generations of Muslims, but which are required by social exigencies that did not exist in their time. Such courtesies are, according to al-Qarāfī, also required by the *sharī'a*; had circumstances so dictated, the earliest Muslims would have practiced them as well. Standing in honor of dignitaries falls into this category, as does the use of honorific titles.[115]

Unsurprisingly, Ibn Taymīya (d. 728 AH/1328 CE) adopted a contrasting position. His questioner notes that people are accustomed (*ya'tāduhu al-nās*) to stand at the arrival of a distinguished person. Apparently aware of the lack of positive precedents in the *sunna*, he wonders whether it is nevertheless permissible to stand if refraining to do so is likely to cause embarrassment and hurt feelings, which "may lead to dislike, antagonism, and enmity." Ibn Taymīya replies that it was not the custom (*'āda*) of the Companions to stand in honor of the Prophet, because they knew that he disliked it; however, they did on occasion stand to receive persons returning after an absence. It is incumbent on people, Ibn Taymīya continues, to make adherence to the example of the early Muslims into their custom. Thus, authority figures ought to instruct their associates not to stand in their honor. However, if people are accustomed to standing and unaware of the "custom" established by the *sunna*, it may be that failing to stand in someone's honor will be interpreted as an insult. In this case it is better to stand, because it is conducive to good relations and prevents the creation of enmities. In such cases, adhering to the prevalent social practice is preferable because it avoids the greater of two harms (that is, the creation of social antipathies is more harmful than a minor infraction of the *sunna*).[116]

It is unclear precisely when the debate over evolving standards of social comportment was applied to the *qiyām* performed in the context of the *mawlid*. We do not have medieval renditions of this argument from the point of view of the practice's supporters, but its outline is clear from the account of the *qiyām* opponent Ibrāhīm al-Ḥalabī. As for those who hold the *qiyām* to be obligatory, he states,

> The utmost extent of their proof for that is that that standing is [an expression of] reverence (*ta'ẓīm*) of the Prophet, and everything that [expresses] reverence for him is obligatory, so it is obligatory to perform this standing. I say, as for the major premise (*al-kubrā*), it is granted by every Muslim (*fa-musallam 'inda kull muslim*). As for the minor premise, there is no legal proof for it. How could there be, when [the Prophet] forbade standing at his own physical approach and at the sight of him?[117]

Al-Ḥalabī proceeds to argue this point at some length, thoroughly analyzing the most important *ḥadīth* in which the Prophet forbids standing.[118]

On a more fundamental level, al-Ḥalabī denies the cogency of the analogy itself, on the grounds that the meaning of such a gesture is based on nothing more than social convention. Such conventions, however, can never take precedence over the model behavior of the Prophet himself.

> There remains no proof for this standing being a form of reverence except what has established itself in their minds (*mā istaqarra fī nufūsihim*) based on what they have become accustomed to and what they have passed on to each other, as the Prophet indicated. This is similar to the additional circlings and movements in the *dhikr* to which the ṣūfīs have accustomed themselves, and which they have come to consider a part of worship (*fa''taqadūhu 'ibāda*)

> based on habit and inheritance (*al-'āda wa'l-tawāruth*). If they say, "We express reverence for [the Prophet] based on the forms of reverence that are customary among us," we say, "In addition to the fact that this involves giving precedence to your custom over [the Prophet's] statement and over his custom, you have no grounds to object against us, because refraining [from standing] is our custom, in addition to its being in conformity with [the Prophet's] custom, in adherence to his prohibition, and in obedience to him – which is [true] veneration of him."

As for standing at the mere mention of the Prophet's arrival, it has no basis at all. No one ever stood up at the recitation of the Qur'ānic verse "There has come to you a messenger from among you" (9:128).

> If they say, "Then why is it that you stand up for someone who comes to you whom you wish to honor?" I say, "To avoid the bad consequences that might result from failing to stand, based on his custom; [the Prophet] commanded us to behave with mutual kindness and to act in ways that foster cordiality and affection, and forbade us to engage in hatred and grudges and the like."[119]

Supporters of the *qiyām* argue on the basis of a fundamental equation between ritual action and social interaction. Despite the fact that the Prophet is deceased, one's relationship with him is cultivated and expressed through the same social conventions shaping one's interactions with living individuals. The only distinction between the two fields of action is that the Prophet's status is immeasurably higher than that of other human beings. If one stands to honor one's fellow men, then *a fortiori* one must stand to honor him. If one stands in honor of the physical approach of a distinguished man, then one might well stand at the mere mention of the Prophet. al-Ḥalabī, in contrast, envisions two sharply distinguished fields of action. In interaction with the Prophet, the varying customs and conventions of human beings are replaced with the single binding "custom" of the Prophet's *sunna*. All of the possible modes of expressing subordination and respect are supplanted by one form of deference, that of obedience to the Prophet's command. Interactions among living persons, in contrast, are governed by the inherited but mutable conventions of social life. If standing at a visitor's approach is understood to express respect, it must be done in order to avoid ill-feeling.

Occasional references make it clear that the *qiyām* continued to be widely performed in subsequent centuries. 'Alī ibn Ibrāhīm ibn Aḥmad al-Ḥalabī, a Shāfi'ī who (despite his *nisba*) was born in Egypt and died in Cairo in 1044 AH/1635 CE, states in his biography of the Prophet that "it is customary among many people (*jarat 'ādat kathīr min al-nās*), when they hear mention of [the Prophet's] birth, to stand up in honor of him (*ta'ẓīman lahu*)." He describes this practice as "an innovation for which there is no [textual] basis," but affirms that it is a "good innovation" (*bid'a ḥasana*), citing the precedent of Taqī al-Dīn al-Subkī.[120] In the eighteenth century, al-Barzanjī refers to the *qiyām* as a commendable practice agreed upon by religious scholars, one justified by the intention to express reverence for the Prophet. "Leading scholars who have mastered textual transmission and analysis have deemed it commendable to stand at the mention of his noble birth," he declares in his prose *mawlid*; "So blessed is he who has the exaltation of [the Prophet] as his utmost desire and aim!"[121]

Premodern discussions of the legitimacy of the *qiyām* generally elide one issue which became central in modern polemics, that of the actual presence of the Prophet. Debates over the legitimacy of applying evolving standards of social propriety to one's relations with the Prophet appear to skirt a more basic question, whether such interactions are applicable to one who is both physically deceased and geographically remote. It is possible that this issue may have been raised in texts that have not survived, such as the missing portions of al-Ḥalabī's work or the lost essay on the subject by Ibn Ḥajar al-Haytamī. However, it may also be that medieval Muslims were generally accustomed to the idea that the Prophet was somehow available and conscious of their actions regardless of their location. In any case, post-medieval texts indicate that at least in some circles, the practice of the *qiyām* reflected a genuine belief in the Prophet's presence at the *mawlid* ceremony. In this view, particularly prevalent among ṣūfīs and those whom they influenced, the transhistorical reality of the Prophet was not withdrawn from creation by his earthly demise. A *fatwā* request directed to the Yemenī scholar Muḥammad ibn 'Alī al-Shawkānī (d. 1250 AH/1834 CE) vividly reflects this belief. His scandalized questioner describes how the guests at a *mawlid* in the home of a Ṣan'ānī merchant "stood as if they were awaiting the arrival of the Master of Humankind," the Prophet Muḥammad, singing "Welcome, O light of my eyes!" According to this informant, the ordinary people (*al-'awāmm*) looked eagerly to see the Prophet. al-Shawkānī, who is fully aware of the practice, confirms that at the moment of the *qiyām* "they do not doubt that the Messenger of God has come to them."[122]

The case described by al-Shawkānī's questioner is not unique. Some form of belief in the presence of the Prophet at the moment of the "standing" (*qiyām*) is suggested by many of the verses composed for performance at that point in the ceremony. The refrain of another such poem begins, "O Aḥmad, o Chosen One, welcome! Greetings!" (*Yā Aḥmad, yā mujtabā, ahlan wa-sahlan, marḥaban*).[123] The verse rendition of al-Barzanjī's *mawlid* mentions the Prophet's presence in a spirit of confident affirmation; *mawlid* participants stand in honor of the Prophet's self/essence (*dhāt*), he writes, "because he is present in any place where he is mentioned" (*huwa ḥāḍir bi-ayyi maqām fīhi yudhkar*).[124] The personal involvement of the Prophet in the origins and performance of a *mawlid* text is prominently discussed by the ṣūfī Muḥammad 'Uthmān al-Mīrghanī (d. 1268 AH/1852 CE), who recounts that the Prophet appeared to him in a dream, directing him to compose a *mawlid* and instructing him about its rhyme scheme. "He gave me the good tidings," recounts al-Mīrghanī, "that he would be present when it was recited . . . and that prayers would be answered when [his] birth was mentioned and when [the *mawlid*] was finished."[125]

In the late-nineteenth and early-twentieth century, when the *qiyām* became the object of much more aggressive critique, it elicited more sustained argumentation from prominent scholars. The historical context of the attacks will be discussed in Chapter 5; here, we will be concerned with the content of the arguments in favor of the *qiyām*. One such discussion was produced by the Egyptian Azharī scholar Muḥammad ibn Khalīl al-Hijrasī, a Shāfi'ī and ṣūfī who settled in the Ḥijāz and died in 1328 AH/1910 CE,[126] in response to enquiries from the Holy Cities.[127] While al-Hijrasī's questioners claim to be unaware of opposition to the celebration of the *mawlid* among mainstream scholars, they point out that even some orthodox scholars (*ba'ḍ 'ulamā' al-sunna*) disapprove of standing when the reciter of the *mawlid* reaches the statement "she gave birth to him." In fact, opponents of the *qiyām* allege that it is forbidden (*ḥarām*), arguing that the Prophet disapproved of people's standing in honor of him when he was alive. If it was not acceptable to stand in his living presence, how can one perform this objectionable action at the mere mention of his birth?[128]

al-Hijrasī argues that the Prophet's reluctance to have his Companions stand up in his honor is to be interpreted as an instance of his compassionate concern to spare them effort. It does not indicate that standing is in itself objectionable (*makrūh*) or forbidden. Were this the case, the Prophet would not have instructed them to stand in honor of his companion Sa'd, an incident recorded in the *ḥadīth*. Because the Prophet was aware of his place in the hearts of his Companions, who honored and exalted him perfectly, he had no need of a manifestation of honor and respect such as their standing at his approach. It was precisely because they did not have comparable regard for Sa'd that the Prophet sought evidence of their respect by instructing them to stand. "The matter of standing being an emblem of respect is an elementary matter which is agreed on by generality of people, both elite and common," argues al-Hijrasī. It is particularly appropriate in these times, when people have fallen far short of the standard established by the Companions of the Prophet.[129]

In part, al-Hijrasī here draws on a common element in apologetics for activities regarded as "good innovations." Much in the spirit of al-Qarāfī, he argues that the decline of religious sentiment in latter-day Muslims necessitates the practice of new forms of devotion. While the Companions had no need to cultivate or reinforce their love and reverence for the Prophet, such means are vital for the lukewarm Muslims of the present day. (Opponents of such activities invert this argument by arguing that no innovated practice can possibly express love or reverence for the Prophet, because it would be impossible to discover a practice of this nature that his pious Companions had neglected to perform.) In another respect, however, al-Hijrasī simply reflects the underlying assumption of Islamic devotionalism, that individual believers can cultivate a relationship with the Prophet through the same forms of social behavior practiced in their everyday lives. While al-Hijrasī refers to standing up as an "elementary" or "innate" (*badīhī*) mode of expressing respect, his evidence for this fact is based on social consensus; everyone agrees that it is true. "I implore you by God, you who object to this standing," al-Hijrasī exclaims later in his *fatwā*, "if you approached a gathering and most of those in it stood up to greet you while some refrained from standing, would you not have the feeling – nay, would not [even] others have the feeling – that those who did not stand up for you disdained you and did not show deference to you, in contrast to those who greeted you and stood up for you?"[130]

Another elaborate apologia for the *qiyām* was produced in the early-twentieth century by the Indian scholar ʻAyn al-Quḍāt al-Ḥaydarābādī (d. 1343 AH/1925 CE) in response to an incident when a religious functionary refused to stand at a *mawlid* where he was presiding.[131] According to ʻAyn al-Quḍāt, the meaning of the *qiyām* is determined not by social convention but by the subjective intentions of the person performing it. What is at stake is not merely the performance of a correct social relationship, but the external manifestation of an otherwise invisible emotion. ʻAyn al-Quḍāt justifies the *mawlid* celebration as a whole as an expression of reverence (*taʻẓīm*) for the Prophet. This reverence is divided into four categories, the first of which is verbal (*qawlī*) and the rest consisting of actions. "The true nature of the reverence (*taʻẓīm*) intended here is the expression of awe (*iẓhār al-ʻaẓama*)," he writes. "This is something that requires to be brought forth (*amr intizāʻī*); it does not exist externally without something to bring it forth, which is either speech or action." Either speech or action can be an expression of respect, "but speech is a[n expression of] reverence without the mediation of the intent and action is a[n expression of] reverence by mediation of intent." It is for this reason that the Prophet said that actions are according to their intentions ("*Innamā al-aʻmāl bi'l-nīyāt*").

There are three kinds of actions used to express reverence for the Prophet in the context of the *mawlid*: the *qiyām*, the distribution of sweets and food, and "licit worldly adornment" (*al-zīna al-dunyawīya al-sharʻīya*), such as fine clothes, pretty furnishings, perfumes, and lamps used to decorate the place where the *mawlid* is held. The *qiyām*, as in itself it is an act devoid of inherent reverence for the Prophet (*li-kawnihi fiʻlan ʻāriyan fī nafsihi ʻan al-taʻẓīm al-nabawī*), becomes such only if it is accompanied by the appropriate intent, just as the *qiyām* in the canonical prayers becomes a veneration of God only if accompanied by the appropriate intent. In addition to expressing reverence for the Prophet, the *qiyām* expresses joy and thanks to God; all of these aspects are compatible and, indeed, linked.[132]

Although al-Hijrasī's questioners at least imply their concern that standing in honor of the Prophet might be doubly inappropriate because he was not literally arriving in the *mawlid* gathering, similar to his premodern predecessors al-Hijrasī avoids addressing this issue. ʻAyn al-Quḍāt confronts the issue directly, if somewhat opaquely. It is commendable to stand up in veneration of the Prophet, he writes,

> not because [the Prophet] has arrived in the gathering and is literally (*bi'l-ḥuḍūr al-aṣlī*) present in it when [the reciter] says this, but because he has been arriving in the physical world from the world of light before this from the time of his noble birth and is present with the one who says [this] with a shadow presence (*ḥuḍūr ẓillī*) which is closer than his physical presence.[133]

In explaining the sense in which the Prophet is "arriving" ʻAyn al-Quḍāt, as is his wont, establishes a complex taxonomy involving several different variables. Having used a *ḥadīth* text to establish that the Prophet instructed a group of people to stand in honor of his Companion Sa'd, 'Ayn al-Quḍāt attempts to demonstrate that the Prophet is actually "arriving" in a sense more essential and profound than that of a simple physical arrival like Sa'd's. Characterizing the Prophet as the impetus for the creation of all beings, he describes how "by virtue of these attributes of his he became their master from the beginning of his formation, directing himself towards them from within himself and pouring forth blessings upon them." Thus, "his manifest presence among them through birth became a spiritual/abstract, essential, absolute, necessary arrival (*qudūman ma'nawīyan aṣlīyan muṭlaqan iḍṭirārīyan*)." This arrival far exceeds Sa'd's arrival, which was merely "external, subsidiary, relative, and voluntary."[134] Although 'Ayn al-Quḍāt's argumentation is typically turgid, it is clear that for him the physical, time- and place-bound arrival of Sa'd is merely an inferior counterpart of the timeless and placeless outpouring of essence that constitutes the eternal "arrival" of the Prophet.

Even if the Prophet is in some sense always "arriving," however, it is less than obvious to 'Ayn al-Quḍāt's imagined interlocutor that he is visibly present. Since perceptible presence is the second condition for the obligation to stand, 'Ayn al-Quḍāt must demonstrate that it is also met. In this passage, he seems to retreat somewhat from his stronger claims for the Prophet's transhistorical "arriving." Because certain actions are particularly desirable, he argues, God has waived or weakened some of the conditions of their performance. For instance, in order to facilitate and encourage the performance of prayers He has allowed *tayammum* in place of *wuḍū'*, and the approximation of the *qibla* when its exact direction is unknown. The invocation of blessings upon the Prophet is similarly desirable. Because of this, God has encouraged this practice by giving people wide latitude in its performance. Specifically, when invoking blessings on the Prophet it is permissible to address him in the second person, even though this would ordinarily be acceptable only if he were physically present. By analogy, the same latitude would be permissible in the case of the *qiyām*.

Furthermore, 'Ayn al-Quḍāt argues, there is a natural connection between the physical presence of the Prophet and the fictional assumption of his presence when invoking blessings upon him or standing in his honor. Because the Prophet's incomparable virtues are so well established in the hearts of the believers, he argues, the Prophet's "intellectual presence" (*ḥūḍūruhu al-'ilmī*) is very near to his visible presence (*ḥuḍūruhu al-baṣarī*).[135] When the narrative of the Prophet's light, his ancestry and his birth are recounted in the *mawlid* ceremony, "by means of these remembrances a detailed intellectual image of him is drawn powerfully in the mind. ... By means of [this image] the soul (*nafs*) is completely directed to him, to the point that in its extreme detail that image becomes a perfect mirror for [the Prophet] and reveals him completely." This reaches the point where "it is as if you saw him." When the mind is prepared by the mention of the things that are recited in the *mawlid*,

> the soul becomes affected by the image of these praiseworthy characteristics that are drawn in the mind and begins to anticipate and long for the mention of his radiant birth. Then, when the reciter says, "The Prophet was born," this

> strong intellectual presence becomes connected with the Noblest Prophet who is arriving in the physical world from the world of light.[136]

Standing is not merely a spontaneous response to one's subjective experience of the Prophet's imaginative presence, however. It is impossible to produce this affect among all participants in the *mawlid* simultaneously, and the decorum of the ceremony demands that the action of standing be synchronized. Therefore, the mention of the Prophet's birth is made the occasion for everyone to stand because it is the juncture at which most are likely to experience the Prophet's intellectual presence.

Even as opposition to the *qiyām* was spreading in the late-nineteenth and early-twentieth centuries, proponents continued to disseminate the practice, apparently quite aggressively. The Moroccan scholar al-Mahdī al-Wazzānī (d. 1342 AH/1923 CE) was asked for a juristic opinion by an enquirer who had experienced a disturbing incident. A group of jurists (*fuqahā'*) had engaged in a religious gathering where one of their numbers

> held a book in his hand which he was reciting (*yasruduhu*); when he reached [the Prophet's] birth and his mother's giving birth to him, he stood up and they stood up with him, except for one jurist among them. He did not stand up, and they objected to his behavior (*ankarū 'alayhi*).

The questioner asked whether the jurist's objection was well-founded. In reponse, al-Wazzānī first remarks that the *qiyām* is not a customary practice in the Maghrib, where *mawlid* celebrations traditionally involve the recitation of devotional poetry, the burning of colored candles, the donning of festive clothing, "and other things that indicate joy, as if it were a festival (*'īd*)." al-Wazzānī argues that it is not blameworthy to follow the customs of one's own locality. He complains that the practice of *qiyām* has recently been introduced by unnamed parties who wish to impose it on the people and who abuse anyone who refrains from performing it; "it is one of them who brought that book to those jurists and started to read it."[137]

al-Wazzānī retorts to the proponents of *qiyām* that "refraining from standing because of the fact that it is a reprehensible innovation (*bid'a makrūha*) is true reverence (*'ayn al-ta'ẓīm*)." He cites Ibn Ḥajar al-Haytamī's opinion about the illegitimacy of the *qiyām*, and dismisses the opinions of its supporters. Nevertheless, he is not willing to reject all instances of *qiyām*. While he does not regard al-Subkī's leaping to his feet upon hearing al-Ṣarṣarī's verses as a sound juristic precedent, he cites the example without disapproval. He follows it with a similar example, recounted by an author who visited the Prophet's grave in 1143 AH/1735 CE. As poetry was recited, the chanter came to the line "Standing on their feet in honor of a master / reverenced by angels, spirits and men." "The next thing we knew," the author recounts, "we, the people, and the vast crowd at the Prophet's magnificent mosque were all standing up and reciting the aforementioned verse; praise be to God, great elation (*uns 'aẓīm*) ensued." Finally, al-Wazzānī cites a ṣūfī authority who encouraged dancing and leaping out of joy in the Prophet's birthday. All of this, al-Wazzānī concludes, falls under the ṣūfī maxim that "an intoxicated person is not reproached while he is in a state of intoxication." al-Wazzānī's legal evaluation of the *qiyām* is ultimately qualified by his statement that it applies only to intentional standing (*fī fi'lihi ikhtiyāran*); "as for someone who is overcome by love and stands, is moved by emotion, dances, and is robbed of his senses, there is nothing to say to him (*lā kalām ma'ahu*)."[138]

In addition to expressing his concern for the integrity of local custom, al-Wazzānī strictly distinguishes the two elements that are ordinarily intertwined in the justification of *qiyām*. One, which he rejects, is a devotional element based on the construction of a right relationship with the Prophet through the performance of a conventional act of deference. The other, which he endorses (or at least declares himself incapable of condemning) is a mystical element based on the spontaneous expression of intense subjective states of emotional arousal. His emphasis on a specifically mystical construal of the *qiyām* reflects his North African environment, where ṣūfī practices predominated in the celebration of the *mawlid*. A similar emphasis on ecstatic joy is reflected in the comments of al-Wazzānī's Fāsī contemporary Muḥammad ibn Ja'far al-Kattānī (d. 1345 AH/ 1927 CE). Unlike al-Wazzānī, al-Kattānī is a proponent of the *qiyām* who is aware that the implication of the Prophet's literal presence exposes the practice to criticism. "In reality," he writes, "it is not in honor of (*li-*) Muḥammad's essence/self (*al-dhāt al-Muḥammadīya*), as some people imagine, so that they object at length and denounce its performance. Rather, it is standing up out of joy and pleasure (*faraḥ wa-surūr*), gladness and delight in his appearance in this world and the dawning of his light on everything in existence."[139] Having defined the *qiyām* as an expression of joy, al-Kattānī supports its legitimacy by citing a number of *ḥadīths* in which the Prophet encourages or condones various types of celebration or entertainment, including dancing, singing, and hopping.[140]

Conclusion

Outside of a ṣūfī context, *mawlid* authors tend to envision the emotional involvement elicited by the *mawlid* in terms of a relatively elementary level of religious engagement. It is significant that both al-'Azafī and al-Raṣṣā' discuss the celebration of the *mawlid* in connection with the religious formation of children (as well as, to a lesser extent, women). Emotions such as joy and love play a key role in motivating and reinforcing religious knowledge and behavior. Most *mawlid* texts (with the exception of some that bear a distinct ṣūfī flavor), however, do not appear to seek any profound or prolonged development in the emotional makeup of the participant. As is appropriate to a devotional form that is usually limited in size and intermittent in performance, it seeks the more modest goal of performing and rehearsing certain basic religious emotions that are considered desirable in themselves. These emotions are understood to be inherently salvific; as one version of *Mawlid al-'arūs* declares, "Glory be to God, who . . . gave those who rejoice in [the Prophet's] birth a veil and covering from the Fire."[141]

Particularly in the case of joy, the *mawlid* literature suggests that the emotion itself is coterminous with its expression. It is not simply that feasting causes one to feel joy, or that it expresses the joy that one feels (although both of these are also true); rather, feasting is defined as a form of rejoicing. Because the emotion of joy is understood in terms of concrete and conventional behavioral manifestations, in the view of *mawlid* proponents it can be used as the basis for substantive legal arguments about the legitimacy of specific actions. Where supporters and opponents of the *mawlid* celebration differ is not in their shared belief that emotions are subject to the strictures of religious law, but in their acceptance or rejection of the principle that a sanctioned emotion may form the legal basis for a novel behavioral form. *Mawlid* supporters tend to argue that there may be different behavioral manifestations of the same religiously valid sentiment. Detractors, in contrast, argue that only the specific behaviors modeled by the Prophet and the early Muslims are legitimate expressions of religiously required emotions. Despite his acknowledgment of the meritorious nature of love for the Prophet, for instance, Ibn Taymīya does not regard joyful gatherings on the occasion of his birth as a legitimate form of expression for this sentiment. The earliest Muslims (*al-salaf*) loved and revered the Prophet more than his contemporaries could possibly do, argues Ibn Taymīya, and yet they did not celebrate the *mawlid*. The most perfect expression of love and reverence for the Prophet (*kamāl maḥabbatihi wa-ta'ẓīmihi*) consists in following and propagating his *sunna*.[142]

Commenting on the commandments to "rejoice before the Lord" in the Pentateuch, Gary Anderson has remarked that "the association of joy with the activity of eating at seasonal festivals is so strong that the preferable translation in these settings may be 'to celebrate.'"[143] More generally, the biblical text has a "tendency to concretize the experience of joy into its performable aspect."[144] In addition to feasting, the activities identified with joy in the Pentateuch include sexual intercourse, singing songs of praise, and anointing with oil. The "behavioral expression" of joy, Anderson argues, is the inverse of the behavioral correlates of mourning. While joy is expressed through eating, sexual relations, praise of God, anointing with oil, and donning festal garments, mourning is expressed through the inverse behaviors of fasting, sexual continence, lamentation, putting dust on one's head, and donning sackcloth or torn clothes.[145] In some ways, the behavioral vocabulary of joy in the *mawlid* literature parallels that of the Pentateuch. Particularly notable is the integral role of feasting in the *mawlid* tradition; as in the context of a marriage celebration, it is largely the meal that constitutes the rejoicing. The important role of praise is also notable. As in the biblical case, the *mawlid* literature reflects a concrete and behavioral understanding of emotion, one that allows emotions to be incorporated into a framework of obligation.

The balanced opposition of the behavioral manifestations of joy and mourning suggested by Anderson for the Bible, however, has no direct parallel in the Islamic literature on celebrations (such as the *mawlid*) and occasions of mourning (such as 'Āshūrā'). A deep ambiguity is produced by the basic principles of Islamic theology, which no longer decisively oppose the joy of birth with the sorrow of death or the joy of feasting with the sorrow of fasting. Death, like birth, is appropriately met with praise of God; fasting, rather than a distasteful deprivation, can also be regarded as a joyful act of thanks.

It was a widespread idea among premodern legal scholars that emotions are acts which may be religiously meritorious or even legally obligatory. The most obvious example of this is the obligation to love the Prophet, which is supported by many *ḥadīth* texts. The recognition of an obligation to love led to a reflection on the nature of this emotion and the means by which it might be elicited. Premodern Muslim legal scholars did not regard emotions as purely personal, subjective, or spontaneous; rather, they believed that correct emotion could and should be cultivated as a matter of proper religious practice. While ṣūfīs are perhaps the Islamic group best known for their concern with the emotional life of the individual spiritual aspirant, theirs was not the theoretical framework most appropriate to the development of Islamic devotionalism. Unlike legal scholars and traditionists, ṣūfīs emphasized the obstinacy of the baser inclinations and the treacherous and complex nature of the self. The elusiveness of the proper emotional attitudes demanded an intensive and all-consuming scrutiny of one's own impulses, and the lengthy path to subjugation of the self was fraught with paradoxes and reversals. The devotional literature of the *mawlid*, on the other hand, posits that at least a minimal degree of correct emotion is natural and attainable by the ordinary believer. While few can achieve the heights of self-abnegating devotion to the Prophet attained by the generation of his Companions, the necessary quantum of emotion is within the reach of all believers. In the class formulations of Ibn al-Jazarī and Ibn Nāṣir al-Dīn as well as in widespread popular belief, the expression of joy and love becomes a key to salvation.

Rejoicing is an indispensable element in the grateful recognition of God's benefactions, and maintains the proper relationship between the individual and the Creator. Like the tender love of Āmina and Ḥalīma for the infant Prophet, the individual's devotion to the Prophet places him in a relationship of mutuality and affection with an inexhaustible source of blessing. Whether directed to God or to the Prophet, thanking (in the form of greeting, blessing, loving, and rejoicing) is expected to yield further blessings from the infinitely magnanimous benefactor. The performance of the *qiyām* is also a means of emotional expression. Whether understood as a spontaneous expression of joy or a more conventional expression of social deference, the *qiyām* generates a sense of immediacy that transcends technical argumentation about the presence or absence of the Prophet. As in a face-to-face encounter, the participant performs a physical action that expresses an affective relationship.

For supporters of the *qiyām*, it serves to perform sentiments of deference and awe within the framework of socially determined standards of conduct. Just as standing in deference to persons in one's immediate social environment serves to maintain relationships of cordiality and respect and to avoid ruptures in relations, the *qiyām* serves to express and maintain a relationship between the believer and the Prophet. Whether debating the legitimacy of rejoicing as a form of thanks to God or of the *qiyām* as an expression of reverence for the Prophet, *mawlid* supporters understood the *sharī'a* to mandate the cultivation of relationships through the performance of right emotions. Opponents, in contrast, tended to understand the *sunna* (and more broadly, the *sharī'a*) in terms of concrete behavioral norms. Nevertheless, the importance of affect could not be completely denied; while Ibn Taymīya affirmed the meritoriousness of expressing love for the Prophet, al-Haytamī conceded that the *qiyām* expressed appropriate sentiments of reverence for the Prophet. Even those who questioned the legitimacy of the *mawlid* and the *qiyām* had to acknowledge the primacy of emotion.

Gary Ebersole has argued that tears can "serve a variety of social purposes, including marking out social and hierarchical relationships at times, dissolving them at others, inviting or demanding specific social relationships, or marking/protesting the abrogation of social and moral contracts."[146] Ebersole cites the biblical account of the behavior of King David, who is said to have wept and fasted as his young son lay sick and to have arisen and eaten as soon as he was informed of the child's death. Questioned about his behavior, he replied that he wept and fasted as long as he had hope of the child's recovery, thinking, "Perhaps [God] will take pity on me and the child will live. But now he is dead, why should I fast?" Tears, Ebersole concluded, in the ancient Near East were "weapons of the weak, which could at times coerce a social superior to play his or her part in a sanctioned social and moral relationship."[147] In some ways, the performances of love and rejoicing in the *mawlid* celebration can be understood as a positive complement to the implicit protest of public mourning. While weeping could signal a violation of a king or deity's role as patron and protector to elicit some form of redress, acts of rejoicing and love dramatize the proper functioning of a hierarchical relationship, affirming the benevolent care of God and the Prophet. While King David hopes to elicit mercy by "adopt[ing] the inferior position of the prostrate weeping petitioner before [God]," *mawlid* participants adopt the position of the satisfied recipient of divine grace. By enacting one's role as a grateful, joyous, and loving recipient of divine favor, one reinforces the relationship within which such favors are bestowed.

4 Time and merit in the celebration of the *mawlid*

The idea that time is inherently patterned, with some days or months intrinsically privileged over others, is deeply rooted in the Islamic tradition and is addressed by the earliest *mawlid* authors. The author of one of the earliest *mawlid* texts, Ibn Diḥya al-Kalbī (d. 633 AH/1235 CE), is also known to have been the author of a work entitled *al-ʿAlam al-manshūr fī faḍl al-ayyām wa'l-shuhūr*, "The unfurled banner on the virtues of [special] days and months."[1] The assumption that time is non-homogeneous, and that some times in the Islamic calendar are particularly spiritually advantageous, would have been natural to a *ḥadīth* scholar such as Ibn Diḥya because of the large number of *ḥadīth* texts extolling the special virtues of specific months, dates, days of the week, and times of the day. Such reports were sufficiently numerous to inspire a minor genre; in addition to Ibn Diḥya's work, the traditionist al-Bayhaqī (d. 458 AH/1066 CE) authored a *Kitāb faḍā'il al-awqāt* ("Book on the virtues of [special] times").[2] The Shāfiʿī scholar Ibn ʿAbd al-Salām al-Sulamī (d. 660 AH/1262 CE) was merely affirming a widely acknowledged truth when he stated that some times and places were distinguished by this-worldly advantages (such as salubrious weather or a profusion of fruits), while others enjoyed a religious pre-eminence "that derives from the fact that in them God generously bestows upon His worshipers a preferential reward for those who perform [pious] acts in them." As examples of the disproportionate divine rewards accruing to acts of worship performed at specific special times, Ibn ʿAbd al-Salām cites (among others) the examples of fasting in the month of Ramaḍān or on the days of ʿĀshūrā' and the tenth of Dhū'l-Ḥijja.[3]

Ṣūfī circles were also particularly alert to the religious benefits of specific points in time, and carefully identified privileged windows of opportunity for special spiritual exertions. al-Ghazālī, for one, is in no doubt that certain nights of the year are "distinguished by enhanced virtue" (*makhṣūṣa bi-mazīd al-faḍl*). The main distinguishing feature of special times, again, is the vastly multiplied degree of religious merit reaped from acts of worship performed at those times. Speaking specifically of the fifteen nights during the year when it was considered desirable to hold religious vigils (*iḥyā'*), al-Ghazālī remarks that it behooves the religious aspirant (*al-murīd*) not to neglect them, because "they are the fairs of blessings and the times when good deals can be made; if a merchant neglects the fairs he will not prosper, and if the religious aspirant neglects the virtues of [special] times he will not succeed."[4]

The belief in special times could also extend to a more general concern with the distinctive themes, events, and religious duties associated with the cycle of the Islamic calendar. The Damascene scholar Ibn Rajab al-Ḥanbalī (d. 795 AH/1392 CE) composed a work especially devoted to the religious observances and reflections specific to various months of the Islamic calendar and seasons of the year, entitled *Laṭā'if al-ma'ārif fīmā li-mawāsim al-'ām min al-waẓā'if*. The book, which includes two chapters on the remembrance of the Prophet's birthday, is intended both as an aid to personal devotion and as a handbook for aspiring preachers.[5] "God gave some months superiority (*faḍl*) over others," affirms Ibn Rajab in the book's introduction; He also favored some special days and nights. "There is none of these special times of the year (*al-mawāsim al-fāḍila*)," he writes,

> but that God has one of the duties of obedience to Him (*waẓīfa min waẓā'if ṭā'ātihi*) at [that time] by which it is possible to seek proximity to Him (*yutaqarrabu bihā ilayhi*) and God has one of His subtle waftings (*nafaḥātihi*) through which He bestows His favor and grace upon whomever He wills. Happy is the one who seizes the special times of the months, days and years and seeks the proximity of his Lord at [those times] through the duties of obedience that are in them; perchance he may receive one of those waftings (*nafaḥāt*) and achieve a felicity after which he will be safe from the Fire and its scorchings (*lafaḥāt*).[6]

Interest in the Prophet's birthday as an occasion for pious observances emerged too late for the successful circulation of alleged Prophetic statements about the special virtues of acts of piety performed on that occasion. Nevertheless, as we have seen in Chapter 2, spurious statements about the vast harvests of merit to be generated by *mawlid* celebrations did eventually gain some degree of popularity. Furthermore, the Prophet's statement that he fasted on Mondays because it was the day on which he had been born was taken by many as an indication of the special nature of the day of his birth. Ultimately, the special status of the Prophet's birth date depended on a general belief that auspicious events occurred at auspicious times. The time of the Prophet's birth could be defined in a number of different ways; its numinous quality was variously associated with Monday, with the entire month of Rabī' al-Awwal, and specifically with the twelfth of the month. The special quality of the month of Rabī' al-Awwal is particularly frequently celebrated in *mawlid* texts. The *mawlid* of Ibn Jābir al-Andalusī (d. 780 AH/ 1378 CE) begins by discussing the date of the Prophet's birth, and notes that

> In that year Rabī' corresponded to April; his birth occurred when the sun entered Aries and time was in balance (*i'tadala al-zamān*).[7] So Rabī' al-Awwal is the source of blessings, the spring of hearts, and the month of miracles; whoever is sincere in his love of this noble Prophet honors this month to the utmost extent.[8]

Khalīl ibn Aybak al-Ṣafadī's (d. 764 AH/1363 CE) *mawlid* text begins by praising "God, who distinguished this blessed month with the noblest of births"; the body of the text commences with the statement that the month of Rabī' al-Awwal "was distinguished by this miracle, and it enjoyed precedence over the rest of the months."[9]

The Cairene Mālikī jurist Ibn al-Ḥājj (d. 737 AH/1336 CE) presents a particularly extravagant treatment of the special qualities of the time of the Prophet's birth. Ibn al-Ḥājj's attitude towards the *mawlid* is somewhat ambivalent. On the one hand, as a stern adversary of *bida'* he is adamantly opposed to formal *mawlid* celebrations, which he believes to be inherently in violation of the *sharī'a*. On the other, he depicts the Prophet's birthday as an extraordinarily luminous and auspicious time of the year. His solution to this conflict is that the *mawlid* is a fit occasion for intensification of one's personal piety, but not for the performance of any specific rituals.[10] Similar to Ibn Jābir al-Andalusī (whose remarks he may possibly have inspired), he re-invests a month of the Islamic calendar with the content and character of a season of the year, a linkage that is ordinarily lacking in a purely lunar calendar. Ibn al-Ḥājj ponders the wisdom (*ḥikma*) of the Prophet's birthday falling precisely in Rabī' al-Awwal, and on a Monday, rather than in one of the times of year already established as holy: in Ramaḍān – when the Qur'ān was first revealed, in which *laylat al-qadr* occurs, and which has many other virtues – or one of the sacred months, or on *laylat niṣf Sha'bān*, or on a Friday. His solution first refers to the idea, reported in a *ḥadīth*, that God created trees on a Monday. This circumstance contains a "great admonition (*tanbīh*)," because the fruits of trees and the sustenance they represent are a source of comfort and joy to people, who know upon seeing them that they will be able to nourish themselves and maintain their lives. Similarly, the coming into being of the Prophet is a source of delight because of the great benefits and comprehensive blessings that he brought to his community.

Second, Ibn al-Ḥājj argues that the Prophet's appearance in the month of Rabī' al-Awwal contains a reference to the etymology of the word *rabī'* ("spring"), which contains an auspicious omen for the Muslim community. The spring season is when the sustenance and provisions by which people are sustained burst forth from the earth; it is when seeds sprout, delighting those who see them and mutely proclaiming the coming season. This is an allusion to the rejoicing caused by the beginning of God's gifts represented by the birth of the Prophet. Third, there is a parallel with the nature of the law (*sharī'a*) borne by Muḥammad; it is the mildest and most moderate of divine laws, just as spring is the mildest and most moderate of seasons. Finally, Ibn al-Ḥājj argues that the birth of the Prophet did not occur at any of the times in the calendar already recognized as special, because God wished to demonstrate that times and places were honored by the Prophet, rather than vice versa. Had the Prophet been born on a date that was already hallowed, people might have imagined that this was an honor to him, rather than the other way around.[11]

According to Ibn al-Ḥājj, the special virtue of the time of the Prophet's birth is also linked with a heightened degree of divine responsiveness to human worship. It is established in a *ḥadīth* that there is a period of time on Friday when, were a Muslim to find it, he would not ask God for anything but that He would grant it to him. This period of time is said to fall between the mid-afternoon prayer and sunset, based on a *ḥadīth* stating that Adam was created on a Friday at this time of the day. Ibn al-Ḥājj concludes that if the time in which Adam was created is such that no Muslim's petition is denied by God, there is no doubt that prayers at the hour of the Prophet Muḥammad's birth will similarly be fulfilled. Since the Prophet Muḥammad is superior to Adam, the virtue of the hour of his birth must be correspondingly greater.[12]

The night of the *mawlid* and *laylat al-qadr*

The idea of non-homogeneous time, which posited the inherent superiority of some times in the Islamic calendar over others, naturally gave rise to the question of hierarchy. What was the best time in the Islamic year, and what was the ranking of the various times of blessing and reward? Ibn Rajab, for instance, is preoccupied with establishing hierarchies among various favored periods of time in the Islamic calendar, carefully balancing different reports against each other to determine precisely which times in the lunar year are most auspicious for the performance of specific acts of piety.[13] Because it was widely believed that the Prophet had been born at night (or perhaps at dawn), the question was often framed in terms of identifying the best night of the year. Aside from the night of the *mawlid*, the obvious contender for supremacy in the Islamic year was the Night of Destiny (*laylat al-qadr*), whose extraordinary virtues are extolled in the Qur'ān. According to verse 97:3, "The Night of Destiny is better than a thousand months." How, then, did the night of the Prophet's birth measure up? Perhaps surprisingly, *mawlid* enthusiasts were quite soon prepared to affirm the superiority of the night of the *mawlid* even over the Night of Destiny.

Probably the most elaborate defense of this position was produced by Abū 'Abd Allāh Muḥammad ibn Aḥmad ibn Muḥammad ibn Marzūq. Ibn Marzūq, an eighth-century AH/fourteenth-century CE maghribī scholar who spent the end of his spectacularly successful career in Cairo, seems to have been particularly interested in devotion to the Prophet. In addition to significant work in the discipline of *fiqh*, he is the author of a commentary on the *Shifā'* of al-Qāḍī 'Iyāḍ and of a poem in honor of the Prophet's birth recited at Granada before the sultan in 763 AH/1362 CE.[14] In his composition entitled *Jany al-jannatayn fī faḍl al-laylatayn*, Ibn Marzūq enumerates twenty-one different ways of demonstrating that the night of the *mawlid* is superior to *laylat al-qadr*.[15] The hypertrophied nature of this work suggests that the argument over the comparative status of these two festivals had reached a rather advanced stage by the author's time, approximately a century and a half after the rise of *mawlid* celebrations among Sunnī Muslims.

Ibn Marzūq begins by arguing, as his first proof, that "loftiness and exaltation (*al-'ulūw wa'l-rif'a*) are relative attributes (*nisbatān iḍāfīyatān*); the honor (*sharaf*) of each night depends on that with which it was honored. The night of the *mawlid* was honored with the birth of the best of God's creation; this establishes its superior status, upon consideration." All of the remaining proofs constitute a rather dry and repetitive set of variations upon this principle, comparing various aspects of the honor constituted by the birth of the Prophet to the special favors associated with *laylat al-qadr*. Some of them became classic arguments in the literature on the *mawlid*, particularly number two: "The night of the *mawlid* is the night of [the Prophet's] coming into existence (or 'appearance', *ẓuhūr*), and the Night of Power was given to him...; that which was honored by the very existence of the one for whose sake it is honored, is more honorable than that which is honored by reason of what was given to him." A somewhat different formulation of the same point is presented as the fifteenth proof, in which Ibn Marzūq states simply that "the Night of Power is a derivative (*far'*) of [the Prophet's] coming into existence, and a derivative is not as strong as the fundament (*aṣl*)."

The question of the comparative virtues of the night of the *mawlid* and the Night of Power is one that recurs fairly regularly in the *mawlid* literature. Even Ibn al-Ḥājj, whose guarded attitude toward the legitimacy of *mawlid* celebrations has already been mentioned, affirms in praise of the Prophet's birthday that the Prophet is "the axis of the circle of the universe, and the one for whose sake all in existence was created; he is the one through whose blessing (*baraka*) times become superior, and the one for whose sake his community was honored with the Night of Destiny."[16]

The contention that the night of the *mawlid* is the best of the Islamic year was not always accepted, even by *mawlid* authors and other supporters of the *mawlid* celebration. Ibn Ḥajar al-Haytamī considers this claim in a quite critical light in his *Itmām al-ni'ma al-kubrā*.[17] Aḥmad ibn Muḥammad al-Suḥaymī al-Azharī (d. 1178 AH/1765 CE), the author of the *mawlid* text *al-Zahr al-fā'iq fī mawlid ashraf al-khalā'iq*, affirms that the Night of Destiny is in fact the best night of the year, despite the claims advanced for the nights of the *mawlid* and the *isrā'*.[18] In other circles, particularly ṣūfī ones, the doctrine of the pre-eminence of the night of the *mawlid* was fervently embraced. In *al-Mawāhib al-ladunīya*, al-Qasṭallānī (d. 923 AH/1517 CE) affirms this doctrine with rationales drawn from the work of Ibn Marzūq.[19] Over time, an elaborate (if contested) hierarchy of sacred nights emerged, at least in certain quarters, in which non-canonical festivals such as the *mawlid* played a leading role. The Syrian jurist Ibn 'Ābidīn (d. 1258 AH/1842 CE) reports an opinion attributed simply to "a Shāfi'ī" (*ba'ḍ al-shāfi'īya*) "that the best of nights is the night of [the Prophet's] birth, then the Night of Destiny, then the night of the *isrā'* and the *mi'rāj*, then the night of 'Arafa, then Friday night [i.e., Thursday night], then the night of *niṣf Sha'bān*, then the night of the *'īd*."[20]

Special times and their uses

Belief in the existence of special times in the Islamic calendar was not merely an abstraction. Rather, it had concrete implications for religious practice and met specific popular needs. The surviving essays and sermons of Ibn Nāṣir al-Dīn al-Dimashqī (d. 842 AH/1438 CE), one of the most prolific and influential authors in the history of the *mawlid* genre, give a vivid sense of the conception of non-homogeneous time that informed the celebration of *mawlid*s. Among his preserved works are a piece on the virtues (*faḍl*) of 'Āshūrā' and one on the day of 'Arafa. The ornate opening invocation of his *al-Lafẓ al-mukarram bi-faḍl 'āshūrā' al-muḥarram* establishes his major underlying theme, that one of the primary blessings bestowed by God is the existence of special times yielding enhanced merit to devout worshipers:

> Praise be to God... Who bestowed and enriched, gave and sufficed, presented and provided, conferred and granted, blessed and favored. Among his favors is the blessing of the holy 'Āshūrā', which God made a season for the striving of worshipers, a prize for the acquisition of ascetics, and a sign of the acceptance of the repentance of [God's] creatures. The reward for action in it is magnified; blessed is the one who is among the humble then, and victory to the one who renounces [sins] then and is among the repentant, because it is a day on which God had mercy on some people and on which He will have mercy on other people. Glory be to Him; how broad is His forgiveness, and how abundant and indulgent His favor. We praise Him for the gifts which He has conferred and the presents which He has bestowed, among which is the coming of favored times to created beings in order that He may pour forth their blessings upon those whom He desires and knows.[21]

Ibn Nāṣir al-Dīn begins his discussion of the day of 'Āshūrā' by presenting a series of *ḥadīth* texts emphasizing the profuse rewards accruing to those who fast on that day. Several versions recount the Prophet's declaration that fasting on the day of 'Āshūrā' is equivalent to fasting for an entire year, or expiates the sins of the previous year. Yet other reports state that "Whoever fasts on 'Āshūrā' is credited with sixty years' worship, including fasting and holding vigils" or that if someone fasts on 'Āshūrā', it is equivalent to fasting continuously throughout his life. Another *ḥadīth* declares that "All good is poured out on the Night of the Sacrifice, the Night of Fastbreaking, the night of *niṣf Sha'bān*, and the Night of 'Āshūrā'." Fasting on 'Āshūrā' is even represented as one of the only actions one can perform that will evoke divine gratitude: "On the Day of Resurrection, God will thank [His creatures] only for the fast of Ramaḍān and the Day of Adornment (*yawm al-zīna*)[22] – that is, the day of 'Āshūrā'."[23]

In these traditions, the fast of 'Āshūrā' carries fabulous quantities of merit, equivalent to vast numbers of acts of worship at other times of year. Typically, the extraordinary holiness of the day is expressed in terms of a fantastically inflated "exchange rate" as compared with worship in ordinary time. Interestingly, the same astronomical multiplication of reward is invoked in Ibn Nāṣir al-Dīn's treatment of other sacred occasions; he seems completely unconcerned by any implicit conflict between the superlatives he applies to different blessed times. For instance, discussing the first ten days of the month of Dhū'l-Ḥijja, he declares that "There are no days in the world in which God more loves to receive acts of worship than the days of the Ten; fasting one day of them is equivalent to fasting for a year."[24]

The fundamental principle that Ibn Nāṣir al-Dīn derives from his discussion of fasting on the ninth of Muḥarram is "that if the performance of good works occurs at a noble time their reward is multiplied, because if anyone fasts for a day in the path of God, God will remove the Fire from his face for seventy autumns; if the fasting of the day occurs at a noble time, the removal from the Fire will be greater."[25] The author makes a similar argument in his piece on the Day of 'Arafa, remarking that "[the rewards for pious] works increase by virtue of the nobility of the time [at which they are performed], just as they increase by virtue of the nobility of the place [at which they are performed] and by the inherent nobility [of the action]."[26]

Ibn Nāṣir al-Dīn's conviction that certain exceptional times in the Islamic calendar offer privileged opportunities for the earning of religious merit is also linked to the idea that these times were the occasions of extraordinary events in sacred history. Having established that there are noble times when the reward for pious action is vastly enhanced and that the day of 'Āshūrā' (and the month of Muḥarram in general) is among these special times, Ibn Nāṣir al-Dīn turns to a recital of the many auspicious events that are associated with this date. These include Noah's disembarkation from the Ark, the salvation of the Israelites from Pharaoh, and the martyrdom of the Prophet's grandson al-Ḥusayn, which he regards as merely further evidence of the numinous quality of 'Āshūrā'. In recounting these events, Ibn Nāṣir al-Dīn gives the special quality of 'Āshūrā' support and substance through a wealth of religious narrative.[27] The occurrence of extraordinary events and the enhancement of religious merit are but two manifestations of the inherent power of the day.

Some sense of the popular desires that were met by the identification and celebration of special times in the Islamic calendar is provided by al-Ṭurṭūshī (d. ca. 520 AH/1126 CE) and by Abū Shāma (d. 665 AH/1268 CE). Ṭurṭūshī was an Andalusian Mālikī who spent time in Syria and settled in Egypt; Abū Shāma was a Syrian, and presents one of the earliest scholarly endorsements of the celebration of the Prophet's *mawlid* in his book *al-Bā'ith 'alā inkār al-bida'*. Both scholars are particularly concerned with those innovations that are widely considered to be religiously legitimate, particularly among the common people (*al-'awāmm*). One of these is the *alfiya*, or "thousand" prayer, that is performed on the eve of the fifteenth of Sha'bān (*laylat niṣf Sha'bān*) and consists of one hundred cycles of prostration, in each cycle of which the first chapter of the Qur'ān is recited once and the 112th chapter ten times. Abū Shāma notes that despite the fact that there are only weak or fabricated *ḥadīth*s on the subject, the common people (*al-'awāmm*) are enchanted by the practice; mosques are illuminated for the occasion, crowds of men and women participate (to the obvious detriment of public order), and many people consider the practice to be one of the greatest rites of the Islamic faith (*min ajall sha'ā'ir al-muslimīn*).[28]

According to al-Ṭurṭūshī, despite its popularity the *alfiya* prayer was a relative latecomer among Islamic ritual practices. He recounts the report of an informant from Jerusalem:

> The first time it was performed among us was in the year 448 [AH/1056 CE]. A man from Nablus by the name of Ibn Abī'l-Ḥamrā' came to us in

> Jerusalem; he recited [the Qur'ān] nicely. He stood and prayed in the Aqṣā Mosque on the night of *niṣf Sha'bān*; a man began to pray (*aḥrama*) behind him, then a third joined the two of them, and a fourth. By the time he finished [the prayer], they were in a large group. Then he came in the next year, and a big crowd (*khalq kathīr*) prayed with him. [The prayer] became well-known in the mosque, and... spread in the Aqṣā Mosque and in people's houses and homes. Then it became established as if it were a *sunna* until this day.

Al-Ṭurṭūshī's informant admits that he himself has performed this prayer in a congregation, a lapse for which he asks God's forgiveness.[29]

About the prayer in Rajab, al-Ṭurṭūshī states that it was performed in Jerusalem only after the year 480 [AH/1087 CE], and that no one had ever seen or heard of it before that date.[30] The *raghā'ib* prayer was performed between the sunset and evening prayers on the evening of the first Friday in the month of Rajab, and was promoted by means of a highly suspect *ḥadīth*. *Raghā'ib*, Abū Shāma explains, is the plural of *raghba*, which means "bounteous gift." "It was probably named this," he infers, "because of the gifts which accrue to the one who prays it, according to the person who forged the *ḥadīth*."[31] The individual suspected of the forgery by scholars is one Abū'l-Ḥasan 'Alī ibn 'Abd Allāh ibn Jahḍam, d. 414 AH/1023–4 CE[32] Ibn al-Jawzī laments the fact that in his time, the common people (*al-'awāmm*) consider this prayer "greater and more pleasant" (*a'ẓam wa-aḥlā*) than the *tarāwīḥ* prayers performed during Ramaḍān; people attend them who do not bother to attend the communal prayers on the canonical festivals. Abū Shāma speculates that this may be because of the copious rewards and expiation of sins that are promised by the forged *ḥadīth*.[33]

The controversy over some of these disputed ritual practices seems to have been particularly acute at the very time and place when the Sunnī *mawlid* festival (and the *mawlid* genre) originated. According to Abū Shāma, Abū 'Amr ibn al-Ṣalāḥ issued a *fatwā* in Damascus "before 620" stating that the *raghā'ib* prayer was based on a forged *ḥadīth* and that the practice was an innovation that arose after the year 400 AH, first appearing in Syria and then spreading to all other countries. There is no inherent harm in a person's performing this prayer, he argues, based on the fact that it is always desirable to pray between the *maghrib* and *'ashā'* prayers; but it is an objectionable innovation to make communal performance of the *raghā'ib* into a *sunna* and regard it as a religious duty. He issued a second *fatwā* to the same effect in response to an enquiry about the oil that is used for the illuminations associated with this prayer, which would be an illegitimate expenditure if the prayer itself were considered baseless.[34]

Abū Shāma notes that when Ibn 'Abd al-Salām became the *khaṭīb* and *imām* of the (Ummayad) mosque of Damascus in 637 AH/1239–40 CE, he was highly concerned with the revivification of *sunna*s and the suppression of innovations. When the beginning of the month of Rajab drew near, he preached against the *raghā'ib* prayer during the Friday congregation, stating that it was an objectionable innovation and that the relevant *ḥadīth* was forged. His efforts to abolish the prayer was upsetting both to the common people and to the sultan and his retinue; Ibn al-Ṣalāḥ himself relented, producing a work supporting the practice and categorizing it as a "good innovation" (*bid'a ḥasana*). Abū Shāma witheringly remarks that he reversed his original position to support "what conformed to the whims of the sultan and the common people of the age," despite being a distinguished and pious scholar.[35]

This incident suggests the fervency of the popular response to these invented festivals and the vast harvests of blessing supposedly to be gained from their observance. At least in the case of the *raghā'ib* prayer, the impetus seems to have come from below (with the support of the political authorities), and the expansion of the practice (and its unwilling embrace by more learned figures) to have been driven by demand. Abū Shāma remarks,

> I have seen one of the common people castigate the *imām* of a mosque and rebuke him because he did not know how to pray it right. I asked [the *imām*] about that, and he said that he led them in praying the *raghā'ib* prayer and did not know how to perform the two cycles of prostration after it. I saw the commoner teach it to him, expressing wonderment that he was the *imām* of a mosque and not well informed about it – the *imām* being like a prisoner in his hands, unable to say that it was an objectionable innovation or that it was not a *sunna*. How many an *imām* has said to me that he prays it only to keep the hearts of the common people by it and in order to keep hold of his mosque, fearing that it might be seized from him.[36]

Based on Abū Shāma's horrified descriptions of the disorders occurring in connection with some of these observances, they must have attracted vast crowds. His main concern in his discussion of the innovations in this category is the anarchic potential of the night-time public festival. The illumination of the mosques, he argues, attracts crowds of men and women who may take advantage of the situation to engage in various kinds of misbehavior, including the fondling of women pressed into dense crowds. He states that anyone who has attended the prayers of the night of *niṣf Sha'bān* in Damascus or someplace similar to it knows the "immorality, sins, commotion, abduction (*khatf*), theft, and the soiling of places of worship" that they occasion.[37]

The wide popularization of at least two other noncanonical festivals in the century and a half preceding the rise of the *mawlid* festival suggests that such observances met an important need in the wider public. Although the chronology of its popularization is somewhat less clear, the celebration of the anniversary of the Prophet's night journey and ascension (*isrā'* and *mi'rāj*) is another example of a post-classical festival that became widely popular in this era. Abū Shāma is probably correct in inferring that the generation of vast quantities of religious merit in a single night presented an irresistible incentive for the minimally observant. The statement that enthusiasts of the *raghā'ib* prayers sometimes neglected obligatory observances, while an obvious polemic, probably also reflects a simple truth: persons whose religious attainments were limited by normative standards would have particularly treasured the opportunity to reap divine blessings on occasional nights of extraordinary blessing. The role potentially played by noncanonical festivals is particularly poignantly suggested by the *ta'rīf*. This practice involved gathering on the evening of 'Arafa, the day on which pilgrims to Mecca stand in prayer on the Mount of Mercy, and performing similar devotions in imitation of the pilgrims in whatever locality one might be. This seems to be a very early innovation, one that was noted (and deplored) by a number of early authorities.[38] Sometime before Abū Shāma's time, however, it seems to have taken on a popular significance threatening the principles of orthodox religion. al-Ṭurṭūshī describes the celebration as it existed in his own time in Jerusalem. The people of the countryside (*al-sawād*) and many of the inhabitants of the city gathered in the mosque and stood facing the *qibla*, raising their voices in invocation as if they were in 'Arafa. More sinister than the popularity of the celebration, however, was the growth of a popular tradition about its significance; al-Ṭurṭūshī reports that there was a rumor in wide circulation that four "standings" in Jerusalem were the equivalent of the *ḥajj* to Mecca, a belief that (he feared) could easily lead to the neglect of the canonical pilgrimage.[39] While it is certainly the case that no one could attend the *ḥajj* every year of his or her life, it seems likely that the practice of *ta'rīf* enjoyed wide popularity because it made some of the spiritual benefits of the pilgrimage available to those who might never fulfill this most rigorous of ritual obligations.

Ibn Nāṣir al-Dīn's piece on the Day of 'Arafa may in fact be an example of the *ta'rīf* condemned by Abū Shāma. Given his emphasis on the added virtues of the Day of 'Arafa when it falls on a Friday, it may also simply be a Friday sermon delivered on the occasion of such a convergence. In any case, in terms of its content it is clearly intended to offer a vicarious experience of the *ḥajj* to those who have not made the journey, and to console them with the thought that the bounteous rewards of worship in God's privileged windows of time will provide them with equal rewards. It exemplifies the ways in which special times could assuage feelings of religious inadequacy or exclusion. The piece climaxes in a series of vivid evocations of the emotional and spiritual states of the pilgrims standing at 'Arafāt. "The delegation to God has departed, and we have stayed home," Ibn Nāṣir al-Dīn laments; "they have approached His presence, and we remain distant." However, "if we have a share with them in our hearts, we have triumphed – by God – and achieved felicity."[40] Rather than promising a mere semi-automatic harvest of blessing, Ibn Nāṣir al-Dīn demands genuine spiritual participation from his audience; yet the effort required – whether financially or physically – is small in comparison with those of an actual pilgrimage.

Both through imaginative participation in the rites of the *ḥajj* and through invocation of the special blessings bestowed by God on this particular day, Ibn Nāṣir al-Dīn provides alternative forms of religious achievement for people who may otherwise feel themselves excluded. His address seems to offer a "little path" to religious merit and salvation for those who may never be real pilgrims. There is no way of knowing whether the audience so addressed was being excluded from the more rigorous forms of Islamic observance by social class, by education, by gender, or by lack of personal commitment. What is clear, however, is that by substituting the category of time for that of place Ibn Nāṣir al-Dīn has paralleled the onerous journey to a distant place with a calendrical occasion that comes to all alike, once in every year.

Within the context of the problematic popular demand for special religious occasions, the *mawlid* festival held an intermediate position. While not expressly mandated by the Prophet's *sunna*, it was based not on blatantly spurious *ḥadīth* but on a historical event of widely accepted religious significance. Similar to the commemoration of the *mi'rāj*, it was thus acceptable to some scholars who roundly condemned the celebrations of Sha'bān and Rajab. Abū Shāma is not the only scholar known to have encouraged the newly introduced celebration of the *mawlid* while condemning these competing, and religiously even more suspect, occasions for popular devotion. Ibn Diḥya himself wrote not only a work condemning forged *ḥadīth* texts about the month of Rajab[41] but a *Kitāb mā jā'a fī shahr Sha'bān* ("Book on What is Reported about the Month of Sha'bān"), in which he argues that there are no reliable *ḥadīth*s about the night of *niṣf Sha'bān*. In this work, Ibn Diḥya argues that it is the duty of the sultan to forbid such celebrations and that of scholars to rebuke those who engage in them.[42] Abū Shāma states that Ibn Diḥya's arguments about the prayers of Rajab and Sha'bān were the stimulus for the sultan of Egypt to abolish the celebrations there.[43] Given Ibn Diḥya's apparent activism in this regard, it is significant that he was willing to promote the celebration of the *mawlid* by composing a devotional work in honor of the occasion. He was also the author of a work in commemoration of the Prophet's ascension to heaven (*mi'rāj*), although it is unclear from that text what attitude he took towards the popular commemoration of this event; a degree of skepticism may be suggested from his brisk dismissal of the popular belief that it occurred in the month of Rajab.[44] It may be that, as a traditionist, he was consoled by the many passable *ḥadīth* texts dealing with the wondrous events surrounding the birth of the Prophet and his ascension to heaven – even if none of them specifically warranted a celebration of the event.

Homogeneous and non-homogeneous time

The idea of special times, although widely popular, was not uncontested among medieval Islamic scholars. On a theoretical level, the idea of non-homogeneous time (and its corollary, non-homogeneous space) was most thoughtfully opposed by the 'Abd al-'Azīz ibn 'Abd al-Salām al-Sulamī, the same Syrian scholar who issued a *fatwā* condemning the *raghā'ib* prayers in the face of strong political pressure. In his consideration of the problem of time and space, Ibn 'Abd al-Salām starts out with the textually incontrovertible fact that the religious merit accruing to a given act of piety could vary widely according to the circumstances of its performance. The implication of this fact is, of course, that the reward is not strictly proportional to the effort expended; in fact, in some cases it may be inversely proportional. He writes,

> It is not improbable (*ba'īd*) of God's favor that He recompense the lesser of two acts of the same kind more than He recompenses the greater of them, just

> as He made the reward of this community (despite the small amount of its work) greater than the reward of the Jews and the Christians (despite the great amount of their work), and as He made the reward of obligatory [acts of worship] greater than that for equivalent acts of supererogation, as a favor to whom He will of His servants; and as holding a vigil on the Night of Destiny causes the forgiveness of sins, despite the fact that it is [in itself] equivalent to holding a vigil on any other night of Ramaḍān. Similarly, acts performed on the Night of Destiny are superior to the acts of a thousand months, despite the fact that they are [in themselves] equivalent (*ma'a al-tasāwī*); similarly, prayer in the Two Mosques [of Mecca and Medina] is superior to prayer in other mosques, despite their equivalence in everything that is required in them.[45]

Since acts of worship such as prayer are uniform in content regardless of the circumstances of their performance, the fact that their rewards are not also equal requires explanation. Ibn 'Abd al-Salām's explanation is simply that this is the unmotivated decree of God:

> God favors His servants at some times with things with which he does not favor them at other times, even if it is definitely known that they are equivalent; this is nothing but the grace of God, since there is no difference between one time and another. Similar to this is God's favoring [acts performed] in some places with multiplication of rewards, as He made prayer in the mosque of Medina superior to a thousand prayers in any other most but the Sacred Mosque, despite the equivalence of the prayers.[46]

As an Ash'arī, Ibn 'Abd al-Salām is not dismayed by the apparent arbitrariness or inequity of God's apportionment of rewards. He need not posit that there is something inherently more meritorious about acts of piety performed at special times or places that might rationally justify the multiplication of merit. In fact, he explicitly rejects this option by asserting the strict homogeneity of both time and space. "Know," he writes,

> that places and times are all equivalent; they are distinguished by virtue of what happens in them, not through attributes that inhere in them. Their preferential status (*tafḍīl*) derives from the grace and favor that God bestows on [His] servants in them, for God punishes without disbelief or disobedience, and He favors without obedience or faith.[47]

Ibn 'Abd al-Salām further specifies that the divine "grace and favor" of such times by stating that "in them God generously bestows upon His servants a preferential reward for those who act in them."[48]

In his invocation of God's "grace and favor," Ibn 'Abd al-Salām alludes to the Ash'arī denial that God's actions need conform to any human standard of justice. Indeed, God's inscrutable apportionment of punishment and reward extends far beyond the bestowal of excess merit for fasting on 'Āshūrā'; even salvation is bestowed without regard for just desserts. Ibn 'Abd al-Salām drives home his argument by stating bluntly, "It is authoritatively reported (*qad ṣaḥḥa*) that [God] creates some people in Paradise and others in Hell; similar are the pure houris (*al-ḥūr al-'īn*) whom He created in the Gardens." In his denial that times and places are distinguished "by attributes that inhere in them," he refers to the Ash'arī doctrine of atoms and accidents.

The theological context of Ibn 'Abd al-Salām's arguments is underlined by the contribution of Ibn Qayyim al-Jawzīya, another Damascene who lived a century later. While Ibn al-Qayyim does not identify the object of his polemic, it is clear that he is engaging either with Ibn 'Abd al-Salām himself or with those who shared his opinions on this subject. In contrast with Ibn 'Abd al-Salām, Ibn al-Qayyim takes the position that different times are not inherently equivalent, and that some special times are qualitatively distinct. His arguments about time appear in the context of a broader discussion of the principle of *qiyās* (analogical consistency). Ibn al-Qayyim argues at great length that there is no element in the *sharī'a* that violates *qiyās*, meaning that there is a cogent and logically consistent rationale for each of the provisions of the law.[49] He then addresses a lengthy list of apparently irrational or anomalous features of the *sharī'a* and attempts to explain the underlying coherence of each one. Each of the examples attributed to his opponents is intended to demonstrate that in the *sharī'a* God has treated various items differentially without any grounds for differentiation; in each case, Ibn al-Qayyim strives to demonstrate that there is a valid distinction to be made. One of the instances in which *sharī'a*, according to Ibn al-Qayyim's hypothetical debate partners, "has distinguished between equivalent things" (*qad farraqat bayna al-mutamāthilayn*) is time. God

> distinguished some times from others and some places from others with special qualities (*khaṣā'iṣ*), despite the fact that they are equivalent; He made the Night of Destiny better than a thousand months, made the month of Ramaḍān the master of months and Friday the master of days, and the Day of 'Arafa, the Day of the Sacrifice, and the Days of Minā the best of days, and made the House [i.e., the Ka'ba] the best spot on earth.[50]

Ibn al-Qayyim comments on this claim,

> As for his stating, "[God] distinguished some times and places, and favored some of them over others, despite the fact that they are equivalent, etc.," the first premise is correct, and the second is false (*kādhiba*). [God] favored some [times and places] over others only because of special qualities inherent in them that occasioned the distinction. [God] never distinguishes anything without a distinguishing factor (*mā khaṣṣa subḥānahu shay'an illā li-mukhaṣṣiṣ*), but it may be evident and it may be hidden.[51]

Ibn al-Qayyim goes on to polemicise vigorously against the unnamed party that holds all times and places to be equivalent, describing it as "the most corrupt school of thought in the world" (*afsad madhhab al-'ālam*). It would seem from the content of the refutation that the party in question is the Ash'arites. In order to demonstrate the offensiveness of their position, he points out that it implies that the essence (*dhāt*) of Gabriel is equivalent to that of Iblīs and that the substance (*jism*) of musk is the same as that of urine and dung, distinguished from them only by accidental attributes. Ibn al-Qayyim concludes that this is a completely irrational position which contradicts sensory data and the common sense of all peoples and religions.[52]

At another point, Ibn al-Qayyim offers a concrete example of his understanding of the differences among different times. In this case, he is responding to the contention that "[God] prohibited fasting on the first day of [the month of] Shawwāl and made it obligatory to fast on the last day of Ramaḍān, despite the fact that they are equivalent." Ibn al-Qayyim responds,

> The two days are not equivalent, even if they share in the rising and setting of the sun. The latter is a day of the month of fasting which God made obligatory for His servants, and the former is their day of celebration and rejoicing, which God made [a time] to give thanks for their fasting and complete it. On it they are His guests; someone who is magnanimous and generous likes his guest to accept what he serves and dislikes for him to refrain from accepting his hospitality by fasting or anything else; it is disapproved for a guest to fast without the permission of the master of the house.[53]

For Ibn al-Qayyim, individual days in the Islamic calendar are invested by God with special values and meanings that make the differential duties imposed on them comprehensible and beneficial.

Theoretically, the issue of whether times and places are inherently homogeneous or non-homogeneous need have no great implications for Islamic devotionalism. Both the text of the Qur'ān and well-authenticated *ḥadīth* affirm the extraordinary rewards accruing to pious actions performed on certain occasions, such as the Night of Destiny; no party to the debate could (or did) deny the existence of such times. However, the view that all times were inherently equivalent tended to reduce "special times" to chronological indicators for the performance of textually specified acts of worship. Furthermore, if the only distinguishing feature of such privileged times and places was the enhanced rewards textually established for the performance of certain forms of piety, there was no way to identify a special time in the absence of such a text. Of course, no specific acts of piety were textually specified for the night of the *mawlid*.[54] This implication is made clear by Ibn Ḥajar al-Haytamī, who writes in his discussion of the relative merits of the night of the *mawlid* and the Night of Destiny that "even if we were to grant that [the night of the Prophet's] *mawlid* was superior, it would have no benefit (*lam yakun lahu fā'ida*), because there is no benefit in attributing superiority to [specific] times except by virtue of the actions that are performed in them. Attributing superiority to the time itself, in which there is no action, is of little benefit."[55]

Authors of a devotionalist cast saw a deeper significance in distinctions among times and places, a tendency that overshadowed issues of formal theological allegiance. A case in point is Tāj al-Dīn al-Subkī who, although a Shāfi‘ī Ash‘arī like Ibn ‘Abd al-Salām, took a divergent view on the issue of special times and places. al-Subkī addresses Ibn ‘Abd al-Salām's thesis on the homogeneity of time and space in the context of his *fatwā* about illumination of the mosque of Medina. Acknowledging the argument that times and places are distinguished not by any inherent qualities specific to them but by virtue of the magnified rewards which God chooses to bestow upon those who engage in pious actions in them, al-Subkī writes:

> I say that it might be for that reason, and it might be because of something else [that exists] in [those times and places], even if no action occurs. Mercy, favor (*riḍwān*), and angels descend upon the grave of the Prophet, and God has a love for it and for its inhabitant that is impossible for intellects to comprehend, and which no other place possesses. So how could it not be the best of places? Yet it is not the site of action for us, because it is not a mosque, nor is it the equivalent of a mosque. Rather, it is a prerogative of the Prophet. This is a factor other than the multiplication of [the rewards for] actions in it.[56]

Just as authors of a devotionalist tendency emphasized the existence of specially blessed times and places, regardless of their formal theological affiliation, others denied it without regard to theology. Unsurprisingly Ibn Taymīya took the most outspoken position in this regard. By denying the existence of special times other than those defined by divinely mandated acts of piety, he reduced such times to neutral indicators of the proper occasions for textually established acts of obedience. Time, like space, for Ibn Taymīya had no inherent value or modulation.

Ibn Taymīya deals with the modulation of time and space in his book-length polemic against religious innovations inspired by non-Muslim practices, *Iqtiḍā' al-ṣirāṭ al-mustaqīm*. Its second-half is devoted to the subject of *a‘yād* (singular *‘īd*), here a concept somewhat too broad to be covered by the ordinary translation "festivals." Ibn Taymīya defines an *‘īd* as any time or place in which there is a gathering, and the activities associated with that time or place.[57] Thus, the category includes places and practices of pilgrimage as well as the various forms of Sabbath and holiday. Ibn Taymīya qualifies *a‘yād* as either "spatial" or "temporal" (*al-a‘yād al-zamānīya*/*al-a‘yād al-makānīya*). Time and space appear as analogous categories; the question at stake is in what ways, and on what basis, individual times or places can be distinguished from others and associated with distinctive ritual practices. Here Ibn Taymīya's argument is not that time and space are strictly homogenous, but that no time or place can be singled out for special religious observance without the explicit instruction of God. "Temporal *ay‘ād*" are subdivided into those days which the *sharī‘a* has not glorified (*ta‘ẓīm*) at all, those on which a great event occurred, and those which are glorified by the *sharī‘a* but to which extraneous forms of worship have accreted.[58]

The celebration of the *mawlid*, naturally, falls into the category of festivals commemorating some date on which an important event occurred. This category may have been particularly problematic to Ibn Taymīya for sectarian reasons; his first example is the Shī'ite observance of the day of Ghadīr Khumm, the occasion on which the Prophet allegedly named his son-in-law 'Alī as his successor in leadership of the community. Unlike Ibn Nāṣir al-Dīn, however, who contents himself with critiquing the deviations and excesses in the Shī'ite commemoration of 'Āshūrā', Ibn Taymīya identifies the whole phenomenon of commemorative observance as a sectarian or non-Muslim phenomenon. There are many events in the life of the Prophet that would richly merit yearly commemoration, he points out, but their anniversaries are not holidays. The only legitimate foundation for the celebration of a festival is an explicit divine command.

> The Prophet had sermons, pacts, and battles on many different days, such as the days of Badr, Ḥunayn, and the Trench, the conquest of Mecca, the time of his hijra, his entry into Medina, and many sermons of his in which he mentioned the principles of the religion. This did not make it necessary to take the anniversaries of those days as festivals; this is the kind of thing that is done by the Christians, who take the anniversaries of the events [in the life] of Jesus as festivals, or by the Jews. Rather, festivals are [a matter of] the divine law (*wa-innamā al-'īd sharī'a*); whatever God has legislated must be followed, and otherwise one must not innovate in the religion what does not belong to it.[59]

Interestingly, in one *fatwā* Ibn Taymīya does implicitly accept the idea that the relative merit of different times might be indicated by the extraordinary nature of the events that occurred in them, rather than by direct textual statement. Asked which is superior (*afḍal*), the Night of Destiny or the night of the Prophet's miraculous night journey (*laylat al-isrā'*), Ibn Taymīya replies that the night of the *isrā'* is superior with respect to the Prophet, while the Night of Destiny is superior with respect to the Muslim community. This is because the Prophet has a greater share (*ḥaẓẓ*) in the night of the *isrā'*, when he personally achieved incomparable honor and rank; the community, on the other hand, has a greater share in the Night of Destiny.[60] Ibn Taymīya's argument about the relative merits of these two nights, however, must be understood to apply only to two unique occasions in the historical past. The occurrence of an extraordinary event, Ibn Taymīya insists, does not in itself constitute a divine warrant for distinguishing the corresponding date on an ongoing, yearly basis.

For Ibn Taymīya, the fundamental problem is specification (*takhṣīṣ*) – attributing some distinction to a specific day or time without proper textual warrant.[61] This alone is enough to render a practice corrupt. According to Ibn Taymīya, the Prophet forbade the believers to distinguish specific times (*takhṣīṣ awqāt*) for prayer or fasting, but allowed supererogatory prayer and fasting if no specific time was established. He illustrates this with a *ḥadīth* in which the Prophet says, "Do not single out (*lā takhuṣṣū*) Friday night for vigils over other nights, and do not single out Friday for fasting over other days, unless it falls within a [period of] fasting that one of you is observing."[62] Given that Friday is, in fact, textually established to have a special status (unlike non-Islamic or noncanonical festivals), there is another inference to be drawn from the Prophet's prohibition on specifying it as a day for fasting.

> Since Friday is a special day (*yawm fāḍil*) on which prayers, invocations, remembrance [of God], recitation [of the Qur'ān], purification, perfume and adornment are desirable (*mustaḥabb*) that are not desirable on other days, it is to be expected that someone might fancy that fasting on that day was superior to [fasting on] other [days].... Thus, the Prophet forbade the specification [of Friday as a day for fasting] in order to avert this harm, which arises only from specification.[63]

The problem with human specification (*takhṣīṣ*) of set times for acts of piety is not merely that it gives rise to baseless ritual practices and (presumably) unfounded expectations of reward. Rather, the issue goes beyond questions of external practice to enter the domain of interior belief. One of the most pernicious elements of the celebration of innovated festivals, according to Ibn Taymīya, is that they entail false beliefs about the times when they occur. "Someone who performs an innovated action on a [specific] day," he argues,

> like the innovation of fasting the first Thursday in Rajab and praying on the night of that Friday, which the ignorant call the "*raghā'ib* prayer," for instance, and the things that accompany that, including the innovation of foods and adornment, additional expenditures (*tawsī' fī 'l-nafaqa*), and the like – inevitably these actions will be followed by a belief in the heart.... because if it were not for the existence of this belief in his heart – or in the heart of the one he is emulating – his heart would not be moved to distinguish this day and night. It is impossible to distinguish [between two things] without a factor distinguishing [between them].[64]

Belief in the special nature of a time which has not been specified by the Qur'an or the sunna is misguidance (*ḍalāl*); if a person does not harbor such a belief, on the other hand, "inevitably he is motivated by conformity with other people, by adherence to custom, by fear of censure, or the like."[65]

Ibn Taymīya was not the only scholar to deny that human beings could institute religious observances of special times in the Islamic calendar without explicit divine instruction. The Andalusian jurist Abū 'Abd Allāh al-Ḥaffār (d. 811 AH/ 1408 CE) expressed similar sentiments in response to a question about the validity of a *waqf* dedicated to the expenses of the yearly *mawlid* celebration. al-Ḥaffār argues that the earliest Muslims (the *salaf*) clearly did not engage in any supererogatory worship in honor of the night of the Prophet's birth; had they done so, the precise date would have been passed down to later generations. The prevalent uncertainty about the actual date of the *mawlid*, then, demonstrates that early Muslims were unconcerned with it. al-Ḥaffār goes on to argue that it is illegitimate to engage in supplementary acts of worship on the *mawlid* simply because it is a special time. "Don't you see," he asks rhetorically, "that Friday is the best day on which the sun ever rose, and the best thing that can be done on an exceptional day (*yawm fāḍil*) is to fast it; [yet] the Prophet forbade fasting on Friday, despite its great merit? This demonstrates that no act of worship can be innovated in a time or place unless it is legislated."[66]

Interestingly, a similar position was adopted by Abū Shāma. He argues in his *Bā'ith 'alā inkār al-bida'* that "One should not assign acts of worship to specific times that were not assigned to them by the sacred law; rather, all pious acts are capable of being performed at all times, without one time having any superiority over another, except those [times] that the sacred law favored and specified for some act of worship."[67] Like Ibn Taymīya, what he fears is the process of ritualization and the emergence of false beliefs. Abū Shāma notes that holding vigils is desirable on all nights of the year, including the night of *niṣf Sha'bān*. What is objectionable is not simply staying up to pray on any given night but specifying a particular night of the year for a particular prayer that is to be performed in a particular way, just as special prayers are stipulated for the Friday congregational prayers, for the two canonical festivals (of the Sacrifice and the end of the Ramaḍān fast), and for the nights of Ramaḍān. The result of establishing such a set prayer, Abū Shāma fears, is that it will become customary among the people; children will be brought up to perform it, and will see their parents adhering to it as strictly as they do to the canonical prayers, or even more so. They will see that the decorations, illuminations, and expenditures devoted to these festivals are equal or greater than those associated with the canonical festivals, as is already observable among the common people (*al-'awāmm*); thus, the light of truth will be contaminated with the darkness of error.[68] It is difficult to discern, in light of these opinions, how Abū Shāma justified his enthusiastic support for the *mawlid* celebration; it may be that its very newness had at that time prevented the emergence of ritualized forms of the kind that he condemned.

In contrast, supporters of the *mawlid* celebration generally affirmed that the occurrence of the Prophet's birthday in itself sufficed as an indication of the special quality of the time, even in the absence of divinely mandated acts of worship. Ibn al-Ḥājj (whose ambivalence towards the *mawlid* has already been discussed) notes that while the special virtues of the Night of Destiny are known through the word of the Qur'ān delivered by the Prophet, "As for the month of Rabī' al-Awwal and Monday, we know of their virtue through his appearance in them."[69] Ibn al-Ḥājj acknowledges that no specific acts of worship have been imposed on Muslims in honor of the Prophet's birthday. However, this does not refute the special quality of the day or the appropriateness of performing voluntary acts of piety in its honor (albeit without the specific intent of celebrating the *mawlid*). The only reason that the Prophet did not engage in special devotions during the month of his own birth was that, in his great compassion for his community, he feared that it would become an obligation for them. In matters pertaining to himself the Prophet always made things easy for his community. Thus, God refrained from imposing any special duties on the day of his birth as an honor to the Prophet; Muḥammad was sent as a mercy to the worlds, and this includes refraining from imposing additional obligations. However, the Prophet did indicate the special virtue of the month of his birth by explaining that he fasted on Monday because it was the day of his birth; this implies that the month of his birth is worthy of similar honor.[70]

A somewhat similar argument is made by the eighteenth-century CE Moroccan scholar Muḥammad ibn Aḥmad Banīs, who argues that "The superiority of *laylat al-qadr* was established textually (*nuṣṣa 'alā*) so that its superiority would be known, because it can be known only from the text; the night of [the Prophet's] appearance does not need its superiority to be established textually because it is so very obvious and extremely manifest; it would be like informing someone of something that is already known – and God knows best."[71]

As we have seen, the issue of special times was inextricably linked to the issue of special places. Arguments about the hierarchical ranking of different days or nights in the Islamic calendar frequently stimulated reflections about a cognate problem, that of the ranking of special places. The assumption that time and space are parallel categories is prevalent, if rarely explicitly addressed, and arguments about one frequently have implications for one's beliefs about the other. This assumption is reflected in Ibn Marzūq's arguments for the superiority of the night of the *mawlid* over the Night of Destiny. His fourteenth argument is that just as the place distinguished by the Prophet (*al-buq'a allatī ikhtaṣṣat bihi*) is agreed to be the best of places, the time distinguished by his birth must be the best of times.[72] More fundamentally, it tacitly reflects the idea that the dimensions of time and space are in some sense interchangeable.

As a North African, Ibn Marzūq was rooted in the one school of law (the Mālikī) that promoted the doctrine that Medina was superior to Mecca.[73] Despite the fact that the relative status of Mecca and Medina was a *madhhab*-based issue, the exaltation of Medina had a devotionalist appeal extending beyond the Mālikī school. The Shāfi'ite Taqī al-Dīn al-Subkī, without explicitly embracing the Mālikī view of the superiority of Medina as a whole, was able to assert that the Prophet's burial chamber was a supremely superior site by virtue of the Prophet's physical presence. For al-Subkī, the factor of propinquity to the Prophet outweighs the differential reward textually established for acts of devotion performed in the two locations. While prayers in the mosque of Mecca are agreed to be more richly rewarded, according to al-Subkī this does not mean that the mosque of Mecca is superior.[74] From the devotionalist point of view exemplified by al-Subkī, proximity to the Prophet sanctifies a place more powerfully than any other factor.

Muḥammad al-Raṣṣā' evokes a similar belief in his discussion of the sanctity of the night of the *mawlid*. After evoking the cosmic wonders of the night of the Prophet's birth al-Raṣṣā' declares, "His birth was on the noblest of nights and days, and in the best time, night, and place; for he is the noblest person ever created by God. How could that night not be the most blessed and best of nights?" In general, "every special merit and miracle God has created, and every place, locale, or time in which He sent down blessings, all of it is in honor of the Master of Created Beings." Everything God has honored, He has honored for the sake of the Prophet.[75]

The underlying principle, and its equal applicability to the dimensions of time and space, is made even more explicit in a passage by Muḥammad Banīs. While his terminology is explicitly ṣūfī, the sentiment would be shared by many *mawlid* authors. He writes:

> The correct [position] is what was established by our teachers' teacher Ibn Zakarī, which is that we say: everything that has honor (*sharaf*) has obtained it and acquired it only from [the Prophet], it is through him that times, places, and other things have become honorable (*tasharrafa*), because he is the intermediary (*wāsiṭa*) through which every benefaction (*ni'ma*) reaches its beneficiary (*mun'am 'alayhi*). In his hands are the keys of the Divine treasuries (*al-khazā'in al-ilāhīya*), and no distinctions (*khuṣūṣiyāt*), lights or secrets emerge from them except by his hands. The honor (*sharaf*) of every honorable thing is according to its propinquity (*qurb*) to him and proportional to it; there is no doubt that the night of his birth is closer to him than *laylat al-qadr*.[76]

Ibn Taymīya expresses his own attitude toward the comparative sacredness of different places in a *fatwā* responding to a query about the supposed superiority of residence in Syria over that in other lands.[77] Much as he does with respect to the analogous category of time, he maintains that places do not have any inherent virtue or superiority independent of the acts of obedience and piety that may be performed in them. Some places do, it is true, afford circumstances which are more conducive to pious behavior than others. However, their conduciveness to good behavior is not to be equated with any intrinsic virtue. After all, a land of disbelief and sin may be more favorable to meritorious action than a land of piety and faith if the individual who dwells there busies himself with jihād and moral exhortation.[78] Furthermore, the status of different locations varies over time; between the hijra and the Conquest, even Mecca – the noblest spot on earth – was a land of disbelief and war where it was forbidden for Muslims to reside. "As for enduring virtue (*al-faḍīla al-dā'ima*) in every time and place, it is in faith and good works."[79] Ibn Taymīya's pithiest textual witness to his position is a tradition in which the Prophet's Companion Abū'l-Dardā' writes to the Companion Salmān al-Fārisī, inviting him to Syria: "Come to the holy (lit., "sanctified") land!" Salmān replies, "Land does not sanctify anyone; a man is sanctified only by his actions."[80] If al-Subkī and Banīs locate holiness in propinquity to the Prophet, Ibn Taymīya locates it exclusively in acts of obedience.

The question of the homogeneity or the hierarchical differentiation of time was only one aspect of the problem. Another basic issue was its linearity or circularity. Even if some times (such as the occasions of the Prophet's birth and of his ascension to heaven) were distinguished by special blessings, their auspicious nature was available to latter-day believers only if they recurred cyclically.

Although this issue was rarely the subject of explicit debate, some authors did deny that this was the case. As we have seen, Ibn Taymīya's statements about the night of the Prophet's ascension indicate that it was a time of vast divine favor, but that its blessings applied to the Prophet himself rather than to the community at large. Its lack of relevance to the community may well have resulted from the fact that, in Ibn Taymīya's view, it was a one-time event experienced by the Prophet at some point in the past; the Night of Destiny, in contrast, was a yearly occasion whose blessings could be reaped by all believers. (Another possible explanation is that, like Friday, it was a recurring holy time; yet no specific acts of worship were mandated as a means of accessing its blessings.)

Indeed, the yearly recurrence of the Night of Destiny itself was occasionally questioned; the Qur'ānic commentator al-Fakhr al-Rāzī (d. 606 AH/1209 CE) cites the statement of al-Khalīl that "Anyone who says that the virtue of [the Night of Destiny] is because of the Qur'ān having been revealed on it says that it has ceased and happened [only] once (*inqaṭaʿat wa-kānat marra*); the majority holds that it remains."[81] In fact, a *ḥadīth* text both raises and resolves the question of whether the Night of Destiny is an ongoing cyclical event, or whether it has been discontinued. In the report, Abū Dharr asks the Prophet a series of questions about the Night of Destiny, including the following: "Does it exist with the prophets as long as they exist, and when they are withdrawn it is withdrawn (*wa-takūn maʿa al-anbiyāʾ mā kānū, fa-idhā rufiʿū rufiʿat*)?" The Prophet replies, "No; it will remain until the Resurrection Day."[82] While this text explicitly affirms that the Night of Destiny will recur until the end of time, it implies that times of special blessing are gifts of God that may be withdrawn, rather than intrinsic and permanent features of the revolving year. This raised the general question of whether the dates of noteworthy events were inherently recurring yearly events or merely points receding in the irrecoverable past.

The issue of whether the Prophet's birthday was an annual occasion or simply a unique, bygone historical event is clearly one that had already been raised and disputed by the time of Ibn Marzūq. "Know that there should be no dispute that the specific night on which the Messenger of God was born is superior to every other night, categorically, by reason of that which occurred on it," Ibn Marzūq declares.

> The discussion is, rather, about the nights of [each] year corresponding to it; this is what is being considered in comparison to the Night of Destiny. If you were to say, "Evidence demonstrates that that which distinguishes the Night of Destiny is present every year, based on the predominant opinion that it remains and has not been withdrawn; [in contrast], with respect to the night of the *mawlid* no evidence has been established that it must be considered [to occur] every year. Thus, one must consider the Night of Destiny superior," I would say: "There is evidence demonstrating that its virtue must be observed on the basis of its time recurring."

Ibn Marzūq then cites the *isnād* and text of the *ḥadīth* in which the Prophet is asked why he fasts on Monday and replies that it is the day on which he was born and on which he first received revelation (and according to another version cited by Ibn Marzūq, also the day on which his Prophetic mission began). After supplying a number of references for the *ḥadīth*, Ibn Marzūq concludes, "This *ḥadīth* establishes that the virtue of the night of the *mawlid* and its morning continues, and its honor remains." Ibn Marzūq emphasizes that the *ḥadīth* in question is indisputably authentic. In fact, he concludes, the continuing existence of the night of the *mawlid* is better authenticated than that of the Night of Destiny, about which there is some debate.[83]

A much more critical stance is adopted by Ibn Ḥajar al-Haytamī, who frames his *mawlid* text both as a model for the celebration of the *mawlid* and as a critique of the wilder claims made on its behalf. Responding to the arguments in favor of the superiority of the night of the *mawlid* over the Night of Destiny, he argues that

> if it is intended that this night and its anniversary in every year until the Resurrection is superior to the Night of Destiny, these proofs do not [logically] demonstrate that, as is evident; if what is intended is that particular night, the Night of Destiny did not exist at that time.... They never occurred together (*lam yakun ijtimā'uhā*) so that it would be possible to judge which one of them was superior. Rather, that [i.e., the *mawlid*] is a narrative (*qiṣṣa*) [about a past event], and this [i.e., the Night of Destiny] remains until the Resurrection; the Lawgiver has explicitly stated its superiority, and He did not mention the superiority of the night of [the Prophet's] birth or its anniversaries at all.

al-Haytamī concludes that it is permissible to say, in view of the sublimity of the Prophet, that the night of the *mawlid* itself (i.e., the unique event that occurred at the beginning of his earthly life) had honor (*sharaf*), even over the Night of Destiny. This does not entail that it is inherently (*min ḥaythu dhātihā*) superior to the Night of Destiny. Regardless, great favors will accrue to anyone who witnesses the appearance of God's benefaction in creating the Prophet on the anniversary of its occurrence and holds it as a vigil.[84]

Conclusion

J.Z. Smith cites a Christian scholar's observation that before the fourth century "Christian worship had been supra-historical in its relationship to [Jesus's] humanity." Up to that time, the single paramount festival of Easter "commemorated simultaneously the Incarnation, the Redemption, the Resurrection, and the Ascension." From the fourth century onwards, the development of sacred sites in Palestine led to increasing interest in Jesus's earthy career; the result was the proliferation and differentiation of festivals commemorating individual events in his life.[85] As a result, Smith argues, "Christian ritual, once brought into contact in the fourth century with the *loca sancta* of Palestine, turned from the vertical dimension of the associative to the linear dimension of the syntagmatic, to an emphasis on narrative and temporal relations."[86]

Of course, there is no direct parallel between the Christian and Muslim cases; Muslims never lacked access to the holy places of the Hijaz, and there was no historical juncture at which they discovered or rediscovered the sites of the Prophet's life and activity. Muslims also never developed an elaborate liturgical calendar. However, in the development of the *mawlid* celebration it is possible to detect in embryonic form both trends Smith describes.

The proliferation of "special times" of popular celebration and devotion in the Islamic calendar was paralleled by a tendency to commemorate the most important events of the Prophet's life. Chief among these were the *mawlid* itself and the anniversary of the Prophet's miraculous night journey to Jerusalem and ascension to heaven, the *isrā'*, and *mi'rāj*. In addition, *mawlid* texts display a strong tendency to identify the first Friday of Rajab – the occasion for the performance of the *raghā'ib* prayers – as the date of the Prophet's conception. As we have seen in Chapter 1, popular narratives depicted the beginning of Āmina's pregnancy as an event surrounded by miraculous happenings. Among Shī'ites, the Prophet's conception was cited by Ibn Bābawayh as an appropriate occasion for religious commemoration. Among Sunnīs, the idea that the Prophet was conceived amidst cosmic rejoicing on a Friday in Rajab is circulated in the *mawlid* literature as early as al-Qurṭubī (d. 671 AH/1273 CE); he attributes the story to the mystic Sahl al-Tustarī (d. 283 AH/896 CE) through the traditionist al-Khaṭīb al-Baghdādī (d. 463 AH/1071 CE).[87] The identification of the night of the *raghā'ib* with the conception of the Prophet does not seem to have successfully asserted itself in the mainstream scholarly literature, even in the context of condemnations of the practice. It did not completely prevail even in the popular literature; al-Bakrī's *Anwār*, for instance, places the event on a Friday that fell on the eve of 'Arafa (i.e., in Dhū'l-Ḥijja).[88] However, it is a widespread idea within the *mawlid* genre.[89]

Nevertheless, to adopt Smith's terminology, in Islamic piety the "horizontal" dimension never overcame the vertical. There was always a tendency to associate one occasion with an entire set of salvific events, rather than differentiating them into a series of separate observances. This tendency to conflate the dates of different acts of divine mercy was aided by the uncertainty in dating many important events. We have seen how, in his treatment of the Day of 'Āshūrā', Ibn Nāṣir al-Dīn emphasizes the occurrence of multiple significant events on the same day of the year. This convergence both intensifies the numinous nature of the day and gives it a transhistorical quality; its special blessings are manifested in different ways throughout the sweep of Islamic salvation history, from Noah's flood to the martyrdom of al-Ḥusayn. al-Qasṭallānī attributes a similarly dense convergence of blessed events to the day of the Prophet's birth in his discussion of the legitimacy of the *mawlid*. He cites a *ḥadīth* of Ibn 'Abbās from the *Musnad* of Aḥmad ibn Ḥanbal stating that the Prophet was born on a Monday, was commissioned as a prophet (*ustunbi'a*) on a Monday, departed Mecca for the hijra on a Monday, arrived in Medina on a Monday, and (an event that here appears out of chronological order) lifted the Black Stone into place in the Ka'ba on a Monday. al-Qasṭallānī adds that the Conquest of Mecca and the revelation of Sūrat al-Mā'ida (Chapter 5 of the Qur'ān) similarly occurred on Mondays.[90] A later *mawlid* author made similar claims for the month of the Prophet's birth, opening his text by praising "God, who honored Rabīʿ al-Awwal with the birth of His Prophet, commissioned him in it as a prophet and a messenger to all peoples, commanded him in it to emigrate to Medina, completed His noble law, and took him to Himself in it at the end of his allotted lifespan."[91]

In the development of the *mawlid* festival, one can also trace a transition in Sunnī devotionalism from sacred points distributed in space to powerful moments distributed in time. When Ibn Jubayr visited Mecca in 579 AH/1184 CE, the birthplace of the Prophet was the most important in a set of holy birthplaces identified and embellished for veneration, including those of his daughter Fāṭima and his grandsons, al-Ḥasan and al-Ḥusayn.[92] These birthplaces were themselves only one category of a broad set of sacred places associated with events, large and small, in the life of the Prophet. Ibn Jubayr characterizes the birthplace of the Prophet himself as "the pure ground that was the first ground to touch his pure body."[93] Ibn Jubayr's account of his own visit to the Prophet's birthplace emphasizes the idea of physical contact with the location of the newborn Prophet's bodily presence. "We rubbed our cheeks on that sacred spot which is the birthplace of the most gracious newborn on the earth, and the spot touched by the purest and noblest of offspring."[94] The Prophet's birthplace thus paralleled a large number of other sites where pilgrims sought physical contact with places or objects that the Prophet had touched.

By Ibn Jubayr's day, there was also a time component in the veneration of the Prophet's birthplace. Ibn Jubayr describes how this "blessed place," as well as the other holy sites of Mecca, was opened on Mondays during the month of Rabīʿ al-Awwal so that the people could enter and enjoy its *baraka*.[95] It seems that the site may also have been open on Mondays in the other months of the year, as Ibn Jubayr visited and touched the spot on a Monday in Dhū al-Qaʿda. A category including all Mondays and an entire month of the year, however, was probably too diffuse to generate a strong sense of sacred time. The source of *baraka* at these times, furthermore, continued to be the location of the Prophet's birth; the ruling category was spatial. This fact is reflected in a shift in the primary usage of the word "*mawlid*." For Ibn Jubayr, the word quite clearly means "birthplace"; he uses it to designate the Prophet's birthplace as well as those of other venerated figures. A century later, of course, the word "*mawlid*" would refer first and foremost to the time of the Prophet's birth.

Given that a mosque was built over the Prophet's birthplace by the ʿAbbāsid queen mother Khayzurān (d. 173 AH/789 CE), it seems that its veneration preceded even the earliest calendrical observances of the Prophet's birth.[96] The celebration of the *mawlid* as a temporal festival commemorating a specific event in the Prophet's life seems to be rooted in the embellishment and veneration of a complex of holy sites in the sacred territory of the rise of Islam. The extension of the *baraka* of the Prophet's birth from a unique geographical location to a universally recurring time (whether of the week or of the year) made it available to ordinary Muslims in all regions of the Islamic world.

J.Z. Smith notes Stefan Czarnowski's finding that "in the process of forming a national [Irish] community, the celebrations of those heros whose feast days are marked out in time, rather than being distributed in different places, supply the unifying occasions."[97] Both the practice of *ta'rīf* and that of invoking blessings on the Prophet in contexts such as the *mawlid* (which emphasized the latter's accessibility and responsiveness to those distant from his actual grave), opened up opportunities for meritorious action to those physically distant from the sacred centers of the Islamic world or without means for travel. Both the *ḥajj* to Mecca and the visit to the Prophet's grave that frequently accompanied it must have presented insuperable obstacles to many individuals limited in resources, feeble in body, or tied by responsibilities to children and spouses. Only the rare religious virtuoso could achieve these experiences on a regular basis. The dates of the "standing" at 'Arafa and the birth of the Prophet, in contrast, reliably returned with their gifts of blessing for persons of all stations. As long as the Prophet's *mawlid* was a location, it could be relevant only to that minority of Muslims who were able to visit Mecca; when it was redefined as a point in time as well as in space, it eventually became a ubiquitous (if disputed) element of Muslim practice around the globe.

It is frequently observed that the Islamic calendar's paucity of canonical festivals and its intentional de-coupling from the seasons of the solar year generate an unusually spare ritual calendar. Hava Lazarus-Yafeh has observed that Islam's "festival culture is rather meagre," and that even its two canonical festivals "lack specific ritual observances and specific associations with the seasons of the year or with historical or religious events."[98] Works such as Ibn Rajab's illustrate the extent to which some scholars invested the months and seasons of the Islamic year with texture and content, endowing the cycle of time with a rich religious significance. The widespread thirst for supplementary festivals did not, however, merely represent a popular desire for variety and diversion (although this may certainly have been a factor). It also reflected a desire for supplementary means to salvation, perhaps particularly for those whose adherence to the canonical requirements of Islamic law was less than flawless. Abū Shāma's remarks about the *raghā'ib* prayers illustrate how popular demand drove the observance of special occasions for the generation of religious merit.

In several insightful pieces, Tilman Nagel has suggested that the linear time of Islamic salvation history presents a disturbingly stark prospect for the ordinary believer cherishing hopes for salvation. Unlike the cyclical conceptions of time that prevailed before the rise of Jewish prophetic teachings, Islamic time proceeds ineluctably towards a single end, the fearsome events of the Day of Judgment. "In the face of this judgment," Nagel writes, "all of a human being's acts and omissions take on a unique and unalterable meaning. For it is the implication of a world history that tends towards (*zustrebenden*) the Last Day that good deeds are recorded for ever and errors can never be erased or corrected." Nagel argues that the "merciless linearity" of this historical progression is "intolerable" for the ordinary believer, who – unlike the small elite of spiritual virtuosi – is unable to devote his life to the fulfillment of the divine commandments. The unrepeatable and uncorrectable nature of actions in a unilinear, unidirectional salvation history is bearable only for a minority of believers, and the three Abrahamic monotheisms deal with the resultant tensions in varying ways, including the festival of Yom Kippur and the sacrament of confession.[99]

Elsewhere, Nagel has argued that the genre of *ḥadīth* itself represents a context in which the Prophet's actions are made imaginatively present, giving the individual believer access to the salvific power of his life and person.[100] Islamic debates over the nature of special times and the issue of their cyclical recurrence also address the questions raised by the relentless linearity of Islamic salvation history. However, the celebration of the *mawlid* (and that of analogous holidays, such as the *mi'rāj*) never implied a truly cyclical conception of time. *Mawlid* authors never envisioned the actual recapitulation of the Prophet's birth. When participants were invited to imagine the Prophet as present at the moment of the *qiyām*, they seem to have envisioned the adult Prophet rather than a newborn infant. To the extent that the devotional conception of time envisioned a cyclical element, it can be understood as an ascending spiral rather than a circle: while proceeding inexorably into the future, it also had a circular component which cyclically brought close the blessings of great events at corresponding times of the week, month, or year. The *mawlid* did not represent the return of the time of the Prophet's birth, but the availability of its blessings.

Vast harvests of blessing and merit could wipe clean the sins of ordinary believers whose daily lives fell far short of the ideal demands of the *sharī'a*. The content of the invocations appended to *mawlid* texts, as well as the narratives of conversion and blessing they often contain, suggest the integral connection of the *mawlid* celebration with the hope for individual salvation. *Mawlid*s represent a "little path" to salvation, one far more accessible than the rigors of strict daily adherence to the *sharī'a* (although it certainly did not release believers from these obligations); and this alternative path is fundamentally linked to a modification of the relentless linearity of the Islamic conception of time. The single line of Islamic history, with the salvific acts of the life of the Prophet receding inexorably in the past as the Day of Judgment approached ineluctably in the future, might well fill the ordinary believer with terror. A festival that brought the events of the Prophet's life within reach, recovering them from their temporal remoteness and making accessible their abundant blessings, redressed the imbalance. No longer did redemption recede into the distance while judgment loomed ever closer; the intimate accessibility of the Prophet closed the gap.

5 *Mawlids* under attack

In the eighteenth and nineteenth century CE, the celebration of the Prophet's birthday and the recitation of *mawlid* texts were ubiquitous practices endorsed by the majority of mainstream Sunnī scholars. As we have seen, the legal status of *mawlid* observances was disputed from quite early in the history of the Sunnī celebration, and dissenters never ceased to exist. However, by the modern period the celebration of the *mawlid* was overwhelmingly accepted and practiced by Muslims at all levels of religious education and authority. Prominent elite scholars continued to contribute to the development of the tradition. The author of one of the most beloved *mawlid* texts in history, Ja'far ibn Ḥasan ibn 'Abd al-Karīm al-Barzanjī (d. 1177 AH/1764 CE), was a respected jurist who served as the Shāfi'ī *muftī* of Medina.[1] While it is relatively brief and avoids the more extreme excesses of the popular *mawlid* tradition, al-Barzanjī's text incorporates elements of the popular tradition that had clearly become the common coin of *mawlid* narrative. Thus, for instance, his *mawlid* refers to the attendance of Āsiya, Maryam, and other heavenly handmaidens at the Prophet's birth.[2] al-Barzanjī also affirms the practice of standing at the mention of the Prophet's birth, although the pointedness with which he does so suggests that the custom must have had its detractors.[3] Another of the most popular *mawlid* works of the modern period was composed by Aḥmad al-Dardīr (d. 1201 AH/1786 CE), a Mālikī jurist and Khalwatī *shaykh* who also produced an influential legal handbook.[4] al-Dardīr reproduces a full spectrum of traditional *mawlid* material, including the cosmogonic narrative attributed to Jābir al-Anṣārī.[5]

The degree of seriousness with which *mawlid* texts were regarded is indicated by the composition of commentaries (*shurūḥ*) on the more important works. Barzanjī's *mawlid*, for instance, was the subject of commentaries by his descendant Ja'far ibn Ismā'īl al-Barzanjī (1317 AH/1899–1900 CE), a Shāfi'ī muftī of Medina, and by Muḥammad 'Ulaysh (d. 1299 AH/1881 CE), the Mālikī muftī of Egypt; one nineteenth-century author went so far as to remark that "all of the most accomplished scholars engaged in commenting on it."[6] The *mawlid* of al-Dardīr was the subject of a commentary by Ḥusayn ibn Ibrāhīm ibn Ḥusayn ibn 'Āmir, who became the Mālikī muftī of Mecca in 1262 AH/1846 CE,[7] and another by the rector of al-Azhar, Ibrāhīm al-Bājūrī (d. 1276 AH/1859–60 CE), who also produced a commentary on the *mawlid* of Ibn Ḥajar al-Haytamī.[8] al-Haytamī's *mawlid* was the object of at least four more commentaries in the eighteenth- and nineteenth-centuries CE, including one by the Syrian muftī Aḥmad ibn ʿĀbidīn (d. 1307 AH/1889 CE).[9]

The celebration of the *mawlid* also flourished on the official level throughout the nineteenth century. A state celebration of the day was introduced in Tunis by the modernizing Bey Aḥmad I (ruled 1253–71 AH/1837–55 CE). It included the illumination of minarets, the distribution of gifts and alms by the bey, and a procession of scholars and notables from the palace to the Great Mosque. The ceremony in the mosque featured a reading of a *mawlid* text by the distinguished North African Mālikī scholar Ibrāhīm al-Riyāḥī (d. 1266 AH/1850 CE).[10] At the line "So stand, O you who desire to gain intercession," the bey and all present rose to their feet; as they intoned "amen," a 101-gun salute rang out. The *mawlid* reading closed with a recitation of the first chapter of the Qur'ān and the distribution of sugared and perfumed water. After Aḥmad Bey's death, Aḥmad Jamāl al-Dīn al-Tūnisī reports, he appeared in a dream to declare, "I have been forgiven [my sins] because of my celebration of the Prophet's birthday." His successor ʿAlī Bey (ruled 1299–1320 AH/1882–1902 CE) added a second *mawlid* reading in a mosque that he had founded, using the *mawlid* text of al-Barzanjī.[11]

An even more elaborate celebration is described in Cairo in the reign of Khedive Tawfīq (ruled 1296–1309 AH/1879–92 CE), one that apparently both continued and enhanced the practices of his predecessors. The influential government minister ʿAlī Pasha Mubārak approvingly recounts a lavish twelve-day festival involving the erection of pavilions representing the various ṣūfī orders in a place and order determined by the government, night-time performances of *dhikr* and recitations of the Prophet's *mawlid*, illumination with candles, and the bestowal of robes of honor by the supreme ṣūfī *shaykh*. On the last day of the *mawlid* celebration, the khedive bestowed a visit on the tent of the head *shaykh* and bestowed upon him a robe of honor "from the government." On the final night, the *mawlid* was recited in the presence of the khedive, the leading figures of the government, the religious scholars, and other dignitaries. The legitimizing role of these festivities is apparent, particularly when ʿAlī Pasha Mubārak enthusiastically describes the erection of tents representing the various ministries of the government along with those of the ṣūfī orders.[12] The Ottoman sultan Abdülhamid also used the Prophet's birthday as an occasion to enact his own benevolence and religious legitimacy, among other things by having candy distributed to schoolchildren and cash bonuses to personnel of the Education Ministry.[13] Overall, in the nineteenth century the celebration of the Prophet's birthday was a widespread practice endorsed and sponsored by the mainstream religious and political establishments of the Middle East.

Wahhābī opposition

At the same time, a new challenge to the legitimacy of *mawlid* celebrations arose with the emergence of the religious trend initiated by Muḥammad ibn ʿAbd al-Wahhāb (d. 1206 AH/1792 CE). Opposing all religious innovations (*bidaʿ*), he and his followers naturally objected to the celebration of the Prophet's birthday and the recitation of *mawlid* narratives. They also argued that devotional expressions of veneration for the Prophet (as well as other holy personages) sometimes violated the stringent demands of monotheism by infringing on God's exclusive right to worship. On the occasion of the conquest of Mecca in 1218 AH/1803 CE, his son 'Abd Allāh issued a proclamation that outlined the movement's positions on a number of issues, including objectionable innovations. "Among them," he wrote,

> is gathering at a specific time around someone who recites the story of the noble birth (*sīrat al-mawlid al-sharīf*), believing that it is a prescribed and required act of piety, distinct from knowledge of the [other] events of the Prophet's life (*qurba makhṣūṣa maṭlūba dūna 'ilm al-siyar*); that has not been transmitted [from the Prophet].

He also objected to more elaborate *mawlid* ceremonies, with which he was apparently familiar only by hearsay from other locations:

> Among them is the custom in some countries of reciting the Prophet's *mawlid* with verses set to music, and interspersed with the invocation of prayers upon him, *adhkār*, and [Qur'ānic] recitation. It occurs after the *tarāwīḥ* prayers [at night, during Ramaḍān], and they believe that performing it in this fashion is an act of piety (*min al-qurab*); the common people even believe that that is a *sunna* transmitted [from the Prophet], so that should be forbidden.[14]

Saudi control of the Ḥijāz was short-lived, however, and in the nineteenth century Wahhābī opposition did not succeed in marginalizing the performance of *mawlid*s even within Mecca. In fact, mainstream scholarly antipathy towards the Wahhābīs seems to have invigorated support for the practice, particularly among the Ḥijāzī establishment. It may not be completely coincidental that, as discussed earlier, a number of *mawlid*s and commentaries on *mawlid*s were produced by *muftī*s of Mecca and Medina in the nineteenth century CE. A *fatwā* in support of the *mawlid* celebration is attributed to the Ḥanafī *muftī* of Mecca, Jamāl ibn 'Umar al-Makkī (d. 1284 AH/1867 CE.), an opinion which was reportedly endorsed by the Mālikī and Shāfi'ī *muftī*s. A similar opinion is reported from a subsequent Ḥanafī *muftī* of Mecca, 'Abd al-Raḥmān Sirāj (d. 1314 AH/1896 CE).[15] The latter is also reported to have produced a polemic in support of the practice of *qiyām*, stating that it had become an emblem of membership in the Sunnī community (*ṣāra shi'āran li-ahl al-sunna wa'l-jamā'a*) and that failing to perform it was a sign of religious deviation. This opinion as well is supposed to have been endorsed by several prominent scholars, suggesting that it was an issue of public interest.[16]

The social and religious centrality of *mawlid* ceremonies also emerges from the writings of the Dutch Orientalist Snouck Hurgronje, whose rich descriptions are based on a half year's residence in Mecca in 1884–5. The annual public celebration of the Prophet's birthday involved an unusual mass attendance of women and children at prayers in the mosque, a recitation of the *mawlid* in the presence of government dignitaries, and a torchlit procession to the house where the Prophet was born.[17] Hurgronje recounts that in Meccan households, *mawlid* ceremonies were a routine feature of the celebration of joyful family occasions, to the point that "It is not all the guests that know whether it is a circumcision, a marriage, a happy return from a journey, or what else may have occasioned the invitation. 'It is a *môlid*': that is enough.... In short the *môlid* is appropriate to all festivities."[18]

A particularly strong endorsement of *mawlid* celebrations and narratives was expressed by Hurgronje's contemporary, the influential Shāfi'ī *muftī* of Mecca, Aḥmad ibn Zaynī Daḥlān (d. 1304 AH/1886 CE).[19] In his widely read biography of the Prophet, he supports the legitimacy of both the *mawlid* ceremony and the practice of *qiyām* with a survey of affirmative opinions by classical scholars.[20] In a series of *fatwā*s issued to Indonesian questioners, Aḥmad Daḥlān expresses reservations only about the casual spirit in which some *mawlid* readings were conducted. He objects to smoking, chatting, and other forms of diversion during the reading, and recommends that participants should listen in a humble spirit of reflection. In response to a question about the precise point at which one should stand in honor of the Prophet's birth, he replies that this may occur at any point where the event is alluded to in the text. The question suggests that his listeners, at least, considered the *qiyām* a legitimate ritual action potentially subject to detailed legal prescriptions.[21]

Similar to al-Barzanjī, Daḥlān also knew and disseminated noncanonical narratives about the Prophet's birth. In his biography of the Prophet, he recounts the following:

> [It is transmitted] from Āmina, the mother of the Prophet, that she said: When I went into labor,[22] I saw women as tall as palm trees resembling the daughters of 'Abd Manāf surrounding me. I have never seen anyone with faces as luminous as theirs. It was as if one of the women came forward to me; I leaned against her and went into labor, and my birth pangs became intense. It was as if one of them came forward to me and handed me a drink of water whiter than milk, colder than ice, and sweeter than honey. She said to me, "Drink!" and I drank. Then the second one said, "Take more!" and I took more. Then she rubbed my belly with her hand and said, "In the name of God, come out with the permission of God!" Then they – those women – said to me, "We are Asiya, the wife of Pharaoh and Maryam, the daughter of 'Imrān, and those are some of the wide-eyed houris."[23]

Interestingly, this passage precisely reproduces no literary source for this popular narrative; rather, it probably reflects oral retelling of a ubiquitous story about the Prophet's birth. The fact that a religious authority of the stature of Daḥlān reproduces it in a historical work bespeaks the essential continuity between folk and learned attitudes to the *mawlid* in his time.

Daḥlān's enthusiasm for the *mawlid* was clearly only invigorated by Wahhābī attacks; some of his most energetic argumentation in support of the celebration appears in an anti-Wahhābī polemic. In his diatribe *al-Durar al-sanīya*, he deplores the fact that the Wahhābīs denounce all expressions of veneration (*ta'ẓīm*) for the Prophet as manifestations of polytheism (*shirk*). Daḥlān argues that, on the contrary, it is religiously legitimate to honor the Prophet in any way that does not ascribe to him the attributes of Godhead (*al-rubūbīya*). On the contrary, in the Qur'ān God has both exalted the Prophet and instructed us to honor him. This commandment is contained in verses 22:32 ("Whoever honors the symbols of God, it is of the piety of hearts") and 22:30 ("Whoever honors the sacrosanct things of God, it is a good thing for him in the sight of his Lord"). As long as the Prophet is not described with the attributes of divinity, exalting him is thus "among the greatest of acts of obedience and devotion" to God (*min a'ẓam al-ṭā'āt wa'l-qurubāt*). The first example that Daḥlān adduces of the exaltation of the Prophet that he believes to be enjoined by these verses is "rejoicing in the night of his birth, reciting the *mawlid*, standing up at the mention of his birth, serving food, and the other kinds of good deeds that people are accustomed to perform."[24]

Daḥlān does not cite sources for this argumentation, and it is unclear whether this line of reasoning originates with him. However, it seems to reflect a significant strengthening and reframing of arguments in favor of the *mawlid* celebration. By construing the *mawlid* celebration as a direct fulfillment of a Qur'ānic commandment, Daḥlān secures it a much more central place in the schema of Islamic legal obligation than had been envisioned by premodern *mawlid* apologists. The argument reflects a new and de-contextualized understanding of the two Qur'ānic verses in question, which are traditionally understood to refer specifically to the rites of the ḥajj.

The continuing marginality of Wahhābī opposition to the *mawlid* within the Ḥijāz in the late-nineteenth century is suggested by an enquiry from "many of the people of the two Noble Sanctuaries" (i.e., Mecca and Medina) to the Shāfi'ī scholar Muḥammad al-Hijrasī in 1303 AH/1886 CE. The questioners express their concern that the *mawlid* festival (*mihrajān*) may fall within the purview of the *ḥadīth* stating that "every innovation is misguidance" (*kull bid'a ḍalāla*). On the one hand, they are aware that the *mawlid* celebration began in the seventh-century AH, and would thus seem to be an innovation. On the other hand, they find it so ubiquitous and uncontroversial that they are incredulous that it might be illegitimate. "What is the legal status (*ḥukm*)," they ask, "of this thing that has spread to all regions of the Islamic world, in the presence of the *'ulamā'*, for nine centuries [*sic*] past and to this time, with no opposition except from the Wahhābī sect, which has departed from the religion by declaring the majority of Muslims unbelievers . . . .?" al-Hijrasī reassures them that not all innovations are illegitimate.[25]

Much more than the *mawlid* celebration itself, the *qiyām* was consistently subject to criticism in scholarly circles. In contrast to their claim that only the Wahhābīs oppose the celebration of the *mawlid*, al-Hijrasī's questioners point out that even some orthodox scholars (*ba'ḍ [al-]'ulamā' min ahl al-sunna*) disapprove of standing when the reciter of the *mawlid* reaches the statement "she gave birth to him"; indeed, some go yet further and claim that the *qiyām* is forbidden (*ḥarām*).[26] However, opposition seems only to have intensified the commitment of the practice's supporters. al-Hijrasī replies forcefully, underlining his positions with oaths: "By God, if the gate of *ijtihād* were not closed I would rule that this standing was a religious obligation, particularly in this time, in which faith has come to be in people's eyes and not in their hearts." He continues, "By God, I am of the opinion that anyone who refrains from standing out of disdain and arrogance is without doubt openly proclaiming his disbelief (*fa-huwa lā shakk mu'lin bi'l-kufr jihāran*)." In fact, he claims that the performance of the *qiyām* was once strictly enforced by the authorities. "It seems to me (*yukhayyalu ilayya*)," he muses,

> that I heard from [one of] the great *muftī*s of Medina the Radiant that he heard from the teachers of his teachers that a learned man refrained from standing when the birth of the Master of Mankind was mentioned. They asked him about [the reason for] his failure to stand and he said that it was because he disapproved. They issued a legal opinion that he was an unbeliever (*aftaw bi-kufrihi*) and subjected him to the dire penalty he deserved (*adhāqūhu wabāla 'āqibat amrihi*).[27]

The increasingly assertive endorsement of *mawlid* celebrations by early-twentieth-century scholars confronted by the rise of Wahhābism is also illustrated by the example of Muḥammad 'Alī ibn Ḥusayn al-Mālikī (d. 1368 AH/1949 CE). A scholar in the fields of Arabic language and pedagogy as well as of Islamic law, he served as the Mālikī *muftī* of Mecca. In his anti-Wahhābī polemic *al-Ṣārim al-mubīd li-munkir ḥikmat al-taqlīd*, al-Mālikī declares the celebration of the *mawlid* desirable (*mustaḥabb*) according to the *sharī'a*.[28] al-Mālikī goes even farther in his commentary on al-Qarāfī's *Furūq*, completed during a visit to Indonesia around the time of the Saudi conquest of the Holy Places in 1924.[29] He cites an opinion attributed to the sixteenth-century CE Ottoman *muftī* Abū al-Su'ūd, stating that the practice of standing at the mention of the Prophet's birth has become such a prevalent expression of respect that omitting to perform it is a sign of indifference and disdain towards the Prophet; thus, failing to stand is a form of *kufr* (unbelief). al-Mālikī qualifies this extreme opinion only by noting that it is *kufr* only if the one failing to stand is conscious that his inaction is a form of contempt.[30]

Modernist critiques

Outside of the Arabian Peninsula, the first sustained and effective modern critiques of the *mawlid* celebration were presented by reformist thinkers in the early-twentieth century. They shared the Wahhābīs' concern with strict fidelity to the practice of the earliest Muslims (and thus may share the broad designation of *salafīya*), but combined it with a concern for the advancement of Muslim religion and society in the modern world. Similar to ʻAbd Allāh ibn Muḥammad ibn ʻAbd al-Wahhāb, they recognized the *mawlid* to be formidably well established, particularly among ordinary believers. In 1918, Rashīd Riḍā expressed his concern that the majority of Egyptians regarded standing at the mention of the Prophet's birth during the *mawlid* recitation a legitimate ritual mandated by Islamic law.

> It may be that most common people (*al-ʻawāmm*) believe that this standing is obligatory, because the religious scholars and everyone else adhere to it. If they became aware that someone was omitting it, they would consider him a sinner making light of the religion or an unbeliever abandoning it. If you were to suggest to a group of religious scholars who attend the recitation of the story of the *mawlid* that they omit [to stand] some of the time so that the common people would know that it was not obligatory, they might not dare to do so.[31]

In Riḍā's time, the Prophet's *mawlid* continued to be observed not merely as a private devotional ceremony, but as a major state celebration. After presenting a summary of Ibn Khallikān's eyewitness account of Kökbürī's celebration of the *mawlid*, Riḍā writes that he has done so "because what is done in Egypt now resembles what used to be done in Irbil, except that it is lesser in pomp and in cost." His description of the state-sponsored festivities (which featured pavilions erected for government ministries, some of which were now illuminated with electric lights, feasting involving both ṣūfīs and dignitaries of the state, the recital of the *mawlid* in the presence of the ruler, and a display of fireworks) largely resembles that of ʻAlī Pasha Mubārak.[32] Riḍā is surely correct in perceiving a resemblance between the Egyptian government's patronage of the *mawlid* festival in his own day and the tradition of government largesse established early in the history of the Sunnī *mawlid* festival. As the example of the Tunisian beys illustrates, the *mawlid* remained a prime occasion for the performance of religious ideals of benevolence and piety, as well as for the display of governmental pomp. Riḍā also notes that the popularity of the *mawlid* extends far beyond the sphere of governmental patronage. The masses of Muslims throughout the world approve of the celebration of the *mawlid*. They gather to hear recitations of the *mawlid* narrative (*qiṣṣa*) in mosques, and hold private gatherings for this purpose in their homes – even on dates other than the birthday of the Prophet.[33]

Unfortunately, Riḍā does not identify the *mawlid* narrative (*qiṣṣa*) that was recited on the occasion of the Egyptian state *mawlid* celebration in his day, nor does he single out specific texts in popular use in Egypt. In general, he limits his criticism to a blanket condemnation of the genre. "Many people," he notes, "have written *mawlid* narratives (*mawālid*) that they stuffed with fabricated and deviant *ḥadīth* texts; some of them [even] contain improper descriptions of the Prophet, such as amorous descriptions of his beauty."[34] It is possible that Riḍā was unfamiliar with the *mawlid* genre, or that he simply did not desire to dignify what he considered disreputable texts with more formal citations. It seems more likely, however, that the popular Egyptian *mawlid* tradition was a rather fluid one in which individual performers collected, selected, and presented materials from a common stock of well-known narratives.

An example of this phenomenon is provided by a somewhat earlier *fatwā*, written by Riḍā in response to a query sent from Dimyāṭ in 1905. The questioner, an instructor in one of the local schools, wrote in response to an event that had recently transpired in the town's main mosque on the occasion of the night of *niṣf Sha'bān* (itself a noncanonical festival). Taking advantage of the large audience afforded by the crowds gathered for the occasion, an unnamed individual with pretensions to religious learning took his place on the elevated seat reserved for formal instruction. "He began by enumerating copious benefits of listening to the story of the Prophet's *mawlid*," then presented a long *mawlid* narrative, only some of which the scandalized questioner was able to remember. Among the points he did recall and reproduce were the claim that the Prophet's light was the first thing created by God, and that from it all other things were created; that Adam paid Eve's *mahr* by invoking blessings upon the Prophet; that all of the animals of the land and sea congratulated each other on the night of the Prophet's conception, speaking in clear Arabic; that Maryam, Sārah, and Āsiya attended the Prophet's birth because they will be his wives in Paradise; that all the prophets were born through an opening in their mothers' right side, and that anyone who believes that they were born through the vagina is a *kāfir*; and that Muḥammad and all of the prophets are alive in their graves.[35]

The details of these motifs, all of which (with the exception of the denial of the prophets' vaginal birth) are sufficiently familiar from the *mawlid* texts of the premodern tradition, suggest that they were subject to improvisation and elaboration in the Egyptian folk context. For instance, this particular version of the motif of Adam's *mahr* states that God initially set a bridal payment of one hundred prayers upon the Prophet. Adam complied, but was able to perform only seventy of the blessings; God remitted the remaining thirty. This, the story concludes, was the basis for the custom of dividing the bridal payment into prompt and delayed portions. Similarly, the motif of the heavenly handmaidens who assisted at the Prophet's birth was subject to elaboration; this individual recounted that some scholars claim that Āsiya never died, but was raised alive to heaven when she appealed for God's protection from Pharaoh. A *mawlid* such as this one probably had no formal title or authorship, and was probably fluid in its details. However, it represented a rich and continuous tradition of *mawlid* narrative. Although Riḍā's questioner provides no specifics about the "copious benefits of listening to the story of the Prophet's *mawlid*" that were presented by this individual, it is tempting to suspect that he recited some version of the text on the "virtues of the *mawlid*" that had already been in circulation for at least a century (if not much longer), as described in Chapter 2. Modern Egyptians thus continued the tradition of *mawlid* narration that we have observed for earlier centuries, combining an element of flexibility and improvisation with a high degree of stability and consensus on the core elements of the *mawlid* story.

Riḍā responded to the fabulous content of popular *mawlid* narratives by composing an alternative text of his own. He embarked on this enterprise with some misgivings. Riḍā had no inherent objection to the presentation of material about the Prophet on the occasion of his birth. "As for the recitation of the story of the Prophet's birth (*al-mawlid*)," he writes, "it involves reading some *ḥadīth* and some of the life story of the Prophet (*al-sīra al-nabawīya*), as al-Suyūṭī said." The problem, he argues, is that people have composed texts known as "*mawlid*s" that are full of spurious and inappropriate material. "For years, I have wished that people had at their disposal essays (*rasā'il*) on this subject in which care was exercised to select correct and edifying [material], which might take the place of some of that harmful [*mawlid* literature] that exercises a bad influence," Riḍā writes. Nevertheless, "I wanted to avoid writing anything on that subject under the title of '*mawlid*', so that I would not be an innovator or an abettor or endorser of things that were not done by the pious early Muslims (*al-salaf al-ṣāliḥ*)."[36]

Riḍā recounts that he was finally persuaded to compose a work in honor of the Prophet's birthday on the occasion of *mawlid* celebration at the home of the supreme *shaykh* of the ṣūfī orders of Egypt, 'Abd al-Ḥamīd al-Bakrī, in 1916. After a banquet and a reading of the *mawlid* narrative, Riḍā approached al-Bakrī to discuss the *mawlid* texts that were in popular circulation and the need to change them. If Riḍā were to produce an alternative text, he asked, would al-Bakrī use it in place of the received narratives in the Egyptian state *mawlid* celebration and other observances of the *mawlid*? al-Bakrī replied in the affirmative, and Riḍā immediately set to work, doing much of his writing at al-Bakrī's home and regularly consulting him about the contents.[37] Since the resulting text was excessively long, Riḍā condensed it for recitation in the official *mawlid* celebration. It was presented in place of the traditional *mawlid* at the state celebration that very year. He then agreed to its publication, first in *al-Manār* and then as a separate book.[38]

Riḍā's *mawlid* text, published in extended form in *al-Manār* in 1916, represents an interesting but unstable religious and literary hybrid. The opening lines of the text carefully refer to it as an essay (*risāla*), the same word Riḍā used in expressing his hopes that new texts would be composed to replace traditional *mawlid*s. The word "essay," evoking a genre of expository writing, studiously avoids the ritual and performative connotations of the word "*mawlid*." However, the text itself cautiously deploys several of the formal markers of the traditional *mawlid* genre. The work proper opens with a brief rhymed introduction (*dībāja*) which, although quite truncated by traditional standards, would have responded to the established expectations of popular *mawlid* audiences. The opening passage finishes with the invocation of prayers upon the Prophet, framed in the first person plural (and thus possibly intended for audience participation).[39]

The extent to which such elements perpetuated popular *mawlid* practice is perhaps suggested by a critique of Riḍā's work published in the pages of *al-Manār*. The anonymous critic complains that Riḍā did well initially to refrain from composing an example of the *mawlid* genre, and accuses him of ultimately doing just that. He begins his detailed list of objections with the observation that each of the sections of Riḍā's composition closes with a "truncated" invocation of blessings on the Prophet. It would have been better, he argues, to print the text with instructions that it be read in the style of a sermon; this would have been more appropriate, and more distant from "the familiar form" (*al-ṣūra al-ma'lūfa*), presumably of traditional *mawlid*s.[40] (Riḍā somewhat weakly replies that there are, in fact, sections of the work that open without such blessings.[41]) What is clearly at stake in this exchange, outwardly picayune as it might seem, is the genre of the text. While traditional *mawlid* works are performative texts that, among other things, generate merit for participants through the invocation of blessings on the Prophet, the word "essay" (*risāla*) evokes the non-performative goal of communicating information. The critic's invocation of the form of a speech or sermon (*khiṭāba*) suggests an equally unproblematic model. By drawing attention to Riḍā's incorporation of the *ṣalāt 'alā al-nabī* into his new composition, the opponent associates it with the devotional model familiar from traditional *mawlid* celebrations.

Riḍā's effort to eliminate the ritual dimension from the recitation of *mawlid* texts reflects his overall critique of *mawlid* celebrations, which is based less on a general rejection of the celebration of the Prophet's birthday than on the fear of introducing illegitimate religious rituals (*'ibādāt*). Riḍā understands the Prophet's condemnation of *bida'* (innovations) to apply to religious rituals performed in a specific way, at a specific time or place. As long as such ritualization is avoided, and common people are not led to believe that the celebration of the *mawlid* in some prescribed fashion is a requirement of the religion, Riḍā has no objection to the commemoration of the day.[42] The fact that he incorporates some elements of the traditional *mawlid* genre into his new text, however, reflects the difficulty of making a clean break with a highly popular tradition; despite his reservations about traditional *mawlid*s, Riḍā undoubtedly hoped to legitimate his new text for a popular audience by adapting their customary form.

Riḍā writes that the objective of his work is "to remind people of a summary of the Prophet's history, so that the believers will remember God's favor (*minna*) in sending him and their spirits will be nourished with an increase in faith and perfect love for him, and will strive to establish his religion and revive his *sunna*."[43] In content, the text is a modernist biography of the Prophet that eliminates most of the supernatural and miraculous elements of the traditional story to emphasize the ethical and social progressiveness of the Prophet's mission. For instance, in place of the familiar narrative of the Light of Muḥammad there is a discussion of the reasons for God's placement of the Prophet's ancestry among the Arabs. Riḍā argues that the Arabs were distinguished for their independence of thought and their personal liberty, at a time when other peoples blindly followed the teachings of priests and kings. Arab society was also more egalitarian and less stratified than others of the day.[44] The version of the work originally presented at the Egyptian state *mawlid* apparently focused, like traditional *mawlid*s, on the Prophet's ancestry, birth, and youth; in the published version, Riḍā extended the story to include the Prophet's migration to Medina and the revelation of the Qur'ān. This was a significant shift away from popular *mawlid* conventions, and Riḍā noted that those presenting the work to uneducated audiences might wish to omit the section on God's selection of the Arabs, due to its difficulty of comprehension; in the interests of brevity, readers might also omit the story of the Prophet's migration.[45]

Riḍā's initial effort to appropriate some dimensions of the traditional *mawlid* genre was probably proven futile by his work's limited success in displacing popular texts. Fifteen years later, he wrote in the pages of *al-Manār* that his essay had "spread slowly" in the Islamic world, and that "its influence in reforming previous customs was weak." Riḍā's reformational efforts were refocused by an initiative started in India, which called for the observance of the Prophet's birthday as an occasion for international Islamic outreach.[46] This development fostered a shift away from the traditional focus on the auspicious cosmic event of the Prophet's birth, and towards general efforts at Islamic education. In 1931, for instance, a call was issued from Lahore for the submission of essays in honor of the *mawlid* on the rights of women in Islam; Riḍā produced a composition on this theme.[47]

Riḍā's original *mawlid* work displayed strong continuities with the tradition of scholarly *mawlid* writing that had flourished since the eighth-century AH, although he was apparently unaware of the existence of this older tradition of *mawlid* reform. Neither his determination to eliminate ill-authenticated reports nor his desire to shift the narrative focus to the events of Muḥammad's prophetic mission and the content of his message was new. In many ways, his adaptation of the *mawlid* genre (aside from his Islamic modernism) echoes the work of the "Damascus school" of *mawlid* composition (see Chapter 1). His later contributions, however, represent a complete departure from the premodern *mawlid* tradition. The subject of the Prophet's actual birth loses its appeal, and the performative genre of the premodern *mawlid* disappears in favor of the journal article and the conference speech. The modern, secular quality of these genres absolved them of the taint of ritualization – and thus, of religious innovation – that attached to traditional *mawlid*s.

Rashīd Riḍā was neither the first nor the last modern author to produce an alternative *mawlid* text. As early as 1904, *al-Manār* warned its readers against the *mawlid* texts in circulation, "of which we have seen none free of lies and forgeries." As a substitute, the journal urged its readers to obtain (by mail order or from its own bookstore) a new narrative composed by the Syrian reformist scholar Jamāl al-Dīn al-Qāsimī (d. 1332 AH/1914 CE), entitled *Shadhara min al-sīra al-muḥammadīya*.[48] Almost two decades after Riḍā produced his own composition, however, the Egyptian religious establishment was still in search of an ideal *mawlid* text for official use. A national competition judged by a committee from the Committee of Senior Scholars (*Hay'at Kibār al-'Ulamā'*) resulted in the selection of a work by 'Abd Allāh 'Afīfī (d. 1363 AH/1944 CE). The Ministry of Endowments designated it for use in official religious celebrations, and the rector of al-Azhar directed that it be broadcast on the radio and used in place of "the old *mawlid*s" (*al-mawālid al-qadīma*) – which evidently had yet to be superseded by the efforts of al-Qāsimī and Riḍā.[49]

Even more than Riḍā's *mawlid*, 'Afīfī's work draws on the formal conventions of traditional *mawlid* texts. It begins with a rhymed *dībāja*, and is interspersed at regular intervals with the invocation of prayers upon the Prophet and interludes of devotional verse. The rhymed couplet used as a *ta'ṭīra* adheres to the traditional form, but in content evokes more activist Islamic values: "O God, keep eternally alive his noble memory," the first line implores, "and give victory to his upright religion." The work ends with an "Islamic anthem" (*nashīd islāmī*) to be sung by Islamic organizations (*al-jamā'āt al-islāmīya*) after listening to the *mawlid* narrative. The verb used in the introduction to these verses (*tahtifu*) suggests that they are less a song than a cheer, evoking the atmosphere of an Islamic rally rather than a devotional gathering. The persistence of more traditional performative conventions is suggested, however, by the inclusion at the end of the printed text of an abridged version of the *mawlid*. The author notes that its composition was requested by the *shaykh* of the Qur'ān reciters (*al-muqri'īn*), who asked that selections of the work be rendered in rhymed prose so that they could be chanted to the traditional tune (*bi-naghmihā al-qadīm*).[50]

Reformist *mawlid*s were composed by a number of other authors; Syrian scholars were particularly productive in this regard. Such works continued to adapt the traditional forms of the *mawlid* genre while transforming its content. In their determined focus on the Prophet's mission, its impact on society, and the imperative for individual believers to emulate his example, such texts radically de-emphasized the significance of his birth. The Syrian Muḥammad Ṣāliḥ ibn Aḥmad al-Ḥalabī begins his "Contemporary *mawlid*" (*al-Mawlid al-'aṣrī*), composed in 1352 AH/1933 CE, by observing that despite constant progress and revision in science and other areas of life, *mawlid* narratives have scarcely changed. He offers his new *mawlid* to those who love scientific progress and Islamic reform (*iṣlāḥ*).[51] The body of the text begins by stating that "the prime objective of this splendid celebration is to remind (*tadhkīr*) those who celebrate of a summary of the history of [the Prophet's] life, so that they can emulate him and follow his *sunna*."[52] There follows a didactic recitation of the events of the Prophet's life, emphasizing his exemplary moral qualities and his reformation of society. Rather than the invocation of blessings on the Prophet, the work's refrain (presumably recited responsively by the participants) is the affirmation that "Muḥammad is a light that vanquished all darkness and illuminated all regions of the inhabited world." The piece culminates with the birth of the Prophet, while determinedly minimizing its inherent importance. Its final lines read, "[The Prophet's] gestation was normal, and the length of his gestation was normal; his birth was also normal. When God permitted that he appear in this human world, his mother went into labor and gave birth to him; he was a mercy to the worlds."[53]

Similar objectives are pursued by another Syrian *mawlid* author, Khayr al-Dīn al-Wānilī. (His work, although undated, bears an endorsement by the Ḥanbalī *muftī* of Damascus Muḥammad al-Shaṭṭī, who died in 1379 AH/1959 CE.) al-Wānilī states that because most *mawlid* texts do not fulfill the needs of the time, he has composed a new version of the Prophet's biography (*sīra*) "from which the reader will draw lessons and guidance." He notes that he has followed the "old style" (*al-nahj al-qadīm*) of *mawlid* composition, using rhymed prose to facilitate the work's recitation and memorization.[54] The work is organized in short sections dealing with the Prophet's ethical qualities and achievements. Similar to al-Ḥalabī's work, it culminates in a section on the Prophet's birth but succeeds in reducing the event to irrelevance; after several lines hailing the Prophet's achievements in civilizing and enlightening the world, it abruptly concludes, "Nine lunar months of Āmina's pregnancy were completed, and she gave birth to Muḥammad, the seal of the pure Prophets."[55]

While modern *mawlid*s such as al-Ḥalabī's and al-Wānilī's rather cleverly attempt to adapt the forms of the traditional genre and take advantage of its enduring popularity, the authors' religious objectives make their works' connection with traditional *mawlid* piety tenuous and problematic. Because they consider the Prophet Muḥammad a teacher and reformer rather than a figure in a cosmic drama of salvation, the events of his life before his commissioning as a prophet – including his birth – are of little interest to them. Because they are concerned with the ethical content of the Prophet's message rather than with the acquisition of merit by loving, blessing, and greeting him, the traditional conventions of the *mawlid* genre lose their significance. Once the *mawlid* has been re-defined as a purely educational endeavor, there is no reason why it should retain a specific ceremonial form or a link with the date of the Prophet's birthday; as al-Wānilī notes in his introduction, the Prophet's life story should not merely be recited on specific occasions, but should be studied from trustworthy sources at all times.[56] Of course, instructing ordinary believers in the basic facts of the Prophet's biography had been an objective of *mawlid* composition as early as al-'Azafī. In an era of widespread formal religious education and popular literacy, however, the recitation of *mawlid*s was no longer a necessary or efficient means of dissemination.

Perhaps unsurprisingly, as they had in previous centuries, reformist appropriations of the *mawlid* genre failed to displace the time-honored devotional narratives. A *mawlid* published in a modern (although undated) Egyptian collection of "contemporary tales and songs" (*qiṣāṣ wa-anāshīd 'aṣrīya*) suggests the continuing vigor of the popular *mawlid* tradition in the late-twentieth century. Its content, rendered in charmingly naïve rhymed prose, reproduces the basic narrative established by such early works as al-Bakrī's *Anwār*. It includes the central cosmogonic role of the Light of Muḥammad, the creation of Adam and his use of blessings on the Prophet to pay Eve's *mahr*, the transmission of Adam's pact to deposit the Light only in the purest of women, the attendance of Āsiya and Maryam at Āmina's labor, and other identifying features of the traditional popular *mawlid* narrative.[57] Although less fancifully embellished, the basic content varies little from that which shocked Riḍā's questioner from Dimyāṭ in 1905. Indeed, most of the material presented in this *mawlid* was the object of scholarly objections many centuries ago. Although persistently critiqued by scholars, the central motifs of the popular *mawlid* tradition have displayed a high degree of stability from the medieval period to the present. In their consistency and durability, they constitute a well-established alternative canon that has proven its ability to withstand the intermittent hostility of scholarly authorities.

New rationales for the celebration of the *mawlid*

The rise of opposition to the celebration of the *mawlid* also stimulated spirited defenses framed in terms of more traditional models of piety. Unlike al-Qāsimī and Riḍā, whose perpetuation of the *mawlid* genre masked a fundamental shift in religious sensibilities, some twentieth-century authors went to new lengths in elaborating rationales for the religious significance of the celebration, in the process generating polemics far more voluminous and detailed than those of their premodern predecessors. One of the earliest and most elaborate twentieth-century defenses of the *mawlid* celebration (and, more specifically, of the practice of *qiyām*) was produced by an Indian scholar, 'Ayn al-Quḍāt al-Haydarābādī, at around the same time that Rashīd Riḍā was framing his critiques of such customs. Although written in South Asia, it was framed in Arabic and proved influential in the Middle East. 'Ayn al-Quḍāt's defense of the practice of standing (*qiyām*) at the mention of the Prophet's birth has already been discussed in Chapter 3. A ṣūfī of the Naqshbandī order and the head of a Qur'ānic school founded by his father, 'Ayn al-Quḍāt is reported to have held lavish yearly *mawlid* ceremonies where two hundred sheep and goats were slaughtered to feed both local and regional guests.[58] His work *Nihāyat al-irshād bi-laylat iḥtifāl al-mīlād* was published in India in 1337 AH/1918–19 CE; 150 pages long in a lithographed edition, it was one of the longest apologias for the celebration of the *mawlid* ever composed, vastly exceeding the magnitude of premodern defenses of the practice.

Building on the traditional (if controversial) distinction between "good" and "bad" innovations, 'Ayn al-Quḍāt points to religious developments of undisputed legitimacy including the collection and vowelling of the Qur'ān, the compilation of *ḥadīth* texts, and the development of schools of law. "Thus, in every age things were added that filled in the deficiencies of [God's] chosen religion." One of the religious needs that emerged after the era of the Prophet was a deficiency in devotion to his person. Through the passage of time, the generation of the Prophet became so remote that the believers' awe (*'aẓama*) and love (*maḥabba*) for the Prophet began to decrease. Since both of these were important elements of the religion and basic supports of people's faith, this development undermined the foundations of Islam. Thus, God took pity on His servants and led them to develop the celebration of the *mawlid* in order to reinforce their feelings of awe and love for the Prophet.[59]

In 'Ayn al-Quḍāt's view, "good" innovations are not merely tolerated human extensions of God's legislation. Rather, they represent the natural unfolding of the inherent content of the law. A bad innovation (*bid'a sayyi'a*), he argues, is a practice that is added to the religion and is not generated from it through any of the forms of proof recognized by the science of jurisprudence. A good innovation (*bid'a ḥasana*), in contrast, is newly introduced in the religion (*muḥdath fī 'l-dīn*) but is generated from it; matters of constructive legal reasoning (*al-ijtihādīyāt*) fall into this category. Good innovations are in reality latent (*kāmina*) in the religion and are simply made manifest (*iẓhār*), rather than being invented (*ikhtirā'*). The religion is already complete before the manifestation of good innovations, as is indicated by verse 5:6 of the Qur'ān ("Today I have completed for you your religion"), although they are as yet simply potentialities waiting to be brought forth.[60] The celebration of the *mawlid*, like other good innovations, is thus grounded in the divine mandate; it was merely hidden (*makhfī*) in the legal proofs and was not apparent until it was extracted.[61]

Consistently with his position that valid religious practices can be newly derived from authoritative texts that implicitly mandate them, 'Ayn al-Quḍāt discovers new textual proofs for the legitimacy of the *mawlid*. Premodern *mawlid* proponents had not grounded the practice in the Qur'ān, sufficing themselves with *ḥadīth* texts such as the story of the Medinian Jews who fasted on 'Āshūrā'. In an age when the *mawlid* was under much more aggressive attack and the Qur'ān was increasingly regarded as a fully self-sufficient and comprehensive statement of Islamic faith, modern apologists discerned new Qur'ānic foundations for the celebration.[62] According to 'Ayn al-Quḍāt, the textual basis for the observance of the Prophet's birthday is the Qur'ānic verse 93:11, "As for the benefactions of your Lord, speak of them!" (*wa-ammā bi-ni'mat rabbika fa-ḥaddith*).[63] The Prophet is the greatest benefaction, exceeding all other benefactions bestowed on the universe. If the Prophet is the greatest benefaction, then speaking about his arrival in the world is incumbent upon us *a fortiori*.[64]

'Ayn al-Quḍāt's defense of the *mawlid* displays all of the basic components of the premodern model of devotional action. By grounding his justification of the practice in the commandment to speak about God's blessings, he displays a basically performative approach to *mawlid* recitation. Such recitation is a speech act that functions as a response to God's act of bestowing the Prophet. In 'Ayn al-Quḍāt's opinion, the one indispensable element of the *mawlid* is the narration of the Prophet's birth; it is the point of the gathering, and if the leader of the *mawlid* omits it he has betrayed his trust.[65] As a performance of thanks, it is paralleled by other, non-verbal acts, particularly the distribution of sweets and food. "Since it is a means of thanking God," he writes, "this distribution of food is obligatory as a matter of juristic preference in the sacred law" (*yajibu wujūban istiḥsānīyan shar'īyan*), based on the Qur'ānic verses 31:14 ("thank Me and your parents; to Me is the return") and 14:7 ("If you give thanks, I will increase [your blessings]").[66]

'Ayn al-Quḍāt also justifies the *mawlid* celebration and its component practices in terms of emotional expression. The basic objective of the celebration, he argues, is to perform licit verbal and physical acts of veneration (*ta'ẓīm*) of the Prophet to the greatest extent possible. Of the distribution of food following the recitation of the *mawlid*, he argues that it is legally recommended because it is an expression of joy; a parallel in the sacred law is the scattering (*nathr*) of dates at the end of a wedding. This is a *sunna*, and its rationale (*'illa*) is the expression of joy. If the purely profane joy of a wedding is the rationale for the scattering of dates, then *a fortiori* the purely religious rejoicing associated with the *mawlid* is an *'illa* for the distribution of food.[67]

'Ayn al-Quḍāt's work clearly circulated in the Arab world. His arguments were reproduced by the Meccan *muftī* Muḥammad 'Alī al-Mālikī in his anti-Wahhābī polemic *al-Ṣārim al-mubīd*,[68] as well as by an Azharī scholar by the name of ʻAbd Rabbih ibn Sulaymān al-Qalyūbī, whose six-volume refutation of Wahhābī doctrines was published in Egypt in 1958–65. Similar to ʻAyn al-Quḍāt, al-Qalyūbī believes that divine guidance for the celebration of the *mawlid* was latent in a Qur'ānic verse; otherwise, he argues, it would have been impossible for learned Muslims to reach consensus (*ijmāʻ*) on its legitimacy. He identifies the text in question as verse 93:6, in which God says to the Prophet, "Did He not find you an orphan, and give you shelter?" He strives to demonstrate that all of the elements of traditional *mawlid* narrative are examples of God's "sheltering" (*īwā'*) of the Prophet.

After describing the miracles and wonders accompanying the Prophet's birth, al-Qalyūbī argues that they constitute a universal rejoicing and celebration held by God Himself. The magnitude of the miracles that occurred indicates the extent to which God honored the Prophet's birthday; is it not, then, appropriate for Muslims to emulate their Creator by celebrating this event? From the events of the Prophet's birth, it is possible to elicit a "general universal principle" (*qāʻida kullīya ʻāmma*): celebration and rejoicing are the correct response to any of God's inexhaustible benefactions. An example of this is the *ʻaqīqa* sacrifice which the Prophet prescribed at the birth of a baby. This principle is also alluded to in the Qur'ānic injunction to "remember God's benefaction upon you" (repeated in a number of different verses). Anyone who celebrates and rejoices is thanking God for the blessing he celebrates; God has stated, "If you thank, I will give you more" (verse 14:7), and a *ḥadīth* declares, "By means of thanking, benefactions increase."[69]

The marginalization of the *mawlid* in the late-twentieth century

In the final decades of the twentieth century, the ascendancy of an oil-rich Saudi regime and the Saudi religious establishment's newly aggressive condemnation of the *mawlid* celebration shifted the terms of the debate. No longer merely a determined minority, opponents of the *mawlid* were able to marginalize its proponents at home and place them in a defensive posture throughout the Islamic world, and particularly the Arab Middle East. Perhaps the most prominent defender of the *mawlid* celebration in this period was Muḥammad ibn ʻAlawī al-Mālikī, a Saudi Arabian scholar and ṣūfī whose work is known far beyond his homeland. al-Mālikī addressed the subject of the *mawlid* in a number of different works. A systematic defense of its celebration appears in his work *al-Dhakhā'ir al-muḥammadīya*,[70] and has been published separately in pamphlet form[71]; privately produced xerox copies of the pamphlet are in wide circulation in receptive circles. He has also produced annotated editions of several *mawlid* works by respected authors of previous centuries, in a clear effort to establish the scholarly credentials of the genre.[72] al-Mālikī published these, along with a selection of other *mawlid* texts and devotional verse, in a collection entitled *Bāqa ʻaṭira min ṣiyagh al-mawālid wa'l-madā'iḥ al-nabawīya al-karīma*.[73] A descendant of the

Prophet (*sayyid*), al-Mālikī came from a family of distinguished scholars and educators in Mecca.[74] Born in 1947, he received a PhD from al-Azhar with a dissertation on *ḥadīth*. In 1970 he was appointed as a professor at Umm al-Qurā University, Mecca; in 1971, after his father's death, he was invited to succeed him as the instructor of a study circle at the Sacred Mosque of Mecca.[75]

Despite al-Mālikī's distinguished lineage and his scholarly credentials, however, his religious views – including advocacy of the *mawlid* celebration – eventually earned him the censure of the Saudi authorities. At the beginning of the 1980's, in the wake of the Iranian Revolution and the takeover of the Meccan sanctuary by extremists, the Saudi establishment took a hard line on religious dissent. In 1400 AH/1980 CE, the council (*majlis*) of the Committee of Senior Scholars (*Hay'at Kibār al-'Ulamā'*) examined a series of accusations against al-Mālikī. In addition to alleging that al-Mālikī was involved in subversive and heretical international ṣūfī networks, the complaint denounced the contents of his book *al-Dhakhā'ir al-muḥammadīya*.[76] The council agreed that al-Mālikī's book was full of "superstitions and propaganda for polytheism and paganism" and resolved to work to reform him and move him to repent. After al-Mālikī declined to make a public recantation, the council decided to turn the matter over to the authorities. They prepared a report listing the "polytheistic" and "innovative" elements in al-Mālikī's book *al-Dhakhā'ir*. Among the items to which they objected was the claim that the night of the Prophet's *mawlid* was superior to the Night of Destiny.[77] al-Mālikī was banned from teaching at both the Sacred Mosque and the university, and began to offer religious instruction in his home.[78] Rather than withdrawing from his more controversial positions, he published a critique of Wahhābī doctrine entitled *Mafāhīm yajib an tuṣaḥḥaḥ* ("Concepts that must be corrected").

The campaign against al-Mālikī gave rise to a lengthy exchange of polemics, including a series of book-length works by his supporters and detractors. The celebration of the *mawlid* was a major theme in the debate. In 1983 a member of the Committee of Senior Scholars, 'Abd Allāh ibn Sulaymān ibn Manī', produced a book-length refutation of al-Mālikī's *al-Dhakhā'ir al-muḥammadīya* entitled *Ḥiwār ma'a al-Mālikī fī radd munkarātihi wa-ḍalālātihi* ("Dialog with al-Mālikī in refutation of his deviant and misguided opinions").[79] At least three books were in turn published in refutation of Ibn Manī''s *Ḥiwār*.[80] All of these works prominently feature discussions of the legitimacy or illegitimacy of the *mawlid* celebration. Yet another book primarily concerned with the refutation of Ibn Manī''s positions was produced by Abū'l-Ḥasanayn 'Abd Allāh ibn 'Abd al-Raḥmān al-Makkī under the simple title, *al-Iḥtifāl bi'l-mawlid al-nabawī* ("The celebration of the Prophet's birthday").[81]

In addition to the dispute over the views of al-Mālikī, which prominently featured arguments over the legitimacy of the *mawlid* celebration in addition to other aspects of his teachings, the early 1980s saw a flurry of legal opinions and polemical writings separately addressing the issue of the *mawlid* celebration. The debate occurred on both the scholarly and the popular level. This was not the first time, of course, that the Saudi religious establishment declared the practice illegitimate.[82] However, a far greater response seems to have been elicited by an anti-*mawlid fatwā* issued in 1401 AH/1981 CE by ʿAbd al-ʿAzīz Ibn Bāz (d. 1420 AH/1999 CE). The year after the promulgation of Ibn Bāz's anti-*mawlid fatwā*, in Rabīʿ al-Awwal 1402 AH/1982 CE, the controversy flared with new intensity. Yūsuf al-Rifāʿī published a refutation of Ibn Bāz's *fatwā* in the Kuwaytī newspaper *al-Siyāsa* in the month of Rabīʿ al-Awwal; an anonymous adaptation of the defense of the *mawlid* from al-Mālikī's *Dhakhā'ir* appeared in the Kuwaytī journal *al-Mujtamaʿ* the following month.[83] A Saudi scholar, Ḥammūd ibn ʿAbd Allāh al-Tuwayjirī (d. 1413 AH/1992 CE), published a blistering book-length refutation of both of them.[84] Also in Rabīʿ al-Awwal of 1402, the Jidda daily newspaper *al-Madīna* published what seems to have been a lively epistolary debate about the *mawlid* celebration; one aspiring contributor, who submitted his anti-*mawlid* essay after the editors formally closed the debate, was so eager to air his views that he published them in book form.[85] The exchange was initiated by the publication in the newspaper of an article calling for the celebration of the *mawlid*.[86] The Saudi debate of 1982 was so intense that a pro-*mawlid* article in the newspaper *al-Nadwa* suggested that an international conference be convened in which supporters and opponents could discuss the issue objectively.[87]

On the scholarly level, the *mawlid* debate generally pitted Saudi scholars against both independent and official religious authorities of the other countries of the region. The volume of Saudi *fatwā*s and polemics against the *mawlid* was such that in 1998 the Saudi Bureau of Scholarly Research and Legal Opinions (*Idārat al-Buḥūth al-ʿIlmīya wa'l-Iftā'*) published a collection of such works running to two volumes and 975 pages, entitled "Essays on the legal status of the celebration of the Prophet's birthday" (*Rasā'il fī ḥukm al-iḥtifāl bi'l-mawlid al-nabawī*).[88] It is not without reason that the editors of a defense of the *mawlid* celebration lament that their Wahhābī opponents have made the question of the *mawlid* "the shibboleth between Islam and heresy."[89] The sheer number of anti-*mawlid* polemics and the high pitch of their denunciations suggest that the *mawlid* celebration had become a key symbolic point of contention between *salafī*s and traditionalists.

Pro-*mawlid fatwā*s and polemics were produced by scholars in other parts of the Arabian Peninsula from the beginning of the 1980s. In Jumādā al-Thāniya 1401 (April-May 1981), a *fatwā* in support of *mawlid* celebrations was published by the head of the Islamic court system (*ra'īs al-qaḍā' al-sharʿī*) in the United Arab Emirates.[90] A heated response to the Saudi attack on *mawlid* celebration was issued by the Administration of Legal Opinions and Research of the Bureau of Endowments and Islamic Affairs of Dubai (*Dā'irat al-Awqāf wa'l-Shu'ūn al-Islāmīya, Idārat al-Iftā' wa'l-Buḥūth*).[91] Although frequently identified only as the "Dubai *fatwā*" or by the name of the government agency under whose auspices it was issued, it also sometimes appears under the name of ʿĪsā ibn ʿAbd Allāh al-Ḥimyarī, the president of the bureau. The same author produced a book-length work in defense of the *mawlid* celebration, elaborating many of the points familiar from the work of al-Mālikī and adding additional arguments.[92] Another book-length defense of *mawlid* ceremonies was produced by Muḥammad ibn

Aḥmad ibn Ḥasan al-Khazrajī, the Minister of Endowments and Islamic Affairs of the United Arab Emirates.[93] In Yemen, a book in defense of the *mawlid* celebration under the title "Celebrating the memory of [God's] blessings is obligatory" (*al-Iḥtifāl bi-dhikr al-ni'am wājib*) was composed by Ḥāmid al-Miḥḍār (b. 1323 AH/1905–6 CE), an Azhar-educated notable from Hadramawt; although undated, it cites sources as late as 1981.[94]

Opposition to the *mawlid* was not, of course, limited to Saudi Arabia. The year (1983) following the *mawlid* debate in the newspaper al-Madīna, saw the publication of anti-*mawlid* works in both Morocco and Indonesia.[95] Within the Gulf region, a booklet arguing that the celebration of the Prophet's birthday was an illegitimate innovation was published in the 1980s by the president of the courts and Islamic affairs of Qatar, Shaykh 'Abd Allāh ibn Zayd Āl Maḥmūd.[96] In addition, *salafī*-minded individuals and organizations throughout the Sunnī Muslim world opposed the celebration of *mawlid*s with increasing vigor and success. The response of *mawlid* supporters was also international. A particularly elaborate apologia for the celebration of the *mawlid* was published in response to Ibn Bāz's *fatwā* in 1982 by a South African *muftī*, M.A. Awwary. Drawing on Arabic and Urdu sources, it presents no fewer than seventy-one proofs for the legitimacy of the *mawlid* and of the associated practices of *qiyām* and of addressing the Prophet in the second person. Boldly asserting that the commemoration of the *mawlid* was established by the Companions of the Prophet, Awwary concludes that anyone who rejects its observance "is lost, astray, leads astray, and there is fear of disbelief."[97]

By the 1990s, the debate over the legitimacy of the *mawlid* within Saudi Arabia seems to have died down; official opposition to the celebration seems to have marginalized its proponents so thoroughly that the issue was no longer relevant (at least in the public arena). In the introduction to his *mawlid* pamphlet, which probably reflects the heightened polemical atmosphere of the early 1980s, al-Mālikī describes the legal status of the *mawlid* is "this side issue whose discussion has become a practically annual affair that is read every season and published every year, to the point that people have grown bored of hearing this kind of talk."[98] In contrast, in a survey of the Saudi dailies *al-Riyāḍ* and *al-'Ukāẓ* for the month of Rabī' al-Awwal, 1413 (August/September, 1992), Aviva Schussman found that the newspapers "did not publish a single word about the *mawlid* celebrations. ... Although the newspapers published *fatwā*s on different religious subjects, none dealt with the *mawlid*, not even to condemn it."[99]

The intense debate of the early 1980s over the legitimacy of *mawlid* celebrations radiated outwards from Saudi Arabia, a country with a high religious prestige that possessed the resources to project its religious agendas internationally. The strongest voices raised against the *mawlid* emanated from the Saudis (although their sentiments were shared by *salafī*-minded Muslims internationally), and the most vigorous defense was staged by their immediate neighbors. Outside of the Arabian Peninsula, an alternative center of Sunnī legitimacy was represented by Egyptian religious establishment centering on al-Azhar. Throughout the controversy of the 1980s the celebration of the *mawlid* continued to be endorsed by the

Egyptian religious establishment, although less vigorously and confrontationally than was the case in the UAE. The scholars of al-Azhar do not seem to have produced elaborate polemical defenses of the *mawlid* celebration, but they continued to celebrate the occasion and support its observance. Articles and poems in honor of the Prophet's birthday continued to appear in *Majallat al-Azhar* on an annual basis, although their content tended to revolve more around the general glorification of the Prophet's mission than around the traditional devotional themes of the *mawlid* tradition.[100]

On the rare occasions when the issue of the celebration's legal status was addressed in the journal's *fatwā* column, the scholars calmly affirmed its permissibility. In Rabīʿ al-Thānī 1304 AH/January 1982, a month after the debate over *mawlid*s raged in the pages of *al-Madīna*, al-Azhar's *Fatwā* Committee responded to a query from an Islamic organization from Mozambique. The questioners asked about the "opinion of religion" (*ra'y al-dīn*) regarding recitation and *samāʿ* in commemoration of the Prophet's birthday, whether in a mosque or elsewhere; the inclusion of praise (*madḥ*), religious songs (*inshād*), and the mention of the Prophet's miracles in the context of the celebration; the adornment of the place where the gathering was held; the serving of food; and the "manifestation of joy." The committee affirmed that all of these things were licit, provided that the *ḥadīth* texts involved were well authenticated, the decorations were free of wasteful ostentation (*isrāf*), and all contributions for the costs of food and drink were made willingly.[101]

The Azhar's acceptance of *mawlid*s did not change over the following decade, although its concern to emphasize adherence to the *sunna* may have grown in a climate increasingly hostile to perceived *bidaʿ*. In 1993, *Majallat al-Azhar* published a *fatwā* in support of the celebration of the *mawlid* in response to a query received from an individual in Saudi Arabia. In harmony with the other *mawlid*-related materials featured in the journal, it offered a moderate affirmation of the legitimacy of the holiday combined with a set of studiously reformist proposals for its observance. The best way to celebrate the Prophet's birthday, the *fatwā* states, is to follow his *sunna*; in order to achieve this, people ought to avoid acts of disobedience, compete with one another in charitable deeds, strive for Islamic unity, and study the lessons of the Prophet's life. Eating sweets on the day of the *mawlid* is an acceptable form of rejoicing, but it is not a religious obligation.[102] Despite its determinedly mild content, the fact that this *fatwā* is expressly directed to a Saudi questioner suggests the Azhar committee's concern to portray their university as a center of Islamic authority exercising influence even in the heartland of their Saudi rivals.

The eclipse of the devotionalist model

The sustained and aggressive attack mounted against the *mawlid* celebration in the 1980s and 1990s led to a retrenchment in the positions of *mawlid* defenders. Modern *mawlid* proponents writing before the ascendancy of Saudi-style salafism, roused to defense of the practice by new trends of opposition but still secure in its overwhelming prevalence, had expressed an unprecedented confidence in its religious legitimacy. al-Hijrasī argues that, while *mawlid* celebrations are in any case legitimate as "good innovations," based on relevant precedents they may in fact be *bona fide* elements of the Prophet's *sunna*. He triumphantly concludes his reasoning by declaring that "my opinion is that it is obligatory to engage in the activities of this celebration at all times when the advent of the Master of Humankind is remembered."[103] al-Qalyūbī resoundingly affirms that celebration of the Prophet's *mawlid* is part of the religion (*min al-dīn*) and is commanded by the Qur'ān (*wa-jā'a bihā kalām rabb al-'ālamīn*).[104] The position that the celebration of the *mawlid* is actually mandated by the *sharī'a* is one from which most late-twentieth-century authors have retreated, assuming a defensive posture in the face of accusations of *bid'a*. al-Mālikī's essay in defense of the *mawlid* begins with a prefatory statement clarifying the position of the author and his followers. "Our opinion," it states, "is that it is permissible to celebrate the noble *mawlid*." A second prefatory point clarifies that the author's followers do not claim that it is a *sunna* to celebrate the Prophet's birth on any specific day, which they concede would be a *bid'a*.[105] The defensive nature of this posture is clear from the content of the body of the text, which strongly suggests that the celebration of the *mawlid* is at least commendable according to the *sharī'a*.[106]

In addition to conceding that the celebration of the *mawlid* is merely neutral (rather than recommended or required by Islamic law), contemporary defenders have also advanced the position that it is not a religious activity at all. This somewhat surprising contention is a response to the *salafī* assertion that as an innovation (*bid'a*), the *mawlid* is inherently illegitimate. Premodern defenders of the *mawlid* relied on the argument that not all *bida'* were condemned by the *sharī'a*, a position that was accepted by many (although by no means all) prominent scholars. This argument is reproduced by many modern authors as well; al-Mālikī, for instance, discusses the concept of the "good innovation" in points 14–19 of his pamphlet in defense of the *mawlid*.[107] Modern *salafī*s' success in establishing the rejection of all *bida'* as a basic premise of the debate, however, has motivated a reframing of the defenders' arguments. Having interpreted the prohibition on innovations as absolute and categorical, *salafī*s open the door to technical and social change by making an unprecedentedly sharp distinction between the sacred and secular realms. Thus, in his discussion of the *mawlid* celebration Ibn Manī' premises his argument on a binary distinction between matters of this world and of the next (*umūr al-dunyā* and *umūr al-ākhira*). If the *mawlid* were a this-worldly matter (one of *umūr al-dunyā*) and its benefits were greater than its harms, it would be valid. As a matter pertaining to the life to come and a form of worship (*'ibāda*), however, its validity can only be based on divine stipulation (*tawqīf*).[108]

In his book *Mafāhīm yajib an tuṣaḥḥaḥ*, published at the height of the campaign against him, al-Mālikī states that "gathering in honor of the Prophet's noble *mawlid* is nothing but a custom, and has nothing to do with worship rituals (*amr 'ādī wa-laysa min al-'ibāda min shay'*)." The only problematic thing, he argues, would be if people were to conflate custom (*'āda*) with worship (*'ibāda*), and become convinced that the *mawlid* celebration was a ritual mandated by the *sharī'a*.[109] In his *mawlid* pamphlet he similarly argues that the *qiyām* is a purely customary matter (*mas'ala 'ādīya*), not a religious one; it is not part of the religion, the *sharī'a*, or the *sunna*.[110]

A similar point is made by another supporter of the *mawlid* celebration, the Syrian Shāfi'ī scholar Muḥammad Sa'īd Ramaḍān al-Būṭī (b. 1350 AH/1931 CE).[111] Basing himself on the definitions of the Mālikī jurist al-Shāṭibī (d. 780 AH/1388 CE), al-Būṭī argues that the concept of "innovation" applies only to the realm of acts of worship (*'ibādāt*). "Thus," he writes, "in order for an activity to partake of the meaning and the legal status of *bid'a*, the person who engages in it must do so in the belief that it enters into the structure of the religion and that it is an integral part of it, when in reality this is not the case."[112] This condition is not met, al-Būṭī argues, in the case of *mawlid* celebrations "because no one who is responsible for them believes that they are part of the essence (*jawhar*) of the religion or that they form part of its foundation and core," or that those who fail to participate in them commit a sin of omission.[113] The concept of *bid'a* does not encompass all areas of life; secular activities are subject to renewal and change in pursuit of the greater good, as defined in the basic objectives of the *sharī'a*.

A similar but somewhat more complex argument is made by Ḥāmid al-Miḥḍār. He argues that the celebration of the Prophet's *mawlid* is actually required by the *sharī'a*, because it is a form of "thanking the benefactor." However, he argues that the way in which the celebration is held is a purely sociocultural matter. "There is no doubt," he states, "that the celebration of the memory of [God's] benefactions is a social matter in terms of its form and mode" (*al-hay'a wa'l-kayf*). Such celebrations develop according to the demands of the social environment. Of course, al-Miḥḍār notes, this rule applies only to cases in which no specific form of celebration is specified by the authoritative texts; if specific forms are mandated by the *sharī'a*, they must be followed in all social and historical circumstances.[114] al-Miḥḍār invokes the example of many civic and national rituals practiced in Islamic nations to honor various kinds of individuals, without becoming the object of accusations of religious innovation and misguidance. His examples include inviting a dignitary to cut a ribbon symbolizing the beginning of an enterprise beneficial to the nation, and erecting victory arches or performing twenty-one gun salutes in honor of a visit by a head of state.[115]

Whether supporters or detractors of the *mawlid*, contemporary authors have come to invoke a newly defined distinction between religious/ritual and secular/social realms. The idea that the category of innovation (*bid'a*) applies distinctively or exclusively to religious practices is an old one, although it was never unproblematic. al-Shāṭibī registers a range of opinion on the applicability of the concept of *bid'a* to mundane affairs (*al-umūr al-'ādīya*), and himself emphasizes the ambiguity of the line between pragmatic secular customs and acts of worship (*'ibādāt*). He demonstrates the porousness of the distinction with the examples of costly decorations in mosques (which, themselves worldly, can come to be considered pious expenditures) and the display of royal pomp and images of rulers (which can similarly come to be regarded as a means of exalting Islam and displaying its insignia).[116] In a *fatwā* defining the concept of *bid'a*, Rashīd Riḍā acknowledges no such ambiguity. He draws a sharp distinction between religious (*dīnī*) and secular (*dunyawī*) matters; while innovations are strictly forbidden in the religious sphere, the sphere of worldly affairs is open to new developments within the guidelines of the *sharī'a*.[117] In another *fatwā* responding to an Arabian query regarding the celebration of the day of the Saudi monarch's ascension to the throne, Riḍā makes a similarly sharp distinction between the religious and secular realms. Citing the *mawlid*s of holy persons as an example of illegitimate religious innovations, he argues that the coronation celebrations held in monarchies and the independence days observed in republics are "political secular festivals" that are subject to no inherent religious objections.[118]

Despite his reservations about the *shar'ī* status of *mawlid* celebrations, however, we have seen that Rashīd Riḍā attempted to avoid the odium of innovation by moving from a mode of *mawlid* observance based on traditional devotional models to one based on modern, secular forms. *Mawlid* defenders of the late-twentieth century were aware of the extent to which such ostensibly secular and non-ritualized forms as the conference and the lecture were being used by their *salafī* opponents as alternative media of religious expression, thus avoiding the accusation of *bid'a*. In 1998 the Naqshbandī *shaykh* Hishām Muḥammad al-Kabbānī, leader of a branch of the order active in the United States of America, wrote a commentary on the "Dubai *fatwā*" centering on this theme. Invoking the supposedly secular celebrations accepted by his opponents, he promotes the idea of the Prophet's birthday as "the Independence Day of the Islamic nation." If the citizens of all Muslim nations commemorate the dates of their liberation from colonialism, he argues, *a fortiori* they ought to celebrate their emancipation from idolatry through the advent of the Prophet Muḥammad.

Furthermore, he notes, all Islamic organizations in the United States of America hold annual conferences, frequently on a fixed day of the year. Such gatherings are considered religiously meritorious, but they are not considered *bida'*. Perhaps somewhat facetiously, al-Kabbānī proposes that the *mawlid* be observed as the "1472nd Annual Global Conference for Commemorating the Birth of the Prophet." Finally, he notes that Islamic organizations frequently hold fundraising dinners, although "if one looks in the *seerah*, the Prophet never held a fundraising dinner." He argues that "No one has ever condemned fundraising dinners as a reprehensible innovation, although it is a newly developed form of worship and an encouragement for worship (donation, *sadaqa*), without precedent in the life of the Prophet, his Companions, or the pious predecessors." There is no valid distinction between fundraisers and traditional *mawlid* ceremonies.[119] al-Kabbānī himself considers the *mawlid* celebration to be *sunna*, and a part of the religion. Similar to al-Miḥḍār, he questions the distinction between secular and religious ritual. In his invocation of supposedly non-ritual Islamic practices that have been embraced by his opponents, however, he displays a keen grasp of the manipulation of the categories of the secular and the sacred in modern Islamic discourse and practice.

At the opposite extreme of the debate, some opponents of the *mawlid* place all commemorative activities in the realm of the sacred, and thus within the exclusive preserve of divine fiat. Although such thinkers recognize a secular realm encompassing technical and scientific innovations, they thus seek to eliminate any traces of civic ritual. According to al-Tuwayjirī, for instance, the prohibition on innovated festivals extends to coronations and inaugurations, revolutionary holidays, and independence days celebrated in Islamic countries in the post-colonial period. All of these, according to al-Tuwayjirī, are illegitimate.[120]

Another distinctive development among contemporary defenders of the *mawlid* is the search for a Qur'ānic basis for the celebration. Premodern justifications of the *mawlid*, as we have seen, were based on analogies with practices documented in the *ḥadīth*. In the twentieth century, the Qur'ān was increasingly perceived as a comprehensive and self-sufficient charter of Islamic practice.[121] The increasingly embattled status of *mawlid* defenders probably also contributed to a search for proof texts in the highest possible source of authority. The new prominence of the Qur'ān in debates over the *mawlid* is apparent in 'Īsā al-Ḥimyarī's work *Bulūgh al-ma'mūl*, in which his proofs for the legitimacy of the celebration are divided into sections on the Qur'ān, the *sunna*, and the consensus of the scholars. He lists nine different Qur'ānic proofs (some based on more than one verse), some paralleling the arguments made by Daḥlān in the nineteenth-century, but others novel. For instance, he appeals to verse 11:120, "All that We relate to you of the stories of the messengers – with it We make firm your heart." The recitation of the *mawlid*, he reasons, involves relating the story of the Prophet Muḥammad; the Qur'ānic verse affirms that this will steady the hearts of the believers. Thus, the Qur'ān encourages the recitation of the *mawlid*.[122] al-Ḥimyarī also appeals to verse 19:33, in which Jesus declares, "Peace is upon me the day I was born, the day I die, and the day I am raised up alive." This verse and many others in the Qur'ān, al-Ḥimyarī argues, celebrate the birth of Jesus; *a fortiori*, the birthday of Muḥammad is worthy of celebration.[123]

Despite the deployment of new textual material, the substance of *mawlid* defenders' arguments has remained the same, emphasizing the principle of reciprocity, the obligation to thank, and the significance of proper emotion. Their opponents respond both by denying the possibility of discovering new meanings in the Qur'ān (while simultaneously advancing their own Qur'ānic readings) and by rejecting the underlying model of reciprocity and meritorious emotion. Presenting an explicit Qur'ānic proof for the specific obligation to thank God for the person of the Prophet (and thus for his birth), the Dubai scholar al-Ḥimyarī cites verse 3:164, which describes God's sending of the Prophet as a benefaction upon the Muslims. Very much like the word *ni'ma*, the verb *manna* (used in this *āya*) refers to a favor imposing an obligation upon its recipient. The only way of discharging this obligation, al-Ḥimyarī argues, is to celebrate and rejoice in the Prophet, "because the favor cannot be reciprocated with any gift; thus, giving thanks for it, celebrating it and praising it are considered a good deed which returns to the one who performs them."[124] The transactional nature of the *mawlid* celebration applies not only to the relationship between the celebrants and God, but (perhaps even more so) to their relationship with the Prophet. al-Mālikī argues that the description of the Prophet and his moral qualities in the context of the *mawlid* is an occasion for the participants to strive to discharge some portion of their obligation to the Prophet (*li-mukāfa'atihi bi-adā' ba'ḍ mā yajibu lahu 'alaynā*). During the Prophet's lifetime, he points out, poets traveled to present the Prophet with poems in his praise; the Prophet rewarded them with favors and gifts. Praising the Prophet in the context of the *mawlid* can similarly be a means of attracting his love and satisfaction.[125]

Ibn Manī' responds indignantly to al-Mālikī's claim that celebration of the *mawlid* represents partial recompense of the debt owed to the Prophet. In several different Qur'ānic verses, he observes, God commands the Prophet to declare that he asks for no reward for delivering God's message (12:104; 25:57; 34:47). No prophet ever sought reward or thanks from the recipients of his message; the only reward would come directly from God. Thus, while it is certainly incumbent upon believers to love and honor the Prophet, "we do not consider any of this to be a favor to him (*lā namannu 'alayhi bi-shay' min dhālika*) on the basis that we are recompensing him; rewarding him is incumbent on God. God will repay him in the best, most complete and perfect way for delivering the message, rendering up the trust, and counseling the community; He is the One in charge of that and the One capable of it."[126]

Mawlid supporters perpetuate a premodern model of devotional practice emphasizing reciprocity and exchange among human beings, God, and the Prophet. In this model, humans' inability to offer any true benefit to the other parties does not invalidate their gifts, but results in a harvest of blessings from infinitely magnanimous beings whose rewards will not fail. In contrast, Ibn Manī' advances a model in which no reciprocity is possible; humans can and should offer nothing to the Prophet, whose mission will be rewarded exclusively by God. While this exchange between al-Mālikī and Ibn Manī' neatly crystallizes the contrast between the two conceptions of religious action, the issue of reciprocity is rarely explicitly addressed in contemporary polemics about the *mawlid*. It is so remote from the conceptions of the *salafī* authors who have succeeded in defining the debate that it generally fades from view altogether.

Closely related to the issue of reciprocity is that of emotion. Contemporary supporters of the *mawlid*, like their premodern predecessors, emphasize that reciprocation can consist primarily in the manifestation of appropriate emotions of gratitude and rejoicing. al-Mālikī's first proof for the permissibility of the practice is "that celebrating the Prophet's noble *mawlid* is an expression of joy and delight (*al-faraḥ wa'l-surūr*) in the Chosen One, and [even] a non-believer has benefited from this." Very traditionally, he then cites the example of Abū Lahab and cites the famous verses of Ibn Nāṣir al-Dīn. Unlike most *mawlid* supporters of earlier eras, who were subject to much less polemical pressure, al-Mālikī enhances the force of this argument by citing al-Bukhārī.[127] al-Mālikī also offers a more novel argument for the legitimacy (or, indeed, the obligatory status) of expressions of rejoicing. In his third proof of the permissibility of the *mawlid*, he cites verse 10:58 of the Qur'ān: "Say: In God's favor and His mercy, in that let them rejoice." God commands us here to rejoice in God's mercy, al-Mālikī reasons, and the Prophet is the greatest of God's mercies. The identity of the Prophet as God's ultimate mercy is textually established by verse 21:107, in which God proclaims to His Messenger, "We have sent you only as a mercy to the worlds."[128] This argument is reiterated by al-Ḥimyarī.[129] al-Mālikī also argues that rejoicing and feasting in honor of the Prophet's birth constitute honoring him (*ta'ẓīm*), which is required by the *sharī'a*.[130]

Both al-Mālikī and al-Ḥimyarī also justify the celebration of the *mawlid* by arguing that it cultivates sentiments of love for the Prophet. In a very traditional mode, al-Mālikī argues that the recitation of the Prophet's good qualities and miracles in the context of the *mawlid* celebration naturally leads to an increase in love for him. By nature human beings love beauty, whether of person, character, knowledge, behavior, or belief; and there is no one more beautiful or perfect than the Prophet. Enhancing one's love and belief for the Prophet are required by the *sharī'a*, and anything that evokes an increase in love and belief is thus required as well.[131] al-Ḥimyarī argues that love and loyalty for the Prophet are the "root and basis of religion; thus, all of religious rituals (*al-'ibādāt*) lead [people] to him and condition their hearts to love him. . . . The celebration of the *mawlid* is nothing but conditioning oneself to invoke blessings upon him frequently, in the hopes that love for him and his family will be impressed on people's hearts, so that that love will form the basis for the pillar of faith."[132] In some cases, *mawlid* supporters update their analysis of the role of emotion by invoking the prestige of modern science. The Moroccan scholars Murād and 'Amrawī, in their defense of al-Mālikī, write that "The study of psychology and modern pedagogy indicates that religious belief (*al-'aqīda*) is established in the minds of children and common people through various means; the celebration of the *mawlid* is of this category."[133]

Opponents of the *mawlid* celebration have little patience for arguments based on the religious value of proper emotion. With respect to the argument about rejoicing, they question the textual premises invoked by *mawlid* supporters. They reject the anecdote about Abū Lahab for the same reasons invoked by premodern scholars.[134] As for verse 10:58, it was interpreted by classical exegetes to refer to the Revelation and not to the Prophet.[135] More importantly, however, *mawlid* opponents do not perceive emotional responses as valid grounds for religious judgments. al-Tuwayjirī responds to the argument that celebrating the *mawlid* is "an expression of joy and delight in the Chosen One" by retorting that "the proofs for something's permissibility or prohibition are not drawn from people's joys and delight, or from their sorrows and griefs; they are drawn only from the Qur'ān, the *sunna*, and the consensus [of the religious scholars]."[136]

In the view of *salafī* authors, the celebratory activities (such as holding festive meals and reciting devotional verse) regarded by *mawlid* supporters as the behavioral expressions of joy are merely deviations from the Prophet's *sunna*. They are judged, not in terms of their expressive dimension as performances of certain appropriate religious statements, but in terms of their conformity or non-conformity to the norms of the prophetic *sunna*. Ibn Manīʿ writes,

> Even if we grant that rejoicing [in the Prophet] is required of the community, the meaning of rejoicing is not that we should invent things in his religion and about him that do not come from him, which entails accusing him of falling short in delivering his message, rendering up what was entrusted to him and counseling the community. ... Rather, rejoicing in the Prophet means adhering to his *sunna* and holding on to it with our teeth, keeping away from inventions and innovations, and worshiping God only in the ways established by [the Prophet]. ... This is rejoicing in the Messenger of God; this is love of the Messenger of God; this is honoring the Messenger of God.[137]

It is notable that in this passage that the author makes no distinction between love (*maḥabba*) and honor (*ta ʿẓīm*); the two are interchangeable, and each of them manifests itself exclusively in emulation and obedience.

In the case of love, as that of joy, the modern opponents of *mawlid* celebrations offer no alternative analysis of the evocation of religiously required emotions. Instead, opponents decisively turn away from the premodern emphasis on issues of emotion. As in the case of joy, their analysis of love of the Prophet is dominated by the concept of conformity to his example, almost to the exclusion of love for his person. In view of the universal acceptance of authoritative texts demanding love of both God and the Prophet, some *mawlid* opponents implicitly take the radical step of denying that "love" is an affective state at all. Specifically, modern Saudi denunciations of the *mawlid* celebration consistently identify love (*maḥabba*) with obedience or following (*ittibāʿ*). Thus, Ibn Bāz notes that supporters of *mawlid* celebrations "have claimed that [celebration of the *mawlid*] is something that realizes the objective of loving and supporting the Messenger of God, and disregard what is obligatory, which is that the love of the Messenger occurs only by means of following him and obeying him (*anna maḥabbat al-rasūl innamā takūnu bi'ttibāʿihi wa-ṭāʿatihi*)."[138] Similarly, Muḥammad ibn Saʿd ibn Shuqayr states that "genuine love for the Messenger of God occurs only through obedience to him and adherence to the divine law which he brought . . . because the roots (*uṣūl*) of love are following (*ittibāʿ*)."[139] al-Tuwayjirī writes that the Companions of the Prophet loved and honored him by following his *sunna* and disseminating his call; "Those are the ones who truly loved the Prophet, and following their path is what expresses love and honor for the Prophet."[140] Ibn Manīʿ states that "Love of [the Prophet] means following his *sunna*, emulating him, and drawing lessons and admonitions from his life and the life of his Companions after him."[141] "Love for [the Prophet]," writes Ṣāliḥ ibn Fawzān, "entails (*taqtaḍī*) being obedient to him and following him."[142] In these passages, as in other similar ones, it is difficult to tell whether love *consists of* obedience or is *achieved through* obedience. What is clear, however, is that the individual believer need concern himself only with obedience; any affective relationship with the Prophet that might arise from such obedience remains undiscussed and undefined.

The equation of love for the Prophet with obedience is not an invention of modern Saudi scholars; verse 3:31 of the Qur'ān ("Say: 'If you love God, follow me.' ") suggested this interpretation to some prominent early scholars. However, the overwhelming premodern consensus was in favor of the interpretation of love as an emotional state. Even Ibn Taymīya, who emphasized the primacy of adherence to the Prophet's example, acknowledged the meritorious nature of expressions of love for the Prophet (see earlier, p. 117). Whereas Ibn Taymīya was willing to accept the expression of love as valid grounds for the celebration of the *mawlid* by Muslims lacking the knowledge or zeal for more orthodox forms of piety, contemporary *salafī*s have rejected all standards but that of adherence to the prophetic *sunna*. Modern *mawlid* opponents also imply an unprecedented sense of distance from the Prophet, one that precludes all forms of adherence but the following of his transmitted example. Ibn Manī' writes with an unwonted poignancy,

> There is no doubt that we love [the Prophet] personally (*fī shakhṣihi*). How we wish that we had been privileged to associate with him, to join with his Companions and to vie with them in following his traces, listening to his statements and sessions (*majālis*) and interacting with him! But nay, nay – we have been separated from him, and all that remains to us as a positive result of our claim to love him and a proof of our sincerity in it is to adhere to his *sunna*.[143]

The question of the emotional, spiritual, and physical availability of the Prophet is most vividly at stake in the debate over the permissibility of the *qiyām*. Although *mawlid* supporters reject the most literalistic forms of folk belief, their arguments are predicated on the idea that he is in some sense present, and that his spiritual or imaginative presence ought rightly to evoke an emotional and behavioral response. al-Mālikī's discussion of this issue suggests the extent to which belief in the literal presence of the Prophet at *mawlid* celebrations has prevailed in the folk imagination. Some ignorant participants, he writes, engage in the *qiyām* in the false belief that the Prophet physically enters the room at that moment. What is worse, some even believe that the incense and perfume are for him, and that the water placed at the center of the gathering is for him to drink. None of these things, al-Mālikī insists, would ever occur to any rational Muslim. These beliefs are an impertinence to the Prophet, who is far too exalted to come forth from his grave in order to attend such-and-such a *mawlid* gathering at such-and-such a time. Rather, al-Mālikī affirms that the Prophet is alive in the liminal realm (*barzakh*) in a mode appropriate to his station, and that his spirit is free to roam throughout God's creation.[144] Although al-Mālikī is not completely explicit, he seems to be arguing that the Prophet may indeed be spiritually present at some *mawlid* gatherings, although it would be below his dignity to appear on command at every such ceremony.

The first edition of al-Mālikī's *mawlid* pamphlet contains a strong, if somewhat ambiguous, affirmation of the Prophet's spiritual presence. The extent of the opposition to this idea is suggested by the fact that the statement is discretely deleted from a later edition of the pamphlet, published under the auspices of a Baḥraynī *shaykh*. In the original version, responding to the objection that one may not stand in honor of the Prophet at a *mawlid* because the Prophet is not present, al-Mālikī declares:

> The answer to that is that the reciter of the noble *mawlid* evokes [the Prophet's] presence (*qāri' al-mawlid mustaḥḍir lahu*) by describing his noble person. He came into the physical world (*al-'ālam al-jismānī*) from the luminous world (*al-'ālam al-nūrānī*) before that time, at the time of his noble birth, and he is present when the reciter says "and he was born" with a shadow presence (*ḥuḍūr ẓillī*) that is closer than his original presence (*ḥuḍūrihi al-aṣlī*).[145]

This rather opaque statement is a direct but unacknowledged borrowing from 'Ayn al-Quḍāt, an author who seems never to be explicitly cited by al-Mālikī but whose influence on him is palpable.

Regardless of the literal attendance of the Prophet's spirit, however, he argues that the Prophet is a vivid emotional presence in the minds of *mawlid* participants. Like the *mawlid* celebration itself, the *qiyām* is for al-Mālikī a matter of emotional response and interpersonal relations. al-Mālikī once again prefaces his remarks by stating that the *qiyām* is not obligatory, nor is it a *sunna*; one must not believe that it is either of these things. "Rather, it is a motion by which people express their joy and delight. When it is mentioned that [the Prophet] was born and went out into the world, in that moment the listener imagines (*yataṣawwaru*) that the entire universe is dancing in joy and delight at that great benefaction (*ni'ma*); he stands up to manifest and express (*muẓhiran . . . mu'abbiran*) that joy and delight."[146] To spring to one's feet expresses not merely one's joy in the advent of the Prophet, but one's honor and respect (*iḥtirāman wa-taqdīran*) for the image of the Prophet that occurs in one's mind. To envision the Prophet in this way, al-Mālikī argues, is not merely praiseworthy but necessary; the Prophet's image must constantly be present in the mind of a sincere Muslim in order that he might properly love and follow him.[147] While this is a purely customary matter and not a religious obligation, failure to stand may be interpreted as an expression of bad manners, poor taste, or emotional rigidity.[148]

The idea that the Prophet may be literally present at *mawlid*s (whether bodily or spiritually is not clear) is indignantly rejected by Ibn Bāz. Some people, he writes,

> fancy (*yaẓunnu*) that the Prophet attends the *mawlid*; for this reason they stand up greeting and welcoming him. This is one of the greatest forms of falsehood and the ugliest kinds of ignorance. The Prophet will not emerge from his grave before the Day of Resurrection; he is not in communication with anyone, and does not attend their gatherings. Rather, he is abiding in his grave until the Day of Judgment, and his spirit is in the highest heaven (*a'lā 'ilīyīn*) with his Lord in the Abode of Grace (*dār al-karāma*).[149]

Similarly, al-Tuwayjirī characterizes claims about the spiritual presence of the Prophet as an example of the "wild utterances of the mystics" (*shaṭaḥāt al-ṣūfīya*), and cites Qur'ān 39:42 to demonstrate that only the spirits of the living can wander freely. Only God knows what becomes of the spirits of the dead, and to claim knowledge of such things without any legitimate evidence is baseless.[150] Ibn Manī', for his part, rejects even the idea of the Prophet's imaginative presence. He finds al-Mālikī's remarks self-contradictory, and clearly suspects him of harboring more extreme and literalistic beliefs than he is willing to admit. However, if he is in fact advocating that people stand up in honor of an imaginary presence that they are conjuring up in their minds, this is delusional and unbalanced behavior that other people should find disturbing. Indeed, like talking to oneself because one imagines one hears voices, it is the beginning of mental illness.[151]

The debate over the *qiyām* reflects a fundamental difference in the two parties' views of the Prophet. For supporters, the Prophet is directly accessible to participants in the *mawlid*. Whether in body, in spirit, or in imagination, he is intimately present to those who love him; it is thus appropriate to engage in physical manifestations of joy and honor, such as rising to one's feet. For opponents, the Prophet is remote from the individual Muslim of the present day. While he is loved and honored as a messenger and will be rejoined on the Day of Judgment, no immediate encounter is possible. In the long interlude of human history between revelation and judgment, only God's word and the Prophet's example remain to sustain our connection with the divine.

The contemporary debate over the legal status of the *mawlid* celebration has also seen significant shifts in interpretations of the significance of time. As we have seen, premodern proponents of the *mawlid* celebration understood it in the context of a non-homogeneous understanding of time, in which copious blessings and rewards accrued to acts of piety performed on auspicious dates in the Islamic calendar. The Prophet's birthday was only one in a series of special times that offered privileged opportunities for the generation of religious merit. While this understanding did not go unchallenged, it was embraced by many scholars and formed part of a pervasive popular Islamic worldview. In the twentieth century, this worldview was challenged with increasing success by *salafī* thinkers who advanced a homogeneous understanding of time. As in other areas of the *mawlid* debate, the initial reaction of *mawlid* supporters was to present uniquely elaborate justifications of positions that had been more summarily accepted for centuries. This initial confidence was followed by a dramatic retreat in the heated polemical atmosphere of the eighties and nineties.

Perhaps the most elaborate theoretical justification of the idea of auspicious times in the history of the *mawlid* debate is offered by 'Ayn al-Quḍāt in his *Nihāyat al-irshād*. He frames his discussion as a response to a hypothetical objection that specifying the month of Rabī' al-Awwal for the celebration of the *mawlid* is a bad innovation:

> Since time is a fluid thing without a stable essence (*dhāt*), it is not possible to bring back the time [of the Prophet's birth] at all; thus, there is no factor rendering any one of the parts of time more appropriate than any other for the

> celebration of the *mawlid*, and specifying one of [time's] parts, which are in truth all the same, for the celebration of the *mawlid* is an arbitrary specification (*tarjīḥ bi-lā murajjiḥ*).[152]

Unsurprisingly, 'Ayn al-Quḍāt vigorously rejects the idea that time is homogeneous and that the time of the Prophet's birth has irrevocably receded into the distant past. His lengthy and elaborate arguments on this subject draw both on ṣūfī concepts and on the vocabulary of traditional Islamic philosophy, to which he was presumably exposed in his studies at Farangi Mahall. He argues that even though the elementary particles of which time is composed (*al-ajzā' al-awwalīya al-taḥlīlīya*) are indistinguishable from the point of view of their essence (*lam tatamāyaz min ḥaythu al-dhāt*), they differ from each other with respect to the perfections that are poured forth upon them from the divine Source. Taking the example of the days of the week, he argues each day exists both as a series of indistinguishable individuals and as "a species recurring each week." Each day is a species (*naw'*) compounded (*murakkab*) from a particle of time and "the specific lights and blessings which are poured form upon it from God to perfect it." The particle of time (*juz' zamānī*) is the material cause (*'illa māddīya*) of the day, while the formal cause (*'illa ṣūrīya*) is the "lights and blessings" bestowed by God. It is these "lights and blessings" which constitute the distinctions (*imtiyāz*) among different times; because of them each day has "effects and benefits" (*āthār wa-fawā'id*) which are different from those of all other days. He offers both rational (*'aqlī*) argumentation and textual (*naqlī*) proof in support of these ideas.[153]

'Ayn al-Quḍāt's textual proof is based on the Qur'ānic verses and *ḥadīth* texts which speak of the virtues of specific nights, days, months, and centuries/generations. These texts imply an underlying principle (*muqaddama*), which is that the time in which something luminous and blessed occurred is itself blessed and luminous. Since the day of the week, the month, and the precise date of an auspicious event all carry different degrees of blessing, there is a corresponding difference in the virtue of acts of worship (*ṭā'āt*) performed in these different times. A *ṭā'a* performed on the twelfth of Rabī' al-Awwal is superior to the one performed on a Monday in that month; a *ṭā'a* performed on a Monday in Rabī' al-Awwal is superior to the one performed on another day of that month, etc. The pinnacle of this hierarchy would, of course, be if the twelfth of Rabī' al-Awwal fell on a Monday. The underlying principle is that the power (*quwwa*) of the "prophetic lights and blessings" varies with the degree of propinquity to the Prophet. This is established by the *ḥadīth* in which the Prophet states that "the best generation is my generation, then those that follow them, then those that follow them." This clearly indicates that closeness to the Prophet is the source of powerful "lights and blessings" which weaken as one becomes increasingly remote from him. The basic principle is that propinquity to the Prophet – whether in space, time, or calendrical date – is the source of powerful prophetic blessings and lights that radiate as far as God wills. Thus, the dust and fruits of Medina are a cure. The virtue of the *mawlid* can be demonstrated by a *qiyās* with the Prophet's grave, the common rationale (*al-'illa al-jāmi'a*) being propinquity to the Prophet.[154]

The specifics of 'Ayn al-Quḍāt's elaborate, pseudo-philosophical analysis of time are somewhat eccentric, and his distinctive educational background supplies him with a technical vocabulary (however quixotically applied) that is alien to his Arab contemporaries. However, his analysis represents a somewhat baroque polemical restatement of ideas that had been prevalent for centuries. Based on texts from the Qur'ān and *ḥadīth*, he believes in a non-homogeneous time in which special occasions (whether days of the week or dates in the calendar) recur cyclically, bearing with them bounteous divine blessings and enhanced opportunities for the generation of merit. His rather odd analysis of the "material" and "formal" causes of days of the week and year is merely a personal interpretation, adapting philosophical terminology, of a very basic Islamic conception of time: moments in time are simultaneously unique (the birth the Prophet and the revelation of the Qur'ān occurred once, and in the past) and recurrent (special days and dates returning cyclically with their harvest of blessing).

Supporters and detractors of the *mawlid* celebration at the end of the twentieth century continued to dispute the nature of time. As in many other areas, however, the grounds of the debate have successfully been re-defined by *mawlid* opponents. Most importantly, some defenders of the *mawlid* have been compelled to respond to the accusation of *takhṣīṣ* ("specification" of a time for a religious observance without mandate from God) by denying that the celebration of the *mawlid* is linked to a specific day of the year at all. In his pamphlet in support of the *mawlid*, al-Mālikī's second introductory point addresses the issue of sacred time. "We do not hold," he writes, "that it is *sunna* to celebrate the aforementioned *mawlid* on a specific night. Whoever believes that has committed an innovation in the religion (*qad ibtada'a fī 'l-dīn*), because remembrance of [the Prophet] and attachment to him must occur at all times."[155] In the expanded second edition, he discusses this issue at greater length. The Prophet's birthday is not a festival (*'īd*), he argues, because "an *'īd* recurs only once per year; as for the celebration of [the Prophet's] birth and the concern with remembering him and his life story, they should be continuous and not limited to any [specific] time or place." Indeed, "We are celebrating the birthday of our master Muḥammad constantly and unceasingly (*dā'iman wa-abadan*), at all times and on every occasion."[156]

There is, of course, some truth to the contention that *mawlid* ceremonies are frequently held in all seasons of the year; however, it represents a major withdrawal from the historical fact that the *mawlid al-nabawī* has long been considered a calendrical festival. These denials of the specificity of the *mawlid* festival (or, indeed, of its being a festival at all) represent a significant shift from the positions taken by *mawlid* supporters of the past. Indeed, traditionally some proponents of the *mawlid* (including Ibn Ḥajar al-'Asqalānī[157] and by Ja'far al-Barzanjī[158]) considered the limitation of *mawlid* celebrations to the actual anniversary of the Prophet's birth important for their validity. Despite the fact that (as we have seen) the homogeneity or non-homogeneity of time was disputed by premodern scholars, the special quality of the date of the *mawlid* was widely accepted; as we have seen, Ibn al-Ḥājj – despite his opposition to the *mawlid* ceremony – affirms the auspicious qualities of the month of the *mawlid* in the most effusive terms.[159] Modern *mawlid* supporters, although they do wish to affirm some kind of rationale for the celebration of the Prophet's actual birth date, tend to do so on much more limited grounds. Rather than a recurring occasion of divine grace and blessing, the birthday is interpreted simply as a convenient and conventional opportunity for the commemoration of the Prophet's life.

al-Mālikī follows up his denial that it is a *sunna* to celebrate the *mawlid* on any particular date by remarking, "Yes; in the month of his birth there is a stronger incentive for people to take an interest and gather, and [for] their intense feeling for the interconnection of time (*shu'ūrihim al-fayyāḍ bi'rtibāṭ al-zamān ba'ḍihi bi-ba'ḍ*); by means of the present they remember the past, and they proceed from what is present to what is absent."[160] His fourth rationale for the celebration of the *mawlid* is

> That the Prophet used to observe the connection (*irtibāṭ*) of time with great religious events that had gone and passed away. Thus, when the time when such events occurred comes it is an opportunity (*furṣa*) for us to remember them and to venerate the day on which they occurred, for their sake and because [time] is a vessel for them (*li'annahu ẓarf lahā*).[161]

Although some of al-Mālikī's terminology in discussing issues of time (particularly his references to the *naw'*, "species," of the day) seem to reflect unacknowledged borrowings from 'Ayn al-Quḍāt, his claims about the blessings of special times are drastically reduced. His primary theme is commemoration, which he argues is the basis of one of the most fundamental canonical Islamic rituals, the pilgrimage to Mecca. "You see," he writes, "that most of the acts of the *ḥajj* are nothing but revivals of momentous memories and laudable events; the hastening between al-Ṣafā and al-Marwa, the pelting of the *jimār*, and the slaughter at Minā are all bygone events of the past (*ḥawādith māḍiya sābiqa*) whose memory the Muslim revives by recreating their image in the present."[162]

Rather than appearing as a uniquely auspicious occasion promising a rich harvest of religious merit, the *mawlid* is now simply a fitting opportunity for remembrance. The function of such occasions is primarily cognitive, to remind people of "important historical events" and celebrate "reform." al-Mālikī's formulations also emphasize the pastness of the past; the events commemorated by the *ḥajj*, for instance, are recapitulated precisely because they are remote. In al-Mālikī's own, somewhat redundant, words, they are "bygone events of the past" (*ḥawādith māḍiya sābiqa*).

The idea that canonical Islamic rituals are commemorations of historical events, and thus precedents for the celebration of anniversaries such as the Prophet's birthday, is also the basis of the endorsement of the *mawlid* celebration in the Azhar *fatwā* of 1993. The committee notes that a celebration is a means of drawing attention to an important thing and perpetuating its memory, so that people learn lessons from it.

> Islam perpetuated important memories by means of the stories of the noble Qur'ān, and prescribed for the people [for instance] the laws of the pilgrimage (*ḥajj*) to God's house in Mecca in order to perpetuate the memory of its foundation. . . . In the same way He prescribed the laws of fasting (*ṣiyām*) and connected them uniquely to Ramaḍān in order to perpetuate the memory of the revelation (*nuzūl*) of the Qur'ān in it.[163]

The idea that the *ḥajj* rituals commemorate the actions of Hājar, Ismā'īl, and Ibrāhīm is one that has a long history in Islamic thought, but which is not uncontested by premodern authors.[164] As far as I am aware, however, it is only in the twentieth century that the idea that canonical Islamic rituals are acts of commemoration is drawn into the debate over the legitimacy of the *mawlid*. Premodern *fatwā*s focus on the themes of thanking and rejoicing (also invoked by al-Mālikī and the Azhar *fatwā*) rather than that of remembrance; indeed, while the word *dhikrā* ("commemoration") features in modern discussions of the *mawlid*, neither it nor any direct equivalent plays a role in the debates of earlier centuries. Just as a performative model of *mawlid* recitation is eclipsed in the modern period by an informative model in which listeners learn about the Prophet's biography, the concept of "commemoration" emphasizes the didactic dimension of the celebration. The central point is not to do something that yields reward as a result of special divine favor at an auspicious time, but to engage in reflection that reminds one of the lessons of an irrevocable past.

The themes of blessing and merit do not completely disappear from contemporary defenses of the *mawlid*; it may be that such concepts are more likely to be retained in contexts further from the Saudi sphere of influence and those where ṣūfī discourses retain more of their authority. Both of these conditions apply, for instance, to the refutation of Ibn Manī' composed by the Moroccan scholars Murād and 'Amrawī. Referring to a *ḥadīth* in the *Ṣaḥīḥ* of al-Bukhārī, they note that Abū Bakr expressed the wish to die on a Monday because it was the day of the Prophet's death. This is an example of observing special occasions (*murā'āt al-munāsabāt*) and seeking blessings from them (*al-tabarruk bihā*), they argue; celebrating the *mawlid* is another example of the same thing.[165]

In response to the argument that the *mawlid* is an example of commemorative celebration analogous to the example of the ḥajj, *mawlid* opponents simply reject the idea that canonical Islamic rituals are based on commemoration. This is a time-honored argument in the context of debates about the ḥajj. In a traditional vein, al-Tuwayjirī supports this point by citing a *ḥadīth* stating that "the circumambulation of the House and the [hastening] between Safā and Marwa and the stoning of the columns were established only for the remembrance of God" – that is, rather than in commemoration of some specific historical event.[166] Ultimately, identifying the benefits of the *mawlid* with edifying remembrance rather than with automatic blessing or meritorious action eliminates the strongest rationale for the distinctiveness of the date of the *mawlid*. *Mawlid* opponents consistently note that (as observed by Ibn Manī'), reminding people of the Prophet should not be an annual (*ḥawlī*) activity.[167] As another anti-*mawlid* author notes, there is no need for a yearly commemoration of the Prophet, because good Muslims do not ever forget him.[168] Similarly, in a sermon on the Prophet's *hijra*, Ṣāliḥ ibn Fawzān urges his listeners to remember the Prophet's emigration and its lessons at all times, so that they can emulate his steadfast commitment to his mission. They should read the Prophet's biography in order to strengthen their faith and increase their knowledge (*ma'lūmāt*). Above all, they should not neglect the events of the Prophet's life and commemorate them only on the occasion of the new year. The commemoration of the Prophet's *hijra* is a *bid'a*, and the study of his biography should not be associated with any specific time or celebration.[169]

In a short *fatwā* opposing the observation of the *mawlid*, Ibn Bāz states that "teaching the historical reports having to do with the Prophet's birth in the context of the lessons on his life in the schools" and the mosques "makes the celebration of his birth superfluous."[170] Once the *mawlid* celebration has been re-defined as an act of historical commemoration with purely pedagogical aims, it is subsumed into the larger framework of modern Islamic education and loses its character as ritual. This shift exemplifies a broader trend of what might be termed the "de-ritualization" of Islamic study. Whereas in the medieval period a public reading of the *Ṣaḥīḥ* of al-Bukhārī might have shared many of the ritualized aspects of *mawlid* recitation, for instance, in the contemporary world the text is increasingly likely to be studied in ways reflecting the dissemination of modern print technology (which makes owning and consulting copies of the text accessible to large numbers of people) and educational techniques.

The contemporary re-definition of the *mawlid* celebration as an act of edifying commemoration is accompanied by a wider shift in the understanding of the role of the Prophet. Devotion to the Prophet's person is eclipsed by a more systematic emphasis on the content of his message, a change that inevitably casts into doubt the unique significance of the event of his birth. Even the pro-*mawlid* Azhar *fatwā* notes that the Prophet's birth "is one of the greatest historical events in general, because it is a preliminary step to [the delivery of] his message."[171] Muḥammad ibn Aḥmad al-Khazrajī, president of the Heritage and History Committee (Lajnat al-Turāth wa'l-Ta'rīkh) of the United Arab Emirates, states in a sermon in honor of the *mawlid* that "when we celebrate the birth of the Messenger, we are really celebrating the birth of his mission, and celebrating the sublime principles that he brought." Throughout his several sermons on the subject, al-Khazrajī thoroughly conflates Muḥammad's birth with the arrival of Islam; there is no specific mention of the events of his nativity.[172] In view of this conflation, the event of the Prophet's birth loses its special saliency. Ṣāliḥ ibn Fawzān asserts that God's favor to humankind was not Muḥammad's birth, but his commissioning as a prophet. "From his commissioning to his death, every moment of his good life was a blessing to humankind," although its benefits were not associated with any specific day of the year.[173] Of course, this formulation pointedly excludes from consideration the Prophet's early life. Similar to other opponents of the *mawlid* festival, al-Tuwayjirī argues that there are many other worthy occasions in the Prophet's life which he did not choose to commemorate. The greatest events in his life included the revelation of the first verses of the

Qur'ān, the Night Journey, the hijra, the Battle of Badr, and the conquest of Mecca. If the Prophet had been in the habit of commemorating momentous occurrences, surely he would have celebrated these great days.[174]

From the point of view of devotion to the person of the Prophet, of course, all of these events are overshadowed by the Prophet's birth. al-Mālikī writes that the *mawlid* is greater than either of the canonical festivals because "it is what brought all festivals and joys; among its virtues are all the great days in Islam. Were it not for [the Prophet's birth] there would have been no commissioning as a prophet (*bu'tha*), no revelation of the Qur'ān, no *isrā'* or *mi'rāj*, no *hijra*, no victory at Badr, no great conquest [of Mecca] – because all of that is dependent on him and on his birth, which is the father of these great blessings."[175]

However, a sense that the Prophet's birth is not obviously the event in his life most worthy of commemoration emerges even from some modern works in honor of the *mawlid*. We have already seen (see pp. 180–1) that modern *mawlid* texts themselves sometimes de-emphasize the Prophet's actual birth in favor of a greater focus on the events of his adulthood. The overshadowing of the Muḥammad's birthday by other events considered more relevant to his prophetic mission is also evident in the creation of new commemorative occasions in the modern period. Ḥasan al-Shaykha already remarks in a collection of essays in celebration of the *mawlid* published by the Egyptian journal *Minbar al-islām* in 1968 that there are many other events in the Prophet's biography that are worthy of yearly commemoration, including the *hijra*, the Prophet's various military campaigns (*ghazawāt*), the revelation of the Qur'ān, and his reception of delegations from Arab tribes that embraced Islam. al-Shaykha observes that the Prophet himself commemorated none of these events, but Muslims have come to celebrate several of them. The *mawlid* is the most time-honored celebration (al-Shaykha unhesitatingly credits the Fāṭimids with its origination), while others have emerged more recently: the *hijra* has been commemorated at the beginning of the Islamic year only since the beginning of the fourteenth-century AH, and the Battle of Badr and the beginning of the revelation of the Qur'ān have only recently begun to be celebrated.[176] Of the occasions mentioned by Shaykha, the commemoration of the *hijra* on the first of Muḥarram has become the most prevalent; it functions as an Islamic New Year's observance. Writing several decades later, al-Būṭī similarly lists the commemoration of the beginning of the *hijrī* year, the Conquest of Mecca and the Battle of Badr (along with the *mawlid* and the *mi'rāj*) as "good customs" (sunan *ḥasana*) that have been initiated by later generations of Muslims.[177]

The legitimacy of commemorative holidays is emphasized in a work issued by al-Azhar in the mid-eighties, edited and introduced by the rector Jād al-Ḥaqq 'Alī Jād al-Ḥaqq (d. 1416 AH/1996 CE). The discussion opens with the quasi-sociological premise that all societies are concerned with the beneficial or harmful events that befall them, which leads in due course to "the commemoration of events that occurred in specific places or times, which the memory recalls in order to renew their joy and delight or to draw lessons and morals from them."[178] Indeed, the authors argue, the *sharī'a* comprises examples of the commemoration of unforgettable events. For instance, the authors assert, fasting was legislated in Ramaḍān "in order to perpetuate the memory (*takhlīdan li-dhikrā*) of [Muḥammad's] prophetic mission and the coming down of the Qur'ān." Similarly, both the location and the individual rites of the *ḥajj* memorialize great events of the past. The authors also cite the examples of the Jews of Medina fasting for 'Āshurā' and of the Prophet fasting on Mondays. All of this indicates the holy law's (*al-tashrī'*) interest in "the perpetuation of memories" (*takhlīd al-dhikrayāt*). "There are memories in Islamic history that must never be forgotten," the authors remark, and "to celebrate them is to draw strength from them (*fī 'l-iḥtifāl bihā istimdād li 'l-quwwa minhā*)."[179]

Because the *sharī'a* manifests a concern for the commemoration of great events, and because their remembrance is inherently edifying, the authors have no objection to the celebration of other foundational events in the Islamic past.

> Is not the emigration from Mecca to Medina a great historical event by which God distinguished between truth and falsehood, so 'Umar immortalized (*khallada*) it and made it the beginning of the calendar, and after other suggestions were presented to him, he found the *hijra* the best and most appropriate? . . . . Are not the victories of Badr, the Ditch, the Conquest of Mecca, Yarmūk, Qādisīya, Ḥiṭṭīn, and 'Ayn Jālūt, occasions before which we should stop, wondering, thinking, studying, and seeking strength that will help us in the present and the future? We see no harm in the celebration of any religious or worldly/secular (*dunyawī*) occasion, on the condition that the mode of celebration not exceed the boundaries of the *shar'* and that the goal be sound.[180]

While occasions such as the commemoration of the *hijra* may be opportunities for thematically appropriate sermons and articles in Islamic journals, however, newer commemorative holidays such as those associated with the *hijra* and the Battle of Badr have not been incorporated into mass Islamic piety in any significant way. This fact is probably rooted in the scholarly aversion to *bida'*, which prevents the religiously sanctioned emergence of new ritual forms (while exempting more neutral modern conventions including the school assembly or the journal article); it may also reflect the lack of popular appeal in commemorations that evoke abstract Islamic ideals while lacking a lively salvific link with the person of the Prophet.

Despite the modest level of development of this embryonic new cycle of holidays, however, it suggests a shift in modern frameworks of Islamic religiosity. The noncanonical holidays of the medieval period that commemorated events in the life of the Prophet, the *mawlid* and the *mi'rāj*, celebrated the person of the Prophet and his salvific role. In popular (and much scholarly) understanding, for instance, the culmination of the events of the *mi'rāj* was the Prophet's reception of a divine pledge guaranteeing his intercession for his community.[181] *Laylat nisf Sha'bān* was also distinguished primarily by its appeal to the need for personal salvation. The invocations prescribed for the occasion entreated God to alter the worshiper's destiny for the good, eliminating poverty and suffering;[182] the special prayers performed on that night were held to yield bounteous religious merit.[183] In contrast, the new commemorative occasions promoted in the modern period have a purely didactic function, reminding Muslims of the content of the Qur'ānic message and inspiring them with the Prophet's example. This shift is exemplified by the twentieth-century reinterpretation of *laylat nisf Sha'bān*. As discussed by Vardit Rispler-Chaim, since the 1950s Egyptian scholars have promoted the previously rather obscure idea that this date is the anniversary of the change in the *qibla* from Jerusalem to Mecca.[184] An opportunity for the generation of merit and the pursuit of personal salvation has thus been transformed by some modern scholars into an occasion of historical commemoration and edifying reflection.

Hava Lazarus-Yafeh perceptively observes that there has been a shift in interpretation of the canonical festivals; recent sermons and writings on the Feast of the Sacrifice, for instance, display an unprecedented concern with the idea that it commemorates the story of Abraham.[185] In the premodern period, opinion ranged from the austere assertion that Islamic rites and celebrations were pure expressions of obedience to divine fiat, through the affirmation that they commemorated great events of the past, to the devotionalist faith that special times were inherently auspicious and rich in blessings. In the contemporary debates, the third option (the inherent sacredness of special times) has been more or less forced from the mainstream among non-ṣūfī Middle Eastern scholars; *mawlid* supporters now argue for the didactic value of commemorative celebrations, while opponents argue that religious celebrations can be no more or less than the punctilious fulfillment of direct divine commands. In the spectrum from unquestioning obedience through edifying reflection to ritual efficacy, only obedience and reflection remain. Furthermore, the range of appropriate objects for commemorative reflection has shifted to emphasize events directly associated with the revelation and propagation of the divine message. The personal dimension of the Prophet's life, exemplified in his birth, childhood, and marriage – the primary content of classic popular *mawlid*s – are thus eclipsed.

Conclusion

In the second-half of the nineteenth century, a mainstream jurist such as Aḥmad ibn 'Ābidīn could still write with assurance that gathering to hear the story of the Prophet's birth was "one of the greatest acts of piety" (*min a'ẓam al-qurubāt*). He described its religious value in terms of pious gifts and the invocation of blessings and greetings upon the Prophet, all out of "love for him that leads to his proximity."[186] Only a few decades later, the idea that ordinary people considered the celebration of the *mawlid* a "great act of piety" was cause for grave concern among Islamic reformers such as Rashīd Riḍā. Islamic scholars of centuries past had expressed concern (and often dismay) with the religious activities and narratives of "common people" (*al-'awāmm*); by their conscious invocation of standards of ritual correctness and narrative truth, they constituted such activities and stories as "popular Islam." However, even in their appropriation and critique of *mawlid* piety, most scholars before the twentieth century engaged with the same models of pious action that underlay the festive meals and pious invocations of ordinary Muslims. The twentieth century saw a dramatic reversal in the fortunes of *mawlid* piety. The shift arose both from changes in political and economic relations (especially those that brought to prominence the followers of Muḥammad ibn ʿAbd al-Wahhāb) and deeper changes in the religious imaginations of Muslims. The earlier models of pious exchange and expressive devotion were gradually eclipsed in favor of an increasing emphasis on discursive knowledge and systematic conformity to the law.

Conclusion

This study has shown that the celebration of *mawlid*s was not primarily pioneered or dominated by members of ruling dynasties, but cultivated by a wide range of private persons with no political power to legitimate. Furthermore, its emergence and flowering cannot be explained genetically, by a succession of temporally ordered inaugural acts (although this approach was attractive to medieval Muslim authors as well as to modern scholars). The origins of the *mawlid* can be traced, not to the single innovative act of some identifiable authority, but to the slow coalescence of a constellation of devotional narratives and practices that eventually converged to form a single, highly flexible, and attractive form of ritual action.

The development and content of the *mawlid* tradition suggests a complex relationship between "popular" and "normative"modes of religiosity. On the level of narrative, works such as the *sīra* of al-Bakrī have been classified as expressions of "folk" Islam. However, only steadfast commitment to the conviction that certain "historical" texts define the normative content of Islam could lead one to deny that, for large bodies of Muslims (including some scholars) and for long periods of time, the narratives associated with al-Bakrī may well have been in all meaningful senses the normative version of the story of the Prophet's life – that is, the one that was known to most people, accepted as true, and taken as a background for the religious ideas and aspirations of a large body of the faithful.

From this point of view, James Kritzeck's irritable judgment of the selection of the Islamic texts in the Toledo Collection is subject to reconsideration. These texts' translation was sponsored by Peter the Venerable in the twelfth-century CE with the aim of providing Christians with basic information about the Muslim faith; their selection was guided by Spanish informants. While Kritzeck praises the inclusion of the Qur'ān and of the *Fabulae Saracenorum*, which provided historical material about the life of the Prophet and the early caliphs, he complains that the *mawlid* narrative of Ka'b al-Aḥbār was one of the "weakest" choices. In its inclusion of "so much *spurii* and trivia," it "proved an almost total washout in terms of providing accurate information."[1] It is worth considering, on the contrary, whether this work's selection as part of a small corpus of core texts for the comprehension of Islam in twelfth-century Spain may in fact tell us something very important about its centrality to contemporary belief. It constitutees evidence that, at least in the eyes of the Spanish informants who guided the selection, Ka'b's *mawlid* narrative was part of the Islamic canon.[2]

The complex of pious practices associated with the recollection of the Prophet's birth, including the serving of food and the generation and donation of merit, should also be understood as an integral part of normative Islamic piety for much of the pre-modern period. Writing about contemporary Java, Mark Woodward has critiqued Geertz's argument that "ritual meals are characteristic of animism but foreign to Islam," observing that "the Hadith include numerous descriptions of ritual meals and the distribution of blessed food."[3] Appreciation of the central role of feeding and blessing in pre-modern Islam, however, does not necessarily rest on direct appeals to the primary textual sources of Qur'ān and *ḥadīth*; rather, such practices are inextricably integrated into a set of assumptions about human relationships and the means of salvation that prevailed unquestioned for many pre-modern Muslims. Introducing his description of the *mawlid* ceremonies that pervaded Meccan social and religious life in the nineteenth-century CE, Snouck Hurgronje observes that "The Holy Law recommends the faithful to celebrate all sorts of joyful events by festive meals,"[4] and it seems likely that this remark faithfully reflects the views of his Arabian informants. Only later would the legitimacy and centrality of ritualized feeding be broadly and effectively disputed.

The twentieth century saw enormous shifts in Islamic understandings of proper piety and ritual action, changes that can be clearly perceived through the prism of the evolving debate over the legitimacy of *mawlid*s. Already toward the end of the nineteenth century, the resurgence of the Saudi state and the rise of modernist voices led to a reevaluation of traditional pious practices. Both a Wahhābī-inspired desire to purify the faith of idolatrous accretions and an apologetic effort to vindicate its rationality and ethical power in the face of western encroachments encouraged new critiques of Islamic devotionalism. The figure of Rashīd Riḍā, who expressed sympathy for the Wahhābī cause, illustrates the convergence of these two trends. As twentieth-century Muslims increasingly focused on the Prophet's ethical teachings and his effectiveness as a reformer, his trans-historical role as a pre-existent light and an agent of salvation on the Day of Judgment was eclipsed in scholarly discourse. Wahhābīs rejected *mawlid*s categorically, but until the late-twentieth century failed to influence popular practice on a broad scale. Modernist reformers attempted to appropriate and transform the *mawlid* genre, but their exclusive emphasis on the content of the Prophet's adult religious mission rendered their work's connection to the tradition of *mawlid* piety tenuous and artificial. Meanwhile, masses of ordinary Muslims (and many scholars) continued to celebrate the Prophet's birthday in traditional ways and to cherish *mawlid* texts and narratives from centuries past.

The chronic ineffectiveness of scholarly critiques is illustrated by the fact that twentieth-century Muslims continued to transmit and perform *mawlid* narratives that had been denounced by scholars since the medieval period. Rashīd Riḍā's objections to the story of the world's creation from the Light of Muḥammad echoed those of Ibn Taymīya and al-Subkī, and were no more effective. Despite at least seven centuries of scholarly denunciation, the narratives familiar from al-Bakrī's *Anwār* continued to circulate in the Middle Eastern Muslim metropoli of Cairo and Damascus. It is with only moderate hyperbole that J. Knappert, surveying usage from Africa to Indonesia, described *Sharaf al-anām* in 1988 as "the single best-known prayer book in Islam."[5]

While efforts to suppress or transform *mawlid* practices and narratives have generally been unsuccessful, however, the last decades of the twentieth century saw far more radical changes. The unprecedented scale and aggressiveness of Saudi-sponsored polemics have succeeded in shifting the terms of the debate in significant and revealing ways. In part, of course, the vigor and passion of the controversy arise from an underlying conflict over religious authority. The Saudi religious establishment's pursuit of al-Mālikī surely reflected not merely a sincere distaste for the theological implications of his teachings (although this is undoubtedly present), but an effort to marginalize a prominent ṣūfī teacher who offered an alternative to official Saudi doctrines in the heart of the Holy Places. Similarly, Azharī endorsements of the celebration of the *mawlid* reflect the institution's claim to serve as an arbiter of correct Sunnī practice; the contrast with official Saudi doctrine is surely not coincidental. The Azharī position's higher degree of continuity with pre-modern Islamic consenses (tempered with a pious commitment to the reform of popular practice) reflects one of the sources of the institution's legitimacy in the eyes of ordinary Muslims.

However, the transformation of the terms of the *mawlid* debate reflects more than the shifting balance of power in a dispute over religious authority in the Sunnī world. It also reflects a transformation of religious consciousness that is integrally related to the impact of modernity. In many ways, the *mawlid* controversy can serve as a microcosm of the religious implications of modern ideas about the nature of the individual and of the world. The person implied by pre-modern devotional practice was not a bounded individual with exclusive responsibility for his or her own actions and an emotional subjectivity inaccessible to others. Rather, the believer's ethical personhood was constituted by a network of relationships with living and dead relatives, neighbors, and holy persons. His or her religious emotions were publicly constituted, inculcated through appropriate pedagogical conditioning and performed through an accepted repertory of expressive religious activities. The inculcation of religious teachings was inseparable from the emotive and ritual aspects of practice. The believer existed in the context of a religious conception of time that was simultaneously linear and cyclical; while the events of sacred history were past, the cycle of holy days made their numinous power available to him on a regular basis. This synthesis was not universally accepted by Islamic scholars, but it was widely prevalent among the elite and its major lineaments seem to have been shared at a popular level.

The person implied by contemporary polemics against the *mawlid*, and largely accepted by many of its defenders, is very different in nature. He or she is a bounded individual who benefits only from his or her own pious actions, the fruits of which may not be shared with others. The believer's ethical life is rationalized, depending on consistent lifelong adherence to core religious precepts rather than episodic reaping of special divine blessings. Emotions are understood to be private, subjective, and evanescent, not manifest social facts that can be regulated or evaluated by religious law. The acquisition of religious knowledge is understood on the model of modern print culture, as a non-ritual activity involving the mastery of a body of knowledge. The individual exists in the context of a linear time that separates him decisively from the events of the sacred past.

These changes are in many ways reminiscent of the concepts developed by students of religion and modernization. The shift from a model in which an inherently sinful believer episodically generates large quantities of merit to one in which he must systematically exercise ethical discipline suggests Weber's analysis of the "Protestant ethic." Prevalent pre-modern ideas about the generation and transfer of merit were based on non-arithmetic principles according to which gift-giving enhanced rather than depleted resources and well-being was defined within a wide web of earthly and supernatural relationships. Its eclipse may well reflect new economic realities in which the social capital generated by gift-giving and sharing no longer dominates the hard reality of saving and investment.

It is to be emphasized that the logic of the economy of merit underlying *mawlid* celebrations is not to be equated with the logic of a modern, secular economic system. The mathematics of divine reward (*thawāb*) are magically elastic, and their meaning lies in the wondrous and beneficent incommensurability of meager human action and bounteous divine reward, rather than in any numerical equivalency. In an article analyzing *mawlid* performances in modern Turkey, Nancy and Richard Tapper argue that the pursuit of merit through the performance of pious activities is "compatible with the capitalist ethic of contemporary Turkey."[6] Only further evidence about the Turkish villagers studied by Tapper and Tapper could confirm or disprove their contention about this specific cultural milieu. In general, however, it is to be emphasized that the logic of merit and demerit/sin is remote from a modern "capitalist ethic." While the basic *sharʿī* outlook emphasizes the moderacy of the demands of the *sharīʿa* and the consequent viability of adequately fulfilling God's commands, the discourse of *thawāb* emphasizes the sinful inadequacy of the believer and his or her consequent dependence for salvation on bounteous rewards for small acts of piety. The pursuit of *thawāb* assumes, not a calculating modern capitalist subjecting his or her actions to consistent and rigorous scrutiny, but a person who views his or her religious efforts as inevitably inadequate and hopes to reap a bountiful harvest of blessing from occasional acts of piety.

In the mainstream pre-modern model of *mawlid* practice, the transactional nature of the devotional bargain is unproblematic. Snouck Hurgronje, describing the perfunctory and cost-conscious spirit in which *mawlid*s for the dead were sometimes arranged in nineteenth-century Mecca, remarks disparagingly that "In this way business is done in a good commercial fashion with the heavenly bookkeeper." His sensibilities in this regard must have diverged sharply from those of his Arabian informants. For them the effort "to increase the credit in

Heaven of dead relatives" is unquestionably legitimate; as he observes elsewhere, "The heavenly advantages hoped to be won in Mekka are in the prayer-formulae always represented in the guide of a profitable trade."[7] However, his sense of disapproval is increasingly shared by later critics of the *mawlid*. Indeed, transactional modes of piety in which pious deeds are performed (or resources expended) in anticipation of a quasi-quantifiable "return" of merit are subject to increasing criticism in the twentieth century. Anne Betteridge recounts that in the 1970s, women's devotional gatherings in Shiraz, Iran, were sharply criticized on the grounds that their motivation was "contractual, not devotional"; opponents argued that they were "not sponsored out of religious feeling but as payment for services rendered." This critique was grounded partially in the perception that the sponsors of such gatherings increasingly sought concrete material benefits from God; however, it more generally targeted the "mercantile attitude" reflected in vows to perform specific ceremonies on the fulfillment of a wish.[8] Without reaching any conclusions about local developments in Shirazi religious practice, it is worth observing that the practice of performing devotional ceremonies in fulfillment of vows is scarcely new; the association between devotional practices and the expression or fulfillment of hopes for such blessings as "children, spouses, employment, houses, [or] health"[9] reaches far back into the pre-modern period. What is perhaps more novel is that the desire to evoke such blessings through pious practice (or the motivation to perform pious actions in gratitude for receiving them) is perceived in an increasingly negative light. In a study of the Gayo of Sumatra, John Bowen describes the disputation of the meaning of the Feast of Sacrifice in the 1980s. While "most villagers . . . interpret the event as an occasion to generate spiritual benefits for themselves and their ancestors" and "see it as primarily a transaction," town-dwelling Modernists "emphasize their attitude of selfless sacrifice."[10] Increasingly in the twentieth century, practices that had been widely accepted in previous times are deprecated as mercenary and self-interested. Furthermore, the religious merit that had once been shared with kin (and the familial well-being that had once been elicited and acknowledged through pious practice) are increasingly replaced by ideals of obedience and moral edification that apply primarily to the individual. (Bowen notes that the ideal of "selfless sacrifice" is also connected to "Indonesian state ideas about sacrifice for the common good"[11]; the virtuous individual envisioned by the ascendant modern models of piety may also be identified with the good citizen of the modern state.)

Jonathan Parry has argued that in modern society, "Gift-exchange – in which persons and things, interest and disinterest are merged – has been fractured, leaving gifts opposed to exchange, persons opposed to things and interest to disinterest."[12] The "ideology of the 'pure gift' " emerges in contrast with that of the market;

> these gifts are defined as what market relations are not – altruistic, moral and loaded with emotion. As the economy becomes progressively disembedded from society, as economic relations become increasingly differentiated from

> other types of social relationship, the transactions appropriate to each become ever more polarized in terms of their symbolism and ideology.[13]

Parry concludes that "an elaborated ideology of the 'pure' gift is most likely to develop in state societies with an advanced division of labour and a significant commercial sector." He also relates it to the belief system of "the major world religions," which emphasize "the merit of gifts and alms, ideally given in secrecy and without expectation of any worldly return."[14]

The increasing marginalization of transactional forms of devotionalism in the twentieth century may reflect this process of disengagement between a market sphere of calculated personal gain and a religious sphere of idealized disinterest. Practices such as the performance of mawlids in fulfillment of vows (or the expectation that pious expenditures will yield this-worldly and otherworldly blessings) may increasingly be rejected as "mercenary" because they smack of the market, and the market is a sphere remote from the realm of religious self-expression (even if subject to the ethical strictures of the *sharīʿa*). However, it would be ill-advised to overdraw this connection. The pre-modern group that most clearly advanced a well-elaborated ideology of "selfless" giving (and thus of religious devotion without hope of worldly, or even otherworldly, reward) was the ṣūfīs, whose distinctive attitudes towards the gift surely arise from their core spiritual agenda rather than from a distinctive experience of the market. The Saudi scholars of Najd scarcely represent the cutting edge of capitalistic development in the Islamic world, yet they are among the most avid advocates of a model of religious rationalization. It is probably best to understand the transformation of prevalent Islamic models of the religious individual in the context of a number of converging factors, some of them structural and some of them reflecting the contingent realities of ongoing ideological conflict and debate.

The pre-modern devotional synthesis envisioned a world pervaded with the sacred. Deceased holy persons, up to and including the Prophet himself, were personally present to the faithful. Neither time nor space prevented the Prophet from being available and responsive to those who blessed and greeted him. The cycle of the Islamic calendar also carried with it periodic opportunities for the reaping of blessings and the generation of merit. The sacred could be accessed by ordinary people with little education and limited commitment to the systematic fulfillment of the requirements of Islamic law. The world envisioned by the contemporary opponents of the *mawlid*, in contrast, is largely devoid of the sacred. Neither special times nor special places are available as means of accessing the sacred; only consistent obedience to divine commandments offers hope of salvation. The Prophet is distant in both time and (except for visitors to his grave) in space; he is not a pervasive transhistorical presence, but a historical individual who passed away centuries ago and will be directly re-encountered only on the Day of Resurrection. In the present, the only connections to the divine are texts and the sacred ordinances they contain; these function as guidelines for behavior, not as salvific talismans. Time is linear and homogeneous. In comparison with the devotionalist worldview exemplified in traditional *mawlid* practices, this vision represents a radical disenchantment of the world.

Pre-modern scholars tended to recognize a distinction between the needs and abilities of elite and ordinary believers. Although all Muslims theoretically had the same basic religious obligations, disparities in religious knowledge and commitment appear to have been acknowledged by scholars on both sides of the controversy. While Ibn Taymīya certainly advocates that Islamic practice be firmly grounded in the Prophet's *sunna*, for instance, he recognizes that it may not be possible to raise all Muslims to this ideal level of practice. Celebrating the Prophet's birthday, like embellishing a Qur'ān with gold (another religiously suspect act of devotion), may be the most sincerely pious act that a given individual is likely to perform. In this case, Ibn Taymīya acknowledges that a noncanonical act of devotion may be genuinely meritorious; he counsels that it may be unwise to prohibit such customs unless a more legitimate alternative can successfully be promoted. "Things may be approved when performed by some people, that would be disapproved if performed by a rightly guided believer (*al-mu'min al-musaddad*)."[15] Similarly, Ibn Ḥajar al-Haytamī makes a distinction between the practices of ordinary and elite Muslims. Acknowledging that the *qiyām* is performed as an expression of reverence for the Prophet, al-Haytamī states that ordinary people are excused for engaging in it (*al-'awāmm ma'dhūrūn li-dhālika*). Learned Muslims, in contrast, must eschew the *qiyām* lest they spread the misconception that it is legally recommended.[16] While Ibn Nāṣir al-Dīn does not explicitly invoke a distinction between elite and ordinary Muslims, as we have seen, his discussion of devotional practice is marked by a populist concern for the needs and desires of the common believer. In discussing the pedagogical value of the *mawlid* celebration, al Raṣṣā' suggests that his readers use the occasion to involve not only children but wives and "commoners" (*al-'awāmm*).[17]

Modern authors, in contrast, tend to assume that all Muslims are subject to the same religious standards. The idea that devotional practice may be a sincere, if imperfect, form of religious expression for the uneducated or the unsophisticated seems to disappear from the debate. Contemporary opponents of the *mawlid* may elide Ibn Taymīya's comments on this subject not merely because they wish to emphasize his more categorical arguments against the *mawlid*, but because they assume that a full *sunna*-based Islamic practice is accessible to all Muslims. If participants in the contemporary *mawlid* debate no longer believe that ordinary Muslims may legitimately engage in lesser (or less well-founded) forms of ritual practice, this may reflect modern developments in literacy and religious education. It is now possible to imagine that scholarly standards of belief and conduct can be disseminated to the entire population.

The emergence and (partial) eclipse of the *mawlid* tradition does not represent a single and unidirectional trajectory. While the broad outlines of the developments described here (which are centered on the Arab world, particularly Egypt, Syria, and Arabia) are likely to be applicable to many other parts of the Islamic world, the legitimacy of *mawlid* celebrations (and of the models of piety that underlie them) are negotiated in different ways in different local contexts. Even in the arena examined here, other factors complicate the overall developments described in Chapter 5. After the September 11 attacks, which inspired the Saudi authorities to re-examine some aspects of their relationship with Wahhābī ideology, both ṣūfism and *mawlid* celebrations were allowed to regain some of their public currency.[18] Muḥammad ibn 'Alawī al-Mālikī was one of the religious scholars who were newly appreciated by the Saudi leadership in the post-9/11 period. After his death in 2004, high Saudi dignitaries made widely publicized condolence visits to his family.[19] Crown Prince 'Abd Allāh (the future king) was quoted as stating that al-Mālikī "was faithful both to his religion and country"[20]; as one western journalist noted, "the rehabilitation of his legacy was almost complete."[21]

Appendix

Mawlid authors to 1000 AH

Name	*Death date (AH)*	*Location*	*Madhhab*	*Discipline*
Muḥammad ibn Salāma al-Quḍāʿī[1]	454	Egypt	Shāfiʿī	Law, *ḥadīth*, history, preaching
ʿIyāḍ ibn Mūsā al-Yaḥṣubī[2]	544	Maghrib, Andalus	Mālikī	*Ḥadīth*, history, law
(Aḥmad ibn Maʿadd al-Iqlīshī[3])	ca. 550	Andalus, mashriq	?	Belles lettres, *ḥadīth*
Ibn Diḥya[4]	633	Maghrib, traveled widely	Ẓāhirī	*Ḥadīth*
Aḥmad al-ʿAzafī[5]	633	Maghrib	Mālikī	
Ibn al-ʿArabī[6]	638	Andalus, Damascus	Mālikī	Mysticism
Ibn Tughrūbek[7]	670	Damascus	Ḥanafī	
Muḥammad al-Qurṭubī[8]	671	Andalus, Cairo	Mālikī	Exegesis
Muḥammad b. ʿAlī b. Saʿīd al-Gharnāṭī[9]	673	Andalus?		History
Muḥammad al-ʿAzafī[10]	677	Maghrib	Mālikī	Law; local ruler
ʿUthmān b. Muḥammad al-Tawzarī[11]	703 or 713	Maghrib, Mecca	Mālikī	*Ḥadīth*
Muḥammad b. ʿAlī al-Zamlakānī[12]	727	Damascus	Shāfiʿī	Law, Mysticism, belles lettres
Ibrāhīm ibn ʿUmar al-Jaʿbarī[13]	732	Baghdād, Damascus	Shāfiʿī	Grammar, *ḥadīth*
Ibn Qayyim al-Jawzīya[14]	751	Damascus	Ḥanbalī	Law, Preaching, theology
Muḥammad ibn Masʿūd al-Kāzarūnī[15]	758	Iran, Medina		*Ḥadīth*, Law
Khalīl ibn Kaykaldī al-ʿAlāʾī[16]	761	Damascus	Shāfiʿī	
Khalīl ibn Aybak al-Ṣafadī[17]	764	Damascus, Aleppo	Shāfiʿī	Belles lettres

(Tāj al-Dīn al-Subkī[18])	769	Cairo, Damascus	Shāfi‘ī	Law, *ḥadīth*
Ibn Kathīr[19]	774	Boṣra, Damascus	Shāfi‘ī	*Ḥadīth*, history, exegesis
al-Ḥasan ibn Ḥabīb[20]	779	Damascus, Aleppo	Shāfi‘ī	Exegesis, belles lettres, preaching, grammar
Muḥammad b. Aḥmad b. Jābir[21]	780	Andalus, Aleppo	Mālikī	Belles lettres, various
‘Abd al-Raḥīm ibn al-Ḥusayn al-‘Irāqī[22]	806	Egypt, traveled in Syria	Shāfi‘ī	*Ḥadīth*
Muḥammad ibn Ya‘qūb al-Fayrūzābādī[23]	817	Iran, traveled widely	Shāfi‘ī	Arabic language, *ḥadīth*
Taqī al-Dīn al-Ḥiṣnī[24]	829	Damascus	Shāfi‘ī	Law
Ibn al-Jazarī[25]	833	Damascus, traveled widely	Shāfi‘ī	Qur’ānic recitation, *ḥadīth*, law
Ibn Nāṣir al-Dīn[26]	842	Damascus	Shāfi‘ī	*Ḥadīth*
Muḥammad al-Dimyāṭī, Ibn al-Faqīh[27]	842–3	Dimyāṭ (Egypt)	Shāfi‘ī	Belles lettres
al-Sayyid ‘Afīf al-Dīn[28]	855	Shīrāz, Mecca	Shāfi‘ī	Mysticism, *ḥadīth*
Ibrāhīm b. Yūsuf al-Fāqūsī[29]	862	Fāqūs, Bilbīs (Egypt)	Shāfi‘ī	Mysticism
Muḥammad b. ‘Uthmān al-Lu’lu’ī[30]	867	Damascus	Shāfi‘ī	*Ḥadīth*, preaching
Abū Bakr b. ‘Alī al-Zunqulī[31]	867	Ta‘izz, Aden (Yemen)	(Shāfi‘ī?)	
‘Abd Allāh al-Harawī[32]	883	Shīrāz, Harāt	Ḥanafī	Preaching
‘Alī b. Sulaymān al-Mardāwī[33]	885	Palestine, Cairo/Damascus	Ḥanbalī	*Ḥadīth*, law, jurisprudence
Abū’l-Ṣafā Ibrāhīm b. ‘Alī[34]	887	Iraq, Jerusalem?	Shāfi‘ī	Mysticism
Burhān al-Dīn al-Nājī[35]	900	Damascus	Shāfi‘ī	
Muḥammad al-Sakhāwī[36]	902	Cairo	Shāfi‘ī	various
al-Ḥusayn b. al-Ṣiddīq al-Ahdal[37]	903	Yemen	(Shāfi‘ī?)	
Ibn Makkīya[38]	907	Nablus, Damascus	Shāfi‘ī	Preaching
‘Ā’isha bt. Yūsuf al-Bā‘ūnīya[39]	922	Damascus, Cairo		Mysticism, belles lettres, law

(continued)

Continued

Name	*Death date* (AH)	*Location*	*Madhhab*	*Discipline*
Muḥammad Baḥraq[40]	930	Ḥaḍramawt, Zabīd (Yemen)	Shāfi‘ī	Mysticism
Abū Bakr al-Ḥubayshī al-Bisṭāmī[41]	930	Aleppo	Shāfi‘ī	Mysticism
Muḥammad al-Bilbīsī[42]	937	Bilbīs, Damascus	Shāfi‘ī	Preaching
‘Abd al-Raḥmān b. ‘Alī al-Dayba‘[43]	944	Zabīd (Yemen)	Shāfi‘ī	*Ḥadīth*, Law
Muḥammad ibn ‘Alī ibn Ṭūlūn[44]	953	Damascus		
Ibn Ḥajar al-Haytamī[45]	973	Egypt, Mecca	Shāfi‘ī	Law
Muḥammad al-Ghayṭī[46]	984	Alexandria, Cairo	Shāfi‘ī	*Ḥadīth*, mysticism
Shaykh ibn ‘Abd Allāh al-‘Aydarūs[47]	990	Tarīm (Yemen)	(Shāfi‘ī?)	Mysticism

Notes
[1]Ṣalāh al-Dīn al-Munajjid, *Mu‘jam mā ullifa ‘an rasūl allāh*, Beirut: Dār al-Kitāb al-Jadīd, 1402 AH/1982 CE, p. 45; [2]‘Abd al-‘Azīz ibn Rāshid ibn ‘Abd al-Karīm al-Sunaydī, *Mu‘jam mā ullifa ‘an makka*, n.p., 1420 AH/1999 CE, pp. 165, 172; [3]Ismā‘īl Bāshā al-Baghdādī, *Īḍāḥ al-maknūn fī al-dhayl ‘alā Kashf al-ẓunūn ‘an asāmī al-kutub wa'l-funūn*, Istanbul: Milli Egitim Basimevi, 1945, 1:451; [4]Ibn Khallikān, *Wafayāt al-a‘yān wa-anbā' abnā' al-zamān*, ed. Iḥsān ‘Abbās, Beirut: Dār al-Thaqāfa, n.d., 3:449; Ibn Kathīr, *al-Bidāya wa'l-nihāya*, Beirut: Dār al-Fikr, n.d., p. 13:137; Brockelmann, *GAL*, GI, pp. 311, 312; [5]See N.J.G. Kaptein, *Muḥammad's Birthday Festival*, Leiden: E.J. Brill, 1993, p. 76, and references mentioned there; Brockelmann, *GAL*, SI, p. 626; [6]There is more than one *mawlid* text attributed to Ibn al-‘Arabī. See Ḥajjī Khalīfa, *Kashf al-ẓunūn ‘an asāmī al-kutub wa'l-funūn*, Istanbul, Milli Egitim Basimevi, 1943, 2:1910; Osman Yahia, *Histoire et Classification de l'Oeuvre d'Ibn ‘Arabī*, Damascus: Institut Français de Damas, 1964, 2:358, 379; Wilhelm Ahlwardt, *Verzeichnis der arabischen Handschriften*, Hildesheim: Georg Olms Verlag, 1981, 9:117–18; Brockelmann, *GAL*, GI, p. 448; [7]Ismā‘īl Bāshā al-Baghdādī, *Hadīyat al-‘ārifīn: Asmā' al-mu'allifīn wa-āthār al-muṣannifīn*, Istanbul: Milli Egitim Basimevi, 1951, 1:787; al-Sakhāwī, *al-Jawāhir wa'l-durar fī tarjamat Ibn Ḥajar*, ed. Ibrāhīm Bājis ‘Abd al-Majīd, Beirut: Dār Ibn Ḥazm, 1419 AH/1999 CE, 3:1253;

[8]*al-I'lām fīmā yajib 'alā al-anām min ma'rifat mawlid al-Muṣṭafā 'alayhi al-salām*, ms. Istanbul, Topkapı, no. 6031 M 443; [9]Ḥajjī Khalīfa, *Kashf*, 2:115; Baghdādī, *Hadīya*, 1:97. There is some possibility that al-Baghdādī simply assumed that the Muḥammad ibn 'Alī ibn Sa'īd who composed the *mawlid* (whose *nisba* and death date are not specified by Ḥajjī Khalīfa) is al-Gharnāṭī; [10]See Kaptein, *Muḥammad's Birthday*, pp. 76–9; [11]al-Sakhāwī, *Jawāhir*, 3:1253; [12]Ahlwardt, *Verzeichnis*, 9:120; Brockelmann, *GAL*, GII, p. 71; [13]*Kitāb maw'id al-kirām fī mawlid al-nabī 'alayhi al-salām*, ms. Damascus, Asad Library, no. 4771; Muḥammad ibn Shākir al-Kutubī, *Fawāt al-wafayāt*, ed. Iḥsān 'Abbās, Beirut: Dār Ṣādir, 1973–4, 1:39; Ḥajjī Khalīfa, *Kashf*, 2:1909; Baghdādī, *Hadiya*, 1:14; [14]al-Shawkānī, *al-Badr al-ṭāli'*, Damascus: Dār al-Fikr, 1419 AH/1998 CE, p. 660; [15]Ibn Ḥajar al-'Asqalānī, *al-Durar al-kāmina*, Beirut: Dār al-Jīl, 1414 AH/1993 CE, 4:256 (under title *al-Mawlid al-nabawī*); *Kashf*, 2:1851; *al-Muntaqā fī mawlid al-muṣṭafā*, ms. Istanbul, Fayd Allah 1536, Hājī Bashar Āghā 174; Brockelmann, *GAL*, GII, p. 195, SII, p. 262; published as *al-Muntaqā min siyar al-nabī al-muṣṭafā*, ed. Luṭfī Manṣūr, Kafr Qari' [Israel] : Markaz Dirāsāt al-Adab al-'Arabiī wa-Dār al-Hudā li'l-Ṭibā'ah wa'l-Nashr, 2001; [16]al-Suyuti, *al-Rasā'il al-'ashar*, Beirut: Dār al-Kutub al- 'Ilmīya, 1409 AH/1989 CE, p. 54; 'Alī ibn Tāj al-Dīn al-Sinjārī, *Manā'iḥ al-karam fī akhbār Makka wa'l-bayt wa-wulāt al-ḥaram*, ed. Jamīl 'Abd Allāh al-Miṣrī, Mecca: Wizārat al-Ta'līm al-'Ālī, 1419 AH/1998 CE, 1:443; [17]*al-Faḍl al-munīf fī'l-mawlid al-sharīf*, Princeton University Islamic manuscripts, Garrett Yahuda no. 3570; [18]*Sharaf al-ānām fī man ẓallahu al-ghumām*, ms. Cairo, Dār al-Kutub, Ta'rīkh Khalīl Āghā no. 8. This text does not seem to be attributed to al-Subkī elsewhere; [19]Princeton University Islamic manuscripts, Garrett Yahuda no. 4098; published as Ibn Kathīr, *Mawlid rasūl allāh*, ed. Ṣalāḥ al-Dīn al-Munajjid (Beirut: Dār al-Kitāb al-Jadīd, n.d.); [20]Ahlwardt, *Verzeichnis*, 2:623; [21]*Mawlid al-nabī*, ms. Istanbul, Süleymaniye no. 344/1; ms. Istanbul, *Irtishāf al-ṭarab fī mawlid sayyid al-'ajam wa'l-'arab*, Suleimaniye, Shahīd 'Alī Bāshā, no. 361; [22]Ibn Fahd, *Laḥẓ al-alḥāẓ bi-dhayl Tadhkirat al-ḥuffāẓ*, Damascus, 1348 AH, p. 231; al-Sakhāwī, *Jawāhir*, 3:1253; Ḥajjī Khalīfa, *Kashf*, 2:1911; [23]Sakhāwī, *al-Ḍaw al-lāmi' li-ahl al-qarn al-tāsi'*, Beirut: Dār Maktabat al-Ḥayāt, n.d., 10:82; Ḥajjī Khalīfa, *Kashf*, 2:1969; [24]Sakhāwī, *Jawāhir*, 3:1253; Ibn al-'Imād, *Shadharāt al-dhahab*, Beirut: Dār al-Kutub al-'Ilmīya, n.d., 7:189; [25]Shawkānī, *Badr*, p. 776; Ḥajjī Khalīfa, *Kashf*, 1:534; 2:1559, 1901, 1910; Brockelmann, *GAL*, GII, p. 203, SII, p. 277; [26]Sakhāwī, *Jawāhir*, 3:1253; idem., *Ḍaw'*, 8:104; Ibn Ḥajar al-'Asqālānī, *al-Majma' al-mu'assis li'l-mu'jam al-mufahras*, Beirut: Dār al-Ma'rifa, 1415 AH/1994 CE, 3:286, 287; al-Shawkānī, *Badr*, p. 715; Ḥajjī Khalīfa, *Kashf*, 1:534; 2:1559, 1901, 1910; Brockelmann, *GAL*, GII, p. 77, SII, p. 83; [27]Sakhāwī, *Ḍaw'*, 7:257; [28]Sakhāwī, *Ḍaw'*, 9:126; Ḥajjī Khalīfa, *Kashf*, 2:1910; [29]Sakhāwī, *Ḍaw'*, 1:181; Ḥajjī Khalīfa, *Kashf*, 2:1911; [30]Sakhāwī, *Ḍaw'*, 8:142; Ibn al-Ḥimṣī, *Ḥawādith al-zamān wa-wafayāt al-shuyūkh wa'l-aqrān*, Ṣaydā/Beirut: al-Maktaba al-'Aṣrīya, 1419 AH/1999 CE, 1:162; Ḥajjī Khalīfa, *Kashf*, 1:735; [31]Sakhāwī, *Ḍaw'*, 11:61; Ḥajjī Khalīfa, *Kashf*, 2:1911; [32]Ḥajjī Khalīfa, *Kashf*, 1:745; Baghdādī, *Hadīya*, 1:470; published as *al-Mawrid al-rawī fī mawlid al-nabī wa-nasabihi al-ṭāhir*, ed. Mabrūk Ismā'īl Mabrūk, Cairo: Maktabat al-Qur'ān, n.d.; [33]Sakhāwī, *Ḍaw'*, 5:227; Baghdādī, *Hadīya*, 1:736; [34]Ḥajjī Khalīfa, *Kashf*, 2:1911, 1231; [35]Ibn al-Ḥimṣī, *Ḥawādith*, 1:384; Baghdādī, *Hadīya*, 1:23; Ḥajjī Khalīfa, *Kashf*, 2:1517; Brockelmann, *GAL*, GII, p. 98, SII, p. 117; [36]Ḥajjī Khalīfa, *Kashf*, 2:1911; Baghdādī, *Hadīya*, , 2:221; [37]*Bughyat al-ẓarīf fī'l-mawlid al-sharīf*, ms. Cairo, Dār al-Kutub, Ḥadīth no. 1418; under title *Kitāb al-mawlid al-sharīf*, ms. Tarīm, Aḥqāf Library; [38]*Durar al-biḥār fī mawlid al-mukhtār*, ms. Cairo, Dār al-Kutub, Tārīkh no.3807; [39]*Mawlid al-nabī*, Damascus, 1884; [40]'Umar Riḍā Kaḥḥāla, *Mu'jam al-mu'allifīn*, Beirut: Mu'assasat al-Risāla, 1414 AH/1993 CE, 3:565; [41]Ḥajjī Khalīfa, *Kashf*, 2:1522; Baghdādī, *Hadīya*, 1:238; [42]Kaḥḥāla, *Mu'jam*, 3:40; [43]'Abd al-Qādir ibn Shaykh ibn 'Abd Allāh al-'Aydarūs, *al-Nūr al-sāfir*, n.p., n.d., p. 220; Brockelmann, *GAL*, SII, p. 549; [44]Muḥammad ibn Ṭūlūn, *al-Fulk al-mashḥūn fī aḥwāl Muḥammad ibn Ṭūlūn*, ed. Muḥammad Khayr Ramaḍān Yūsuf, Beirut: Dār ibn Ḥazm, 1416 AH/1996 CE, p. 132; [45]Brockelmann, *GAL*, GII, p. 389, SII, p. 528; [46]Brockelmann, *GAL*, GII, p. 339, SII, p. 467; [47]Brockelmann, *GAL*, GII, p. 419.

Notes

Introduction

1 Two possible cases of earlier *mawlid* celebrations have been mentioned in the secondary literature, but do not seem to sustain further scrutiny. The *Encyclopaedia of Islam* mentions that "The fires lit at Isfahān about 313/935 to celebrate Muhammad's birthday seem to have been inspired by Zoroastrian winter fire festivals" (EI², s.v. "Majus"). The source of this statement is Bertold Spuler's study *Iran in früh-islamischer Zeit*, Wiesbaden: Franz Stiener Verlag GMBH, 1952, p. 189, which states that "in 935 the birthday of the Prophet was celebrated in Isfahān by the burning of bonfires according to Zoroastrian custom." (I thank Michael Morony for graciously supplying me with this reference.) Spuler's reference for this statement is to Ibn al-Athīr's account of the year 323 AH, in which he discusses the events leading to the assassination of the Iranian warlord Mardāwīj ibn Ziyār. Ibn al-Athīr states that "when the Night of the Birthday (*laylat al-mīlād*) of that year came, which is the Night of Kindling Fires (*laylat al-wuqūd*)," Mardāwīj commanded that firewood be collected for a vast bonfire that covered the sides of an entire valley and was ignited by birds whose feet were dipped in naphtha; he also prepared a banquet of prodigious size ('Alī ibn Muḥammad Ibn al-Athīr, *al-Kāmil fī 'l-ta'rīkh*, Beirut: Dār Ṣādir, 1386 AH/1966 CE, 8:298–9). Was the "Night of the Birthday" mentioned by Ibn al-Athīr really the birthday of the Prophet Muḥammad? One possible piece of supporting evidence is that Muḥammad ibn 'Abd al-Malik al-Hamdānī states in his *Takmilat tārīkh al-Ṭabarī* that Mardāwīj was killed in the month of Rabī' al-Awwal. (Muḥammad ibn 'Abd al-Malik al-Hamdānī, *Takmilat tārīkh al-Ṭabarī*, ed. Albert Yūsuf Kan'ān, Beirut: Catholic Press, 2nd printing, 1961, 1:90). C.E. Bosworth states in his article "Mardāwīdj ibn Ziyār" in the EI² that the assassination occurred in Ṣafar (i.e., the month before Rabī' al-Awwal); I have so far been unable to identify the source of this information.

However, another source places in doubt the idea that the bonfires kindled at the command of Mardāwīj were really in honor of the Prophet's birthday. Miskawayh's *Kitāb tajārib al-umam* identifies the "Night of Kindling Fires" as the festival of *sadhaq*. (Miskawayh, *al-Qism al-akhīr min Kitāb tajārib al-umam*, in *The Eclipse of the 'Abbasid Caliphate: original chronicles of the fourth Islamic century*, ed. and trans. H.F. Amedroz and D.S. Margoliouth, Oxford: Basil Blackwell, 1920, 1:310.) The identification of the holiday during which Mardāwīj was killed as "*sadhaq*" is very plausible, as the festivities described in the historical sources are completely compatible with the nature of that day in the Zoroastrian calendar. The eastern Iranian scholar al-Bīrūnī (d. 440 AH/1048 CE) describes the relevant holiday as follows: "The Night of Alsadhak. They fumigate their houses to keep off mishap, so that finally it has become one of the customs of the kings to light fires on this night and to make them blaze, to drive wild beasts into them, and to send the birds flying through the flames, and to drink and amuse themselves round the fires." (al-Bīrūnī, *The Chronology of Ancient Nations*, trans. and ed. C. Edward Sachau, London: Published for the Oriental Translation Fund of Great Britain and Ireland by William H. Allen and Co., 1879, p. 213.) One possible solution is that there was some conflation of the two festivals at the time of Mardāwīj's death. This is at least marginally possible, since Rabī' al-Awwal of the year 323 AH roughly coincided with February. The festival of *sadhaq* occurs in the month of Bahman, which al-Bīrūnī describes as occurring in his time at the end of winter (its place in the solar year having shifted as a result of the Persians' neglect of intercalation) (Ibid., p. 213). In any case, Ibn al-Athīr's isolated reference to "*al-mīlād*" seems to be frail evidence of early celebration of the Prophet's birthday. The article "*Mawlid*" in the first *Encyclopaedia of Islam* also echoes F. Wüstenfeld's statement ("Die gelehreten Schâfi'íten des IV. Jarh. d. H.," *Abhandlungen der historischen-philologischen Klasse der Königlichen Gesellschaft der Wissenschaften zu Göttingen*, XXXVII, p. 41) that the *faqīh* Abū'l-'Abbās Muḥammad ibn 'Alī al-Karajī broke his fast only "an den beiden grossen Festtagen (Geburt des Propheten und ende der Fasten) und an den drei Tagen nach dem Opferfeste am 10. Dhu'l-Ḥijja." Since al-Karajī died in 343 AH/955 CE, this would be a very early instance of Sunnī observance of the day. In fact, however, the original sources merely state that al-Karajī broke his fast "on the two days of the festival" (*yawmay al-'īd*); the reference to the Prophet's birthday appears to be an anachronistic interpretation by Wüstenfeld. (The relevant passage is presented most fully in 'Alī ibn Yūsuf al-Qifṭī, *Inbāh al-ruwāt 'alā anbāh al-nuḥāt*, ed. Muḥammad Abū'l-Faḍl Ibrāhīm, Cairo: Maṭba'at Dār al-Kutub al-Miṣrīya, 1374 AH/1955 CE, 3:185–6.)

2 N.J.G. Kaptein, *Muḥammad's Birthday Festival*, Leiden: E.J. Brill, 1993, p. 26; see also Paula Sanders, *Ritual, Politics and the City in Fatimid Cairo*, Albany: State University of New York Press, 1994, p. 35.

3 Cf. Ibn Ṭuwayr's account, cited in Kaptein, *Muḥammad's Birthday*, pp. 13–15.

4 Ibid., pp. 21–4.

5 Kaptein argues that the celebrations did indeed persist, and thus represent the immediate forerunners of the later Sunnī celebrations. His arguments (*Muḥammad's Birthday*, pp. 28–9) consist of (a) a grammatical argument that an apparent reference to the demise of *mawlid* celebrations refers to the observance of the other birthdays, not that of the Prophet; (b) the inference that, given that all the *mawlid*s were apparently observed identically, Ibn Ṭuwayr's choice to use the example of the Prophet's *mawlid* suggests that it continued in his day; and (c) the assumption that, by this time, Egyptians would have become too accustomed to the festival to relinquish it. While an ingenious use of meager evidence, none of this can be considered compelling.

6 'Abd al-Raḥmān ibn Ismā'īl Abū Shāma, *Kitāb al-rawḍatayn fī akhbār al-dawlatayn al-nūrīya wa 'l-ṣalāḥīya*, ed. Ibrāhīm al-Zaybaq, Beirut: Mu'assasat al-Risāla, 1418 AH/1997 CE, 1:279, 285; 2:315. See Kaptein, *Muḥammad's Birthday*, pp. 31–2.

7 Kaptein, *Muḥammad's Birthday*, p. 35.

8 Ismā'īl Bāshā al-Baghdādī, *Hadīyat al-'ārifīn: asmā' al-mu'allifīn wa-āthār al-muṣannifīn*, Istanbul: Milli Egitim Basimevi, 1951–5, 1:784; Ḥajjī Khalīfa, *Kashf al-ẓunūn 'an asāmī al-kutub wa 'l-funūn*, Istanbul: Milli Egitim Basimevi, 1360–2 AH/1941–3 CE, 2:2010; Carl Brockelmann, *Geschichte der arabischen Litteratur*, 2nd edn, Leiden: E.J. Brill, 1943–9, SI: 784.

9 For a description of the manuscript of *Wasīlat al-muta'abbidīn*, see Maulavi Muinuddin Nadwi, *Catalogue of the Arabic and Persian Manuscripts in the Oriental Public Library at Bankipore*, Patna, 1929, 15:47–62. For the inscription recording the public reading of the text, see ibid., 15:52.

10 In addition to its unwieldy length, the work does not seem to be primarily narrative in character. The preserved sections cover various aspects of the Prophet's personal

practices and activities, arranged in no particular chronological order, although it does end with a section on his medical treatments, final illness, and death. Unfortunately, the first, second, and third sections of the work are not preserved, so it is not possible to determine whether the beginning of the book featured any narrative or discussion of the Prophet's birth. This seems fairly likely, given the prominence given to the Prophet's illness and death at the end of the book, but in the absence of the relevant sections it is impossible to know whether the Prophet's birth was a highly elaborated feature of the composition.

11 Muḥammad ibn Aḥmad ibn Jubayr, *Riḥlat Ibn Jubayr*, Beirut: Dār Ṣādir / Dār Bayrūt, 1384 AH/1964 CE, p. 92.

12 Aḥmad ibn Muḥammad ibn Khallikān, *Wafayāt al-a'yān wa-anbā' abnā' al-zamān*, ed. Iḥsān 'Abbās, Beirut: Dār al-Thaqāfa, n.d., 4:117–19.

13 Ibid., 4:449.

14 Kaptein, *Muḥammad's Birthday*, p. 42.

15 Ibid., pp. 69–73.

16 Ibn Ṭuwayr's account describes an ordinary sermon, after which the preacher declared, "And this is the day on which he was born to fulfill his mission by which God has blessed the Religion of Islam (*millat al-islām*)" (Kaptein, *Muḥammad's Birthday*, p. 15.)

17 'Alī ibn Mūsā ibn Ṭāwūs, *Iqbāl al-a'māl*, Beirut: Mu'assasat al-A'lamī li'l-Maṭbū'āt, 1417 AH/1996 CE, p. 110.

18 Cited in ibid., p. 82. Ibn Ṭāwūs cites the passage from al-Mufīd's work *Ḥadā'iq al-riyāḍ wa-zahrat al-murtāḍ wa-nūr al-mustarshid*. A parallel passage appears in Muḥammad ibn Muḥammad al-Mufīd's *Masārr al-shī'a*, in *Muṣannafāt al-shaykh al-Mufīd*, al-Mu'tamar al-'Ālamī li-Alfīyat al-Shaykh al-Mufīd, 1413 AH, 7:50–1.

19 Muḥammad ibn al-Ḥasan al-Ṭūsī, *Tahdhīb al-aḥkām fī sharḥ al-Muqni'a li'l-shaykh al-Mufīd,* Beirut: Dār al-Aḍwā', 1406 AH/1985 CE, 4:305–6.

20 Mufīd, *Masārr*, 7:53.

21 Ibid., 5:54.

22 See Kaptein, *Prophet's Birthday*, pp. 9–10.

23 See earlier, note 16.

24 Kaptein, *Prophet's Birthday*, pp. 21, 31.

1 The emergence of *mawlid* narratives

1 See 'Umar Riḍā Kaḥḥāla, *Mu'jam al-mu'allifīn*, Beirut: Mu'assasat al-Risāla, 1414 AH/ 1993 CE, 4:79; Ibn al-Nadīm, *al-Fihrist*, ed. Yūsuf 'Alī Ṭawīl, Beirut: Dār al-Kutub al-'Ilmīya, 1416 AH/1996 CE, p. 161; Muḥammad ibn Aḥmad al-Dhahabī, *Mīzān al-i'tidāl fī naqd al-rijāl*, ed. 'Alī Muḥammad al-Bijāwī, Cairo: 'Isā al-Bābī al Ḥal-ābī wa-Shurakā'uhu', 1388 AH/1963 CE, 4:353–4; Yāqūt al-Ḥamawī, *Mu'jam al-udabā'*, Beirut: Dār al-Kutub al-'Ilmīya, 1411 AH/1991 CE, 5:577.

2 Aḥmad ibn 'Alī al-Najāshi, *Kitāb al-rijāl*, n.p.: Markarz-i Nashr-i Kitāb, n.d., p. 336; Aḥmad ibn 'Alī al-Khaṭīb al-Baghdādī, *Ta'rīkh Baghdād aw madīnat al-salām*, Beirut: Dār al-Kitāb al-'Arabī, n.d., 7:419. Other sources fail to mention this work, although such general titles such as Shādhān ibn Jibrā'īl al-Qummī's *Kitāb al-faḍā'il* (n.p.: Manshūrāt Maktabat al-'Irfān, n.d.) might well apply to it.

3 Ibn al-Nadīm, *Fihrist*, p. 158.

4 Najāshī, *Rijāl*, p. 306.

5 'Alī ibn Mūsā ibn Ṭāwūs, *al-Yaqīn bi'khtiṣāṣ mawlānā 'Alī bi'imrat al-mu'minīn*, Beirut: Mu'assasat al-Thaqalayn, 1410 AH/1989 CE, p. 191.

6 Najāshī, *Rijāl*, p. 306.

7 Āghā Buzurg al-Ṭihrānī, *al-Dharī'a ilā taṣānīf al-shī'a*, Beirut: Dār al-Aḍwā', n.d., 23:277.

8 'Alī ibn Mūsā ibn Ṭāwūs, *Iqbāl al-a'māl*, Beirut: Mu'assasat al-A'lamī li'l-Maṭbū'āt, 1417 AH/1996 CE, pp. 76, 77, 81 (and elsewhere in the same work).

9 Ibn Ṭāwūs, *Yaqīn*, pp. 191–2.

10 Muḥammad ibn al-Ḥasan al-Fattāl, *Rawḍat al-wā'iẓīn*, Najaf: al-Maktaba al-Ḥaydarīya, 1386 AH/1966 CE, pp. 77–81. For a discussion of al-Fattāl's identity and dating, see Muḥammad Bāqir al-Mūsawī al-Khwānsārī, *Rawḍāt al-jannāt fī aḥwāl al-'ulamā' wa'l-sādāt*, Qum, n.d., 6:253–5. al-Fattāl was a teacher of Ibn Shahrāshūb (d. 588 AH/1192 CE).

11 The same story, also attributed to Jābir, is presented by al-Qummī in his *Faḍā'il*, p. 54; he states in the *isnād* that it was transmitted to him in the year 633 AH.

12 For al-Quḍā'ī's biography, see Aḥmad ibn Muḥammad Ibn Khallikān, *Wafayāt al-a'yān wa-anbā' abnā' al-zamān*, ed. Iḥsān 'Abbās, Beirut: Dār al-Thaqāfa, n.d., 4:212–13; Khalīl ibn Aybak al-Ṣafadī, *al-Wāfī bi'l-wafayāt*, Wiesbaden: Franz Steiner Verlag, 1394 AH/1974 CE, 3:116–17; Kaḥḥāla, *Mu'jam*, 3:327.

13 Sūhāj library, no. 77 Tārīkh. See Ṣalāḥ al-Dīn al-Munajjid, *Mu'jam mā ullifa 'an rasūl allāh*, Beirut: Dār al-Kitāb al-Jadīd, 1402 AH/1982 CE, p. 45.

14 Aḥmad ibn 'Abd al-Ḥalīm Ibn Taymīya, *Majmū' fatāwā shaykh al-islām Aḥmad ibn Taymīya*, collected and arranged by 'Abd al-Raḥmān ibn Muḥammad ibn Qāsim al-'Āṣimī al-Najdī, n.p., n.d., 18:367.

15 See Shīrawayh ibn Shahradār al-Daylamī, *al-Firdaws bi-ma'thūr al-khiṭāb*, Beirut: Dār al-Kutub al-'Ilmīya, 1406 AH/1986 CE, Introduction, p. ṣ.

16 See Muḥammad ibn Salāma al-Quḍā'ī, *Kitāb al-inbā' bi-anbā' al-anbiyā' wa-tawārīkh al-khulafā' wa-wilāyāt al-umarā'*, Beirut: al-Maktaba al-'Aṣrīya, 1418 AH/1998 CE.

17 Boaz Shoshan, *Popular Culture in Medieval Cairo*, Cambridge: Cambridge University Press, 1993, pp. 23–39.

18 Ibid., p. 99, n. 15; p. 36.

19 Ibn Taymīya, *Majmū' fatāwā*, 18:355, 357.

20 In addition to the Vatican manuscript (ms. Borg. no. 125), lengthy selections from al-Bakrī's work appear in the early *mawlid* work *al-Durr al-munaẓẓam fī al-mawlid al-mu'aẓẓam*, by Abū'l-'Abbās al-'Azafī (d. 633 AH/1236 CE), which I consulted in the manuscript held at Princeton University Library, Garrett Yehuda no. 256. A large proportion of it is also reproduced in the voluminous *Biḥār al-anwār* of Muḥammad Bāqir al-Majlisī (Tehran, d. 1110 AH/1698 CE). I have also consulted modern printed versions of *al-Anwār*, including one published by Muṣṭafā al-Bābī al-Ḥalabī, Cairo, in 1379 AH/1959 CE and one published by al-Maṭba'a al-Ḥaydarīya, Najaf (undated).

21 Dhahabī, *Mīzān*, 1:112. al-Dhahabī remarks that various books by al-Bakrī "are read in the booksellers' market" (*yuqra' lahu fī sūq al-kutubīyīn*).

22 See Shoshan, *Popular Culture*, p. 23; p. 107, n. 160.

23 See Majlisī, *Biḥār*, 15:307; Abū'l-Ḥasan Aḥmad ibn 'Abd Allāh al-Bakrī, *al-Anwār wa-miṣbāḥ al-surūr wa'l-afkār*, [Cairo]: Muṣṭafā al-Bābī al-Ḥalabī, 1379 AH/1959 CE, pp. 68–9. This anecdote does not seem to appear in the Vatican manuscript, but must have been incorporated into the corpus of al-Bakrī's work by the sixteenth-century AH.

24 Majlisī, *Biḥār*, 1:41.

25 Bakrī, *Anwār*, Cairo, p. 4.

26 There is some unclarity about the dating of al-Qummī's lifetime. Majlisī states in the *Biḥār* that his work on the direction of the *qibla* was composed in 558 AH (an interlinear note that, according to the editor, is in the handwriting of the original manuscript; *Biḥār*, 81:72). The work itself, which Majlisī reproduces in full, states that it was composed at the request of the prince Farāmarz ibn 'Alī al-Jurjānī (*Biḥār*, 82:73). The latter may be the same Farāmarz ibn 'Alī, 'Aḍud al-Dīn, who is mentioned by Ibn al-Athīr as having built a wall to protect worshipers at the tomb of the eighth

Imām ʻAlī al-Riḍā in Ṭūs in 515 AH Ibn al-Athīr, *al-Kāmil fī al-ta'rīkh*, Beirut: Dār Ṣādir, 1386 AH/1966 CE, 10:523.

27 Qummī, *Faḍā'il*, p. 54.

28 Ibid., p. 18; Majlisī, *Biḥār*, 15:287.

29 Qummī, *Faḍā'il*, pp. 12–49.

30 Ibid., p. 14; Majlisī, *Biḥār*, 15:283.

31 Qummī, *Faḍā'il*, pp. 14, 25; Majlisī, *Biḥār*, 15:283, 343.

32 Qummī, *Faḍā'il*, pp. 16–17; Majlisī, *Biḥār*, 15:286.

33 Fattāl, *Rawḍa*, pp. 67–8.

34 ʻAbd al-Malik ibn Muḥammad al-Kharkūshī, *Sharaf al-Muṣṭafā*, ed. Nabīl ibn Hāshim Bā ʻAlawī, Mecca: Dār al-Bashā'ir al-Islāmīya, 1424 AH/2003 CE, 1:188–92; Aḥmad ibn al-Ḥusayn al-Bayhaqī, *Dalā'il al-nubūwa wa-ma ʻrifat aḥwāl ṣāḥib al-sharī ʻa*, ed. Aḥmad Ṣaqr, [Cairo]: al-Majlis al-Aʻlā li'l-Shu'ūn al-Islāmīya, Lajnat Iḥyā' Ummahāt Kutub al-Sunna, 1389 AH/1970 CE, 1:355–60; Muḥammad ibn ʻAlī al-Karājikī, *Kanz al-fawā'id*, Beirut: Dār al-Aḍwā', 1405 AH/1985 CE, pp. 187–91.

35 Qummī, *Faḍā'il*, pp. 38–44.

36 al-Tirmidhī, *Sunan*, *Kitāb al-manāqib*, *ḥadīth* no. 3968. All *ḥadīth* references to the six books are to *Jam' jawāmi' al-aḥādīth wa'l-asānīd*, Vaduz, Liechtenstein: Thesaurus Islamicus Foundation, 2000. Also see references in Muḥammad Saʻīd Zaghlūl, *Mawsūʻat aṭrāf al-ḥadīth al-nabawī al-sharīf*, Beirut: Dār al-Kutub al-ʻIlmīya, n.d., 6:398.

37 See references in Zaghlūl, *Mawsūʻa*, 6:508.

38 See references in ibid., 6:504–5. For a critical overview of the references for this and related *ḥadīth* texts see Muḥammad ibn ʻAbd al Raḥmān al-Sakhāwī, *al-Maqāṣid al-ḥasana fī bayān kathīr min al-aḥādīth al-mushtahira ʻalā al-alsina*, Beirut: Dār al-Kutub al-ʻIlmīya, 1399 AH/1979 CE, p. 327.

39 ʻAbd al-Malik ibn Hishām, *al-Sīra al-nabawīya*, Beirut: Dār al-Jīl, 1411 AH/1991 CE, 1:292–3. An exhaustive survey of the various themes and permutations associated with the Light of Muḥammad is provided by U. Rubin, "Pre-existence and light: aspects of the concept of Nūr Muḥammad," *Israel Oriental Studies* V, 1975, pp. 62–117.

40 Ibn Hishām, *Sīra*, 1:293, 302. See also references in Zaghlūl, *Mawsūʻa*, 2:518 (*ḥadīth* beginning "*Anā daʻwat [abī] Ibrāhīm wa-bishārat [bushrā] ʻĪsā* ... ").

41 See Sakhāwī, *Maqāṣid*, p. 327.

42 See Muḥammad ibn Yūsuf al-Ṣāliḥī al-Shāmī, *Subul al-hudā wa'l-rashād fī sīrat khayr al-ʻibād*, ed. ʻĀdil Aḥmad ʻAbd al-Mawjūd and ʻAlī Muḥammad Muʻawwaḍ, Beirut: Dār al-Kutub al-ʻIlmīya, 1414 AH/1993 CE, 1:80; Sakhāwī, *Maqāṣid*, p. 327.

43 U. Rubin writes that "the Shīʻa is ... the Muslim sect that has made the utmost use of light" (Rubin, "Pre-existence," p. 65); Louis Massignon states that "among the Shīʻīs, this doctrine [of the Light of Muḥammad] appears earlier and with more logical coherence" (EI[1], s.v. "nūr Muḥammadī"; see also Ignaz Goldziher, "Neuplatonische und gnostische Elemente im Ḥadīth," *Zeitschift der Assyrologie* 22, 1908, pp. 326–8, reprinted in *Gesammelte Schriften*, ed. Joseph Desomogyi, Hildesheim: Georg Olms Verlagsbuchhandlung, 1970, 5:118–20; Tor Andrae, *Die Person Muhammads in Lehre und Glauben seiner Gemeinde*, Stockholm, 1918, p. 320.

44 ʻIyāḍ ibn Mūsā al-Yaḥṣubī, *al-Shifā bi-taʻrīf ḥuqūq al-Muṣṭafā*, ed. ʻAlī Muḥammad al-Bijāwī, Cairo: ʻĪsā al-Bābī al-Ḥalabī, n.d., 1:109. Rubin presents another Sunnī tradition in which the Prophet avers that "God created me from His light, Abū Bakr from my light, ʻUmar from Abū Bakr's light, and the Muslim community from ʻUmar's light..." (Rubin, "Pre-existence," p. 113; see Dhahabī, *Mīzān,* 1:166, where the tradition is indignantly rejected as a forgery.)

45 ʻIyāḍ, *Shifā*, 1:20–1. Cited in Andrae, *Person*, p. 320.

46 Abū Ṭālib al-Makkī, *'Ilm al-qulūb*, ed. 'Abd al-Qādir Aḥmad 'Aṭā', Cairo: Maktabat al-Qāhira, 1384 AH/1964 CE, pp. 93–4. Paraphrased in Rubin, "Pre-existence," pp. 113–14. al-Tustarī is also supposed to have transmitted from the deathless spiritual guide Khiḍr that "God created the Light of Muḥammad from His light; He shaped it and sent it forth by His hand. That light remained before God for one hundred thousand years. He looked at it and regarded it seventy thousand times every day and night; with every look, He wrapped it in new light. Then He created from it all beings." (Louis Massignon, *Recueil des Textes Inédits Concernant l'Histoire de la Mystique en Pays d'Islam*, Paris: Librairie Orientaliste Paul Geuthner, 1929, p. 39; for this citation, and also a general discussion of al-Tustarī's treatment of the Light of Muḥammad, see Gerhard Böwering, *The Mystical Vision of Existence in Classical Islam*, Berlin: Walter de Gruyter, 1980, pp. 149–50.)

47 Abū Ḥāmid al-Ghazālī, *Nafkh al-rūḥ wa'l-taswiya*, ed. Aḥmad Ḥijāzī al-Saqā, [Cairo]: Maktabat al-Madīna al-Munawwara, 1399 AH/1979 CE, pp. 38–9.

48 Ibn Taymīya, *Majmū' fatāwā*, 18:367.

49 Taqī al-Dīn 'Alī ibn 'Abd al-Kāfī al-Subkī, *Fatāwā al-Subkī*, Beirut: Dār al-Ma'rifa, n.d., 1:39.

50 'Umāra ibn Wathīma al-Fasawī al-Fārisī, *Kitāb bad' al-khalq wa-qiṣaṣ al-anbiyā'*, in Raid Georges Khoury, *Les Légendes Prophétiques dans l'Islam depuis le Ier jusqu'au IIIe Siècle de l'Hégire d'après le Manuscript d'Abū Rif ā'a 'Umāra b. Wathīma b. Mūsā b. al-Furāt al-Fārisī al-Fasawī Kitāb bad' al-Khalq wa-Qiṣaṣ al-Anbiyā'*, Wiesbaden: Otto Harrassowitz, 1978, p. 138.

51 Fārisī, *Bad'*, Arabic text, p. 341.

52 The Fārisī text reads "handful"; the emendation is from the text of Majlisī, *Biḥār*, 15:27 and Bakrī, *Anwār*, Cairo, p. 5. The text of this line is illegible in my copy of the Vatican manuscript.

53 Fārisī, *Bad'*, Arabic text, p. 342.

54 Ibid., pp. 346–7.

55 The passage from al-Bakrī begins with an *isnād* that ends with the statement, "I heard Ka'b al-Aḥbār, and I asked him about the beginning of the Prophet in the foreknowledge of God, what God honored him with, his proofs, the origins of his [prophetic] mission, and the events of his life (*ayyāmihi*)." However, no narrative follows. There follows the statement, "Wahb ibn Munabbih and Ibn 'Abbās both said..." (Fārisī, *Bad'*, Arabic text, p. 343). However, later in the passage, the phrase "Ka'b said" recurs several times (pp. 343, 345, 347). See also al-Bakrī, Abū'l-Ḥasan Aḥmad ibn 'Abd Allāh, *Kitāb al-anwār*, ms. Vatican, Borg. Ar. no. 125, 2a; Majlisī, *Biḥār*, 15:26; Bakrī, *Anwār*, Cairo, pp. 4, 5.

56 Charles Pellat writes that "In spite of elements which militate in favour of this identification, it is doubtful whether the *Ithbāt al-waṣiyya* comes from the pen of the author of the *Murūj*; but the question remains open, and is unlikely ever to be settled definitively." By Shī'ite authors, the work is listed as early as the *Rijāl* of al-Najāshī. See EI^2, s.v. "Mas'ūdī, Abū'l-Ḥasan 'Alī ibn al-Ḥusayn."

57 'Alī ibn al-Ḥusayn al-Mas'ūdī (attributed), *Ithbāt al-waṣīya li'l-imām 'Alī ibn abī Ṭālib*, Beirut: Dār al-Uṣūl, 1409 AH/1988 CE, p. 287.

58 Ibid., pp. 99–124.

59 Ibid., pp. 104–5.

60 Ibid., p. 99.

61 For a discussion of Abū Sa'd/Abū Sa'īd 'Abd al-Malik ibn abī 'Uthmān al-Kharkūshī and his works, see John C. Lamoreaux, *The Early Muslim Tradition of Dream Interpretation*, Albany: State University of New York Press, 2002, pp. 64–5. For a biographical notice see 'Abd al-Karīm ibn Muḥammad al-Sam'ānī, *al-Ansāb*, Haydarabad, 1385 AH/1966 CE, 5:101–2; for further references see Lamoreaux, *Early Muslim Tradition*, p. 200.

62 al-Kharkūshī, 'Abd al-Malik ibn Muḥammad, *Kitāb Sharaf al-nabī*, ms. London, British Library, no. OR 3014, 7b; Kharkūshī, *Sharaf al-Muṣṭafā*, 1:297–300.

63 Mas'ūdī, *Ithbāt*, p. 104.
64 Kharkūshī, *Sharaf al-Muṣṭafā*, 1:312–13.
65 Ibid., pp. 314–15.
66 The various transformations of this narrative have been analyzed by Oleg Grabar and Mika Natif, "The story of the portraits of the Prophet Muḥammad," *Studia Islamica* 96, 2003, pp. 19–37 (especially pp. 19–23). In the versions of the story transmitted by al-Bayhaqī and al-Iṣfahānī in their respective works entitled *Dalā'il al-nubūwa*, the images of the prophets are in the possession of the Byzantine emperor Heraclius, who displays them to a delegation of Muslims. Returning to Mecca, the envoys recount the incident to Abū Bakr, "who cried upon hearing it and confirmed for them that the Prophet had told him that Christians and Jews had in their possession descriptions of [the Prophet's] characteristics (*na't*)." As Grabar and Natif note, "the purpose of the story was to demonstrate that Christians knew well that the final revelation of Islam was coming" (p. 22).
67 For biographical sources on al-Kāzarūnī, see Kaḥḥāla, *Mu'jam*, 3:715.
68 Muḥammad ibn Mas'ūd al-Kāzarūnī, *al-Muntaqā fī siyar al-nabī al-muṣṭafā*, ed. Luṭfī Manṣūr, Kafr Qari', [Israel]: Markaz Dirāsāt al-Adab al-'Arabī, 1422 AH/2001 CE, 2:70.
69 Ibid., 2:81.
70 Bakrī, *Anwār*, Cairo, p. 42; Mas'ūdī, *Ithbāt*, pp. 115–16; Kharkūshī, *Sharaf al-Muṣṭafā*, 1:338; Kāzarūnī, *Muntaqā*, 2:94.
71 Bakrī, *Anwār*, Cairo, p. 42 (the garment is in the possession of Jews, and no attack immediately follows); Mas'ūdī, *Ithbāt*, pp. 116–17 (the garment is in the possession of the Arab clans); Kharkūshī, *Sharaf al-Muṣṭafā*, 1:339; Kāzarūnī, *Muntaqā*, 2:95–6.
72 See the Qur'ān, 12:23–32. Bakrī, *Anwār*, Cairo, p. 43; Mas'ūdī, *Ithbāt*, p. 117; Kāzarūnī, *Muntaqā*, 2:96.
73 Bakrī, *Anwār*, Cairo, pp. 54–7 (longer rendition, significantly divergent from other versions); Mas'ūdī, *Ithbāt*, pp. 117, 118; Kharkūshī, *Sharaf al-Muṣṭafā*, 1:339–40; Kāzarūnī, *Muntaqā*, 2:97.
74 Mas'ūdī, *Ithbāt*, p. 118; Kharkūshī, *Sharaf al-Muṣṭafā*, 1:347; Kāzarūnī, *Muntaqā*, 2:98. al-Kāzarūnī attributes this report to 'Abd Allāh ibn 'Abbās (reporting from his father, al-'Abbās).
75 Walid Saleh, *The Qur'ān commentary of Tha'labī (d. 427 / 1035)*, PhD dissertation, Yale University, 2001, Appendix C, p. 70 (Arabic numbering).
76 James Kritzeck, *Peter the Venerable and Islam*, Princeton, New Jersey: Princeton University Press, 1964, p. 85.
77 Ibid., p. 87.
78 Ibid., p. 88.
79 Karājikī, *Kanz*, pp. 164–6.
80 See Bakrī, *Anwār*, ms. Vatican, 21a; Majlisī, *Biḥār*, 15:78; Bakrī, *Anwār*, Cairo, p. 43; Mas'ūdī, *Ithbāt*, pp. 116–17.
81 Abū'l-Faraj 'Abd al-Raḥmān ibn al-Jawzī, *al-Wafā' bi-aḥwāl al-Muṣṭafā*, Riyadh: al-Mu'assasa al-Sa'īdīya bi'l-Riyāḍ, n.d., 1:70.
82 Ibn al-Ḥājj, *al-Madkhal*, [Cairo]: Sharika wa-Maṭba'at Muṣṭafā al-Bābī al-Ḥalabī wa-Awlādihi, 1380 AH/1960 CE, 2:33–4. This passage occurs within a rendition of the "white handful" narrative that Ibn al-Ḥājj cites from the *Shifā' al-ṣudūr* of one Abū Rabī'. The latter is identified by Ḥājjī Khalīfa as al-Imām al-Khaṭīb Abū'l-Rab' [*sic?*] Sulaymān al-Sabtī, known as Ibn al-Sab'. (Ḥajjī Khalīfa, *Kashf al-ẓunūn 'an asāmī al-kutub wa'l-funūn*, Istanbul: Milli Egitim Basimevi, 1362 AH/1943 CE, 2:1050.) Ismā'īl Bāshā al-Baghdādī identifies him as Sulaymān ibn Dāwūd Tāj al-Islām Abū'l-Rabī' al-Sabtī al-Suwārī and lists three works by him. (*Hadīyat al-'ārifīn, asmā' al-mu'-allifīn wa-āthār al-muṣannifīn*, Istanbul: Milli Egitim Basimevi, 1951, 1:401.) Unfortunately, his death date is left blank, and Abū'l-Rabī' al-Sabtī seems to be unidentifiable through the standard biographical sources.

83 Muḥammad ibn Aḥmad ibn Faraj al-Anṣārī al-Andalusī [al-Qurṭubī], *Kitāb al-i'lām bi-mā yajib 'alā al-anām min ma'rifat al-nabī 'alayhi al-salām*, ms. Istanbul, Topkapı, no. 6031 M443, 6a.

84 Abū Mikhnaf (attributed), *Mawlid baṭal al-islām amīr al-mu'minīn 'Alī ibn abī Ṭālib* in the recension of Ḍiyā' al-Dīn Abū'l-Alā' al-Ḥasan ibn Aḥmad ibn Yaḥyā al-Azdī, Najaf: Manshūrāt al-Maktaba al-Ḥaydarīya, n.d., p. 11. The *isnād* attached to this text (p. 6) is clearly corrupt; it seems to have been borrowed (in a mangled form) from the Jābir *ḥadīth* cited by al-Qummī (*Faḍā'il*, p. 54), and cannot be used as an indicator of the age of the text as a whole. See also Majlisī, *Biḥār*, 15:34, cited in Rubin, "Pre-existence," pp. 97–8, n. 81.

85 Aḥmad ibn Muḥammad al-Tha'labī, *Qiṣaṣ al-anbiyā' al-musammā 'Arā'is al-majālis*, Sūsa, Tunisia: Dār al-Ma'ārif, 1989, p. 26.

86 Muḥammad Ibn Sa'd, *Kitāb al-ṭabaqāt al-kubrā*, ed. Eduard Sachau, Leiden: E.J. Brill, 1918, VII.2:154.

87 For a study of the narrative of Ka'b's conversion, see Moshe Perlmann, "A legendary story of Ka'b al-Aḥbār's conversion to Islam," in *Joshua Starr Memorial Volume*, New York: Conference on Jewish Relations, 1953, pp. 85–9. See also Kharkūshī, *Sharaf al-Muṣṭafā*, 1:275–7.

88 Kharkūshī, *Sharaf al-Muṣṭafā*, 1:137–57.

89 Cf. *The Book of the Thousand Nights and a Night*, trans. Richard F. Burton, n.p., 1885, 5:304–28, 383–96.

90 Steven Wasserstrom, *Between Muslim and Jew*, Princeton: Princeton University Press, 1995, pp. 178–9.

91 Jonathan Berkey, *Popular Preaching and Religious Authority in the Medieval Islamic Near East*, Seattle: University of Washington Press, 2001, pp. 39–40.

92 See Kharkūshī, *Sharaf al-Muṣṭafā*, pp. 312; Rubin, "Pre-existence," p. 117, n. 29. The reference to Kharkūshī seems (although full bibliographic references are lacking in Rubin's article) to be to ms. London, British Library, no. OR 3014, 8b–9a. Kharkūshī also supplies another report with an elaborate rendition of the motif of the veils, without the division of the light and the creation of the cosmos (pp. 305–11). Rubin also states that this narrative is found in the *sīra* of al-Bakrī (as cited in Majlisī, *Biḥār*, 15:27–9). However, Majlisī's citation from al-Bakrī is here interrupted by a lengthy interlude attributed to 'Alī ibn abī Ṭālib, which does not correspond to any other version of al-Bakrī; the editor notes that the manuscript on which he based his text omits this interpolation (15:27, n. 6).

93 *Mawlid al-nabī 'alayhi al-ṣalāt wa'l-salām li'l-shaykh Muḥyī al-Dīn al-'Arabī* [*sic*] *qaddasa allāh sirrahu*, ms. Istanbul, Süleymaniye, Ashir Efendi no. 434, 10a–11a. Muḥammad 'Abd al-'Azīz al-Khālidī states in his notes to al-Zurqānī's commentary to al-Qasṭallānī (*Sharḥ al-'allāma al-Zurqānī 'alā al-Mawāhib al-ladunīya bi'l-minaḥ al-muḥammadīya li'l-'allāma al-Qasṭallānī*, Beirut: Dār al-Kutub al-'Ilmīya, 1417 AH/1996 CE, 1:89, n. 1) that Ibn al-'Arabī cites the Jābir report and attributes it to 'Abd al-Razzāq in his work *Talqīḥ al-adhhān*. This would corroborate the fact that the report was known to Ibn al-'Arabī, and perhaps provide some additional support for the attribution of his *mawlid*; however, I have not been able to consult a copy of the *Talqīḥ* to confirm it. For the *Talqīḥ*, see Osman Yahya, *Histoire et Classification en l'Oeuvre d'Ibn al-'Arabī*, Damascus: Institut Français de Damas, 1964, 2:498–9.

94 Kāzarūnī, *Muntaqā*, 2:32–3. al-Diyārbakrī's version is cited by Ismā'īl ibn Muḥammad al-Anṣārī, "*al-Qawl al-faṣl fī ḥukm al-tawassul bi-khayr al-rusul*," in *Rasā'il fī ḥukm al-iḥtifāl bi'l-mawlid al-nabawī*, Riyadh: Ri'āsat Idārat al-Buḥūth al-'Ilmīya wa'l-Iftā', 1419 AH/1998 CE, 2:720–2. For the identity of al-Diyārbakrī, see Kaḥḥāla, *Mu'jam*, 1:635.

95 Shaykh al-Ḥurayfīsh, *al-Rawḍ al-fā'iq fī'l-mawā'iẓ wa'l-raqā'iq*, [Cairo]: Maktabat al-Jumhūrīya al-'Arabīya, n.d., pp. 301–2.

96 In Kāzarūnī, *Muntaqā*: "after that He created every evil thing" (2:32).
97 The translation is from the version of al-Diyārbakrī. I do not have a verbatim copy of Ibn al-'Arabī's version, although my notes indicate almost complete correspondence in details such as the names and ordering of the "stations" and "veils." al-Kāzarūnī's version corresponds to al-Diyārbakrī's precisely, but is slightly garbled (containing an obvious omission) in at least one point.
98 Kharkūshī, *Sharaf al-Muṣṭafā*, pp. 310–11; *Sharaf al-nabī*, 8b–9b.
99 Aḥmad ibn Muḥammad al-Qasṭallānī, *al-Mawāhib al-ladunīya bi'l-minaḥ al-muḥammadīya*, ed. Ṣāliḥ Aḥmad al-Shāmī, Beirut: al-Maktab al-Islāmī, 1412 AH/1991 CE, pp. 171–2. This report does not appear in the published text of 'Abd al-Razzāq's *Muṣannaf*, nor does it appear to be attributed to 'Abd al-Razzāq in any early or independent source.
100 Jalāl al-Dīn 'Abd al-Raḥmān ibn Abī Bakr al-Suyūṭī, *al-Ḥāwī li'l-fatāwā*, Beirut: Dār al-Kutub al-'Ilmīya, 1395 AH/1975 CE, 1:323, 325.
101 Ibn Taymīya, *Majmū' fatāwā*, 18:355, 357.
102 Ibid., 18:367.
103 *Mawlid al-nabī*, attributed to Abū'l-Faraj 'Abd al-Raḥmān Ibn al-Jawzī, Princeton University Arabic manuscripts, Third Series, no. 209, 11b–12b. A Shī'ite rendition of this motif appears in *Mawlid baṭal al-islām amīr al-mu'minīn 'Alī ibn abī Ṭālib*, pp. 6–9.
104 Kharkūshī, *Sharaf al-Muṣṭafā*, p. 312; *Sharaf al-nabī*, British Library, OR 3014, 8b–9b.
105 This is the number in the published text, although it may originally have been 124,000 (the traditional number of prophets).
106 Kāzarūnī, *Muntaqā*, 2:31–2.
107 Peter Burke, *Popular Culture in Early Modern Europe*, New York: New York University Press, 1978, p. 125.
108 Muḥammad ibn 'Abd Allāh al-Kisā'ī, *Qiṣaṣ al-anbiyā'*, Leiden: Brill, 1922, 2:6–7. The author of this work, although named, has remained unidentifiable and undatable; similar to the mysterious al-Bakrī, the material attributed to him is regarded by scholars as representing an example of popular medieval storytelling. The earliest manuscripts of al-Kisā'ī's *Qiṣaṣ* date to the seventh-century AH/thirteenth-century CE. See T. Nagel, EI², s.v. "al-Kisā'ī, Ṣāḥib Qiṣaṣ al-anbiyā'."
109 Qurṭubī, *I'lām*, 19a–b; Qasṭallānī, *Mawāhib*, 1:118.
110 Mas'ūdī, *Ithbāt*, pp. 118–9; Kharkūshī, *Sharaf al-Muṣṭafā*, pp. 347–8; Kāzarūnī, *Muntaqā*, 2:99–100.
111 Kritzeck, *Peter the Venerable*, p. 87.
112 Qasṭallānī, *Mawāhib*, 1:119.
113 Kāzarūnī, *Muntaqā*, 2:98–100.
114 Abū Nu'aym Aḥmad ibn 'Abd Allāh al-Iṣbahānī, *Dalā'il al-nubūwa*, Aleppo: Dār al-Wa'y, n.d., pp. 535–38; see also Kharkūshī, *Sharaf al-Muṣṭafā*, 1:349.
115 Ibn Hishām, *Sīra*, 1:293.
116 The fact that the skeptical remark derives from Ibn Isḥāq rather than from his redactor, Ibn Hishām, is suggested by the parallel text in Ṭabarī's history (Muḥammad ibn Jarīr al-Ṭabarī, *Ta'rīkh al-Ṭabarī*, ed. Muḥammad Abū'l-Faḍl Ibrāhīm, Beirut: Dār al-Turāth, n.d., 2:156).
117 See Qasṭallānī, *Mawāhib*, 1:120–1.
118 Iṣbahānī, *Dalā'il*, pp. 94–5.
119 Ismā'īl ibn 'Umar Ibn Kathīr, *Mawlid rasūl allāh*, ed. Ṣalāḥ al-Dīn al-Munajjid, Beirut: Dār al-Kitāb al-Jadīd, n.d., p. 15; Ismā'īl ibn 'Umar Ibn Kathīr, *al-Bidāya wa'l-nihāya*, Beirut: Dār al-Fikr, 1402 AH/1982 CE, 1:293.
120 Ṣāliḥī, *Subul*, 1:329.
121 Kāzarūnī, *Muntaqā*, 2:102.
122 Other versions read "the daughters of 'Abd Manāf."

123 Iṣbahānī, *Dalā'il*, pp. 535–8. For parallels to this story, see the following note.

124 Transmitted from Abū Nu'aym al-Iṣbahānī in Jalāl al-Dīn al-Suyūṭī, *al-Khaṣā'iṣ al-kubrā aw kifāyat al-ṭālib al-labīb fī khaṣā'iṣ al-ḥabīb*, ed. Muḥammad Khalīl Harās, [Cairo]: Dār al-Kutub al-Ḥadīthīya, n.d., 1:120–1. Parallels in Bakrī, *Anwār*, ms. Vatican, 36a–37a; Mas'ūdī, *Ithbāt*, p. 122; Kharkūshī, *Sharaf al-Muṣṭafā*, 1:354–5, 359–60; Fattāl, *Rawḍa*, pp. 68–9 (transmitted from Āmina by the sixth Imām, Ja'far al-Ṣādiq).

125 The text here continues "and that there was no sign of childbirth on her," which does not fit sequentially into the narrative.

126 Mas'ūdī, *Ithbāt*, pp. 123–4; parallels in Khakūshī, *Sharaf al-Muṣṭafā*, 1:361–3; Bakrī, *Anwār*, ms. Vatican, 37a–b; Fattāl, *Rawḍa*, pp. 69–70.

127 Muḥammad ibn Qāsim al-Raṣṣā', *Tadhikrat al-muḥibbīn fī asmā' sayyid al-mursalīn*, ed. Muḥammad Riḍwān al-Dāya, Abu Dhabi: al-Majma' al-Thaqāfī, 1423 AH/2002 CE, pp. 150–1.

128 Bakrī, *Anwār*, ms. Vatican, 34a.

129 Nūr al-Dīn 'Alī ibn Nāṣir al-Shāfi'ī al-Ash'arī al-Makkī, "*'Unwān al-sharīf*," in *Mawlid Sharaf al-'Ālamayn*, distributed by Dār al-Fikr, n.p., n.d., pp. 74–5.

130 al-Ḥurayfīsh, *Rawḍ*, pp. 303–4.

131 Anonymous, *Mawlid*, ms. Cairo, Dār al-Kutub, Tārīkh no. 704, 15a-16a. Compare anonymous, untitled *Mawlid*, ms. Cairo, Dār al-Kutub, Majāmī' Ṭal'at no. 293, 13a–b; anonymous, "*Hādhā mawlid jawharī*," ms. Cairo, Dār al-Kutub, Tārīkh Ṭal'at no. 1962, 36a–37a.

132 Qummī, *Faḍā'il*, pp. 17–18.

133 For instance, in one narrative the mother of 'Uthmān ibn al-'Āṣ recounts her attendance at the Prophet's birth. See Ṭabarī, *Ta'rīkh*, 2:156–7.

134 Muḥammad ibn 'Alī ibn Bābawayh al-Qummī, *Amālī al-Ṣadūq*, Najaf: Manshūrāt al-Maṭba'a al-Ḥaydarīya, 1379 AH/1980 CE, pp. 531–3; parallel in Fattāl, *Rawḍa*, pp. 143–4.

135 Fattāl, *Rawḍa*, pp. 79–80. This passage forms part of the Jābir narrative that, as discussed above (p. 7), was very likely transmitted by Ibn Bābawayh in his work *Mawlid mawlānā 'Alī*. An even more elaborate version of this narrative of 'Alī's birth is presented in the anonymous (and truncated) manuscript *Kitāb al-anwār bi'l-mu'jizāt*, ms. London, British Library, no. OR 4281, 3a–4b.

136 Aḥmad Zaynī Daḥlān, *al-Sīra al-nabawīya wa'l-āthār al-muḥammadīya*, printed in the margins of 'Alī ibn Burhān al-Dīn al-Ḥalabī, *Insān al-'uyūn fī sīrat al-amīn al-ma'mūn*, [Cairo]: Maṭba'at Muḥammad Efendī Muṣṭafā, n.d., 1:41.

137 The version that recounts the birth of 'Alī rather than that of the Prophet Muḥammad is, however, supplied with an *isnād* in Shī'ite sources.

138 This account, somewhat confusingly, seems to imply that both Chosroes and the high priest had disquieting dreams.

139 Ṭabarī, *Ta'rīkh*, 2:166–8.

140 Muḥammad ibn Mukarram, known as Ibn Manẓūr, *Mukhtaṣar Tārīkh madīnat Dimashq li-Ibn 'Asākir*, ed. Ma'mūn al-Ṣāghirjī, Damascus: Dār al-Fikr, 1405 AH/1985 CE, 8:297; Ibn Kathīr, *Bidāya*, 1:270.

141 The Saṭīḥ narrative does not seem to be included in the Vatican manuscript, but it must have been incorporated into the framework of *al-Anwār* at least by the eleventh-century AH/seventeenth-century CE, as it appears in the version presented by al-Majlisī (*Biḥār*, 15:299–324). The story occupies twenty pages of the Cairo edition of *al-Anwār* (pp. 62–82).

142 Ibn Hishām, *Sīra*, 1:298–302; see also Ṭabarī, *Ta'rīkh*, 2:158–60 (Ṭabarī has it from Yūnus ibn Bukayr and from al-Muḥāribī, both from Ibn Isḥāq); and in Muḥammad ibn Ḥibbān al-Bustī, *al-Sīra al-nabawīya*, ed. 'Abd al-Salām 'Allūsh, Beirut: al-Maktab al-Islāmī, 1420 AH/2000 CE, pp. 42–3. The editor of Ibn Ḥibbān's *Sīra* states that it is also found in the *Musnad* of Abū Ya'lā, the *Ṣaḥīḥ* of Ibn Ḥibbān,

the *Sīra* of Ibn 'Asākir, the *Mu'jam al-kabīr* of al-Ṭabarānī, the *Dalā'il al-nubūwa* of al-Bayhaqī, *al-Bidāya wa'l-nihāya*, and other sources.

143 Bayhaqī, *Dalā'il*, 1:77.

144 Kāzarūnī, *Muntaqā*, 2:208–21.

145 See Bakrī, *Anwār*, Cairo, pp. 89–103; Majlisī, *Biḥār*, 15:371–82.

146 Kāzarūnī, *Muntaqā*, 2:208–9.

147 Bakrī, *Anwār*, Cairo, p. 90; parallel in Majlisī, *Biḥār*, 15:372.

148 Qummī, *Faḍā'il*, pp. 24–8.

149 Bayhaqī, *Dalā'il*, 1:80; parallel in Kāzarūnī, *Muntaqā*, 2:218. A close parallel to this dialogue appears in Ṭabarī, *Ta'rīkh*, 2:163, although it is set within a different framing narrative.

150 Bayhaqī, *Dalā'il*, 1:80–4; Kāzarūnī, *Muntaqā*, 2:219–22.

151 Saleh, *Qur'ān Commentary*, Appendix C, p. 71 (Arabic numbering).

152 Bakrī, *Anwār*, ms.Vatican, pp. 45a–b; Kritzeck, *Peter the Venerable*, p. 88. In the Toledo version, the young Prophet is finally "discovered in the midst of a vast multitude of evil spirits who were accusing him of having been born 'for our ruination'."

153 Qummī, *Faḍā'il*, p. 36.

154 Ibn Hishām, *Sīra*, 1:304. It is likely that here again the skeptical language originates with Ibn Hishām rather than Ibn Isḥāq, as it does not appear in al-Ṭabarī's citation of the story from Ibn Isḥāq (Ṭabarī, *Ta'rīkh*, 2:158).

155 Saleh, *Qur'ān Commentary*, Appendix C, p. 70 (Arabic numbering).

156 Ibn Ḥajar al-'Asqalānī, *Lisān al-mīzān*, Beirut: Dār al-Fikr, 1407 AH/1897 CE, 5:190.

157 Muḥammad ibn Ḥibbān al-Bustī, *Kitāb al-thiqāt*, Haydarabad: Dā'irat al-Ma'ārif al-'Uthmānīya, 1403 AH/1983 CE, 9:154.

158 Kāzarūnī, *Muntaqā*, 2:10.

159 Ibn al-Ḥājj, *Madhkal*, 2:14.

160 Ibn Ḥajar al-Haytamī, *Itmām al-ni'ma al-kubrā 'alā al-'ālam bi-mawlid sayyid wuld Ādam*, ed. 'Abd al-'Azīz Sayyid Hāshim al-Ghazūlī, Beirut: Dār al-Kutub al-'Ilmīya, 1422 AH/2001 CE, p. 28.

161 Bakrī, *Anwār*, Cairo, p. 25; Majlisī, *Biḥār*, 15:43.

162 Bakrī, *Anwār*, Cairo, p. 28; Majlisī, *Biḥār*, 15:44.

163 Bakrī, *Anwār*, Cairo, p. 31; Majlisī, *Biḥār*, 15:46.

164 Bakrī, *Anwār*, Cairo, p. 38; Majlisī, *Biḥār*, 15:49–50.

165 See Qur'ān 2:117, 3:47, 3:59, 6:73, 16:40, 19:35, 36:82, 40:68.

166 They are located in the manuscript section of the Central Library of Jāmi'at al-Imām Muḥammad ibn Sa'ūd al-Islāmīya (nos. 1752 and 6535). See 'Abd al-'Azīz ibn Rāshid al-Sunaydī, *Mu'jam mā ullifa 'an makka*, Riyadh, 1420 AH/1999 CE, pp. 165, 172.

167 It is described as being divided into ten sections and beginning "*al-Ḥamdu li'llāh al-maḥmūd bi-kull lisān*..." (Baghdādī, *Īḍāḥ*, 1:451).

168 There seems to be some possibility that the *Īḍāḥ*'s listing on Iqlīshī's *mawlid* reflects a confusion with the same author's *al-Durr al-manẓūm fīmā yuzīl al-ghumūm wa'l-humūm*, also listed in the same work (1:452). A surviving manuscript of the latter is described in *Majallat Ma'had al-Makhṭūṭāt al-'Arabīya* 3, Rabī' al-Thānī 1377/November 1957, p. 236, as being divided into ten sections and beginning "al-Ḥamdu li'llāh al-maḥmūd bi-kull lisān al-karīm al-mannān ... " The fact that these details are identical to the *Īḍāḥ*'s description of al-Iqlīshī's *mawlid* suggests the possibility of confusion. Given the fact that the *Īḍāḥ* provides separate entries for the two works, however, it seems unlikely (although not impossible) that the whole entry on the *mawlid* is merely a garbled reference to the book on the alleviation of sorrows; the author clearly believed that there were two different books involved.

169 Ibn al-'Abbār, *Kitāb al-takmila li-kitāb al-ṣila*, al-Qism al-awwal al-mafqūd min ṭab'at al-shaykh Qadāra Zaydīn, Algiers, 1337 AH/1919 CE, p. 75.

170 For bibliographical information on all of these works, see the Appendix.

171 In classical Arabic the word *'arūs* can refer to either a bride or groom; in the text in question, the *'arūs* is a metaphorical presence that appears to be feminine in grammatical gender, but figuratively represents the Prophet Muḥammad.

172 Nūrā Abū'l-Fatḥ, *al-Mutāḥ min al-mawālid wa'l-anāshīd al-milāḥ*, n.p., 1416 AH/ 1995 CE, 1:78.

173 'Abd al-Qādir ibn Shaykh al-'Aydarūs, *al-Nūr al-sāfir 'an akhbār al-qarn al-'āshir*, n.p., n.d., pp. 217–18.

174 Fatḥ Allāh al-Bannānī, *Fatḥ allāh fī mawlid khayr khalq allāh*, [Cairo], 1323 AH, p. 110. The Javanese scholar Muḥammad Nawawī al-Bantanī (d. 1316 AH/1898 CE), who wrote a commentary on the *mawlid* of Ibn al-Jawzī or al-Ḥarīrī, appears to have acknowledged both attributions. His commentary has been printed under the title *Fatḥ al-ṣamad al-'ālim 'alā mawlid ibn al-Qāsim*.

175 Ḥajjī Khalīfa, *Kashf al-ẓunūn*, 2:115.

176 Ḥurayfīsh, *Rawḍ*, pp. 303, 369, 370. For this figure see Berkey, *Popular Preaching*, p. 18. The practice of appropriating and adapting passages of rhymed prose is also illustrated by three manuscripts preserved in Cairo (all of them, unfortunately, anonymous and undated) where the *dībāja* familiar from *Mawlid al-'arūs* is subsumed into a longer passage of rhymed prose that begins with a complex set of celestial and floral images. (Ms. Cairo, Dār al-Kutub, Tārīkh Ṭal'at no. 1962, 1a; Tārīkh no. 704, 1a; Majāmī' Ṭal'at no. 293, 1b.)

177 Ibrāhīm ibn 'Umar al-Ja'barī, *Kitāb maw'id al-kirām fī mawlid al-nabī 'alayhi al-salām*, ms. Damascus, Asad Library, no. 4771, 1a.

178 Ibn Kathīr, *Mawlid*, p. 13.

179 Ibid., p. 17.

180 Ja'barī, *Maw'id*, 1b.

181 Muḥammad ibn 'Alī al-Zamlakānī, *Mawlid*, ms. Berlin, Staatsbibliothek, Ahlwardt no. 9527, 12b–15a.

182 Ibn Kathīr, *Mawlid*, pp. 26–30.

183 Muḥammad ibn Muḥammad ibn al-Jazarī, *al-Mawlid al-kabīr*, ms. London, British Library, OR 3608, 3a–7b.

184 Ibid., 9b.

185 Ibid., 12a.

186 Ibn Ḥabīb, *Mawlid al-nabī*, ms. Berlin, Staatsbibliothek, Ahwardt no. 2617, 84b.

187 Ibn al-Jazarī, *al-Mawlid al-kabīr*, 13a.

188 Ibn al-Ḥājj, *Madhkal*, 2:14.

189 Ibid., 2:15.

190 Ibn Kathīr, *Mawlid*, p. 13.

191 Haytamī, *Itmām*, p. 28.

192 On Zayn al-Dīn's polemic, see Berkey, *Popular Preaching*, pp. 32–3.

193 Jalāl al-Dīn 'Abd al-Raḥmān ibn Abī Bakr al-Suyūṭī, *Taḥdhīr al-khawāṣṣ min akādhīb al-quṣṣāṣ*, ed. Muḥammad al-Ṣabbāgh, n.p.: al-Maktab al-Islāmī, 1392 AH/ 1972 CE, pp. 4–5.

194 Kāzarūnī, *Muntaqā*, 2:10.

195 Ibid., 2:10–11.

196 Ibn Ḥajar al-'Asqalānī, *al-Durar al-kāmina fī a'yān al-mi'a al-thāmina*, Beirut: Dār al-Jīl, n.d., 4:256.

197 Burke, *Popular Culture*, p. 63.

198 Ibid., p. 63.

199 A partial recording of this work by the Syrian chanter Nūr al-Dīn Khurshīd recounts two such episodes, both associated with the Prophet's journey to Syria as Khadīja's commercial agent. In one of them, the Prophet's malevolent uncle Abū Lahab encounters a fearsome serpent while attempting to pass through a valley. Craftily, Abū Lahab withdraws from the road, hoping that Muḥammad will soon arrive at the head of his section of the caravan and be slain by the serpent. Upon sighting the Muḥammad,

however, the serpent hails him as a prophet. The serpent reveals that he is no ordinary snake, but the son of the king of the jinn, who recognized God in the time of Abraham. In the second episode, a Jewish merchant insists on inviting the Prophet to lunch. Seeking to kill Muḥammad, he conspires with his wife to drop a millstone on his head from the roof of their house. Through divine intervention, however, she crushes her own children instead. Although these incidents occur after the abrupt end of the medieval manuscript of *al-Anwār*, they appear in the citations of al-Bakrī by Muḥammad Bāqir al-Majlisī (Majlisī, *Biḥār*, 16:35–6, 45). See also Nadhīr Muḥammad Maktabī, *al-Inshād wa'l-munshidūn: dirāsa adabīya shar'īya*, Damascus: Dār al-Maktabī, 1420 AH/2000 CE, p. 141.

200 One particularly vivid example of the continuing efflorescence of popular narratives is the *mawlid* attributed to Nūr al-Dīn 'Alī ibn Nāṣir al-Shāfi'ī (d. ca. 915 AH/1509 CE) and published under the title *Mawlid sharaf al-'ālamayn*, n.p.: Dār al-Fikr, n.d. The work begins with an elaborate rhymed-prose introduction and continues with a lengthy, composite cosmogonic narrative. It includes both elements familiar from the *mawlid* tradition and ones drawn from the broader storytelling tradition. For instance, one extended passage recounts how the seven layers of the earth are supported by the hands of an angel, whose feet are supported on a bull, which rests on a green boulder "as thick as the seven heavens and the seven earths," which lies upon the back of a great whale (pp. 54–5).

201 Tāj al-Dīn al-Subkī (attributed), *Kitāb sharaf al-anām fī mawlid man ẓallahu al-ghumām*, ms. Cairo, Dār al-Kutub, Ta'rīkh Khalīl Āghā no. 8.

202 Ms. Cairo, Dār al-Kutub, Tārīkh no. 3807.

203 Najm al-Dīn al-Ghazzī, *al-Kawākib al-sā'ira bi-a'yān al-mi'a al-'āshira*, Beirut: Manshūrāt Dār al-Āfāq al-Jadīda, 2nd edn, 1979, 1:136.

204 Ms. Cairo, Dār al-Kutub, Tārīkh Ṭal'at no. 1962, 19b–21a; Majāmī' Ṭal'at no. 293, 8b; Tārīkh no. 705, 14a–15a.

205 Abū Mikhnaf (attributed), *Mawlid baṭal al-islām*, pp. 189–215.

2 Gifts and reciprocity in the celebration of the *mawlid*

1 'Abd al-Raḥmān ibn Ismā'īl, known as Abū Shāma, *al-Bā'ith 'alā inkār al-bida' wa'l-ḥawādith*, ed. 'Uthmān Aḥmad 'Anbar, n.p.: Dār al-Hudā, 1398 AH/1978 CE, pp. 23–4.

2 Ibn Rajab al-Ḥanbalī, *Kitāb laṭā'if al-ma'ārif fīmā li-mawāsim al-'ām min al-waẓā'if*, Beirut: al-Maktab al-Islāmī, 1414 AH/1993 CE, pp. 105–6.

3 Jalāl al-Dīn 'Abd al-Raḥmān ibn Abī Bakr al-Suyūṭī, *Ḥusn al-maqṣid fī 'amal al-mawlid*, ed. Muṣṭafā 'Abd al-Qādir 'Aṭā', Beirut: Dār al-Kutub al-'Ilmīya, 1405 AH/ 1985 CE, pp. 63–4 (translated in N.J.G. Kaptein, *Muḥammad's Birthday Festival*, Leiden: E.J. Brill, 1993, pp. 63–4). This *fatwā* is also reproduced in Alī ibn Sultān Muḥammad al-Qāri' al-Harawī, *al-Mawrid al-rawī fī mawlid al-nabī wa-nasabihi al-ṭāhir*, ed. Mabrūk Ismā'īl Mabrūk, Cairo: Maktabat al-Qur'ān, n.d., pp. 12–13. al-Harawī cites it from Muḥammad al-Sakhāwī, a student and enthusiastic disciple of Ibn Ḥajar al-'Asqalānī; this quotation is one of the many passages attributed to Sakhāwī that appear throughout al-Harawī's text. It appears that al-Sakhāwī's lost *mawlid* work may have been one of al-Harawī's major sources for his own composition. The version of al-'Asqalānī's *fatwā* reproduced in Ibn Ḥajar al-Haytamī, *Itmām al-ni'ma al-kubrā 'alā al-'ālam bi-mawlid sayyid wuld Ādam*, ed. 'Abd al-'Azīz Sayiid Hāshim al-Ghazūlī, Beirut: Dār al-Kutub al-'Ilmīya, 1422 AH/2001 CE, pp. 23–4, suggests that al-Suyūṭī's citation is somewhat free and does not include the entire opinion.

4 Suyūṭī, *Ḥusn al-maqṣid*, pp. 64–5.

5 Ibn al-Ḥājj, *al-Madkhal*, Cairo: Sharikat wa-Maṭba'at Muṣṭafā al-Bābī al-Ḥalabī wa-Awlādihi, 1380 AH/1960 CE, 1:288.

6 Ibid., 1:302.
7 Ibid., 2:3.
8 Aḥmad ibn Yaḥyā al-Wansharīsī, *al-Mi'yār al-mu'rib wa'l-jāmi' al-mughrib 'an fatāwā ahl ifrīqīya wa'l-andalus wa'l-maghrib*, [Ribāṭ]: Wizārat al-Awqāf wa'l-Shu'ūn al-Islāmīya li'l-Mamlaka al-Maghribīya, 1401 AH/1981 CE, 7:114. The same sentiment is reflected in an incident involving the Tunisian Mālikī jurist Muḥammad ibn 'Abd al-Salām al-Munastīrī (d. 749 AH/1348 CE). Having ostentatiously walked out of a royal *mawlid* celebration, the scholar expresses his disapproval of the proceedings by remarking that "This is the blessed night for which it is obligatory to thank God," yet the Prophet would not have permitted the frivolity and singing with which it was being observed. Chastened, the sultan in later years distributed food to the needy and provided aid to the poor (or perhaps the *ṣūfīs*: *al-fuqarā'*), "as thanks to God." Abū'l-Hasan 'Alī ibn 'Abd Allāh al-Nubāhī al-Māliqī al-Andalusī, *Ta'rīkh quḍāt al-andalus*, known as *Kitāb al-marqaba al-'ulyā fī-man yastaḥiqq al-qaḍā' wa'l-futyā*, ed. E. Levy-Provencal, Cairo: Dār al-Kātib al-Miṣrī, 1948 CE, pp. 162–3.
9 A. Kevin Reinhart, *Before Revelation: the boundaries of Muslim moral thought*, Albany: State University of New York Press, 1995, p. 118.
10 Ibid., p. 120.
11 al-Qāri' al-Harawī, *al-Mawrid al-rawī*, p. 17.
12 Ismā'ī ibn 'Umar Ibn Kathīr, *al-Bidāya wa'l-nihāya*, Beirut: Dār al-Fikr, 1402 AH/ 1982 CE, 13:137.
13 Aḥmad ibn Muḥammad Ibn Khallikān, *Wafayāt al-a'yān wa-anbā' abnā' al-zamān*, ed. Iḥsān 'Abbās, Beirut: Dār al-Thaqāfa, n.d., 4:118.
14 Cited in Ibn Kathīr, *Bidāya*, 13:137.
15 Muḥammad ibn Muḥammad ibn al-Jazarī, *al-Mawlid al-kabīr*, ms. London, British Museum, no. OR 3608, 13b.
16 Kaptein, *Muḥammad's Birthday*, p. 43.
17 Ibn Khallikān, *Wafayāt*, 4:116.
18 Ibn Kathīr, *Bidāya*, 13:137.
19 Muḥammad ibn Yūsuf al-Ṣāliḥī al-Shāmī, *Subul al-hudā wa'l-rashād fī sīrat khayr al-'ibād*, ed. 'Ādil Aḥmad 'Abd al-Mawjūd and 'Alī Muḥammad Mu'awwaḍ, Beirut: Dār al-Kutub al-'Ilmīya, 1414 AH/1993 CE, 1:363–4.
20 Ibid., 1:364.
21 Ibn al-'Imād al-Ḥanbalī, *Shadharāt al-dhahab fī akhbār man dhahab*, Beirut: Dār al-Masīra, 1399 AH/1979 CE, 4:253.
22 al-Ṣāliḥī himself seems to be unsure of the attribution of the passage. He first cites "*al-'allāma* Ibn Ẓufar" and then writes "or rather (*bal*) in *al-Durr al-muntaẓam*." There are several early *mawlid* texts with similar names, although none with this precise title.
23 Ṣāliḥī, *Subul*, 1:363.
24 Shams al-Dīn Abū 'Abd Allāh Muḥammad ibn Mūsā ibn al-Nu'mān al-Fāmī al-Mālikī died in 683 AH/1284–5 CE. He was a follower of Ḍiyā' al-Dīn Abū'l-Ḥasan 'Alī ibn abī'l-Qāsim, known as Ibn Qufl. (Ibn al-Mulaqqin 'Umar ibn 'Alī', *Ṭabaqāt al-awliyā'*, ed. Nūr al-Dīn Shuraybah, Cairo: Maktabat al-Khānjī bi'l-Qāhira, 1393 AH/ 1973 CE, pp. 501–2.)
25 See 'Umar Riḍā Kaḥḥāla, *Mu'jam al-mu'allifīn*, Beirut: Mu'assasat al-Risāla, 1414 AH/ 1993 CE, 3:942.
26 Ṣāliḥī, *Subul*, 1:366.
27 The *fatwā* is cited in its entirety in Suyūṭī, *Ḥusn al-maqṣid*, pp. 45–9, and translated in Kaptein, *Muḥammad's Birthday*, pp. 51–4.
28 Suyūṭī, *Ḥusn al-maqṣid*, pp. 46–8.
29 Ibn al-Ḥājj, *Madkhal*, 2:11.
30 Ibid., 2:12.
31 Ibid., 2:27.

32 Haytamī, *Itmām*, p. 24.
33 Aḥmad ibn ʻAbd al-Ḥalīm Ibn Taymīya, *Majmūʻ fatāwā shaykh al-islām Aḥmad ibn Taymīya*, collected and arranged by ʻAbd al-Raḥmān ibn Muḥammad al-ʻĀṣimī al-Najdī, n.p., n.d., 25:298.
34 Ibn Ṭawq, *al-Taʻlīq*, Damascus: al-Maʻhad al-Faransī li'l-Dirāsāt al-ʻArabīya bi-Dimashq, 2000, 1:156–7.
35 Ibid., 1:234, 239.
36 Ibid., 1:234.
37 Ibid., 1:358, 379.
38 See ibid., 1:60; 3:1195 (another apparent reference to a wedding *mawlid* on 3:1193).
39 Muḥammad ibn ʻAlī ibn Ṭūlūn al-Ṣāliḥī, *Mufākahat al-khillān fī ḥawādith al-zamān*, Beirut: Dār al-Kutub al-ʻIlmīya, 1418 AH/1998 CE, p. 288. Another wedding *mawlid* is mentioned on p. 37.
40 Ibid., p. 313.
41 Ibid., p. 404.
42 Wansharīsī, *Miʻyār*, 7:99–101, 102–3, 114; 9:252; see also discussion in Kaptein, *Muḥammad's Birthday*, pp. 135–7.
43 Ibn Ḥajar al-Haytamī, *al-Fatāwā al-kubrā al-fiqhīya*, ed. ʻAbd al-Laṭīf ʻAbd al-Raḥmān, Beirut: Dār al-Kutub al-ʻIlmīya, 1417 AH/1997 CE, 4:330.
44 Muḥammad ibn Jābir al-Andalusī, *Kitāb mawlid rasūl allāh*, ms. Istanbul, Süleimaniye, no. 344, 14a–15a.
45 The language here is Qur'ānic. The Prophet is referred to in a number of different verses as "*nabī karīm*," and the reference to his "lofty character" is from the Qur'ān 68:4.
46 Nūrā Abū'l-Fatḥ, *al-Mutāḥ min al-mawālid wa'l-anāshīd al-milāḥ*, n.p., 1416 AH/1995 CE, 2:273–4. In addition to the considerable popularity of *Sharaf al-ānām* itself, this story has been circulated by a number of the many authors who compiled their own *mawlid*s from pre-existing materials. It seems to have enjoyed a degree of acceptance independent of its attribution to any particular *mawlid* text or author. Ibn Makkīya credits it in *Durar al-Biḥār* to a Muḥammad ibn Ḥātim, rather than to (the equally unidentifiable) ʻAbd al-Wāḥid ibn Ismāʻīl (ms. Cairo, Dar al-Kutub, Ta'rīkh no. 3807, 14b). Whatever its ultimate origin, this tale has been recounted with a frequency that renders it an established trope of the *mawlid* genre. It clearly resonates with authors and audiences alike; interviewing an elderly ritual chanter in Yemen in the early stages of my research, I heard it presented so factually and compellingly that I initially took it for a tale of the recent local past.
47 al-Qāri' al-Harawī, *al-Mawrid al-rawī*, p. 14.
48 Ibid., pp. 14–15.
49 Abū'l-Fatḥ, *Mutāḥ*, 1:85.
50 Ṣāliḥī, *Subul*, 1:364.
51 Ibid., 1:364. There is some ambiguity about al-Ṣāliḥī's attribution of this *fatwā*. The editor of another edition of the text states that some manuscripts have "al-Shirbīnī" instead of "al-Tizmantī." (Muḥammad ibn Yūsuf al-Ṣāliḥī, *Subul al-hudā wa'l-rashād*, ed. Muṣṭafā ʻAbd al-Wāḥid, Cairo: al-Majlis al-Aʻlā li'l-Shu'ūn al-Islāmīya, Lajnat Iḥyā' al-Turāth al-Islāmī, 1392 AH/1972 CE, 1:442, n.1.)
52 Suyūṭī, *Ḥusn al-maqṣid*, p. 48.
53 Ibn al-Ḥājj, *Madkhal*, 2:3, 6–10.
54 Ibn Taymīya, *Majmūʻ fatāwā*, 25:298.
55 Ibn al-Ḥājj, *Madkhal*, 2:26.
56 Ṣāliḥī, *Subul*, 1:364.
57 Ibid., 1:364.
58 See Constance E. Padwick, *Muslim Devotions*, Oxford: Oneworld, 1996, pp. 152–7; Fritz Meier, *Bausteine II*, Istanbul: Franz Steiner Verlag, 1992, pp. 837–75.

59 Jalāl al-Dīn 'Abd al-Raḥmān ibn Abī Bakr al-Suyūṭī, *Ḥusn al-muḥāḍara fī ta'rīkh miṣr wa'l-qāhira*, ed. Muḥammad Abū'l-Faḍl Ibrāhīm, Cairo: Dār Iḥyā' al-Kutub al-'Arabīya, 1387 AH/1968 CE, 2:306.
60 Muḥammad ibn Aḥmad al-Lakhmī al-'Azafī, *al-Durr al-munaẓẓam fī'l-mawlid al-mu'aẓẓam*, Princeton University Islamic manuscripts, Garrett Yahuda no. 256, 160b.
61 Ibid., 160b.
62 Muḥammad ibn 'Abd al-Raḥmān al-Sakhāwī, *al-Qawl al-badī' fī'l-ṣalāt 'alā'l-ḥabīb al-shafī'*, Medina: al-Maktaba al-'Ilmīya, 1397 AH/1977 CE.
63 Ibid., pp. 43, 44, 109, 116, 123, 126, 132. The printed text (p. 43) has Abū'l-Qāsim al-Bustī, but this is clearly a mistake for al-Sabtī. Interestingly, al-Sakhāwī failed to find any source for most of al-'Azafī's traditions.
64 Sakhāwī, *al-Qawl al-badī'*, p. 12.
65 Ibid., p. 25.
66 Ibid., p. 25. A similar point is made by al-Fakhr al-Rāzī (*al-Tafsīr al-kabīr*, [Tehran], n.d., 25:228) in his discussion of verse 33:56. "If God and His angels bless [the Prophet]," he asks, "what need has he of our blessings? Our answer is that we do not bless him because he is in need of it; otherwise, there would be no need for the angels' blessings in addition to God's. Rather, [blessing him] is ... so that we will manifest [our] reverence for him, so that in his solicitude for us He can reward us for it. For this reason [the Prophet] said, 'Whoever blesses me once, God will bless him ten times.'"
67 'Azafī, *Durr*, 161a.
68 Sakhāwī, *al-Qawl al-badī'*, pp. 102–10.
69 Abū'l-Fatḥ, *Mutāḥ*, 1:92–3.
70 'Abd al-Salām ibn Ibrāhīm al-Laqānī, *Tarwīḥ al-fu'ād bi-mawlid khayr al-'ibād*, ms. Cairo, Dār al-Kutub, Majāmī' mīm no. 6, 5a–6a.
71 See Abū'l-Fatḥ, *Mutāḥ*, 1:188–2–7, passim. For a discussion of *ta'ṭīras* as performed by modern Egyptian *maddāḥūn*, see Kamal Abdel-Malek, *Muḥammad in the Modern Egyptian Popular Ballad*, Leiden: E.J. Brill, 1995, pp. 106–7.
72 Ja'far ibn Ismā'īl al-Barzanjī, *al-Kawkab al-anwar 'alā 'Iqd al-jawhar fī mawlid al-nabī al-azhar*, n.p.: al-Maṭba'a al-Wahbīya, 1290 AH, p. 32. Ja'far al-Barzanjī (d. 1317 AH/1899 CE) was a descendant of the author of the *mawlid* he comments on; he is specifically describing the customs prevalent in Medina.
73 For various versions of this narrative, see al-Qāri' al-Harawī, *al-Mawrid al-rawī*, p. 24; al-Qāḍī al-Dimyāṭī, *Mawlid al-rasūl al-karīm*, ms. Cairo, Dār al-Kutub, Ta'rīkh no. 280, 7b; Anonymous, *Mawlid*, ms. Cairo, Dār al-Kutub, Ta'rīkh Ṭal'at no. 2050, 3b; Anonymous, *Mawlid al-nabī*, ms. Cairo, Dār al-Kutub, Ta'rīkh no. 705, 4b; Anonymous, *Mawlid*, ms. Cairo, Dār al-Kutub, Ta'rīkh Ṭal'at no. 1963, 5b; Muḥammad al-Amīr al-Ṣaghīr, *Mawlid*, ms. Cairo, Dār al-Kutub, Ḥadīth no. 1677, 10b.
74 Abū'l-Faraj 'Abd al-Raḥmān Ibn al-Jawzī (attributed), *Mawlid al-nabī*, Princeton University Arabic manuscripts, Third Series, no. 209, 20b–21a.
75 Ibn al-Jazarī, *al-Mawlid al-kabīr*, 13a.
76 Muḥammad ibn Muḥammad ibn al-Jazarī, *Kitāb 'Urf al-ta'rīf bi'l-mawlid al-sharīf*, Princeton University Islamic manuscripts, Garrett Yehuda no. 225, 142b.
77 Fakhr al-Dīn al-Rāzī (d. 606 AH/1209 CE) was a prominent Ash'arī theologian and Qur'an commentator. Although it is chronologically plausible that he was aware of the celebration of the Prophet's birthday, this passage bears no apparent resemblance to his thought or style.
78 A Baghdādī ṣūfī who died in 253 AH/867 CE; see EI^2, s.v. "Sarī al-Saqaṭī."
79 al-Wāḥidī, *Bayān faḍā'il mawlid al-nabī*, Princeton Islamic Arabic manuscripts, Third Series, no. 198, 1b–2b (also found in Ibn al-Jawzī, *Mawlid al-nabī*, 1b–6a; *Sharḥ faḍā'il al-mawlid al-Nabī* [*sic*], ms. Damascus, Asad Library, no. 11044; *Faḍā'il al-mawlid al-sharīf*, ms. Cairo, Dār al-Kutub, Taṣawwuf wa-akhlāq dīnīya no. 2582; *al-Mawlid*, apocryphally attributed to Ibn Ḥajar al-Haytamī, published in Aleppo and reproduced in Abū'l-Fatḥ, *Mutāḥ*, 1:148).

80 Fatḥ Allāh al-Bannānī, *Fatḥ allāh fī mawlid khayr khalq allāh*, [Cairo]: al-Maṭba'a al-Ḥamīdīya al-Miṣrīya, 1323 AH/[1905–6]CE, pp. 153–7.
81 Muḥammad Nawawī al-Bantanī, *Madārij al-ṣu'ūd ilā iktisā' al-burūd*, n.p., n.d., pp. 18–19.
82 Wāḥidī, *Bayān*, 2b–3a; Bannānī, *Fatḥ allāh*, pp. 154–5.
83 Wāḥidī, *Bayān*, 2b–3a; Bannānī, *Fatḥ allāh*, p. 155.
84 Wāḥidī, *Bayān*, 3a; Bannānī, *Fatḥ allāh*, pp. 155–6.
85 Cited in Yūsuf ibn Ismā'īl al-Nabhānī, *Jawāhir al-biḥār fī faḍā'il al-nabī al-mukhtār*, ed. Muḥammad Amīn al-Ḍannāwī, Beirut: Dār al-Kutub al-'Ilmīya, 1419 AH/1998 CE, 3:395.
86 Ibn al-Jawzī, *Mawlid al-nabī*, 16b–17a.
87 al-Wāqidī (attributed), *Mawlid al-nabī*, Princeton University Arabic manuscripts, New Series, no. 163, 41b–42a.
88 For the incident in which Abraham is cast into the fire, see Qur'ān 21:68–9. For the motif of the "fire-fighting frogs" and its midrashic antecedents, see Shari Lowin, *The Making of a Forefather: Abraham in Islamic and Jewish exegetical narratives* (PhD dissertation, University of Chicago, 2002), pp. 206–45.
89 al-Shaykh Yaḥyā, *Rawḥ al-nufūs fī mawlid rūḥ al-nufūs*, ms. London, British Library, no. OR 11083, 169a.
90 Ibn Ṭūlūn, *Mufākaha*, p. 397.
91 Anonymous, *Mawlid al-nabī*, ms. Cairo, Dār al-Kutub, Ta'rīkh no. 704, 30a–b.
92 Ibid., 31b. Rather similarly, but without explicitly invoking the idea of *thawāb*, a manuscript of *Mawlid al-'arūs* copied in 1206 AH ends with the prayer, "May God forgive [the sins of] him who was the cause of the recitation of this noble *mawlid*, him, his parents, his friends, his neighbors and his relatives, [as well as] us, our parents and teachers, and all who are present and their parents, our brothers [*ikhwān*], friends and neighbors." Anonymous, *Kitāb al-'arūs*, ms. Damascus, Asad Library, no. 10114, 36b.
93 Abū'l-Fatḥ, *Mutāḥ*, 1:142.
94 'Alī ibn Nāṣir al-Makkī, in *Mawlid sharaf al-'ālamayn*, p. 87.
95 *Hādhā al-khatm yuqra'u ba'da itmām mawlūd al-sharīf*, n.p., n.d., private library of Ja'far Muḥammad al-Saqqāf, Tarīm, Yemen. I thank Ja'far al-Saqqāf for graciously granting me access to his library.
96 *Sharḥ faḍā'il al-mawlid*, ms. Damascus, Asad Library no. 11044, 10a–b.
97 Other relevant verses include 2:48, 6:52, 28:55, 29:12, 31:33, 82:19.
98 *Jam' jawāmi 'al-aḥādīth wa'l-asānīd*, Vaduz, Liechtenstein: Thesaurus Islamicus Foundation, 2000, Muslim, *Ṣaḥīḥ*, no. 4310 (Kitāb al-waṣīya, Bāb mā yalḥaq al-insān min al-thawāb ba'd mamātihi); Abū Dāwūd, *Sunan*, no. 2882 (Kitāb al-nikāḥ, bāb tazwīj man lam yūlid); al-Nasā'ī, *Sunan*, no. 3666 (Kitāb al-waṣāyā, Bāb faḍl al-ṣadaqa 'an al-mayyit).
99 The Mālikīs are the only school categorically denying the possibility of performing the *ḥajj* on behalf of another living person. The other three Sunnī schools (and a minority of Mālikīs) allow a deputy to perform the pilgrimage on behalf of someone whose chronic or terminal illness makes it impossible to perform in person. The Ḥanbalīs and Shāfi'īs hold that the obligation to perform the pilgrimage expires with the death of the individual if he or she was never capable of undertaking it; if the person was capable but failed to perform it, it must be performed on his or her behalf and the expenses paid from the estate. The Ḥanafīs and Mālikīs hold that the obligation to perform the ḥajj expires with the individual's death in all cases; the ḥajj must only be performed on behalf of the deceased (and financed from the estate) if he or she has made a bequest to that effect. *al-Mawsū'a al-fiqhīya*, al-Kuwayt: Wizārat al-Awqāf wa'l-shu'ūn al-islāmīya, 1414 AH/1993 CE, 2:335–6.
100 For *ḥadīth* supporting the principle that the dead benefit from the pious actions of the living, see Ibn al-Qayyim al-Jawzīya, *Kitāb al-Rūḥ*, third printing, Haydarabad: Maṭba'at

Majlis Dā'irat al-Ma'ārif al-'Uthmānīya, 1357 AH, pp. 206–7 (almsgiving); 207–9 (fasting); 209–10 (*ḥajj* pilgrimage).

101 *al-Mawsū'a al-fiqhīya*, 29:259.

102 Ibid., 29:258–60.

103 Muḥammad ibn Muḥammad al-Ḥaṭṭāb al-Ru'aynī, *Mawāhib al-jalīl li-sharḥ Mukhtaṣar Khalīl*, ed. Zakarīyā 'Umayrāt, Beirut: Dār al-Kutub al-'Ilmīya, 1416 AH/1995 CE, 3:521.

104 Muḥammad 'Alī ibn Ḥusayn al-Mālikī, *Tahdhīb al-furūq wa'l-qawā'id al-sanīya fī'l-asrār al-fiqhīya,* printed in the margin of Aḥmad ibn Idrīs al-Qarāfī, *Anwār al-burūq fī anwā' al-furūq,* 4 vols, ed. Khalīl al-Manṣūr, Beirut: Dār al-Kutub al-'Ilmīya, 1418 AH/1998 CE, 3:344.

105 Ibid., 3:223.

106 The equivalence between *thawāb* and wealth may be considered an analogy (*qiyās*), or *thawāb* may be considered an asset literally encompassed within the meaning of the *shar'ī* regulations governing economic transactions. See Ibrāhīm ibn Mūsā al-Shāṭibī, *al-Muwāfaqāt*, ed. Mashhūr ibn Ḥasan Āl Sulaymān, al-Khubar: Dār Ibn 'Affān, 1417 AH/1997 CE, 2:402.

107 Ibn al-Qayyim, *Rūḥ*, pp. 210–11. Ibn al-Qayyim is very emphatic on this point; a few lines earlier he argues that there is "no difference" between donating one's religious merit to a deceased person and forgiving him a monetary debt, because "the merit of the action belongs to the giver and donator; if he assigns it to the deceased it is transferred to him, just as any debts or other [monetary] obligations carried by the deceased are purely rights/possessions (*ḥaqq*) of the living person, and if he forgives the debt the forgiveness reaches [the deceased] and [the debt] ceases to be his obligation. Each of them [i.e., the money owed and the merit earned] is a possession of the living person; what text, analogy or legal principle dictates that one of them reaches [the dead] person and the other does not?"

108 Ibn al-Qayyim, *Rūḥ*, pp. 228–9.

109 Muḥammad Amīn Ibn 'Ābidīn, *Ḥāshiyat Radd al-muḥtār 'alā al-Durr al-mukhtār sharḥ Tanwīr al-abṣār*, Cairo: Sharikat Maktabat wa-Maṭba'at Muṣṭafā al-Bābī al-Ḥalabī wa-Awlādihi, second printing, 1386 AH/1966 CE, 2:595.

110 Ibid., 2:244.

111 Ibn al-Qayyim, *Rūḥ*, p. 212.

112 al-Shāṭibī, *Muwāfaqāt*, 2:401–2.

113 Abū'l-Ḥusayn 'Alī ibn Aḥmad ibn Yūsuf al-Qurashī al-Umawī al-Hakārī, *Kitāb Hadīyat al-aḥyā' ilā'l-amwāt wa-mā yaṣilu ilayhim min al-thawāb 'alā mamarr al-awqāt*, ms. Sanaa, Western Library, Majmū' no. 84, 26a-31b (quotation from 26b).

114 Ibid., 26b.

115 Ibid., 30a.

116 Ibid., 27a.

117 Ibid., 28a.

118 Ibid., 30b.

119 Ibn al-Qayyim, *Rūḥ*, p. 213.

120 Ibn Ḥusayn, *Tahdhīb al-Furūq*, in margin of Qarāfī, *Furūq*, 3:343.

121 Ibn al-Qayyim, *Rūḥ*, p. 220.

122 Ibn al-Qayyim, *Rūḥ*, pp. 221–2.

123 This is not the only passage in which Ibn al-Qayyim presents interdependence as the foundation of the moral order. In response to the argument that religious duties are tests of the faith and obedience of the individual and are inherently non-transferable, he argues that both the *sharī'a* and the cosmic order are based not only on justice but on acts of kindness (*iḥsān*) and mutual benevolence (*al-ta'āruf*). God has set the angels to implore forgiveness for the believers and the Prophet to intercede for them, as well as allowing individual believers to do many things on each other's behalf. In the end, "is acting kindly towards another religiously responsible individual

(*mukallaf*) by donating merit to him anything but an imitation of God's kindness? God loves those who perform acts of kindness. All of creation is dependent on God, and God loves most those of them who are most beneficial to His dependents" (Ibn al-Qayyim, *Rūḥ*, pp. 231–2).

124 Bantanī, *Madārij*, pp. 2–3.

125 Muḥammad al-Majdhūb, *al-La'ālī al-zāhirāt wa'l-fuṣūṣ al-fā'iqāt fī dhikr mawlid al-nabī dhī al-mu'jizāt*, in *Majmū'a taḥtawī 'alā qiṣṣat al-mi'rāj al-musammā bi'l-Jumāna al-yatīma wa'l-Nūr al-sāṭi' fī mawlid al-nabī al-jāmi'* ... [etc.], [Cairo]: Muṣṭafā al-Bābī al-Ḥalabī, 1339 AH, p. 55.

126 Ibn al-Qayyim, *Rūḥ*, p. 247.

127 Ru'aynī, *Mawāhib*, 3:520.

128 Ibid., 3:521.

129 Ru'aynī, *Mawāhib*, 3:519–21.

130 Aḥmad al-Budayrī al-Ḥallāq, *Ḥawādith Dimashq al-yawmīya*, [Cairo]: al-Jam'īya al-Miṣrīya li'l-Dirāsāt al-Ta'rīkhīya, 1959, p. 112.

131 Ibn 'Ābidīn, *Ḥāshiyat Radd al-muḥtār*, 2:440. The printed text reads *manāyir* (minarets), which is probably a misprint; *manābir* (pulpits) appears in a citation of this passage in Abū'l-Fatḥ, *Mutāḥ*, 1:244. Ibn 'Ābidīn was not categorically opposed to the donation of merit to the Prophet; in support of its legitimacy, he cites both the idea that such a donation constitutes thanks (*shukr*) to the Prophet for salvation from misguidance and the belief that the Prophet's station, while exalted, was subject to further enhancement. (*Ḥāshiyat Radd al-muḥtār*, 2:244.)

132 Muḥammad Aḥmad 'Ulaysh, *Fatḥ al-'alī al-malik fī'l-fatwā 'alā madhhab al-imām Mālik*, Beirut: Dār al-Ma'rifa, n.d., 1:205.

133 Bio-bibliographical information on Ibn Nāṣir al-Dīn is found in Muḥammad ibn 'Abd al-Raḥmān al-Sakhāwī, *al-Ḍaw' al-lāmi' li-ahl al-qarn al-tāsi'*, Beirut: Dār Maktabat al-Ḥayāt, n.d., 8:103–6; Ibn al-'Imād al-Ḥanbalī, *Shahdarāt*, 7:243–5; Muḥammad ibn 'Alī al-Shawkānī, *al-Badr al-ṭāli' bi-maḥāsin man ba'd al-qarn al-sābi'*, Damascus: Dār al-Fikr, 1419 AH/1998 CE, pp. 715–16; 'Abd al-Qādir Muḥammad al-Nu'aymī al-Dimashqī, *al-Dāris fī Ta'rīkh al-madāris*, ed. Ja'far al-Ḥasanī, [Cairo]: Maktabat al-Thaqāfa al-Dīnīya, n.d., 1:41–3.

134 Ibn Nāṣir al-Dīn, *Majālis fī qawlihi ta'ālā "La-qad manna Allāh 'alā al-mu'minīn idh ba'atha fīhim rasūlan min anfusihim,"* Beirut: Mu'assasat al-Rayyān, 1420 AH/2000 CE, p. 30.

135 Ibid., pp. 31–4.

136 Ibid., p. 36.

137 Ibid., pp. 37–8.

138 Ibid., p. 51.

139 Ibid., p. 54.

140 Ibid., p. 45.

141 Ibid., pp. 38–65.

142 Ibid., p. 73.

143 Ibn Nāṣir al-Dīn al-Dimashqī, *Minhāj al-salāma fī mīzān al-qiyāma*, ed. Mash'al ibn Bānī al-Jabrīn al-Muṭayrī, Beirut: Dār Ibn Ḥazm 1416 AH/1996 CE, pp. 50–1.

144 *Jam' jawāmi' al-aḥādīth*, Bukhārī, *Ṣaḥīḥ*, no. 851 (Kitāb al-ādhān, Bāb al-dhikr ba'd al-ṣalāt); see also Muslim, *Ṣaḥīḥ*, no. 1375 (Kitāb al-masājid, Bāb istiḥbāb al-dhikr ba'd al-ṣalāt wa-ṣifatihi); Ibn Māja, *Sunan*, no. 580 (Kitāb iqāmat al-ṣalāt wa'l-sunna, Bāb mā yuqāl ba'd al-taslīm).

145 al-Wāqidī (attributed), *Mawlid al-nabī*, Princeton University Arabic manuscripts, New Series, no. 1963, 42a.

146 Muḥammad 'Alī ibn 'Allān al-Bakrī, *Kitāb al-Nafaḥāt al-'anbarīya fī mawlid sayyid al-barīya*, ms. Sanaa, Awqāf Library, 4b. For the identity of the author, see Ismā'īl Bāshā, *Hadīya*, 2:283–4. By "the morrow," the final line refers to the Day of Resurrection.

147 Fransciso Rodriguez-Manas, "Charity and deceit: the practice of the *iṭ'ām al-ṭa'ām* in Moroccan ṣūfism," *Studia Islamica* 91, 2000, p. 66.
148 Marcel Mauss, *The Gift*, New York, London: W.W. Norton & Company, 1967, p. 72.
149 Ibid., p. 70.
150 Muḥammad ibn Ja'far al-Kattānī, *al-Yumn wa'l-is'ād bi-mawlid khayr al-'ibād*, Casablanca: al-Maktaba al-Sharqīya, 1345 AH/1927 CE, p. 17.
151 Dina Rizk Khoury, "Slippers at the entrance or behind closed doors: domestic and public spaces for Mosuli women," in Madeline C. Zilfi, ed., *Women in the Ottoman Empire*, Leiden New York, Köln: Brill, 1997, p. 117.

3 Emotion, law, and the celebration of the *mawlid*

1 Muḥammad ibn Yūsuf al-Ṣāliḥī al-Shāmī, *Subul al-hudā wa'l-rashād fī sīrat khayr al-'ibād*, ed. 'Ādil Aḥmad 'Abd al-Mawjūd and 'Alī Muḥammad Mu'awwaḍ, Beirut: Dār al-Kutub al-'Ilmīya, 1414 AH/1993 CE, 1:363.
2 Ibid., 1:364.
3 Ibid., 1:365.
4 Ibn Ḥajar al-Haytamī, *Itmām al-ni'ma al-kubrā 'alā al-'ālam bi-mawlid sayyid wuld Ādam*, ed. 'Abd al-'Azīz Sayyid Hāshim al-Ghazūlī, Beirut: Dār al-Kutub al-'Ilmīya, 1422 AH/2001 CE, p. 24.
5 Ṣāliḥī, *Subul*, 1:363.
6 Ibn 'Abbād, *Lettres de Direction Spirituelle, Collection Majeur (ar-Rasā'il al-kubrā)*, ed. Kenneth L. Honerkamp, Beirut: Dar el-Machreq, 2005, pp. 180–1 and 448–9 of Arabic text.
7 Ibid., p. 180.
8 Ibid., pp. 218–9.
9 See Qur'ān 111:1.
10 Muḥammad ibn Aḥmad al-Lakhmī al-'Azafī, *al-Durr al-munaẓẓam fī'l-mawlid al-mu'aẓẓam*, Princeton University Islamic manuscripts, Garrett Yahuda no. 256, 84b.
11 Ibn Ḥajar al-'Asqalānī, *Fatḥ al-bārī bi-sharḥ Ṣaḥīḥ al-Bukhārī*, ed. Muḥammad 'Abd al-Mu'ṭī, Mustafā Muḥammad al-Harāwī, and Tāhā 'Abd al-Ra'uf Sa'd, [Cairo]: Maktabat al-Kullīyāt al-Azharīya, 1398 AH/1977–8 CE, 19:174.
12 *Jam' jawāmi 'al-aḥādīth wa'l-asānīd*, Vaduz, Liechtenstein: Thesaurus Islamicus Foundation, 2000, Bukhārī, *Ṣaḥīḥ*, no. 5157.
13 An intermediate stage in the evolution of the anecdote may be reflected by the version presented by Ibn Hishām's commentator 'Abd al-Raḥmān al-Suhaylī (d. 581 AH/1185 CE). In sources "other than al-Bukhārī" (*fī ghayr al-Bukhārī*), he states, it is specified that the relative who saw Abū Lahab in a dream was his brother al-'Abbās; he then recounts the anecdote in a form that represents the freeing of Thuwayba as a reaction to her announcing Muḥammad's birth, but does not suggest that it was Abū Lahab's joy (as opposed to his act of manumission) that merited the later alleviation of his punishment. ('Abd al-Raḥmān al-Suhaylī, *al-Rawḍ al-unuf fī sharḥ al-Sīra al-nabawīya li-Ibn Hishām*, ed. 'Abd al-Raḥmān al-Wakīl, n.p.: Dār al-Kutub al-Ḥadītha, n.d., 5:191–2.)
14 Abū-Khaṭṭāb Ibn Diḥya, *Nihāyat al-sūl fī khaṣā'iṣ al-rasūl*, ed. Ma'mūn al-Ṣāghirjī and Muḥammad Adīb al-Jādir, Damascus: Dār al-Bashā'ir, 1420 AH/1999 CE, p. 95.
15 Ibn Ḥajar al-'Asqalānī, *Fatḥ al-bārī*, 19:174–5.
16 Muḥammad ibn Muḥammad ibn al-Jazarī, *Kitāb 'Urf al-ta'rīf bi'l-mawlid al-sharīf*, Princeton University Islamic manuscripts, Garrett Yehuda no. 225, 145a.
17 Ibn Nāṣir al-Dīn al-Dimashqī, *Mawrid al-ṣādī fī mawlid al-hādī*, ms. Dublin, Chester Beatty, no. 4658, 3a.
18 Aḥmad ibn 'Abd al-Raḥmān Ibn Makkīya, *Durar al-biḥār fī mawlid al-mukhtār*, ms. Cairo, Dār al-Kutub, Ta'rīkh no. 3807, 14a–b.
19 Interestingly, the comments of Ibn al-Jazarī and Ibn Nāṣir al-Dīn in their *mawlid* texts were so influential that they eventually became standard elements of legal discussions

of the topic. Both are cited by Jalāl al-Dīn ʻAbd al-Raḥmān ibn Abī Bakr al-Suyūṭī (*Ḥusn al-maqṣid fī ʻamal al-mawlid*, ed. Muṣṭafā ʻAbd al-Qādir ʻAṭā', Beirut: Dār al-Kutub al-ʻIlmīya, 1405 AH/1985 CE, pp. 65–6). The popularity of the texts and the stature of their authors may have sufficed to overshadow the weakness of the legal argument.

20 ʻAbd al-Raḥmān ibn Ismāʻīl Abū Shāma, *al-Bāʻith ʻalā inkār al-bidaʻ wa'l-ḥawādith*, ed. ʻUthmān Aḥmad ʻAnbar, n.p.: Dār al-Hudā, 1398 AH/1978 CE, pp. 23–4.

21 Suyūṭī, *Ḥusn al-maqṣid*, p. 64. The anonymous author of ms. Cairo, Dār al-Kutub, Ta'rīkh Ṭalʻat no. 2051, whose title page is missing, writes: "It is appropriate to observe the noble *mawlid* by manifesting joy and delight (*iẓhār al-faraḥ wa'l-surūr*), feeding people, giving charity to the poor, reciting the Glorious Qur'ān, mentioning (*dhikr*) God, and reciting poems in honor of the Prophet with all respect and honor, invoking prayers and blessings upon him, and reading the story of the noble birth and the wonders, miracles, and supernatural events that it included." The author then relates the celebration of the *mawlid* to *shukr al-niʻma*, and cites the story of the Jews fasting in honor of the deliverance of Moses (5b).

22 Suyūṭī, *Ḥusn al-maqṣid*, pp. 64–5.

23 Muḥammad ibn Muḥammad al-Ghazālī, *Iḥyā' ʻulūm al-dīn*, Beirut: Dār al-Fikr, 1414 AH/1994 CE, 4:86.

24 Ibid., 4:87–8.

25 Ibid., 4:89.

26 Ibid., 4:89.

27 Suyūṭī, *Ḥusn al-maqṣid*, p. 49. A similar opinion is attributed to Ibn al-Jazarī, who is said to have argued that Muslims do not take the night of the Prophet's birth as a festival (*ʻīd*), as the Christians have done with Jesus's birthday, because festivals are a matter of divine stipulation (*tawqīfīya*) and only two festivals have been stipulated in the *sharīʻa*; or, alternatively, that "since the day of [the Prophet's] birth is the day of his death, they are equivalent, and joy is canceled out by mourning (*takāfa'a al-surūr bi'l-ʻazā'*)." Cited in Yūsuf ibn Ismāʻīl al-Nabhānī, *Jawāhir al-biḥār fī faḍā'il al-nabī al-mukhtār*, ed. Muḥammad Amīn al-Ḍannāwī, Beirut: Dār al-Kutub al-ʻIlmīya, 1419 AH/1998 CE, 3:425. This position seems difficult to reconcile with the sentiments expressed in Ibn al-Jazarī's preserved *mawlid* works; for instance, in his *Mawlid al-kabīr* (13a) he remarks without apparent censure that the people of Mecca celebrate the Prophet's *mawlid* more than the official festivals (*yawm al-ʻīd*).

28 Ibn al-Ḥājj, *al-Madhkhal*, [Cairo]: Sharikat wa-Maṭbaʻat Muṣṭafā al-Bābī al-Ḥalabī wa-Awlādihi, 1380 AH/1960 CE, 2:16–17.

29 Suyūṭī, *Ḥusn al-maqṣid*, pp. 54–5.

30 ʻAlī ibn Sulṭān al-Qāri' al-Harawī, *al-Mawrid al-rawī fī mawlid al-nabī wa-nasabihi al-ṭāhir*, ed. Mabrūk Ismāʻīl Mabrūk, Cairo: Maktabat al-Qur'ān, n.d., pp. 11–12.

31 Ibn Rajab at Ḥanbālī, *Kitāb laṭa'if al-maʻārif fīmā li-mawāsin al-ʻām min al-waẓā'if*, Beirut: al-Maktab al-Islāmī, 1414 AH/1993 CE, pp. 108–24.

32 Ibn Nāṣir al-Dīn al-Dimashqī, *Salwat al-ka'īb bi-wafāt al-ḥabīb*, ed. Ṣāliḥ Yūsuf Maʻtūq, Dubai: Dār al-Buḥūth li'l-Dirāsāt al-Islāmīya wa-Iḥyā' al-Turāth, n.d.

33 Muḥammad ibn ʻAbd al-Raḥmān al-Sakhāwī, *al-Jawāhir wa'l-durar fī tarjamat Ibn Ḥajar*, ed. Ibrāhīm Bājis ʻAbd al-Majīd, Beirut: Dār Ibn Ḥazm, 1419 AH/1999 CE, p. 1253.

34 One exception to this observation is documented for modern India. The book *Qānūn-i-Islām*, composed by the Deccani Muslim Ja'far Sharif for the benefit of a British colonial audience and translated by G.A. Herklots, describes the rites and customs of Indian Muslims in the early-nineteenth century. According to this source, at that time among Indian Muslims the month Rabīʻ al-Awwal was "commonly called that of the twelve days of sickness ending in death, *Bārah Wafāt*, because on the twelfth day His Excellency the Prophet, Muhammad Mustafā ... departed this life." Sharif describes the twelfth of Rabīʻ al-Awwal as "one of the three days on which Sunnīs mourn, the others being the Muharram and the *Shab-i-Qadr*, or Night of Power." (Ja'far Sharif, *Islam in India or the*

Qānūn-i-Islām, the customs of the Musalmāns of India, ed. and trans. G.A. Herklots, rev. and with additions by William Crooke, London and Dublin: Curzon Press, 1972, p. 188.) S. Inayatullah notes that this situation has not survived into the modern day; most of the ceremonies described in Sherif's work having fallen into desuetude, *Bāra Wafāt* "is now a day of rejoicing rather than mourning for the Muslims, who consider 12th Rabī' I at the same time as the birthday of the Prophet." (EI², s.v. "Bāra wafāt.")

35 N.J.G. Kaptein, *Muḥammad's Birthday Festival*, Leiden: E.J. Brill, 1993, p. 68.

36 Aḥmad ibn 'Abd al-Ḥalīm Ibn Taymīya, *Majmū' fatāwā shaykh al-islām Aḥmad ibn Taymīya*, collected and arranged by 'Abd al-Raḥmān ibn Muḥammad ibn Qāsim al-'Āṣimī al-Najdī, n.p., n.d., 25:299.

37 Ibn Nāṣir al-Dīn al-Dimashqī, *Majmū' fīhi rasā'il li'l-ḥāfiẓ Ibn Nāṣir al-Dīn al-Dimashqī*, Beirut: Dār Ibn Ḥazm, 1422 AH/2001 CE, pp. 51–108, especially 98–106.

38 Mahmoud Ayoub, *Redemptive Suffering in Islam, a study of the devotional aspects of 'Āshūrā' in Twelver Shī'ism*, The Hague, Paris, New York: Mouton Publishers, 1978, p. 150 (cited from Ibn Bābawayh's *'Ilal*).

39 Ibn Nāṣir al-Dīn, *Majmū'*, pp. 97–8.

40 For a discussion of the life and teachings of 'Abd al-Qādir, see Alexander Knysh, *Islamic Mysticism, a short history*, Leiden: Brill, 2000, pp. 179–83.

41 Ibn Nāṣir al-Dīn, *Majmū'*, p. 98.

42 Abū'l-'Abbās Aḥmad ibn Muḥammad ibn 'Umar, Moroccan ṣūfī and patron saint of Salé, d. 764, 765 AH/1362–3 CE. See EI², s.v. "Ibn Āshir."

43 Ibn 'Abbād, *al-Rasā'il al-kubrā*, Arabic text, p. 180.

44 This opinion is expressed by Aḥmad ibn Muḥammad al-Dardīr (d. 1201 AH/1786 CE), in his *al-Sharḥ al-kabīr*, in *Ḥāshiyat al-Dasūqī 'alā al-Sharḥ al-kabīr*, 'Īsā al-Bābī al-Ḥalabī, n.d., 1:518, and Aḥmad ibn Muḥammad al-Ṣāwī (d. 1241 AH/1825 CE) in his commentary on al-Dardīr's *al-Sharḥ al-ṣaghīr 'alā Aqrab al-masālik ilā madhhab al-imām Mālik*, Cairo: Dār al-Ma'ārif bi-Miṣr, n.d., 1:693. This position seems to have been standard among eighteenth and nineteenth-century CE Mālikī commentators on the *Mukhtaṣar of al-Khalīl*; see list of Mālikī endorsers of the *mawlid* celebration from 'Abd al-Jabbār al-Mubārak, *al-Barāhīn al-jalīya fī jawāz al-iḥtifāl bi-mawlid khayr al-barīya*, excerpted in Ḥāmid al-Miḥḍār, *al-Iḥtifāl bi-dhikr al-ni'am wājib*, n.p.: Maktabat al-Muṭī'ī, n.d., p. 55.

45 Ibn Taymīya, *Majmū' fatāwā*, 25:308–9.

46 Ibid., 25:309–10.

47 Ibid., 25:311–12.

48 Haytamī, *Itmām*, p. 29.

49 Aḥmad ibn 'Abd al-Ḥalīm ibn Taymīya, *Iqtiḍā' al-ṣirāṭ al-mustaqīm li-mukhālafat aṣḥāb al-jaḥīm*, Riyadh: Dār al-'Āṣima, 1419 AH/1998 CE, 2:123.

50 Among the many sources that discuss the obligation to love the Prophet and present Qur'ānic and *ḥadīth* texts in its support are Muslim ibn Ḥajjāj al-Qushayrī, *Ṣaḥīḥ Muslim bi-sharḥ al-imām Muḥyī al-Dīn al-Nawawī al-Minhāj sharḥ ṣahiḥ Muslim ibn al-Ḥajjāj*, Beirut: Dār al-Ma'rifa, 1414 AH/1994 CE, 2:205–6; Abū Bakr Aḥmad ibn al-Ḥusayn al-Bayhaqī, *Shu'ab al-īmān*, ed. Muḥammad al-Sa'īd Zaghlūl, Beirut: Dār al-Kutub al-'Ilmīya, 1410 AH/1990 CE, 2:129–32; al-Qāḍī 'Iyāḍ ibn Mūsā al-Yaḥṣubī, *al-Shifā bi-ta'rīf ḥuqūq al-muṣṭafā*, ed. 'Alī Muḥammad al-Bijāwī, [Cairo]: 'Īsā al-Bābī al-Ḥalabī, n.d., 2:563–4.

51 Anonymous *Qiṣṣat al-mawlid al-nabawī al-sharīf*, ms. Damascus, Asad Library, no. 11251, 4a. The author also affirms that love for the Prophet brings the believer close to him, leads to the fulfillment of wishes and hopes, washes away sins, and even protects against the evil eye.

52 al-Shaykh Qāsim al-Shāfi'ī al-Qādirī, known as al-Ḥallāq, *Mawrid al-nāhil bi-mawlid al-nabī al-kāmil*, ms. Damascus, Asad Library, no. 11400, 4a. al-Ḥallāq died in 1284 AH/1806 CE; see 'Umar Riḍā Kaḥḥāla, *Mu'jam al-mu'allifīn*, Beirut: Mu'assasat al-Risāla, 1414 AH/1993 CE, 2:643.

53 Muḥammad Ṣāliḥ ibn Muḥammad al-Dasūqī, known as al-Shāfi'ī al-Ṣaghīr, *al-Manhal al-awfā fī mīlād al-muṣṭafā*, ms. Damascus, Asad Library, no. 11402, 39a. al-Dasūqī died in 1242 AH/1830 CE; see Kaḥḥāla, *Mu'jam*, 1:834.

54 The reference is presumably to al-Ḥusayn ibn al-Ḥasan al-Ḥalīmī (d. 403 AH/1012 CE), the author of *Minhāj al-dīn fī shu'ab al-īmān*. See Kaḥḥāla, *Mu'jam*, 1:607.

55 Bayhaqī, *Shu'ab*, 2:133.

56 'Azafī, *Durr*, 3b–4a, 7a. The section of the text dealing with Muslims' involvement in Christian festivals is printed in F. de la Granja, "Fiestas cristianas en Al-Andalus," *al-Andalus* 34, 1969, pp. 19–32.

57 Ibid., 4a.

58 Ibid., 4b.

59 This word is unclear in the manuscript; I am reading "*anfusihim*."

60 Ibid., 13a–b.

61 Ibid., 13b. I am reading this sentence as "Inna talaṭṭuf al-qulūb wa-tansīyatuhā bi-hādhā hawāhā huwa'l-maṭlūb," ignoring the floating "hā" at the beginning of line 12 as a copyist's mistake.

62 The "Day of Bu'āth" was a battle in 617 CE between the two Medinian clans of Aws and Khazraj. See EI^2, s.v. "Bu'āth." This event occurred before the Emigration of the Prophet and the conversion of the Aws and Khazraj to Islam, so it exemplifies the tribal chauvinism of the *jāhilīya* (pre-Islamic period).

63 Ibid., 13b–14a.

64 al-Raṣṣā' served as a *qāḍī* and as the *imām* and *khaṭīb* of the Zaytūna Mosque of Tunis. He was known for his knowledge of *fiqh*, *uṣūl al-fiqh*, *kalām*, and logic. See Kaḥḥāla, *Mu'jam*, 3:593.

65 Muḥammad ibn Qāsim al-Raṣṣā', *Tadhikrat al-muḥibbīn fī asmā' sayyid al-mursalīn*, ed. Muḥammad Riḍwān al-Dāya, Abu Dhabi: al-Majma' al-Thaqāfī, 1423 AH/2002 CE, pp. 152–4.

66 Ibid., p. 148.

67 'Iyāḍ, *Shifā*, 2:579.

68 Ibid., 2:580–1.

69 For references see Muḥammad Sa'īd Zaghlūl, *Mawsū'at aṭrāf al-ḥadīth al-nabawī al-sharīf*, Beirut: Dār al-Kutub al-'Ilmīya, n.d., 4:491.

70 Ibn Ḥajar al-'Asqalānī, *Fatḥ al-bārī*, 1:116.

71 Raṣṣā', *Tadhkira*, p. 160.

72 Anonymous *Mawlid*, ms. Cairo, Dār al-Kutub Ta'rīkh Ṭal'at no. 2051 (title page missing), 2b–5a.

73 Joseph Norment Bell, *Love Theory in Later Ḥanbalite Islam*, Albany: State University of New York Press, 1979, p. 119.

74 Nawawī, *Ṣaḥīḥ Muslim bi-sharḥ al-imām Muḥyī al-Dīn al-Nawawī*, 2:205.

75 Muḥammad ibn 'Abd al-Raḥmān al-Sakhāwī, *al-Maqāṣid al-ḥasana fī bayān kathīr min al-aḥādīth al-mushtahira 'alā al-alsina*, Beirut: Dār al-Kutub al-'Ilmīya, 1399 AH/1979 CE, pp. 171–2.

76 See Ghazālī, *Iḥyā'*, 4:314–18.

77 Another, unnamed author held that such statements could be made only in an instructional context (presumably, as opposed to that of popular preaching). Some Mālikīs apparently held that anyone who stated in a public religious gathering (*fī'l-majālis*) that the Prophet was an orphan was guilty of apostasy. Nabhānī, *Jawāhir*, 3:429, 430. al-Nabhānī cites the report from al-Zurqānī (Muḥammad ibn 'Abd al-Bāqī, d. 1122 AH/1710 CE), who states that it was quoted by al-Suyūṭī. The attribution to al-Suyūṭī indicates that the Ibn Ḥajar in question must be al-'Asqalānī, rather than al-Haytamī.

78 Cited in Nabhānī, *Jawāhir*, 3:394. The author of the remark appears to be Burhān al-Dīn al-Ḥalabī (d. 956 AH/1549 CE), although the attribution is somewhat unclear and the original source is unavailable.

79 Anonymous, *Mawlid*, ms. Cairo, Dār al-Kutub, Ta'rīkh Ṭal'at no. 2051, 2b.

80 Muslim, *Ṣaḥīḥ Muslim bi-sharḥ al-imām Muḥyī al-Dīn al-Nawawī*, 3:74.
81 *Jam' jawāmi 'al-aḥādīth*, Abū Dāwūd, *Sunan*, no. 3236 (Kitāb al-Janā'iz, Bāb fī ziyārat al-qubūr); Ibn Māja, *Sunan*, no. 1639 (Kitāb al-janā'iz, Bāb mā jā'a fī ziyārat qubūr al-mushrikīn); al-Nasā'ī, *Sunan*, no. 2046 (Kitāb al-janā'iz, Bāb ziyārat qabr al-mushrik).
82 See 'Alī ibn Sulṭān Muḥammad al-Qāri' al-Harawī, *Adillat mu'taqad Abī Ḥanīfa al-a'ẓam fī abaway al-rasūl 'alayhi al-ṣalāt wa'l-salām*, ed. Mashhūr ibn Ḥasan ibn Salmān, Medina: Maktabat al-Ghurabā' al-Atharīya, 1413 AH/1993 CE, pp. 71–4.
83 Ibid., pp. 64–70.
84 'Alī ibn Sulṭān Muḥammad al-Qāri' al-Harawī, *Sharḥ al-fiqh al-akbar li-Abī Ḥanīfa al-Nu'mān*, ed. Marwān Muḥammad al-Sha''ār, Beirut: Dār al-Nafā'is, 1417 AH/1997 CE, p. 220.
85 See earlier, note 82.
86 See al-Qāri' al-Harawī, *Sharḥ*, p. 220.
87 Jalāl al-Dīn 'Abd al-Raḥmān ibn Abī Bakr al-Suyūṭī, *al-Rasā'il al-'ashar*, Beirut: Dār al-Kutub al-'Ilmīya, 1409 AH/1989 CE, pp. 7–179.
88 See al-Qāri' al-Harawī, *Sharḥ*, p. 220.
89 See Suyūṭī, *Rasā'il*, pp. 27–9.
90 Ibid., pp. 12, 28. The verse version of al-Barzanjī's *mawlid* also cites al-Ash'arī for the position that the Prophet's parents were saved; see Nūrā Abū'l-Fatḥ, *al-Mutāḥ min al-mawālid wa'l-anāshīd al-milāḥ* , n.p., 1416 AH/1995 CE, 1:220–1.
91 Ṣalāḥ al-Dīn al-Munajjid, *Mu'jam mā ullifa 'an rasūl allāh*, Beirut: Dār al-Kitāb al-Jadīd, 1402 AH/1982 CE, p. 51; Sakhāwī, *Maqāṣid*, p. 25; Muḥammad ibn 'Alī ibn Ṭūlūn al-Ṣāliḥī, *al-Fulk al-mashḥūn fī aḥwāl Muḥammad ibn Ṭūlūn*, ed. Muḥammad Khayr Ramaḍān Yūsuf, Beirut: Dār ibn Ḥazm, 1416 AH/1996 CE, p. 134.
92 See, for instance, the extensive discussion of the issue in Aḥmad ibn Muḥammad al-Suḥaymī al-Azharī, *al-Zahr al-fā'iq fī mawlid ashraf al-khalā'iq*, ms. Cairo, Dār al-Kutub, no. B 27998, 5a.
93 See Suyūṭī, *Rasā'il*, p. 31.
94 Ibn Taymīya, *Majmū' fatāwā*, 4:324.
95 Suyūṭī, *Rasā'il*, p. 10.
96 Ibid., p. 11.
97 Sakhāwī, *Maqāṣid*, p. 25. Despite al-Sakhāwī's enthusiasm for Ibn Nāṣir al-Dīn's verses on the subject, he expresses skepticism about the authenticity of the *ḥadīth*, ultimately concluding that "it is best to refrain from addressing this subject, whether to affirm or deny." See also 'Abd al-Raḥmān ibn 'Abd al-Mun'im al-Jurjāwī, *Mawlid*, ms. Cairo, Dār al-Kutub, Ta'rīkh no. 218, 16b.
98 Haytamī, *Itmām*, pp. 106–18.
99 Abū'l-Fatḥ, *Mutāḥ*, 1:220–1.
100 Ṣāliḥī, *Subul*, 1:382–4; Ibn 'Abd al-Barr, *al-Istī'āb fī ma'rifat al-aṣḥāb*, printed in margins of Ibn Ḥajar al-'Asqalānī, *al-Iṣāba fī tamyīz al-ṣaḥāba*, Baghdad: Maktabat al-Muthannā, n.d., 4:270; al-'Asqalānī, *al-Iṣāba*, 4:274. Based on the difference of opinion over her faith status, some authors counted her as a Companion of the Prophet, while others did not.
101 See Ṣāliḥī, *Subul*, 1:382.
102 Ibid., 1:384.
103 On the controversial issue of Abū Ṭālib's death as a non-believer, see Fred McGraw Donner, "The death of Abū Ṭālib," in *Love & Death in the Ancient Near East, essays in honor of Marvin H. Pope*, ed. John H. Marks and Robert M. Good, Guilford, Connecticut: Four Quarters Publishing Co., 1987, pp. 237–45. For a passionate book-length defense of Abū Ṭālib's status as a Muslim composed by a strong supporter of the *mawlid* celebration, see Aḥmad ibn Zaynī Daḥlān, *Asnā al-maṭālib fī najāt Abī Ṭālib*, n.p.: 'Alī Muḥammad al-Ḥaḍirī wa-Awlāduhu, n.d.

104 Yūsuf ibn Ismā'īl al-Nabhānī, *al-Hamzīya al-alfīya al-musammā Ṭaybat al-gharrā' fī madḥ sayyid al-anbiyā'*, Beirut: al-Maṭba'a al-Adabīya, 1314 AH, p. 21. The conviction that the Prophet's parents were saved frequently extends to all of his ancestors. Because the pre-existence of the Prophet's light and its migration through the generations of his ancestors was an integral part of the traditional *mawlid* narrative, it was important to affirm that all of his forebears had been worthy vessels. For a discussion of the doctrine that all of the Prophet's ancestors were believers, see U. Rubin, "Pre-existence and light: aspects of the concept of Nūr Muḥammad," *Israel Oriental Studies* 5, 1975, pp. 75–9.

105 Tāj al-Dīn 'Abd al-Wahhāb ibn 'Abd al-Kāfī al-Subkī, *Ṭabaqāt al-shāfi'īya al-kubrā*, ed. 'Abd al-Fattāḥ Muḥammad Ḥilw and Maḥmūd Muḥammad al-Ṭināḥī, [Cairo]: 'Īsā al-Bābī al-Ḥalabī, n.d., 10:208.

106 Ms. Berlin, Ahlwardt no. 9546, 287^{Bb}. Ahlwardt lists the title as *al-Qawl al-tamām 'inda dhikr wilādatihi 'alayhi al-salām*. The upper portion of the leaf is damaged and difficult to read, but there is a partially effaced word between "*tamām*" and "*'inda*" that, I believe, must be read as "*fī 'l-qiyām*" in order to yield a comprehensible title that fits the content of the text.

107 Abū'l-Su'ūd's alleged *fatwā* was cited by two Meccan scholars of the modern period, 'Abd Allāh ibn 'Abd al-Raḥmān Sirāj and Muḥammad 'Alī al-Mālikī. See Muḥammad ibn Sālim ibn Ḥafīẓ, *Qurrat al-'ayn bi-jawāb as'ilat wādī al-'ayn*, printed in Muḥammad ibn 'Alawī al-Mālikī, *Bāqa 'aṭira min ṣiyagh al-mawālid wa'l-madā'iḥ al-nabawīya al-karima*, n.p., 1403 AH/1983 CE, p. 32; Muḥammad 'Alī ibn Ḥusayn al-Mālikī, *Tahdhīb al-furūq wa'l-qawā'id al-sannīya fī al-asrār al-fiqhīya*, printed in the margin of Aḥmad ibn Idrīs al-Qarāfī, *Anwār al-burūq fī anwā' al-furūq*, ed. Khalīl al-Manṣūr, Beirut: Dār al-Kutub al-'Ilmīya, 1418 AH/1998 CE, 4:428.

108 See Kaḥḥāla, *Mu'jam*, 3:83.

109 *Mawlid al-nabī*, ms. Cairo, Dār al-Kutub, Ta'rīkh no. 645, 10b–11a.

110 Ismā'īl Bāshā al-Baghdādī: *Hadīyat al-'ārifīn: asmā' al-mu'allifīn wa-āthār al-muṣannifīn*, Istanbul: Milli Egitim Basimevi, 1951–5, 1:146.

111 Ibn Ḥajar al-Haytamī, *al-Fatāwā al-ḥadīthīya*, [Cairo]: Muṣṭafā al-Bābī al-Ḥalabī, 1356 AH/1937 CE, p. 69.

112 Ms. Damascus, Asad Library, no. 11402, 17b.

113 See Yaḥyā ibn Sharaf al-Nawawī, *al-Tarkhīṣ bi'l-qiyām li-dhawī al-faḍl wa'l-mazīya min ahl al-islām*, ed. Aḥmad Rātib Ḥammūsh, Damascus: Dār al-Fikr, 1402 AH/1982 CE, pp. 34–47.

114 See note 113.

115 Qarāfī, *Anwār al-burūq*, 4:426–9.

116 Aḥmad ibn 'Abd al-Ḥalīm Ibn Taymīya, *Fatwā fī'l-qiyām wa'l-alqāb*, in *Rasā'il wa-nuṣūṣ*, vol. 3, ed. Ṣalāḥ al-Dīn al-Munajjid, Beirut: Dār al-Kitāb al-Jadīd, 1963, pp. 9–12.

117 Ḥalabī, *Qawl*, 287^{Bb}.

118 This is a text transmitted by Abū Dāwūd, in which the Prophet says, "Do not stand up as the Iranians do, some of them exalting others" (*lā taqūmū kamā yaqūm al-a'ājim yu'aẓẓimu ba'ḍuhum ba'ḍan*). He counters his opponents' anticipated argument that the Prophet declined this honor out of modesty. While there are some cases in which the Prophet appeared to deny his own high status (as in the case of his saying, "Do not prefer me over Moses"), al-Ḥalabī replies, "we say that is it permissible to deviate from the literal meaning [of a text] only on the basis of a proof." For instance, there are multiple texts in the Qur'ān and the *ḥadīth* indicating that the Prophet Muḥammad was preferred by God over all other prophets. In the case of the Prophet's prohibition of standing in his own honor, however, there is no such countervailing proof. Had he said this out of modesty, no doubt his Companions would have discerned that fact.

119 Ḥalabī, *Qawl*, 293[ab].
120 'Alī ibn Burhān al-Dīn Ibrāhīm al-Ḥalabī, *Insān al-'uyūn fī sīrat al-amīn al-ma'mūn*, [Cairo]: Maṭba'at Muḥammad Efendī Muṣṭafā, n.d., 1:90.
121 Abū'l-Fatḥ, *Mutāḥ*, 1:193.
122 Muḥammad ibn 'Alī al-Shawkānī, *al-Fatḥ al-rabbānī min fatāwā al-imām al-Shawkānī*, ed. Muḥammad Ṣubḥī ibn Ḥasan Ḥallāq, Sanaa: Maktabat al-Jīl al-Jadīd, 1423 AH/2002 CE, 2:1083, 1090. I thank Bernard Haykel for providing me with this fascinating text.
123 Muḥammad Fawzī Efendī, *Qudus al-kalām fī mawlid al-nabī 'alayhi al-salām*, ms. Cairo, Dār al-Kutub, Ta'rīkh Ṭal'at no. 1996, 5a.
124 Abū'l-Fatḥ, *Mutāḥ*, 1:224.
125 Muḥammad 'Uthmān al-Mīrghanī, *Mawlid al-nabī al-Asrār al-rabbānīya*, Ta'izz, Sanaa, Ḥudayda: Maktabat Dār al-Fikr, n.d., pp. 6–7.
126 See Kaḥḥāla, *Mu'jam*, 3:282.
127 His response forms the second-half of his work *al-Manẓar al-bahī fī ṭāli' mawlid al-nabī wa-mā yatba'uh min al-a'māl al-mawlid wa-ḥukm al-qiyām 'inda dhikr mawlidihi*, n.p., n.d.
128 Ibid., pp. 12–13.
129 Ibid., p. 16.
130 Ibid., pp. 16–18.
131 For a biographical reference on 'Ayn al-Quḍāt al-Ḥaydarabādī, see 'Abd al-Ḥayy ibn Fakhr al-Dīn al-Ḥasanī, *al-I'lām bi-man fī ta'rīkh al-Hind min al-a'lām*, Beirut: Dār Ibn Ḥazm, 1420 AH/1999 CE, 8:1316–17. He was a Naqshbandī ṣūfī and a scholar who was trained at Farangi Maḥall. He inherited the direction of a school of Qur'ānic recitation from his father.
132 'Ayn al-Quḍāt al-Ḥaydarābādī, *Nihāyat al-irshād ilā iḥtifāl al-mīlād*, Lucknow: Nāẓir Press, n.d, pp. 12–13.
133 Ibid., p. 10.
134 Ibid., p. 63.
135 Ibid., pp. 93–4.
136 Ibid., pp. 96–7.
137 Abū Īsā al-Mahdī al-Wazzānī, *al-Nawāzil al-jadīda al-kubrā fīmā li'ahl Fās wa-ghayrihim min al-badw wa'l-qurā*, [Rabat]: al-Mamlaka al-Maghribīya, Wizārat al-Awqāf wa'l-Shu'ūn al-Islāmīya, 1417–21 AH/1996–2000 CE, 12:469–70.
138 Ibid., 12:472–3.
139 Muḥammad ibn Ja'far al-Kattānī, *al-Yumn wa'l-is'ād bi-mawlid khayr al-'ibād*, Casablanca: al-Maktaba al-Sharqīya, 1345 AH/[1926–7 CE], p. 20.
140 Ibid., pp. 21–4.
141 Abū'l-Fatḥ, *Mutāḥ*, 1:85.
142 Ibid., 2:123–4.
143 Gary A. Anderson, *A Time to Mourn, a Time to Dance: the expression of grief and joy in Israelite religion*, University Park, Pennsylvania: The Pennsylvania State University Press, 1991, p. 20.
144 Ibid., p. 21.
145 Ibid., p. 49.
146 Gary L. Ebersole, "The function of ritual weeping revisited: affective expression and moral discourse," *History of Religions* 39, 2000, p. 214.
147 Ibid., pp. 241–2.

4 Time and merit in the celebration of the *mawlid*

1 Cited in Aḥmad ibn Yaḥyā Ibn Abī Ḥajala, *Sukurdān al-sulṭān*, ed. 'Alī Muḥammad 'Umar, Cairo: Maktabat al-Khānjī, 1421 AH/2001 CE, pp. 9–10.

2 Abū Bakr Aḥmad ibn al-Ḥusayn al-Bayhaqī, *Kitāb faḍā'il al-awqāt*, ed. Khilāf Maḥmūd 'Abd al-Samī', Beirut: Dār al-Kutub al-'Ilmīya, 1417 AH/1997 CE.
3 'Izz al-Dīn 'Abd al-'Azīz ibn 'Abd al-Salām, *al-Qawā'id al-kubrā al-mawsūm bi-Qawā'id al-aḥkām fī iṣlāḥ al-anām*, ed. Nazīh Kamāl Ḥammād and 'Uthmān Jum'a Ḍamīrīya, Damascus: Dār al-Qalam, 1421 AH/2000 CE, 1:62.
4 Abū Ḥāmid Muḥammad ibn Muḥammad al-Ghazālī, *Iḥyā' 'ulūm al-dīn*, Beirut: Dār al-Fikr, 1414 AH/1994 CE, 1:426.
5 Ibn Rajab al-Ḥanbalī, *Kitāb laṭā'if al-ma'ārif fīmā li-mawāsim al-'ām min al-waẓā'if*, Beirut: al-Maktab al-Islāmī, 1414 AH/1993 CE, p. 13.
6 Ibid., p. 11.
7 This is probably a reference to the spring solstice and the equal length of the day and night.
8 Muḥammad ibn Jābir al-Andalusī, *Kitāb mawlid rasūl allāh*, ms. Istanbul, Süleymaniye, no. 344, 3b.
9 Khalīl ibn Aybak al-Ṣafadī, *al-Faḍl al-munīf fī'l-mawlid al-sharīf*, Princeton University Islamic manuscripts, Garrett Yahuda no. 3570, 8a, 8b.
10 Ibn al-Ḥājj, *al-Madkhal*, [Cairo]: Sharikat wa-Maṭba'at Muṣṭafā al-Bābī al-Ḥalabī wa-Awlādihi, 1380 AH/1960 C.E, 2:3–4.
11 Ibid., 2:28–31.
12 Ibid., 2:31.
13 See, for instance, Ibn Rajab, *Laṭā'if*, pp. 36–7. Unlike Ibn Nāṣir al-Dīn, however, Ibn Rajab does not seem particularly interested in the quantification of merit (*thawāb*); he simply speaks of the virtue/superiority (*faḍl, faḍīla*) of a given period of time.
14 EI^2, s.v. "Ibn Marzūq."
15 The text of this composition is preserved in a later work, Abū'l-'Abbās Aḥmad ibn 'Ammār, *Nubdha min al-kitāb al-musammā Niḥlat al-labīb bi-akhbār al-riḥla ilā'l-ḥabīb*, Algiers: Maṭba'at Fūntāna, 1320 AH/1902 CE, pp. 103–11. Ibn 'Ammār reproduces the entire list, with the exception of one lacuna in the manuscript from which the printed edition was prepared. Ibn Marzūq's work was produced in the context of a debate over the comparative statuses of the night of the *mawlid* and *laylat al-qadr* that took place at the caliphal court in Tunis. See Aḥmad ibn Yaḥyā al-Wansharīsī, *al-Mi'yār al-mu'rib wa'l-jāmi' al-mughrib 'an fatāwā ahl ifrīqīya wa'l-andalus wa'l-maghrib*, [Ribāṭ]: Wizārat al-Awqāf wa'l-Shu'ūn al-Islāmīya li'l-Mamlaka al-Maghribīya, 1401 AH/1981 CE, 8:255.
16 Ibn al-Ḥājj, *Madkhal*, 2:35. The superiority of the night of the *mawlid* is similarly affirmed in the *mawlid* text *Minḥat al-ṣafā wa-nafḥat al-shifā bi-mawlid al-muṣṭafā*, composed by the Syrian *shaykh* Muṣṭafā ibn Muḥammad al-'Araḍī (ms. Damascus, Asad Library, no. 9771, 4a; ms. dated 1296 AH).
17 Ibn Ḥajar al-Haytamī, *Itmām al-ni'ma al-kubrā 'alā al-'ālam bi-mawlid sayyid wuld Ādam*, ed. 'Abd al-'Azīz Sayyid Hāshim al-Ghazūlī, Beirut: Dār al-Kutub al-'Ilmīya, 1422 AH/2001 CE, pp. 30–1.
18 Ms. Cairo, Dār al-Kutub, B no. 27998, 9b. For al-Suḥaymī, see 'Umar Riḍā Kaḥḥāla, *Mu'jam al-mu'allifīn*, Beirut: Mu'assasat al-Risāla, 1414 AH/1993 CE), 1:280.
19 Aḥmad ibn Muḥammad al-Qasṭallānī, *al-Mawāhib al-ladunīya bi'l-minaḥ al-muḥammadīya*, ed. Ṣāliḥ Aḥmad al-Shāmī, Beirut: al-Maktab al-Islāmī, 1412 AH/1991 CE, 1:145.
20 Muḥammad Amīn ibn 'Ābidīn, *Ḥāshiyat Radd al-muḥtār 'alā al-Durr al-mukhtār sharḥ Tanwīr al-abṣār*, Cairo: Sharikat Maktabat wa-Maṭba'at Muṣṭafā al-Bābī al-Ḥalabī wa-Awlādihi, second printing, 1386 AH/1966 CE, 2:511.
21 Ibn Nāṣir al-Dīn al-Dimashqī, *Majmū' fīhi rasā'il li'l-ḥāfiẓ Ibn Nāṣir al-Dīn al-Dimashqī*, Beirut: Dār Ibn Ḥazm, 1422 AH/2001 CE, p. 51.
22 'Āshūrā' is identified with the *yawm al-zīna* referred to in verse 20:59 of the Qur'ān, in the story of Pharaoh and the Israelites.
23 Ibn Nāṣir al-Dīn, *Majmū'*, pp. 62–5.

24 Ibid., p. 145.
25 Ibid., p. 79.
26 Ibid., p. 165.
27 Ibid., pp. 82–97.
28 'Abd al-Raḥmān ibn Ismā'īl Abū Shāma, *al-Bā'ith 'alā inkār al-bida' wa'l-ḥawādith*, ed. 'Uthmān Aḥmad 'Anbar, n.p.: Dār al-Hudā, 1398 AH/1978 CE, pp. 34–5.
29 Muḥammad ibn al-Walīd al-Ṭurṭūshī, *Kitāb al-ḥawādith wa'l-bida'*, Tunis: al-Maṭba'a al-Rasmīya li'l-Jumhūrīya al-Tūnisīya, 1959, pp. 121–2; Abū Shāma, *Bā'ith*, p. 35.
30 Ṭurṭūshī, *Ḥawādith*, p. 122; Abū Shāma, *Bā'ith*, p. 35.
31 Abū Shāma, *Bā'ith*, pp. 41–2. The term "*raghā'ib*" was at one time apparently also used to refer to the special prayer of *niṣf Sha'bān*.
32 Ibid., p. 42.
33 Ibid., p. 43.
34 Ibid., p. 44.
35 Ibid., pp. 45–6.
36 Ibid., p. 67.
37 Ibid., p. 40.
38 Ṭurṭūshī, *Ḥawādith*, pp. 115–16; Abū Shāma, *Bā'ith*, pp. 32–4.
39 Ṭurṭūshī, *Ḥawādith*, pp. 116–17; Abū Shāma, *Bā'ith*, p. 33.
40 Ibn Nāṣir al-Dīn, *Majmū'*, p. 179.
41 Abū'l-Khaṭṭāb ibn Diḥya, *Adā' mā wajab min bayān waḍ' al-waḍḍā'īn fī rajab*, Beirut: al-Maktab al-Islāmī, 1419 AH/1998 CE.
42 Abū Shāma, *Bā'ith*, pp. 35–6.
43 Ibid., p. 43.
44 Abū'l-Khaṭṭāb ibn Diḥya, *al-Ibtihāj fī aḥādīth al-mi'rāj*, ed. Rif'at Fawzī 'Abd al-Muṭṭalib, Cairo: Maktabat al-Khānjī, 1417 AH/1996 CE, p. 9.
45 Ibn 'Abd al-Salām, *Qawā'id*, 1:44.
46 Ibid., 1: 45.
47 Ibid., 1:62.
48 Ibid., 1:62
49 Ibn al-Qayyim al-Jawzīya, *I'lām al-muwaqqi'īn 'an rabb al-'ālamīn*, ed. Ṭāhā 'Abd al-Ra'ūf Sa'd, Cairo: Maktabat al-Kullīyāt al-Azharīya, 1388 AH/1968 CE, 2:71.
50 Ibid., 2:73–4.
51 Ibid., 2:170.
52 Ibid., 2:170–1.
53 Ibid., pp. 151–2.
54 Not all authors interpreted Ibn 'Abd al-Salām's arguments to mean that the superiority of a given time must be based on enhanced rewards for the pious actions appointed to be performed in it. Ibn Marzūq cites extensively from Ibn 'Abd al-Salām's arguments regarding the equivalence of all places and times and argues that the latter's reasoning actually supports his own view, which is that the night of the *mawlid* is rendered superior to the Night of Power by the pre-eminence of the blessing that occurred upon it. (Ibn 'Ammār, *Niḥla*, pp. 110–11.)
55 Haytamī, *Itmām*, pp.30–1.
56 Taqī al-Dīn 'Alī ibn 'Abd al-Kāfī al-Subkī, *Fatāwā al-Subkī*, Beirut: Dār al-Ma'rifa, n.d., 1:279.
57 Aḥmad ibn 'Abd al-Ḥalīm Ibn Taymīya, *Iqtiḍā' al-ṣirāṭ al-mustaqīm li-mukhālafat aṣḥāb al-jaḥīm*, Riyadh: Dār al-'Āṣima, 1419 AH/1998 CE, 2:5.
58 Ibid., 2:121–2, 129.
59 Ibid., 2:122–3.
60 Aḥmad ibn 'Abd al-Ḥalīm Ibn Taymīya, *Majmū' fatāwā shaykh al-islām Aḥmad ibn Taymīya*, collected and arranged by 'Abd al-Raḥmān ibn Muḥammad ibn Qāsim al-'Āṣimī al-Najdī, n.p., n.d., 25:286. Ibn Taymīya also produced *fatwā*s on the

comparative ranking of the first ten days of Dhū'l-Ḥijja and the last ten days of Ramaḍān, and of the days of 'Arafa, Friday, the breaking of the fast (at the end of Ramaḍān) and the Day of the Sacrifice (on the tenth of Dhū'l- Ḥijja). Asked about the "best of days," he responded that Friday was the best day of the week, while the Day of the Sacrifice was the best day of the year (25:287–9).

61 Ibn Taymīya, *Iqtiḍā'*, 2:113.
62 Ibid., 2:111.
63 Ibid., 2:113.
64 Ibid., 2:107.
65 Ibid., 2:114–15.
66 Wansharīsī, *Mi'yār*, 7:99–100.
67 Abū Shāma, *Bā'ith*, p. 51.
68 Ibid., p. 38.
69 Ibn al-Ḥājj, *Madkhal*, 2:34–5.
70 Ibid., 2:3–4, 32.
71 Muḥammad ibn Aḥmad Banīs, *Lawāmi' anwār al-kawkab al-durrī fī sharḥ Hamzīyat al-imām al-Būṣīrī*, printed in the margins of Muḥammad ibn Qāsim Jasūs, *Sharḥ al-Shamā'il al-Tirmidhīya*, Cairo: Maktabat wa-Maṭba'at Muḥammad 'Alī Ṣibīḥ wa-Awlādihi, 1346 AH/1927 CE, 1:23–4.
72 Ibn 'Ammār, *Niḥla*, p. 105.
73 See Subkī, *Fatāwā al-Subkī*, 1:279.
74 Ibid., 1:277–9.
75 Muḥammad ibn Qāsim al-Raṣṣā', *Tadhkirat al-muḥibbīn fī asmā' sayyid al-mursalīn*, ed. Muḥammad Riḍwān al-Dāya, Abu Dhabi: al-Majma' al-Thaqāfī, 1423 AH/2002 CE, p. 147.
76 Banīs, *Lawāmi'*, 1:23.
77 Ibn Taymīya, *Majmū' fatāwā*, 27:39–47.
78 Ibid., pp. 39–40.
79 Ibid., p. 45.
80 Ibid., pp. 44–5.
81 al-Fakhr al-Rāzī, *al-Tafsīr al-kabīr*, [Tehran]: n.p., n.d., 32:29.
82 Aḥmad ibn Muḥammad al-Ṭaḥāwī, *Sharḥ ma'ānī al-āthār*, ed. Muḥammad Zuhrī al-Najjār, Cairo: Maṭba'at al-Anwār al-Muḥammadīya, n.d., 3:85. The tradition also appears in al-Bayhaqī's *al-Sunan al-kubrā*, Ibn Ḥajar al-Haytamī's *Majma' al-zawā'id*, and Ibn 'Abd al-Barr's *Tamhīd*; see Muḥammad Sa'īd Zaghlūl, *Mawsū'at aṭrāf al-ḥadīth al-nabawī al-sharīf*, Beirut: Dār al-Kutub al-'Ilmīya, n.d., 4:283.
83 Ibn 'Ammār, *Niḥla*, p. 106.
84 Haytamī, *Itmām*, pp. 30–1.
85 F.L. Cross, cited in Jonathan Z. Smith, *To Take Place: toward theory in ritual*, Chicago and London: The University of Chicago Press, 1987, p. 88.
86 Smith, *To Take Place*, p. 88.
87 Muḥammad ibn Aḥmad ibn Faraj al-Anṣārī al-Andalusī [al-Qurṭubī], *Kitāb al-I'lām bi-mā yajibu 'alā al-anām min ma'rifat mawlid al-muṣṭafā 'alayhi al-salām*, ms. Istanbul, Topkapi no. 6031 M443, 19a–b.
88 Bakrī, *Anwār*, Cairo, p. 62.
89 See, for instance, 'Abd al-Raḥmān ibn 'Abd al-Mun'im al-Khayyāṭ al-Yamanī, *Mawlid*, ms. Cairo, Dār al-Kutub, Ta'rīkh no. 218, 5b; anonymous, *Mawlid al-nabī*, ms. Cairo, Dār al-Kutub, Ta'rīkh no. 705, 14a, 14b; Muḥammad Fawzī Efendī, *Qudus al-kalām fī mawlid al-nabī 'alayhi al-salām*, ms. Cairo, Dār al-Kutub, Tārīkh Ṭal'at no. 1996, 3a; Muḥammad Ṣāliḥ ibn Muḥammad al-Dasūqī, *al-Manhal al-awfā fī mīlād al-muṣṭafā*, ms. Damascus, Asad Library, no. 11402, 14a.
90 Qasṭallānī, *Mawāhib*, 1:143.
91 al-Khayyāṭ al-Yamanī, *Mawlid*, 2a.

92 Muḥammad ibn Aḥmad Ibn Jubayr, *Riḥlat Ibn Jubayr*, Beirut: Dār Ṣādir / Dār Bayrūt, 1384 AH/1964 CE, p. 91.
93 Ibid., pp. 91–2.
94 Ibid., p. 141.
95 Ibid., p. 92.
96 See Abū'l-Walīd Muḥammad ibn 'Abd Allāh ibn Aḥmad al-Azraqī, *Akhbār Makka*, ed. F. Wüstenfeld, Göttingen, 1858; reprinted Beirut: Maktabat al-Khayyāṭ, n.d., p. 422. Spatial and temporal veneration of the birth of the Prophet (as well as those of members of his family) clearly co-existed over time; the Prophet's birth site was renovated by several different rulers in the era of the rise of the *mawlid* celebration. See Taqī al-Dīn Muḥammad ibn Aḥmad al-Fāsī, *Shifā' al-gharām bi-akhbār al-balad al-ḥarām*, Beirut: Dār al-Kutub al-'Ilmīya, n.d., 1:270.
97 Smith, *To Take Place*, p. 94.
98 Hava Lazarus-Yafeh, *Some Religious Aspects of Islam*, Leiden: E.J. Brill, 1981, pp. 38, 42.
99 Tilman Nagel, "Der islamische Prinz Karneval," *XXIV. Deutscher Orientalistentag*, ed. Werner Diem and Abdoljavad Falaturi, Stuttgart: Franz Steiner Verlag, 1990, pp. 247–8. Translation mine.
100 Tilman Nagel, "Hadīth – oder: Die Vernichtung der Geschichte," *XXV Deutscher Orientalistentag*, ed. Cornelia Wunsch, Stuttgart: Franz Steiner Verlag, 1994, pp. 125–8.

5 *Mawlids* under attack

1 A vivid sense of al-Barzanjī's scholarly and religious stature is provided by Aḥmad ibn Muḥammad al-Ḥaḍrāwī, *Nuzhat al-fikr fīmā maḍā min al-ḥawādith wa'l-'ibar*, Damascus: Manshūrāt Wizārat al-Thaqāfa, 1996, 1:247–51, who lauds both his intellectual accomplishments and his performance of *karāmāt* (miracles), both before and after his death. al-Barzanjī's *mawlid* is entitled *'Iqd al-jawhar fī mawlid al-nabī al-azhar* (Kaḥḥāla gives the title as *'Iqd al-jawhar fī mawlid ṣāḥib al-hawḍ wa'l-kawthar*, and it is generally known simply as *Mawlid al-Barzanjī*) . al-Barzanjī also produced a verse rendition of his *mawlid*, which remains in circulation. Although al-Barzanjī's death date is variously given as 1179, 1184, and 1187 (apparently a misprint in Kaḥḥāla, who gives the Gregorian date correctly), the most specific information (including the month and day of his death, as well as a verse whose numerical value yields its year) is provided by al-Ḥaḍrāwī, who states that he died in 1177 AH. See 'Umar Riḍā Kaḥḥāla, *Mu'jam al-mu'allifīn,* Beirut: Mu'assasat al-Risāla, 1414 AH/1993 CE, 1:490; 'Abd al-Raḥmān ibn Ḥasan al-Jabartī, *'Ajā'ib al-āthār fī'l-tarājim wa'l-akhbār*, Cairo: al-Hay'a al-'Āmma li-Dār al-Kutub wa'l-Wathā'iq al-Qawmīya, 1997–8, 1:569–70; Muḥammad Khalīl al-Murādī, *Silk al-durar fī a'yān al-qarn al-thānī 'ashar*, Beirut: Dār al-Bashā'ir al-Islāmīya, 1408 AH/1988 CE , 1:9; Ismā'īl Bāshā al-Baghdādī, *Hadīyat al-'ārifīn, asmā' al-mu'allifīn wa-āthār al-muṣannifīn*, Istanbul: Milli Egitim Basimevi, 1951–5, 1:255; Brockelmann, *GAL,* GII, p. 384, S II, p. 517.
2 See Nūrā Abū'l-Fatḥ, *al-Mutāḥ min al-mawālid wa'l-anāshīd al-milāḥ*, n.p., 1416 AH/ 1995 CE, 1:192, 222.
3 See ibid., 1:193, 224.
4 See Ḥaḍrāwī, *Nuzha*, 1:128–32; Jabartī, *'Ajā'ib*, 2:223–5; Baghdādī, *Hadīya*, 1:181.
5 Abū'l-Fatḥ, *Mutāḥ*, 1:238.
6 Ḥaḍrāwī, *Nuzha*, 1:248. Ja'far al-Barzanjī's commentary is titled *al-Kawkab al-anwar 'alā 'iqd al-jawhar fī mawlid al-nabī al-azhar*, and 'Ulaysh's commentary is titled *al-Qawl al-munjī 'alā mawlid al-Barzanjī*; see Brockelmann, *GAS*, GII,

pp. 353, 384, 486. For al-Barzanjī see al-Ḥaḍrāwī, *Nuzha*, 1:252–5; ʻAbd al-Razzāq al-Bayṭār, *Ḥilyat al-bashar fī ta'rīkh al-qarn al-thālith ʻashar*, Damascus: Majmaʻ al-Lugha al-ʻArabīya, 1961–3, 1:452–4; Baghdādī, *Hadīya*, 1:256–7. For ʻUlaysh, see Kaḥḥāla, *Muʻjam*, 3:104; Baghdādī, *Hadīya*, 2:382–3. Another commentary on al-Barzanjī, *Madārij al-ṣuʻūd ilā iktisā' al-burūd*, was produced by the Javanese scholar Muḥammad Nawawī al-Bantanī (d.1316 AH/1898 CE), a Shāfiʻī *faqīh* and ṣūfī who settled in Mecca (see Kaḥḥāla, *Muʻjam*, 3:754).

7 See al-Ḥaḍrāwī, *Nuzha*, 1:345–6.

8 See Ḥaḍrāwī, *Nuzha*, 1:41, 42; Baghdādī, *Hadīya*, 1:41–2; Bayṭār, *Ḥilya*, 1:7–11; Brockelmann, *GAS*, SII, p. 741.

9 Yūsuf ibn Ismāʻīl al-Nabhānī, *Jawāhir al-biḥār fī faḍā'il al-nabī al-mukhtār*, ed. Muḥammad Amīn al-Ḍannāwī, Beirut: Dār al-Kutub al-ʻIlmīya, 1419 AH/1998 CE, 3:391; Kaḥḥāla, *Muʻjam*, 1:172. Commentaries on al-Haytamī's *mawlid* were also produced by Muḥammad b. Muḥammad al-Khayyāṭ (d. 1166 AH/1753 CE), Muḥammad ibn ʻUbāda al-ʻAdawī (d. 1193 AH/1779 CE), and ʻAbd Allāh b. ʻAlī al-Damlījī (d. 1234 AH/1819 CE); see Brockelmann, *GAS*, GII, p. 388.

10 For Ibrāhīm al-Riyāḥī, see Baghdādī, *Hadīya*, 1:42 (who describes him as the leading Mālikī scholar and jurisconsult in Tunis); Kaḥḥāla, *Muʻjam*, 1:37; Bayṭār, *Ḥilya*, 1:67–8 (gives death date as 1263 AH). As demonstrated by an enquiry by a Tunisian received by Muḥammad Rashīd Riḍā in 1905, the *mawlid* of Ibrāhīm al-Riyāḥī was still the "official" *mawlid* used in Tunisia (*al-riwāya al-muʻtamada rasmīyan*) at the beginning of the twentieth century. (Muḥammad Rashīd Riḍā, *Fatāwā al-imām Muḥammad Rashīd Riḍā*, ed. Ṣalāḥ al-Dīn al-Munajjid and Yūsuf Q. Khūrī, Beirut: Dār al-Kitāb al-Jadīd, 1390 AH/1970 CE, 1:339.)

11 Aḥmad Jamāl al-Dīn al-Tūnisī, *Mawlid al-nabī al-maʻrūf bi-khtiṣār Mawlid al-Barzanjī*, Kano, Nigeria: al-Dār al-Ifrīqīya, n.d., pp. 29, 31 (pages 29 and 30 are reversed and misnumbered in this pamphlet).

12 ʻAlī Bāshā Mubārak, *al-Khiṭaṭ al-tawfīqīya al-jadīda li-miṣr al-qāhira*, Cairo: al-Hay'a al-Miṣrīya al-ʻĀmma li'l-Kutub, 1983; facsimile of the second printing, Cairo, 1970, 3:444–6.

13 Benjamin C. Fortna, *Imperial Classroom: Islam, the state, and education in the late Ottoman Empire*, Oxford: Oxford University Press, 2002, pp. 109, 138.

14 ʻAbd al-Raḥmān ibn Muḥammad al-ʻĀṣimī al-Qaḥṭānī al-Najdī, *al-Durar al-sanīya fī al-ajwiba al-najdīya*, Beirut: Dār al-ʻArabīya li'l-Ṭibāʻa wa'l-Nashr, 1402 AH/1982 CE, 1:158–9.

15 The opinions of Jamāl ibn ʻUmar and of ʻAbd al-Raḥmān Sirāj are cited in a *fatwā* that is abridged in Atif Sabri, "The ruling according to Islamic law in justification of: (1) Meelad-un-nabi (2) Meelad feast (3) Qiyam. . ." in circulation on the web on various Islamic web sites. The original *fatwā*, by the South African *muftī* M.A. Awwary, was published in *Muslim Digest* 32 (1982). See Annemarie Schimmel, *And Muhammad Is His Messenger*, Chapel Hill: The University of North Carolina Press, 1985, pp. 295–6, n. 20. For bio-bibliogaphical information on Jamāl ibn ʻUmar al-Makkī, see al-Ḥaḍrāwī, *Nuzha*, 1:268–72; Baghdādī, *Hadīya*, 1:257; Kaḥḥāla, *Muʻjam*, 1:501. For ʻAbd al-Raḥmān al-Sirāj, see Ḥaḍrāwī, *Nuzha*, 2:142–3; Baghdādī, *Hadīya*, 1:558; Kaḥḥāla, *Muʻjam*, 2:96.

16 Muḥammad ibn Sālim ibn Ḥafīẓ, *Qurrat al-ʻayn bi-jawāb as'ilat wādī al-ʻayn*, printed in Muḥammad ibn ʻAlawī al-Mālikī al-Makkī al-Ḥasanī, *Bāqa ʻaṭira min ṣiyagh al-mawālid wa'l-madāiḥ al-nabawīya al-karīma*, n.p., 1403 AH/1983 CE, p. 32.

17 C. Snouck Hurgronje, *Mekka in the Latter Part of the 19th Century*, trans. J.H. Monahan, Leiden: E.J. Brill, 1970, pp. 46–8.

18 Ibid., p. 117.

19 For Daḥlān, see Ḥaḍrāwī, *Nuzha*, 1:186–90; Baghdādī, *Hadīya*, 1:191; Bayṭār, *Ḥilya*, 1:181–3; Zakī Muḥammad Mujāhid, *al-Aʻlām al-sharqīya fī'l-mi'a al-rābiʻa ʻashara al-hijrīya*, Cairo: Dār al-Ṭibāʻa al-Miṣrīya al-Ḥadītha, 1369 AH/1950 CE, 2:75–6.

20 Aḥmad ibn Zaynī Daḥlān, *al-Sīra al-nabawīya wa'l-āthār al-muḥammadīya*, printed in the margins of ʻAlī ibn Burhān al-Dīn al-Ḥalabī, *Insān al-ʻuyūn fī sīrat al-amīn al-ma'mūn*, [Cairo]: Maṭbaʻat Muḥammad Efendī Muṣṭafā, n.d., 1:47–9.

21 N.J.G. Kaptein, "The *Berdiri Mawlid* issue among Indonesian Muslims in the period from circa 1875 to 1930," *Bijdragen Tot de Taal-, Land- en Volkenkunde* 149, 1993, pp. 129–31.

22 Literally, "when there befell me what befalls women, that is, when giving birth."

23 Daḥlān, *Sīra*, 1:41.

24 Aḥmad ibn Zaynī Daḥlān, *al-Durar al-sanīya fī al-radd ʻalā al-wahhābīya*, Cairo: Dār Jawāmiʻ al-Kalim, n.d., pp. 63–4.

25 Muḥammad ibn khalīl al-Hijrasī, *Kitāb al-Manẓar al-bahī fī ṭāliʻ mawlid al-nabī wa-mā yatbaʻuhu min aʻmāl al-mawlid wa-ḥukm al-qiyām ʻinda dhikr mawlidihi ʻalayhi al-ṣalāt wa'l-salām*, [Cairo]: al-Maṭbaʻ al-ʻIlmī, 1312 AH/[1895 CE], pp. 12–13.

26 Ibid., p. 13.

27 Ibid., pp. 17–18.

28 Cited in Ḥasan al-Khazrajī, *al-Qawl al-wāḍih al-mufīd fī qirā'at al-mawlid fī kull ʻām jadīd*, excerpted in introduction to Ḥāmid al-Miḥḍār, *al-Iḥtifāl bi-dhikr al-niʻam wājib*, n.p.: Maktabat al-Muṭīʻī, n.d., pp. 6–7.

29 Muḥammad ʻAlī ibn Ḥusayn al-Mālikī, *Tahdhīb al-furūq wa'l-qawāʻid al-sannīya fī al-asrār al-fiqhīya*, printed in the margin of Aḥmad ibn Idrīs al-Qarāfī, *Anwār al-burūq fī anwā' al-furūq*, ed. Khalīl al-Manṣūr, Beirut: Dār al-Kutub al-ʻIlmīya, 1418 AH/1998 CE, 4:428. The author states that the work was completed in Sumatra in 1343 AH/1924 CE (ibid., 4:493).

30 Ibid., 4:428. Although unusually extreme, al-Hijrasī's and al-Mālikī's affirmation of the practice of *qiyām* was not isolated. Several Syrian scholars of the early-twentieth century also seem to have written in its support. According to the editors of Abū'l-Ḥasanayn ʻAbd Allāh ibn ʻAbd al-Raḥman al-Ḥasanī al-Makkī al-Hāshimī, *al-Iḥtifāl bi'l-mawlid al-nabawī bayna mu'ayyidīn wa-muʻāriḍīn*, n.p., 1417 AH/1996 CE, p. 82, n. 1, writings in support of the *qiyām* are also attributed to Maḥmūd al-ʻAṭṭār (d. 1362 AH/1944 CE), a Damascene religious scholar who served as a *muftī* in Kerak and taught at the Great Mosque of Damascus, and to Jamāl al-Dīn al-Qāsimī (d. 1332 AH/1914 CE). al-ʻAṭṭār is supposed to have held that the *qiyām* was legally desirable (*mustaḥabb*), and al-Qāsimī to have argued that it was obligatory (*wājib*). The editors state that they have published these treatises, but I have been unable to obtain either text. The persistence of doubts about the legitimacy of the *qiyām* is reflected by Saʻīd Ramaḍān al-Būṭī's comments on his father. Although the senior al-Būṭī attended *mawlid*s, his son recalls, for the first years of his residence in Damascus he did not participate in the *qiyām*; perhaps basing himself on the *fatwā* of Ibn Ḥajar al-Haytamī, he considered it a *bidʻa*. Later, however, he began to engage in the *qiyām*; his son speculates that he may have changed his judgment based on his observation that people performed it in a spirit of reverence for the Prophet (Cited in Hāshimī, *Iḥtifāl*, p. 44). al-Būṭī's change of heart would have occurred sometime in the 1930s.

31 Muḥammad Rashīd Riḍā, "Muqaddima li-dhikrā al-mawlid al-nabawī," *al-Manār* 20, 1335 AH/1917 CE, p. 28.

32 Ibid., pp. 24–5.

33 Ibid., p. 25.

34 Ibid., p. 30.

35 Riḍā, *Fatāwā*, 2:439–40.

36 Riḍā, "Muqaddima," p. 30.

37 Ibid., p. 31.

38 Ibid., p. 31.

39 Muḥammad Rashīd Riḍā, "Dhikrā al-mawlid al-nabawī," *al-Manār* 19, 1334 AH/1916 CE, pp. 408–10.

40 "Ṣāḥib al-imḍā' al-ramzī," "Naqḍ Dhikrā al-mawlid al-nabawī," *al-Manār* 20, 1336 AH/1918 CE, p. 345.
41 Muḥammad Rashīd Riḍā, "Radd al-Manār 'alā al-nāqid li-Dhikrā al-mawlid al-nabawī," *al-Manār* 20, 1336 AH/1918 CE, p. 395.
42 Riḍā, "Muqaddima," p. 28.
43 Riḍā, "Dhikrā," p. 410.
44 Ibid., pp. 412–13.
45 Riḍā, "Muqaddima," p. 32.
46 Muḥammad Rashīd Riḍā, "Dhikrā al-mawlid al-nabawī," *al-Manār* 34, 1353 AH/1934 CE, p. 130.
47 Riḍā's work was published under the title *Nidā' li'l-jins al-laṭīf yawm al-mawlid al-nabawī al-sharīf*, Cairo: Maṭba'at al-Manār, 1932.
48 Muḥammad Rashīd Riḍā, "al-Mawlid al-nabawī," *al-Manār* 7, 1322 AH/1904 CE, p. 199.
49 'Abd Allāh 'Afīfī, *al-Mawlid al-nabawī al-mukhtār, wa-huwa al-qiṣṣa al-fā'iza fī' l-mubārāt al-islāmīya al-'āmma*, [Cairo]: Majallat al-Islām, second printing, 1356 AH/ 1937 CE.
50 Ibid., p. 74.
51 Abū'l-Fatḥ, *Mutāḥ*, 1:385.
52 Ibid., 1:386.
53 Ibid., 1:394.
54 Ibid., 2:117.
55 Ibid., 2:127.
56 Ibid., 2:117.
57 *Mūjaz al-Asrār fī mawlid al-mukhtār*, in *al-Anwār al-badrīya fī'l-mu'jizāt al-nabawīya*, Ṭanṭā: Maktabat Nahḍat Miṣr, n.d., pp. 123–36. Traditional attitudes persisted even within the Egyptian religious establishment; Muḥammad ibn 'Abd al-Salām al-Munayyar, a religious official in the areas of religious instruction and preaching (*murshid 'āmm* and *wā'iẓ 'āmm*), composed a very traditional *mawlid* entitled *al-Fayḍ al-midrār 'alā mawlid al-mukhtār*, [Cairo]: Maktabat al- Ādāb, 1415 AH/ 1994 CE, in the 1940s.
58 'Abd al-Ḥayy ibn Fakhr al-Dīn al-Ḥasanī, *al-I'lām bi-man fī ta'rīkh al-Hind min al-a'lām*, Beirut: Dār Ibn Ḥazm, 1420 AH/1999 CE, 8:1316.
59 'Ayn al-Quḍāt al-Ḥaydarābādī, *Nihāyat al-irshād ilā iḥtifāl al-mīlād*, Lucknow: Nāẓir Press, n.d., p. 3.
60 Ibid., p. 6.
61 Ibid., p. 24.
62 For a discussion of the modern understanding of the Qur'ān as a fully independent and complete source of Islamic doctrine, see Daniel Brown, "The triumph of scripturalism: the doctrine of *naskh* and its modern critics," Earle H. Waugh and Frederick M. Denny, eds, *The Shaping of an American Islamic Discourse, a memorial to Fazlur Rahman*, Atlanta, Georgia: Scholars Press, 1998, pp. 49–66.
63 'Ayn al-Quḍāt, *Nihāya*, p. 7.
64 Ibid., p. 8.
65 Ibid., pp. 20–1.
66 Ibid., p. 11.
67 Ibid., p. 11.
68 Cited in Ḥasan al-Khazrajī, *al-Qawl al-wāḍih al-mufīd fī qirā'at al-mawlid fī kull 'ām jadīd*, excerpted in introduction to Miḥḍār, *Iḥtifāl*, pp. 6–7.
69 'Abd Rabbih ibn Sulaymān, known as al-Qalyūbī, *Fayḍ al-wahhāb fī bayān ahl al-ḥaqq wa-man ḍalla 'an al-ṣawāb*, n.p.: Dār al-Qawmīya al-'Arabīya li'l-Ṭibā'a, 1383 AH/1964 CE, 5:104–7.
70 Muḥammad ibn 'Alawī al-Mālikī al-Ḥasanī, *al-Dhakhā'ir al-Muḥammadīya*, with notes and commentary by Jamāl Fārūq Jibrīl Maḥmūd al-Daqqāq, Cairo: Dār Jawāmi' al-Kalim, n.d., pp. 319–27.

71 The pamphlet is entitled "Ḥawl al-iḥtifāl bi-dhikrā al-mawlid al-nabawī al-sharīf."
72 al-Mālikī's annotated editions of the *mawlids* of Ibn al-Dayba' and Ibn Kathīr (in the versified version of Muḥammad ibn Sālim ibn Ḥafīẓ) are published in his compilation *Bāqa 'aṭira* (see next note). al-Miḥdār mentions the edition of Mullā 'Alī al-Qāri's *al-Mawrid al-rawī* in *al-Iḥtifāl bi-dhikr al-ni'am wājib*, p. 59.
73 al-Mālikī al-Ḥasanī, *Bāqa 'aṭira*. The introduction to this collection, which is appropriate for use as a sourcebook for *mawlid* performance, includes the complete text of his apologia for the celebration of the *mawlid*, as well as a pro-*mawlid fatwā* issued by the Ḥaḍramī scholar Muḥammad ibn Sālim ibn Ḥafīẓ.
74 For a biography of his father, see Muḥammad 'Alī Maghribī, *A'lām al-Ḥijāz fī'l-qarn al-rābi 'ashar li'l-hijra*, n.p., 1404 AH/1984 CE, 2:275–6.
75 Ibn Naqīb al-Miṣrī, *Reliance of the Traveler*, trans. and ed. by Nuh Ha Mim Keller, rev. edn, Beltsville, Maryland: Amana Publications, 1994, pp. 1074–5; 'Ātiq ibn Ghayth al-Bilādī, *Nashr al-rayāḥīn fī ta'rīkh al-balad al-amīn*, Mecca: Dār Makka, 1415 AH/1994 CE), 2:669–72.
76 'Abd Allāh ibn Sulaymān ibn Manī', *Ḥiwār ma'a al-Mālikī fī radd munkarātihi wa-ḍalālātihi*, Riyadh: al-Ri'āsa al-'āmma li-idārat al-buḥūth al-'ilmīya wa'l-iftā' wa'l-da'wa wa'l-irshād, 1403 AH/1983 CE, pp. 9–10.
77 Ibid., pp. 11–15.
78 Ibid Naqīb, *Reliance*, p. 1075.
79 Riyadh, 1403 AH/1983 CE.
80 1 Yūsuf Hāshim al-Rifā'ī, *Adillat ahl al-sunna wa'l-jamā'a aw al-radd al-muḥkam al-manī' alā munkarāt wa-shubuhāt Ibn Manī' fī tahajjumihi 'alā al-sayyid Muḥammad 'Alawī al-Mālikī al-Ḥasanī* ("The proofs of the people of the *sunna* and the community, or the decisive and unassailable refutation of Ibn Manī''s deviant and dubious opinions in his attack on *al-sayyid* Muḥammad 'Alawī al-Mālikī al-Ḥasanī"), published in several different editions in Cairo (1985), Kuwait (1988), and Casablanca (1989). al-Rifā'ī (b. 1351 AH/1932 CE), a Shāfi'ī scholar and ṣūfī *shaykh*, served as a member of parliament and a government minister in Kuwait (Ibn Naqīb, *Reliance*, pp. 1112–13).
2 'Abd al-Karim Murad and 'Abd al-Hayy al-'Amrawi, *al-Tahdhir min al-ightirar bi-ma ja'a fi kitab al-Hiwar* ("A warning against being deceived by what is stated in the book *al-Hiwar*"), Fez, 1404 AH/1984 CE.
3 A third refutation of Ibn Manī''s work was published by the Baḥraynī scholar Rāshid ibn Ibrāhīm al-Marīkhī under the title *Raf' al-astār 'an shubuhāt wa-ḍalālāt ṣāḥib al-Ḥiwār* ("Lifting the coverings from the insinuations and aberrations of the author of *al-Ḥiwār*"). I have been unable to obtain this book. It is cited by Yūsuf ibn Hāshim al-Rifā'ī in his 1420 AH/1999 CE work "Advice to our brothers the scholars of Najd," available on the web in English translation at http://mac.abc.se/home/onesr/d/absn_e.pdf, accessed on June 12, 2006. al-Marīkhī also reissued al-Mālikī's pamphlet on the permissibility of the *mawlid* celebration.
81 Hāshimī, *Iḥtifāl*.
82 For instance, the *muftī* Muḥammad ibn Ibrāhīm Āl Shaykh had produced a polemic against the *mawlid* celebration in 1383 AH/1963 CE (printed in *Rasā'il fī ḥukm al-iḥtifāl bi'l-mawlid al-nabawī*, 1:17–43).
83 *Rasā'il fī ḥukm al-iḥtifāl bi'l-mawlid al-nabawī*, 1:66, 244.
84 Ḥammūd ibn 'Abd Allāh al-Tuwayjirī, *al-Radd al-qawī 'alā al-Rifā'ī wa'l-majhūl wa-Ibn 'Alawī wa-bayān akhṭā'ihim fī al-mawlid al-nabawī*, 1:65–324.
85 'Alī ibn Muḥammad al-'Īsā, *al-'Aqlīya al-islāmīya wa-fikr al-mawlid*, Riyadh: Maktabat al-Kharījī, 1405 AH); he discusses the exchange of letters in the newspaper *al-Madīna* on pp. 15–16.
86 Ibid., p. 15; see also N.J.G. Kaptein, *Muḥammad's Birthday Festival*, Leiden: E.J. Brill, 1993, p. 45, n. 1.

87 Hāshimī, *Iḥtifāl*, p. 50.
88 Various authors (Majmū'a min al-'ulamā'), *Rasā'il fī ḥukm al-iḥtifāl bi'l-mawlid al-nabawī*, Riyadh: Ri'āsat Idārat al-Buḥūth al-'ilmīya wa'l-iftā', 1419 AH/1998 CE.
89 *fayṣal al-tafriqa bayna'l-islām wa'l-zandaqa*, an allusion to the title of a work by the medieval authority al-Ghazālī on the boundaries of Islamic orthodoxy. (Hāshimī, *Iḥtifāl*, p. 7.)
90 Aḥmad 'Abd al-'Azīz al-Mubārak, *"Ḥukm al-iḥtifāl bi-mawlid al-rasūl,"* *Manār al-islām* 6, Jumādā al-Ākhira, 1401 AH/April–May 1981 CE, pp. 6–11.
91 This *fatwā* is still widely circulated internationally by supporters of the *mawlid*, often as an informally copied Xerox pamphlet; it is also currently available on the internet, in both Arabic and English. I was given a Xerox copy at a shop called *al-Tasjīlāt al-Islāmīya* in Say'ūn, Hadramawt, Yemen, in the summer of 2000; a note on the cover sheet says, "Dear Brother! After you have read this essay, give it to someone else so that he can benefit from it." This suggests the informal distribution networks through which such pamphlet literature is disseminated.
92 'Īsā ibn 'Abd Allāh al-Ḥimyarī, *Bulūgh al-ma'mūl fī'l-iḥtifā' wa'l-iḥtifāl bi-mawlid al-rasūl*, Dubai: Dā'irat al-Awqāf wa'l-Shu'ūn al-Islāmīya, n.d. The popularity of the work is suggested by the fact that the copy available to me was from the "expanded and revised" seventh printing.
93 al-Khazrajī's work was entitled *al-Qawl al-wāḍiḥ al-mufīd fī qirā'at al-mawlid fī kull 'ām jadīd*. A long passage from it is presented in the introductory matter to Ḥāmid al-Miḥḍār, *al-Iḥtifāl bi-dhikr al-ni'am wājib*, n.p.: Maktabat al-Muṭī'ī, n.d., pp. 5–8.
94 See n. 93.
95 Kaptein, *Prophet's Birthday*, p. 45, n. 1.
96 *Mawlid al-rasūl wa-'umūm barakat ba'thatihi*, translated into French as *La Naissance du Prophète et la Bénédiction Universelle de sa Mission*, trans. M. Ibrahim Nuckcheddy, Qatar: La Présidence des tribunaux et affaires islamiques, 1407 AH/1987 CE.
97 For a discussion of Awwary's *fatwā*, see Schimmel, *And Muhammad Is His Messenger*, pp. 295–6, n. 20. It appeared in the South African journal *Muslim Digest*, vol. 32, 1982.
98 Mālikī, "Ḥawl al-iḥtifāl," in *Bāqa*, p. 5.
99 Aviva Schussman, "The legitimacy and nature of *mawlid al-nabī* (analysis of a *fatwā*)," *Islamic Law and Society* 5, 1998, p. 223.
100 A generally conciliatory attitude towards *mawlid* celebrations, combined with a concern to curb excesses, is also expressed in earlier opinions by mainstream Egyptian scholars. See 'Alī Maḥfūẓ, *al-Ibdā' fī maḍārr al-ibtidā'*, Cairo: al-Maktaba al-Maḥmūdīya al-Tijārīya, n.d., pp. 258–65; Ḥasanayn Muḥammad Makhlūf, *Fatāwā shar'īya wa-buḥūth islāmīya*, second printing, Cairo: Muṣṭafā al-Bābī al-Ḥalabī, 1385 AH/1965 CE, 1:150–1.
101 *Majallat al-Azhar*, 54, Rabī' al-Thānī 1402 AH/January 1982 CE, p. 651.
102 Translated in Schussman, "Legitimacy," pp. 218–21.
103 Hijrasī, *Manẓar*, p. 15.
104 Qalyūbī, *Fayḍ*, p. 109.
105 al-Mālikī al-Ḥasanī "Ḥawl al-iḥtifāl," in *Bāqa*, p. 5.
106 Ibid., pp. 8, 9, 11.
107 Ibid., pp. 10–11.
108 Ibn Manī', *Ḥiwār*, p. 32.
109 Muḥammad ibn 'Alawī al-Mālikī al-Makkī al-Ḥasanī, *Mafāhīm yajib an tuṣaḥḥaḥ*, Cairo: Dār al-Insān, 1405 AH/1985 CE, p. 224.
110 Mālikī, "Ḥawl al-iḥtifāl," in *Bāqa*, p. 16.
111 For a biographical entry on al-Būṭī, see Miṣrī, *Reliance*, p. 1079.
112 Muḥammad Sa'īd Ramaḍān al-Būṭī, *Raddan 'alā al-ladhīna yunkirūn al-iḥtifāl bi'l-mawlid al-nabawī: Lays kull jadīd bid'a*, published in Miḥḍār, *Iḥtifāl*, p. 62.
113 Ibid., p. 64; also cited in Murād and 'Amrawī, *Taḥdhīr*, pp. 65–6.

114 Miḥḍār, *Iḥtifāl*, p. 29.
115 Ibid., p. 37.
116 Ibrāhīm ibn Mūsā al-Shāṭibī, *Kitāb al-i'tiṣām*, Beirut: Mu'assasat al-Kutub al-Thaqāfīya, 1416 AH/1996 CE, 1:22, 2:52–8.
117 Riḍā, *Fatāwā*, 1:91–3.
118 Ibid., 6:2221–4.
119 Shaykh Hisham Muhammad Kabbani, "An explanation of the Dubai Fatwa," accessed online at http://www.sunnah.org/publication/index.htm on June 3, 2006.
120 Tuwayjirī, "Radd," in *Rasā'il fī ḥukm al-iḥtif āl*, 1:107.
121 See Brown, "Triumph," passim.
122 Ḥimyarī, *Bulūgh*, p. 25.
123 Ibid., pp. 26–7.
124 Ibid., p. 34.
125 Mālikī, "Ḥawl al-iḥtifāl," in *Bāqa*, p. 8.
126 Ibn Manī', *Ḥiwār*, pp. 78–80.
127 Mālikī, "Ḥawl al-iḥtifāl," in *Bāqa*, p. 6.
128 Ibid., p. 7.
129 Ḥimyarī, *Bulūgh*, pp. 23–4.
130 Mālikī, "Ḥawl al-iḥtifāl," in *Bāqa*, p. 8.
131 Ibid., p. 8.
132 Ḥimyarī, *Bulūgh*, pp. 34–5.
133 Murād and 'Amrawī, *Taḥdhīr*, p. 88.
134 Tuwayjirī, "Radd," in *Rasā'il fī ḥukm al-iḥtifāl*, 1:121–5.
135 Ibn Manī', *Ḥiwār*, p. 52.
136 Tuwayjirī, "Radd," in *Rasā'il fī ḥukm al-iḥtifāl*, 1:120.
137 Ibn Manī', *Ḥiwār*, p. 54.
138 Quoted in Ismā'īl ibn Muḥammad al-Anṣārī, "al-Qawl al-faṣl fī ḥukm al-tawassul bi-khayr al-rusul," in *Rasā'il fī ḥukm al-iḥtifāl*, 2:393–4.
139 Muḥammad ibn Sa'd ibn Shuqayr, "al-Iḥtifāl bi'l-mawlid bayna al-ittibā' wa'l-ibtidā'," in *Rasā'il fī ḥukm al-iḥtifāl*, 2:925.
140 Tuwayjirī , "Radd," in *Rasā'il fī ḥukm al-iḥtifāl*, p. 89.
141 Ibn Manī', *Ḥiwār*, p. 80.
142 Ṣāliḥ ibn Fawzān Āl Fawzān, al-*Khuṭab al-minbarīya fī al-munāsabāt al-'aṣrīya*, Beirut: Mu'assasat al-Risāla, 1414 AH/1993 CE, 1:125.
143 Ibn Manī', *Ḥiwār*, p. 40.
144 Mālikī, "Ḥawl al-iḥtifāl," in *Bāqa*, pp. 14–15.
145 Ibid., pp. 17–18.
146 Ibid., p. 15.
147 Ibid., p. 16.
148 Ibid., p. 16.
149 'Abd al-'Azīz ibn 'Abd Allāh ibn Bāz, "Ḥukm al-iḥtifāl bi'l-mawlid al-nabawī," in *Rasā'il fī ḥukm al-iḥtifāl*, p. 62.
150 Tuwayjirī , "Radd," in *Rasā'il fī ḥukm al-iḥtifāl*, p. 289.
151 Ibn Manī', *Ḥiwār*, pp. 174–5.
152 'Ayn al-Quḍāt, *Nihāya*, p. 32.
153 Ibid., pp. 32–5.
154 Ibid., pp. 44–6.
155 Mālikī, "Ḥawl al-iḥtifāl," in *Bāqa*, p. 5.
156 Cited in Hāshimī, *Iḥtifāl*, pp. 10, 11.
157 Jalāl al-Dīn 'Abd al-Raḥmān ibn Abī Bakr al-Suyūṭī, *Ḥusn al-maqṣid fī 'amal al-mawlid*, ed. Muṣṭafā 'Abd al-Qādir 'Aṭā', Beirut: Dār al-Kutub al-'Ilmīya, 1405 AH/1985 CE, p. 64; Ibn Ḥajar al-Haytamī, *Itmām al-ni'ma al-kubrā 'alā al-'ālam bi-mawlid sayyid wuld Ādam*, ed. 'Abd al-'Azīz Sayyid Hāshim al-Ghazūlī, Beirut: Dār al-Kutub al-'Ilmīya, 1422 AH/2001 CE, p. 24.

158 Ja'far ibn Ismā'īl al-Barzanjī, *al-Kawkab al-anwar 'alā 'iqd al-jawhar fī mawlid al-nabī al-azhar*, n.p.: al-Maṭba'a al-Wahbīya, 1290 AH/[1873–4] CE, p. 6.
159 Ibn al-Ḥājj, al-*Madkhal*, [Cairo]: Sharikat wa-Maṭba'at Muṣṭafā al-Bābī al-Ḥalabī wa-Awlādihi, 1380 AH/1960 CE, 2:4–5, 28–31.
160 Mālikī, "Ḥawl al-iḥtifāl," in *Bāqa*, p. 6.
161 Ibid., p. 7.
162 Ibid., p. 11.
163 Schussman, "Legitimacy," pp. 218–19.
164 Marion Katz, "The ḥajj and the study of Islamic ritual," forthcoming; see also Hava Lazarus-Yafeh, *Some Religious Aspects of Islam*, Leiden: E.J. Brill, 1981, p. 45.
165 Murād and 'Amrawī, *Taḥdhīr*, p. 71.
166 Tuwayjirī, "Radd," in *Rasā'il fī ḥukm al-iḥtifāl*, p. 172.
167 Ibn Manī', *Ḥiwār*, p. 30.
168 Abū Bakr Jābir al-Jazā'irī, "al-Inṣāf fīmā qīla fī'l-mawlid min al-ghulūw wa'l-ijḥāf," in *Rasā'il fī ḥukm al-iḥtifāl*, 1:364–5.
169 Āl Fawzān, *Khuṭab*, 1:118.
170 'Abd al-'Azīz ibn 'Abd Allāh ibn Bāz, Muḥammad ibn 'Uthaymīn, 'Abd Allāh ibn Jabrīn, *Fatāwā islāmīya*, Beirut: Dār al-Qalam, 1408 AH/1988 CE, 1:148.
171 Schussman, "Legitimacy," p. 219.
172 Muḥammad ibn Aḥmad al-Khazrajī, *Khuṭab minbarīya*, UAE: Lajnat al-Turāth wa'l-Ta'rīkh, 1400 AH/1980 CE, 1:110.
173 Āl Fawzān, *Khuṭab*, 1:126.
174 Tuwayjirī , "Radd," in *Rasā'il fī ḥukm al-iḥtifāl*, pp. 133–4.
175 Cited in Hāshimī, *Iḥtifāl*, p. 11, from the expanded second edition of al-Mālikī's "*Ḥawl al-iḥtifāl*. . . ."
176 Ḥasan al-Shaykha, "Fī dhikrā al-mawlid al-nabawī," in *Mawlid sayyidinā Muḥammad, ṣallā allāhu 'alayhi wa-sallam, nabī al-hudā wa-rasūl al-salām*, n.p., [Cairo, 1968], p. 63.
177 Cited in Miḥdār, *Iḥtifāl*, p. 64; Hāshimī, *Iḥtifāl*, p. 39.
178 Cited in Hāshimī, *Iḥtifāl*, p. 16.
179 Ibid., pp. 18–21.
180 Ibid., p. 21.
181 See Frederick Stephen Colby, *Constructing an Islamic Ascension Narrative: the interplay of official and popular culture in pseudo-Ibn 'Abbās*, PhD dissertation, Duke University, 2002, pp. 267–8.
182 Vardit Rispler-Chaim, "The 20th century treatment of an old *bid'a*: *Laylat al-niṣf min Sha'bān*," *Der Islam* 72, 1995, p. 93.
183 Some argued that *laylat niṣf Sha'bān* was the "blessed night" upon which the Qur'ān had been revealed (verse 44:1), but scholarly opinion favored *laylat al-qadr* for this distinction (see Muḥammad ibn al-Walīd al-Ṭurṭūshī, *Kitāb al-Ḥawādith wa'l-bida'*, Tunis: al-Maṭba'a al-Rasmīya li'l-Jumhūrīya al-Tūnisīya, 1959, pp. 117–21). In any case, the popular medieval observance of *laylat niṣf Sha'bān* does not seem to have revolved primarily around edifying reflection on the revelation of Scripture.
184 Rispler-Chaim, "20th century treatment," pp. 90–2.
185 Lazarus-Yafeh, *Some Religious Aspects*, pp. 44–5.
186 Nabhānī, *Jawāhir*, 3:394.

Conclusion

1 James Kritzeck, *Peter the Venerable and Islam*, Princeton, New Jersey: Princeton University Press, 1964, p. 109.
2 Similarly, although he categorizes al-Bakrī's work as a manifestation of " popular" Islam, Boaz Shoshan recounts that when the Qarāmānid ruler 'Alā' al-Dīn Khalīl

commissioned a biography of the Prophet from Muṣṭafā ibn Yūsuf Ḍarīr in the later-fourteenth-century CE, the latter consulted one of the leading scholars of Anatolia, who advised him to base his work on that of al-Bakrī. (Boaz Shoshan, *Popular Culture in Medieval Cairo*, Cambridge: Cambridge University Press, 1993, pp. 38–9.)

3 Mark Woodward, "The *Slametan*: textual knowledge and ritual performance in central Javanese Islam," *History of Religions* 28, 1988, p. 62.

4 Snouck Hurgronje, *Mekka in the Latter Part of the 19th Century*, trans. J.H. Monahan, Leiden: E.J. Brill, 1970, p. 116.

5 Knappert conflates *Sharaf al-anām* with the *mawlid* of al-Barzanjī. Based on my own familiarity with *mawlid* pamphlets similar to those he describes, they probably contained both *Sharaf al-anām* and the prose and poetry versions of the *mawlid* of al-Barzanjī. J. Knappert, " The Mawlid," *Orientalia Lovaniensia Periodica* 19, 1988, p. 212.

6 Nancy Tapper and Richard Tapper, "The Birth of the Prophet: ritual and gender in Turkish Islam," *Man*, n.s. 22, 1987, p. 83.

7 Hurgronje, *Mekka*, pp. 3, 148.

8 Anne H. Betteridge, "The controversial vows of urban Muslim women in Iran," in Nancy Auer Falk and Rita M. Gross, eds, *Unpsoken Worlds: women's religious lives in non-Western cultures*, San Francisco: Harper & Row, 1980, pp. 144–5.

9 Ibid., p. 145.

10 John R. Bown, *Muslims Through Discourse*, Princeton: Princeton University Press, 1993, p. 273.

11 Ibid., p. 273.

12 Jonathan Parry, "The gift, the Indian gift and the 'Indian gift', " *Man* (N.S.) 21, 1986, p. 458.

13 Ibid., p. 466.

14 Ibid., p. 467.

15 Ibn Taymīya, *Iqtiḍā' al-ṣirāṭ al-mustaqīm li-mukhālafat aṣḥāb al-jaḥīm*, Riyadh: Dār al-'Āṣima, 1419 AH/1998 CE, 2:126.

16 Ibn Ḥajar al-Haytamī, *al-Fatāwā al-ḥadīthīya*, [Cairo]: Muṣṭafā al-Bābī al-Ḥalabī, 1356 AH/1937 CE, p. 69.

17 See Muḥammad ibn Qāsim al-Raṣṣā' , *Tadhkirat al-muḥibbīn fī asmā' sayyid al-mursalīn*, ed. Muḥammad Riḍwān al-Dāya, Abu Dhabi: al-Majma' al-Thaqāfī, 1423 AH/2002 CE, pp. 152–4.

18 Faiza Saleh Ambah, "In Saudi Arabia, a Resurgence of Sufism," *Washington Post*, May 2, 2006, p. A13.

19 See Khālid ' Abd Allāh, " al-Amīr Sulṭān yazūru usrat al-Duktūr Muḥammad 'Alawī al-Mālikī mu'azziyan," *Jarīdat al-Riyāḍ*, 19 Ramaḍān 1425 (accessed at www.alriyadh.com/Contents/02-11-2004/Mainpage/LOCAL1_24136.php on May 25, 2006).

20 See P.K. Abdul Ghafour, "Abdullah Lauds Noble Efforts of Al-Malki," *Arab News*, November 2, 2004 (accessed at www.arabnews.com/?page=1&section=0&article=53834&d=2&m=11&y=2004 on May 25, 2005).

21 Ambah, "In Saudi Arabia," p. A13.

Bibliography

Sources in Western languages

Abdel-Malek, Kamal, *Muḥammad in the Modern Egyptian Popular Ballad*, Leiden: E.J. Brill, 1995.

Abou-Zahra, Nadia, "Rites of spiritual passage and the anthropology of Islam: a response to Tapper and Tapper," *Révue d'Histoire Maghrebine* 19, 1992, pp. 9–30.

—— *The Pure and Powerful, studies in contemporary Muslim society*, Reading, UK: Ithaca Press, 1997.

Ambah, Faiza Saleh, "In Saudi Arabia, a resurgence of Sufism," *Washington Post*, May 2, 2006, p. A13.

Anderson, Gary A., *A Time to Mourn, a Time to Dance: the expression of grief and joy in Israelite religion*, University Park, Pennsylvania: The Pennsylvania State University Press, 1991.

Andrae, Tor, *Die Person Muhammads in Lehre und Glauben seiner Gemeinde*, Stockholm: P.A. Norstedt, 1918.

Ayoub, Mahmoud, *Redemptive Suffering in Islam, a study of the devotional aspects of 'Āshūrā' in Twelver Shī'ism*, The Hague, Paris, New York: Mouton Publishers, 1978.

Bell, Joseph Norment, *Love Theory in Later Ḥanbalite Islam*, Albany: State University of New York Press, 1979.

Berkey, Jonathan, *Popular Preaching and Religious Authority in the Medieval Islamic Near East*, Seattle: University of Washington Press, 2001.

Betteridge, Anne H., "The controversial vows of urban Muslim women in Iran," in Nancy Auer Falk and Rita M. Gross, eds, *Unpsoken Worlds: women's religious lives in non-Western cultures*, San Francisco: Harper & Row, 1980, pp. 141–55.

Bowen, John R., *Muslims Through Discourse*, Princeton: Princeton University Press, 1993.

Böwering, Gerhard, *The Mystical Vision of Existence in Classical Islam*, Berlin: Walter de Gruyter, 1980.

Brockelmann, Carl, *Geschichte der arabischen Litteratur*, Second edition, Leiden: E.J. Brill, 1943–9.

Brown, Daniel, "The triumph of scripturalism: The doctrine of *naskh* and its modern critics," in Earle H. Waugh and Frederick M. Denny, eds, *The Shaping of an American Islamic Discourse, a memorial to Fazlur Rahman*, Atlanta, Georgia: Scholars Press, 1998, pp. 49–66.

Burke, Peter, *Popular Culture in Early Modern Europe*, New York: New York University Press, 1978.

Burton, Richard F., trans., *The Book of the Thousand Nights and a Night*, 10 vols, n.p., 1885.

Colby, Frederick Stephen, *Constructing an Islamic Ascension Narrative: the interplay of official and popular culture in pseudo-Ibn 'Abbās*, PhD dissertation, Duke University, 2002.

Donner, Fred McGraw, "The death of Abū Ṭālib," in *Love & Death in the Ancient Near East, essays in honor of Marvin H. Pope*, ed. John H. Marks and Robert M. Good, Guilford, Connecticut: Four Quarters Publishing Co., 1987, pp. 237–45.

Ebersole, Gary, "The function of ritual weeping revisited: affective expression and moral discourse," *History of Religions* 39, 2000, pp. 211–46.

Fortna, Benjamin C., *Imperial Classroom: Islam, the state, and education in the late Ottoman Empire*, Oxford: Oxford University Press, 2002.

Goldziher, Ignaz, "Neuplatonische und gnostische Elemente im Ḥadīth," Zeitschift der Assyrologie 22, 1908, reprinted in *Gesammelte Schriften*, ed. Joseph Desomogyi, Hildesheim: Georg Olms Verlagsbuchhandlung, 1970, pp. 107–34.

Grabar, Oleg, and Natif, Mika, "The story of the portraits of the Prophet Muḥammad," *Studia Islamica* 96, 2003, pp. 19–37.

Granja, F. de la, "Fiestas cristianas en Al-Andalus," *al-Andalus* 34, 1969, pp. 1–53.

Ḥadj-Ṣadok, Maḥammad, "Le mawlid d'après le mufti-poète d'Alger Ibn 'Ammar," in *Mélanges Louis Massignon*, Damascus: Institut Français de Damas, 1957, 2:269–91.

Hurgronje, C. Snouck, *Mekka in the Latter Part of the 19th Century*, trans. J.H. Monahan, Leiden: E.J. Brill, 1970.

Kabbani, Shaykh Hisham Muhammad, "An Explanation of the Dubai Fatwa," accessed online at <http://www.sunnah.org/publication/index.htm> on June 3, 2006.

Kaptein, N.J.G., "Materials for the history of the Prophet Muḥammad's birthday celebration in Mecca," *Der Islam* 69, 1992, pp. 193–246.

—— *Muḥammad's Birthday Festival*, Leiden: E.J. Brill, 1993.

—— "The *Berdiri Mawlid* issue among Indonesia Muslims in the period from circa 1875 to 1930," *Bijdragen Tot de Taal-, Land- en Volkenkunde* 149, 1993, pp. 124–53.

Khoury, Dina Rizk, "Slippers at the entrance or behind closed doors: domestic and public spaces for Mosuli women," in Madeline C. Zilfi, ed., *Women in the Ottoman Empire*, Leiden, New York, Köln: Brill, 1997, pp. 105–27.

Knappert, J., "The Mawlid," *Orientalia Lovaniensia Periodica* 19, 1988, pp. 209–15.

Knysh, Alexander, *Islamic Mysticism, a short history*, Leiden: Brill, 2000.

Kritzeck, James, *Peter the Venerable and Islam*, Princeton, New Jersey: Princeton University Press, 1964.

Lazarus-Yafeh, Hava, *Some Religious Aspects of Islam*, Leiden: E.J. Brill, 1981.

Lowin, Shari, *The Making of a Forefather: Abraham in Islamic and Jewish exegetical narratives*, PhD dissertation, University of Chicago, 2002.

Massignon, Louis, *Recueil des Textes Inédits Concernant l'Histoire de la Mystique en Pays d'Islam*, Paris: Librairie Orientaliste Paul Geuthner, 1929.

Mauss, Marcel, *The Gift*, New York: W.W. Norton and Company, 1967.

Meier, Fritz, *Bausteine II*, Istanbul: Franz Steiner Verlag, 1992.

Munajjid, Ṣalāḥ al-Dīn, *Mu'jam mā ullifa 'an rasūl allāh*, Beirut: Dār al-Kitāb al-Jadīd, 1402 AH/1982 CE.

Nadwi, Maulavi Muinuddin, *Catalogue of the Arabic and Persian Manuscripts in the Oriental Public Library at Bankipore*, vol. 15, Patna, 1929.

Nagel, Tilman, "Der islamische Prinz Karneval," *XXIV Deutscher Orientalistentag*, ed. Werner Diem and Abdoljavad Falaturi, Stuttgart: Franz Steiner Verlag, 1990.

—— "Ḥadīth – oder: Die Vernichtung der Geschichte," *XXV Deutscher Orientalistentag*, ed. Cornelia Wunsch, Stuttgart: Franz Steiner Verlag, 1994.

Padwick, Constance E., *Muslim Devotions*, Oxford: Oneworld, 1996.
Paret, Rudi, *Die legendäre maghāzī-Literatur*, Tübingen: Verlag von J.C.B. Mohr, 1930.
Parry, Jonathan, "The Gift, the Indian gift and the 'Indian gift'," *Man*, New Series 21, 1986, pp. 453–73.
Perlmann, Moshe, "A legendary story of Ka'b al-Aḥbār's conversion to Islam," in *Joshua Starr Memorial Volume*, New York: Conference on Jewish Relations, 1953, pp. 85–9.
Reinhart, A. Kevin, *Before Revelation: the boundaries of Muslim moral thought*, Albany: State University of New York Press, 1995.
al-Rifā'ī, Yūsuf ibn Hāshim, "Advice to our brothers the scholars of Najd," available in English translation at http://mac.abc.se/home/onesr/d/absn_e.pdf, accessed on June 12, 2006.
Rispler-Chaim, Vardit, "The 20th century treatment of an old *bid'a*: *Laylat al-niṣf min Sha'bān*," *Der Islam* 72, 1995, pp. 82–97.
Rodriguez-Manas, Francisco, "Charity and deceit: the practice of *iṭ'ām al-ṭa'ām* in Moroccan ṣūfism," *Studia Islamica* 91, 2000, pp. 59–90.
Rubin, U., "Pre-existence and light: aspects of the concept of Nūr Muḥammad," *Israel Oriental Studies* 5, 1975, pp. 62–117.
Saleh, Walid, *The Qur'ān commentary of Tha'labī (d. 427 / 1035)*, PhD dissertation, Yale University, 2001.
Sanders, Paula, *Ritual, Politics and the City in Fatimid Cairo*, Albany: State University of New York Press, 1994.
Schimmel, Annemarie, *And Muhammad Is His Messenger*, Chapel Hill: The University of North Carolina Press, 1985.
Schussman, Aviva, "The legitimacy and nature of *mawlid al-nabī* (analysis of a *fatwā*)" *Islamic Law and Society* 5, 1998, pp. 214–33.
Sharif, Ja'far, *Islam in India, or the Qānūn-i-Islām, the customs of the Musalmāns of India*, ed. and trans. G.A. Herklots, rev. William Crooke London and Dublin: Curzon Press, 1972.
Shoshan, Boaz, *Popular Culture in Medieval Cairo*, Cambridge: Cambridge University Press, 1993.
Smith, Jonathan Z., *To Take Place: toward theory in ritual*, Chicago and London: The University of Chicago Press, 1987.
Spuler, Bertold, *Iran in früh-islamischer Zeit*, Wiesbaden: Franz Steiner Verlag GMBH, 1952.
Tapper, Nancy, and Tapper, Richard, "The birth of the Prophet: ritual and gender in Turkish Islam," *Man*, New Series 22, 1987, pp. 69–92.
Wasserstrom, Steven, *Between Muslim and Jew*, Princeton: Princeton University Press, 1995.
Weber, Max, *The Protestant Ethic and the Spirit of Capitalism*, trans. Talcott Parsons, New York: Charles Scribner's Sons, 1958.
Woodward, Mark, "The *Slametan*: textual knowledge and ritual performance in central Javanese Islam," *History of Religions* 28, 1998, pp. 54–89.
Yahya, Osman, *Histoire et Classification de l'Oeuvre d'Ibn al-'Arabī*, 2 vols, Damascus: Intitut Français de Damas, 1964.

Sources in Arabic

Abū'l-Fatḥ, Nūrā, *al-Mutāḥ min al-mawālid wa'l-anāshīd al-milāḥ*, 2 vols, n.p., 1416 AH/ 1995 CE.

Abū Mikhnaf (attributed), *Mawlid baṭal al-islām amīr al-mu'minīn Alī ibn abī Ṭālib*, Najaf: Manshūrāt al-Maktaba al-Ḥaydarīya, n.d.

Abū Nu'aym al-Iṣbahānī, Aḥmad ibn 'Abd Allāh, *Dalā'il al-nubūwa*, Aleppo: Dār al-Wa'y, n.d.

Abū Shāma, 'Abd al-Raḥmān ibn Ismā'īl, *al-Bā'ith 'alā inkār al-bida' wa'l-ḥawādith*, ed. 'Uthmān Aḥmad 'Anbar, n.p.: Dār al-Hudā, 1398 AH/1978 CE.

—— *Kitāb al-rawḍatayn fī akhbār al-dawlatayn al-nūrīya wa'l-ṣalāḥīya*, 5 vols, ed. Ibrāhīm al-Zaybaq, Beirut: Mu'assasat al-Risāla, 1418 AH/1997 CE.

al-'Afīfī, 'Abd Allāh, *al-Mawlid al-nabawī al-mukhtār, wa-huwa al-qiṣṣa al-fā'iza fī'l-mubārāt al-islāmīya al-'āmma*, [Cairo]: Majallat al-Islām, second printing, 1356 AH/1937 CE.

Āl Fawzān, Ṣāliḥ ibn Fawzān, al-*Khuṭab al-minbarīya fī al-munāsabāt al-'aṣrīya*, 4 vols, Beirut: Mu'assasat al-Risāla, 1414 AH/1993 CE.

al-Amīr al-Ṣaghīr, Muḥammad, *Mawlid*, ms. Cairo, Dār al-Kutub, Ḥadīth no. 1677.

Anonymous, *al-Anwār al-badrīya fī'l-mu'jizāt al-nabawīya*, Ṭanṭā: Maktabat Nahḍat Miṣr, n.d.

Anonymous, *Faḍā'il al-mawlid al-sharīf*, ms. Cairo, Dār al-Kutub, Taṣawwuf wa-akhlāq dīnīya no. 2582.

Anonymous, *Kitāb al-'arūs*, ms. Damascus, Asad Library, no. 10114.

Anonymous, *Mawlid*, ms. Cairo, Dār al-Kutub, Majāmī' Ṭal'at no. 293.

Anonymous, *Mawlid*, ms. Cairo, Dār al-Kutub, Ta'rīkh Ṭal'at no. 1963.

Anonymous, *Mawlid*, ms. Cairo, Dār al-Kutub, Ta'rīkh Ṭal'at no. 2050.

Anonymous, *Mawlid al-nabī*, ms. Cairo, Dār al-Kutub, Ta'rīkh no. 704.

Anonymous, *Mawlid al-nabī*, ms. Cairo, Dār al-Kutub, Ta'rīkh no. 705.

Anonymous, *Qiṣṣat al-mawlid al-nabawī al-sharīf*, ms. Damascus, Asad Library, no. 11251.

'Ayn al-Quḍāt al-Ḥaydarābādī, *Nihāyat al-irshād ilā iḥtifāl al-mīlād*, Lucknow: Nāẓir Press, n.d.

al-'Azafī, Abū'l-'Abbās, *al-Durr al-munaẓẓam fī al-mawlid al-mu'aẓẓam*, Princeton University Arabic Manuscripts, Garrett Yehuda 256.

al-Azraqī, Abū'l-Walīd Muḥammad ibn 'Abd Allāh ibn Aḥmad, *Akhbār Makka*, ed. F. Wüstenfeld, Göttingen, 1858; reprinted Beirut: Maktabat al-Khayyāṭ, n.d.

al-Baghdādī, Ismā'īl Bāshā, *Īḍāḥ al-maknūn fī al-dhayl 'alā Kashf al-ẓunūn 'an asāmī al-kutub wa'l-funūn*, 2 vols, Istanbul: Milli Egitim Basimevi, 1945–7.

—— *Hadīyat al-'ārifīn: asmā' al-mu'allifīn wa-āthār al-muṣannifīn*, 2 vols, Istanbul: Milli Egitim Basimevi, 1951–5.

al-Bakrī, Abū'l-Ḥasan Aḥmad ibn 'Abd Allāh, *Kitāb al-anwār*, ms. Vatican, Borg. Ar. no. 125.

—— *al-Anwār wa-miṣbāḥ al-surūr wa'l-afkār*, [Cairo]: Muṣṭafā al-Bābī al-Ḥalabī, 1379 AH/1959 CE.

al-Bakrī, Muḥammad 'Alī ibn 'Allān, *Kitāb al-Nafaḥāt al-'anbarīya fī mawlid sayyid al-barīya*, ms. Sanaa, Awqāf Library.

Banīs, Muḥammad ibn Aḥmad, *Lawāmi' anwār al-kawkab al-durrī fī sharḥ Hamzīyat al-imām al-Būṣīrī*, printed in the margins of Muḥammad ibn Qāsim Jasūs, *Sharḥ al-Shamā'il al-Tirmidhīya*, 2 vols, Cairo: Maktabat wa-maṭba'at Muḥammad 'Alī Ṣibīḥ wa-Awlādihi, 1346 AH/1927 CE.

al-Bannānī, Fatḥ Allāh, *Fatḥ allāh fī mawlid khayr khalq allāh*, [Cairo]: al-Maṭba'a al-Ḥamīdīya al-Miṣrīya, 1323 AH/[1095–6 CE].

al-Bantanī, Muḥammad Nawawī, *Madārij al-ṣu'ūd ilā iktisā' al-burūd*, n.p., n.d.

al-Barzanjī, Ja'far ibn Ismā'īl, *al-Kawkab al-anwar 'alā 'Iqd al-jawhar fī mawlid al-nabī al-azhar*, n.p.: al-Maṭba'a al-Wahbīya, 1290 AH/[1873–4 CE].

al-Bayhaqī, Abū Bakr Aḥmad ibn al-Ḥusayn, *Dalā'il al-nubūwa wa-ma'rifat aḥwāl ṣāḥib al-sharī'a*, ed. Aḥmad Ṣaqr, [Cairo]: al-Majlis al-A'lā li'l-Shu'ūn al-Islāmīya, Lajnat Iḥyā' Ummahāt Kutub al-Sunna, 1389 AH/1970 CE.

—— *Shu'ab al-īmān*, 7 vols, ed. Muḥammad al-sa'īd Zaghlūl, Beirut: Dār al-Kutub al-'Ilmīya, 1410 AH/1990 CE.

al-Bayṭār, 'Abd al-Razzāq, *Ḥilyat al-bashar fī ta'rīkh al-qarn al-thālith 'ashar*, 3 vols, Damascus: Majma' al-Lugha al-'Arabīya, 1961–3.

al-Bīrūnī, *The Chronology of Ancient Nations*, trans. and ed. C. Edward Sachau, London: Published for the Oriental Translation Fund of Great Britain and Ireland by William H. Allen and Co., 1879.

al-Bukhārī, Muḥammad ibn Ismā'īl, al-Qushayrī, Muslim ibn al-Ḥajjāj, al-Tirmidhī, Muḥammad ibn *et al.*, *Jam' jawāmi' al-aḥādīth wa'l-asānīd*, 12 vols, Vaduz, Liechtenstein: Thesaurus Islamicus Foundation, 2000.

Daḥlān, Aḥmad ibn Zaynī, *al-Durar al-sanīya fī al-radd 'alā al-wahhābīya*, Cairo: Dār Jawāmi' al-Kalim, n.d.

—— *al-Sīra al-nabawīya wa'l-āthār al-muḥammadīya*, printed in the margins of 'Alī ibn Burhān al-Dīn al-Ḥalabī, *Insān al-'uyūn fī sīrat al-amīn al-ma'mūn*, [Cairo]: Maṭba'at Muḥammad Efendī Muṣṭafā, n.d.

al-Dardīr, Aḥmad ibn Muḥammad, *al-Sharḥ al-kabīr*, in *Ḥāshiyat al-Dasūqī 'alā al-Sharḥ al-kabīr*, 4 vols, 'Īsā al-Bābī al-Ḥalabī, n.d.

—— *al-Sharḥ al-ṣaghīr 'alā Aqrab al-masālik ilā madhhab al-imām Mālik*, 4 vols, Cairo: Dār al-Ma'ārif bi-Miṣr, n.d.

al-Dasūqī, Muḥammad Ṣāliḥ ibn Muḥammad, *al-Manhal al-awfā fī mīlād al-muṣṭafā*, ms. Damascus, Asad Library, no. 11402.

al-Daylamī, Shīrawayh ibn Shahradār, *al-Firdaws bi-ma'thūr al-khiṭāb*, 6 vols, Beirut: Dār al-Kutub al-'Ilmīya, 1406 AH/1986 CE.

al-Dhahabī, Muḥammad ibn Aḥmad, *Mīzān al-i'tidāl fī naqd al-rijāl*, 4 vols, ed. 'Alī Muḥammad al-Bijāwī, Cairo: 'Īsā al-Bābī al-Ḥalabī wa-Shurakā'uhu, 1388 AH/ 1963 CE.

al-Dimyāṭī, al-Qāḍī, *Mawlid al-rasūl al-karīm*, ms. Cairo, Dār al-Kutub, Ta'rīkh no. 280.

al-Fārisī, 'Umāra ibn Wathīma al-Fasawī, *Kitāb bad' al-khalq wa-qiṣaṣ al-anbiyā'*, in Raid Georges Khoury, *Les légendes prophétiques dans l'Islam depuis le 1er jusqu'au IIIe siècle de l'Hégire d'après le Manuscript d'Abū Rifā'a 'Umāra b. Wathīma b. Mūsā b. al-Furāt al Fārisī al-Fasawī Kitāb bad' al-Khalq wa-Qiṣaṣ al-Anbiyā'*, Wiesbaden: Otto Harrassowitz, 1978.

al-Fāsī, Taqī al-Dīn Muḥammad ibn Aḥmad, *Shifā' al-gharām bi-akhbār al-balad al-ḥarām*, 2 vols, Beirut: Dār al-Kutub al-'Ilmīya, n.d.

al-Fattāl, Muḥammad ibn al-Ḥasan, *Rawḍat al-wā'iẓīn*, Najaf: al-Maktaba al-Ḥaydarīya, 1386 AH/1966 CE.

Fawzī Efendī, Muḥammad, *Qudus al-kalām fī mawlid al-nabī 'alayhi al-salām*, ms. Cairo, Dār al-Kutub, Tārīkh Ṭal'at no. 1996.

al-Ghayṭī, Najm al-Dīn, *Mawlid al-nabī*, ms. Cairo, Dār al-Kutub, Tārīkh no. 645.

al-Ghazālī, Abū Ḥāmid Muḥammad ibn Muḥammad, *Nafkh al-rūḥ wa'l-taswiya*, ed. Aḥmad Ḥijāzī al-Saqā, [Cairo]: Maktabat al-Madīna al-Munawwara, 1399 AH/1979 CE.

—— *Iḥyā' 'ulūm al-dīn*, 5 vols, Beirut: Dār al-Fikr, 1414 AH/1994 CE.

al-Ghazzī, Najm al-Dīn, *al-Kawākib al-sā'ira bi-a'yān al-mi'a al-'āshira*, 3 vols, Beirut: Manshūrāt Dār al-Āfāq al-Jadīda, 1979.

al-Ḥaḍrāwī, Aḥmad ibn Muḥammad, *Nuzhat al-fikar fīmā maḍā min al-ḥawādith wa'l-'ibar*, 2 vols, Damascus: Manshūrāt Wizārat al-Thaqāfa, 1996.

Ḥajjī Khalīfa, *Kashf al-ẓunūn 'an asāmī al-kutub wa'l-funūn*, 2 vols, Istanbul: Milli Egitim Basimevi, 1360–2 AH/1941–3 CE.

al-Hakārī Abū'l-Ḥusayn, 'Alī ibn Aḥmad ibn Yūsuf al-Qurashī al-Umawī, *Kitāb Hadīyat al-aḥyā' ilā'l-amwāt wa-mā yaṣilu ilayhim min al-thawāb 'alā mamarr al-awqāt*, ms. Sanaa, Western Library, Majmū' no. 84, 26a–31b.

al-Ḥalabī, 'Alī ibn Burhān al-Dīn Ibrāhīm, *Insān al-'uyūn fī sīrat al-amīn al-ma'mūn*, 3 vols, [Cairo]: Maṭba'at Muḥammad Efendī Muṣṭafā, n.d.

al-Ḥalabī, Ibrāhīm ibn Muḥammad, al-*Qawl al-tamām [fī al-qiyām] 'inda dhikr wilādatihi 'alayhi al-salām*, ms. Berlin, Staatsbibliothek, Ahlwardt no. 9546, 287^{B}, 293^{B}.

al-Ḥallāq, Aḥmad al-Budayrī, *Ḥawādith Dimashq al-yawmīya*, [Cairo]: al-Jam'īya al-Miṣrīya li'l-Dirāsāt al-Tārīkhīya, 1959.

al-Ḥallāq, al-Shaykh Qāsim al-Shāfi'ī al-Qādirī, *Mawrid al-nāhil bi-mawlid al-nabī al-kāmil*, ms. Damascus, Asad Library, no. 11400.

al-Ḥasanī, 'Abd al-Ḥayy ibn Fakhr al-Dīn, *al-I'lām bi-man fī ta'rīkh al-Hind min al-a'lām*, 8 vols in 3, Beirut: Dār Ibn Ḥazm, 1420 AH/1999 CE.

al-Hāshimī, Abū'l-Ḥasanayn 'Abd Allāh ibn 'Abd al-Raḥman al-Ḥasanī al-Makkī, *al-Iḥtifāl bi'l-mawlid al-nabawī bayna mu'ayyidīn wa-mu'āriḍīn*, n.p., 1417 AH/1996 CE.

al-Ḥaṭṭāb al-Ru'aynī, Muḥammad ibn Muḥammad, *Mawāhib al-jalīl li-sharḥ Mukhtaṣar Khalīl*, 8 vols, ed. Zakarīyā 'Umayrāt, Beirut: Dār al-Kutub al-'Ilmīya, 1416 AH/1995 CE.

al-Hijrasī, Muḥammad ibn Khalīl, *Kitāb al-Manẓar al-bahī fī ṭāli' mawlid al-nabī wa-mā yaṭba'uhu min a'māl al-mawlid wa-ḥukm al-qiyām 'inda dhikr mawlidihi 'alayhi al-ṣalāt wa'l-salām*, [Cairo]: al-Maṭba' al-'Ilmī, 1312 AH/[1895 CE].

al-Ḥimṣī al-Baṣīr, 'Abduh, *Mawlid al-nabī*, n.p., n.d.

al-Ḥurayfīsh, Shaykh, *al-Rawḍ al-fā'iq fī'l-mawā'iẓ wa'l-raqā'iq*, [Cairo]: Maktabat al-Jumhūrīya al-'Arabīya, n.d.

Ibn 'Abbād, *Lettres de Direction Spirituelle, Collection Majeur (ar-Rasā'il al-kubrā)*, ed. Kenneth L. Honerkamp, Beirut: Dar el-Machreq, 2005.

Ibn 'Abd al-Salām, 'Izz al-Dīn, *al-Qawā'id al-kubrā al-mawsūm bi-Qawā'id al-aḥkām fī iṣlāḥ al-anām*, 2 vols, ed. Nazīh Kamāl Ḥammād and 'Uthmān Jum'a Ḍamīrīya, Damascus: Dār al-Qalam, 1421 AH/2000 CE.

Ibn Abī Ḥajala, Aḥmad ibn Yaḥyā, *Sukurdān al-sulṭān*, ed. 'Alī Muḥammad 'Umar, Cairo: Maktabat al-Khānjī, 1421 AH/2001 CE.

Ibn 'Ābidīn, Muḥammad Amīn, *Ḥāshiyat Radd al-muḥtār 'alā al-Durr al-mukhtār: sharḥ Tanwīr al-abṣār*, 8 vols, Cairo: Sharikat Maktabat wa-Maṭba'at Muṣṭafā al-Bābī al-Ḥalabī wa-Awlādihi, second printing, 1386 AH/1966 CE.

Ibn 'Ammār, Abū'l-'Abbās Aḥmad, *Nubdha min al-kitāb al-musammā Niḥlat al-labīb bi-akhbār al-riḥla ilā al-ḥabīb*, Algiers: Maṭba'at al-Fūntāna, 1320 AH/1902 CE.

Ibn al-'Arabī, Muḥyī al-Dīn, *Mawlid al-nabī*, ms. Istanbul, Süleymaniye, Ashir Efendi no. 434.

Ibn al-Athīr, 'Alī ibn Muḥammad, *al-Kāmil fī'l-ta'rīkh*, 13 vols, Beirut: Dār Ṣādir, 1386 AH/1966 CE.

Ibn 'Aydarūs, 'Abd al-Qādir, *Ta'rīkh al-nūr al-sāfir 'an akhbār al-qarn al-'āshir*, n.p., n.d.

Ibn Bābawayh al-Qummī, *Amālī al-Ṣadūq*, Najaf: Manshūrāt al-Maṭba'a al-Ḥaydarīya, 1379 AH/1970 CE.

Ibn Bāz, 'Abd al-'Azīz ibn 'Abd Allāh, Ibn 'Uthaymīn, Muḥammad, and 'Abd Allāh Ibn Jabrīn, 'Abd Allāh, *Fatāwā islāmīya*, 3 vols, Beirut: Dār al-Qalam, 1408 AH/1988 CE.

Ibn Diḥya, Abūl-Khaṭṭāb, *al-Ibtihāj fī aḥādīth al-mi'rāj*, ed. Rif'at Fawzī 'Abd al-Muṭṭalib, Cairo: Maktabat al-Khānjī, 1417 AH/1996 CE.

Ibn Diḥya, Abūl-Khaṭṭāb, *Adā' mā wajab min bayān waḍ' al-waḍḍā'īn fī rajab*, Beirut: al-Maktab al-Islāmī, 1419 AH/1998 CE.

—— *Nihāyat al-sūl fī khaṣā'iṣ al-rasūl*, ed. Ma'mūn al-Ṣāghirjī and Muḥammad Adīb al-Jādir, Damascus: Dār al-Bashā'ir, 1420 AH/1999 CE.

Ibn Ḥabīb, *Mawlid al-nabī*, ms. Berlin, Staatsbibliothek, Ahlwardt no. 2617, 76b-83a.

—— *Mawlid al-nabī*, ms. Berlin, Staatsbibliothek, Ahlwardt no. 2617, 83a-92a.

—— *Mawlid karīm badī'*, ms. Berlin, Staatsbibliothek, Ahlwardt no. 2617, 92a-94b.

Ibn Ḥajar al-'Asqalānī, *al-Durar al-kāmina fī a'yān al-mi'a al-thāmina*, 4 vols, Beirut: Dār al-Jīl, n.d.

—— *al-Iṣāba fī tamyīz al-ṣaḥāba*, 4 vols, Baghdad: Maktabat al-Muthannā, n.d.

—— *Fatḥ al-bārī bi-sharḥ Ṣaḥīḥ al-Bukhārī*, 28 vols in 14, ed. Muḥammad 'Abd al-Mu'ṭī, Mustafā Muḥammad al-Harāwī, and Tāhā 'Abd al-Ra'ūf Sa'd, [Cairo]: Maktabat al-Kullīyāt al-Azharīya, 1398 AH/1977–8 CE.

Ibn Ḥajar al-Haytamī, *al-Fatāwā al-ḥadīthīya*, [Cairo]: Muṣṭafā al-Bābī al-Ḥalabī, 1356 AH/1937 CE.

—— *al-Fatāwā al-kubrā al-fiqhīya*, 4 vols, ed. 'Abd al-Laṭīf 'Abd al-Raḥmān, Beirut: Dār al-Kutub al-'Ilmīya, 1417 AH/1997 CE.

—— *Itmām al-ni'ma al-kubrā 'alā al-'ālam bi-mawlid sayyid wuld Ādam*, ed. 'Abd al-'Azīz Sayyid Hāshim al-Ghazūlī, Beirut: Dār al-Kutub al-'Ilmīya, 1422 AH/ 2001 CE.

Ibn al-Ḥājj, *al-Madkhal*, 4 vols in 2, [Cairo]: Sharikat wa-Maṭba'at Muṣṭafā al-Bābī al-Ḥalabī wa-Awlādihi, 1380 AH/1960 CE.

Ibn Ḥibbān al-Bustī, Muḥammad, *Kitāb al-thiqāt*, 9 vols, Haydarabad: Dā'irat al-Ma'ārif al-'Uthmānīya, 1393–1403 AH/1973–83 CE.

—— *al-Sīra al-nabawīya*, 6 vols in 3, ed. 'Abd al-Salām 'Allūsh, Beirut: al-Maktab al-Islāmī, 1420 AH/2000 CE.

Ibn Hishām, 'Abd al-Malik, *al-Sīra al-nabawīya*, Beirut: Dār al-Jīl, 1411 AH/1991 CE.

Ibn al-'Imād al-Ḥanbalī, *Shadharāt al-dhahab fī akhbār man dhahab*, Beirut: Dār al-Masīra, 1399 AH/1979 CE.

Ibn Jābir al-Andalusī, Muḥammad, *Mawlid al-nabī*, ms. Istanbul, Süleymaniye no. 344/1.

Ibn al-Jawzī, Abū'l-Faraj 'Abd al-Raḥmān, *al-Wafā' bi-aḥwāl al-Muṣṭafā*, 2 vols, Riyadh: al-Mu'assasa al-Sa'īdīya bi'l-Riyāḍ, n.d.

—— (attributed), *Mawlid al-nabī*, Princeton University Arabic manuscripts, Third Series, no. 209.

—— (attributed), *Sharḥ faḍā'il al-mawlid al-nabī* [*sic*], ms. Damascus, Asad Library, no. 11044.

Ibn al-Jazarī, Muḥammad ibn Muḥammad, *al-Mawlid al-Kabīr*, ms. London, British Library, no. OR 3608.

—— *Kitāb 'Urf al-ta'rīf bi'l-mawlid al-sharīf*, Princeton University Islamic manuscripts, Garrett Yehuda no. 225.

Ibn Jubayr, Muḥammad ibn Aḥmad, *Riḥlat Ibn Jubayr*, Beirut: Dār Ṣādir Dār Bayrūt, 1384 AH/1964 CE.

Ibn Kathīr, Ismā'īl ibn 'Umar, *Mawlid rasūl allāh*, ed. Ṣalāḥ al-Dīn al-Munajjid, Beirut: Dār al-Kitāb al-Jadīd, n.d.

—— *al-Bidāya wa'l-nihāya*, Beirut: Dār al-Fikr, 1402 AH/1982 CE.

Ibn Khallikān, Aḥmad ibn Muḥammad, *Wafayāt al-a'yān wa-anbā' abnā' al-zamān*, 8 vols, ed. Iḥsān 'Abbās, Beirut: Dār al-Thaqāfa, n.d.

Ibn Makkīya, Aḥmad ibn 'Abd al-Raḥmān, *Durar al-biḥār fī mawlid al-mukhtār*, ms. Cairo, Dār al-Kutub, Ta'rīkh no. 3807.

Ibn Manīʻ, ʻAbd Allāh ibn Sulaymān, *Ḥiwār maʻa al-Mālikī fī radd munkarātihi wa-ḍalālātihi*, Riyadh: al-Riʼāsa al-ʻāmma li-idārat al-buḥūth al-ʻilmīya wa'l-iftāʼ wa'l-daʻwa wa'l-irshād, 1403 AH/1983 CE.

Ibn Manẓūr, Muḥammad ibn Mukarram, *Mukhtaṣar Taʼrīkh madīnat Dimashq li-Ibn ʻAsākir*, 29 vols, ed. Maʼmūn al-Ṣāghirjī, Damascus: Dār al-Fikr, 1404–8 AH/1984–8 CE.

Ibn al-Mulaqqin, ʻUmar ibn ʻAlī, *Ṭabaqāt al-awliyāʼ*, ed. Nūr al-Dīn Shuraybah, Cairo: Maktabat al-Khānjī bi'l-Qāhira, 1393 AH/1973 CE.

Ibn al-Nadīm, *al-Fihrist*, ed. Yūsuf ʻAlī Ṭawīl, Beirut: Dār al-Kutub al-ʻIlmīya, 1416 AH/ 1996 CE.

Ibn Nāṣir al-Dīn al-Dimashqī, *Mawrid al-ṣādī fī mawlid al-hādī*, ms. Dublin, Chester Beatty, no. 4658.

—— *Salwat al-kaʼīb bi-wafāt al-ḥabīb*, ed. Ṣāliḥ Yūsuf Maʻtūq, Dubai: Dār al-Buḥūth li'l-Dirāsāt al-Islāmīya wa-Iḥyāʼ al-Turāth, n.d.

—— *Minhāj al-salāma fī mīzān al-qiyāma*, ed. Mashʻal ibn Bānī al-Jabrīn al-Muṭayrī, Beirut: Dār Ibn Ḥazm, 1416 AH/1996 CE.

—— *Majmūʻ fīhi rasāʼil li'l-ḥāfiẓ Ibn Nāṣir al-Dīn al-Dimashqī*, Beirut: Dār Ibn Ḥazm, 1422 AH/2001 CE.

Ibn Qāsim, ʻAbd al-Raḥmān ibn Muḥammad, *al-Durar al-sanīya fī'l-ajwiba al-najdīya*, 6 vols, Beirut: Dār al-ʻArabīya li'l-Ṭibāʻa wa'l-Nashr, 1402 AH/1982 CE.

Ibn al-Qayyim al-Jawzīya, *Kitāb al-rūḥ*, Haydarabad: Maṭbaʻat Majlis Dāʼirat al-Maʻārif al-ʻUthmānīya, 1357 AH/[1938–9 CE].

—— *Iʻlām al-muwaqqiʻīn ʻan rabb al-ʻālamīn*, 4 vols, ed. Ṭāhā ʻAbd al-Raʼūf Saʻd, Cairo: Maktabat al-Kullīyāt al-Azharīya, 1388 AH/1968 CE.

Ibn Rajab al-Ḥanbalī, *Kitāb laṭāʼif al-maʻārif fīmā li-mawāsim al-ʻām min al-waẓāʼif*, Beirut: al-Maktab al-Islāmī, 1414 AH/1993 CE.

Ibn Saʻd, Muḥammad, *Biographien Muhammeds, seiner Gefährten und der späteren Träger des Islams, bis zum Jahre 230 der Flucht*, 9 vols in 15, ed. Edward Sachau, Leiden: E.J. Brill, 1904–40.

Ibn Ṭawq, *al-Taʻlīq*, 3 vols, Damascus: al-Maʻhad al-Faransī li'l-Dirāsāt al-ʻArabīya bi-Dimashq, 2000.

Ibn Ṭāwūs, ʻAlī ibn Mūsā, *al-Yaqīn bi'khtiṣāṣ mawlānā ʻAlī bi'imrat al-muʼminīn*, Beirut: Muʼassasat al-Thaqalayn, 1410 AH/1989 CE.

—— *Iqbāl al-aʻmāl*, Beirut: Muʼassasat al-Aʻlamī li'l-Maṭbūʻāt, 1417 AH/1996 CE.

Ibn Taymīya, Aḥmad ibn ʻAbd al-Ḥalīm, *Majmūʻ fatāwā shaykh al-islām Aḥmad ibn Taymīya*, 37 vols, collected and arranged by ʻAbd al-Raḥmān ibn Muḥammad ibn Qāsim al-ʻĀṣimī al-Najdī, n.p., n.d.

—— *Fatwā fī'l-qiyām wa'l-alqāb*, in *Rasāʼil wa-nuṣūṣ*, vol. 3, ed. Ṣalāḥ al-Dīn Munajjid, Beirut: Dār al-Kitāb al-Jadīd, 1963.

—— *Iqtiḍāʼ al-ṣirāṭ al-mustaqīm li-mukhālafat aṣḥāb al-jaḥīm*, 2 vols, Riyadh: Dār al-ʻĀṣima, 1419 AH/1998 CE.

Ibn Ṭūlūn al-Ṣāliḥī, Muḥammad ibn ʻAlī, *al-Fulk al-mashḥūn fī aḥwāl Muḥammad ibn Ṭūlūn*, ed. Muḥammad Khayr Ramaḍān Yūsuf, Beirut: Dār ibn Ḥazm, 1416 AH/1996 CE.

—— *Mufākahat al-khillān fī ḥawādith al-zamān*, Beirut: Dār al-Kutub al-ʻIlmīya, 1418 AH/1998 CE.

al-ʻIrāqī, Abū Zurʻa, *Sharḥ al-ṣadr bi-dhikr laylat al-qadr*, ed. Muḥammad Subḥī Ḥallāq, Beirut: Muʼassasat al-Rayyān, 1412 AH/1992 CE.

ʻIyāḍ ibn Mūsā al-Yaḥṣubī, al-Qāḍī, *al-Shifā bi-taʻrīf ḥuqūq al-muṣṭafā*, 2 vols, ed. ʻAlī Muḥammad al-Bijāwī, [Cairo]: ʻĪsā al-Bābī al-Ḥalabī wa-Shurakāʼuhu, n.d.

al-Ja'barī, Ibrāhīm ibn 'Umar, *Kitāb maw'id al-kirām fī mawlid al-nabī 'alayhi al-salām*, ms. Damascus, Asad Library, no. 4771.

al-Jabartī, 'Abd al-Raḥmān ibn Ḥasan, *'Ajā'ib al-āthār fī'l-tarājim wa'l-akhbār*, 4 vols, Cairo: al-Hay'a al-'Āmma li-Dār al-Kutub wa'l-Wathā'iq al-Qawmīya, 1997–8.

Kaḥḥāla, 'Umar Riḍā, *Mu'jam al-mu'allifīn*, 4 vols, Beirut: Mu'assasat al-Risāla, 1414 AH/1993 CE.

al-Karājikī, Muḥammad ibn 'Alī, *Kanz al-fawā'id*, 2 vols, Beirut: Dār al-Aḍwā', 1405 AH/1985 CE.

al-Kattānī, Muḥammad ibn Ja'far, *al-Yumn wa'l-is'ād bi-mawlid khayr al-'ibād*, Casablanca: al-Maktaba al-Sharqīya, 1345 AH/[1926–7 CE].

al-Kāzarūnī, Muḥammad ibn Mas'ūd, *al-Muntaqā fī siyar al-nabī al-muṣṭafā*, 4 vols, ed. Luṭfī Manṣūr, Kafr Qari', [Israel]: Markaz Dirāsāt al-Adab al-'Arabī, 1422 AH/2001 CE.

al-Kharkūshī, 'Abd al-Malik ibn Muḥammad, *Kitāb Sharaf al-nabī*, ms. London, British Library, no. OR 3014.

—— *Sharaf al-Muṣṭafā*, 6 vols, ed. Nabīl ibn Hāshim Bā 'Alawī, Mecca: Dār al-Bashā'ir al-Islāmīya, 1424 AH/2003 CE.

al-Khaṭīb al-Baghdādī, Aḥmad ibn 'Alī, *Ta'rīkh Baghdād aw madīnat al-salām*, 14 vols, Beirut: Dār al-Kitāb al-'Arabī, n.d.

al-Khayyāṭ al-Yamanī, 'Abd al-Raḥmān ibn 'Abd al-Mun'im, *Mawlid*, ms. Cairo, Dār al-Kutub, Tārīkh no. 218.

al-Khurashī, Muḥammad ibn 'Abd Allāh, *Ḥāshiyat al-Khurashī 'alā Mukhtaṣar sayyidī Khalīl*, Beirut: Dār al-Kutub al-'Ilmīya, 1417 AH/1997 CE.

al-Khwānsārī, Muḥammad Bāqir, *Rawḍāt al-jannāt fī aḥwāl al-'ulamā' wa'l-sādāt*, 8 vols, Qum, n.d.

al-Kisā'ī, Muḥammad ibn 'Abd Allāh, *Qiṣaṣ al-anbiyā'*, Leiden: Brill, 1922.

al-Laqānī, 'Abd al-Salām ibn Ibrāhīm, *Tarwīḥ al-fu'ād bi-mawlid khayr al-'ibād*, ms. Cairo, Dār al-Kutub, Majāmī' mīm no. 6, 4bff.

Maḥfūẓ, 'Alī, *al-Ibdā' fī maḍārr al-ibtidā'*, Cairo: al-Maktaba al-Maḥmūdīya al-Tijārīya, n.d.

al-Majlis al-A'lā li'l-Shu'ūn al-Islāmīya, *al-Mawlid al-nabawī al-sharīf*, Hadīyat Majallat *Minbar al-Islām*, [Cairo], 1398 AH/[1977–8 CE].

al-Majlisī, Muḥammad Bāqir, *Biḥār al-anwār*, 111 vols, Tehran, d. 1110 AH/1698 CE.

Makhlūf, Ḥasanayn Muḥammad, *Fatāwā shar'īya wa-buḥūth islāmīya*, second printing, Cairo: Muṣṭafā al-Bābī al-Ḥalabī, 1385 AH/1965 CE.

al-Makkī, Abū Ṭālib, *'Ilm al-qulūb*, ed. 'Abd al-Qādir Aḥmad 'Aṭā', Cairo: Maktabat al-Qāhira, 1384 AH/1964 CE.

al-Maktabī, Nadhīr Muḥammad, *al-Inshād wa'l-munshidīn: dirāsa adabīya shar'īya*, Damascus: Dār al-Maktabī, 1420 AH/2000 CE.

al-Mālikī al-Makkī al-Ḥasanī, Muḥammad ibn 'Alawī, *al-Dhakhā'ir al-Muḥammadīya*, notes and commentary by Jamāl Fārūq Jibrīl Maḥmūd al-Daqqāq, Cairo: Dār Jawāmi' al-Kalim, n.d.

—— *Bāqa 'aṭira min ṣiyagh al-mawālid wa'l-madā'iḥ al-nabawīya al-karīma*, n.p., 1403 AH/1983 CE.

—— *Mafāhīm yajib an tuṣaḥḥaḥ*, Cairo: Dār al-Insān, 1405 AH/1985 CE.

al-Mālikī, Muḥammad 'Alī ibn Ḥusayn, *Tahdhīb al-furūq wa'l-qawā'id al-sannīya fī al-asrār al-fiqhīya*, printed in the margin of Aḥmad ibn Idrīs al-Qarāfī, *Anwār al-burūq fī anwā' al-furūq*, 4 vols, ed. Khalīl al-Manṣūr, Beirut: Dār al-Kutub al-'Ilmīya, 1418 AH/1998 CE.

al-Māliqī al-Andalusī, Abū'l-Ḥasan 'Alī ibn 'Abd Allāh al-Nubāhī, *Ta'rīkh quḍāt al-andalus*, known as *Kitāb al-marqaba al-'ulyā fī-man yastaḥiqq al-qaḍā' wa'l-futyā*, ed. E. Levy-Provencal, Cairo: Dār al-Kātib al-Miṣrī, 1948 CE.

al-Mas'ūdī, 'Alī ibn al-Ḥusayn (attributed), *Ithbāt al-waṣīya li'l-imām 'Alī ibn abī Ṭālib*, Beirut: Dār al-Uṣūl, 1409 AH/1988 CE.

al-Mawsū'a al-fiqhīya, 41 vols (ongoing), Kuwait: Wizārat al-Awqāf wa'l-shu'ūn al-islāmīya, 1414 AH/1993 CE.

al-Miḥḍār, Ḥāmid, *al-Iḥtifāl bi-dhikr al-ni'am wājib*, n.p.: Maktabat al-Muṭī'ī, n.d.

al-Mīrghanī, Muḥammad 'Uthmān, *Mawlid al-nabī al-Asrār al-rabbānīya*, Ta'izz , Ṣan'ā', Ḥudayda: Maktabat Dār al-Fikr, n.d.

Miskawayh, Aḥmad ibn Muḥammad, *al-Qism al-akhīr min Kitāb Tajārib al-Umam*, in *The Eclipse of the 'Abbasid Caliphate: Original Chronicles of the Fourth Islamic Century*, ed. and trans. H.F. Amedroz and D.S. Margoliouth, vol. 1, Oxford: Basil Blackwell, 1920.

al-Miṣrī, Aḥmad ibn Naqīb, *Reliance of the traveler*, trans. and ed. Nuh Ha Mim Keller, rev. edn, Beltsville, Maryland: Amana Publications, 1994.

al-Mubārak, Aḥmad 'Abd al-'Azīz, "Ḥukm al-iḥtifāl bi-mawlid al-rasūl," *Manār al-islām* 6, Jumādā al-Ākhira, 1401 AH/April–May 1981, pp. 6–11.

Mubārak, 'Alī Bāshā, *al-Khiṭaṭ al-tawfīqīya al-jadīda li-miṣr al-qāhira*, 11 vols, Cairo: al-Hay'a al-Miṣrīya al-'Āmma li'l-Kutub, 1983; facsimile of the second printing, Cairo, 1970.

al-Mufīd, Muḥammad ibn Muḥammad, *Masārr al-shī'a*, in *Muṣannafāt al-shaykh al-Mufīd*, al-Mu'tamar al-'Ālamī li-Alfīyat al-Shaykh al-Mufīd, 1413 AH, vol. 7, pp. 1–63.

Muḥammad al-Majdhūb, *Majmū'a taḥtawī 'alā qiṣṣat al-mi'rāj al-musammā bi'l-Jumāna al-yatīma wa'l-Nūr al-sāṭi' fī mawlid al-nabī al-jāmi'* ... [etc.], [Cairo]: Muṣṭafā al-Bābī al-Ḥalabī, 1339 AH/[1920–1 CE].

Muḥsin al-Ḥusaynī al-'Āmilī, *Mawlid al-nabī*, Damascus, 1338 AH/[1919–20 CE].

al-Munayyar, Muḥammad ibn 'Abd al-Salām, *al-Fayḍ al-midrār 'alā mawlid al-mukhtār*, [Cairo]: Maktabat al-Ādāb, 1415 AH/1994 CE.

Murād, 'Abd al-Karīm, and al-'Amrawī, 'Abd al-Ḥayy, *al-Taḥdhīr min al-ightirār bi-mā jā'a fī kitāb al-Ḥiwār*, Fez, 1404 AH/1984 CE.

al-Murādī, Muḥammad Khalīl, *Silk al-durar fī a'yān al-qarn al-thānī 'ashar*, 4 vols in 2, Beirut: Dār al-Bashā'ir al-Islāmīya, 1408 AH/1988 CE.

Muslim ibn Ḥajjāj al-Qushayrī, *Ṣaḥīḥ Muslim bi-sharḥ al-imām Muḥyī al-Dīn al-Nawawī al-Minhāj sharḥ Ṣaḥīḥ Muslim ibn al-Ḥajjāj*, 18 vols in 9, Beirut: Dār al-Ma'rifa, 1414 AH/1994 CE.

al-Nabhānī, Yūsuf ibn Ismā'īl, *al-Hamzīya al-alfīya al-musammā ṭaybat al-gharrā' fī madḥ sayyid al-anbiyā'*, Beirut: al-Maṭba'a al-Adabīya, 1314 AH/[1896–7 CE].

—— *Jawāhir al-biḥār fī faḍā'il al-nabī al-mukhtār*, 4 vols, ed. Muḥammad Amīn al-Ḍannāwī, Beirut: Dār al-Kutub al-'Ilmīya, 1419 AH/1998 CE.

al-Najāshi, Aḥmad ibn 'Alī, *Kitāb al-rijāl*, n.p.: Markarz-i Nashr-i Kitāb, n.d.

al-Nawawī, Yaḥyā ibn Sharaf, *al-Tarkhīṣ bi'l-qiyām li-dhawī al-faḍl wa'l-mazīya min ahl al-islām*, ed. Aḥmad Rātib Ḥammūsh, Damascus: Dār al-Fikr, 1402 AH/1982 CE.

Nūr al-Dīn 'Alī ibn Nāṣir al-Makkī, *'Unwān al-sharīf*, in *Mawlid sharaf al-'ālamayn*, distributed by Dār al-Fikr, n.p., n.d.

al-Qalyūbī, 'Abd Rabbih ibn Sulaymān, *Fayḍ al-wahhāb fī bayān ahl al-ḥaqq wa-man ḍalla 'an al-ṣawāb*, 6 vols, n.p.: Dār al-Qawmīya al-'Arabīya li'l-Ṭibā'a, 1383 AH/ 1964 CE.

al-Qāri' al-Harawī, 'Alī ibn Sulṭān Muḥammad, *al-Mawrid al-rawī fī mawlid al-nabī wa-nasabihi al-ṭāhir*, ed. Mabrūk Ismā'īl Mabrūk, Cairo: Maktabat al-Qur'ān, n.d.

—— *Adillat mu'taqad Abī Ḥanīfa al-a'ẓam fī abaway al-rasūl 'alayhi al-ṣalāt wa'l-salām*, ed. Mashhūr ibn Ḥasan ibn Salmān, Medina: Maktabat al-Ghurabā' al-Atharīya, 1413 AH/ 1993 CE.

al-Qāri' al-Harawī, *Sharḥ al-fiqh al-akbar li-Abī Ḥanīfa al-Nu'mān*, ed. Marwān Muḥammad al-Sha"ār, Beirut: Dār al-Nafā'is, 1417 AH/1997 CE.

al-Qasṭallānī, Aḥmad ibn Muḥammad, *al-Mawāhib al-ladunīya bi'l-minaḥ al-muḥammadīya*, 4 vols, ed. Ṣāliḥ Aḥmad al-Shāmī, Beirut: al-Maktab al-Islāmī, 1412 AH/1991 CE.

al-Qifṭī, 'Alī ibn Yūsuf, *Inbāh al-ruwāt 'alā anbāh al-nuḥāt*, 4 vols, ed. Muḥammad Abū'l-Faḍl Ibrāhīm, Cairo: Maṭba'at Dār al-Kutub al-Miṣrīya, 1374 AH/1955 CE.

al-Qummī, Shādhān ibn Jibrā'īl, *Kitāb al-faḍā'il*, n.p.: Manshūrāt Maktabat al-'Irfān, n.d.

[al-Qurṭubī] Muḥammad ibn Aḥmad ibn Faraj al-Anṣārī al-Andalusī, *Kitāb al-i'lām bi-mā yajib 'ala al-anām min ma'rifat al-nabī 'alayhi al-salām*, ms. Istanbul, Topkapı no. 6031 M443.

al-Raṣṣā', Muḥammad ibn Qāsim, *Tadhkirat al-muḥibbīn fī asmā' sayyid al-mursalīn*, ed. Muḥammad Riḍwān al-Dāya, Abu Dhabi: al-Majma' al-Thaqāfī, 1423 AH/2002 CE.

al-Rawāḥī, Nāṣir ibn Sālim, *al-Mawlid al-musammā bi'l-nūr al-muḥammadī*, n.p., n.d.

al-Rāzī, al-Fakhr, *al-Tafsīr al-kabīr*, 32 vols in 16, [Tehran], n.p., n.d.

Ri'āsat Idārat al-Buḥūth al-'Ilmīya wa'l-Iftā' wa'l-Da'wa wa'l-lrshād, *Rasā'il fī ḥukm al-iḥtifāl fī'l-mawlid al-nabawī, li-majmū'a min al-'ulamā'*, 2 vols, Riyadh: Dār al-'Āṣima, 1419 AH/1998 CE.

Riḍā, Muḥammad Rashīd, "al-Mawlid al-nabawī," *al-Manār* 7, 1322 AH/1904 CE, p. 395.

—— "Dhikrā al-mawlid al-nabawī," *al-Manār* 19, 1334 AH/1916 CE, pp. 408–25, 473–85, 607–18.

—— "Muqaddima li-dhikrā al-mawlid al-nabawī," *al-Manār* 20, 1335 AH/1917 CE, pp. 23–32.

—— "Radd al-Manār 'alā al-nāqid li-Dhikrā al-mawlid al-nabawī," *al-Manār* 20, 1336 AH/1918 CE, pp. 395–403.

—— "Dhikrā al-mawlid al-nabawī," *al-Manār* 34, 1353 AH/1934 CE, pp. 129–31.

—— *al-Wāfī bi'l-wafayāt*, 3 vols, Wiesbaden: Franz Steiner Verlag, 1962-.

—— *Fatāwā al-imām Muḥammad Rashīd Riḍā*, 6 vols, ed. Ṣalāḥ al-Dīn al-Munajjid and Yūsuf Q. Khūrī, Beirut: Dār al-Kitāb al-Jadīd, 1390 AH/1970 CE.

al-Ṣafadī, Khalīl ibn Aybak, *al-Faḍl al-munīf fī'l-mawlid al-sharīf*, Princeton University Islamic manuscripts, Garrett Yahuda no. 3570.

al-Sakhāwī, Muḥammad ibn 'Abd al-Raḥmān, *al-Ḍaw' al-lāmi' li-ahl al-qarn al-tāsi'*, 12 vols in 6, Beirut: Dār Maktabat al-Ḥayāt, 1394 AH/1974 CE.

—— *al-Qawl al-badī' fī'l-ṣalāt 'alā al-ḥabīb al-shafī'*, Medina: al-Maktaba al-'Ilmīya, 1397 AH/1977 CE.

—— *al-Maqāṣid al-ḥasana fī bayān kathīr min al-aḥādīth al-mushtahira 'alā al-alsina*, Beirut: Dār al-Kutub al-'Ilmīya, 1399 AH/1979 CE.

—— *al-Jawāhir wa'l-durar fī tarjamat Ibn Ḥajar*, 3 vols, ed. Ibrāhīm Bājis 'Abd al-Majīd, Beirut: Dār Ibn Ḥazm, 1419 AH/1999 CE.

al-Ṣāliḥī al-Shāmī, Muḥammad ibn Yūsuf, *Subul al-hudā wa'l-rashād fī sīrat khayr al-'ibād*, 12 vols, ed. 'Ādil Aḥmad 'Abd al-Mawjūd and 'Alī Muḥammad Mu'awwaḍ, Beirut: Dār al-Kutub al-'Ilmīya, 1414 AH/1993 CE.

al-Shāṭibī, Ibrāhīm ibn Mūsā, *Kitāb al-i'tiṣām*, 2 vols in 1, Beirut: Mu'assasat al-Kutub al-Thaqāfīya, 1416 AH/1996 CE.

—— *al-Muwāfaqāt*, 6 vols, ed. Mashhūr ibn Ḥasan Āl Sulaymān, al-Khubar: Dār Ibn 'Affān, 1417 AH/1997 CE.

Shawkānī, Muḥammad ibn 'Alī, *al-Badr al-ṭāli' bi-maḥāsin man ba'd al-qarn al-sābi'*, Damascus: Dār al-Fikr, 1419 AH/1998 CE.

—— *al-Fatḥ al-rabbānī min fatāwā al-imām al-Shawkānī*, 12 vols, ed. Muḥammad Ṣubḥī ibn Ḥasan Ḥallāq, Sanaa: Maktabat al-Jīl al-Jadīd, 1423 AH/2002 CE.

al-Shaykha, Ḥasan, "Fī dhikrā al-mawlid al-nabawī," in *Mawlid sayyidinā Muḥammad, ṣallā allāhu 'alayhi wa-sallam, nabī al-hudā wa-rasūl al-salām*, n.p., [Cairo, 1968], n.d.

al-Shītānī, 'Aṭīya ibn Ibrāhīm, *Mawlid al-muṣṭafā al-'adnānī*, n.p.: al-Maṭba'a al-'Ilmīya, 1311 AH/[1893–4 CE].

al-Subkī, Tāj al-Dīn 'Abd al-Wahhāb ibn 'Abd al-Kāfī, *Ṭabaqāt al-shāfi'īya al-kubrā*, 10 vols, ed. 'Abd al-Fattāḥ Muḥammad Ḥilw and Maḥmūd Muḥammad al-Ṭināḥī, [Cairo]: 'Īsā al-Bābī al-Ḥalabī, n.d.

—— (attributed), *Kitāb sharaf al-anām fī mawlid man ẓallahu al-ghumām*, ms. Cairo, Dār al-Kutub, Ta'rīkh Khalīl Āghā no. 8.

al-Subkī, Taqī al-Dīn 'Alī ibn 'Abd al-Kāfī, *Fatāwā al-Subkī*, 2 vols, Beirut: Dār al-Ma'rifa, n.d.

al-Suhaylī, 'Abd al-Raḥmān, *al-Rawḍ al-unuf fī sharḥ al-Sīra al-nabawīya li-Ibn Hishām*, 7 vols, ed. 'Abd al-Raḥmān al-Wakīl, n.p.: Dār al-Kutub al-Ḥadītha, n.d.

al-Suḥaymī al-Azharī, Aḥmad ibn Muḥammad, *al-Zahr al-fā'iq fī mawlid ashraf al-khalā'iq*, ms. Cairo, Dār al-Kutub, B 27998.

al-Sunaydī, 'Abd al-'Azīz ibn Rāshid, *Mu'jam mā ullifa 'an Makka*, Riyadh: 1420 AH/1999 CE.

al-Suyūṭī, Jalāl al-Dīn 'Abd al-Raḥmān ibn Abī Bakr , *al-Khaṣā'iṣ al-kubrā aw kifāyat al-ṭālib al-labīb fī khaṣā'iṣ al-ḥabīb*, ed. Muḥammad Khalīl Harās, [Cairo]: Dār al-Kutub al-Ḥadīthīya, n.d.

—— *Ḥusn al-muḥāḍara fī ta'rīkh miṣr wa'l-qāhira*, 2 vols, ed. Muḥammad Abū'l-Faḍl Ibrāhīm, Cairo: Dār Iḥyā' al-Kutub al-'Arabīya, 1387 AH/1968 CE.

—— *Taḥdhīr al-khawāṣṣ min akādhīb al-quṣṣāṣ*, ed. Muḥammad al-Ṣabbāgh, n.p.: al-Maktab al-Islāmī, 1392 AH/1972 CE.

—— *al-Ḥāwī li'l-fatāwā*, 2 vols, Beirut: Dār al-Kutub al-'Ilmīya, 1395 AH/1975 CE.

—— *Ḥusn al-maqṣid fī 'amal al-mawlid*, ed. Muṣṭafā 'Abd al-Qādir 'Aṭā', Beirut: Dār al-Kutub al-'Ilmīya, 1405 AH/1985 CE.

—— *al-Rasā'il al-'ashar*, Beirut: Dār al-Kutub al-'Ilmīya, 1409 AH/1989 CE.

al-Ṭabarī, Muḥammad ibn Jarīr, *Ta'rīkh al-Ṭabarī*, 11 vols, ed. Muḥammad Abū'l-Faḍl Ibrāhīm, Beirut: Dār al-Turāth, n.d.

al-Ṭaḥāwī, Aḥmad ibn Muḥammad, *Sharḥ ma'ānī al-āthār*, 4 vols, ed. Muḥammad Zuhrī al-Najjār, Cairo: Maṭba'at al-Anwār al-Muḥammadīya, n.d.

al-Tha'labī, Aḥmad ibn Muḥammad, *Qiṣaṣ al-anbiyā' al-musammā 'Arā'is al-majālis*, Sūsa, Tunisia: Dār al-Ma'ārif, 1989.

al-Ṭihrānī, Āghā Buzurg, *al-Dharī'a ilā taṣānīf al-shī'a*, 26 vols, Beirut: Dār al-Aḍwā', n.d.

al-Tūnisī, Aḥmad Jamāl al-Dīn, *Mawlid al-nabī (ṣ) al-ma'rūf bi'Ikhtiṣār Mawlid al-Barzanjī*, Kano, Nigeria: al-Dār al-Ifrīqīya, n.d.

al-Ṭurṭūshī, Muḥammad ibn al-Walīd, *Kitāb al-ḥawādith wa'l-bida'*, Tunis: al-Maṭba'a al-Rasmīya li'l-Jumhūrīya al-Tūnisīya, 1959.

al-Ṭūsī, Muḥammad ibn al-Ḥasan, *Tahdhīb al-aḥkām fī sharḥ al-Muqni'a li'l-shaykh al-Mufīd*, 10 vols, Beirut: Dār al-Aḍwā', 1406 AH/1985 CE.

'Ulaysh, Muḥammad Aḥmad, *Fatḥ al-'alī al-malik fī'l-fatwā 'alā madhhab al-imām Mālik*, 2 vols, Beirut: Dār al-Ma'rifa, n.d.

al-Wāḥidī, *Bayān faḍā'il mawlid al-nabī*, Princeton Islamic Arabic manuscripts, Third Series, no. 198.

al-Wansharīsī, Aḥmad ibn Yaḥyā, *al-Mi'yār al-mu'rib wa'l-jāmi ' al-mughrib 'an fatāwā ahl ifrīqīya wa'l-andalus wa'l-maghrib*, 13 vols, [Ribāṭ]: Wizārat al-Awqāf wa'l-Shu'ūn al-Islāmīya li'l-Mamlaka al-Maghribīya, 1401 AH/1981 CE.

al-Wāqidī (attributed), *Mawlid al-nabī*, Princeton University Arabic manuscripts, New Series, no. 163.

al-Wazzānī, Abū ʿĪsā al-Mahdī, *al-Nawāzil al-jadīda al-kubrā fīmā li-ahl Fās wa-ghayri-him min al-badw wa'l-qurā*, 12 vols, [Rabat]: al-Mamlaka al-Maghribīya, Wizārat al-Awqāf wa'l-Shu'ūn al-Islāmīya, 1417–21 AH/1996–2000 CE.

Yaḥyā, al-Shaykh, *Rawḥ al-nufūs fī mawlid rūḥ al-nufūs*, ms. London, British Library, no. OR 11083, 148a–78b.

Zaghlūl, Muḥammad Saʿīd, *Mawsūʿat aṭrāf al-ḥadīth al-nabawī al-sharīf*, 11 vols, Beirut: Dār al-Kutub al-ʿIlmīya, n.d.

al-Zamlakānī, Muḥammad ibn ʿAlī, *Mawlid*, ms. Berlin, Staatsbibliothek, Ahlwardt no. 9527.

Zurqānī, Muḥammad ibn ʿAbd al-Bāqī, *Sharḥ al-ʿallāma al-Zurqānī ʿalā al-Mawāhib al-ladunīya bi'l-minaḥ al-muḥammadīya li'l-ʿallāma al-Qasṭallānī*, 12 vols, Beirut: Dār al-Kutub al-ʿIlmīya, 1417 AH/1996 CE.

Index

'Abd Allāh (father of Prophet Muḥammad) 11, 13, 18–20, 25, 30, 55, 61, 127, 185–7
'Abd Allāh ibn Salām 23
'Abd al-Muṭṭalib 12, 18–19, 25, 33–6, 45, 98, 247 n.4
Abdülhamid, Sultan 170
Abraham 13, 18, 34, 36, 54, 87–8, 168, 202, 206, 232 n.199, 236 n.88
Abū Bakr 18, 21, 22, 83, 119, 202, 226 n.66
Abū'l-Bukhturī 6
Abū Ḥanīfa 126
Abū Lahab 106–9, 193–4, 231 n.199, 239 n.13
Abū Shāma 2, 63, 110, 150–3, 160, 167
Abū Ṭālib 11, 128, 243 n.103
Adam 12–26, 34, 38, 40, 81–2, 114, 145–6, 176, 181, 230 n.160, 232 n.3, 239 n.4, 246 n.17, 255 n.157
'Afīfī, 'Abd Allāh 179
Aḥmad I, Bey of Tunis 170
alfiya prayer 149
'Alī ibn Abī Ṭālib 6–7, 114
Āmina 11, 19, 25, 29–39, 41, 43, 45–6, 48–9, 53–4, 60–1, 108, 125–8, 141, 165, 172, 181, 229 n.124
Anderson, Gary 140
angels 11–13, 15–16, 19–21, 24–5, 30, 35, 42, 49, 54–5, 58, 76–7, 82, 85, 87, 94, 138, 157, 235 n.66, 237 n.123
'aqīqa sacrifice 112, 184
Arabian Nights 22
'Arafa 147–8, 152, 155, 167, 248 n.60
'Āshūrā' 5, 64, 97, 110, 113–16, 140, 143, 148–9, 154, 158, 165, 183, 205, 241 n.38, 246 n.22
Āsiya 36–7, 39, 169, 172, 176, 181
Awwary, M.A. 187
'Ayn al-Quḍāt al-Ḥaydarābādī 136–7, 182–3, 198–200
al-'Azafī, Abū'l-'Abbās 10, 51, 56, 77–9, 101, 106–8, 118–19, 139
al-Azhar 169, 184, 188

al-Baghdādī, al-Khaṭīb 6, 29, 165
al-Bājūrī, Ibrāhīm 169
al-Bakrī, Abū'l-Ḥasan 9, 16, 35, 44, 46, 48–9, 54, 56, 57, 81, 165, 181, 208
Banīs, Muḥammad ibn Aḥmad 161–2
al-Bannānī, Fatḥ Allāh 52–3, 85
banquets *see* food
al-Bantanī, Muḥammad Nawawī 85, 94
baraka 42, 47, 50, 61, 82–4, 86, 88, 91, 108, 147, 166
al-Barzanjī, Ja'far ibn Ḥasan 61, 81, 85, 108, 127, 133, 134, 169
al-Barzanjī, Ja'far ibn Ismā'īl 169, 200
al-Bayhaqī, Aḥmad ibn al-Ḥusayn 12, 35, 43–6, 54, 117–18, 143
Bell, Joseph Norment 123
bequests 73
Berkey, Jonathan 23
Betteridge, Anne H. 212
bid'a 119, 129, 130, 133, 135, 138, 145, 150–1, 157, 158, 170, 173, 178, 182–3, 189–91, 200, 203
blessings, invoked upon Prophet *see ṣalāt 'alā al-nabī*
Bowen, John R. 212
bridal payment 49, 82, 176
al-Budayrī, Aḥmad 95
al-Bukhārī 100, 107–8, 193, 203, 239 n.13
Burke, Peter 28, 48
Buṣrā 31, 43
al-Bustī, Muḥammad ibn Ḥibbān 46
al-Būṭī, Muḥammad Sa'īd 190, 251 n.30

Chosroes 40, 229 n.138
Christian festivals 118–19, 242 n.56
Christians 53, 117, 154, 208, 226 n.66, 240 n.27
commemoration 4–5, 29, 64–5, 111–14, 116, 153, 158, 165, 178, 187, 201–6

Daḥlān, Aḥmad Zaynī 39, 172–3
"Damascus school" of *mawlid* texts 54, 56–7, 59, 179
al-Dardīr, Aḥmad 169
al-Dasūqī, Muḥammad Ṣāliḥ 117, 131
David 34, 114, 142
Day of Judgment 15–16, 74, 80, 89, 93, 99, 121, 167–8, 197–8
Day of Resurrection 15–16, 25, 77, 79, 83–4, 87, 148, 163, 197, 213, 238 n.146
al-Daylamī, Shīrawayh 8
al-Diyārbakrī, Ḥusayn ibn Muḥammad 24, 28
"Dubai *fatwā*" 186, 191, 255 n.119

Ebersole, Gary L. 142
emotions 47, 104, 111, 115, 116, 124, 130, 139–42, 183, 193, 195, 210–11
Eve 38, 81, 89, 176, 181

al-Fākihānī, Tāj al-Dīn 70–1, 100, 111–12, 116
Farangi Mahall 199, 245 n.131
al-Fārisī, ʻUmāra ibn Wathīma 15, 20, 162, 225 n.50
fasting 4, 63–4, 108, 115–17, 140–1, 148–9, 154, 156, 158–60, 202, 205, 237 n.100, 240 n.21
Fāṭima 4, 6–7, 21, 37–9, 60, 166
Fāṭimid dynasty 1, 2, 3, 5, 6, 8, 113
al-Faṭṭāl al-Nīsāpūrī 7, 12
fatwās 14, 28, 64, 66, 69–70, 73, 76, 104, 110–11, 113, 116, 129, 131, 134, 150, 153, 157–8, 162, 171–2, 176, 186–8, 191, 201–3, 232 n.3, 233 n.27, 234 n.51, 238 n.132, 244 nn.107, 116, 247 n.60, 250 n.15, 251 n.30, 253 n.73, 254 nn.91, 97, 99, 255 n.119
feasting *see* food
Feast of the Sacrifice 206
food 4, 65, 67–76, 78, 81–7, 92–3, 101–2, 104–6, 110, 113, 170, 175, 188, 202, 209, 233 n.8

Gabriel 8, 16, 20–1, 28, 30, 58, 156
al-Ghayṭī, Najm al-Dīn 129–30
al-Ghazālī, Abū Ḥāmid 14, 110–11, 123, 143
Granada 146

al-Ḥaffār, Muḥammad 66, 73, 159–60
ḥajj pilgrimage 72, 94, 202, 236 n.99
al-Hakārī, ʻAlī ibn Aḥmad 92–3
al-Ḥalabī, Ibrāhīm ibn Muḥammad 129–30, 132–4, 244 n.118
al-Ḥalabī, Muḥammad Ṣāliḥ 180–1
Ḥalīma al-Saʻdīya 11, 19, 41–9, 50–3, 55, 61, 124–5, 127, 141
al-Harawī, al-Qāri' 67, 75, 102, 112, 126–7
Hāshim 17, 49
hashish 76, 104
al-Haytamī, Ibn Ḥajar 48, 57, 62, 73, 117, 124, 130, 134, 138, 142, 147, 156, 164, 169, 214
"heavenly handmaidens" 37–9, 61, 169, 176
Ḥijāz 135, 165, 171, 173, 225 n.47, 253 n.74
al-Hijrasī, Muḥammad ibn Khalīl 135–6, 173–4, 189
al-Ḥimyarī, ʻĪsā 186, 192, 194
al-Ḥurayfīsh, Shaykh 24, 36, 53
Hurgronje, C. Snouck 171–2, 209, 211
al-Ḥusayn ibn Abī Ṭālib 6, 68, 78, 114, 116–17, 149, 165–6, 224 n.34, 225 nn.56, 57, 241 n.50, 242 n.54, 246 n.2

Ibn ʻAbbād 105–6, 115
Ibn ʻAbbās 13, 16, 22, 30, 33, 40, 43–4, 46–7, 80, 165, 225 n.55, 226 n.74, 256 n.181
Ibn ʻAbd al-Salām al-Sulamī 78, 131, 143, 150, 153–5, 157, 247 n.54
Ibn ʻAbd al-Wahhāb, Muḥammad 170, 207
Ibn ʻĀbidīn, Aḥmad 86, 147, 170, 206
Ibn ʻĀbidīn, Muḥammad 96
Ibn al-ʻArabī, Muḥyī al-Dīn 24, 28, 29, 51, 79
Ibn ʻAsākir 40
Ibn Bābawayh 3, 6–7, 29, 37, 38, 165
Ibn Bāz, ʻAbd al-ʻAzīz 186, 195, 203
Ibn al-Daybaʻ 52–3, 88
Ibn Diḥya al-Kalbī, Abū'l-Khaṭṭāb 2, 51, 108–9, 143, 153
Ibn Fawzān, Ṣāliḥ 203
Ibn Ḥabīb, al-Ḥasan 56

Ibn Ḥajar al-ʻAsqalānī 64, 108–10, 114–15, 122, 124, 200, 232 n.3
Ibn al-Ḥājj 21, 48, 56–7, 62, 65, 71, 72, 76, 77–8, 87, 100, 111, 145–7, 160, 201
Ibn Hishām 8, 31, 46
Ibn al-ʻIrāqī, Abū Zurʻa 71, 104
Ibn Isḥāq 10, 13, 41, 46, 47, 54, 55, 57, 61
Ibn Jābir al-Andalusī 74, 95, 144–5
Ibn al-Jawzī 27, 51, 88
Ibn al-Jazarī 56, 67, 82, 109, 141, 240 n. 27
Ibn Jubayr 2, 166
Ibn Kathīr 32, 54–5, 57, 61, 128
Ibn Khallikān 2, 67–8
Ibn Makkīya, Aḥmad ibn ʻAbd al-Raḥmān 60, 109
Ibn Manīʻ, ʻAbd Allāh 185, 189, 193, 195–6, 202
Ibn Marzūq 146–7, 161, 163–4
Ibn Nāṣir al-Dīn al-Dimashqī 96–100, 109, 112, 114–15, 127, 141, 147–9, 152–3, 165, 193
Ibn Qayyim al-Jawzīya 91, 93–5, 155–6, 237 nn.107, 123
Ibn Rajab al-Ḥanbalī 63–4, 112, 114, 144, 146, 167
Ibn Saʻd 22
Ibn al-Ṣalāḥ 150, 151
Ibn al-Ṭabbākh 68–9, 76, 104–5
Ibn Ṭawq 72
Ibn Ṭāwūs 3, 7
Ibn Taymīya 8, 9, 14, 27, 72, 115–17, 127, 132, 140, 142, 157–60, 162–3, 196, 210, 214, 247 n.60
Ibn Ṭūlūn al-Ṣāliḥī 72, 88
Ibrahim *see* Abraham
Imāmī Shīʻites *see* Shīʻism
India 136, 179, 182, 240 n.34
innovation, religious *see bidʻa*
al-Iqlīshī, Aḥmad ibn Maʻadd 51, 230 n.168
al-ʻIrāqī, Zayn al-Dīn 32, 58
al-Iṣfahānī, Abū Nuʻaym 30, 32, 33, 35
ʻIyāḍ ibn Mūsā al-Yaḥṣubī, al-Qāḍī 51, 121–2, 146

al-Jaʻbarī, Ibrāhīm ibn ʻUmar 54–6, 61
Jābir ibn ʻAbd Allāh al-Anṣārī 7, 12, 24, 26–9, 53, 58, 169
al-Jazarī, Mawhūb ibn ʻUmar 104–5
al-Jazarī, Muḥammad ibn Muḥammad 56, 70
Jerusalem 149–50, 152, 165, 206
Jesus 34, 117–18, 128, 158, 164, 192, 240 n.27
al-Jīlī, ʻAbd al-Qādir 114–15
Job 34
John the Baptist 19, 118
Joseph 34

Kaʻb al-Aḥbār 12, 15–24, 30, 46–7, 53, 58, 208, 225 n.55, 227 n.87
al-Kabbānī, Hishām 191
Kaptein, N.J.G. 1, 2, 5, 67, 113
al-Karajī, Muḥammad ibn ʻAlī 221 n.1
al-Karājikī, Muḥammad ibn ʻAlī 12, 19–20
al-Kattānī, Muḥammad ibn Jaʻfar 102, 139
al-Kāzarūnī, Muḥammad ibn Masʻūd 18, 24, 27, 28, 30, 32, 44–6, 48, 58
Khadīja 10, 37, 48–9, 55, 60–1, 231 n.199
al-Kharkūshī, Abū Saʻd 12, 17–18, 23, 24, 26, 27, 30
al-Khazrajī, Muḥammad ibn Aḥmad 187, 203
al-Kisāʼī 29
Knappert, J. 210
Kökbürī, Muẓaffar al-Dīn 2, 3, 67–9
Kritzeck, Peter 19

al-Laqānī, ʻAbd al-Salām ibn Ibrāhīm 80
laylat al-qadr 146–7, 154–6, 158, 160–4, 185, 240 n.34, 247 n.54
Lazarus-Yafeh, Hava 167, 206
Light of Muhammad 10, 12–15, 17–18, 20, 24, 26, 28–9, 34, 49, 54, 58, 61, 178, 181, 209, 224 nn.39, 43, 225 n.46, 244 n.104
"light verse" of the Qurʼān 14

al-Majdhūb, Muḥammad 95
al-Majlisī, Muḥammad Bāqir 10
al-Makkī, ʻAlī ibn Nāṣir 36, 89
al-Mālikī, Muḥammad ʻAlī 174, 183
al-Mālikī, Muḥammad ibn ʻAlawī 184–7, 189, 193–4, 196–8, 200–1, 204, 210, 215
Mardāwīj ibn Ziyār 220 n.1
Maryam 36, 38–9, 169, 172, 176, 181
al-Masʻūdī 17
Mauss, Marcel 101–2
Mecca 2, 34, 37, 40–2, 44–5, 68–9, 85, 94, 101, 152, 154, 158, 161–2, 165–7, 169, 171–4, 183, 185, 201–2, 204–6, 209, 211, 224 n.34, 226 n.66, 240 n.27, 250 n.6, 253 n.75

Medina 18, 55, 64, 116, 154, 157–8, 161, 165–6, 169, 171, 173–4, 178, 199, 205, 235 nn.62, 72, 243 n.82
merit, religious 73, 82–3, 87, 89–95, 97–101, 108, 143, 148, 149, 151–3, 167, 198, 201, 206, 211–12, 236 nn.92, 98, 237 nn.106, 107, 246 n.13
al-Miḥḍār, Ḥāmid 187, 190
mi'rāj 55, 97, 151, 153, 158, 165, 204, 205
Mubārak, 'Alī Pasha 170
al-Mufīd, al-Shaykh 3–4, 7
al-Munastīrī, Muḥammad 233 n.8

al-Nabhānī, Yūsuf 128
Nagel, Tilman 167–8
al-Najāshī 6
Nebuchadnezzar 87
Night Journey *see mi'rāj*
Night of Destiny *see laylat al-qadr*
Night of Power *see laylat al-qadr*
nisf Sha'bān 145, 148–9, 153, 160, 205–6
Noah 13, 16, 34, 64, 114, 149, 165
Nūr al-Dīn 1, 2, 101

Palestine 164
paradise 7, 16, 20–1, 25, 29, 38, 75, 80, 83–5, 87, 92, 98, 155, 176
Parry, Jonathan 213–14
Peter the Venerable 19, 208
Pharaoh 36, 65, 149, 172, 176, 246 n.22
popular storytelling 9, 11–12, 20, 22–3, 26–9, 31–2, 46–9, 57–9, 107, 169, 176, 181, 208, 228 n.108, 232 n.200
pre-existence of the Prophet 10, 12, 14–15, 29, 47, 54, 58, 112, 224 nn.39, 43, 44, 225 n.46, 227 n.92, 244 n.104
"Protestant ethic" 211
pseudo-Wāqidī text 12, 46–7

al-Qalyūbī, 'Abd Rabbih 184, 189
al-Qarāfī, Aḥmad 90, 131
al-Qāsimī, Jamāl al-Dīn 179, 182
al-Qasṭallānī, Aḥmad ibn Muḥammad 26, 30, 112, 147
qiyām 128–39, 141–2, 168, 171–4, 182, 187, 190, 196–8
al-Quḍā'ī, Muḥammad ibn Salāma 8, 51
al-Qummī, Shādhān ibn Jibrā'īl 11, 44, 223 n.26
Qur'ān 3, 8, 14, 16, 19, 21, 27–9, 45, 50–1, 55, 67, 72, 75–6, 81–2, 85, 89, 91–3, 95, 97, 102, 106, 108–9, 126, 128, 130, 145–6, 149–50, 156, 159–60, 163, 173–4, 178, 180, 182–3, 189, 192–4, 196, 198–200, 204–6, 208–9, 214, 226 nn.72, 75, 230 nn.151, 155, 165, 232 n.3, 234 n.45, 235 n.77, 236 n.88, 239 n.9, 240 nn.21, 30, 244 n.118, 246 n.22, 252 n.62, 256 n.83
al-Qurṭubī, Muḥammad ibn Aḥmad 21, 51, 127, 165

raghā'ib prayer 150–1, 153, 159, 165, 167
Ramaḍān 72, 143, 145, 148, 150, 154–6, 160, 171, 190, 202, 205, 243 n.91, 248 n.60, 251 n.30, 254 n.112, 257 n.19
al-Raṣṣā', Muḥammad ibn Qāsim 35, 119–20, 122, 139, 161, 214
al-Rāzī, Fakhr al-Dīn 84, 163, 235 n.66
recitation 3, 6, 10, 52, 56, 64, 67, 72, 75–6, 80–4, 86–92, 96, 100, 110, 113, 117, 124, 128, 133, 138, 159, 169–72, 175, 177, 180–1, 183, 188, 192, 194, 202–3, 236 n.92, 245 n.131
Reinhart, A. Kevin 66
Riḍā, Muḥammad Rashīd 175–9, 181, 182, 191, 206, 209
Rispler-Chaim, Vardit 206
al-Riyāḥī, Ibrāhīm 170
Rodriguez-Manas, Francisco 101

al-Ṣafadī, Khalīl ibn Aybak 145
al-Sakhāwī, Muḥammad 78–80, 95, 123, 127, 232 n.3
salafī authors 193–4
ṣalāt 'alā al-nabī 76–82, 100, 177–8, 180
ṣalāt al-tasbīḥ 99–100
al-Ṣāliḥī al-Shāmī, Muḥammad ibn Yūsuf 32, 68–9, 127
salvation 37–8, 75, 86–7, 93, 95, 100, 114, 121, 125–8, 141, 149, 152, 154, 165, 167–8, 181, 205–6, 209, 211, 213, 238 n.131
samā' 76
Saṭīḥ 39–41, 48–9, 54
Saudi Bureau of Scholarly Research and Legal Opinions 186
Sayf ibn Dhī Yazin 12
Schussman, Aviva 187
Seth 16, 20, 25
al-Shāṭibī, Abū Isḥāq 73, 91, 190
al-Shawkānī, Muḥammad ibn 'Alī 134
al-Shaykha, Ḥasan 204
Shī'ism 3–5, 6, 11, 13, 17, 19–20, 21, 37, 60, 113–16, 158
Shoshan, Boaz 9, 256 n.2

Smith, J.Z. 164–5, 167
soothsayers 9, 32, 40, 45, 48, 54–5
standing (in honor of the Prophet Muḥammad) *see qiyām*
al-Subkī, Tāj al-Dīn 59, 95, 128–30, 157
al-Subkī, Taqī al-Dīn 15, 128, 130, 133, 161, 210
sūfīs/sūfism 13, 70, 73, 75, 89, 101–3, 105, 106, 112, 115, 123, 130–2, 134, 139, 141, 143, 175, 215, 233 n.8, 238 n.147, 257 n.18
Suhaylī, ʻAbd al-Raḥmān 239 n.13
Sunnī *mawlid* celebrations 5, 12, 76, 82, 95
Sunnīs 1–2, 4, 7, 9–10, 13, 19–20, 50, 114–15, 165, 240 n.34
al-Suyūṭī, Jalāl al-Dīn 26, 58, 64, 77, 110, 112, 127
Syria 2, 13, 31, 40, 43, 54–5, 149–50, 162, 171, 214, 231 n.199

al-Ṭabarī, Muḥammad ibn Jarīr 39–40, 54, 57
Tapper, Nancy and Richard 211
Tawfīq, Khedive 170
al-Thaʻlabī, Aḥmad ibn Muḥammad 19, 21, 45, 46
thanking 63–7, 109–11
thawāb see merit, religious
al-Tizmantī, Jaʻfar 76
Toledo Collection 208
al-Ṭurṭūshī, Muḥammad ibn al-Walīd 149–50, 152
al-Tustarī, Sahl 13–14, 25, 29, 61, 165, 225 n.46
al-Tuwayjirī, Ḥammūd 186, 192, 197, 202

ʻUlaysh, Muḥammad 96, 169
ʻUmar al-Mallāʼ 1–3, 101
United Arab Emirates 186–7, 203

vows 95–6, 106

Wahhābīs 170–4, 209
al-Wānilī, Khayr al-Dīn 180–1
al-Wansharīsī, Aḥmad 73
al-Wāqidī 11–12, 37
Wasserstrom, Steve 22–3
al-Wazzānī, al-Mahdī 138–9
"white handful" 16–18, 20–3, 226 n.82
women 11, 19, 32, 33, 35–9, 41, 44–5, 48–50, 56–7, 60, 72, 75, 100, 102, 105, 119, 124, 149–51, 172
Woodward, Mark 209

al-Zamlakānī, Muḥammad ibn ʻAlī 55
al-Zarqāʼ 41, 48
Zoroastrianism 220 n.1

CPSIA information can be obtained at www.ICGtesting.com
Printed in the USA
BVOW06s1950280616

453820BV00005B/37/P

9 780415 551878